W9-BUY-947

Advances in Argumentation Theory and Research

EDITED BY J. ROBERT COX & CHARLES ARTHUR WILLARD

Published for the American Forensic Association

BY

Southern Illinois University Press

Carbondale and Edwardsville

Printed in the United States of America

Edited by H. L. Kirk

Designed by David Ford

Production supervised by John DeBacher

Library of Congress Cataloging in Publication Data

Main entry under title:

Advances in argumentation theory and research.

  Bibliography: p.
  Includes index.
   1. Reasoning—Addresses, essays, lectures.
I. Cox, J. Robert. II. Willard, Charles Arthur.
BC177.A43   001.54   82-5496
ISBN 0-8093-1050-3   AACR2

85 84 83 82   5 4 3 2 1

To Wayne Brockriede

Contents

Acknowledgments   xi

Introduction: The Field of Argumentation   xiii
J. Robert Cox and Charles Arthur Willard

Part One: Conceptual Foundations

[1]   The Concepts of Argument and Arguing   3
Daniel J. O'Keefe

[2]   Argument Fields   24
Charles Arthur Willard

[3]   Perelman's Concept of "Quasi-logical Argument": A
Critical Elaboration   78
Ray D. Dearin

[4]   Bilaterality in Argument and Communication   95
Henry W. Johnstone, Jr.

Part Two: Reasoning and Reasonableness

[5]   Rationality and Reasonableness in a Theory of Argument   105
Ray E. McKerrow

[6]   Knowledge in Time: Toward an Extension of Rhetorical
Form   123
Thomas B. Farrell

[7]   Children's Arguments   154
Barbara J. O'Keefe and Pamela J. Benoit

[8]   Values and Beliefs: A Systematic Basis for Argumentation   184
        Malcolm O. Sillars and Patricia Ganer

Part Three: Methodological Issues

[9]   Conversational Argument: A Discourse Analytic
        Approach   205
        Scott Jacobs and Sally Jackson

[10]   Argumentation and the Critical Stance: A Methodological
        Approach   238
        V. William Balthrop

[11]   Modeling Argument   259
        Dale Hample

Part Four: Uses of Argument

[12]   Philosophy and Rhetoric   287
        Ch. Perelman

[13]   Argument and Historical Analysis   298
        E. Culpepper Clark

[14]   Foreign Policy: Decision and Argument   318
        Robert P. Newman

[15]   Argument in Drama and Literature: An Exploration   343
        Walter R. Fisher and Richard A. Filloy

[16]   Argumentation in the Legal Process   363
        Richard D. Rieke

        Reference List   379
        Glenda Rhodes and Jack Rhodes

        Notes on Contributors   405

        Index   409

Tables

6.1   The Languages of Authority as Social Knowledge   135
14.1 Decision Arenas   321
14.2 Decision Stages   325
14.3 Flow of Cuba II Decision   328

Figures

8.1   Beliefs, attitudes, and values in an argument   193
11.1 Schematic illustration of Brockriede's essay   276
13.1 Linguistic possibilities qua historical tradition   301

Acknowledgments

The editors are indebted for the assistance and advice of many individuals in preparing this volume. Manuscript commentators were Bill Balthrop, G. Thomas Goodnight, Michael Hyde, James F. Klump, Ray E. McKerrow, Trevor Melia, Dale Newman, Barbara O'Keefe, Daniel J. O'Keefe, Yves de la Queriere, Otis M. Walter, Julia T. Wood, and David Zarefsky.

In the inception stage of this project the editors benefited from the advice of Joseph McAdoo, Robert L. Scott, Malcolm O. Sillars, Joseph W. Wenzel, and George W. Ziegelmueller.

Permission to publish an English translation of Chaim Perelman's "*Philosophie et Rhétorique*" was granted by the author and by A. De Brie, Rédacteur en Chef, *Tijdschrift voor Filosofe*; the original French text appeared in *Tijdschrift voor Filosofe*, no. 3, 1979.

The editors received support from Dean Fred Berthold of Dartmouth College, Beverly W. Long of the University of North Carolina at Chapel Hill, and Jack Matthews of the University of Pittsburgh.

Anthony Derosby, Nancy Keeshan, Antonio C. Piggee and Judith Woloschuk served as research assistants.

The editors also express their appreciation to Gerald R. Sanders of the College of Wooster, President of the American Forensic Association, for his strong personal and official support for this project. Professor Farrell is much indebted to G. Thomas Goodnight for painstaking criticism of chapter six. Professor Clark expresses appreciation to Michael Hyde for insights into the relationship between hermeneutics and the inquiry in chapter thirteen.

J. ROBERT COX AND CHARLES ARTHUR WILLARD

Introduction: The Field of Argumentation

One way to take the measure of an intellectual tradition is to assess the importance of the problems it addresses. By this yardstick, argumentation has become increasingly important. From its beginnings in late nineteenth-century forensics pedagogy, the field has grown to include the study of argument in various forms and contexts. Scholars have come to claim as subject matter the study of practical argument in jurisprudence, politics, social controversy, art, and ordinary conversation; and the role of argument in epistemology has become a core concern. Studies of practical discourse have come to be regarded as fertile resources for understanding rationality, reasonableness, and how ideas pass muster as knowledge.

Another measure of intellectual traditions is their vigor. By this standard, argumentation has become an enormously fertile domain in the past decade. During this period the *Journal of the American Forensic Association* (1976, 1977, 1980), *Speaker and Gavel* (1980), and the *Western Journal of Speech Communication* (1981) devoted special issues to argumentation. The American Forensic Association and the Speech Communication Association established biennial conferences on argumentation, the first held in 1979 in Alta, Utah. Nearly a hundred panels, programs, and short courses touching at least in part on argumentation were conducted at regional and national conventions and at doctoral honors seminars. Such sustained inquiry during this decade marks the beginnings of disciplinary maturity—the self-conscious examination of the field's assumptions, rationales, and scholarly methods.

This growth has not proceeded from agreed-upon assumptions about what argumentation theory is about or is supposed to accomplish. There are now sharp disputes about what the notions of "argument," "arguing," and "rationality" should be taken to mean (Brockriede, 1975; O'Keefe, 1977; Willard, 1976, 1978, 1979; McKerrow, 1977, 1980b, 1980c). Historical-critical studies of particular orators, debates, or documents—long the dominant focus of argumentation scholars (Dovre, 1965; Gronbeck, 1972)—have been gradually replaced by philosophical and theoretical examinations of the field's assumptions and methods. Natanson (1965, 10) insisted that argumentation's subject matter was argument *as such* rather than any particular argument. An argument "is the naive content of daily life; argument as such is the theme for a disciplined inquiry which must stand outside of common-sense affairs; and theory of argumentation is a distinctively philosophical entertainment." In reviewing these and earlier contributions (Toulmin, 1958; Johnstone, 1965; Perelman and Olbrechts-Tyteca, 1958), Cox (1977, 117) noted: "greater concern has been displayed in viewing argument as a distinct form of human communication—as a set of interrelationships among audiences, social values, and the giving of reasons for claims."

Efforts to construct theories of argumentation have been a relatively recent development. Despite occasional journal essays (Rowell, 1932, 1934; Yost, 1917; Woolbert, 1917; Baird, 1924; Simmons, 1960; Wallace, 1963) and anthologies (Miller and Nilsen, 1966; Anderson and Dovre, 1968), publications in the field through the mid-1960s were largely pedagogical. The upsurge of interest in theoretical matters has ensued from the efforts of many scholars to redefine argument principles in terms of "working logics" (Anderson and Mortenson, 1967), constructivist psychology (Delia, 1976; Willard, 1978), cognitive psychology (Hample, 1980a, 1981), discourse analysis (Jackson and Jacobs, 1980), and symbolic interaction theory (Willard, 1978; Jacobs and Jackson, 1981). Sharp disputes have resulted from analytic attempts to define or exemplify the main concepts of the field (O'Keefe, 1977; McKerrow, 1977; Burleson, 1979, 1980; Willard, 1981).

The essays commissioned for this volume are attempts not merely to inventory recent developments and disputes but also to sharpen them by carrying them as far as current thinking permits. These essays show that argumentation scholars are still a far cry from rallying around a single unifying theory. The field is, in Toulmin's (1972) terms, a "would-be discipline" because it contains paradigmatic disputes. Not all these disputes reflect the historical schools of thought in the field, but enough are historically rooted to necessitate a review of the development and present status of the "field" of argumentation. Here we shall trace (1) the philosophical foundations of early argumentation scholarship; (2) the criticisms of "applied formalism" made in the 1960s and 1970s; and (3) the recent philosophic and theoretical work which the essays in this volume attempt to clarify and sharpen.

The Philosophical Traditions

The seeds of this disciplinary growth were modest enough. Interscholastic debating, which grew out of the literary societies of British and American universities, made few theoretical demands on its practitioners. The early textbooks—George Pierce Baker's landmark *Specimens of Argumentation* (1893) and *Principles of Argumentation* (1895) were perhaps the most influential—were specialized public-speaking manuals that combined models of famous debates and recipelike instruction for research, case-building, and refutation (Gronbeck, 1972; Hochmuth and Murphy, 1954).

The textbooks by Baker and early twentieth-century writers such as Foster (1908), O'Neill, Laycock, and Scales (1917), and Shaw (1922) made no elaborated commitments to philosophical principles. Debate was thought to be a practical training device, an analogue of broader decision-making processes, especially law and politics. Nevertheless, the emphasis on debate as a *method of inquiry*—a kind of truth-seeking—evolved from philosophic traditions that would influence argumentation theorists for many years. Close scrutiny of the early textbooks in argumentation reveals a view of argument grounded in a duality of conviction and persuasion, monism, and a belief in the natural power of truth. Debate was consequently felt to be the appropriate instrument for critical decision-making in human affairs.

Conviction–Persuasion Duality

Early writers drew heavily on British rhetorical theory in describing debate as a mode of rational discourse and decision-making. Nearly all of the argumentation textbooks of this period reflected the "faculty" psychology in the theories of Campbell, Whately, and Priestly: strict distinctions were drawn between reason and passion, logic and emotion, or (to use the authors' terms) between "conviction" and "persuasion." Conviction was thought to issue from logical processes while persuasion resulted from appeals to the passions. Thus Baker rigorously distinguished "pure conviction," which issued from "appeals only to the intellect," and persuasion, which came from the arousal of emotion or from appeals to a person's special interests, prejudices, or idiosyncrasies (Baker, 1895; Baker and Huntington, 1905).

Persuasion was an appropriate part of argumentation's subject matter only insofar as one focused upon the ways the power of emotional appeals could be brought to the service of logical positions. What Aristotle had called "the depraved character of the audience" was an unquestioned assumption. Ordinary persons were thought to be slaves of passion; argument was a critical *rigor* that could inform ordinary thought. Only when rational inquiry shows the way, however, should persuasion be used. Persuasion is a necessary evil because, for ordinary people, it is a more powerful instrument of social influence. Thus writers such as McElligott (1868), Alden (1900), Perry (1906), and Foster (1908) defended the primacy of reason and urged that persuasion only be used to augment the power of reason's conclusions.

Some subsequent writers focused less on the inquiry function of debate and more on its suasory powers. One of these influential textbooks was Laycock and Scales' *Argumentation and Debate* (1913). The conviction–persuasion duality, however, remained a central feature of their thinking: "Successful argumentation . . . must always be of a two-fold nature: it must contain an appeal to the intellect and an appeal to the will; or, in other words, it must contain both conviction and persuasion" (Laycock and Scales, 1913; O'Neill and McBurney, 1932). Baird (1928) also believed that both rational and emotional appeals were essential to effective argument, which, "in addition to satisfying the understanding as to the truth of a proposition, must also reckon with human prejudices, impulses, motives, and emotions. . . . Your argument . . . to be effective should become a series of emotional concepts." Baird nevertheless assumed that "reflective thinking" differed in kind from the "fundamentally disorganized and random" aspects of emotion (1943). The assumption undergirding the pedagogical advice of these textbooks was that the most rational decisions occurred when people were moved not by persuasion but by understanding (conviction).

The value judgment implied in the conviction–persuasion duality has been perennially endorsed in argumentation textbooks. Kruger's condemnation of "unreasonable appeals" (1960) typifies this literature from roughly 1893 to 1965. Argumentation was a moral art, as Winans and Utterback said, because it consisted primarily of appeals addressed to the reason and only secondarily of "psychological appeals" (1930). The tawdry necessity of persuasion was never to be the central focus of the domain: Argumentation's core was the analysis of the truth or falsity of propositions (Pelsma, 1937). Pattee similarly wrote: "Argumentation is the art of presenting truth so that others will accept it and act in accordance with it. Debate is a special form of argumentation . . ." (1920). Normatively, argumentation was *the study of the proper or "best" grounds for conviction*—the truth conditions of propositions, the requirements for valid reasoning, and the rational selection of belief or action from among the expressed alternatives.

Though the conviction–persuasion duality stood at the core of the field's self-definition, some criticism appeared quite early in the journals of the speech profession. Yost (1917) attacked the foundations of the duality by surveying psychological theories of the time and urged that dualism be replaced with a holistic view of mind. Yost wanted argumentation theorists to focus upon the different *functions* of mind on the assumption of organic wholeness. Woolbert (1917) advocated a behavioristic posture; that is, a focus on behavior should replace the traditional focus on the nature of appeals. The emphasis these theorists placed on *listener responses* influenced only a few textbooks: "Psychological monism" (Rowell, 1934; Thonssen and Baird, 1948) became the rubric under which responses were studied holistically. Cronkhite (1964) concluded that many textbook writers had "effected a compromise: they have argued that, while [conviction and persuasion] cannot be separated in reality, they can be separated in theory for pedagogical purposes" (13). Cronkhite objected to the imprecision of this thinking by saying that faculty psychology had given way to "factor psychology"—a judgment that seems entirely fair when one reads Rowell's (1934) influential exposition of psychological monism or many of the important essays of this period (Woolbert, 1917; Graham, 1924; Utterback, 1925; Wichelns, 1925).

Cronkhite (1964) attempted to dislodge the assumption of dualism by locating logical and emotional "proofs" in a theory of attitudes. He argued that verbal stimuli may elicit distinguishable "cognitive" and "arousal" responses *if* one recognizes that the nervous system operates holistically, that *all* responses to symbolic stimuli require cognitive mediation. What is distinguished by this view is the responses of the audience, not the argumentative appeals. Whatever the merits, this helped lay the groundwork for an "audience-centered" argumentation.

Monism

For the Greeks, especially Aristotle, logic and ontology—Knowledge and Being—were indissoluble. The formal relationships expressed by syllogistic logic were believed to replicate the essential realities of the world. The syllogism was an instrument of discovery: it could reveal the hidden nature of things because it was itself a fact of nature. Mind, in thinking of events in the world, literally could become one with the events; it was assumed to be endowed by nature with the capacity to reveal all aspects of natural processes.

As an applied logic, argumentation took on the airs of formal logic. Debate was, after all, a testing process. Aristotle's claim that debating both sides of a proposition gave insight into its truth or falsity was widely believed and, indeed, became a cornerstone of forensic competition as a pedagogical device. The claim was thus widely made that debate could be a form of research, inquiry, or even scientific testing (Shurter, 1908). It was a rational process, permitting disputants to function at their optimum as humans, facilitating the search for truth.

At the root of this thinking was the idea that debate was a forum of *discovery* (knowing) and that analyses of the logical *form* of arguments offered a guide to correct patterns of thought and decision. Delia has described the monistic assumptions of this thinking:

> In its traditional treatment, *logos*, or reasoned argument, is defined in terms of message characteristics, and form and structure are viewed as possessing the mystical power to transmit meaning. Thus, the theory goes, the structure of a piece of discourse controls how it affects the hearer. This is so because, to state a crucial traditional assumption, the laws of logical form correspond to the operation of the thinking or reasoning process [Delia, 1970, 140].

The majority of argumentation textbooks distinguished their subject matter from that of formal logic essentially in terms of the *probability* versus the *certainty* of knowing in practical affairs. Their reasoning echoed Aristotle's view that people deliberate about probable, contingent affairs rather than the "necessary" conclusions of syllogisms.

Despite this modest caveat, the process of debate was believed to issue in something closely resembling the truth of analytical modes of thought. Debaters deal, after all, with the "facts of the case at hand." These "facts" could be ascertained—albeit at the level of probability—and the truth or falsity of propositions of belief and action could be more or less conclusively determined through the "clash of ideas." This body of theory had, in a sense, *no* theory of perception: traditional argumentation scholars had little or nothing to say about mediational processes; they seemed to have assumed, as did Aristotle, that the facts more or less spoke for themselves.

Some of the theorists of the 1930s and 1940s saw argumentation as a discipline closely allied with (and in limited respects equivalent to) science. Wagner, for example, wrote that "the principles of argumentation are derived from scientific proof, as found in logic, chiefly" (1936). He subsequently lamented that, with respect to ordinary affairs, even the most intelligent individuals were not "logic machines" and that they were sometimes influenced by emotions. The most appropriate way for debaters to balance logical and psychological appeals, Nichols and Baccus urged, was through the "scientific attitude" (1936).

Scientific procedures were understood to be methods applicable to ordinary issues. Several textbooks took traditional positivist descriptions of scientific method and applied them to the practice of debate. Pellegrini and Stirling, for example, saw scientific method as a form of problem-solving closely allied with debate—debate being the archetype of problem-solving in nonscientific spheres of conduct (1936). Whereas earlier argumentation theorists had seen issues merely as critical questions capable of being answered in alternate ways, the scientific adherents defined them as hypotheses put to the test of public argument. The underlying assumption was that propositions are verified through confrontation with the facts they purport to describe.

The Natural Power of Truth

A common theme in the early textbooks was Aristotle's rather unclear idea that truth had a "natural" tendency to triumph over its opposite. That is, whatever the subject, and assuming that the disputants do the best job possible in arguing their cases, "truth will out." Aristotle did not elaborate this idea in the *Rhetoric* but it seems sound to interpret it in terms of his monistic epistemology, *psyche* being naturally endowed to take in (become) true forms or essences. Fair debate allowed one to compare and evaluate alternative arguments, to discover their formal weaknesses, and thus to discern the truth of contingent matters. Arguing both sides of uncertain affairs was a process possessed of special probity, then, because it led the arguers to expose fallacies and to reject them in face of valid serial predications. The truth of contingent matters was not a subjective matter: it was "there" waiting to be discovered.

In this spirit the argumentation textbooks viewed their domain as an applied formalism, standing in the same relation to apodeictic syllogisms that Aristotle assigned to rhetoric. Willhoft's treatment is typical:

> Logic is the science of exact reasoning. Its purpose is to help men discern good and bad reasoning. The purpose of argument is to influence other people's minds to belief or disbelief. Argument uses logical formulae, but the terms of

logic are not the terms of everyday life, so that logic is impractical for debate, while argument is practical [1931].

By "logic" Willhoft means a priori logic. Although practical logic (argument) was sharply distinguished from formal logic, it was presumed to have roughly equivalent effects vis-à-vis knowledge. Properly debated, the most contingent of issues would yield up their truths.

The possibility of securing practical truths has served as the consistent pedagogical rationale for courses in this area. As recently as 1972, Smith and Hunsaker restated their faith in this principle:

> The justification for the teaching of argumentation lies in one crucial assumption: *all things being equal, the truth will prevail.* When given a fair chance, truth should survive because it is more natural, more attractive, and less contrived than falsehood. Argumentation functions to encourage equal defense of ideas, and hence to propagate truth [1972, 3].

The early textbooks assumed that these truth functions of debate operated both for the disputants and for the judge. Yet the idea of an impartial adjudicator has consistently been central to their reasoning. The debaters, after all, were assumed to be hotly involved in the contest; their personal commitments might cause them to miss fallacies that a disinterested judge could light upon. This judge could render an impartial verdict because he or she was not one of the contending parties. Hence the language of the early textbooks closely approximates passages of the *Rhetoric* describing adjudication of forensic and deliberative disputes. It was to be the judge who was the efficient cause of truth's triumph.

Critical Decision-Making

The description of argument in these and later textbooks seemed ideally adapted to the assumptions of liberal democracy. "Argument" was a practical method (*techne*) available to participants in the marketplace of political, social, and judicial controversies. Practical argument referred to the process of "ideas in conflict" and "reason in controversy" (Mills, 1968; Dick, 1972; Freely, 1966; Ehninger and Brockriede, 1963; Thompson, 1971).

Because of the attributes assigned in these textbooks, argument was believed to produce "critical" decisions. Such decision resulted from "primarily logical appeals," use of natural faculties for discovering or knowing reality, and a belief that—through rational deliberation—truth was more likely to emerge than its opposite. Thus, critical decisions were superior to noncritical ones (Ehninger and Brockriede, 1978; Kruger, 1964; McBath, 1963; McBurney and Mills, 1964) and debate was seen as the paradigm of rational decision-making.

As a theoretical and practical domain, then, argumentation focused on appeals to "conviction." It was an applied logic, differentiated from formal logic mostly by virtue of its applied status. The philosophical tradition behind the early textbooks helped to shape not only a view of "argument," then, but also of the objectives and methods appropriate for analyzing particular arguments. The field of argumentation had become *the study of the logical forms underlying ordinary language claims, disputes, and debates.*

Reductionism

The analysis of argument, from this tradition, was seen as an identification of essential structures, that is, as *logical*, which authorized the belief or action the argument purported to support. "Logical structure" was distinguished from the social and linguistic contexts and the use to which an argument was put. As recently as 1965, Fisher and Sayles insisted that "argument has a dual nature: (1) its structure is logical, and (2) its content, the context in which it is used, and the consequences sought by its use are essentially rhetorical" (2–3). An "argument," then, could exist independently of the disputants or the process of interaction between arguer and respondent. "All that is necessary for an argument to exist logically is that a statement or a series of statements be made which requires or rationally authorizes another statement" (Fisher and Sayles, 1965, 3).

The objective of analysis under such assumptions, therefore, was to "uncover" the essential (logical) structure of an argument—to *reduce* the manifest rhetorical appearance to its underlying (real) form. Such reductionism often was accomplished through the use of artificial or formal languages such as symbolic logic or various descriptions of inductive and deductive modes of reasoning. One hoped-for result was *control*: The critic "can control the number of terms in the 'vocabulary' of the language, the significance of those terms, and the basic ways in which the terms can be combined to form statements" (Fisher and Sayles, 1965, 7).

Once an argument was reduced to its logical form—whether analytical form or a calculus of probabilities—the task of argument analysis was determination of the a priori acceptability of the knowledge claim. Such evaluation proceeded independently of arguers' construal of "meaning" or acceptance of the claim. "Acceptance" was a normative concern: respondents ought to accept only those claims whose supporting statements conformed to a priori structures of "correct," "valid," or "rational" inference.

Thus, during the period roughly from late nineteenth century to the mid-1960s argumentation was viewed as an applied formalism—a view grounded in a priori assumptions about Being and Knowledge. The mission of argumentation scholars was essentially prescriptive: an application of a priori criteria both in forensics pedagogy and in historical-critical studies of public discourse. But by the mid-1960s this mission had come under strong criticism.

Rejection of Applied Formalism

The beginnings of this criticism first appeared in the writings of scholars who were outside the field of argumentation proper. The two publications that had the greatest influence upon American argumentation scholars in the 1960s and 1970s appeared in the same year: Stephen Toulmin's *The Uses of Argument* (1958) and Chaim Perelman and L. Olbrechts-Tyteca's *La Nouvelle Rhétorique: Traité de l'Argumentation* (1958; tr. as *The New Rhetoric*, 1969). A second broad source of influence emerged in the studies of rhetorical processes by such American scholars as Charles Sears Baldwin, Lane Cooper, Herbert A. Wichelns, Marie Hochmuth Nichols, Karl R. Wallace, Donald C. Bryant, and Carroll Arnold. Such studies raised concern for the role of the *audience* and for "*good reasons*" in judgments of arguers' claims. Arnold (1970) observed that this tradition of American scholarship in rhetoric "antedated *La Nouvelle Rhétorique* by as much as thirty-five years but [was] unknown to its authors" (89).

The writings of Toulmin (1958), Perelman and Olbrechts-Tyteca (1958; 1969), and such American rhetoricians as Wallace (1963) provided a basis for reconceptualizing "argument" and the aims of argumentation theory. In the decades of the 1960s and 1970s, scholarship in this area would be concerned less with *prescription* than with the description of *argument-in-use*. Toulmin (1958) suggested that a working logic "may have to become less of an *a priori* subject than it has recently been; so blurring the distinction between logic itself and the subjects whose arguments the logician scrutinizes" (257). Instead, inquiry would focus on contextual and/or audience-dependent sources of a claim's correctness, reasonableness, or acceptance:

Accepting the need to begin by collecting for study the actual forms of argument current in any field, our starting point will be confessedly empirical. . . . This will seem a matter for apology only if one is completely wedded to the ideal of logic as a purely formal, *a priori* science. But not only will logic have to become more empirical; it will inevitably tend to become more historical. . . . We must study the ways of arguing which have established themselves in any sphere, accepting them as historical facts . . . [257].

O'Keefe (1977) reaffirmed this goal when he urged that students of argument should "undertake the task of 'seeing and describing the arguments in each field as they are, recognizing how they work; not setting oneself up to explain why, or to demonstrate that they necessarily must work'" (127, citing Toulmin, 1958, 258).

Toulmin's (1958) location of criteria for reasonableness or well-formedness of an argument in relevant *fields* proved a heuristic proposition for many scholars. Assumptions of audience- or context-dependent meaning signaled a departure from "applied formalism" in argumentation studies. Delia (1970), for example, observed that the "traditional equation of 'rational' and 'logical' is simply inaccurate." Theorists in the past had been "committed to the 'logic fallacy' of demanding that reasoned discourse correspond to abstract form or predetermined criteria, rather than recognizing that logic, like reality, truth, and meaning, does not exist independent of the listener" (141). In an attack upon the reductionist assumptions of this tradition, Anderson and Mortensen (1967) argued:

Once context-invariant connectives, with their presumptions of stability and fixed lexical meanings, are made to replace less stable connectives in ordinary language, important shifts occur. The critic may well end up determining the validity of forms having little syntactical resemblance to the ordinary language propositions for which they are supposed to be equivalents [146].

Anderson and Mortensen (1967) insisted that "rhetorical acts are defined by context, both linguistic and social, and hence must be understood and judged with careful attention to context" (146).

The reassessment of the place of logic in "marketplace argumentation" offered by Anderson and Mortensen (1967) marked a period of intensive questioning. Other critics included Shepard (1966; 1969), Mudd (1959), Mills and Petrie (1968), and Petrie (1969). Perhaps the culmination of this period came with the English translation of Perelman and Olbrechts-Tyteca's *The New Rhetoric: A Treatise on Argumentation* (1969) and its more extensive distribution in paperback form (1971).

Perelman and Olbrechts-Tyteca announced "a break with a concept of reason and reasoning due to Descartes which has set its mark on Western philosophy for the last three centuries" (1). "Rational" belief, the authors explained, has been associated (in this tradition) with formal logic, that is, with "the study of the methods of proof used in the mathematical sciences" (2). Central to this concept of reason was the idea of *self-evidence*—of analytical or empirical assuredness. "It is the *idea of self-evidence* as characteristic of reason, which we must assail, if we are to make place for a theory of argumentation that will acknowledge the use of reason in directing our own actions and influencing those of others" (1971, 3).

In seeking a rapprochement with classical theories of rhetoric (in particular Aristotle's *Topics*), Perelman and Olbrechts-Tyteca (1971) emphasized that "*it is in terms of an audience that an argumentation develops*" (5). The proper domain of argumentation theory, then, is "the study of the discursive techniques allowing us *to induce or to increase the mind's adherence to the theses presented for its assent*" (1971, 4).

Of importance to Perelman and Olbrechts-Tyteca's theory of argumentation has been their identification of "proof" with the quality of minds giving adherence to an argument's claim. The quality or worth of an argument is highest when there is agreement of the "universal audience" (1971, 31). Such an audience is a construction of particular audiences and of the culture or historical epoch in which an audience participates: "Everyone constitutes the universal audience from what he knows of his fellow men, in such a way as to transcend the few oppositions he is aware of. Each individual, each culture, has thus far its own conception of the universal audience" (1971, 33). The basis of critical observation, then, is the sociological construction of "reasonableness" invoked by particular audiences in justifying their adherence to a claim. As Arnold (1970) observed in his review of *The New Rhetoric*, "argumentation is *audience-centered, not form-centered*" (88).

In grounding their description of argument in a rhetorical methodology, Perelman and Olbrechts-Tyteca (1971) sought to return *logos* to its role as a practical art (*techne*) in the realm of action. In this effort they echoed a number of American scholars concerned with what Wallace (1963) called the "substance" of rhetoric—values and value judgments. This concern lies at the heart of recent considerations of rhetorical *logos*, its conduct, consequences, and methods of assessment in studies by Wallace (1963), Booth (1974), Eubanks and Baker (1962), Eubanks (1978), Hardwig (1973), Ehninger (1968), Fisher (1978; 1980), and Cox (1980). The most indispensible need in contemporary rhetoric, Fisher believed, "is a scheme by which values can be identified and their implications critically considered" (1978, 376).

The tradition of applied formalism seemed woefully inadequate for this purpose. Its assumptions and methods of analysis were rooted in an epistemology that excluded values from serious consideration in what constituted "knowledge." What was needed was an account of "good reasons"— "statements, consistent with each other, in support of an *ought* proposition or of a value-judgment" (Wallace, 1963, 247).

Though the concern of many rhetoricians remained pedagogical—that is, offering a reliable, useful guide to practical wisdom and action—their plan of attack was decidedly empirical. "Instead of working out *a priori* possible structures for a logic of value judgments," Perelman (1970, 281) asked whether argument scholars might not do better adopting the methods of Frege, "who, to cast new light on logic, decided to analyze the reasoning used by mathematicians? Could we not undertake, in the same way, an extensive inquiry into the manner in which the most diverse authors in all fields do in fact reason about values?" This willingness to ground argumentation theory in experience—in encounters with arguments-in-use—signaled the demise of applied formalism. Even scholars who took exception to the Belgians' project turned their attention to nonformal matters. By the close of the 1970s two trends had become clear:

1. A shift from a priori to field- and auditor-defined sources of reasoning, reasonableness, plausibility, and rationality
2. An emerging view of argument as *method* in a sociology of knowledge and a related reconsideration of the nature of justification.

These are the recurring themes in otherwise divergent attempts to build theories of argument. Recent scholarship has exhibited unprecedented self-consciousness as theorists have undertaken conceptual clarifications to examine philosophical assumptions and critical methods and to conduct programmatic research.

The past decade has been a period in which scholars have attempted to construct argumentation theories of varying degrees of generality and to engage in skirmishes and sometimes pitched battles with one another over particulars. It is not always possible to tell whether issues thought to be of vital importance today will be similarly viewed in the future; but our aim in the next section is to survey some of these disputes and developments since they comprise the background of the essays in this volume.

Toward Theories of Argumentation

Conceptual Foundations

Theory construction in any domain assumes some minimal agreement regarding the nature of the phenomena that are taken to be the objects of theoretical inquiry. Much of the literature in argumentation has therefore focused in recent years on various senses of the concepts of "argument" and "arguing." In a seminal essay, Brockriede (1975) announced a bias for "a humanist point of view that denies an interest in logical systems, in messages, in reasoning, in evidence, or in propositions—*unless these things involve human activity rather directly*" (179). Similarly, Willard (1976) lamented the assumption that "arguments are 'things' *possessing*, independent of the people who use them, certain formal characteristics" (309). In our haste to describe the concept of inference, he insisted, "we blur over most of the vital and highly complex cognitive processes which coalesce to produce the symbolic phenomenon we call 'argument'" (311).

The views of argument Brockriede and Willard advanced nevertheless contained certain ambiguities. In suggesting that "students of argument rarely acknowledge that the term 'argument' has two importantly different sense," O'Keefe (1977) sought to distinguish these interpretations in a more formal manner:

> In everyday talk the word 'argument' is systematically used to refer to two different phenomena. On the one hand it refers to a kind of utterance or a sort of communicative act. This sense of the term I will call 'argument$_1$.' It is the sense contained in sentences such as 'he made an argument.' On the other hand, 'argument' sometimes refers to a particular kind of interaction. This sense, 'argument$_2$,' appears in sentences such as 'they had an argument.' Crudely put, an argument$_1$ is something one person makes (or gives or presents or utters), while an argument$_2$ is something two or more persons have (or engage in) [121].

Subsequent analyses (see O'Keefe, this volume) have attempted to expand and refine either O'Keefe's subscripted distinctions or the notions of argument-as-product and argument-as-process (or interaction). O'Keefe explicitly rejects an equation of his two senses of argument and the more widely used "product–process" notions. His intention is to *replace* the "product—process" distinction because his subscripted notions and the analytic work undergirding them are *clearer*. Willard (1978, 1979, 1979a, 1979b) proposed that the process view of argument be the "organizing model" since communication theory is increasingly based on a processual view of reciprocal perspective-taking. O'Keefe (1980, chap. 1) has resisted Willard's general claim on grounds of unclarity; and Willard (1981) has modified his claim to be a general statement about the view critics should take of *meaning*; that is, definitions of situation give meaning to utterances, "interaction *organizes* utterance," the study of argument interactions thus being the "organizing" activity by which utterances are analyzed.

Willard's thesis that arguments$_1$ may assume nondiscursive forms has produced perhaps the sharpest controversy. His claim has been that, given the nature of arguments$_2$, arguments$_1$ may display nonlinguistic aspects and that these are nontrivial elements of the meanings of statements. The most extreme version of this thinking is Hample's (1980, 151–152) claim that "argument exists only within the receiver. The message is of secondary importance, if any. Its only function is to *stimulate* the production of an argument within someone's cognitive system." Hample and Willard work from utterly different theoretical frameworks, however; and Willard's hermeneutic view of message analysis (this volume) is different from Hample's psychologistic project. Willard uses sociological concepts to explain fields and messages while Hample is more interested in a cognitive explanation of influence-taking.

Willard's (1981) "nondiscursiveness thesis" takes specific exception to the Belgians' claim that "the object of the theory of argumentation is the study of the *discursive* techniques" for gaining adherence (Perelman and Olbrechts-Tyteca, 1971, 4). In reply to Willard's position, Kneupper (1978, 182) has argued that although nonverbal signs or symbols "may be utilized in communicating an 'argument,' this communication does not *function as argument* until it is linguistically interpreted by the receiver." Burleson (1979, 1980), while disagreeing with Kneupper's equation of argument with linguistic elements, raised methodological and analytic objections to Willard's view. More recently, Balthrop (1980) has suggested that Willard's position "would preclude argument from fulfilling *its symbolic functioning of presenting justification*" (188) (emphasis supplied). Willard (1978a) sharply disputed Kneupper's criticisms but accepted the methodological standards of Burleson and Balthrop with the proviso that the standards did not deny the importance of nondiscursive symbolism. His position thus sinks or swims on its capacity to produce meaningful research and analysis. His field view (chap. 2) puts Balthrop's claims about justification into a different context, with the possibility that the disagreement about justification may not be genuine.

Willard's views are thus outside the mainstream in two respects. Though many theorists have accepted O'Keefe's two senses of argument, they have generally not agreed with Willard's claim that argument-as-interaction be the main object of attention and that analyses of arguments$_1$ cannot (more often than not) succeed without attention to interaction. Thus Burleson (1979, 145) has argued that the methods employed by theorists and critics ought to reflect a central concern with argument$_1$. Jacobs and Jackson (chap. 9) extend this rationale by grounding their conception of "argument" in speech-act theory.

The Jacobs and Jackson view of argument and discourse analytic methodology has been rapidly gaining adherents. They ground an understanding of the communicative functions of argument in their performative structure, their nature as illocutionary acts. Thus "an argument needs to be understood *as an argument* to *be* an argument" (chap. 9). The "fit" between discourse analytic procedures and other theoretical frameworks in argumentation (such as O'Keefe's, Burleson's, McKerrow's, and Willard's) remains insufficiently clear.

Finally, Wenzel (1980) has proposed a third sense of argument— argument-as-procedure; that is, a set of rules or conventions for the conduct of successful dialectic. Undergirding Wenzel's work is a concern for the normative functions of argumentation—an orientation likely to be disputed in coming years.

Underlying these conceptions of argument as process, product, and procedure is the presupposition that arguments exist in the natural attitude, that they are *objects* of study (Zarefsky, 1980). Alternatively, Zarefsky believes, we might regard argument as the point of view of analysts and critics: "Our object of study would not be some *part* of the natural world but all communication behavior. The concept of argument would be hermeneutic; that is, it would be a way to interpret communication" (1980, 234).

While there is consensus that process and product *or* argument$_1$ and argument$_2$ are necessary distinctions, there is little agreement about their relationships. Burleson (1979, 140) has correctly observed that arguments$_1$ and arguments$_2$ are independent constructions; neither sense is derivative and neither is completely reducible to the other (O'Keefe, 1977). O'Keefe's

(1977) caution has proved true: "Very thorny issues immediately arise concerning how one is to delimit arguments$_1$ and arguments$_2$, and how one is to characterize the relation" between them (127).

Ontological Assumptions

Social and rhetorical theorists assume the existence of an arguer, an audience, and the contact of minds as integral to an understanding of the form and function of "argument." Of some importance, then, are *the nature of the relationship between arguers and the implications of this relationship for the constitution and maintenance of arguers' selves*. Such a concern suggests quite different ontological assumptions from the analysis of argument as a thing or product that exists apart from social actors. Johnstone (1965) characterizes this "standard view of argument" as a transaction that has

> no essential bearing on the characters of those who engage in it. The arguer attempts to persuade the listener. If he succeeds, well and good; if he fails, he may either resort to nonargumentative techniques or else give up the effort. But the argument is in no way definitive of either the arguer or the listener. It is simply a kind of communication among minds that already exist and already inhabit the world—a device that they may or may not choose to employ. And *one can always choose argument without simultaneously choosing himself* [5 – 6; emphasis added].

When one turns from the analysis of argument$_1$ to argument$_2$ this view of argument becomes problematic.

In the last decade and a half, several philosophers whose special concern is argumentation as well as argumentation theorists have explored the assumptions underlying a view of argument as *a process of persons' arguing*. We will look briefly at the emergence of this view and a dispute regarding the attribution of *personhood* this view seems to suggest.

The first significant essay in this connection is Perelman and Olbrechts-Tyteca's "Act and Person in Argument" (1951), reprinted in Perelman (1963) and Natanson and Johnstone (1965). The authors focus upon the relation of the person to an act—argument—that is attributed to him or her: "The reaction of the act on the agent is of such a nature as to modify constantly our conception of the person" (cited in Natanson and Johnstone, 1965, 108). "Arguments," then, are significantly associated with the acts of persons. An argument is assessed via inferences about the person (on the assumption of such concepts as "intention" and moral traits); likewise, *person* is constituted (in the mind of the respondent or observer) in the quality of the arguer's acts (cited in Natanson and Johnstone, 1965, 113).

The relationship of person and "self" is put more explicitly in essays by Johnstone and Natanson in *Philosophy, Rhetoric and Argumentation* (1965). In "Some Reflections on Argument" (1965), Johnstone suggests that to argue with another is to regard that person as beyond our control; we give an auditor "the option of resisting us, and as soon as we withdraw that option we are no longer arguing" (1). Thus, *to argue is inherently to risk failure*—the failure to secure adherence to our claim (Johnstone, 1965, 1). "Not only the arguer takes a risk," Johnstone insists; "the person to whom the argument is addressed may or may not elect to run the risk of having his behaviors or beliefs altered by the argument" (1965, 2). By remaining open to the risk of argument, "man transcends the horizons of his own perceptions, emotions, and instincts" (1965, 3).

Johnstone (1965) distinguishes "risk" from "possibility" in that which an auditor "has an interest or stake in the outcome of activity [*sic*] in which he is taking a risk . . ." (3). Thus genuine argument can occur "only when the respondent is himself interested in the outcome of the argument; that is, where the respondent takes a risk, and thus forces a risk upon the arguer" (4).

What is the nature of such a "risk"? Johnstone (1965) explains:

> It is that the respondent, in his belief or conduct, may have to take account of something that he has not had to take account of before. What he would like to maintain is the relative simplicity of his own position. And in general the risk a person takes by listening to an argument is that he may have to change himself. *It is the self, not any specific belief or mode of conduct, that the arguer's respondent wishes to maintain* [4].

Johnstone concludes that "argument is in fact essential to those who engage in it—a person who chooses argument does in fact choose himself" (6).

Natanson (1965) takes exception to the notion (expressed by Johnstone [1965]) that risk is encountered only in nonimmediate claims. "What is at issue, really, in the risking of the self in genuine argument," he explains, "is the immediacy of the self's world of feeling, attitude, and the total subtle range of its affective and cognitive sensibility" (15). The relationship among self, risk, and immediacy is described by Natanson in a striking passage:

> [W]hen I truly risk myself in arguing I open myself to the viable possibility that the consequence of an argument may be to make me see something of the structure of my immediate world. To say that argument is constitutive of a world is right, but it is precisely the meaning of "world" that such an assertion calls into question. I am suggesting that "world" is in the first place the personal and immediate domain of individual experience. When an argument hurts me, cuts me, or cleanses and liberates me it is not because a particular stratum or segment of my world view is shaken up or jarred free but because *I* am wounded or enlivened—*I* in my particularity, and that means in my existential immediacy: feelings, pride, love, and sullenness, the world of my actuality as I live it [1965, 15–16].

In Natanson's view, "belief" is a mode of conduct or action: "Having a belief is a way of organizing a world and a means of participating in a world" (1965, 17). Argument that aims to secure belief, then, invites a respondent to participate in a world of "immediacy"—an engagement of *self*.

Much influenced by Natanson and Johnstone's views is Ehninger (1970). Ehninger believes that, because argument entails the risk of self-modification, it also creates conditions for "person-making." By accepting the risks implied in "restrained partisanship" the arguer "both bestows 'personhood' on his opponent and gains 'personhood' for himself" (109). Ehninger goes on:

> For to enter upon argument with a full understanding of the commitments which as a method it entails is to experience that alchemical moment of transformation in which the ego-centric gives way to the alter-centric; that when, in the language of Buber, the *Ich-Es* is replaced by the *Ich-Du*; when the 'other,' no longer regarded as an 'object' to be manipulated, is endowed with those qualities of 'freedom' and 'responsibility' that change the 'individual' as 'thing' into the 'person' as 'not-thing' [109].

The establishment of the potential for personhood for disputants is, in Ehninger's mind, the ultimate justification of argument as method.

Similarly, Brockriede (1972) places the primary *locus* of the study of argument in a person "in the process of arguing with another person" (2). "Only those argumentative transactions in which all parties have their selves engaged can result in a fully human interaction" (10). What Ehninger (1970) says of an argument in transforming an *Ich-Es* into an *Ich-Du*, argues Brockriede, can be achieved only by the stance of the "lover": "Since only lovers risk selves, only lovers can grow, and only lovers can together achieve a genuine interaction" (1972, 10).

At least one writer has taken specific issue with the view that argument depends upon a special bond between the participants in a social interaction. McKerrow (1977) argues that "'personhood' is a term which implies far more than the mere recognition of another person: it suggests the existence of a special relation between people, typified by terms such as 'communion,' 'consubstantiality,' or 'intersubjectivity'" (139). A view of argument as *pragmatic justification* of belief or action runs counter to the bestowal of personhood (139). McKerrow explains that "the risk enjoined in the argumentative encounter is the product of an objectification of the elements within the dialectical interchange. *Objectification*, in turn, *denies the full potentiality of personhood*—the fullness present in a state of communion with the Other—between the participants" (139; emphasis added).

McKerrow notes that the "risk" of self enjoined in argument is a product of three preconditions for the conduct of argumentative discourse: (1) willingness to "hear each other out," (2) agreement upon a criterion of validity "which can be invoked to evaluate the efficacy of arguments," and (3) agreement—upon a recognition that the other has presented a stronger argument—to acquiesce or at least "recognize the weakness of [one's] own position" (140). Such preconditions are *social* conventions and one can adhere to them without entering a consubstantial state with the other participant. In the process of adhering to these conditions, McKerrow suggests,

> I objectify the Other (my opponent), myself, *and* the standard of validity we choose. From this objectification, a cohesive relationship emerges which makes possible a rational deliberation of a dispute. By thus objectifying the Other, I degrade his Being, as well as my own. *Instead of conferring personhood, I classify and label the other as my opponent in a dialogue, thus denying the full potential of communion between us* [140–141; emphasis added].

Thus, McKerrow believes, arguers are not "lovers" but only "dialecticians seeking to justify their positions only so long as it is rational to do so" (1977, 141).

Aune (1979) offers one response to McKerrow's position that is derived from the critical theory of Jürgen Habermas (1971; 1975). Aune objects in part to the manner in which McKerrow frames his argument regarding the bestowal of personhood. The process of "objectification" of the Other and the common standard of validity requires McKerrow to give unnecessarily negative connotations to social interaction. Aune contrasts the meaning of objectification in Marcel's (1950) existentialist phenomenology, upon which he claims McKerrow relies, with the Hegelian–Marxist tradition. The latter, Aune notes, draws an important distinction between objectification and *alienation*:

> Human creative activity is essentially objectification. Only when such activity becomes separated from conscious decision making by the human actor does alienation occur. Full communion with the Other requires consensus both on social standards for conducting an argument and on the need for reflection upon the ideological and neurotic distortions which each partner in argument brings to the situation [1979, 109].

Drawing upon Habermas' theory, Aune observes that "a given utterance may be rational in itself but may be contradicted and defeated by the irrational social world in which it is grounded" (108). Habermas thus seeks to enlarge the context of genuine (valid) argument "by locating fuller communion with the Other in the ideals of a rational society" (Aune, 108). Whether his concepts of universal pragmatics and the "ideal speech situation" prove to be useful for argument scholars, however, remains to be seen (see Burleson and Kline, 1979; and the entire issue of the *Journal of the American Forensic Association*, Fall 1979).

Modes of Explanation

In saying what an "argument" *is*, one opens up or forecloses certain ways of understanding its occurrence, conduct, and "successes" in social interaction. That is to say, an adequate theory of argumentation must include *a structure of explanation appropriate both to its subject matter and to the ontological assumptions undergirding it.*

Though argumentation theorists have probably been least clear on this particular subject, we can offer one generalization: In rejecting the assumptions of applied formalism, contemporary researchers have tended to steer away from nomological-deductive ("covering law") explanations of argument and arguing. Knowledge of causally contingent, necessary relationships seems of little value in the realm of intentions, reasons, and strategic behavior; that is, argument.

In recent investigations of argument—including several essays in this volume—two modes of explanation seem to be emerging: (1) *second-order descriptions of natural processes and categories* and (2) *the critical reconstruction of public standards of rationality, validity, or reasonableness*—a mode closely resembling what Taylor (1970) has called "reason-giving explanation." Willard (1978) offers this rationale for the description of natural processes in argument and arguing: "If argument is a 'kind of interaction' and, therefore, a kind of 'social relationship,' it is probable that a statement such as 'we are having an argument' will lead social actors to negotiate a definition of situation which embraces certain subjective rules which serve to govern the interaction" (130). Such a conceptualization of "argument" invites a specific mode of explanation that incorporates *discoursive and non-discoursive processes*:

> The argumentation theorist is being urged to inquire into the meanings which social acts have for actors, to discover the routine ways in which actors construe social reality, and to understand the assumptions on which naive actors base their procedural rules for the conduct of argument [Willard, 1978, 132].

For Willard, the *locus* of inquiry becomes the description of the "social interpretations used by actors in day-to-day living" (1978, 132).

Others would locate "argument" in the individual actor's cognitive field and would therefore be more concerned with describing relevant *psychological* processes. Delia (1970), for example, maintains that *logos* should "be understood as based on the natural tendency of the psychological field to maintain a coherent and harmonious relationship among its affective, cognitive, and behavioral elements" (144). Hample (1980) suggests that a "cognitivist" might explain the process of argument/arguing as follows:

> . . . a stimulus impinges on a cognitive system (possibly because the system sought it), and the system then processes, interacts with and integrates its interpretation of the environment (*that is to say, it argues*), so that the system is changed in some respect [152; emphasis added].

What is significant in Hample's view is that *the cognitive system*—not the public, message-based stimulus—"controls the argument" (1980, 152).

Some theorists have taken specific objection to explanations that reduce "argument" to individual reasoning processes (Jackson and Jacobs, 1980). Jacobs and Jackson (chapter 9, this volume) argue that psychological theories ignore the way "argument is experienced as *existing publicly and independently of individuals*. . . ." For them, this distinction is crucial:

> . . . the processes which allow people to construct, evaluate, and make sense of arguments are not at all specific to argument. People bring to bear processes which apply to language comprehension and problem-solving in general. What makes argument unique is not some special reasoning faculty, but the system of rules through which very general processes are adapted to a particular type of activity. *Argument is not a process whereby a single individual privately*

*arrives at a conclusion; it is a procedure whereby two or more individuals publicly
arrive at agreement* [Jacobs and Jackson, chap. 9; emphasis added].

Jacobs and Jackson want to know how argument is *publicly* conducted.
And—as with language "games" generally—they believe "there is a perfectly satisfying type of explanation that comes from a description of the
components and rules which define the game" (chap. 9). Similarly, O'Keefe
and Benoit (chap. 7) focus on the *interactions* that characterize "naturally
occurring arguments" in children's disputes. Such second-order descriptions of natural processes and categories promise insightful explanations of
human argument and arguing.

The period of the last two decades also has been marked by attempts of
argument critics to reconstruct the bases of assent (belief, acceptance, or
adherence) upon which argument depends. Theorists like Wallace (1963),
Fisher (1978; 1980), Perelman and Olbrechts-Tyteca (1969; 1971),
Toulmin, (1958), and McKerrow (1977) have been interested in asking
"What do social actors count as 'good reasons' for belief, judgment, or
decision?" and "What criteria are available to observers/critics for assessing
the 'validity' or 'reasonableness' of claims?" In trying to clarify "those public standards of justification that we all employ in science and in everyday
life" (O'Keefe, 1977, 127), the argumentation theorist thus invokes a particular structure of explanation; that is, the theorist "accounts for" assent by
reconstructing those bases on which an actor grounds his or her belief or action.

Such a mode of explanation closely resembles Taylor's (1970) description
of reason-giving explanations. Monge (1973) notes that

> "Reason-giving explanations" account for why certain phenomena occur by
> showing why a person thought that a particular action or belief was right,
> correct, true, or a good thing to do. It often answers to the question of why a
> person felt that a particular action was a good thing to do rather than why the
> action did in fact occur [7].

Thus, reason-giving explanations characterize the description of actor- or
field-defined standards of "good" arguments *and* the critical process that
theorists themselves engage in when offering normative propositions; that
is, in assessing a particular argument *as* "good." The latter process is modified, importantly, by the assumption that normative propositions "ought to
be regarded as *outgrowths of social definitions*" (Willard, 1978, 133).

Several theorists—along with Toulmin (1958) and Perelman and Olbrechts-Tyteca (1969; 1971)—have attempted to reconstruct the bases of
"rational" or "reasonable" assent. McKerrow (1977) observes: "The criteria

for assessing the validation of good reasons have been variously located in a field dependent conception of relevance [Toulmin, 1958; 1972], in the values of society [Wallace, 1963], in a person's recognition of his own moral obligations [Ehninger, 1968], and in appeal to a universal audience [Perelman and Olbrechts-Tyteca, 1969]" (133). Although the sources of reasonableness vary, each operates "on the assumption that arguments *justify* rather than *verify* their claims" (McKerrow, 1977, 134).

The location of bases of assent in relevant social definitions of reasonableness suggests that argument partakes of more broadly construed features of *rhetorical* discourse. More specifically, theorists have argued that such discourse presupposes a "public" knowledge that validates practical claims and that argument in turn helps to shape. Farrell (1976; 1978) and Carleton (1978) hypothesize that rhetorical discourse is essentially *epistemic* or productive of "knowledge"; Farrell (1976) qualifies such knowledge as "social" and distinguishes it from "technical knowledge." In a careful elaboration of a "public" knowledge, Bitzer (1979) suggests that culturally shared attributions of facts, advisories, or wisdom *authorize* a rhetor's claims.

In summary, the two most promising modes of explanation in recent investigations of "argument" are descriptions of natural processes and categories and the critical reconstruction of bases of "rational" assent. We do not mean to suggest that these are the *only* sources of explanation of argument and arguing. Indeed, a considerable body of research has been generated from assumptions of causal models—particularly in the area of the *behavioral correlates of argument, features*. Much of this research, however, seems inconsistent with the conceptual and ontological foundations of human argument described in this section.

Methodological Issues

In reconceptualizing "argument," scholars face a number of methodological issues that they formerly have not had to address. Among these issues are: (1) operational definitions of argument$_1$ and argument$_2$; (2) observer-critic interaction with the phenomena being studied; (3) the need to generate *public* data; (4) isolation of "argument" or "arguing" from its social and linguistic context; and (5) the use of descriptive/analytical techniques that are relevant to these concerns.

We have already noted the ambiguity in traditional conceptions of "argument" and its related meanings. Central to recent research has been the need operationally to distinguish actors engaged in arguments$_2$, their arguments$_1$ (as interpreted by themselves and others), and the objectification of both forms by the observer-critic. O'Keefe (1977) notes that "very thorny issues" confront the researcher here:

> Do we want to say that an argument$_2$ necessarily involves the exchange of arguments$_1$ and counter-arguments$_1$ (so that what we might call "squabbles" or "quarrels," in which—if we define them this way—arguments$_1$ are not exchanged, are not arguments$_2$)? Or are quarrels genuine arguments$_2$, simply different from arguments$_2$ in which arguments$_1$ are exchanged? Again, would we want to say that someone had made an argument$_1$ if no argument$_2$ took place (so that making an argument$_1$ definitionally involves having an argument$_2$)? Or are we willing to allow that arguments$_1$ can be made even if no argument$_2$ ensues? [127–128]

One illustration of the practical consequences of an issue O'Keefe cites has been the dispute whether an "argument" in analytical form is, in fact, a genuine argument$_1$ (Brockriede, 1975; O'Keefe, 1977; and Burleson, 1979). Failure to arrive at satisfactorily operational specification of such concepts only adds to each of the following issues.

One requisite for descriptions of psychological and social features of "argument" obviously is *a greater involvement of an observer with the phenomenon being observed*. Because "meaning" is *situated*—in various fields, contexts, audiences, and symbolic acts—the observer must enter into, become a participant in those situations he or she hopes to understand.

> *Understanding* in this instance means much more than mere comprehension of symbols being used to transmit perceptions about how reality is or how it should be. Rather, understanding includes an awareness and examination of the modes of thought which lead to attribution of meaning as well as the attempts to attribute meaning to a newly experienced phenomenon or interpretation of reality. . . . Placing an argument into history involves an understanding of both the context in which it is encountered, and from which, for the critic, argument derives its meaning [Balthrop, chap. 10, this volume; emphasis added].

Such "understanding" involves a critic/observer in attributions of both form and meaning of arguments or arguing that are taken to be the *archai* of inquiry. Anderson and Mortensen have pointed out the obvious problems this requirement poses, even in systems such as Toulmin's (1958) field-variant model of argument. "The critical issue," they note, "is whether *the meanings given to the warrant* by a majority of qualified critics have sufficient xxxviii · INTRODUCTION ·

similarity for consistent evaluation of the argument's worth" (1967, 148).

These concerns bring stronger pressures on the researcher to generate *public* data. Ironically, the shift from an essentially normative posture to emphasis on empirical-descriptive methods arises at a point when the *locus* of explanation has shifted from *form-centered* to audience- or field-centered sources. Thus, "data" are often nonpublic in nature. Researchers are forced to rely upon self-reports of naive social actors or upon inferences regarding the rules that govern the conduct and resolution of argument.

The problem of producing public data is further constrained by the reliance upon argument₁ and the process of arguing (argument₂) as *a mode of explanation* for the phenomena of arguments₁ and arguments₂. Argumentation scholars (as Johnstone [1973] has remarked about scientists) must "argue for" certain inferences or interpretations that can neither be deduced analytically nor empirically verified absolutely.

Though reliability can be gained through simplifying the phenomena being investigated, other problems emerge. In particular, techniques that isolate arguments from their linguistic and social contexts face many of the same charges made earlier against formal reductionism. Willard (1976) has argued that "diagrams" such as the Toulmin model suffer from several sources of distortion: (a) the process of translating or reducing symbolic form into analytical form; (b) the linguistic bias of the model; and (c) the model's intrinsic isolation of context—both linguistic and sociopolitical (314 ff.) Both Kneupper (1978) and Burleson (1979), however, have argued for the continued utility of such methods of analysis while acknowledging the methodological dangers. "Properly understood," Burleson says, "the Toulmin diagram leads critics and theorists to consider what may be termed the *substantive context* of an argument" (146).

These concerns have led argumentation scholars in recent years to search for descriptive and critical techniques that are suitably adapted to the nature of the phenomena being studied. Recommended methods have included linguistic analysis (Balthrop, 1980), participant observation (Willard, 1980), discourse analysis (Jacobs and Jackson, chap. 9), as well as criticism (Willard, chap. 2; Balthrop, chap. 10). In developing a model of conversational argument, Jacobs and Jackson (chap. 9) rely on the method of "analytic induction"—a method they suggest is "the method of choice for at least the initial stages of empirical exploration of any domain":

> Analytic induction, as a process, incorporates both the formulation of a hypothesis and the testing of that hypothesis. The first step in the process is the

location or collection of some number of relevant examples of the phenomenon being studied. . . . The second step in the process is the construction of a hypothesis, usually in the form of a rule, convention, or schema. The hypothesis, built inductively from the examples, must of course apply to every case. . . . Having arrived at a hypothesis, the third step in analytic induction is to test the hypothesis through an active search for disconfirming cases. . . . An analysis may be considered "complete" when the analyst arrives at a relatively durable hypothesis, but any hypothesis is continually subject to revisions forced by further observation [chap. 9, 219–220].

Such a process underlies not only Jacobs and Jackson's discourse analytical approach but *most* attempts to provide second-order descriptions of natural processes and categories of argument.

Balthrop (chap. 10), on the other hand, defends a "critical" stance as a legitimate and important perspective from which to understand argument as either process or product. Though criticism has been a much-used method in this area, Balthrop cautions that *different* interpretations of the phenomena being analyzed will emerge, depending upon "what it is that the critic seeks to understand." The critical stance is thus rooted in one's theory of interpretation—one's views of the manner and processes by which meaning is constituted. More broadly, criticism is the appropriate methodology for self-reflexive scrutiny of the assumptions and procedures of the argumentation field. As Willard (chap. 2) says, "fields are frameworks of assumptions," and criticism functions as the study of the effects of these assumptions.

Issues in Argumentation

The essays in this volume display, on the whole, more differences than similarities. For instance, it would be a serious error to read O'Keefe's opening essay on the assumption that all of the following essays share his distinctions. Willard (1981) has objected that O'Keefe's paradigm case argument "loads the dice" in favor of propositional logic; and B. O'Keefe and Benoit (chap. 7) call the generality of paradigm case reasoning into doubt in their survey of children's arguments. It would be equally erroneous to read Willard's rejection of evaluation in criticism on the assumption that it is shared by the other authors, or Hample's mathematical operationism, or Dearin's defenses of Perelman, and so on.

Despite these differences, there emerge in the essays certain recurring themes—"shared problem foci" whose importance is for the most part not disputed. One way to define a field is to point to its recurring problems (Willard, 1981c; Toulmin, 1972), and our aim here is briefly to describe these shared problems.

Justification

Weimer (1979, 2) has argued that all of the traditional philosophic positions (empiricism, rationalism, formalism, idealism) *"are variations of one and the same metatheory.* In short, the traditional distinctions between 'philosophies' are largely epiphenomenal. They are surface level differences between essentially similar positions that share a common deep conceptual structure. All traditional philosophies are *generically related* in the sense that they are variants of the same metatheory."* The metatheory is "justificationism," by which Weimer means epistemic views that equate justification with *proof* and identify knowledge with *authority*.

Of the essays here, only Willard's and Balthrop's use what Weimer calls "nonjustificational" approaches to knowledge. Willard argues that, in cases of interfield disputes, it is often pointless to deliberate about which field is "correct." He replaces that traditional question with a consideration of the fields to which students of knowledge should pay attention. Willard and Balthrop rely on hermeneutical assumptions—which are basically nonjustificational. Both, however, regard justificatory practices as important social phenomena. Their empirical procedures thus square with several other essays that do not enter into epistemological disputes. The research in children's arguments surveyed by B. O'Keefe and Benoit bears upon empirical justificatory practices. It permits the inference that socialization involves, among other things, learning the ways of justifying claims and practices. Put broadly, this squares with Jacobs and Jackson's focus upon particular conversational expansions—especially reason-giving. These otherwise diverse essays thus share a *focus* on justification as an empirical phenomenon.

McKerrow, conversely, takes a strict justificationist line respecting the epistemic mission of the field of argumentation, that justification (as an empirical focus and as a *normative aim*) is the field's core enterprise. Sillars and Ganer take an equally strong line. In different ways, the essays by Dearin, Farrell, Clark, and Perelman impute similar importance to justification. They replace the "justified true belief" of traditional epistemology with rhetorical concerns; but they retain the traditional aim of deriving standards for evaluating justificatory arguments.

Knowledge

Many of the essays, despite profound theoretical differences, are attempts to explain knowing and knowledge. The belief that "rhetoric is epistemic" receives the particular focus that "arguments lead to knowledge." Farrell's extension of his social-knowledge views takes the form of a critical-historical account. Dearin and Perelman focus on the reasonableness of claims and the grounds for judging reasonableness. McKerrow focuses on a coherentist explanation of reasonableness and plausibility, drawing heavily upon Rescher's (1976, 1977, 1979) "plausibility thesis." Clark's claims that argument is the appropriate method of historiography take a similar posture. Willard's field theory is an attempt to explain the sociological grounds of knowledge. His claim that field theory blurs the usual distinction between "Knowledge" and "social knowledge" may spark controversy. Balthrop grounds criticism in a particular hermeneutical view of knowledge. An emerging theme in many of these essays is, in fact, that critical problems *are* epistemic problems.

The recurring themes, then, are that argument can be seen as a *method* of knowledge—in Willard's phrase, a method of "passing muster on knowledge"—and that arguments in differing ways *produce* knowledge. Considerable differences emerge as to how these aspects of argument are to be taken. The symbolic interactionists and constructivists focus on the discourse processes in which knowledge claims are evident and on the interactions between psychological processes and social life (utterances). The cognitive theorists (such as Hample) see knowledge as a cognitive state or orientation. The "analytic theorists"—so named for want of a better term—equate "Knowledge" with the probity of the reasoning processes that produce claims (among them McKerrow, Perelman, Dearin, Newman, Farrell, Clark, and Balthrop).

Ordinary Discourse

Despite differences, many of the essays impute philosophical, theoretical, and empirical importance to ordinary talk. This differs from (but is not necessarily incompatible with) the field's traditional emphasis on formal speech. Discourse analytic work seems to be a genuine departure from traditional foci because it concentrates on everyday conversation rather than dramatic instances of public speaking. Jacobs and Jackson use an arsenal of concepts appropriate to mundane discourse (for example the adjacency pair) that seem to differ in kind from the concepts of traditional speech analysis. While Jacobs and Jackson explicitly contrast their views with "monologic" (psychological) conceptions, it is not obvious that their "structural/functionalist" explanations of conversational structure inevitably must be dichotomized with psychological views. It would depend, we would suggest, upon how exhaustively we think the discourse analytic concepts explain the phenomena argumentation theorists want to explain. If we believe that the structure of conversation buttressed with speech act concepts sufficiently explains all of the important aspects of arguments$_1$ and arguments$_2$, we may well come to regard discourse analysis as an alternative—indeed, competing—paradigm to (say) constructivism, cognitive psychology, and other "psychological" paradigms. It is thus likely that the grounds for dispute about discourse analysis will not concern its focus upon ordinary talk as much as the exhaustiveness or breadth of the explanations it yields.

Rieke likewise urges that studies of legal argument utilize the resources of ordinary talk. Traditional rhetorical studies have obscured the informal aspects of legal communication and ignored the interdependencies between formal and informal structures. Rieke's argument is that such informal communication is the stuff of jurisprudence, proved perhaps by the importance of plea bargaining and other informal legal arrangements. In this respect, his arguments cohere with those of Willard (1980, chap. 2) and Balthrop (chap. 10). Sharp disputes are likely to result from Rieke's historical defense of the importance of ordinary, informal discourse. Dearin and Perelman, for example, locate the rationality and reasonableness of jurisprudential argument in far more formal processes. Unlike the more general conversational focus of Jacobs and Jackson, Rieke's view of legal argument seems incompatible with traditional views of *stare decisis* and the reasoning therefrom.

One effect of the ordinary-discourse focus is to tie argumentation more closely to the broader speech communication discipline. The research survey by B. O'Keefe and Benoit, for instance, leads us to think of arguments as particular kinds of discourse, making argumentation a special focus within the larger framework of rhetorical and communication studies. Jacobs and Jackson's view is but a piece of their larger communication theory; the same can be said of many of the other theorists in this volume, including Farrell, McKerrow, Hample, Sillars and Ganer, Newman, Clark, and Fisher and Filloy. Willard's field theory and Balthrop's critical views are in the same sense "broader" than argumentation theories, although they place great weight on the importance of argument. The general tenor of this rapprochement of argumentation with rhetoric and communication is a genuine departure from traditional thinking. The lines between the genus and the species are fuzzy, to be sure, but it seems clear that the essays here bring argumentation into closer alignment with the theories and practices of the larger discipline.

Rationality, Reasonableness, and Persuasion

It is remarkable, given the historical importance of the rationality notion to argumentation, how little it gets explicitly discussed in these essays. This reflects several developments. It reflects, among other things, the general rejection of a priorism and the logical principles attendant to it. The theorists who used "rationality" to name demonstrative reasoning were forced over time to so narrow the range of operations that could be called "rational" that the term lost its usefulness to students of ordinary utterance. Only Hample uses models drawn from mathematics; and he does not make claims about rationality inhering in mathematical structure. Within philosophy there emerged more expansive views of rationality, some equating it with "reason-giving" without regard to evaluations of the reasons, others equating with consistent reasoning—again without regard to the content of the reasoning per se. Willard (1980c) calls this "a trivialization of rationality" because (a) rationality becomes a redundant word standing for the effects of some other concept (like consistency or reason-giving) and (b) rationality has no particular results: consistent- or reason-based claims are as apt to be as evil, foolish, or unjust as are their opposites. Rationality, for whatever reason, seldom appears in the essays here; perhaps its trivialization is the reason.

The term seems to have taken on an informal and proportionately loose meaning. Newman's model of the "rational actor," for instance, seems to be a loose variant of the consistency and reason-giving views of rationality. The term itself does no philosophic work for Newman, since it is historical judgments of the substance of reasons that arbitrates our views of the values of particular decisions (and the processes producing them). Johnstone's expansion of the "bilaterality" notion *might be* seen as a principle of rationality but he makes no such strong claims for it. His thinking seems more consonant with Newman's than with traditional analytic philosophy.

Dearin and Perelman devote the most attention to rationality. Their rhetorical view of rationality has attracted followers, possibly because they use the concept in a way that does not depend upon the restricting arguments of traditional analytic philosophy (or, for that matter, the narrowing claims of the formalists). Reason-giving is their main criterion, but it remains to be seen whether they will devise a judgmental apparatus for evaluating the content of reasons. Dearin insists that the "universal audience" is not a concept that is central to Perelman's system. Some of the other writers in this volume diverge from this interpretation; this is likely to be source of future dispute. If Dearin and Perelman restrict rationality to the giving of reasons without regard to their content, they may prove open to the triviality objection. If, on the other hand, they open the door to the evaluation of reasons without a lucid account of the universal audience, their prospects for success are uncertain.

McKerrow uses the concepts of reasonableness, plausibility, and persuasion to express his views of argument processes. He seems consistently to use *rationality* in an informal way. His thinking squares with Rescher's (1977) plausibility thesis, which is a search for the *standards* of persuasion. If one can explain why a person of a particular sort is persuaded of a thing, one has explained the plausibility of particular claims. Plausibility for Rescher is not a pale reflection of probability theory but a full-blown theory of coherence which says, among other things, that claims are plausible insofar as they cohere with a person's cognitive arrangements. This leads Rescher (and by implication, McKerrow) to a coherentist epistemology. This entails a search for universal principles of coherence (which include simplicity, regularity, uniformity with other beliefs, and normalcy). While Rescher's theory is too detailed to discuss here adequately, it bears saying that his thinking might prove to be one more avenue by which argumentation is brought more closely into line with the broader rhetorical and communication discipline. It may also prove important by virtue of its stress on debate as a mode of inquiry. It can be seen as a fully articulated defense of debate, both as an epistemic procedure and as a decision-making apparatus. In any case, the McKerrow/Rescher view makes the term *rational* into a general rubric standing for "reasonable" and "plausible." This use represents a distinct shift away from traditional views.

Two universalist lines of thought about rationality are still apparent in argumentation. Toulmin and his followers seek an "impartial standpoint of rationality" derived from recurring themes in field practices respecting conceptual change. Burleson (1979a) has attempted to "complete" this project by using the felicity conditions of discourse in Habermas' critical theory. That claims be redeemable through discourse seems a viable standard, although its implications for particular critical activities remain to be seen. It is arguably the case that Habermas' conditions warrant "warranting"; that is, justify the practice of warranting without warranting particular warrants. Critics will thus have to work out the implications to avoid being open to the triviality objection. A second line (Willard, 1980c, 1981b, chap. 2) involves studying rationality as an ordinary social practice as a term field actors use to express approval of particular argument methods while ignoring searches for universals of rationality. These two lines are not in principle incompatible but they require very different scholarly programs.

Propositional Utterance

Most of the essays here retain propositional utterance as the core object of research and criticism. O'Keefe, for example, carefully restricts his claims to utterance, and in this respect he seems to be defining the mainstream of current thought. "Inference" stands for private psychological processes (thought) while "argument" stands for public utterance (Toulmin, 1958). Dearin and Perelman retain a strict linguistic focus; and Balthrop's hermeneutic critical theory, while it admits nondiscursive elements into the system, focuses mainly on propositional utterance. There seems to be agreement, then, that the paradigm case of arguments$_1$ must be propositional utterance. Aside from a criticism of equating fields with documents, Willard's essay does not address this issue.

Fisher and Filloy present two sustained case studies of "implied" arguments in artistic works—not in the mundane sense that artistic works can be didactic but in the sense that arguments can be inferred from stage directions, nonverbal activities onstage, general plot arrangements, and other elements not clearly "in the talk." By O'Keefe's paradigm case standard, this is a "fringe case" of arguments$_1$; but this does not diminish their importance. Fisher and Filloy have expanded our commonsense understanding of the breadth of the "argument" concept and the range of applicability of traditional argument concepts—the notion of "aesthetic proof" opens the door to a promising line of speculation and research (and ultimately criticism) for argumentation scholars.

Argument Fields

Many of the essays touch on the subject of argument fields. McKerrow has perhaps elaborated the outlines of a theory compatible with Toulmin's (1958, 1972) original aims (McKerrow, 1977, 1980, 1980a, 1980b, 1980c). One might draw from O'Keefe's essay certain conclusions about what a field theory based upon analytic/critical distinctions would look like, although O'Keefe does not spell these out. While McKerrow's view is based on the aim of securing a judgmental logic, O'Keefe's work could be the basis for seeing fields as analytic/critical points of view: alternative perspectives critics and analysts may take. Jacobs and Jackson have referred, usually in footnotes, to the sort of field theory their discourse analytic work implies. While they have not elaborated a field theory, it is plausible to guess that their view of fields will look something like the distinctions between speech acts; that is, it will be a classificatory scheme of particular sorts of act.

Willard's essay here regards fields as real sociological entities and as psychological perspectives (in the Chicago School Interactionist sense that social entities take their existence from the defining activities of their members). Whether his scheme will clash with the other developing views remains to be seen. A likely source of clash is his stress on the relativistic implications of field theory. His conclusions are at odds with those of Toulmin and McKerrow, though perhaps not with the embryonic field theory of Jacobs and Jackson or with the analytic/critical perspective view implied in O'Keefe's distinctions. Field theory is a way of tying together various strands of activity within argumentation, and scholarly interest in the subject is likely to increase in the immediate future.

Conclusion

These essays are checkpoints along a variety of alternative routes. They attempt to assess the field's progress to date and to speculate about the immediate prospects of particular lines of thinking. They also elaborate these prospects by clarifying the grounds for disputing them and by advancing the states of arguments already in progress in the literature.

Although they do not present a unified picture of the field, these essays do yield the sense that argumentation has progressed as a discipline. The status of various internal disputes has advanced considerably in the past decade; these essays are attempts to solidify this progress and move beyond it.

PART ONE

Conceptual Foundations

DANIEL J. O'KEEFE

[1] The Concepts of Argument and Arguing

My aim in this essay is to clarify what one might take to be the fundamental conceptual equipment of students of argumentation: the concepts of argument and arguing. My analysis will be grounded in the common meanings and uses of words such as "argument" and "arguing," but my concerns are not simply linguistic ones. Rather, I take the analytic route I do because I hope that it will lead somewhere useful, specifically to a clearer conception of the phenomena that concern students of argumentation and to an improved understanding of the diverse approaches that may be taken to those phenomena. In what follows I first discuss the terms "argument" and "arguing" with an eye to dispelling some ambiguities and establishing some basic distinctions. I then take up in a more detailed way issues concerning some of the concepts so distinguished, and finally discuss some consequences of my analysis. [1]

Basic Distinctions

The terms "argument" and "arguing" are important to students of argument, but unhappily these words have diverse usages that, if unrecognized, can threaten clear discussion. Thus I think it important to begin by making some obvious but not insignificant distinctions.

I have elsewhere underscored a distinction between two senses that the term "argument" has in everyday talk (O'Keefe, 1977). One sense of the term is that found in sentences such as "he made an argument." The object to which the term "argument" refers in such sentences I have called argument$_1$; an argument$_1$ I have characterized (1977, 121) as "a kind of utterance or a sort of communicative act." A second sense of "argument" is found in sentences such as "we had an argument." The object to which "argu-

[1] I have profited from commentary on earlier versions of this essay by Charles Arthur Willard and Joseph W. Wenzel. Portions of this analysis were presented in O'Keefe (1980).

ment" refers in these sentences I have called argument$_2$; an argument$_2$ is "a particular kind of interaction" (1977, 121). Although this distinction is expressed as one between "two senses of 'argument,'" it is founded on a distinction between two different sorts of things, two different phenomena (arguments$_1$ and arguments$_2$) which are both referred to by the word "argument."

This distinction is so obvious as to be nearly trivial. Nevertheless the distinction is a rather fundamental one, and a failure to recognize it can only lead to unfortunate consequences for argumentation theory and research. For example, an attempt to list the "generic characteristics" of "argument" is unlikely to succeed if only because the characteristics of arguments$_1$ are so different from the characteristics of arguments$_2$. Similarly, to criticize Toulmin's (1958) way of diagramming arguments$_1$ because that method misses the important characteristics of arguments$_2$ is to mistake the phenomena Toulmin's approach is designed to illuminate: "if the Toulmin diagram and similar systems are appropriate only for the analysis of argument$_1$, then criticisms regarding their shortcomings in describing argument$_2$ are irrelevant" (Burleson, 1979, 143).[2]

A distinction similar to that between argument$_1$ and argument$_2$ is reflected in uses of the verb "to argue," and in particular is detectable in the difference between "arguing about" and "arguing that." The sentence "John and Jane argued about which movie to see" implies or suggests that John and Jane had an argument$_2$. Since arguments$_2$ ordinarily involve two

---

[2] I might say, by way of clarifying the distinction between argument$_1$ and argument$_2$, that the numerical subscripts say nothing about which is the more "important," "basic," or "fundamental" sense of "argument." The subscripts were assigned to help keep straight the two senses, in that an argument$_1$ is ordinarily given by *one* person whereas an argument$_2$ involves at least *two* persons. I mention this only because some have apparently taken the ordering of subscripts to mean that I believe argument$_1$ to be the more "important" sense of "argument." In fact, although some have claimed that, for example, the argument$_2$ sense is the most "fundamental sense of the term 'argument'" (Willard, 1979, 169), I cannot imagine what is meant by such a claim—unless etymological matters (which I would think to be of only passing interest to an argumentation theorist) are being raised. After all, which is the more "fundamental," "basic," and "important" sense of "bank," the "financial institution" sense or the "side of the river" sense? And who (besides an etymologist) cares? Perhaps Willard's (1979) phrasing of his claim is inexact; perhaps what he wants to claim is that argumentation theory and research should focus on arguments$_2$ rather than on arguments$_1$. By this view I might be thought (by virtue of the subscripts) to prefer a focus on arguments$_1$, but this inference is also mistaken. Whether one studies arguments$_1$ or arguments$_2$ (or—to introduce a notion to be discussed shortly—the making of arguments$_1$) will depend entirely on one's interests and purposes, and so in my view is not a matter to be either "disputed" or "resolved" through either theoretical or empirical work (see Zarefsky, 1980, for a similar view). Thus on no account should one make many inferences from my assignment of numerical subscripts.

or more persons, it is not surprising that "arguing about" ordinarily takes a plural subject ("they were arguing about nuclear power"). Even in those constructions in which the subject is singular ("John argued about nuclear power") one can always legitimately ask with whom the person was arguing; and indeed when "arguing about" occurs with a singular subject, a "with" clause is typically appended or inserted ("John argued about nuclear power with some protesters"). Hence, the "arguing about" form of "arguing" is one that is concerned with arguments$_2$.

The "arguing that" form of "arguing," on the other hand, is rather more related to the phenomenon of argument$_1$. The sentence "John argued that they should see *Citizen Kane*" can be used to imply or suggest that John made arguments$_1$ to that effect. Notice that I do not claim that the sentence suggests or implies John made arguments$_1$, but only that the sentence can be used so to suggest or imply. My reason lies in my suspicions that (1) for many speakers of English there is (at least in some circumstances) not much difference between "argue that" and "suggest that" (between "John argued that they should see *Citizen Kane*" and "John suggested that they should see *Citizen Kane*"), save perhaps for an implication about the vehemence with which the suggestion is forwarded; and (2) for many speakers of English there is (at least in some circumstances) not much difference between "argue that," "believe that," and "claim that"—so that, for instance, a speaker who says "I argue that P" may be fairly characterized as simply making a belief declaration (akin to "I believe that P") or as enunciating a claim (akin to "I claim that P").

While there are these close connections between "argue that," "suggest that," "claim that," and "believe that," arguments$_1$ presumably are very different from suggestions, claims, and belief declarations. Thus the occurrence of the "arguing that" form of "arguing" is not an altogether reliable indicator of the presence of an argument$_1$. That is why I do not say that sentences of the form "S argued that P" suggest or imply that arguments$_1$ were made, but only that such sentences can be used to so suggest or imply. Nevertheless, it should be clear enough that the "arguing that" form of "arguing" is one related to the phenomenon of argument$_1$.

These distinctions, obvious as they are, nevertheless can serve to clarify and illuminate the concerns of argumentation theorists and researchers. Presumably the domain of the field of argumentation consists of the phenomena of argument$_1$ and argument$_2$, with the aim of argumentation theory and research being to provide an understanding of arguments$_1$ and arguments$_2$.

But traditionally argumentation theorists and researchers have had one of three somewhat narrower concerns, as has been nicely discussed by Wenzel (1980). One concern has been with argument$_2$ as a procedure for reaching critical decisions; a second has been with establishing standards for sound (e.g., logically valid) arguments$_1$; and a third has been with characterizing the features of effective (persuasive) arguments$_1$. Very broadly put, these three traditional concerns can all be seen as "normative" rather than "descriptive." That is, the concern has been with what makes for a "good" argument$_1$ (one that is logically sound or that is successful in persuading hearers) or a "good" argument$_2$ (one that does lead to a more critical decision).

Recently, however, argumentation theorists have turned to more basic descriptive and explanatory concerns, to issues of just what an argument$_1$ is, what an argument$_2$ is, how arguments$_1$ are related to arguments$_2$, and how arguments$_1$ and arguments$_2$ work in everyday human interaction. In the next section I address several questions concerning these more fundamental matters; the several questions all bear on the concepts of argument$_1$ and argument$_2$, and my primary aim is to elucidate these notions further.

Paradigm Cases of Argument

I want to consider the concepts of argument$_1$ and argument$_2$ further, for these are presumably as fundamental to argumentation as any. And the analytic strategy I shall adopt is that of examining the paradigm cases of these concepts, a strategy that requires some explication.

One way of clarifying the meaning of a concept is by giving a definition of the concept. But for clarifying argument$_1$ and argument$_2$ this strategy is not ideal, for definitions typically have sharp edges that include or exclude disputable cases—with consequent disagreement over the acceptability of the definition. For example, a definition of argument$_1$ that included only "purely linguistic serial predications" (Willard, 1979a, 212) would not satisfy Willard, who is concerned that "non-discursive forms" be counted as arguments$_1$; but other theorists might be dubious about Willard's suggestion that "non-discursive forms" are arguments$_1$ and so would be unwilling to accept a broader definition (see Kneupper, 1978). This does not mean that definition-giving is always a fruitless or pointless enterprise. One may come to a better understanding of an author's position if the author provides something like a definition for otherwise unclear terms; disputes over definitions may clarify alternative positions on important issues. But precisely because definitions include or exclude disputable cases more or less by fiat, they do not go far toward *analyzing* the defined concept.

An alternative strategy for clarifying the meaning of a concept involves considering "paradigm cases" of the concept. By "paradigm cases of a concept," I mean to point to those sorts of examples (cases) which would elicit widespread agreement that these *are* in fact examples of the concept in question. By focusing on such cases and by asking ourselves what such cases have in common, we may be able to clarify the concept under discussion. As Minas (1977, 230) explains, paradigm cases "serve a useful function in discussion, explanation, argumentation, and thinking, this function being to clarify meaning. . . . It is sometimes useful in thinking to . . . [examine] situations which (it is believed) certain expressions describe. The believed features of these situations help clarify what these expressions mean."

An example may be helpful here. If I go on television to ask for contributions for my political campaign, my efforts would very likely be called "persuasion" by most persons; that is, this would seem to be a paradigm case of persuasion. By contrast, if I knock someone unconscious and take his wallet, this would not ordinarily be called a case of persuasion. From these and similar examples we might be able to conclude that exemplary (paradigm) cases of persuasion ordinarily involve there being some measure of "freedom of choice" or "free will" on the part of the persuadee—and we thereby would have gone some way toward clarifying the concept of persuasion, by identifying a feature paradigm cases of the concept seem to share. Notice that when such a feature is absent (or only questionably present), one typically has a "borderline case" of the concept. Consider the circumstances of a mugger holding a gun to one's head and demanding one's wallet; I suspect that most would take this to be at best a borderline case of persuasion (as can be detected in the inclination of some to call such an example a case of "coercive persuasion" or "persuasive coercion")—and the reason *why* such a circumstance is a borderline case of persuasion can be elucidated by comparison to the elements shared by paradigm cases of persuasion (in this case, because "freedom of choice" is only questionably present). Hence by focusing on paradigm cases of persuasion one might be able to explicate the "core" of the concept, and thereby also explicate how it is that some circumstances turn out to be disputable (borderline) cases of the concept. Similarly, by focusing on paradigm cases of argument$_1$ and argument$_2$—that is, on cases that would elicit widespread agreement that these *are* cases of the concept in question—and by asking ourselves what these sorts of cases have in common, we may be able to clarify the concepts of argument$_1$ and argument$_2$.

Several aspects of this "paradigm case" way of proceeding are worth clarifying. First, this sort of analysis is not aimed at providing a definition. To say that the circumstance of the mugger with the gun held to one's head is not a paradigm case of persuasion is *not* to say that such a circumstance isn't a case of persuasion; some definitions of "persuasion" might include it, others might exclude it—but precisely because it is a borderline example it is not a paradigm case of persuasion. The point of analyzing the common features of paradigm cases of (say) persuasion is not to arrive at a list of necessary and sufficient conditions for something's being "properly" termed persuasion. The point, instead, is simply to get a better understanding of the concept by examination of the kinds of circumstances in which application of the concept would be largely straightforward and unobjectionable.

Second, to speak of paradigm cases of a concept is different from discussing the empirically most *common* cases of that concept. (I emphasize this because Willard [1979a] uses "paradigm case" and "exemplar" to refer to the most commonly occurring instances of a concept.) To focus on the most commonly occurring instances of a concept *presupposes* something like a definition for the concept; one can't determine what the most common mammal in Africa is unless one already has some way of deciding what is and is not to count as a mammal. Thus, for example, Willard's (1979a) assertion that "*typical* arguments rarely if ever take clear propositional form" (212; emphasis in original) depends directly on Willard's inclusion of "non-discursive forms" as arguments$_1$; someone who defined argument$_1$ in a different way could produce a different tabulation of the frequency of forms of argument$_1$. Hence asking about paradigm cases of a concept, because it does not involve having a definition of the concept, puts aside questions about the "most common cases" of the concept.

Third, this paradigm-case way of proceeding exploits—and rests upon—our common everyday understandings of terms. In a sense, the relevant questions are of the form "Would we ordinarily be inclined to call this a case of X (argument$_1$, argument$_2$)?" And as nothing more than procedural clarification, it may be useful to put the question this way: "If one were explaining the concept of X to a non-native speaker of English, would one offer this example as an aid to understanding?" This latter question, I think, can help one to focus on clear, straightforward examples of the concept in question—just the sorts of examples I am after here. But because my analysis will rest on ordinary understandings, it may sometimes appear as though I am making pronouncements about what is and isn't a paradigm case; and this may leave the unfortunate impression that I regard myself as the sole arbiter of what is and isn't a paradigm case. The ground of my analysis, however, is not any special status I claim for myself alone, but is my appeal to the reader's native sense of the concepts in question: if my intuitions about paradigm cases are idiosyncratic or skewed in some fashion, then my claims will not ring true to the reader's ear, and in that sense the claims advanced here may be said to be intersubjectively confirmable. By way of example: I believe that if one wanted to explain the concept of "furniture" to a non-native speaker, one would not likely use the example of a walnut-encased television set; such an object is not a paradigm case of "furniture" (it *may* be furniture—that depends on a definition—but it's not a paradigm case). The plausibility of my claim here rests on the degree to which my intuitions concretize generally held understandings about the concept of furniture, not on special capability I alone possess. And similarly for my analyses of argument$_1$ and argument$_2$.

So the matter to be pursued is this: What can we learn about our concepts of argument$_1$ and argument$_2$ by examining the sorts of cases that recommend themselves as exemplary cases of those concepts? In a way this may be seen to parallel earlier discussion of the two senses of "argument" (O'Keefe, 1977), for the issue there was: What can we learn about the notion of "argument" by examining the sorts of things to which the term is commonly applied? And the answer there was, roughly, that there is an important distinction to be noticed between arguments$_1$ and arguments$_2$. The present analysis thus can be seen as taking matters another step, by asking now about argument$_1$ and argument$_2$ individually.[3]

Argument$_2$

What is a paradigm case of an argument$_2$? What sorts of example would one offer to a non-native speaker who wished to understand what an argument$_2$ is? It seems to me that exemplary cases of argument$_2$ are simply interactions in which extended overt disagreement between the interactants occurs. Any time there is overt extended expression of disagreement, an argument$_2$ would ordinarily be said to be occurring.

Notice that overt disagreement itself (as against overt *extended* disagree-

---

[3] I should perhaps say explicitly that my use of paradigm cases here is not aimed at showing that the term "argument" has referents, and so is not a "Paradigm Case Argument" in the sense that such has been criticized by, among others, Gellner (1959) and Minas (1977).

ment) would not make for a paradigm case of an argument$_2$. If John says "Let's see a movie tonight," and Jane responds "Let's stay home instead," and John says, "Okay," there my have been overt disagreement, but this is clearly a minimal case of an argument$_2$. It is not the sort of example that recommends itself as useful for instructing the non-native speaker. If this disagreement had been extended (in a childlike way) so that the interaction ran "Let's see a movie tonight," "Let's stay home instead," "No, let's see a movie," "No, I think we should stay home!" "No, we should go to a movie!" then I think one would be more inclined to say that the interactants had been having an argument$_2$. It might not have been a "good" or "productive" or "rational" or "mature" argument$_2$, but I believe that in a perfectly ordinary and everyday sense John and Jane would be said to have been having an argument$_2$.

This explication of the paradigm case of argument$_2$ says nothing about the exchange of arguments$_1$. Now some theorists (such as Brockriede, 1977) would want to say that only interactions in which arguments$_1$ occur are genuine arguments$_2$. But this seems to me to fly in the face of common understandings about arguments$_2$. For instance, one can overhear a conversation being conducted in a foreign tongue and have no difficulty concluding that the interactants are having an argument$_2$—even though one cannot understand the words and hence is not in any position to say whether arguments$_1$ were being made.[4] Or one can see a couple in a restaurant obviously having an argument$_2$ yet not be able to hear what they are saying to each other (and hence not be able to say whether any arguments$_1$ were being made). Or one might see a parent come upon two children who are manifesting extended disagreement over the rights to a toy—yet who are not making arguments$_1$—and one would not be surprised to hear the parent say "Stop arguing!"

I am not suggesting that there are no differences between arguments$_2$ in which arguments$_1$ occur and arguments$_2$ in which arguments$_1$ do not occur. Nor am I suggesting that argumentation theorists and researchers should spend as much energy investigating arguments$_2$ that don't contain arguments$_1$ as they should studying arguments$_2$ that do. I am only pointing to

[4] It is not relevant here (or in the next example) that an observer might be *mistaken* in the judgment that these interactants were having an argument$_2$ (mistaken, say, because of cultural variation in the overt stylistic features of argumentative interactions, such as have been identified by Lein and Brenneis, [1978]). The point instead is that one's decision (mistaken or otherwise) that an argument$_2$ was occurring *did not depend on* one's knowing whether arguments$_1$ were being exchanged; that is, the basis on which one concludes that an argument$_2$ is occurring (the basis on which one relies in labeling an interaction as an argument$_2$) makes no reference to the presence of arguments$_1$.

what I take to be our common everyday understanding of "argument" (understood as argument₂). If one told our hypothetical non-native speaker that cases of overt extended disagreement where no arguments₁ occurred are *not* cases of argument₂, one would, I think, be misleading the non-native speaker about the ordinary meaning of "argument" (as argument₂).

It is perhaps worth re-emphasizing that what I am after is the everyday sense of "argument" (as argument₂). Argumentation scholars may have (for whatever reason) become accustomed to distinguishing "fights," "quarrels," "arguments," "tiffs," "squabbles," and "disputes" from one another on various grounds. But I do not believe that these things are all that carefully distinguished from one another in everyday talk. I cannot imagine, for example, everyday folk trying to decide whether it was a "quarrel" or an "argument" that the next-door neighbors were having; I cannot imagine a family counselor in a crisis center asking a client "Now was it a *dispute* that you were having with your spouse, or was it an *argument?*" I cannot imagine these things precisely because I think that the everyday sense of "argument" (as argument₂) paradigmatically refers simply to those cases in which extended overt disagreement occurs between interactants.[5]

Argument₁

I turn attention now to the question of a paradigm case of argument₁. This matter requires some preliminary ground-clearing, however, concerning the nature of argument₁.

Is argument₁ a speech act? I have previously characterized an argument₁ as "a kind of utterance or a sort of communicative act" (O'Keefe, 1977, 121). A similar characterization has been used by Burleson (1979, 139) and by Wenzel (1980, 113) in describing an argument₁ as "a type of speech act."

I am presently disinclined to think that these ways of characterizing argument₁ are very adequate. The difficulty I see can perhaps be made most clear by considering John Searle's (1969) discussion of speech acts. Searle's

---

[5] Consider, as one additional bit of evidence here, the following local newspaper story, headlined MAN STRUCK WITH BOARD IN ARGUMENT: "A Champaign man was briefly hospitalized Sunday after he reportedly was hit in the head with a board during an argument at a late night party." The man "was outside a party . . . when he began arguing with seven other men," one of whom "hit him in the head with a thick board." When the man called for help, "his assailant threw the board through the window of a car that slowed down in response." I rather much doubt that the reporter for this story, before labeling the interaction an "argument," inquired as to whether the interactants were actually exchanging arguments₁.

examination of speech acts involves examination of a variety of speech act verbs: to promise, to request, to recommend, to apologize, and the like. Thus there are the speech acts of promising, requesting, recommending, apologizing, and so forth. But we also have the notions of "a promise," "a request," "a recommendation." Now a promise is obviously not a speech act; promising is a speech act, and a promise is what is conveyed in that speech act. A recommendation is not a speech act; recommending is a speech act; and a recommendation is what is conveyed in that speech act.

I trust it is now clear why I would not want to say that an argument₁ is a speech act (or any other kind of act). An argument₁, like a promise or a recommendation, is something that is conveyed by some speech act. But what speech act?

If clarity is our aim, it won't do to say that "arguing" is the speech act that conveys an argument₁, for (as noted previously) "arguing" is ambiguous as between "arguing about" and "arguing that." Nor will it be quite satisfactory to say that "arguing that" is the speech act that conveys an argument₁, for (as discussed above) "arguing that" is (at least sometimes) not very different from "claiming that" or "suggesting that." So perhaps the most perspicuous label for the speech act that conveys an argument₁ is the phrase "making an argument."⁶

This distinction—between the speech act "making an argument" and the argument₁ that is conveyed by that speech act—has some important consequences to be discussed later. But for the paradigm-case line of analysis, the implication is that it is one thing to ask "In what sorts of circumstances would we be inclined to say that someone had made an argument₁?" and something very different to ask "What sorts of things would we be inclined to call arguments₁?" That is, we need to keep separate the question of paradigm cases of argument-making and the question of paradigm cases of argument₁.

Argument-making. So what is a paradigm case of someone's making an argument₁? What sorts of examples would one offer to a non-native speaker who wished to understand what it is to make an argument₁?

⁶Quasthoff (1978) has argued that the term "speech act" should not be used to refer to argument-making on the grounds that "argumentation as a form of verbal interaction is more than a sequence of basic speech acts like statements and justifications" (6). Her preferred term is Kallmeyer and Schutze's (1976) "action schema" (*Handlungsschema*), which she takes to be roughly equivalent to Gumperz's (1972) more familiar term "speech event." Argument-making is, she suggests, a "complex action" rather on a par with "telling a story, telling a joke, uttering an invitation, giving a report on something, etc." (7). There is

Perhaps it would be useful to start by noticing that the making of claims or suggestions is by itself a poor candidate. We would not ordinarily be inclined to say that someone who says "Let's see a movie tonight" has made an argument$_1$. Nor would the presentation of counterclaims or counter-suggestions, or the simple expression of disagreement, be good candidates for exemplary cases of argument-making. If John says "Let's see a movie tonight" and Jane responds "Let's stay home instead," we would not usually be inclined to say that Jane had made an argument$_1$. In general it would seem that expressing a position on an issue or offering a claim is, by itself, not sufficient to qualify as a paradigm case of making an argument$_1$ (if, indeed, such cases are even nonparadigmatic cases of argument-making).

What seems to be lacking from the cases discussed thus far is the overt expression of reasons. That is, the considerations expressed thus far would suggest that a paradigm case of making an argument$_1$ is a case in which a person makes a claim and overtly expresses a reason (or reasons) for that claim. But I think that even this is not sufficient, that there is an additional element of paradigm cases of argument-making: that both the claim and the overtly expressed reason(s) be linguistically explicable—which is not to say linguistically explicit. That is, in exemplary cases of argument-making, one should be able to *say what the argument$_1$ was*, to express linguistically both the claim and the overtly expressed reasons. The requirement that the claims and reasons be linguistically explicable is, it seems to me, warranted by the fact that we would surely not want to find ourselves in the position of having to say to our hypothetical non-native speaker "He just made an argument, but I can't tell you what the argument was." That is, paradigm cases of argument-making would seem necessarily to involve the linguistic explicability of the claims and the overtly expressed reasons involved.

This does not mean that paradigm cases of argument-making necessarily involve linguistically explicit claims. Consider, for instance, an exchange in which John says "Let's see a movie tonight" and Jane responds "There's nothing good showing." Surely we would want to say that Jane made an argument$_1$ (that she made a claim *and* that she overtly expressed a reason for that claim), even though all that is linguistically explicit is the overtly expressed reason. The claim is not linguistically explicit but is linguis-

certainly merit in the considerations Quasthoff raises—considerations bolstered by Jacobs and Jackson's (1979) findings concerning the "collaborative aspects" of argument-making—though my own feeling is that neither "action schema" nor "speech event" is completely satisfactory (as indeed Quasthoff acknowledges). Thus although I will use the term "speech act" as describing argument-making, I place no great stock in that usage and would welcome suggestions as to an alternative.

tically explicable: The claim is clearly something on the order of "We shouldn't see a movie tonight" (and the inference *that* such is the claim is warranted for actor and analyst alike by principles such as Grice's [1975] conversational maxims).[7]

This last example is one in which the *claim* is not linguistically explicit. Could there be a case in which the *overtly expressed reasons* were not linguistically explicit? In what sense might a reason be "overtly expressed" but not linguistically explicit? The most plausible cases I can imagine are ones like the following: (1) Imagine a circumstance in which a husband suggests to his wife that they go to a movie that evening and the wife's response is a grimace. Obviously enough, the wife has expressed a position on the issue. But she might also be said to have overtly (but nonverbally) expressed a *reason* for rejecting the suggestion, and that reason would be that she doesn't want to go. This circumstance is one in which the wants and desires of the parties involved are relevant to the decision, and hence nonverbal expressions of wants or desires might be counted as overtly expressed reasons. But I would not think the wife's grimace would be a *paradigm case* of making an argument$_1$. Rather it seems to me to be just the sort of "fringe" case that so often leads to definitional disputes; I don't think this example would be one likely to help our hypothetical non-native speaker. (2) Imagine that two persons have been having an argument$_2$ over the propriety of recombinant DNA research, one defending such research on grounds of its scientific utility, the other criticizing it on grounds of its incompatibility with fundamentalist Christian tenets. At one point, the defender of the research says "But I just don't see any reason why this research should be stopped." And in response the other simply points to a Bible. Now this pointing might well be said to overtly but nonverbally express a reason. But once again, this nonverbal act would not seem to be a *paradigm case* of making an argument$_1$; rather it strikes me as a borderline case similar to the previous example. These examples have led me to conclude that in a paradigm case of argument-making the overtly expressed reason must be not merely linguistically explicable but indeed linguistically explicit.

Thus my view is that a paradigm case of making an argument$_1$ involves the communication of both (1) a linguistically explicable claim and (2) one or more overtly expressed reasons which are linguistically explicit.

[7] Vis-à-vis such inferences, it may be noted that Willard (1976) makes much of analysts' putatively unwarranted "filling in" of missing (nonexplicit) parts of argument diagrams (such as diagrams based on Toulmin's model). What Willard seems to appreciate insufficiently are the conventional and conversational inferences and implicatures warranted—for both actor and analyst—by the very structure of human life, language, and interaction.

In saying that in paradigm cases of argument-making the overtly expressed reasons are linguistically explicit, I am *not* saying that a person's reasons for making a claim must be either linguistically explicit or explicable. Thus there is nothing in my analysis that conflicts with Willard's (1979a, 211) view that "non-discursive elements often reside at the center of a person's reasons and reasonings," so long as "reasons" and "reasonings" are understood as something different from *overtly expressed* reasons. A person may have unexpressed reasons for making a claim, and those unexpressed reasons may or may not be linguistically explicable. But the having of unexpressed reasons (whether linguistically explicable or not) is irrelevant to deciding whether someone has made an argument$_1$. One wouldn't tell the non-native speaker that uttering "Let's see a movie tonight" is an example of making an argument$_1$; and one wouldn't tell the non-native speaker that uttering "Let's see a movie tonight" is an example of making an argument$_1$ *so long as* the speaker was having certain kinds of unexpressed thoughts (reasons). That is, *regardless* of the nature or content of the unexpressed reasons of the speaker, uttering "Let's see a movie tonight" would not count as a paradigm case (if a case at all) of making an argument$_1$. It is not "reasons" in general but overtly expressed reasons that are important for deciding whether someone has made an argument$_1$.

Argument$_1$. What sorts of cases recommend themselves as paradigm cases of argument$_1$? Of what sorts of things would we ordinarily confidently say "That is an argument" (understood as argument$_1$)?

Presumably the answers to these questions cannot be wholly independent of the analysis of argument-making. Just as one's conception of a promise is presumably connected to one's notions about what it means to make a promise, so one's conception of argument$_1$ is likely related to the idea of argument-making. Hence we might profitably start with the possibility that paradigm cases of argument$_1$ are cases involving a claim and an associated reason (or reasons) for that claim. This is a common enough view of argument$_1$. For example, Burleson (1979, 141) holds that "an argument is composed of a claim and a statement or set of statements, adduced in its support," and Rieke and Sillars (1975, 48) define an argument (argument$_1$) as "a statement with the support for it."

But notice that both these explications (Burleson's and Rieke and Sillars') characterize argument$_1$ as in some way involving *statements*, either as the claim (Rieke and Sillars) or as the support/reason (Burleson). This is the sort of thing to which Willard has repeatedly objected:

> Despite their disagreements, most argumentation theorists seem to agree that "arguing" usually consists of making claims and providing reasons to support them. My only objection to this view is that it is usually colored by the assumption that the claims and the reasons must be linguistically serialized [1979a, 212].

But now some confusion has entered as a consequence of failing to distinguish clearly argument$_1$ and argument-making. Willard seems here to object to the assumption that in cases of *argument-making* the claims and reasons must be "linguistically serialized." That is something different from an assumption that in cases of *argument$_1$* the claims and reasons must be of a certain sort. This confusion between the conditions of something's being an argument$_1$ and the conditions under which we would say that someone had engaged in an act of argument-making (that is, that someone had made an argument$_1$) is in fact not uncommon. For example, what Burleson (1979, 141–143) describes as "characteristics of argument$_1$," appear in fact to be characteristics or features of argument-making. One characteristic he identifies begins this way: "Discourse is said to contain an argument [argument$_1$] only if. . . ." That is, it seems that Burleson's analysis is most perspicuously characterized as indicating the conditions under which we would be inclined to say that a bit of discourse contained an argument$_1$, that some speaker had made an argument$_1$.

I mention all this to help clarify the focus of the present section. We are here interested in (if you will) the *abstract object* "argument$_1$" and its features—*not* in the features of the act of argument-making. To draw the parallel: the focus is on *promises* and their features, not on *promising* and its characteristics.

Just as one feature of promises is that they are conveyed in acts of promising, so one feature of arguments$_1$ is that they are conveyed in acts of argument-making. Indeed, just as one feature of promises is that they are the sort of thing that *can* be conveyed in acts of promising, so one feature of arguments$_1$ is that they are the sort of thing that can be conveyed in acts of argument-making. And this in turn suggests that the analysis of paradigm cases of argument-making will indeed be helpful in identifying paradigm cases of argument$_1$. Just as one might inspect paradigm cases of promising to discover paradigm cases of promises, so one might examine paradigm cases of argument-making to discover paradigm cases of arguments$_1$.

The preceding analysis of paradigm cases of argument-*making* suggested that such cases involve the *communication* of both a linguistically explicable claim and one or more overtly expressed reasons that are linguistically explicit. Thus it might seem that a paradigm case of *argument₁* would be a case of both a linguistically explicable claim and one or more overtly expressed reasons that were linguistically explicit. But this is not completely satisfactory, for the requirement of "linguistic explicitness" for the "overtly expressed reasons" is a requirement tied to the behavioral expression of the argument₁ (that is, to the making of the argument₁)—not to the argument₁ qua argument₁. A more satisfactory explication is that paradigm cases of argument₁ involve a linguistically explicable claim and one or more linguistically explicable reasons. This formulation avoids any reference to the way in which an argument₁ is actually made (communicated); that is, this formulation more nearly distinguishes the abstract object "argument₁" from the act of argument-making.

But why the requirement that paradigm cases of argument₁ involve *linguistically explicable* claims and reasons? Why not simply suggest that paradigm cases of argument₁ involve "claims and reasons" *simpliciter?* My reasoning is this: When one points to paradigm cases of argument₁, one should be able to say what the argument₁ is—that is, one should be able to express linguistically both the claim and the reasons. If our hypothetical non-native speaker asked for an example of an argument₁, the most helpful example would presumably be one that involved something more than mere pointing, unintelligible grunting, or wild arm-flapping; one would want to be able to answer the question "What *is* the argument?" That is, my belief is that exemplary cases of argument₁ are ones in which one can *say* "The claim is such-and-such, and the reasons are thus-and-so." Thus my view is that paradigm cases of argument₁ are ones involving a linguistically explicable claim and one or more linguistically explicable reasons.

Some Consequences

The foregoing analysis has several consequences for the study of argument. These can conveniently be broken into those issuing from the distinction between argument-making and argument₁ and those issuing from the analysis of paradigm cases of argument₁ and argument₂.

Argument₁ and Argument-Making

One consequence of the distinction between the speech act "making an argument" and the argument₁ that is conveyed by that speech act is that it permits us to distinguish more clearly different interests one may have in examining the phenomena of argument$_1$. For example, Jackson and Jacobs' studies (1978, 1980; Jacobs and Jackson, 1979) are centered on the act of making arguments, whereas both Toulmin's (1958) model and the tools of the formal symbolic logician are focused on the arguments$_1$ that are (or might be) made.[8]

A second—and more important—consequence of the distinction is that it helps one to see how arguments$_1$ are describable apart from the particulars of their occurrence. Consider the analogy with promises. I can describe the promise that someone made to me apart from the utterances of the promiser in the act of promising; I can, so to speak, abstract the promise from its particular linguistic (or, more broadly, communicative) vehicle and describe it. Obviously the promiser's utterances are related to the promise that is made; but in describing the promise I am not describing the promiser's utterances per se, but rather (if you will) the import of those utterances. Given several acts of promising, I can abstract the several promises and compare them apart from the acts of promising in which they were conveyed; I might, for example, have some notion of the "structural elements" of promises (not to be confused with the structural elements of the act of promising)—perhaps such elements as what action was promised, conditions on fulfillment of the promise, the time at or by which the promised act is to be performed, and so on—and thus I could compare promises with respect to these various elements. I can of course also describe acts of promising (to see, perhaps, the various ways in which the act of promising is accomplished).

All this holds for arguments$_1$ and the making of arguments$_1$. I can describe the argument$_1$ that someone made apart from the utterances of the speaker in the act of making the argument$_1$; I can, that is, abstract the argument$_1$ from its particular communicative vehicle and describe it. Obviously the speaker's utterances are related to the argument$_1$ that is made; but in describing the argument$_1$ I am not describing the speaker's utterances per se but rather the import of those utterances. Given several acts of argument-making, I can abstract the several arguments$_1$ and compare them apart from the acts of argument-making in which they were conveyed; I

[8]It might be useful also to notice that there are different interests one may have in studying argument-making. One might be interested in the kinds of things that go on publicly, that is, in what happens overtly (as Jackson and Jacobs are). Or one might be interested in what happens covertly—in the psychological processes of "reasoning," in the cognitive machinations that lie behind a person's making certain arguments$_1$, or in the cognitive processes involved in what would ordinarily be called the reception of arguments$_1$ made by others (as is Hample, 1980).

might, for example, have some notion of the structural elements of arguments₁ (perhaps claim, warrant, qualifier, etc.?), and thus could compare arguments₁ with respect to those various structural elements. I can, of course, also describe acts of argument-making (to see, perhaps, the various ways in which the act of argument-making is accomplished).

Notice that, from this vantage point, there is nothing about arguments₁ that a priori rules out approaches such as those taken by Toulmin (1958) or the traditional symbolic logician. On the contrary, the very nature of arguments₁ (as versus the act of argument-making) is such as to legitimate their being abstracted from their linguistic (and kinesic, paralinguistic, proxemic) vehicles.

This conclusion is directly at odds with Willard's (1976) claims about "argument diagrams." His view is that such diagrams "have no descriptive value" (309) and that analysts should "eschew the use of descriptive diagrams entirely" (319). But his reasons for these broad claims are rather more limited. For example, he suggests that Toulmin-like diagrams cannot "adequately describe 'what happened'" (313) when an argument₁ was made; and that Toulmin-like diagrams are defective because "many of the forces that impel speakers to certain modes of persuasive behavior . . . are not expressible in language" (315). What these sorts of considerations might show is that Toulmin's model is a poor tool for representing argument-making, but they do not show that Toulmin-like diagrams are poor tools for representing arguments₁. It might be that to abstract acts of argument-making from their communicative vehicles would be objectionable; but, as I think I have shown, the abstraction of arguments₁ from their communicative vehicles— as one might do when using Toulmin-like diagrams—is not something intrinsically faulty.

None of this means that *any* use of (for example) Toulmin's model is legitimate (see, for example, Quasthoff's [1978] remarks on Settekorn [1977]), or indeed that Toulmin's model is itself entirely adequate (see Hample [1977] for a suggestion of the "structural inadequacy" of Toulmin's model). It only shows that there is nothing illegitimate about the *enterprise* in which Toulmin and traditional logicians are engaged, for that enterprise is focused on arguments₁ rather than on the act of making arguments₁.

A third consequence of the distinction between arguments₁ and argument-making is potentially some illumination of just how argument-making works in interaction. It is a commonplace observation that one rarely finds fully explicit arguments₁ in everyday talk ("fully explicit" in the sense that the conclusion and all of the premises—or the claim, data, warrant, and so forth—are all overtly expressed in talk). This has led many researchers to ask why the implicit elements are left implicit (see Jackson and Jacobs, 1980). But Quasthoff (1978) has turned the question around: Why are those argumentative elements that are explicit made explicit? Though the details of her analysis cannot be reproduced here, very broadly put she shows that there are several possible reasons for an argumentative element's being made explicit—some of which turn on the argument$_1$ that is being made (those overt parts that are "primarily logico-semantically motivated") and others of which turn on the interactional aspects of the act of argument-making (the overt parts "primarily motivated by their interactional function"). Thus, for instance, the explicitness of a warrant may be motivated by the fact that "one or more of the other positions of the argument simply have been left out" (30) or by the use of that explicitness as a "device for initiating or structuring" segments of the interaction (35). The important point for my purposes here is this: The observed features of argumentative interactions might be explained by reference to the characteristics of arguments$_1$ or—something rather different—by reference to the characteristics of argument-making (not to suggest that these are the only two possibilities), and hence a recognition of the distinction between argument$_1$ and argument-making seems important. I might parenthetically note that, against Willard's (1976) conclusion that Toulmin-like diagrams have *no* descriptive value whatever, Quasthoff's (1978) use of Toulmin diagrams in depicting arguments$_1$ seems to me to be a case in which the application of the model has proved quite valuable.

What these three consequences show, I think, is that the distinction between arguments$_1$ and argument-making is potentially a useful one in that it not only can help more clearly to distinguish different interests one may have in studying the phenomena of argument$_1$ but also can assist in providing a more careful analysis both of arguments$_1$ and of argument-making.

Paradigm Cases

But the present focus on "paradigm cases" of argument$_1$, argument-making, and argument$_1$ may also prove beneficial. Consider: For what sorts of objects or phenomena should one hold a theory of argument accountable? Where should one's research efforts be focused? These are obviously important questions, for by the answers one will judge the adequacy, powerfulness, and potential fruitfulness of alternative theories and research programs.

One response to questions such as these is that efforts should center on the most common forms of argument₁, that theories unable to account for these common forms are unsatisfactory. For example, Willard has argued that because argument diagrams based on Toulmin's model require the linguistic expression of propositions in arguments₁, "Toulmin's diagram . . . cannot depict one of the most common (therefore, important) genres of argument [argument₁], viz., argument produced through the conjunction of several artistic media [as in television commercials for beer, automobiles, and political candidates]" (Willard, 1976, 315). But this criticism depends on one's already having granted that such things *are* arguments₁; one who did not agree that these things were arguments₁ could hardly be expected to agree that these were "one of the most common genres" of argument₁ and so would not be likely to find much force in Willard's analysis. I think that what this shows is that *if* one has agreement on a definition of argument₁, then the way is cleared for a focus on the "typical" or "most common" cases, but that in the absence of such definitional agreement some alternative strategy is required.

My belief is that focusing on paradigm cases of argument₁, argument-making, and argument₂ provides such an alternative strategy. Paradigm cases are, by their very nature, those cases that elicit widespread agreement as to their being cases of the concept in question. Though it may be arguable whether an adequate argumentation theory will need to be able to account for "non-discursive symbolism" or "nonverbally expressed reasons," surely an adequate theory will need to be able to account for paradigm cases—and hence my view is that it is such cases that should engage one's attention at present. In the context of discussing arguments₁, Balthrop (1980, 203) has made this point nicely:

> Until the beast is better known, I would urge that investigations of argument [argument₁] center upon those items which are clearly identifiable as providing support or justification for claims advanced. It may, in truth, turn out that . . . nonverbal behavior can provide justification. . . . But to concentrate energies upon phenomena which are intuitively borderline is to run the risk that characteristics may be included as belonging to the giving of reasons in specific situations which are not essential to such activity and which might, in fact, obscure those which are. . . . The most effective use of time and intellect would seem to dictate concentration upon clear instances of argument.

Indeed, a focus on paradigm cases may be the most rapid way to improved argumentation theories: A theory that encounters difficulties in handling borderline cases may or may not be badly defective—but a theory that cannot account for paradigm cases is surely a poor one.

In urging a focus on paradigm cases, I would not want to leave the impression that I think something is wrong with focusing on some *subset* of paradigm cases. For example, one's attention might center on those paradigm cases of argument$_2$ in which arguments$_1$ are exchanged. As Burleson (1979a, 126) has noted, the present explication of paradigm cases of argument$_2$ (as interactions in which extended overt disagreement between interactants occurs) "necessarily includes a wide array of phenomena not traditionally of interest to argumentation scholars." It may well be the case, as he suggests, that a focus on those arguments$_2$ in which arguments$_1$ occur will be "more useful" for argumentation theorists' purposes, and nothing in the present analysis is aimed at undermining such a more restricted scope of attention. But I would want to caution that such a restricted focus ought not blind one to the possibility that illumination of arguments$_2$-with-arguments$_1$ might be had by also examining arguments$_2$-without-arguments$_1$. Just as Jackson and Jacobs (1980) have suggested that cases of extended disagreement evolve from fundamental structures found in cases of simple disagreement, so it might be that the characteristics of arguments$_2$-with-arguments$_1$ can be better understood with reference to arguments$_2$-without-arguments$_1$. For instance, what makes argument$_2$ a "rational decision-making procedure" (as it has often been characterized)? Where is the putative "rationality" of argument$_2$ as a decision-making procedure to be located? It surely cannot be something intrinsic to argument$_2$, for (as I think I have shown) it is possible to have—in a perfectly ordinary sense—an argument$_2$ without arguments$_1$ being exchanged, and yet such cases of argument$_2$ would hardly be called examples of rational decision-making procedures at work. Thus I suspect that one clue to the "rationality" of argument$_2$ as a decision-making procedure is likely to be found in a comparison between arguments$_2$-with-arguments$_1$ and arguments$_2$-without-arguments$_1$ (as has already been conducted implicitly, I think, by Burleson, 1979a).

Conclusion

I have taken considerable pains to be careful and clear in my discussions of argument$_1$, argument-making, and argument$_2$ (to the point that I might be accused of pedantry). But it is important to proceed in this way if progress in argumentation theory and research is to be had. Others may find it satisfactory to speak more loosely. But for my own part I cannot see the value of, for example, speaking of a contrast between "argument-as-structure" and "argument-as-interaction" when there is already work (see Boggs, 1978; Goodwin, 1974) displaying the *structural* features of argumentative *interactions* (arguments$_2$). Nor can I discern the utility of speaking of a contrast between "argument-as-product" and "argument-as-process" where this latter phrase is intended as a gloss for the concept of argument$_2$ given that the production of arguments$_1$ obviously has "processual" features (see Jackson and Jacobs, 1980). Yet these ways of speaking are common (see Kneupper, 1978; McKerrow, 1980; Wenzel, 1980; Willard, 1979c; Zarefsky, 1980). Similarly, statements such as "When people argue they typically do X" may not make it clear whether the claim is that persons typically do X in the course of making arguments$_1$ or that persons typically do X in the course of having arguments$_2$—though obviously these are rather different claims. Maintaining clear distinctions is often an inconvenient matter, but the price of convenience may be a hopelessly muddled enterprise. My aim here has been to offer some clarifications that may permit avoidance of such a muddle.

CHARLES ARTHUR WILLARD

[2]   Argument Fields

I want to make some progress toward saying what argument fields are by considering the modes of research and criticism appropriate to their study. Specifically, I will propose a broad methodological stance based on *verstehen* assumptions (Weber, 1949) and a critical posture consistent with (but different from) hermeneutics (Gadamer, 1975, 1976). So proceeding, I hope to be able to say what argumentation's subject matter is. In particular, I hope to make a plausible case for defining argumentation as the branch of epistemics that studies field practices.

Plausible methodological choices, however, presume a coherent theory of fields, for such choices may otherwise be haphazard. The constructivist/interactionist view of argument (Willard, 1978, 1978a, 1978c, 1979, 1979b, 1979c) has already suggested an embryonic field theory (Willard, 1980, 1908c, 1981a, 1981b, 1981c); and the first part of this essay elaborates this view of fields. My aim is to show not that this is the only correct doctrine, but that it is a plausible account of sufficient depth to permit coherent methodological choices.

The second part, proceeding on the theoretic groundwork of the first, considers the methods and practices appropriate to field studies. Since to know a field is to know its practices (Kuhn, 1970), my aim will be to refine and flesh out the theory further, to illuminate the special problems it poses, and to exemplify certain methodological advantages.

In the third section I argue that defining argumentation's subject matter as the study of fields yields a clearer view of argumentation's fit into other intellectual traditions. In particular I suggest that argumentation might be the taproot of "epistemics" (Willard, 1981b), a recently developed interdisciplinary enterprise concerned with the creation, acquisition, and uses of knowledge.

In short, I hope to give a plausible account of what fields are, to refine and elaborate that account by considering the methodological commitments appropriate to it, and to speculate about the utility of this scheme for solving certain traditional problems. My arguments concerning these three aims are concretized through a sustained examination of a paradigm case—the field of cost-benefit analysis.

To forestall an objection: I do not claim that the methodological principles I sketch for the examination of argument fields are completely satisfactory or that they exhaust the possibilities consistent with the theoretical stance I offer. A theory's reach should exceed its grasp, or what's a paradigm for?

The Constructivist/Interactionist View of Fields

If a history of the field concept is ever written, it will record that scholars united around an intuitively attractive but astonishingly vague idea and that, as they hashed out alternatives for clarifying the concept, they gradually replaced the seminal intuition with more elaborate and markedly different theories. The starting point was Toulmin's (1958) straightforward conviction that people organize their affairs around incommensurable bodies of knowledge. From the outset, attempts to elaborate this vision ran into seemingly intractable difficulties, often stemming from paradigmatic differences in what fields were thought to be and in the jobs field theory was supposed to perform. There developed, for instance, disagreements about what sort of work one does in drawing distinctions between fields: is one doing sociology, applied logic, or psychology? These disagreements were exacerbated by the fact that the most promising schemes drawn from sociology, logic, and psychology did not clearly square with the rhetorical and communication principles that were thought to be preconditions of a good field theory. Toulmin, for instance, tied argument fields to logical types. But no one has succeeded in making this account square with conventional wisdom about the context-embeddedness of utterance (Willard, 1981a).

Attempts to equate fields with academic disciplines and impersonal "conceptual ecologies" (Toulmin, 1972; McKerrow, 1980, 1980a) have proved equally uncongenial to communication concepts (Willard, 1981b, 1981c). These accounts work best when the activities of field actors are thought to be trivial and when "progress" is said to be a characteristic not of practices but of the conceptual ecologies themselves. Foucalt's (1972) attempts to define "domains of objectivity" by describing the principles of "the emergence of concepts" has more promise but awaits the development of a full-blown field theory based on the structure of conversation (see Jacobs and Jackson, this volume). The differences between these views are not clearly understood because they are embryonic. As I see it, the main difficulty is that no single agreed-upon encompassing principle is at hand to provide an objective stance while respecting the differences and interrelationships among fields. In various ways, every field uses induction, deduction, arguments from analogy and sign, qualitative and quantitative data, scientific and humanistic arguments, and the like. Their languages have grammar and syntax; their practices depend upon social interaction in similar ways; and their beliefs and practices are sometimes similar enough to make us wonder whether the field notion can be sustained at all.

Quite apart from problems of distinguishing among fields is the problem of labeling our thinking. We have "epistemic communities," "communities of discourse," "rhetorical communities," "groups and organizations," "collective mentalities," "disciplines," "domains of objectivity," and countless permutations of these. These labels reflect different disciplinary orientations and analytic purposes; they draw distinctions that cut rather differently and they focus on different phenomena.

The most striking source of dispute has not been made explicit. It concerns the relationship of field theory to the philosophy of science. Believing the sciences to be the most consistently successful epistemic enterprises, we are tempted to take their conceptual ecologies as models of all communal knowledge. But this is not a straightforward matter. First, there are important differences between scientific "progress" (Laudan, 1977) and progress in ordinary fields (Willard, 1980). Second, there are sharp disputes within science about "sociological versus rational" explanations of progress. This disarray undermines the only justification for tying field theory to the philosophy of science: we tie field theory to the philosophy of science only if we think that "progress" is the main thing we want to explain; thinking this way, we make field theory a footnote to a dispute that is unlikely to be settled. Third, it is now conventional wisdom that the natural sciences cannot serve as models for the social sciences. The arguments favoring this view have proved so strong that it can plausibly be said that the social sciences—and even ordinary activities—are better models for understanding the "hard" sciences (Willard, 1981c, 1981d). Thus, while field theorists agree that field theory must include the sciences, there are sharp disputes about what their status should be.

These disputes are not insoluable, but they are likely to prove obdurate.

For one thing, the best paradigm cases of "knowledge" (the natural sciences or the history of ideas) have not been unqualified successes in exemplifying "knowing." "Knowing" is often equated with entering a domain of objectivity. This is circular as long as the "sociological versus rational" dispute remains unsettled. For another thing, field theorists are trying to settle these disputes by virtue of assumptions that are muddled and contestable. For instance, some theorists want the field idea to do the work of the grand formal systems Toulmin used the field notion to discredit. They seek universal justificatory principles. This makes social practices out to be desiderata, Russell's "layers of misconception" waiting to be peeled away to get at the verities. This trivializes fields just as Plato's cave metaphor trivialized perception (Willard, 1981a). While everyone agrees that field theory describes a relativity, the ways societies are balkanized into distinguishable domains, there are disputes about whether this relativity must result in a relativ*ism*. Because the natural sciences are taken to be the benchmark of epistemic success, the importance of the "sociological versus rational" dispute is taken for granted. Recent disputes have thus borne striking resemblances to the older arguments about the grand formal systems. The search is still for universal guarantors, impartial standpoints, logical principles, or felicity conditions of discourse (Wenzel, 1979, 1980; Burleson, 1979, 1979a, 1979b, 1979c; McKerrow, 1980, 1980a, 1980b, 1980c). When empirical programs are made to serve grand universalistic agendas, they inevitably focus upon stable and precise features of fields while ignoring the sources of instability and change. The intelligence of Toulmin's program is that he seeks recurring themes in the ways of conceptual change. But this requires that the powerful relativity of fields that permitted his critique of absolutism and the "cult of systematicity" be softened and blurred as he seeks his impartial standpoint of rationality (Willard, 1980, 1980c).

But even loose field theories strengthen the arguments that brought the absolutists down. In particular, they fuel the *tu quoque* argument by grounding it empirically.[1] If you make a claim and I reply "How do you

---

[1] The term *tu quoque* is variously used. Strictly put, it is a reply to attacks upon knowledge claims: *you too* are vulnerable. Sometimes called the "two wrongs" argument, the *tu quoque* involves showing that one's critic is open to his own criticism. Skeptics impute irrational bases to formalistic systems; and Weimer (1979, 6) uses *tu quoque* as a label for three claims: (1) that views of rationality are always rooted in irrational commitments, so (2) everyone has a right to make whatever commitments they choose, and (3) these commitments are beyond critique. A looser use of the *tu quoque* involves using it as a label for infinite-regress arguments as relativists and absolutists impute similar weaknesses to one another. A still looser

know?," the bare fact of interfield differences undermines your ability to point to a body of judgmental or veridical standards as a final guarantor of your claim. If you try to stop infinite regress by embracing a standard, I shall confront you with an incommensurable standard from another field to buttress the demand that you further justify your stopping point. And so on—forever. Any universal must succeed in a way consistent with its internal assumptions in refuting or subsuming particular field standards that contradict or bypass it. The grand formal schemes were brought down by the skeptical critique's proof that they could not meet their own standards of justification; field theory attacks universal projects from outside by forcing consideration of empirical differences *in principle*.

I want to bypass all this on the grounds that social practices are worthy of study in themselves. On the assumption that the universalists are unlikely to defeat the combined offensive of the skeptical critique and field theory anytime soon, I have tried in recent essays (1980, 1980c, 1981b, 1981c) to piece together a coherent view of fields that avoids these difficulties. What follows is an attempt to tie these piecemeal sketches together.

1.1   *Fields are real sociological entities.* The field notion can overarch terms such as "groups," "organizations," "frameworks," and "relationships." It can so function if we assume that in making claims about fields we are making three sorts of sociological claims: (1) *Unity is imputed to a social entity*—actors unify around beliefs, standards, rhetorical appeals, relationships, and political aims; (2) *unity is presumed to stem from something*, either from the phenomena mentioned in (1) or from the people themselves, their faith in certain communal standards; and (3) *unity and its sources are presumed to have effects*, we make causal claims (however loose) about the relationships among social phenomena. By virtue of one or all of these implicit sociological claims, fields are said to be distinguishable points of stability.

Think of a field as a constellation of practices organized around one or a few dominant assumptions. It might seem diffuse at first glance if its *Weltanschauungen* are not obvious; its theories and practices might seem strat-

---

version of the argument is as a term for "turning an opponent's argument against him." There are two recurring ideas in these strict and loose uses of *tu quoque*: it is a *process* (or posture) of argument about someone's *presuppositions*. As an expositional convenience, I want to use *tu quoque* as a broad label encompassing all of these ideas. It can stand for the familiar features of the skeptical critique *combined with* the special implications of field theory *as if* these different arguments were a monolithic objection. So viewed, it is a tactic, a posture, and a line of argument often present in *interfield disputes* that turn on absolutistic claims, though it crops up differently as actors adopt different argumentative lines.

ified and compartmentalized; there may be no grand premise out of which all else can be deductively derived. A closer look may reveal recurring themes, especially understandings about the range of events to which certain practices are appropriate and about the degree of fit between practices and events. If enough recurring themes are found to permit the inference that they comprise a tradition of activity, we have a field.

Cost-benefit analysis (CBA) pursues a variety of practices yielding the recurring theme that value claims must be reduced to the same quantitative language used to express fiscal costs—expressing the value of human lives in dollar terms. Another theme is that CBA analysts see themselves in an advisory, not a policy-making capacity.

No obvious sociological threshold of cohesion marks fields off from other communal activities. Social relations vary dramatically in the extent to which they require allegiance, involvement, and frequency of association. "Cohesion" is a term that works best when loosely defined. Apart from the difficulties of framing a definition that fits empirical phenomena (which weakened early attempts to define "groups") is the possibility that a rigid and brittle sense of "cohesion" is beside the point we want to make. One does not become a cost-benefit analyst by virtue of formal memberships. CBA crops us in disciplines ranging from economics to legal philosophy. While memberships in professional guilds *may* bear upon one's practices, we cannot know this without studying the practices. Also, the professional associations are themselves balkanized ("psychology" subsumes "Freudianism," "behaviorism," and "constructivism") whose *practices* are incommensurable.

Nor can we say that fields are "organized" while other domains are not: children's games and cocktail parties are organized. A looser idea like "degrees of organization" does no better if ordinary activities like games are more tightly knit than aggregations we intuitively want to say are fields, such as aesthetics. Toulmin uses such a distinction to separate "rational enterprises" from ordinary assocations by virtue of their professional character. As a sociological claim this has the defect of assuming what it must prove: that formal memberships in guilds are sure guides to understanding practices. In ordinary *and* professional spheres, people exhibit the same variability in their ties to groups; they are "multivalent" (Lee, 1966), moving from group to group, displaying different allegiances, and defining their actions in different ways. Not all economists are CBA analysts and not all CBA actors are economists.

So the field idea will not distinguish among kinds of groups. For sociological purposes, let us say that *field* and *group* are synonymous because they denote the same social boundaries. Terms like "cohesion" and "organization" work best for narrow views of groups and least well for the expansive sense of group I have in mind—an aggregation of any size with a communal sense of "we-ness" embodied in the recurring themes in its practices. On this basis, I have distinguished (1980, 1980c) four senses of "field": (1) *Encounter fields*, relations among strangers, conversations, special understandings created for particular interactions; (2) *relational fields*, sustained clusters of encounters between spouses, friends, lovers, and professional colleagues; (3) *issue fields or schools of thought*, larger groupings based on paradigms, positions on issues ("behaviorism" is a disciplinary school of thought; the proabortion movement is an ordinary issue field; as going concerns, issue fields are made up of encounter and relational fields); and (4) *normative fields*, a reformed version of the "reference group" that overlaps and interplays with the first three senses of field; if someone takes influence from the beliefs of a group while no longer actively involved with the group (as when one follows religious teachings while no longer a church member), one is referring to a normative field. In other ways, normative fields are the same things as issue fields.

Overlaid on these senses of field is the distinction between ordinary and disciplinary activities (Willard, 1980, 1980c). This captures the difference between (say) a group organized around a political-action goal and one centered on an epistemic goal of "getting better." Ordinary fields are apt to take a body of knowledge for granted and to act upon it for political or social aims. Disciplines are apt to focus on making a body of knowledge better. This is not a strict dichotomy, but it is a useful working distinction between ordinary and professional activities.

This list displays the crude outlines of my thinking; we shall doubtless want to narrow or broaden it later. But it suggests the breadth of phenomena I want the field notion to serve. I want "field" to overarch "groups," "social frameworks," "social relationships," "communities of discourse," and so on. In speaking of fields we are referring to *real* social aggregations animated by the activities of flesh-and-blood people whose actions have effects.

Think of fields as living, breathing organisms. People breathe life into them through their defining activities in the sense that Chicago School Interactionists (Blumer, 1966) insist that groups exist in and through the social interactions of their members. They *are* their actions. Communal life is made up of the mutual accommodations actors make to the perspectives of others, their temporary inhibitions of their own actions (Mead's "I") to assess the imported expectations of others (Mead's "me"). The field notion is thus a way of fleshing out Mead's view of the "generalized other" (Jacobs and Jackson, this volume). The assumption is that "this picture of human society as action must be the starting point (and the point of return) for any scheme that purports to treat and analyze human society empirically" (Blumer, 1966, 6).

1.2 *Field theory studies "objectifying," not objectivity*. Objectifying is a "social comparison process" (Festinger, 1954) by which we enter a domain of objectivity to check our thinking. It is synonymous with "passing muster on claims." It is not the sole motive for entering fields (just as we say that young scholars often enter disciplines because they identify with certain professors) but it is an important practice one does once in a field. A Catholic theologian may enter that domain for its authority and a political activist might pick up and use the principles of a discipline to buttress claims. "Objectifying" thus proceeds variously and is differently motivated.

Notice that this thinking fits field theory into the traditional concerns of argumentation; it specifies the indispensible preconditions for success in the analysis of arguments. It stipulates that argumentation be the study of how people pass muster on claims and that if more universal analytic standards for judging arguments are sought they will be derived as recurring themes in such ordinary practices. If theorists want to make broad analytic claims about particular arguments, field theory is a way of specifying what they will have to do to justify their right to make such claims.

This is worth insisting upon: analytic claims have to square with sociological practices; they cannot make impossible demands on arguers; they cannot propose standards no one can meet. This is why I argued that the grand ontological projects need to be set aside. Field theory defines the empirical work necessary to securing universal standards for judging arguments.

Philosophers of science are divided along two lines for explaining "progress," (1) progress is a social-psychological phenomenon, and (2) progress is a "rational" accomplishment of conceptual ecologies (Laudan, 1977). Proponents of (1) focus on uncontroversial social practices—scientists *do* associate and communicate; convention and orthodoxy *are* powerful influences on the willingness of a community to accept change; some theories are devised and gain followers for social, economic, and political reasons. Proponents of (2) do not deny these things happen; they question that such things are "genuine" progress. They sharply distinguish between why such claims are accepted and why they are *worthy* of acceptance. Proponents of (1) focus on *belief* while proponents of (2) focus on something much like the analytic view of justified true belief: A is justified in believing X if and only if A believes X, X is true, and A believes X for the right reasons. If you think the third condition collapses to a social-psychological statement, that "correctness" is inevitably conventional (a matter of the orthodoxies and traditions of fields) you probably side with the proponents of (1). If you believe the third condition *proves* the second (the right reasons prove X is true) you are likely to downgrade the importance of the first condition and to equate correctness with progress—thus siding with those who seek "genuine" standards.

If you entertain the possibility that the third condition is *any* sense socially grounded—even granting that it might be analytically rooted as well—you may believe that the dispute between the "conventionalists" and the "rationalists" is premature. If any claim about the social grounding of a knowledge claim is nontrivial, if it bears upon the probity of the knowledge claim, it is in principle possible that the two are *interdependent*. The "rationalists" inevitably make social practices and orthodoxies trivial in just the way that holding field theory hostage to universalistic schemes trivializes fields. But they cannot do this in a principled way consistent with their own standards of good argument.

By defining fields as constellations of practices, traditions of activity, and recurring uses of theories, we avoid getting bogged down in the "progress" dispute. "Progress" for now becomes just what field actors take it to be—political success would be one sort of progress; the avoidance of some procedural problem in science, social life, and politics would be another.

Think about it this way: every field is a corollary to the traditional dispute between conventionalists and rationalists, a naturally occurring organization of practices by which actors seek to impose order on phenomena and to make their activities seem rational. Whatever "rationality" is, every field displays assumptions about it that are worthy of our attention; and since we do not possess the conceptual equipment for drawing sharp judgments upon field views (that is, we are not equipped to point to this or that theory of rationality as being correct or incorrect), it seems justified to proceed as if field practices and assumptions are important in and of themselves.

The merit of this thinking is that it does social-psychological and analytic work, thus opening the door to holistic claims about the sources of "genuine" claims. In subsuming (or ignoring) the traditional dichotomy of *social versus genuine*, it permits the working assumption that the two views of knowledge are interdependent rather than antagonistic polar opposites.

The progress dispute itself may be a universal; virtually all fields have their special versions. The social comparison notion seems to dovetail into this dispute by its stipulation that fields are communal domains into which people enter to check their thinking or bodies of knowledge people may draw upon to buttress their claims. The field notion is thus a way of talking meaningfully about social life in a way that does justice to the dialectical tension between private points of view and communal standards. Every statement on the order of "A believes X correctly" makes at least two simultaneous judgments: "A believes that he believes X correctly" and "A is by some standard correct." It is arguably the case that each standard is an ephiphenomenon of the other; that is, it is not self-evidently absurd to say "A believes correctly because he is right" and conversely "A is right because this or that standard makes him right." If either case is plausible the sociological view is nontrivial.

1.3   *Fields are psychological perspectives*. Think of fields as alternative ways of construing phenomena. This is consonant with the later Wittgenstein's doctrine that expressions are embedded in language games that are embedded in forms of life. The thrust of this thinking is apparent whenever we plug content into the three conditions of justified true belief mentioned above; instead of making an abstract claim about all knowledge, we make a particular claim about a particular belief, such as "A correctly believes a virus causes cancer because a virus *does* cause cancer." This expression gets meaning from conventional, standardized rules for using such expressions, the language game being played. This narrow enterprise itself takes meaning from a larger tradition of language use, the *field*. Wittgenstein used "forms of life" to say that every expression and language game occurs within the context of a broader tradition of practices.

A cost-benefit analyst might tell a court that "For present purposes, a human life is worth $220,000; this is a workable yardstick for determining damages and awards in this instance of disaster litigation." The expression takes significance from the equations special to CBA—the ways the $220,000 figure was arrived at. The *practice* of reducing value claims to tangible quantities (in this case, equating human lives with dollar amounts) and the broad assumptions justifying it coalesce to form a field of discourse, a "form of life," a general orientation toward activities of a particular sort.

I want to pursue a three-way analogy between cognitive development, socialization into argument fields, and participant observation as a research procedure. There are enough functional similarities among these three processes to illuminate one another; perpsective-taking is central to all three.

Perspective-taking is both a precondition and a product of the symbolic exchanges by which children build interpretive schemes for predicting events (Ryan, 1974; Shotter, 1974; Harré, 1974). Development proceeds "orthogenetically" (Werner, 1957; Crockett, 1965; Delia, 1976) from relative simplicity and lack of differentiation toward cognitive complexity (hierarchic integration of constructs, greater articulation within them, and expanded differentiation among them). As Piaget believed, "decentering" is a precondition of socialization since a child cannot enter a social world without increasing ability to adapt to the perspectives of others (Flavell, 1968; Adams-Weber, 1979; Clark and Delia, 1976; Delia and Clark, 1977). Crudely put, children become more adept at social interaction by recognizing differences between others' perspectives and their own and by expanding their repertoire of constructs for interpreting other people (Livesley and Bromley, 1973; Chandler, 1977) and acquiring interpretive schemes for strategically adapting to the expectations of others (Clark and Delia, 1977).

Socialization into an argument field proceeds in this way, although some of the details of developmental theory do not fit into all cases of entering a field. Consider that the *family* is the group into which children are first socialized and that the family is a *relational argument field*. I am *not* proposing in the manner of Tonnies, Durkheim, Simmel, or Cooley that the family is a "primary" group that endows larger social organizations with informing ideals. The family may be regarded as an argument field because it is organized around background assumptions, routines, and taken-for-granted beliefs to such a degree that it can legitimately be regarded as a community of discourse. If Cooley was correct in saying that a family is organized around "an intense feeling of we-ness," this is so because its members are able to take for granted certain assessments of the perspectives of the other members.

The precondition of entering an argument field is to construe certain phenomena in roughly the way that other actors in the field construe them. Cognitive development proceeds via social comparison processes (Willard, 1979, 1979a); socialization likewise succeeds as a person learns to objectify interpretations in the orthodox ways of a field. Objectivity is thus a subjective accomplishment (Willard, 1979) rather than the antagonistic opposite of subjectivity; it is a stance a person may take, a point of view toward phenomena a person can shift to when one requires a dialectical test of his or her subjective interpretations. Social comparison is thus the importation of the assessed views of a particular other or a generalized other; field theory is a way of describing generalized others.

I have discussed elsewhere the analytic complexities of making claims such as "A is in field X," "A is arguing from field X," and "Field X has N characteristics" (Willard, 1981c). My conclusion was that one can plausibly and coherently plug content into such statements if and only if one's organizing model is the construing person engaged in role-taking and social comparison. An important element of this argument is the assumption that people enter fields by virtue of symbolic interactions with other people—which I take to be a sound reason for defining fields in terms of the ongoing lines of interaction of their members rather than equating them with their documents (Willard, 1980, 1980c). This reinforces the present analogy with development: just as social exchanges with others provide children with the social comparisons necessary to elaborating their interpretive schemes for social life, so interactions with field actors are the bases on which the uninitiated enter fields.

Epistemic betterment is an *effect* of entering a field; it may or may not be a person's reason for entrance. We possess a battery of traditional concepts for explaining the motives people have for social comparison: graduate students may adopt a paradigm because their professors do, as a matter of identification or of authority; they may adopt a perspective because "most people do." In many respects, this parallels the choices children make in development. I have elsewhere spelled out the reasons for adopting a "smidgeon of functionalism" (Willard, 1980c), namely, that people enter into domains because doing so seems to serve some function. If we can pinpoint the "jobs" a field is believed to perform, the reasons people enter it, we will have gone far toward defining the field.

Participant observation is a broad term we often use to describe studying groups by being socialized into them in the way that their members are (Bruyn, 1966). Perspective-taking is thus the core process of research (Denzin, 1970)—the idea being to participate in the social processes of a group as its members do, to see them and to use them just as members do. So proceeding, the researcher aims at personal understanding of a field's practices. While the term *verstehen* has been variously operationalized (by stances ranging from disinterested nonparticipant observation to "wallowing in experience," or becoming a member of a group in *every* sense), here is what I want it to mean (Bruyn, 1966, 13–21): the participant observer aims to make a series of *controlled decisions* for (1) entering into ongoing social events and dealing with a field's actors *as if* one of them—I explain the "as if" maxim below; (2) taking the perspectives of normal members of a field in order to see their practices as they do; (3) producing coherent accounts of being socialized into a field; and (4) while taking a field at face value (that is, at its own definition, taking its assumptions to be true just as its members do) maintaining sufficient detachment to permit description of these assumptions. My core assumption here—which some participant observers do not share—is that one does not need to become a naive actor in a field in order to describe what it is like to be a naive actor; that is, to reflectively assess and monitor the background understandings that permit unreflective action.

There are exemplars of this research that while not directed at the field idea illuminate the analogy I am trying to draw. Znaniecki (1940, 1952, 1955, 1968) defended the "humanistic coefficient"—by which he meant that data always reflect the researcher's assumptions and that the researcher's ties to the people studied are important data. His epic study (Thomas and Znaniecki, 1918–1920) thus attempts to see mundane social practices as their practitioners see them. During the 1920s, researchers following Simmel's lead produced studies of the social interactions animating particular groups (see Bruyn's 1966 review, 10–11); the aim was to recreate the lived experiences of actors in a group (Lindbloom, 1924) and to describe groups as an insider (Kluckhohn, 1940; Schwartz and Schwartz, 1955; Whyte, 1955, Junker, 1960)—prison life, for example, could be described by becoming a prisoner or a guard (Reimer; 1937). More recent work has probed the background awareness of marriages (Berger and Kellner, 1970; Waller and Hill, 1951) and of the physician–patient relationship in gynecological examinations (Emerson, 1970). In each case, the rhetorical force of explicit and implicit rules is said to be the glue binding fields together (Cicourel, 1964, 1970, 1974; Anderson, 1974; Attwell, 1974; Denzin, 1970; Mehan and Wood, 1976; Psathas, 1973). Just as scientists engage in "normal" activities (Kuhn, 1970), actors in all fields organize their practices around conventional procedures to sustain the sense that "nothing unusual is happening" (Emerson, 1970a).

Thus a three-way analogy between cognitive development, field socialization, and participant observation seems plausible. All three similarly depend upon perspective-taking and social comparison; observations of all three illuminate the others. Thus, to understand CBA we observe CBA actors at work: my research has benefited from observing the efforts of undergraduates learning to work with CBA's special assumptions, language, and techniques (Willard, 1980c). CBA comes to life when we try to use it to formulate particular policies. We can study, for instance, how the courts use CBA to assign dollar values to lost lives in disaster litigation— one measure being the "income model," which produces claims such as "the old people don't yield the cash value the young ones do" (Willard, 1980c) in speaking of people killed in an air crash. Young lives are worth more than older ones when measured against potential income.

1.4   *A loose sense of group best serves our aims.* I want to run a loose ship respecting the lines we draw between fields. If fields are real social entities and (as 1.1 above argues) real entities blur together because their boundaries are fuzzy, our theoretical distinctions must reflect this fuzziness. We should not insist upon distinctions that are more rigid than is justified by the "group" literature. Having argued that membership, cohesion, and organization are undependable defining criteria for groups, I need only add that *informal* structures are interdependent with formal structures— making strict demarcations based on formal declarations unwise. Thus we cannot define fields axiomatically: our thinking must respect the loose and fuzzy boundaries, intermittent as well as zealous ties to groups, variations in cohesion and frequency of contact, and differing interactions of formal and informal group structures.

We require a methodological stance that respects the differences between fields, explains their similarities and shared ideas, and captures the continual dialectic between situated actors and conventions. We need defining principles that do justice to the view of *social interaction* that has helped clarify the three preceeding propositions.

1.5   *Fields are "domains of objectivity"* (Foucalt, 1972). To use Searle's (1969) example, I can enter the institution of *promising* to make social affairs predictable and rational; the arguments of philosophers help me assess my obligations when I promise. To make an administrative decision, I might enter CBA. In both cases, I implicitly or explicitly decide to *attend to* the claims made by the fields' main theories. If I must devise a municipal budget that balances the needs of the poor against the costs of public safety (or these demands versus supporting the orchestra or art museum), CBA is an institution of assumptions that helps me clarify my options (by expressing values and their costs in the same language). If this account is plausible, we may speak of people entering domains in order to deal with situations; a decision to "go and get" some objectivity always springs from a definition of situation.

Respecting this claim, there is an important difference between ordinary and disciplinary fields. Ordinary fields may consult many domains of objectivity and make no attempt to combine them in a logically unified whole. Antinuclear power advocates thus refer to the claims of engineers, physicists, biologists, epidemiologists, and physicians; antiabortionists refer to theology, biology, medicine, sociology, and other domains. Disciplines, conversely, seek epistemic betterment—which means that they are more likely reflectively to unify their sources of objectivity.

1.5a   *To enter a field is to be constrained.* It entails a *decision* to surrender a measure of one's freedom. If I enter the institution of promising, I *choose* to abide by its obligations; if I am a CBA analyst, I decide to use its systematic apparatus to make my decisions for me. CBA makes my decisions easier by ruling out broad value disputes; its special constraints permit me to proceed in an ordered way. This succeeds because I surrender to the field that part of my freedom that presented other alternatives. If I treat the field's standards as immutable axioms, I surrender a great deal of my freedom; if I unreflectively take a field's standards for granted, I surrender nearly all of my freedom respecting a given decision.

Kelly's (1955) view of freedom and determinism holds that regnant constructs determine subordinate ones by giving them meaning. Since cognitive elements are hierarchically arranged, it is plausible to say that we are as free as we think we are. Unexamined assumptions are what enslave us. "Each little prior conviction that is not open to review is a hostage [we give] . . . to fortune" (1955, 21–22). People who reflect on their points of view and cast their thinking into broad principles rather than rigid rules are more able and apt to choose alternatives that lead to personal freedom. Theories, Kelly says, are the thinking of actors seeking freedom from events; freedom consists of an actor's control of interpretations: an idea which controls another idea is free of that idea; determinism is the control higher order constructs exert over subordinate ones.

People enter fields because they are "accomplished," because doing so allows them to proceed as if certain things can be taken for granted. One can gain or lose freedom by adopting a theory depending on the decisions one makes about the theory's power. The decision to work with a field's standards, however, is a surrender of private alternatives.

1.5b   *Fields are schools of thought.* I elsewhere (1980, 1980b, 1980c) advocated replacing broad disciplinary names with schools of thought. "Behaviorism" and "constructivism" are better names for people's allegiences than "psychology." A psychologist who is a constructivist has more in common with constructivists in other disciplines than with another psychologist who is a "behaviorist."

1.5c *The "as if" maxim: people treat schools of thought as if they are accomplished bodies of knowledge.* The "objectifying" process requires the *as if* maxim to make sense. Social comparison implies that actors seek points of reference, things taken to be true, and not-to-be-questioned assumptions against which they may check their private constructions. I use the shorthand phrase "judgmental and veridical standards" to denote these checkpoints. We need not assume that everyone enters fields with the same confidence in the outcomes; plausibly, we check our thinking tentatively or axiomatically, as critical users of ideas or as "true believers."

The *as if* maxim is an indispensible precondition of a field's standards being used—which makes the maxim a necessary but not sufficient condition for the existence of a field. It is necessary because even the most modest assumption about the dependability of a standard requires a final bracketing of doubts, a proceeding *as if* certain things are at least provisionally true. The maxim is not a sufficient condition because it does not explain why an actor chooses this or that standard to deal with this or that event.

To ask why I choose this or that standard to guarantee my beliefs is to ask why I have *faith* in the standard. At least part of the explanation lies in a field's "sense of accomplishment." By this I mean that no one will proceed *as if* certain things are true unless one's field seems to be an accomplished body of knowledge. This sense of accomplishment requires that fields be seen as more or less static and "completed" by the actors who enter them.

The *as if* maxim does not depend upon a distinction between the natural attitude and reflective thinking. While the maxim is appropriate to the natural attitude, reflective thinkers would be frozen in inaction unless they could bracket their doubts and proceed *as if* certain things can be taken as true. Nor does the maxim depend upon a distinction between actors "in" a tradition of practices and those who incidentally reach into a tradition to pick up and use its standards. Both disciplinary and incidental actors must bracket their doubts to use a field's standards.

1.6 *Fields are essentially rhetorical.* This means three things: (1) the source of "authority" of a field's standards is the *faith* actors have in its standards and experts; (2) the "retreat to commitment" (Bartley, 1962) occurs in fields when standards and experts are challenged; and (3) fields may be defined as *audiences*. While the previous claims have centered on problems of imputing *unity* to real social entities, the present arguments bear on the *sources* of unity.

The first claim is that the glue which binds fields together is the rhetorical power of its standards and experts. Toulmin's (1972) question is "What is the source of authority of our concepts?" I replace that with *Why do people trust standards and experts?* Toulmin seeks an impersonal standard independent of situations and individuals that requires no further justification. I claim that, if the present field view is plausible, it is doubtful that he can devise such a standard without making it so abstract as to be substantively trivial. We should not define fields with an eye to devising universals, although one can speculate about universals *on the basis of* the present field theory. I have thus argued (Willard, 1980c) that a reformed view of "presumption" tied to Mead's view of "reflexiveness" meets Toulmin's standard for an impartial standpoint of rationality. The universal merely says "eschew randomness"; you are obligated to have reasons. This succeeds because it is trivial, it says nothing about a particular warrant; it warrants "warranting" (as Habermas' felicity conditions of discourse do) but validates no particular warrants. The experts and standards of *fields* are what justify particulars.

Fields are going concerns because people trust their standards and experts. The development of this trust is a phenomenon worthy of study quite apart from issues of "correctness." This is equally true of "rationality"; that is, the surest thing to be said of it is that it is a principle around which actors passionately align themselves—this being true regardless of what rationality's sources are thought to be (Willard, 1980c, 1981b). A claim's authority inheres in the fact that it is believed; belief is legitimized by its conventional fit into a field's standards. This is sociologically true regardless of how the universalistic disputes turn out. Fields often take their standards to be universals; and they usually draw contrasts between private, idiosyncratic views and "rational" (orthodox, conventionally approved) beliefs. The tensions between field standards and individual efforts to apply them to situations is thus a main concern of field studies. If Toulmin succeeds with a nontrivial universal, we shall have done the empirical work necessary to contrasting ordinary practices to it.

There are at least two sources of trust, the first being the most important. I have argued (1980) that the ticket into most fields is interpersonal influence. Actors can enter fields by consulting their documents; but they most often do so by consulting other people: graduate students adopt the views of their professors, political activists the views of their leaders. So I want to say that the main source of trust in a field's standards is the *field's experts*.

Stich and Nisbett (1980) have argued that individuals do not depend solely upon their idiosyncratic constructions since "there is a higher court of appeal." An actor can refer to "the reflective equilibrium of his cognitive betters. There are people in our subject's society who are recognized as *authorities* on one or another sort of inference." "The role of experts and authorities in our cognitive lives has been all but ignored by modern epistemologists. Yet it is a hallmark of an educated and reflective person that he recognizes, consults, and defers to authority on a wide range of topics" (1980, 198–199). Indeed, "it is our suspicion that one of the principal effects of education is to socialize people to defer to cognitive authorities" (1980, 199). Moreover, "deference to authority is not merely the habitual practice of educated people, it is, generally, the right thing to do from a normative point of veiw. The man who persists in believing that his theorem is valid, despite the dissent of leading mathematicians, is a fool" (1980, 199). The obvious conclusion is that we defer to experts on matters outside our spheres of expertise.

The deeper conclusion pertains to *justification*. The reference to authority by itself is inadequate to explain justification because it does not give the "cognitive rebel his due." If we equate this account with justification, we shall have to say that cognitive rebels *contradict* themselves when they reject authority. Stich and Nisbett thus offer an amended view that dovetails elegantly with the present focus on *practices*:

> . . . an attribution of justification to a rule of inference can be unpacked as a claim that the rule accords with the reflective inductive practices *of the people the speaker takes to be appropriate*. But the attribution of justification does not, by itself, *specify* whose reflective equilibrium the speaker takes to be appropriate. That job of specification can be done in varying ways by the context of the utterance. Or it can be left quite open and ambiguous [1980, 201].

So any claim such as "rule *r* is justified" can be unpacked as meaning "rule *r* accords with the reflective inferential practice of the (person or) group of people I (the speaker) think appropriate" (1980, 201). This permits a view of what I shall call (in the third section) interfield disputes:

> Now, most people are cognitive conservatives most of the time. They take the appropriate group to be the socially, consensually, designated authorities. The disagreement between the cognitive rebel and the cognitive conservative is, in effect, a dispute over whose judgment ought to be heeded in the issue at

hand. In our view, such disputes are not exclusively cognitive disputes. They are better viewed on the model of political disputes whose resolution . . . is determined by such factors as social power, personal style and historical accident. . . . [O]ur view leaves abundant room for rational argument about justification *among* cognitive conservatives. Also, there may be rational argument among cognitive rebels who agree about the appropriate authority group. However, if our account succeeds in capturing what we mean when we say an inference is justified, it is to be expected that there will be some disputes over justification that admit of no rational resolution [1970, 201–202].

While I hope to prove the last claim wrong, Stich and Nisbett's account is on the whole a firm foundation for field theory. Fields are *not* impersonal conceptual ecologies and they do not speak for themselves.

A second source of faith in fields can be gleaned from Laudan's (1977) view of research traditions, by which he means a set of ontological and methodological "do's and dont's." Formally, *"a research tradition is a set of general assumptions about the entities and processes in a domain of study, and about the appropriate methods to be used for investigating the problems and constructing the theories in that domain"* (1977, 81). A "field," as viewed here, could contain several research traditions or could be just the same thing as a particular research tradition. I shall not list the important advances Laudan's thinking gives to the philosophy of science. For present purposes, it may suffice to note that "progress" is a source of faith in a field. A successful tradition leads by its component theories (which may be inferentially incompatible) to the adequate solution of an increasing *range* of problems (1977, 82). This range is what creates and sustains faith; I trust X because X solves my problems. This applies equally to ordinary fields, though "success" might not be equated with "range." Thanks to our psychological (Kelly, 1955) and sociological (Willard, 1978) assumptions, we can avoid getting bogged down in disputes about perceived versus actual success; both collapse to our assumptions.

I turn now to the second reason for regarding fields as rhetorical. My aim is to specify and clarify the implications of Bartley's (1962) notion of a "retreat to commitment" for our field theory. Bartley held that defenders of particular doctrines of rationality or justification are always forced (by the *tu quoque*) into passionate and thus contradictory defenses. Our field theory introduces complexities into this. If retreats occur, they doubtless do so along field-dependent lines. At least three versions of this are obvious.

First, fields display an "animal faith" in standards by taking them for granted, making them a not-to-be-questioned framework of assumptions. This happens not in the heat of pointed disputes but as a matter of routine practice. The background awarenesses informing practices (Garfinkle, 1967) exemplify this, as do the commonplace assumptions undergirding talk (Jacobs and Jackson, this volume). Views of rationality, deviance, and verification often recede into the background because they seem so obvious as to require no reflection. CBA actors, for example, take the view that "decisions have to be made" in this way: a society's business must go on; we must temporize; we cannot wait for grand value disputes to be settled. The need for explicitness is another implicit assumption: values must be explicitly rendered in ordinary fiscal language. CBA actors rarely argue these views; they take them as givens; their theory of "rational decision-making" is thus rooted in two assumptions that are not products of CBA theory. Gödel's incompleteness theorem explains why fields import concepts when their implicit assumptions are attacked. I shall elaborate this in part three.

Second, interfield disputes are sometimes intractable if field actors back into *intuitive* defenses of their standards. CBA analysts reduce values to quantities; Kantian and neo-Kantian moral theorists hold that reducing values to quantities is among the worst offenses. These are incommensurable assumptions and could preclude satisfactory settlement of disputes between CBA and Kantian thinkers. Only a principle external to both fields could weigh their competing claims. I shall explore this possibility below. The retreat to intuition occurs when fields claim that they are *hierarchically* prior to other fields, as when analytic philosophers rule certain empirical examples out of disputes because philosophy is hierarchically positioned in a "grand arrangement" of fields to judge the importance of all examples. Consider the general who says "We had to destroy the town to save it" contrasted to the moral theorists (such as Sartre) who condemn "abstracting that which is concrete" (Willard, 1980c). To any criticism, the General can reply with arguments special to the military domain that rule moral criticisms out. If "war is hell," the usual standards of applicability of moral claims do not apply to the conduct of war; so the general and the moral critic retire to intuitive views of the rightness of their own fields.

Our field theory rules out all talk of hierarchies, of ranking fields in order of importance; the third section of this essay makes a special merit of this: it opens the door to using argumentation concepts to understanding interfield disputes. The *tu quoque* will do us in if we try to defend some fields as regnant, others as subordinate, in some Lovejoyian great chain of Being. So it suffices here to claim that fields are rhetorical; the first two senses of this rhetorical dimension stress the brute fact of commitment. The third, to which I now turn, does not.

Think of fields as audiences. The audience is a relatively compact concept that clarifies the claims already made. It implies that one way to define a group is to look at the messages, speakers, journals, and tracts to which its members attend. This squares with our "issue field" definition and applies equally to disciplinary and ordinary fields: the pamphlets of social movements and academic journals can be similarly studied because they serve similar functions. A merit of the audience notion is that it can be static or fluid, thus calling our attention to changes in audiences as well as recurring gatherings.

For *defining* fields, the audience is a superior construct to the "speaker." We can use field knowledge to illuminate a speaker's utterance (and the reverse) and the "appeal to experts" to explain the trust actors place in fields; but, strictly speaking, the speaker cannot help us define the boundaries of a field. There are doubtless cases where a speaker exemplifies a field, but this criterion would fail in other nontrivial cases (does Pauling speak for medicine or physics in defending vitamin C?). Worse, using the speaker to define fields requires reviving the *formal membership* view of groups criticized above because formal memberships are rare, misleading, and irrelevant to situated talk.

Foucalt (1972) uses the idea of the speaker to define fields—his example being that only physicians can "speak medically" because only they have the degrees qualifying them to speak. This has four defects. First, it forces us to ignore the ordinary field of popular medicine. Thanks to recent dissemination of medical information, ordinary folk speak medically *making the correct arguments* (the ones in vogue in medicine) *for the right reasons* (the ones accepted in medicine). Popular medicine is surely as important as the medical discipline; its arguments affect the life prospects of everyone—decisions to seek diagnosis and treatment spring from the ordinary, not the professional, sphere.

Second, Foucalt ignores overlaps in subject matters. Physicians and ordinary folk alike make "medical" arguments that are also psychological, sociological, economic, and legal. It is thus circular and oversimple to take certain people as field exemplars, *then* look to the things they talk about and conclude that a field has been described. Economists Samuelson and Freidman often make claims about psychology, sociology, persuasion, and politics; should we conclude that economics is the master science of which the others are only species?

Third, Foucalt uses the clearest-cut case: medical degrees obviously mark professionals off from ordinary folk; degrees in the social sciences are less clear-cut (behaviorists might have many different degrees); and there are few such distinctions that fit happily into ordinary field studies.

Fourth, Foucalt (like Toulmin) blurs distinctions *within* medicine (Willard, 1980). He selects a broad and proportionately gross disciplinary name, "medicine," and equates the name with a universe of discourse. But that encompassing label subsumes many schools of thought just as most broad disciplines do: some physicians have more in common with electron-microscopists than with general practitioners or surgeons.

These four objections are to using the speaker to define fields. Taking the concept of the audience as our organizing view, we can more clearly point to the important contributions the idea of the speaker can make. There are some fields that are partly defined by *who* shall speak—Catholic theology being largely organized around the appropriateness of certain claims to certain speakers; papal authority and standards for priestly ministries thus display parallels with Foucalt's "speaking medically." Moreover, ethos is clearly part of the glue that binds each field together. Religious sects organize around single personalities; Catholic theology turns on role credibility and authority; political movements form around individuals; and the earlier argument about trusting experts (Stich and Nisbett, 1980) suggests that personalities are not irrelevant in the disciplines. Ethos surely figures in explanations of convention and orthodoxy and it arguably bears upon explanations of progress (to the degree we are willing to say the appeals-to-experts argument is correct). It is fashionable to contrast such "identifications" with "genuine" progress, but this value judgment does not work equally well in all fields. Religions, for instance, close off doubts by virtue of authority and prestige; such closure is progressive in the sense that followers are able to lead happier, more confident lives because they can take certain things on faith. Too, it is by no means clear that there are no parallels between "faiths by fiat" and disciplinary faiths: a faith in scientific method cannot be justified by the method; just as a priest tells his flock to put aside doubt and proceed with life, so scientists pursue their projects on the faith that they are engaged in rational progress.

I have ignored the concept of the message because it is redundant to issue fields. But message analysis is essential to field definitions because messages display favored puzzles, exemplars of success, preferred metaphors, and— generally—the ways fields order their activities. These elements symbolically bind practitioners together in the way Kuhn (1970) says "communities" are brought to life and sustained. The recurring themes in messages coalesce to define the normal activities of a field, its routines and mundane affairs; they sometimes embody the symbols of unity that make the community possible (Burke, 1950). In defining fields as audiences and in emphasizing their rhetorical dimensions, I am using "field" to subsume the sociological notion of "community," which I take to be central to Kuhn's view of scientific organization and progress. Rhetorical practices build and sustain the sense of community, of "we-ness," of belonging that sociologists use to describe how individuals fit into aggregations of activity. The audience notion means that communities are rhetorically achieved and that *this is what they are in the most fundamental sense.* They are other things as well; but they are always rhetorically achieved—this achievement being a necessary but not sufficient condition of a field.

Where is this leading? I have proceeded in a piecemeal way to argue that fields are real sociological entities—*unities* based on *sources* that have *effects.* "Field" thus subsumes terms such as "group" and "community" by doing the work these terms do *and* analytic work as well. If fields are real entities, they are brought to life by the practices of people—these being our object of study. Thus the subject matter of field theory is "objectifying," the social comparison process by which situated actors test their interpretations against communal standards. Fields are thus psychological perspectives—an elaboration of Mead's "generalized other." A field is a stance one can take in dialectically balancing private interpretations against communal standards. "Passing muster on knowledge" is a good way of describing such practices. A three-way analogy between cognitive development, socialization into fields, and participant observation research has been defended as a way of explaining the appropriateness of participant observation research to the subject matter. Fields are domains of objectivity, schools of thought, and "accomplished" bodies of knowledge; they are used "as if" "completed." The "sense of accomplishment" explains how objectivity is a subjective accomplishment and why entrance into a field entails in different ways a loss of freedom. The importance of the sense of accomplishment stems from the rhetorical nature of fields—meaning (1) the "source of authority" of concepts is the faith people have in the guarantors of a field, its experts and standards; (2) the guarantors of a field's concepts often cannot be defended on the field's grounds—they require either imported concepts or a "retreat to commitment"; and (3) fields are *audiences.*

Fields are made up of activities; all activities are *context-embedded;* so fields are recurring definitions of situation. Actors appeal to fields because of definitions of the situation and they use fields to expand or change their definitions of the situation. These decisions are our main objects of study; the ways individuals dialectically balance their own aims and interpretations against communal standards are the best clues to the unity, sources, and effects of fields.

Methods and Practices

I now consider the critical methods appropriate to the study of argument fields. Two assumptions should be kept in mind. First, methodological choices should be outgrowths of theoretic claims about the phenomena to be studied. Our field theory poses questions of a particular sort; since questions frame the horizons of their answers, I now sketch the methodological entailments of the present view. Second, the research and critical methods appropriate to the present view of fields are to a large extent indistinguishable. Their assumptions, procedures, and results are largely the same. Having chosen to define fields as real sociological entities, I now choose a procedural convenience appropriate to the theory: the assumptions that researchers and critics alike will be preoccupied with extended examples.

I shall survey the assumptions and purposes, the techniques and procedures, and the aims and results of argument criticism. Proceeding this way, I hope to flesh out three more propositions about what fields are:

2.1 *Fields are frameworks of assumptions.*
2.2 *Fields cannot be equated with their documents.*
2.3 *Fields are analytic distinctions.*

These claims cohere with the propositions in the first section and should be seen as outgrowths of the methodological choices dictated by the emerging field theory. While these propositions might be construed in many ways that would not square with the present view, I want to proceed with them on the understanding that they must cohere with the earlier claims about the *context-embeddedness* of talk and action.

Assumptions and Purposes of Criticism

Criticism is a mode of epistemology that aims at illuminating the effects of assumptions. It seeks to understand the reality of events by accounting for the alternative constructions that may be placed upon them. Its subject matter is the range of interpretive possibilities presented in situations and the cognitive effects of alternative points of view. "Every form of existence has its source in some peculiar way of seeing, some intellectual formulation and intuition of meaning" (Cassirer, 1946, 8–9). Every interpretation is open to alternative construction, and "it is not a matter of indifference which of a set of alternative constructions one chooses to impose upon his world" (Kelly, 1955, 15). We live in an intersubjective world filled with obdurate objects (Blumer, 1969) and the interpretations of other people. We deal with objects and people by generating from our stock of experience whatever interpretations seem appropriate to particular circumstances. Let us call this "the multiple realities argument" (Schutz, 1945, 1945a, 1951, 1953, 1962, 1967).

The multiple realities argument describes the upshots of field theory. Our theory says that (1) the reality of situations inheres in actors' interpretations—the interpretations they in fact make; (2) the possibilities of situations inhere in the range of envisionable interpretations—all the constructions we might dream up for a particular case; (3) definitions of situation lead to action; (4) people define and act in situations by virtue of a dialectical balancing of conventional expectations (field standards) and their particular intentions; and (5) we best understand fields by understanding how and why actors refer to them, by understanding the purposes they serve. It will not do to contrast conventions and intentions as if convention were a monolithic and singular "other." Field theory describes a multiplicity of (to different degrees) incommensurable conventions.

Criticism is the branch of epistemics concerned with explaining objectifying, how social comparison proceeds, and the relationships between cognitive arrangements (how people structure experience) and epistemic choices. Idiosyncratic personal experience gets objectified by reference to conventions; our working assumption is that one way of knowing conventions is to know the situated choices that refer to them. The multiple realities argument applies as strongly to our understandings of fields as it does to ordinary life—which is why we know fields by spotting recurring themes in *many* acts of objectification.

Every actor, in making situated appeals to a field, participates in the activities that constitute the field and—for our purposes—speaks for the field. The multiple-realities argument tells us to seek a parade of witnesses, *not* because the competing voices coalesce to produce a single account but because the *range* of alternative views is in itself important. In the play *Rashomon*, the succession of witnesses does not produce a single "correct" account of the rape (if it *was* a rape); the reality of the "encounter field" described in the play consists if we trust the witnesses of all of the very different interpretations. The methodological consequences of attending to multiple testimony have been described by Brown (1977, p. 69):

> . . . knowledge is possible only through the interpretive processes which the knower enacts in his encounter with the subjects in question. In this view, objectivity is not depersonalization but a mastery of passion. Through such an attitude, the inquirer is presumed to be able to "accept the other's illusions as real money," and then to ask how such "illusions" are possible. The "bias," rather than being suppressed, is used as a source of understanding. The various voices do not cancel each other out, nor is the truth limited to those points on which they agree; instead, much as the characters in a play, each voice enriches the others, each contributes to the dialectical construction of more and more comprehensive metaperspectives. These metaperspectives are not objective in that they eliminated bias but in that they organize the "biases" of various actors into a structured mimesis of the domain of experience to be explained.

Fields are not things; they are recurring themes in experience.

Let me draw a distinction between understanding situations and understanding fields. We have two different but interdependent projects: using situations to understand fields and using fields to understand situations. I want to restrict my remarks to the first on the assumption that the second presupposes success with the first. Critics proceeding with the first project are, naively or reflectively (Swanson, 1977, 1977a), proceeding "as if" they have an "accomplished" field, a successful theory of fields *and* a fully fleshed-out description of this or that field. The first project tries to secure a theory of fields and fully articulated descriptions of specific fields. There is a circularity here: we use what we know of utterance to yield insights into fields and what we know of fields to tell us what this or that utterance means. What keeps the viciousness out of the circle is that we do not do both simultaneously. Illuminating fields comes first.

With this distinction in mind we are ready to say that the epistemic project of criticism is the study of the effects of definitions of situation. This is an outcome of defining fields as real sociological entities made up of ongoing practices. This sociological view combined with the multiple realities argument suggests that the critical theories based on realism are inappropriate to field studies.

Hermeneutic views of criticism (Balthrop, chap. 10) differ from realistic views in much the same way that *Weltanschauungen* philosophies of science differ from positive or received views. Realistic criticism, like positivism, presupposes that its objects exist in an uninterpreted state and present themselves in a straightforward way. The "received view" of criticism tasks critics with discovering obdurate characteristics of the objects of criticism in a manner analogous to Russell's theory of descriptions (Willard, 1981a). The focus is on characteristics of the objects rather than interpretive processes on the assumption that critical claims are somehow "falsifiable."

Criticisms of realism have paralleled critiques of the received view of science. The assumption that critics do theory-free reserach has been attacked (Hirsch, 1967; Hoy, 1978; Ricoeur, 1965, 1965a, 1966, 1967, 1970; Swanson, 1977, 1977a); and the view that knowing does not affect the known has been rejected vis-à-vis the social world (Psathas, 1973; Bock, 1956; Gurvitch, 1971; Brown, 1977). Criticial realism was thus said to be premised on more doubtful assumptions than was the received view of science; it required a special reductionism, a faith that social processes could be described in physicalist language. For literary criticism this meant there was one correct reading of a text; for rhetorical criticism it meant that there could be one correct reading of situated meaning; and for argument criticism it meant that correct meanings of arguments had to be what could be found in texts.

The criticisms of this thinking are familiar and require no exposition here. Literary and rhetorical critics have moved away from realism largely because they did not want to tread the thin ice required for making claims about "correct" readings of situated meanings. Argumentation critics have not, mainly because they want to retain the right to evaluate critical objects. I have argued elsewhere (Willard, 1981b) that evaluation is a core culprit in argument criticism because it can be defended only by assumptions that make critics omniscient. There are views of evaluation corresponding to different epistemic theories and they suffer roughly the same fates. Corresponding to naive realism is the view that makes criticism a weighing of particular objects against taken-for-granted standards; the object succeeds or fails by virtue of its fit with the standards. The successful critiques of naive realism have amounted to destruction of critical standards based on it. Restricted realistic epistemologies thus produced a more modest critical theory which allowed that evaluative standards were open to dispute and had to be defended before objects could be held up to them. But two untenable assumptions undergirded this: (1) that the principles which justify applying a general standard to a particular instance are straightforward and uncontroversial, and (2) that the object of criticism could not talk back. The model was naive realistic literary criticism, not situated people and the assumption was that texts were straightforward objects. Argument critics following this model glossed over the possibilities that the arguers they studied might dispute their evaluations. The insisted-upon prerogative was the right to say that a particular claim was right or wrong, good or evil, true or false. This was conjoined with more technical senses of evaluation used by rhetorical critics (elaborating standards for rhetorical success and using them to understand success and failure in particular instances); but for the most part evaluation was a process of moral and epistemic judgment.

My (1981b) discussion rejected evaluation as a critical procedure and replaced it with very restricted projects. Following Eliot and others, I claimed that *explication* is the core critical project; unlike Eliot, I was not willing to grant that evaluation might be a "pleasant avocation of critics" tacked onto the important work. My claim was that evaluative aims inevitably distort explication unless evaluation is understood narrowly, in these terms: (1) observation is never theory-free and explication always proceeds by virtue of implicit values and presuppositions; (2) the effects of presuppositions are construed in terms of value systems—this applying equally to critics and their objects of study; (3) fields are value-laden; since all points of view presuppose their own value, their "is's" are grounded in "oughts"; and (4) taking a field at its own definition is an evaluative act, though understanding does not entail approval.

Our field theory describes a relativity that undermines traditional claims that argumentation is a "normative" discipline. The incommensurability of field standards—taken seriously—becomes a formidable roadblock. If a critic cannot *settle*, say, the dispute between the general and the moral theorist, he or she has no credentials for evaluating *either* field. The evaluative posture requires a remarkably immodest assumption, that critics have succeeded where epistemologists failed; they have defeated the *tu quoque*, avoided infinite regress, and thus have the *right* to reject justifications different from their own.

Criticism appropriate to fields seeks to unpack the possibilities of its objects. Hermeneutic criticism probes possibilities for alternative interpretations of texts; argument criticism must study, among other facets, the interpretations actually operating in situations. This expands the hermeneutic project by insisting upon the importance of speakers' intentions. Literary critics can ignore for some purposes an author's intentions; but argument critics must concern themselves with what Gadamer (1976, 88) calls "the vast realm of the occasionality of all speaking that plays an important role in establishing the meaning of what is said; by occasionality I mean dependency on the situation in which an expression is used."

One plausible reading of Gadamer's philosophical hermeneutics is that it is an elaborate theory of role-taking, an attempt to flesh out the views of Goffman and others with an ontology of perspective-taking. The automatic, unreflective mechanisms that facilitate daily life are not of main interest only because hermeneutics is concerned with difficult meanings—ones requiring interpretive effort. For these, it is the structure of the knower's understanding, not the structure of events, that is important. Gadamer's view of critical understanding thus parallels and augments Schutz's view of reflective thinking. We can also press a parallel with Kelly's (1955) view of freedom and determinism discussed above. Kelly's claim that we are enslaved by unexamined assumptions dovetails with Gadamer's belief that prejudices are the "biases of our openness to the world." Kelly's claim that one gains freedom by theorizing squares with Gadamer's claim that a knower's boundedness to a horizon is the ground of all understanding; prejudices are not barriers to understanding: they are doors that open *us* up to the world. Gadamer calls this a "positive concept of prejudice" and equates it with Heidegger's view of historical consciousness. The idea is that prejudices are results of our historicity—in Kelly's terms, the constructs that embody our experience. Prejudices thus comprise the directions of our ability to experience just as Kelly's construct systems are frames of reference that give meaning to events; prejudices are conditions "whereby what we encounter says something to us" (Gadamer, 1976, 9). Understanding is thus rooted in "unsuspendable" historicity and finitude.

Gadamer's views square with Kelly's and Goffman's because all three suppose that role-taking is an interpretive process fueled by the cognitive constitutive processes of the knower. The characteristics and intentions a person attributes to another are characteristics of the attributor's system just as features attributed to texts are aspects of the critics' own interpretive schemes. Herein lies the main difference between Gadamer's views and mine: literary critics do not need to attribute intentions to authors. Where Dilthey and Schleiermacher saw texts as symptoms, ciphers, or even facades *behind which* stood "actual meanings," the author's intentions, Gadamer is preoccupied with the text, with the things it says to successive generations regardless of the author's intentions. Texts have lives of their own; they live by the interpretations placed upon them; hermeneutics is thus the study of the ways texts—as opposed to their creators—communicate. I shall return to this in the third part by considering the field status of *documents*.

I am proposing, in sum, that the critical view appropriate to our field theory is based on perspective-taking as a mode of knowing. Criticism is the epistemic enterprise that studies the effects of assumptions on speech and action. The focus is upon situated activity if it is plausible that fields are traditions of recurring, context-embedded practices endowed with meaning by the "objectifying" of their actors.

2.1 *Fields are frameworks of assumptions.* One can gloss Kelly's (1955) organization corollary to describe fields: each field evolves for convenience in anticipating events a construction system embracing ordinal relationships among constructs. We need only insert "field" in Kelly's (1955, 57–58) view of a person's system to get a parallel between a personal construct system and a communal framework of assumptions: "[W]ithin a construct system there may be many levels of ordinal relationships, with some constructs subsuming others and those, in turn, subsuming still others. . . . Thus man systematizes his constructs by concretely arranging them in hierarchies and by abstracting them further." Try substituting "field" for "person" in this passage: "[A] person must occasionally decide what to do about remodeling his system. . . . How disruptive will a new set of ideas be? Dare he jeopardize the system in order to replace some of its constituent parts? Here is the point at which he must choose between preserving the integrity of the system and replacing one of its obviously faulty parts" (1955, 58–59). Kelly's principle of elaborative choice thus speaks to fields: they choose interpretations that enhance the extension or definition of their systems (Willard, 1979), that narrow the field of vision to get precision or broadening it to embrace more events (while tolerating more uncertainty).

Thus the parallel between *personal* construct theory and field activities yields insights. Since fields *are* their practices and practices take meaning from practitioners, the analogy between personal and communal frameworks can be seen as a parallelism—which has the advantage of explaining fields and the psychological processes of their actors in the same language. This illuminates how fields get referred to, adapted to situations, and changed; it squares in most respects with Kuhn's (1970) sense of "communities"; and it doevtails into our three-way analogy between cognitive development, socialization into fields, and participant observation. The common language also has the advantage of more clearly specifying the dialectical balancing of private and communal expectations and aims: "objectifying" becomes the process by which communal and private interests are accommodated.

Techniques and Procedures

Having chosen to define fields as real sociological entities in the manner of the Chicago School Interactionists, I now consider the main methodological implication of this decision: that it is most fruitful to think in terms of *action* rather than *structure* (Shibutani, 1961, 34). This fixes our attention squarely on situations: it makes the context-embeddedness of action and the meaning-creating importance of definitions of situation the two hard facts to be respected. This is not the road most field theorists had hoped to travel. It seems to propose an extreme situationalism or "radical contextuality" (Johnson, 1977) that subordinates (say) rules, language, discourse, and interaction to idiosyncratic, context-specific interpretations. The result might seem to be a fabric of discontinuous observations testifying to the importance of volition but nothing else. By insisting on the indexicality of expression (Garfinkle and Sacks, 1970; Cicourel, 1970a), we may seem to propose such a fragmentary view of communal life that the question arises whether a field theory can be sustained.

Assembled against these doubts we have the claims associated with proposition *1.1 Fields are real sociological entities*, especially the claim that we know fields by discerning recurring themes in their practices. The intuitive idea is that actors make events seem rational by using their arsenals of objectifying techniques: "the immense generality of members' procedures for assembling and employing the features of a particular setting so as to recognize and account for . . . those scenes within an 'objective societal context'" (Zimmerman and Pollner, 1970, 99) stems from everyone's ability to use different perspectives. Fields are thus "families of practices" having describable features; they are animated when people use them in commonsense ways to deal with events. Were extreme contextualism true, people would greet every situation as utterly new; they would have failed to learn from experience (Kelly, 1955). This does not happen because people have at-the-ready repertoires of interpretive techniques. What *is* utterly situational is any particular adaptation to a situation—which is why fields must be defined in terms of recurring themes.

We know we are looking at a CBA analyst if that actor enters a succession of events on the assumptions that (1) despite unclarity, decisions *will* be made; (2) we cannot dispute values, even when they are relevant; and (3) we generate the best policies by making values as explicit as possible; that is, in the language of fiscal costs. So the practice of expressing the value of life in dollars crosses situations; it is a ready-made paradigm for adapting to situations regardless of their content. The *meanings* of these calculations—in the CBA case, the *outcomes*—are context-specific, however.

As I argued earlier, the merit of participant observation is its focus on perspective-taking and, in particular, the effects of assumptions on the definitions of situation actors choose to use. This assumes a holism of "inner and outer" symbols in two ways: (1) objectivity is subjectively accomplished; and (2) people enter fields to grasp at principles that transcend situations, to make sense of *this* situation by noting its commonalities with *those* situations. The aim is predictability through continuity. It is through participation in events that observers see "the inner and outer worlds of man conjoin to create human fields of knowledge" (Bruyn, 1966, 87); fields are thus *the same things* as their outcomes in particular cognitive uses and situational adaptations.

The objection arises here that this is needlessly complex. One can look at textbooks and the signal documents of disciplines and generalize about the broad shape of fields. By this view, we define fields by discerning recurring themes not in practices but in documents. My only objection to this is that it cannot be the core mode of research; "the literature" does not exhaustively define a field, though it may confirm our impressions of practices. Thus:

2.2 *Fields cannot be equated with their documents.* First, a field-document equation assumes that documents speak for themselves and require no interpretation. This is untenable for several reasons. Consider first that some theoretical works serve as foundational documents for several fields. What, then, could we say of the works of Freud, Skinner, or Kelly when they are used to define problems in psychology, sociology, and communication? We *can* notice differences in the *uses* made of these documents; that is, different practices.

More important is the hermeneutic claim that texts admit of alternative interpretations, that their meanings are "not to be compared with an immovable and fixed point of view. . . . [U]nderstanding the text itself . . . means that the interpreter's own thoughts have also gone into the reawakening of the meaning of the text. In this the interpreter's own horizon is decisive . . . as a meaning and a possibility that one brings into play and puts at risk" (Gadamer, 1975, 350). This "fusion of horizons" means that criticism is possible *because* understanding is interpretive; I understand a text by understanding my interpretations of it and comparing them with those of others. Understanding texts is self-understanding. Just as I cannot objectify self-understanding, I cannot, except dogmatically, objectify a text: its objective meaning consists in all of the interpretations that possibly can be made of it.

This squares with our view of fields because it makes criticism a historical enterprise, a process of locating texts in their appropriate fields of discourse and of understanding the interpretations that *have been made* of them. Like Heidegger, Gadamer sees the historicity of a text as never a fixed state but a progressively elaborated cognitive structure. Criticism is thus an attributive process, a self-conscious form of understanding that is episodic, intersubjective, and transubjective. It is episodic because every interpretive act is historically rooted, becoming part of the historical ecology of the phenomenon thus adding to its possibilities. It is intersubjective because every interpretive act comes from reciprocating attributions. It is transubjective because every interpretive act is a dialectical merger of past and present through language that transcends the knower's control.[2] Understanding texts thus presupposes an accomplished sense of fields—which obviates using documents to *define* fields. My CBA research, for example, reveals gaps between documentary claims about CBA and actual practices. Texts hint that there are limits to how literally one can take the expressions of values in dollar terms (expressing the value of a civic orchestra in "ergs" of aesthetic experience) while in practice such equations are taken literally. The scholarly hedges in the literature are ignored in practice. Thus it seems prudent to assume that every field will be an inference we draw from practices and that documents are secondary sources of information.

Bear in mind that our interests in texts and Gadamer's are not completely parallel; we cannot use Gadamer's distinction between the text and the author's intentions when we want to know what a speaker in a situation *means* by a claim. When texts stand as *records* of events, imputations of intentions to speakers are of central importance. Thus:

2.2a *Texts are unsure records of situated speech.* Gadamer's view of linguistic context is sufficiently pliable to permit this restriction. He says that language always leads behind itself and behind the facade of overt verbal expression; it is not coincident with what it expresses; and there is a proportional limit to objectifying anything that is thought and communicated: "[L]inguistic expressions . . . are not simply inexact and in need of refine-

---

[2] "Transubjectivity" can be variously defined. Since it might be defined as a linguistic determinism, I want to eschew such an interpretation explicitly. I intend "transubjectivity" to cohere with my (1981) "nondiscursiveness thesis."

ment, but rather, of necessity, they always fall short of what they evoke and communicate. For in speaking there is always implied a meaning that is imposed on the vehicle of expression, that only functions as a meaning behind the meaning and that in fact could be said to lose its meaning when raised to the level of what is actually expressed" (Gadamer, 1976, 88). So we have things unsaid but made present in speech and things concealed by speech. The first notion means that "relativity to situation and opportunity constitutes the very essence of speaking. For no statement simply has an unambiguous meaning based on its linguistic and logical construction as such, but, on the contrary, each is motivated" (1976, 88). The notion of things concealed by speech penetrates more deeply, Gadamer believes, into the hermeneutical conditions of language use. Lies conceal things in ways that have no semantic character (Oriental courtesy on the one hand and clear breaches of trust on the other): "[I]n the case of texts, for instance, a modern linguist would speak of lie-signals by virtue of which what is said in the text can be identified by intending to conceal. Here lying is not just the asser- tion of something false; it is a matter of speaking that conceals and knows it." Seeing through a lie is a matter of linking a concealment to the "true intention of the speaker" (1976, 90–91).

Technical expressions, which are of particular concern to defining disci- plinary boundaries, present special obstacles to equating texts with situated speech. They have, Gadamer (1976, 86) says, "a peculiar profile that pre- vents them fitting into the actual life of the language." They live and com- municate in a language, but "they enrich their power of making things clear—a power previously limited to their univocality—with a commu- nicative power of multivocal, vague ways of speaking." The "world orienta- tion" requisite to linguistic orientations to the world thus requires special situational adaptations. This permits a useful sense of linguistic context:

> One of the fundamental structures of all speaking is that we are guided by preconceptions and anticipations in our talking in such a way that these con- tinually remain hidden and that it takes a disruption in oneself of the intended meaning of what one is saying to become conscious of these prejudices as such. In general the disruption comes about through some new experience, in which a previous opinion reveals itself to be untenable. But the basic preju- dices are not easily dislodged and protect themselves by claiming self-evident certainty for themselves, or even by posing as supposed freedom from all prejudice and thereby securing their acceptance [Gadamer, 1976, 92].

Dogmatism is thus explained along the same lines Kelly (1955) uses to explain the unwillingness of persons to jeopardize construct systems.

2.3 *Fields are analytic distinctions.* The important question is what someone means by an utterance. One starts with "A claims X" and gives meaning to this by considering what A means (1) by saying X, and (2) by X. One might also ask what X conventionally can be made to mean—hence the hermeneutic project of textual criticism; but if one is interested in understanding *practices*, situated acts, it is usually proper to start with the question of what A means by saying X. Field theory is a way of proceeding with this question because (1) the idea of a field is an analytic abstraction from many such observations, and (2) an accomplished field notion yields insight into what A means by X.

Both procedures turn upon the critic's ability to attribute intentions to speakers. Whatever X means, A has made situational adaptations and choices among conventional possibilities. If the reality of a text inheres in the range of interpretations we can make of it, this places special demands upon critics who treat texts as records. Out of the interpretations that might be made of a text one particular interpretation must be defended as being just what A had in mind. This makes sense as long as we realize that the imputation is to A, not the text. Textual characteristics will be force-fitted into one's organizing interpretation. Thus explaining and defending such interpretations is the organizing problematic of criticism.

Aims and Purposes of Criticism

Our theory of fields has nontrivial implications for criticism. *Ex hypothesi*, criticism is a disciplinary field—a real sociological entity whose practices reveal recurring themes, a perspective one takes toward events. It proceeds by virtue of an "as if" maxim and explains the things that can be taken for granted by appeal to broad theories of critical action; and it is not monolithic, containing as it does sharply divergent schools of thought. If criticism is a field its practices can be characterized as being explicative, programmatic, and progressive. By "explicative" I mean that critical acts aim at explaining phenomena. By "programmatic" I mean that critical inquiries are tied together by a unifying thread of theory and assumptions; I do not mean that most rhetorical criticism *is* programmatic—only that it ought to be. By "progressive" I mean Laudan's (1977) notion of "cognitive progress," success with problems.

This undermines three pieties of traditional criticism. In ways already discussed, the explication notion forces a redefinition of evaluation. The claim that criticism should be programmatic undermines two *practices* (as opposed to theories). The first practice involves seeing critical acts as disconnected inquiries. This occurs when critics believe that their work bears mainly or solely upon the phenomenon they study. The second practice consists of assuming that the *content* of a particular critical act, what the critic has to say about the phenomenon, is nothing but an expansion of knowledge about the events studied; critics of the anti-nuclear power movement, for example, would say that their work contributes to our understanding of that movement per se. Both practices deny criticism a subject matter of its own; both make programmatic accomplishments unlikely. While a series of inquiries into the rhetoric of the antinuclear movement might produce programmatic development of a body of knowledge, the results would bear upon the movement, not criticism. Moreover, the practical result of the assumption that critical acts *can* be disconnected has been that critics pick and choose among the historical examples they find interesting without regard for the implications of their work for the field of criticism.

In considering the critical theory appropriate to fields, two interdependent programmatic lines suggest themselves. First, since fields are frameworks of assumptions, criticism becomes the study of the effects of assumptions. It follows that critics select their objects of study along lines suggested by their theory of interpretation—the standard being whether a particular study will contribute to the general theory—rather than for their historical interest. Second, the study of the effects of assumptions is facilitated by field studies because fields are conventional institutions actors use to objectify their thinking. Critical inquiries are thus programmatically arranged so as to expand our understanding of the nature, operations, and effects of particular domains of objectivity. In every case, critical attention to a field turns on its importance to broader theoretic claims about the effects of assumptions upon situated action.

The third piety of traditional criticism is that it is founded on "essentially contested concepts" and thus to be contrasted with science on the grounds that it does not "progress." To make sense this belief requires oversimple views of criticism, science, and progress. Laudan's (1977) reformation of the "progress" notion undermines the positivistic equation of progress with "accumulation" and thus destroys the main contrast between criticism and empirical programs of research. By defining "progress" as problem-solving and research traditions in terms of progressive success with problems, Laudan has produced a standard by which we can measure the present theory:

> It is frequently claimed that the sciences alone are progressive and cumulative, while other areas of inquiry exhibit changes of fashion and style which cannot be meaningfully described as progressive. . . . [I]t is sometimes said that the sciences can discover when their assumptions are wrong, but the humanistic disciplines cannot. . . . However the distinction is put (progressive v. non-progressive, rational v. non-rational, empirical v. non-empirical, falsifiable v. non-falsifiable), it will not hold up to detailed scrutiny. Disciplines like metaphysics, theology, even literary criticism exhibit all the features we require for making rational appraisals of the relative merits of competing ideologies within them. The nonsciences, every bit as much as the sciences, have empirical and conceptual problems; both have criteria for assessing the adequacy of solutions to problems; both can be shown to have made significant progress at certain stages of their historical growth [1977, 191].

Laudan attributes the strict dichotomy between the humanities and the sciences to a naive equation of science with experimental control and quantitative work. While the sciences have progressed more quickly than the humanities, "there is no reason in principle why this should be the case. The choice between atheism and theism, between phenomenalism and realism, between intuitionism and formalism, between capitalism and socialism (to cite only a few examples) could be made by appraising the relative progressiveness . . . of these competing research traditions" (Laudan, 1977, 192). We can compare them by noting their successes and failures with problems that interest us. Criticism appropriate to the present field theory will be "progressive" because it will address the conceptual problems posed by the question of the effects of assumptions on justificational practices. It would progressively elaborate a paradigm and a series of specific theories about the relationships between social practices, sociologically based beliefs, and—if such can be defended—"genuine" beliefs.

If there is a single organizing question concerning students of justification it is this: ideas are believed both because they fit field standards in a "rational" (field-countenanced) way and because of social factors (authority, orthodoxy, dogma, and incompetence)—does the first collapse to the second or does it make the second trivial? If we immediately take sides on this question we presuppose that the social groundings of belief are fully understood and that clear contrasts between "rationally" grounded and "merely sociological" beliefs can be sustained. I have proposed that the evidence justifying such comparisons is too thin to permit confident projects based on either side of the question. Field criticism aims to explicate this duality and to make comparisons across fields on the assumption that fields balance standards against practices in interestingly different ways. This posture will produce programmatic research and will assume the burdens of the "progress" standard.

Field Theory and Epistemics

Having fitted the conceptual apparatus of field theory to a critical project appropriate to it, I now turn to speculations about the immediate prospects of this thinking. My aim is to assess the contributions the present view might make to "epistemics." In particular, I want to propose that a successful field theory combined with appropriate critical equipment is a necessary condition of even modest success in the study of knowing.

3.1 *Field theory as construed here explains invariance and dependence in the same terms.* They cannot be antagonistic dichotomies except as people use them in that way. If objectivity is a subjective accomplishment, the recurring themes in fields are situated subjective accomplishments. Moreover, invariance can now be discussed completely apart from issues of determinism. Consider the things tentatively said to be invariant: the importance of language and of nondiscursive symbols, the structure of interaction, and (broadly construed) the structure of communicative *acts*. Theorists have used all three as evidence of determinism, although the complexities entailed in such uses can be avoided by dropping claims of exhaustiveness and (thus) of determination. Hence, *one* defining characteristic of argument products might be a certain adjacency pair; another might be the conventional meaning of someone's words; still another might reside in the structure of the interaction. I add only the caveat that the speaker's intentions are in every case important.

Conventional wisdom has it that a search for invariant principles is the main job of field theory. This trivializes fields (I have argued) by ignoring context-embeddedness. It also shunts us aside onto the determinism dispute: if one stipulates that individual instances are nothing but (say) deductive results of universals, one cannot get around confusing invariance with determinism.

3.2 *Field theory can bracket disputes about theory and practice.* We need settle none of the great disputes to do field studies. We are proceeding on the hunch that fields exist in practice and are thus bound to see theory as cumulative and accumulating, bearing a dialectical relation to practice; just as practice is never theory-free, theory is never practice-free. Practices are, in a shopworn phrase, "theory made flesh." The field theory presented here suggests that we shall find not *a* theory—practice dialectic but many dialectics, possibly differing in kind across fields. CBA, for example, displays a dialectic between broad theoretical proclamations and actual practices that seems unique—the sole standard of sufficiency being a loose utilitarian calculus of success with decisions. The epistemic view advocated here permits bracketing of ontic disputes about theory and practice as well. Since a field exists in activity it evolves the standards for deciding what constitutes a problem and what alternatives are feasible or orthodox out of the situated needs of its actors. So we may well expect to find a continual situated tension between theories and practices that is resolved by specific definitions of situation.

3.3 *The theory usefully poses the problems of interfield argument.* This bears upon two distinct but related matters: (1) the fact that disciplines borrow and evaluate one another's concepts, and (2) the fact that ordinary fields use the arguments of many disciplines and that their boundaries are fuzzy and unstable. These ordinary practices often create intractable problems for field theorists because, when a field borrows or evaluates the ideas of another field, it usually does so for field-dependent reasons. Since such reasons are often incommensurable across fields, "cross-pollination" runs the risk of muddying everyone's conceptual waters. My sustained example of this is ethics, but the arguments to follow apply more broadly.

The present field theory has theoretic resources for making genuine contributions to ethical inquiry by conceptualizing interfield disputes in a useful way. I shall not belabor the obvious problems field theory raises for ethics. Some of them are merely the familiar relativistic arguments stated in an especially blunt way. I can perhaps capsulize their implications with the claim that, *if field theory is true, ethics does not possess the theoretic resources for defending its autonomy from other disciplines except as a theory of argumentation.* This claim is a special case of the central epistemic thrust of field theory, namely that *in principle* no field possesses the theoretic resources for holding another field hostage to its special assumptions and standards. Ethical inductivists (especially, but not exclusively, hedonists and utilitarians, act and rule) may not object to this claim, but most everyone else will, mostly on the basis of Kant's famous argument that inductivist ethics inevitably reduces values to *thingness*—keep the cost-benefit-analysis example in mind—or on the different ground (Scheler, 1973) that any nonformal experiential ethical system must be grounded in some primal intuition of essences. Scheler's argument thus speaks for ethical theorists of many stripes in its stipulation that ethics is not interested in what people *think* is good or evil or in which they think good and evil are, but in what good and evil *in fact* are. As one reads Scheler's great work, *Formalism in Ethics* (1973), one readily discerns a rejection in advance of field theory as the inductive basis of ethical inquiry on the assumption that the intuition of essences does not and cannot depend upon the practices of a society. Scheler's search is for nonformal ethical intuitions that are immediately *given* and cannot be tested or refuted by observation and induction.

I take very seriously Scheler's attacks on "Kant's empty and barren formalism" and his criticism of Kant's implicit assumptions. But Scheler uses presuppositions of his own to advance his case for rigid absolutism and objectivism. You will search in vain for one scintilla of evidence or even argument in that monumental work to justify the conceit that ethical theorists, having intuited essences, possess principles that justify their use. Scheler faces the problem common to all intuitionists of doing one of two things, either positing as Kant did necessary but unknowable entities *or* establishing one's own intuitions as a prioris by virtue of *arguments that rule disagreement out*. Scheler opts for the second line and says—by proclamation, really—that intuition is independent of life experience. This argument, among other things, precludes you or me from confronting him with an example that empirically denies the universality of his intuited principle. Scheler does not grapple with relativity and relativisms—he fiats them out of the dispute.

Explicitly recognizing that any intuitionist scheme that cannot obtain universality is in trouble, Scheler seeks his universally obtaining condition by arguing something like the following: (1) if you reason exactly as I do (that is, if you follow my lines in every respect), you will produce X, and so will everyone else in any society however circumscribed; (2) there can be no evidence for this because social practices are (he asserts) utterly unrelated to intuitions; (3) thus do not give me examples of social or cultural differences since these are serendipitous historical matters bearing no relation to essences; and (4) good and evil are essential features of the world intuited in the same ways by all people however circumstanced, although they may not realize this because their sociocultural circumstances blind them to intuition. This drags us into Plato's cave by establishing a narrow standard of what can be evidence and by ruling out empirical differences on the ground that those who believe in them are blinded by their circumstances. Even granting these claims, what are we to make of the procedure?

First, it is perfectly useless. It says nothing to anyone in a field who must decide something. It possesses only two choices for principles that allow us to apply universals to situations—either a principle of application is itself intuited, universal, and immune to field standards, *or* principles of application are field-dependent. The first makes it impossible to apply intuitions to field practices; the second makes them trivial.

Second, Scheler's procedure is circular. The claim is its own warrant. The argument that essences are universals depends on the strict separation of intuition and experience, which is in turn justified by the claim that intuitions are universals.

Third, Scheler's view does not argue counterintuitions away. If I intuit that while intuition is universal its contents are not, Scheler can only say that I am blinded by my milieu and that social differences are artifacts of traditions and orthodoxies. But how on earth can he know this? By the conventions of traditional academic argument, Scheler could prove this position only by pointing to the specific facts of *my* world that in fact blind me; but if he embarked on that project, he inevitably would ground his universals in the facts of some field. The proof of his position would inhere in the refutation of mine.

If you or I intuit that intuition is nothing but the effects of regnant constructs on cognitive systems (Willard, 1979, 1979a) and that people take these to be "mystical" processes because they are unreflective and forgetful, Scheler would reject our reasoning qua reasoning. This result is bad enough, since it says that it does not matter whether my arguments are better than his. Worse, however, is that in face of my claims Scheler can only lament my delusions. He cannot convince anyone not already convinced of my errors; nor can he argue with me. Given *Scheler's* definition of the field of ethics we have a drawn game. Given the present field theory, however, this is no draw at all; Scheler is in *zugzwang*. By his own view, he cannot ignore situations counter to his own, so he must either counter with arguments and examples, which he is loath to do, or he must prove the autonomy of intuition from reasons and factual experience *in a way that does not use reason or factual experience.*

To draw this problem as sharply as possible, recall the cost-benefit-analysis assumption that values are useless to decision-makers unless expressed in quantitative language. Its field definition is a mirror opposite of Scheler's definition of the ethical field. By Scheler's view, values would be meaningless expressed quantitatively; CBA theorists want to express values in dollar terms. Since no ethical theorists can defeat these views on CBA's grounds (since CBA insists that such disputes be resolved in quantitative terms), they will try to do so on grounds special to ethics.

But this cuts no ice if ethics is a self-contained field. Why should CBA theorists or anyone listen to ethical claims if ethics is a nonempirical field? Formalism was an attempt to justify such projects; but if our field theory is *in any way* plausible, formalism will be unsuccessful. The better question is by what enabling assumption Scheler can speak to the CBA issues. The only answer I can see him making would require the assumption that his intuitional insights are *right* (not demonstrably but *given*). If CBA theorists claim intuitional orientations to the views, they are *wrong*; and this is *given* to anyone not blinded by milieu. CBA actors do claim intuitional affinities to their thinking just as positivists sometimes make self-evidence their ultimate metaphysical ground; and *I* intuitively believe that many people embrace quantitative orientations on intuitive grounds (a hatred of ambiguity or abstraction). So we have a conflict of intuitions so extreme as to be almost a caricature: Scheler and Kant reject grounding values in *things*: CBA theorists insist on doing nothing but grounding values in things; Scheler has rejected the thing orientation only by two arguments, (1) the unexplained claim that Kant *rightly* rejected this orientation and (2) the claim that if one does equate values with the things often associated with them, the arguments (for *ethics*) do not work out.

Scheler thus does not defeat the CBA theorists; and, more to the point, he does not defeat relativisms—he only snubs them. Given his assumptions, he has nothing of interest to say *to* the CBA theorists or anything of value to say *about* them. Theology might be his deus ex machina since it is possible cogently to argue that one's intuitions *are* tuned into the harmonies of the universe since, thanks to revelation, God is the guarantor of one's intuitions. I shall not attempt to confront this line of reasoning here on the grounds that the reader who has stayed with me this far is probably not in a temper to think this way and the Lord helps those who help themselves: we ought not pray unless we are sure we are in trouble.

Here then is the problem. Ethics, if defined as a self-contained study of intuited essences, stands silent to circumstances, cannot answer examples, and in the face of sincere claims of opposed intuitions can only arbitrarily shut them out of the field of ethics. Ethics so viewed cannot engage in a dispute with any other field. We have two examples that expose the serious consequences of this: the moralist has nothing to say to the general who speaks within the field of military science; and we have seen that Scheler cannot reply to sincere intuitional claims about CBA except dogmatically. This alienates ethics from other fields by vitiating its claims to priority, its rights to evaluate. As far as I can see, it means that ethics can speak only to itself. Scheler's views typify this: Kant's empty, barren formalism is replaced with an equally empty and barren pure phenomenology owing no debt to empirical abstractions. As Scheler addresses Kant, we have a dialogue about how best to ground a *shared* assumption that the "movement of the moral law within" (which Scheler makes out to be part of the essence of egoness, its link to the *one world being*) is but a special case of the movement of planets. From this lofty perch, relativity is a mere happenstance of empirical processes.

It might be said that I proceed more dogmatically than Scheler by replacing his insistence on essences with insistence on the importance of fields. I have but sketched a theory; my evidence is admittedly thin and my examples are inclusive. Nonetheless, the most modest inferences permitted by my exposition are that there *are* such things as fields; their discourse is often incommensurable; and interfield differences must be understood to make sense of empirical examples. This is less dogmatic than Scheler's claim that values are nonempirical; it uses no a priorism and it is testable; if there is a standoff, the testable theory is arguably the better one.

Can field theory adequately explain and resolve interfield disputes? Or has an insoluble problem been posed? Does taking fields at their own definition entail so extreme a relativism as to obviate comparative judgments? The present theory makes evaluation a datum, not an accomplished right; but formalists could grant this without surrendering their nonempirical stance. However, they cannot defend the nonempirical posture if, all other things being equal, we have a standoff and the empirical corpus bears against formalism. If I have made plausible arguments here, formalists have to meet the examples head-on or disengage from the dispute. In disengaging, they would admit that they have nothing to say to other fields; in engaging with the data, they would abandon formalism—*zugzwang* revisited.

If there is nothing more to be said than this, we are where Sartre left us; alternativism in ethics and knowledge are the hard facts we have to work with. This is the worst that can come from our theory; and it is not all that bad. It vitalizes philosophic concerns with the practical world; it casts "in principle" arguments under suspicion; and field theorists would have to have something of value to say to situated actors.

But perhaps we can do better than this. If one grants that practical reasoning can be considered "grappling with situations in a philosophic way," argumentation might turn out to do philosophic work. Several claims come to mind that may combine to display a useful solution to interfield disputes.

3.3a *Fields are not hierarchically arranged.* Aristotle constructed his philosophical system the way he thought the world was arranged; the subclaims of metaphysics thus became organizing paradigms for subordinate realms. But such hierarchical arrangements are mischievous unless a thorough-going teleology can be taken for granted. It is thus unlikely that the moral theorist in our recurring example will be able to refute the general's claim that military science does not need to listen to ethics by claiming that ethics is "prior" or "superordinate" to military discourse.

Our field theory is grounded on the idea that interfield discourse stems from activities within the fields. Since fields are *social* entities, they must have "fields of attention" analogous to a person's field of attention; the flow of interfield influence would thus be horizontal, not vertical. Lived experience attends first to this, then to that; individuals thus appeal to fields by glancing, as it were, sideways. Our model here is the person taking influence as a constructive accomplishment of his field of attention.

This is not an ontological argument. People and their fields may so arrange things that epistemic realms *are* hierarchically, temporally, or spatially related. This is a convenience of thinking that might not be shared by others who pursue different analytic purposes. The "history of ideas" will arrange fields temporally just as the great systematizers saw their systems "plodding through time intact." This accomplishes purposes for them, but tracing the ebb and flow of ideas is not central to the present theory.

An advantage of our theory is that it discourages all talk of hierarchies and focuses instead on the ways fields take influence from one another. It implies that interfield disputes (between ethics and CBA or ethics and military discourse) can be settled only by appeal to practices every field uses in taking influence. I hope to show below that these are argument practices.

3.3b *The "invariant–field dependent" dichotomy is unproductive.* The principles most easily said to be invariant do not settle interfield disputes. Universals succeed when unrestrained by particularities—which is why I argued that the most successful of them are substantively trivial. If the precondition of success for universals is *just that* they be unable to justify any particular warrant or claim, dichotomizing invariant and field-dependent principles will not help us understand or settle interfield disputes. The grounds for this sort of success will be field-dependent.

Ignoring the invariant–dependent dichotomy, we can ask about the *range* and *focus of convenience* (Kelly, 1955) of argument principles. The idea of presumption (Willard, 1980c) becomes a universal by virtue of its broad focus and virtually limitless range of convenience. It "works best" (focus) for public argument practices within and between fields and can be made to work (range) for all of the practices we can imagine. Presumption does not by itself settle (say) ethics' disputes with CBA analysts or with military discourse. We might decide which side *had* presumption by considering which side's practices cohered with the practices of other fields. CBA might be the loser because its standards do not square with those of most other fields; that is, it would have the burden of proof if outnumbered this way. So we have broadened "presumption's" focus and range of convenience to include such disputes on the assumption that a principle *like* presumption is foundational to every field's conceptual and procedural ecology. People trust ideas when they think they have been proved. But this does not get us beyond Toulmin's impasse since it is not impossible that a majority of fields would side with CBA's quantifying practices; counting noses, we might get a 603-to-28 vote that values are nothing but quantities (*for all practical purposes*). This in fact happens when decision-makers in conditions of uncertainty opt for the side with the most votes. Decision-makers also reject the consensuses available to them—which means we need a mediating principle derived from field practices, built up from recurring themes in fields' procedures, to settle interfield disputes. Defending universals requires defending principles of application to particular fields. The application principles are just as difficult as the universals themselves. The most successful ones are procedural principles—principles of argument. The more successful they are, the more they make universals redundant or, worse, excess baggage.

The procedural feature common to every field I can conjure is borrowing, using the concepts of other fields to get beyond impasses in a field. Gödel's incompleteness theorem thus has a parallel in procedural ecologies. Inside and across fields, change occurs when someone decides, often by a crude utilitarian calculus, that a new idea does more good than harm. Such thinking may stem from methodological preferences, intolerance of inconsonant findings, simple followership, or intuition. The parallel already drawn between Kelly's views of *personal* constructive processes and field procedures suggests the range of conditions under which a field's actors might decide to jeopardize their system by importing new ideas. Avoiding impasses is often worth considerable risks.

While there are differences between these reasons for change, they all entail appeals to principles *outside* a given field. Taking CBA and ethics at their own definitions, we cannot resolve the value-versus-quantity dispute; neither field can be defeated on its own ground. In resolving this dispute, we will not be saying that one or the other field is "right" but that *people in other fields should look at the dispute in a certain way*. To do this, we need principles outside both fields that nonetheless cohere with the procedures of both. I am pursuing this interfield example because it is a difficult case; if we adequately say how other fields should see it, we shall have gone far toward explaining intrafield change as well.

Let us try two argumentation principles on for size to see if their ranges and foci of convenience make them appropriate for mediating the disputes we have been considering. I shall start with a principle whose focus is too narrow: Johnstone's (chap. 4) "bilaterality" notion. By this he means that one cannot deny one's own argument strategy to an opponent; this is an epistemic test because valid reasoning requires that we not argue in any way we cannot *in principle* allow an interlocutor to argue. While this principle doubtless succeeds in many fields as a professional and pragmatic standard of good debating, our interfield disputes seem to fall outside its focus and range of convenience. Formalists and CBA theorists do just the opposite of denying their own strategies to their opponents: they insist that the only way to refute their claims is to use *only* their strategies. The CBA theorist will listen only to value claims couched quantitatively; the formalist likewise rules empirical and quantitative claims out of discourse.

Let me use the term "closure" to stand for the practice of refusing an argument strategy to an opponent on the grounds that one's own strategy rules it out, as in "formal arguments cannot be refuted by empirical claims." In advance one is told "you may argue only as I do." CBA theorists thus "close" arguments by stipulating the language of quantity as the only useful one for their purposes. They may do this as a procedural convenience by way of simplifying their obligations and burdens of proof; they may also do this because it has the salutary effect of making it impossible for some views to be refuted at all. CBA thus will not be defeated on its own grounds; formalists often get defeated on their own grounds, but by virtue of arguments that make no sense in any other fields.

"Closure" does not mean that an advocate has gotten an idea fallaciously. It is not strictly speaking a fallacy, but an arbitrary dismissal of a procedural nicety. We thus say to the formalist and CBA theorist "you have reached a *stasis* that makes further dispute useless; this is bad because dispute is presumptively good; you achieved this stasis because both theories are too rigid and arbitrary, too self-contained, and too innocent of the facts of other fields; both theories will be improved if you rethink not their substance but your assumptions about the argument standards they have to meet." What is new here is that an argument principle explains the incapacities of both theories.

It is plausible to claim that closure is a sin everywhere. No scientist would deny a theorist the right to analyze his or her data and no theorist would in principle deny the importance of someone's data; but we cannot say the same of the fields that wrestle with "essentially contested concepts." The "progress" dispute discussed in the second part of this essay often turns on the ways schools of thought in the nonsciences use principles and practices held to be refutable only on their own terms. They do what Scheler would call a "Copernican turn," so designing their practices that consensus is dispreferred. The traditional rejections of the possibility of "progress" (discussed above) thus depend upon *closure*. Laudan's (1977) arguments depend upon a nonclosure principle. Fields ignore this nonclosure principle at the risk of being arbitrary; they are not "wrong" about their claims, but they make counterproductive assumptions about their argument obligations.

This thinking coheres with consensualism: its argument principles are not a prioris; argumentation has not been made hierarchically superior to other fields; the only demand is that we make comparative judgments about the argument practices that recurringly work out for the best. Relativity being the case, this is a useful relativism. The comparative study of argument practices aims to assess the strengths and weaknesses of different practices from the perspectives of different fields. The common source of such observations is the practice of interfield borrowing (though there are surely others as well). Given the prevalence of this practice, a field that finds itself alienated from all others by virtue of its argument practices is presumably one that needs to rethink its methods of conducting disputes.

3.3c *Borrowing incurs obligations.* I have modeled fields on interaction and interaction in specific persons. Thus just as individuals enter fields for social comparison, so fields borrow concepts to check their thinking against new standards. One way for a field to resolve its determinism-versus-free-will debate might be to import Gödel's proof, Heisenberg's Uncertainty Principle, or the Second Law of Thermodynamics. Such importation amounts to risking one's ideas against the checks of another field to reap the benefits of progress. The motive is "getting epistemically better." It has thus been common in philosophy's history for particular thinkers to use selected aspects of the physical theories in vogue: Kant appropriated Newtonian space and time to create the a prioris of cognition (Feinberg, 1972, 33) just as contemporary thinkers wrestled with the Copenhagen Interpretation. This is interesting because thinkers who hitched their wagons to this or that physical model did so by virtue of arguments that forced them to share the physical model's fate. The positivists used realism rather than quantum theories to argue, for instance, that psychology should be based on the language of physics. This made them *accountable to the arguments of physics* and vulnerable to the doom of their philosophy of science at the hands of Bohr and others: "if the inherent realism of classical physics showed the sheer irrelevance of idealistic epistemologies, then the idealism espoused by Neils Bohr and others of the Copenhagen school showed the folly of trying to base philosophical positions on current science" (Fine, 1972, 3).

When fields import concepts they *transform* them in ways dictated by their traditional assumptions. But there are limits to such transformations. Imported concepts have no value unless they have to some extent their own meanings. Fields borrow concepts to transcend local obstacles; this would not succeed unless the whole apparatus of the borrowed concept were imported. This permits the inference that a field that wants the advantages of importation assumes the *logical* burdens of the imported concept. If one uses the Uncertainty Principle, one buys into the assumptions that produced it and the conditions under which it might be changed; if the concept is devised by fallibilists, its use entails fallibilism; if the concept presupposes realism, its use entails the demands of realism. I am not resurrecting a priorism here; I am making a claim about how borrowing traditionally works out. An act of importation implies that a field dispute's internal logic cannot work itself out in a satisfactory way; the virtue of importation is that a concept is hauled in intact to point to new lines of argument, implications, and truths that were obscured by the logic being used. While imported concepts get transformed by their new paradigms, their attractiveness and power reside in their capacity to transform the disputes at hand.

While we might see this as a logical principle, it is also a communication principle. Fields borrowing from other fields do, as a practical matter, obligate themselves to attend to the arguments of the fields borrowed from. They hold themselves accountable to the outcomes of arguments in the raided fields. Thus thinkers who ground their theories of knowledge on physical models attend carefully to disputes among physicists; they feel obligated to do so by the internal logic of their procedures.

3.3d *The attention obligation: Fields observing the nonclosure principle command our attention; fields that depend on closure do not.* For purposes of defining the field of epistemics, the question is not whether a field is right but *whether we should pay attention to it.* This question might be asked by anyone in any field for any number of purposes. For our purposes, it is the organizing question of epistemics. First, if concept importation is widespread as I have said, "attending to" other fields must be a fundamental element of every field's epistemic posture. Bear in mind that one part of our field definition is the notion of the *audience*: one way of defining fields is by virtue of how they see themselves as audiences, by the sources of influence they choose to attend to. One way of defining "epistemics" is by pointing to the fields that can and do speak to us and whose procedures and practices are capable of being argued about. Perhaps an analogy will clarify this claim: some fields function like autistic children, being self-contained and unwilling or unable to communicate with others. While we might (being very liberal in granting some premises) grant that autism is an unpainful way of dealing with the world, we would never grant that an autistic person (assuming that we might enter that world) demanded our attention and followership. Just as a naive social actor would never go to an autistic child for social comparison, no sensible field will go to another whose internal definitions make it incapable of speaking or being understood. Our field-defining question, then, is whether we shall take counsel from autistic fields.

If CBA and formalism so define things that they owe no social-comparison obligations to any outsiders, they have no obvious claim on our attention. Their disputes are of no special interest *to us* except as instances of stases that cannot be transcended except by changing modes of argument—in our examples, eschewing closure is what is needed. We have three ways of looking at such stases:

1. Can a field's epistemic views be defeated by its own logic?
2. Does this or that field succeed only by closure?
3. Does the act of borrowing incur an obligation to attend to all arguments pertaining to the borrowed concept?

Respecting (1) we have familiar arguments. We might say to decision-makers, "if you deem decision-making a free enterprise, giving full and fair play to all competing claims, CBA is a data source incompatible with your belief." Respecting (2) we would add "CBA works *only* by virtue of closure; it gets its results in no other way; closure is presumptively bad because it has worked out poorly in most fields." Respecting (3) we would conclude that "CBA is a field based on an assumed right to speak to other fields—especially those involved with decision-making; this, by *its* logic incurs the obligation of attending to counterarguments that do not fit its own quantitative language; if decision-makers are asked to attend to CBA, CBA surely must attend to other fields.

To some formalist theories, the arguments would be the same. Respecting (1) we would survey the *tu quoque* and infinite regress arguments—our skeptical critique being fueled by formalistic assumptions. Respecting (2) we would point to the obvious: "If you in principle rule empirical claims out of discourse, no empirical field in principle owes you its attention. Respecting (3) we would conclude that fields that live by physical concepts can die by them as well.

As to our example of moral versus military claims. Respecting (1) we observe that the general has imported other political concepts ("better dead than Red") and thus has no in principle arguments for rejecting counterclaims out-of-hand. Respecting (2) we say that closure is the *only* recourse the general possesses; by military logic, once the door is opened to value judgments from outside, the "war-is-hell, anything-goes" paradigm is beset. Respecting (3) we say that claims such as "We had to destroy the town in order to save it" *are* imported value concepts; thus military science has no rationale—by its own logic—for ignoring outside critiques. It does not matter whether we can settle the rightness of the general's claim; what matters is that political policymakers in a free society can decide by virtue of the general's mode of argument whether military claims merit serious attention.

3.4 *Argumentation principles are deontological.* Epistemics founded on the sort of field theory presented here is a relativism that respects interfield differences while explaining interfield influences. The three questions we have used to resolve the examples thus dovetail into the critical posture presented in the second part of this essay. They suggest that the study of knowledge be based on what Weimer (1979) calls "comprehensively critical rationalism." Weimer argues that science is a comprehensively critical endeavor because "*all* its conjectures, including the most fundamental standards and basic positions are always . . . open to criticism. Nothing in science is immune to criticism or justified fideistically, by appeal to authority" (1979, 40). This may be an empirical overstatement, but as a normative principle it has much to recommend it. It gives epistemics a way of proceeding with the study of disputes in and among fields without using "justificationist" principles. "The nonjustificational philosophies of criticism locate rationality in criticism rather than in justification. One can be rational without attempting to prove—by criticizing or testing (as severely as necessary)—every position that one entertains" (1979, 41).

Since argument procedures are foundational to knowing (Willard, 1980c, 1981b), the field of argumentation buttresses epistemics by considering the principles and practices that work out for the best. Argument principles do not get their justification *within* argumentation but from their successes in the fields using them. While epistemics is not "justificational" in Weimer's sense, *most fields are.* But the study of justificational practices does not require a commitment to justificationism. So argumentation becomes the study of the accumulated wisdom of fields (in general) respecting their argument practices. As fields change, their practices change; and the test of argument principles is how well they withstand new uses. They are not conjured from thin air or empty logic; they come from practices and are judged in something like an act-utilitarian way—fields evaluate the usefulness of principles by assessing whether their recurring problems fall within their ranges and foci of convenience. There is thus a continual dialectic between argumentation and the fields it studies (and presumably serves).

3.5 *Stability and change are thus explained in the same terms.* Toulmin (1972) attaches such importance to doing this that we might call it the main aim of his field theory. The present project replaces his "conceptual ecologies" with "procedural ecologies" to capture the importance of ordinary practices. The intuitive idea is that stability and change inhere in practices, especially argument practices. In arguments we find what concepts mean by noting their functions and strategic fits into broader arguments; the working hypothesis is that it is their strategic fit that determines their stability or vulnerability to change. A concept's survival factor is not exhaustively contained in its own characteristics but in its fit into broader strategies. Just as monistic epistemologies were critiqued by saying that objects do not "go about the world with their meanings engraved on their backs," so we can say that concepts rarely have their uses carved on their faces. This may explain why, when a field might use two equally good concepts but chooses one over the other, one appeared better. Perhaps the "better" concept was more easily argued, more compatible with other arguments, more socially or politically orthodox, or more powerfully advocated.

I shall not belabor this vis-à-vis other argumentation principles such as bilaterality, clash obligations, burdens of proof, and ethical demands on arguers. If my exposition has been clear and plausible, the reader can work out how these arguments would go. In every case, a nonjustificational interpretation is preferred and one would proceed in a way consistent with the present field theory.

Conclusions

An embryonic theory of argument fields has been proposed and a methodological apparatus appropriate to it has been defended. I have labored to prove not that this is the only viable doctrine but that it is a theoretical view of sufficient clarity and depth to permit coherent methodological choices, useful research, and a plausible sense of the outcomes of taking fields seriously.

I have proposed that fields are real sociological entities whose unity stems from practices. Consistent with Chicago School thinking, I have defined fields as existing in the actions of their members; field theory thus studies "objectifying," not objectivity. The sociological sense of fields is thus elaborated by understanding them also as psychological perspectives; field theory becomes a fleshing out of Mead's "general other." To explain this, I used a three-way analogy between cognitive development, socialization into argument fields, and participant observation. All three depend upon perspective-taking and social comparison processes; and all three help us make sense of the context-embeddedness of action and utterance. Attendant to these claims, I have urged acceptance of fuzziness and blurred distinctions between fields (1) on the sociological assumption that fields in fact relate to each other this way, and (2) on the psychological assumption that "domains of objectivity" get referred to incidentally. This permitted introduction of the notion that we enter fields by accepting their constraints (and a loss of freedom). The "as if" maxim was thus proposed to explain the epistemic advantages of treating schools of thought as if they are ideally "completed" or "accomplished." The "as if" maxim was claimed to be a basic precondition of a field's standards being used—the condition for people taking it seriously.

I proposed in a way consistent with these claims that fields are essentially rhetorical. This means that every field's standards take their authority from the faith people have in them, that a retreat to commitment occurs when standards are challenged, and that fields can be seen as *audiences*. I ruled the concept of the speaker out as a way of *defining* fields but accorded the role of experts and authorities great importance. Contrary to many traditional views, I placed appeals to authority at the very center of epistemics.

The methodology section added three propositions to the developing picture of fields, that they are frameworks of assumptions, that they cannot be equated with their documents, and that they are analytic distinctions. I sought a methodological posture that does justice to what I take to be the one hard fact to respect: the context-embeddedness of action. The multiple realities argument led to the conclusion that justificationism is inappropriate to field criticism and that evaluating the claims of fields is beside the point. I thus adopted a modified hermeneutic posture—unique only in the sense that a speaker's intentions are of central importance in field studies.

I glossed Kelly's view of personal constructive change to describe how fields change—which captures both stability and change in the same language. This procedure also yields insight into why social frameworks and private processes cannot be usefully dichotomized: the dichotomy is pointless. Objectivity is a subjective, constructive accomplishment; field theory is a way of generalizing about this process.

Criticism, as defined here, is an issue field that can secure "progress" in Laudan's sense. The field concept is a focal point that can permit cumulative work and empirically grounded claims about knowledge and knowing, and the range of critical problems can be progressively expanded.

Threaded into these discussions have been examples of interfield differences which I claim other views cannot adequately explain or resolve. I hope to have explained and resolved them. I advanced the principles of nonclosure and of the imported concept to establish the obligations borrowers place upon themselves *by their own standards*. In each case I have been uninterested in saying that a particular field is right or wrong; this would return us to justificationism and its familiar dead ends. Instead I proposed that our organizing question should concern which fields merit our attention as we study knowledge and knowing. This question opens the door to seeing interfield disputes in a more productive way.

If I have succeeded with these examples, we can put forth the claim that argumentation, understood as the study of fields, can be the taproot of epistemics. This doubtless looks like disciplinary imperialism, but consider that argumentation—as defined here—can mount a three-pronged offensive against problems of knowledge: it can study (1) how people pass muster on knowledge, (2) how their communal arrangements and practices affect passing muster, and (3) how people use the things they take to be knowledge in arguments. Strictly put, argumentation can be seen as the theory and criticism of all three.

The "attention obligation" is a two-edged sword. It conveniently allows us to pick and choose our principles; but it likewise obligates the field to succeed with the conceptual problems it takes to be appropriate. Sustained critical work is thus needed to flesh out examples. This theory is not a granite citadel but a gossamer cobweb, and only empirical successes can firm it up.

RAY D. DEARIN

[3] Perelman's Concept of "Quasi-logical" Argument: A Critical Elaboration

The question posed by the present inquiry is whether elements of Perelman's "new rhetoric" (Perelman and Olbrechts-Tyteca, 1969) elucidate the central issues of argumentation or resolve any of its conundrums. Perelman's philosophic mission—to elaborate a nonformal "logic" that brings decision-making within the embrace of an enlarged conception of reason—is so sweeping that any implications for argumentative practice or pedagogy will be secondary or incidental. Nevertheless, this expansiveness of view and detachment from the internecine controversies of communication scholars may provide a vantage point for a new look at the place of logic in the argumentative enterprise. Although this has been called a "pseudo-problem" (Wenzel, 1980) arising from a failure to distinguish the various perspectives from which an argument may be viewed, it is a persistent one indeed. For well over a half-century the cleavage between logic and argumentation has been disputed (Graham, 1924: Anderson and Mortensen, 1967; Mills and Petrie, 1968). Perhaps Perelman's "new rhetoric," which is both a "logic of value judgments" and a "theory of argumentation," can yield fresh insights.

Although Perelman has written extensively on the relationship between logic and rhetoric, this essay will eschew a discussion of these writings in favor of an approach more directly relevant to practical argumentation: a critical examination of certain schemes of argument that appear formally valid, but which, when submitted to analysis, turn out to be specimens of nonformal reasoning. These structures, which Perelman calls "quasi-logical" arguments, can provide a focal point for our discussion, since they exhibit characteristics of both the logical and the rhetorical modes of rationality.

To clarify the idea of quasi-logical argument is, therefore, the primary purpose of this paper; a subsidiary goal is to see what incidental light is cast on the role of logic in argumentation. As a working hypothesis, it is suggested that logic and argumentation have distinct but complementary roles and that this view harmonizes with the audience-centered preoccupation of the "new rhetoric."

This essay first reviews the features of Perelman's theory most relevant to the present inquiry. Second, it explains the nature of quasi-logical arguments. Third, it distinguishes these techniques of argumentation from the structures of formal logic. And fourth, it brings the insights thus gained to bear on certain issues facing modern theorists and researchers in argumentation.

Argumentation and the New Rhetoric

The "new rhetoric" is closely identified with argumentation. *"In my conception,"* Perelman writes (1968, 168), "the techniques of argumentation constitute *a part* of rhetoric, which I explicitly define as 'the study of . . . techniques of non-demonstrative argument, its end being to support judgments and thereby win or reinforce the assent of other minds'" (see also Perelman, 1965, 103). Perelman considers all argumentation rhetorical, from the marketplace variety to philosophical controversy. His oft-repeated definition holds that argumentation studies *"the discursive techniques which make it possible to evoke or further people's assent to the theses presented for their acceptance"* (1963, 155; 1968, 503). It seeks to "convince or persuade." Furthermore, argumentation is exclusively concerned with *discursive* means: "anything done to win adherence falls outside the field of argumentation to the extent that language is not used to support or interpret it" (Perelman, 1957, 8).

The "old rhetoric" of Graeco-Roman antiquity constituted only a special case of argumentation. The "new rhetoric" differs in two important respects: (1) It is concerned with "argument itself" and not its method of communication, and (2) it does not limit the idea of audience to a gathering in the marketplace, but "conceives the possibility of an infinite variety of audiences—starting from anyone who deliberates in secret up to the concrete universality (that is, the whole of mankind)" (Perelman, 1955, 800). This indifference to the mode of presentation and enlarged notion of audience broadens argumentation beyond the conception held by many, perhaps most, argumentation theorists. In Willard's (1978) view, argument is a social relationship based on dissensus, whereas for Perelman no fundamental difference of opinion is implied, the goal sometimes being to *increase* or *reinforce* the adherence of an audience to a thesis. And Crable views the process of argumentation as supporting "a questioned statement by reasoned discourse" (1979, 1)—an unnecessary limitation as far as Perelman is concerned.

In evaluating particular features of Perelman's theory, it is necessary to remember his encompassing philosophical purpose: "[T]his effort to put an end to the absolute supremacy of formal logic takes the form of the elaboration of a rhetorical reason which is more supple, historical, valid in the behavioral sciences and laying claim to being the law of a logic of value judgments" (Loreau, 1965, 458). This is the grand design of *The New Rhetoric*, from its "starting points" (agreements ranging from uncontested facts to disputed loci) through the discursive "techniques" of argumentation (the techniques of association and dissociation). To one kind of associative technique, the quasi-logical argument, we now turn for a concrete expression of Perelman's nonformal reasoning and for a clarification of the practical relationship between logic and argumentation.

Quasi-logical Arguments

Having concluded that modern logic has become a narrow field with little or no application to practical argumentation, Perelman nonetheless recognizes that "logic" enjoys a certain prestige. The term is frequently invoked in the courts, philosophical discussions, and other arenas of nonformal dialogue and persuasion. How are we to reconcile the irrelevance of logic with its obvious rhetorical power? Perelman answers that while strict logical procedures have no application outside formal systems, the *notion of logic* has much persuasive force. In fact, quasi-logical arguments are a species of nonformal argument that owe their effect to their similarity to formal procedures. But they are not formal, "for only an effort of reduction or specification of a nonformal character makes it possible for these arguments to appear demonstrative" (Perelman and Olbrechts-Tyteca, 1969, 193).

Quasi-logical arguments must not be understood as merely deceptive or imprecise versions of the real thing: "formal reasoning results from a process of simplification which is possible only under special conditions, within isolated and limited systems. But, since there are formal proofs of recognized validity, quasi-logical arguments derive their persuasive strength from their similarity to these well-established modes of reasoning" (1969, 193; see Dearin, 1970). It is thus unnecessary to reduce quasi-logical arguments to formal structures and doing so may arouse disagreement, in which case other forms of argument besides quasi-logical ones must be used.

Quasi-logical arguments include those based on logical relations—contradiction, total or partial identity, transitivity—and those depending on mathematical relations—the part and the whole, the smaller and the larger, and frequency. Perelman's examples "can be understood and analyzed differently by different hearers, and logical structures can be regarded as mathematical and *vice versa*" (1969, 194). Although these arguments could have been analyzed according to other planes of cleavage—despite, that is, the arbitrariness of the classification scheme—the specimens of reasoning offered by the Belgians share the common feature that their quasi-logical character is readily perceived.

Quasi-logical Arguments and Formal Logic

Because rhetoric seeks the adherence of an audience, not formal validity, argumentation does not consist of a chain of reasoning in which some ideas are derived from others according to accepted rules of inference; rather, it consists of "a web formed from all the arguments and all the reasons that combine to achieve the desired result" (Perelman, 1970, 18). Let us observe how the strands of this web can be spun out of resemblances to "well-known" principles of logical and mathematical reasoning.

Nowhere is Perelman's view of the similarities and distinctions between logic and argumentation more clearly expressed than in his discussion of contradiction and its rhetorical counterpart, incompatibility. Because logical contradiction must be inescapable within a framework of preassigned conventions and because argumentation uses premises that are inexplicit, "it is permissible only in exceptional cases . . . to claim the presence of a contradiction in an opponent's system. Usually the line of argument tries to show that the theses one is disputing lead to an *incompatibility*, which resembles a contradiction in that it consists of two assertions between which a choice must be made . . ." (1969, 196). Closed systems of thought cannot tolerate inconsistency, but argumentation unfolds openly over time and uses various stratagems (fiction, falsehood, or silence) to avoid inconsistency; incompatibilities exist only in circumstances. We have an incompatibility when two principles apply "simultaneously to the same reality. As soon as the incompatibility can be spread out in time, as soon as it appears possible to apply the rules successively rather than simultaneously, the sacrifice of one of them can be avoided" (1969, 200).

This difference between incompatibility and contradiction underscores the role played by the technique of ridicule: "it is the ridiculous and not the absurd which is the principal weapon of argumentation" (1969, 205). The "most characteristic" form of ridicule consists of "accepting a statement contradictory to that one wishes to defend, deducing its consequences, showing their incompatibility with what is accepted on other grounds, and thereby inferring the truth of the proposition being defended" (1969, 207). Accepting certain objections against the scriptures as established, Whately used this technique to arrive at a denial of the existence of Napoleon.

Arguments based on total or partial *identity* include definitions that, when they claim to identify *definiens* and *definiendum*, are quasi-logical. This is so because relations of identity are not formally valid in argumentation but are merely asserted by the speaker.

Another group of arguments based on the relation of identity includes those that appear to be analytic or tautological. In argumentation analysis, "*all* analysis is directional, in the sense that it tends in a certain direction" and, insofar as it is not strictly conventional, it is quasi-logical (1969, 215). Genuine tautologies likewise rarely arise in argument; and when they do, they are "figures." "Use is made of a formal identity between two terms which cannot be identical if the statement is to be of any interest" (1969, 217). Tautologies are quasi-logical because, at first sight, the terms seem univocal and capable of being identified, whereas differences arise after interpretation. The identities are never complete and they depend on the *context* for their meaning (1969, 218).

Two distinctions can be drawn from this view of tautology as quasi-logical: (1) In the depersonalized calculations of demonstrative reasoning, the mind itself is eliminable from the context of proof whereas, as Zyskind points out, "the mind has an unavoidable and, further, a governing role when the thought is not calculative or experimentally determined. It is most evident in argumentative processes of criticizing and justifying; persuading, convincing, and so on" (1979, x). It is in line with Perelman's theory to say that argumentation is noncalculative, noncompelling, and audience-dependent; in short, it is a *behavioral* matter (Zyskind, 1979, x). (2) Unlike a logical calculus using an artificial language of univocal signs, an argument employs a natural language in which words have various meanings (Perelman, 1970, 19). This thinking supports the claim of Anderson and Mortensen (1967, 143) that, "given the full powers of language, much rhetorical argument may simply be beyond logic."

The final group of quasi-logical arguments modeled after logical relationships consists of those based on transitivity. "Transitivity is a formal property of certain relations which makes it possible to infer that because a relation holds between *a* and *b* and between *b* and *c*, it therefore holds between *a* and *c*; the relations of equality, superiority, inclusion, and ancestry are transitive" (Perelman and Olbrechts-Tyteca, 1969, 227). Transitivity allows formal demonstrations, but it may also be debatable and thus quasi-logical. Syllogistic reasoning is obviously based on transitivity, and it appears that *all* of Aristotle's enthymematic "lines of thought" are quasi-logical (Dearin, 1970).

In brief review, one sees that arguments based on contradiction, identity, or transitivity are never strictly formal; these arguments derive their force from their similarity to formal structures. In each case, the differences between logic and argumentation—the association of the former with a closed system of predetermined instruments and defined methods of procedure, and of the latter with an open system, with language that is seldom univocal, and with temporality—account for the quasi-logical character of these arguments.

Now that the drift of Perelman's thought is becoming evident, we may consider the other kind of quasi-logical structures—those based on mathematical relations. Some of these deal with the inclusion of the parts in a whole; others say that the whole is the sum of its parts; and others draw comparisons stated as facts, whereas the relation of equality or inequality "is often nothing more than a claim of the speaker" (1969, 242). These arguments are not purely formal because they require personal knowledge and because one's interlocutor is under no compulsion to agree with them.

To summarize, Perelman believes that rhetoric and argumentation operate in specific contexts where logic in the strict sense has no place. He nonetheless believes that "the prestige of logic is frequently invoked in argumentation. Moreover, there are techniques of argument whose persuasive force derives from their similarity to recognized logical structures" (Dearin, 1970, 164–165). These are the quasi-logical arguments.

Implications for Argumentation Theory

First, *the idea of quasi-logical argument is useful for the light it sheds on the nature of "validity" in argumentation.* A traditional distinction has been made between the validity of an argument and the truth value of its premises. "If validity is at issue, then criticism concerns the logical connectives between premises and conclusion. The question of validity can be resolved by the principles of logic. If the truth is at issue, however, the question must be decided by whatever inquiries may be necessary for establishing the truth value of a set of premises" (Simmons, 1960, 348). As we saw, argumentative structures bear striking resemblances to logical relationships—resemblances made possible only by a reduction of thought. Analysis reveals their quasi-logical character. The temporality of an argument, its expression in language, and the role of the audience in interpretation combine to give a cast to the notion of rhetorical validity that is quite different from its logical counterpart. Farrell (1977, 148) says that, "given the traditional restrictions upon the usage of the term 'validity,' it might be asked if the conditions for determining rhetorical validity are not so foreign to traditional usage . . . as to undermine all continuity of meaning. Put another way: perhaps we need a term other than validity."

The views of other contemporary writers harmonize with Perelman's notion of rhetorical validity. The late Douglas Ehninger's investigation dismissed six tests that have been propounded for determining the validity of an argumentative case: its internal consistency or noncontradiction, its persuasibility, its comparison with cases earlier judged to be valid, its workability, the number or kind of facts adduced in support of it, and the prestige of its proponent. Ehninger proposed instead that "as an appropriate test of its validity we ask whether a case, assuming it is competently presented, forces a fundamental readjustment in the thinking of the person to whom it is addressed—whether . . . it 'strikes home' in such a way that this person either must abandon or revise in a radical fashion the position to which he previously adhered" (Ehninger, 1968, 219). It must cause the person to do this "out of necessity rather than choice" and must make him "fully aware of the adjustments he is effecting and of the reasons why these adjustments are required" (Ehninger, 1968, 220; Johnstone, 1964). This position comports well with Perelman's notion that the adherence of the audience, a standard internal to the rhetorical *situation* but not internal to the argument itself, is the standard for evaluating rhetorical appeals. The idea that the interlocutor be fully aware of the readjustment is not necessary to Perelman's thinking because for him the efficacy of an argument itself becomes a test of its rationality, the degree of which will be a function of the quality of the audience whose adherence is gained. In this sense, Perelman's view parallels McKerrow's (1977, 135) notion that *"an argument is valid if and only if it serves as a pragmatic justification for the adoption of a belief."* This can mean that quasi-logical arguments are complementary to logic: "if rhetoric were a mere counterpart of formal logic and not complementary to it then the standard of rhetoric could be the establishment of what is probable or has verisimilitude. The standard here, however, in the new view, is not truth. It is the adherence of the judge" (Zyskind, 1979, x).

This discussion of quasi-logical arguments and rhetorical validity indicates that the dichotomy expressed by Simmons between validity and truth in argumentation is misleading. "How we argue a point of view depends on the audience we want to convince and the techniques we must use to make this conviction valid," says Kluback and Becker. "There is no truth apart from its communicability. Truth is a social and political reality. This point is the profound difference between Perelman and Hegel. This was the same difference that separated Socrates from Plato" (Kluback and Becker, 1979, 39). Nowhere is the inextricability of rhetorical validity and truth more evident than in Perelman's quasi-logical arguments.

Beyond this broadened view of rhetorical rationality encompassing the notions of validity and truth, *another area highlighted by Perelman's treatment of these quasi-logical techniques is the role of the audience generally in the process of argumentation.* "Rhetoric," as Robert Feys follows Perelman in pointing out, "differs from logic in that it is occupied not with abstract, categorical or hypothetical truth, but with adhesion" (1961, 12). This emphasis on adaptation to the audience (Crable, 1979, note 8) "pervades literally all his writing that occurred during and after his 'discovery' of the 'new' rhetoric." Indeed the choice of the term "rhetoric" rather than "dialectics" to characterize his emergent theory of argumentation was made largely as a result of the centrality of the audience in the ancient theories of rhetoric: connecting argumentation with rhetoric in this way underlines the fact that argumentation is developed in relation to an audience. Submitting quasi-logical arguments to analysis reveals clearly, as we have seen, the role of the mind in the argumentative process. The so-called "prestige associated with rigorous thought" is nothing else than an accumulation of mental associations an audience in our culture might hold as a result of the generally assumed credibility of modern logic, or the unchallenged success of mathematical reasoning in certain well-delineated areas of knowledge. The process of association whereby a linkage is made between the quasi-logical structures and their formal counterparts is also, of course, a psychological or behavioral activity. In short, the workings of these quasi-logical arguments reveal clearly that mental activity is occurring which differs appreciably from the mechanical operations within the closed system of a formal logic.

Given the Belgian writers' preoccupation with the audience as the central element in their theory of argumentation, it is ironic that Perelman's concept of quasi-logical argument should come under criticism for its alleged continuation of the outdated "will–intellect" dualism (and its rhetorical counterpart, the "conviction–persuasion" dichotomy). This seems to be the concern of Willard, who writes from a "constructivist" perspective:

> We may owe to Perelman and Olbrechts-Tyteca the notion, however vague, of "quasi-logical" arguments. This notion seems intuitively attractive, but the Belgians have hardly pinned the notion down. If my arguments here are sound, we surely do not wish to define quasi-logical arguments as formal serials which are somehow "contaminated" by the emotional spewings of animal soul. Argumentation theorists can reformulate the idea of logic with reference to movements in construct systems, needing no appeal to dualities of logic and emotion, conviction and persuasion, or (possibly) even form and matter [Willard, 1980a, 171].

Although the distinction between conviction and persuasion is recognized in *The New Rhetoric*, it does not involve the psychological faculties of an auditor but results from the *sort of audience* being addressed. Writing of this dichotomy, Perelman and Olbrechts-Tyteca (1969, 28) say:

> However, even if one refuses, as we do, to adopt these distinctions in actual thought, one must recognize that our language makes use of two notions, convincing and persuading, and that there is a slight and perceptible difference in the meaning of the two terms.
>
> We are going to apply the term *persuasive* to argumentation that only claims validity for a particular audience, and the term *convincing* to argumentation that presumes to gain the adherence of every rational being. The nuance involved is a delicate one and depends, essentially, on the idea the speaker has formed on the incarnation of reason.

It is not necessary here to discuss the merits of Perelman's "universal audience" as a rhetorical concept; one can simply acknowledge that in Perelman's scheme the "will–intellect" distinction is transcended as he shifts the distinction to the type of audience addressed: the particular is persuaded, the universal is convinced. As Zyskind says, "Thus we have a confrontation of opinions instead of a knowledge–will separation" (1979, xiv). The role of emotional factors in argumentation is far from that of a "contaminant." To be sure, for Aristotle personal factors and extra-logical considerations (stylistic figures, volitions, time pressure) were undesirable but necessary elements in rhetoric. "Aristotle recognized the unavoidability of emotive involvement," writes Zyskind, "but he sought to minimize this by making his quasi-logical forms the body of rhetoric and dealing with the emotions in a separate popular psychology; and in the *Topics* very little consideration is given them." Zyskind continues:

> Perelman's premises and method are different. Relying on discourse to which the new rhetoric is restricted to carry an initial sense of order, he tends as much as possible to assimilate feeling into the quality of thought itself, thickening it with an extra dimension. Although when writing as a logical empiricist he used C. L. Stevenson's separation of cognitive belief from adventitious emotion in the use of a term, he shifts from that position in rhetoric: "the 'emotive meaning' is an integral part of the notion's meaning, not just an adventitious addition." It belongs to the symbolic character of language; and its role in meaning is important argumentatively because it influences the ambiguity of a notion's meaning [1979, xiii–xiv].

In the quasi-logical arguments of *The New Rhetoric* one sees, indeed, the inseparability of the part of an argument's appeal that derives from its approximation to a "recognized" logical form (which part is based itself on an "emotional" attachment to the notion of logic and its forms) and the other part of its appeal deriving from the context, language, or other attributes of the argumentation.

Perhaps by pressing the matter at issue we may see in a new light the effect of "soundness" or "validity" as an ingredient of an argument's appeal. Mills and Petrie bring this question into focus:

> Why do some rhetoricians . . . deny that logic has any significant place in rhetoric? Such a denial may have stemmed from a crucial ambiguity in the original Aristotelian formulation. *The Rhetoric* does not say whether logic persuades through its "proper" or its "accidental" features. For instance, logic may effect persuasion through its own "proper" nature of providing logically compelling reasons for belief and the concomitant recognition of the rationality of such belief by the audience. Or logic may stimulate belief through external or "accidental" features of formal argument such as style or emotional involvement, irrespective of its formal correctness [1968, 260].

In Perelman's view, the "formal correctness" of an argument is always an elusive phenomenon. The similarity of an argumentative structure to an analogous relation in formal thought disappears as the argument is shown to have meaning. Only in the closed universe of a logic whose terms are univocally expressed, and whose rules and procedures are pre-fixed, can formal validity be achieved. But this is not to say that arguments can only stimulate belief in the second sense spoken of by Mills and Petrie— through external or "accidental" features of formal argument. The persuasion exerted by logic through its "proper" nature of providing "logically compelling reasons" recognized by the audience is also a rhetorical matter. Both instances are included in the enlarged rationality of the new rhetoric, and, although Mills and Petrie use the term "logic," the Belgian writers would assign both these modes of appeal to the realm of rhetoric. For Perelman and Olbrechts-Tyteca,.the ambiguity attached to the notion of logic in Aristotle's *Rhetoric* has resolved itself clearly as modern-day logic has become a purely formal affair, a condition that leaves correspondingly more room for the scope and reach of the "new rhetoric." And these quasi-logical structures constitute a reminder that logic was once a broad, embracing discipline that included forms of reasoning which can now be seen to have been rhetorical all along. Hence these arguments should not be considered fallacious or sham versions of "the real thing"; their soundness rests, as it does with other rhetorical techniques, upon the degree and nature of the adherence they elicit from their audience.

As a corollary, the resulting elucidation of the relation of (present-day) logic to rhetoric makes clear that some of the commonly perceived "fallacies in logic" are actually rhetorical deficiencies. "Begging the question," for example, is an error not in logic but in rhetoric: "The orator who builds his discourse on premises not accepted by the audience commits a classical fallacy in argumentation—a *petitio principii*. This is not a mistake in formal logic, since formally any proposition implies itself, but it is a mistake in argumentation, because the orator begs the question by presupposing the existence of an adherence that does not exist and to the obtaining of which his efforts should be directed" (Perelman, 1970, 14–15). Instead of *assuming* the truth of a proposition, this fallacy actually presumes in advance that the assent of the interlocutor has already been gained. Such an insight could only emerge from a theory of argumentation in which the audience is never forgotten and in which the restricted role of logic is rightly understood and carefully spelled out.

Not only does the concept of quasi-logical argument illuminate the nature of "validity" in argumentation and highlight the role of the audience, but *it also contributes to a unified theory of argumentation by linking the common world of social controversy with the most intricate and formalistic reasonings of philosophers*. The tendency has been to focus on the differences between everyday reasoning and philosophical argument. Thus, McKerrow (1980, 214–227) says that "The stock of argument forms commonly employed in social argument may be characterized as less formal than those utilized in the philosophical community. While the basic element of 'reason plus claim' is the same in both arenas, the standards governing the relationship between reasons and claims differ radically." With such a statement one should perhaps not take issue, although Perelman would emphasize the differing audiences applying those "standards." However, McKerrow goes on to add that "Perelman and Olbrechts-Tyteca's treatment of quasilogical arguments such as incompatibility exemplifies the difference between social and philosophical argument." Actually, one might argue more plausibly that quasi-logical arguments demonstrate the *continuity* between the two fields of argument. A charge of *contradiction* is no more appropriate to an inconsistency in a philosophical argument than in the lowliest of ordinary squabblings; unless the point at issue is a purely formal error, the proper label is *incompatibility*. Philosophers, like other reasoners, employ quasi-logical arguments, as any analysis of the ambiguity of their terms or the temporality and contextual dependency of their arguments will attest. This is not to say that philosophers do not aspire to convince the "universal audience" by presenting arguments which (they think) *ought* to gain the adherence of all reasonable men. In practice, however, a reduction of even their most "formalistic" arguments (assuming they are not chains of thought borrowed entirely from a formal proof) will reveal their quasi-logical character. In this respect, a thread of similarity is shown to run throughout the field of argumentation. Quasi-logical arguments give support to the thesis propounded in the opening pages (1969, 7–8): "We shall show that the same techniques of argumentation can be encountered at every level, at that of discussion around the family table as well as that of debate in a highly specialized environment."

It has recently been charged that Perelman's theory of argumentation is not as unified as it purports to be, and that Perelman occasionally has recourse to the very concepts of formal validity and self-evidence which his new rhetoric seeks to overthrow. One line of criticism advanced by Wenzel concerns the "universal audience," a concept that has received far more attention than its place in Perelman's theory warrants. Objecting to the critical perspective engendered by the "idealized conception of the critic that follows from a purely formal logic," Wenzel writes that:

> An uncharacteristic slip into that formalism seems to be the cause of Perelman and Olbrechts-Tyteca's remark that "Argumentation addressed to a universal audience must convince the reader that the reasons adduced are of a compelling character, that they are self-evident, and possess an absolute and timeless validity. . . ." and ". . . maximally efficacious rhetoric, in the case of a universal audience, is rhetoric employing nothing but logical proof." The conception of the logical critic that emerges from such a formalistic notion of

logic is not so much that of a human exercising judgment as a "logic machine" applying some invariant rules of validity. Moreover, one wonders what sort of propositions and arguments (excluding mathematical statements) could possibly be "self-evident" and "possess an absolute and timeless validity." So Perelman and Olbrechts-Tyteca seem to lapse into that uncharacteristic formalism because at that point they focus on the nature of the *appeals* as the ultimate grounding of validity and soundness [1980, 123].

Wenzel argues for a much broader conception of logical criticism—one that would emphasize the *persons* making up the universal audience, not formal structure and self-evidence of the arguments.

Because Perelman's whole philosophical enterprise culminates in the new rhetoric as a rebellion against the Cartesian notions of the uniqueness of truth and self-evidence, and against the influence of the mathematical logicians on the modern state of logic, Wenzel's comments would seem to uncover a serious inconsistency (an incompatibility, no doubt, not a contradiction) in Perelman's theory of argumentation. However, two things need to be pointed out: (1) The universal audience is a highly idealized conception (addressed only by philosophers or others who seek to convince an "incarnation of reason") that never exists in the form of a specific audience (except as "floating incarnations"); (2) more significantly, Wenzel (1980, 123) believes logic can be something other than the purely formal logic Perelman believes it has, in fact, become. Wenzel argues for "a much broader conception of logical criticism than that implied in *traditional, formal logic*" (italics mine). In Perelman's view, logic has today been reduced to an entirely formal affair whether we like it or not, and what Wenzel would like to call "logical soundness":—that is, the winning of the approbation of the universal audience as all *qualified* judges—is actually "rhetorical soundness." The new rhetoric, as we have seen, has expanded to encompass the territory left by a glacially receding modern logic.

Another criticism more directly relevant to the concept of quasi-logical argument has been offered by Willard, who agrees with the Belgians that "formal reasoning results from a process of simplification that is possible only under special conditions, within isolated and limited systems." But Willard (1980b, 271) disagrees with what follows:

The Belgians, however, follow the above statement with a pronouncement I believe to be false, viz., that "since there are formal proofs of recognized validity, quasi-logical arguments derive their persuasive strength from their similarity with these well-established modes of reasoning." True, they are

persuasive to philosophers, logicians, and argumentation theorists of formalist inclination. But as a statement about the persuasive impact of ordinary
arguments, this proposition is demonstrably false.

Like Wenzel, Willard finds an excessive formalism in Perelman's thought.
Unlike Wenzel, who writes from the standpoint of a logical critic of argumentation, however, Willard seems to be concerned with the psychological
soundness of Perelman's conception of quasi-logical argumentation (that is,
whether there is *really* any similarity to formal patterns of thought that
actually persuades people). Willard (1980b, 276) says expressly: "The belief
of Perelman and Olbrechts-Tyteca . . . that arguments take their persuasive force from their correspondence to logical form is profoundly erroneous. . . ." First, it should be said that quasi-logical arguments *are used* in
all argumentative settings, not just in discussions with philosophers, logicians, and certain theorists of argumentation. One hears them in daily
conversation ("Boys will be boys," "Any friend of John's is a friend of
mine."). Second, Perelman is not concerned with how arguments actually
work on minds, as though argumentation were a branch of psychology.
Whether or not the persuasiveness of these arguments, if indeed they are
effective at all, is due to their similarity to logical relations is certainly open
to discussion (and, perhaps, experimentation). Because most quasi-logical
arguments could also be examined from another perspective (plane of cleavage), it would be difficult in given cases to identify the actual characteristics that make them persuasive. Certainly it would be hard to isolate their
quasi-logical character from other elements. About all that can be said here
is that Perelman is a logician of thought seeking a unified theory of argumentation, not a communication theorist or pedagogue.

If Willard objects to the idea that "there are formal proofs of recognized
validity," however, this is a more serious philosophical issue that cannot be
resolved by rhetorical or communication theorists. Any recourse to actual
arguments outside formal systems cannot disconfirm their existence. However, it could be posited that a natural inclination exists impelling arguers
to seek to develop arguments that approximate the standards of validity
that *do exist* (by definition) in formal logic. Evidently Crable has this tendency in mind:

> Human agents seem almost universally to act upon the impulse to reason
> "correctly." What we do not seem to agree upon is the nature of "correct-
> ness"—the criterion or criteria that operationalize correct reasoning. Formal
> logic was—and in some respects, is—an attempt to create a universal stan-

dard of correctness. And, to the extent one argues about A's, B's and C's or other contentless symbols, the relationship between argument and this particular kind of logic is simple and straightforward [1979, 7].

That practically all argumentation deals with symbols rich with content, and in which the context plays a deciding part, does not diminish the fervency with which arguers try to construct their unassailable arguments. Nor is this a conscious proclivity to which only logicians, metaphysicians, or a certain breed of argumentation theorists are susceptible. Indeed, a careful reading of any scholarly paper (including, one suspects, Willard's) reveals assumptions implying the existence of "valid" patterns (laws of identity, noncontradiction, and the like), as would the analysis of the arguments of any "naive social actor." But the actual existence of these "forms of recognized validity," or the sense in which they exist, is a matter not for the theorist but for the philosopher of argumentation.

There is reason to believe, finally, that this investigation of Perelman's concept of quasi-logical argument *can contribute to a clarification of the argumentation "discipline" itself.* The sharpened distinctions concerning the concept of rhetorical validity demonstrate how the forms of logic can be invoked in argumentation, even as the field of logic itself has become remote from the concerns of most persuaders. The reasserted place of the audience links argumentation inextricably with rhetoric, as that field was understood by the ancient Greeks and Romans. And the acknowledgment of the essential unity of the argumentative enterprise, irrespective of the setting or audience, should go a long way toward eliminating unnecessary distinctions between social and philosophical argument.

Naturally theorists and researchers will be enthusiastic about stressing the insights to be gained by viewing argumentation from their own disciplinary perspectives. In recent years, for example, Willard's (1978, 125) research shows that a cornucopia of intriguing results can flow from the constructionist and interactionist paradigms of the communication theorists. Taking an "argument-as-process" model based upon a "processual view of reciprocal perspective-taking," Willard has proposed that *"argument is a kind of interaction in which two or more people maintain what they construe to be mutually exclusive propositions."* By defining argument as a specific kind of social relationship or encounter, he rejects the "traditional view of argument as serial predication." This theoretical stance leads Willard to denounce the idea that argument can be dealt with as a "unit of proof" or "unit of reasoning." As a consequence, he attacks the utility of a diagrammatic model of argument of the kind developed by Toulmin. Says Willard (1976, 43), "an argument, as the communication theorist looks at it, and as the argumentation theorist ought also to regard it, is a psychological phenomenon having no existence apart from the individuals who use it. It is not a 'thing' endowed by nature with substance and properties." Perhaps it is not a "thing" *as the communication theorist views it*, but, as this investigation of quasi-logical arguments has shown, a particular kind of argument can profitably be viewed as a structure bearing a certain resemblance to an identifiable, "recognized" relation in formal logic. Following the "logic of value judgments" approach yields results quite different from those of the communication theorist employing a paradigm such as constructivism or interactionism. Put another way, the adherent of the new rhetoric and the communication theorist address differing conceptions of the universal audience.

One's disciplinary perspective determines, in large part, how one understands the nature—or indeed the *existence*—of discrete, isolable arguments. A good effort at clarifying these alternative perspectives is made by Wenzel:

> From the standpoint of rhetoric, a good argument is an *effective* one; from the standpoint of logic, it is a *sound* one; and from the standpoint of dialectic it is a *candid* and *critical* interchange. The failure to distinguish those critical perspectives, grounded in different disciplines, has given rise to a number of issues in the literature that I would characterize as "pseudo-problems." One of these was the debate over the relevance of logic to rhetoric that involved most notably Mortensen and Anderson on one side, and Mills and Petrie on the other [1980, 126].

Without arguing the matter in any great detail, one might propose that the insights of the interactionist could contribute to the dialectical evaluation of the "candid and critical interchange," while the enlarged notion of reason espoused by Chaim Perelman can embrace both the "logical soundness" and "rhetorical effectiveness" of an argument.

As our scrutiny of quasi-logical arguments shows, however, the reduced scope of modern logic and the test of audience adherence as a measure of effectiveness cause the logical and rhetorical perspectives to merge; that is, today's rhetorician becomes essentially a logician of thought. Even so, as Simmons (1960, 350) has said, "We must sharply distinguish between the argu*ment* and the argu*ing*. Arguing, the social function of argumentation, needs persuasion for it needs clear communication and inducement to understanding." As to whether any discipline purporting to investigate the process of argumentation can effectively dispense with the idea that "arguments" exist, the observation by Brockriede (1977, 129) rings true: "Although persons can make arguments without engaging in the process of arguing, I do not see how they can argue without making arguments." However one views the *process* of argumentation, in conclusion, it is undeniable that there are *products* also. Moreover, it has been the purpose of this paper to show that an analysis of certain of these products, the quasi-logical arguments described by Perelman, clarifies the relationship between logic and rhetoric as it sheds light on some of the persistent, recurring issues facing contemporary theorists and researchers.

HENRY W. JOHNSTONE, JR.

[4]   Bilaterality in Argument and Communication

For many years I have been claiming that a philosophical argument cannot be valid unless it is bilateral (1978, chap. 3), which is to say that the arguer must use no device of argument he could not in principle permit his interlocutor to use. This claim now seems to me to apply to discourse of a more general sort than philosophical argument. In particular, it seems applicable to some kinds of communication, including the most important kinds. I shall develop the case for the bilaterality of communication, then compare my conclusion with my earlier views on philosophical argument.

Language is not restricted to communication. Yet communication does seem an indispensable core of linguistic activity. A creature that used language in every way that man does except to communicate would not be human. The grunts and growls by which he established authority and vented emotions would not distinguish him from subhuman animals of many kinds.

It might be argued that every grunt or growl is in fact an act of communication. It tells others about the dispositions of the utterer. It seems to me, however, that it does so only in an abstract way. A rival recoils from the snarl of an ape; isn't it stretching things to say that the ape has communicated anger to his rival? And yet if my reader wishes to suppose that every linguistic act is an act of communication, I have no essential quarrel. Instead of working toward a philosophy of communication, I shall be elaborating a philosophy of language in general.

To be human is to be able to communicate. (The converse is not true; animals such as bees communicate without being human.) It follows that if there are motives for becoming human or maintaining one's humanity, it is from these same motives that one communicates. Under such circumstances, a pragmatic account of communication is not sufficient. By "a pragmatic account" I mean one according to which we communicate in order to achieve the satisfaction of particular needs. For example, I make known my hunger in order to be fed, or I tell the traveler the way to his destination that he may arrive there. But if there is an imperative to become or be human and communication is an aspect of being human, then we communicate not merely to achieve the satisfaction of our needs but in order to participate in humanity.

The imperative to become or be human must, I think, be established by something like an ontological argument. One version of the latter is the consideration that if there are to be arguments at all, whatever is presupposed by the possibility of arguing must exist. The ontological argument is thus an argument for the existence of the ground of all arguments. If, for example, language is presupposed by argument, any argument is itself the premise of an argument for the existence of language. Similarly, any imperative presupposes conditions under which imperatives are possible and thus presupposes the imperative to maintain such conditions. Only humans (or, as Kant would say, rational beings) are responsive to imperatives. The humanity of the addressee is thus a condition under which any imperative is possible. It follows that it is an imperative to maintain this condition.

I have so far put the matter very abstractly. As I proceed I hope to make it clearer what I mean by "humanity" and how I think it might be enhanced or maintained. Such clarification depends on a further discussion of communication.

We must ask what *sorts* of communication maintain humanity. For obviously not all sorts do; one example is the honey-dances of bees. And what can be communicated to a computer is certainly no contribution to humanity. And what a computer communicates, in the form of output, is not likely to enhance the humanity of its audience, although it may facilitate his or her choice of a course of action.

It can in fact be doubted whether a computer can engage in communication at all. Elsewhere (1978, 130–131) I have argued that while communication presupposes an interface, no genuine interface presents itself as we feed information to a computer. It is claimed, of course, that there is an interface between the punched card and the electronic impulses generated by the machine. But the punched card, the card-reader, and the processing of the impulses generated by the latter are all part of the same system; there is no break in it, no gulf to be crossed. Or if there are any gulfs, everything is a gulf—not only the relation of the punched card to the sensing circuits of the card-reader but also the relation between those circuits and whatever electronic element receives their output in turn. The point is that there can be no mechanical model of the sort of gulf that is crossed at an interface—a genuine gulf the peculiarity of which is that it can be crossed. If an interface is a frontier at which impulses propagated through a medium of one kind must be converted to impulses of a radically different kind, propagated through a different medium, then we must look to something other than the design of computers for examples of a genuine interface. The best place to look would be the human percipient. There is an interface between the energy impinging upon one's sense organs and what occupies one's attention. Sometimes this interface is absent, as it is when the percipient is paying no attention to the signals reaching him or her from the external world. On such occasions there is presumably no interruption of the train of energy transfers from the world to the sensorium. That train is as continuous as is the train that leads from the input of information to the computer to ultimate output. But if sensory energy is to register as information, as a message, a gulf must be crossed. The percipient must begin to notice the noises being heard, and to interpret them as, say, the ticks of a clock or the ringing of the telephone. Otherwise, background sensations are devoid of informative content. (To be sure, subliminal stimulation can be construed as unnoticed information and is clearly a case in which a percipient responds just as a computer does; but here I am talking about stimulation which is superliminal—in principle perceptible.)

One way to put my point is to say that the process through which a person consciously receives information is mediated. The information does not pass directly from its source to the storage facilities of the receiver. It must first be acknowledged by the individual, whose capacity to acknowledge the information received can be thought of as the medium of that information. In more general terms, the medium of communication is language, whether it is the privately addressed language in which I acknowledge that the phone is ringing or the intersubjective announcement through which someone else calls the ringing to my attention. It is likely that situations of the latter type are antecedent to those of the former—that I could never tell myself that the phone was ringing unless on a previous occasion someone else had told me.

The situation I am attempting to describe is similar to the one Aristotle had in mind in one of his criticisms of Democritus (*De Anima*, 419ᵃ, 15–17). Democritus had declared that if the distorting medium of air were replaced by void, we could see an ant in the sky. Aristotle's impatient retort "But it is impossible" rests on his conviction that in the absence of a medium we could see nothing at all. Sight presupposes a medium that makes visible. (We mustn't be too harsh on Aristotle for failing to know that the void can make visible.) The communication of information similarly presupposes a medium that makes explicit, that rescues a message from the shadowy darkness of the background. In either case, the medium mediates. It intervenes between stimulus and experience. Aristotle is fond of telling us that an object placed directly on the eye cannot be seen (see *De Anima*, 419^a, 11–13). The visual medium must separate the object from the eye. Language, the medium of communication, likewise must separate the message from its recipient. Otherwise it would be as if we had opened a person's skull and simply placed the information on the brain as one might place an object on the eye.

Sometimes we attempt to communicate with others as if they were computers. We feed information to them in the expectation that they will process it appropriately. But there is something paradoxical about an effort of this sort. For it can succeed only when the other is not a computer—when that person is in a position to acknowledge what is told him or her, to rescue the information from the background noises that surround it. Communication is successful only when mediation is invoked.

Now I am in a better position than before to deal with the question of what I mean by "humanity" and how I think it might be enhanced or maintained. For one way to obey the imperative to be or become human is to engage in mediation. Man* is the mediating animal, the animal capable of reflecting on his own experience and thus of holding it at a distance. (While the honey-dance indicates the distance of the pollen, it does not hold the pollen at a distance; it simply triggers a response.) Furthermore, a person is humanized or maintains humanity if he or she addresses the capacity of another to mediate. For the process as it occurs in oneself is not independent of the result of one's dealings with others. As I have already pointed out, the latter process is antecedent to the former. More generally, furthermore, part of being or becoming human is maintaining or encouraging humanity in others. This is true in particular because the mediation that one invites in another is likely to take the form of a move in a dialogue in which the initiator will himself be addressed through language.

It is reflective communication that humanizes. Communication is reflec-

---

*"Man" here and in the rest of this discussion of course means the human being of either gender, and "his" connotes his *or* her or his *and* her. This long-used communicative shortcut appears here consciously and without prejudice; the thrust is defining being and becoming *human*.

tive when the person addressed can hold at a distance the message he has received, maintaining the distinction between that message and himself. I do not mean to suggest that he regards the message as false or that his stance toward it is critical. It is sufficient just that there be a gap between the message and its recipient. The latter must be conscious of the former as originating outside himself. A computer cannot enjoy such consciousness, because it has no notion of an "outside." All the impulses it processes are impulses internal to it.

I am trying to circumscribe the relation between communication and humanity—to circle around it so as to see it from all sides. One link that it is now relevant to mention is bilaterality. I have already argued that one aspect of our becoming or being human is to encourage humanity in others. Communication that is bilateral does this. By "bilateral communication" I mean the transmission of messages to another in such a way that it is clear that he is entitled to transmit messages to me in the same way. In other words, my transmission does not deprive him of any mode of transmission. Examples of unilateral communication—that is, communication that is not bilateral—include pronouncements of those claiming authority, suggestion, hypnosis, brainwashing, and, in general, situations in which a speaker puts extraordinary presence and personality behind the utterance of a message. Such a speaker cannot afford to permit replies supported by a magic equivalent to those of his utterances, for such replies would totally neutralize the messages he was trying to get across. There is never room for two disagreeing authorities in the same auditorium.

In bilateral communication, each interlocutor speaks as if the others were capable of propagating a message fully as credible as his own. He treats his hearers with respect rather than as merely means to the end of their own credulity. A typical situation involving bilateral communication is a classroom discussion. If the teacher makes it clear by his very manner of addressing the class that he supposes that any of his students is in as good a position to communicate credible messages as he is, he is, in effect, making available to them all the techniques of transmission he can avail himself of. This situation contrasts sharply with the authoritative lecture in which the teacher in effect withholds from his students the devices of presentation he uses. This teacher is not, in his communication, enhancing the humanity of his students—although I shall comment further on this point. Nor is he enhancing his own. For the more he manipulates the belief of his audience the less is he engaged in the spiritual exercise of mediation. His language tends no longer to serve as a medium that separates him from his topic, enabling him to reflect upon it, but simply becomes an auditory aura of his body, an extension of his face that touches his hearers directly like the object on the eyeball. His voice becomes a sensory field like his odor as it impinges on his dog—immediate and offering no option of reflection either to his audience or to himself.

Bilateral communication, on the other hand, is reflective communication. If I am fully prepared for your not accepting my message, I am prepared also to go along with your nonacceptance. I am prepared for the contingency that I might myself have to withdraw my own acceptance of my message.

By "reflective communication" I mean communication in which both communicator and communicatee can entertain the possibility that the message might be subject to revision. They are, in other words, able to reflect upon the message. This means in turn that a space intervenes between the message and those who consider it. The communication is mediated; the message does not directly assault the mind of either party. Hence "reflective," "bilateral," and "mediated" all come to pretty much the same thing when they qualify communication.

In this discussion I am moving to a generalized version of a position I have been advocating for many years, that valid argumentation in philosophy must be bilateral. As early as 1959 I held that in a philosophical argument in which the arguer did not make available to his audience exactly the techniques of argumentation that he himself used he was arguing invalidly. I see now that the concern I had in mind was of much wider application. If the autonomy of one's interlocutor in an argument must be respected, why not also the autonomy of any person with whom one is communicating? And why should such autonomy be restricted to the exercise of philosophy? Just as no valid philosophical argument ought to strong-arm its audience, so no valid communication about anything—shoes or ships or sealing-wax—ought to enlist belief by means unavailable in turn to the audience.

The extension of my view to communication, at least of certain kinds, forces me to re-evaluate the role of rhetoric and indeed to understand its nature in a different way. Hitherto I had thought of rhetoric as the use of one-sided arguments, the ones that withheld from the audience the franchise to employ them. Rhetoric was thus tantamount to unilateral argumentation. I see now, however, that even if there is a rhetoric of that sort, another rhetoric is precisely the instrument needed to open up bilateral argumentation and communication. This is the rhetoric that drives a wedge between a message and a mind to which it is addressed. It is the rhetoric that calls to my attention the fact that the telephone is ringing or, to choose a less trivial example, that separates out of the confused background of my unexamined assumptions the assumption that the Shah was good for Iran, now that this assumption has been forcefully challenged. Before we can think about any issue, we must first attend to it. The rhetoric that forces it on our attention is the rhetoric of bilaterality, because no one can, in the nature of the case, have a monopoly on it. If I can point out your unnoticed assumptions, you can point out mine.

If I include certain kinds of communication in my list of activities that I recommend carrying out bilaterally, I imply a kinship between communication of these kinds and valid philosophical argument. Perhaps what is central to both is that neither is a use of force. A philosophical argument, even of impeccable validity, cannot compel its hearer to abandon willy-nilly the position he espouses; it cannot charm or psych him out of it. If he does abandon it in view of the argument, his will, his consent, is involved; he must himself see how the argument exposes hitherto hidden defects in his position. Similarly, communication of the kind I have in mind cannot see truth as a club. It must get me to see the truth in my own way. To choose a simplistic example, a phone bill is a communication. But the mere statement "You owe $34.05" does not enlist my belief. If I am to accept this dun, I must see an itemization, and know that I can take exception to it if it is wrong. The communication is bilateral because I am free to use the same arithmetic that the phone company does. One effect of recent Truth in Lending legislation has been to render bilateral certain previously unilateral kinds of communication. A unilateral bill is tantamount to a creditor's simply helping himself to some of my bank balance; the transaction need not even register in my consciousness. (Unfortunately this procedure does seem to be in the offing as computers take over more and more of the work of banking. Unilateral billing is much cheaper than bilateral.)

I have been arguing that bilateral communication implements the imperative to be or become human. Of course not all communication is bilateral; we must consider what other sorts there are. We shall find that some unilateral forms of communication can also be humanizing.

It has been remarked that in a university lecture the notes of the professor pass into the notebook of the student without going through the mind of either. This old joke in fact states the essence of unilateral communication: that it should bypass minds. Small wonder that it can most efficiently be carried out by machines, since it requires no interface, no medium. One can think of many similar examples. Teletype messages tumbling into a stockbroker's office are only intermittently present to a mind, and when they are they are not likely to trigger a bilateral response. They enlist consciousness at its dimmest and most automatic level. But even a communication of which one is fully conscious need not exhibit the possibility of bilaterality. A letter from a journal editor accepting a manuscript of mine needs no reply. Directions to my friend's house given by an obliging native must be held in mind as I count the traffic lights but not challenged.

Some unilateral communications not only evoke consciousness but do so in a way that can clearly be regarded as humanizing. If the university lecturer is authoritative in his grasp of his field, his one-way communication to a student can open for the latter a new world of experience, a world of fascinating ideas. In more general terms peremptory communication can serve to structure a life, as sometimes happens when a parent "lays down the law" or a charismatic preacher lays the foundation for a basic decision.

Unilateral communication verges on force; indeed, the soft-sell, suggestion, subliminal stimulation, and hypnosis are forms of force. There is a place for force in human life, if only because if all possibilities of bilateral communication were realized, people would talk forever and nothing would get done. Philosophy, however, cannot be carried out by force, and neither can the kind of communication that shares with it its bilaterality. This kind of communication is necessary to human life even if to some extent the other kind is also necessary.

PART TWO

Reasoning and Reasonableness

RAY. E. McKERROW

[5]   Rationality and Reasonableness
in a Theory of Argument

Reason, the source of human being, is a colorless thing to
contemplate. It cannot be characterized in itself, but only
when subjected to the limitation and particularity of a character. Conceived in its perfection, it is nothing but an empty
image, but seen in its reality, it is everything that constitutes
the dignity of man. It is never complete in time, for it is
merely man's path uphill. Its essence is to grow greater, not to
be greater to begin with [Jaspers, quoted in Natanson, 1974,
337–348]

Jaspers' view encompasses two visions of reason. It is a perfect but cold,
sterile instrument "indifferent to our needs and desires" and a "living
force," a "historically continuous matrix within which the individual is
able to confront and analyze, doubt and defend, consider and reconsider the
meaning and implication of the central terms of his existence" (Natanson,
1974, 337). Tillich (1953–60, 73–75) aptly terms these visions *technical
reason* and *ontological reason*. The former, separated from values, is inextricably linked to method as a systematic, unvarying adherence to rules of procedure. The latter is "cognitive and aesthetic, theoretical and practical,
detached and passionate, subjective and objective" (Tillich, 73). An argument theory solely reliant on *technical* reason cannot be sustained. Argument, conceived of as "organization" (Cowan, 1972, 333) is nothing more
than a sterile product of cognition. Unconnected to values, such a conception of reason—and the theory of argument it would dictate—is "subject
to a deterioration of outlook—'specialists without spirit or vision,' in
Weber's formulation" (Natanson, 1974, 338). *Ontological* reason, conversely, provides a broader basis for a theory of argument. Focused on the

concerns of daily life, it allows us to proceed, however imperceptibly, on "man's path uphill."

Consideration of reason, whether technical or ontological, inexorably leads to a concern for the rationality of enterprises with which reason is connected. In the case of argument, conclusive reasoning is the exception rather than the norm, and the personal values of the arguers are as integral to the outcome as the method of arguing. What ensures the rationality of this reason-giving activity? If rationality is ensured, can we presume that the argument and its acceptance or rejection are reasonable? Does rationality entail reasonableness? Finally, does reasonableness mean that *good reasons* have been presented for belief or action? These questions suggest three topics as requisites in an elaboration of the role of reason in argument theory: (1) reason and rationality, (2) rationality and reasonableness, and (3) reasonableness and good reasons.

Reason and Rationality

Rationality has historically been associated with the employment of reason in accord with an internally coherent set of agreed-upon rules or procedures. The essence of Cartesian rationality, and the paradigm for modern science, is *method* (Gadamer, 1979, 7). Going further, one might assert that this conception of rationality is, or should be, the paradigm case for all reasoning, including public argumentation. Decision and procedural rules independent of the substance of argument and of the arguers provide an impartial standpoint from which to ensure the rationality of human discourse. The appeal of scientific reason, with its concern for precision and clarity, is *almost* irresistible. Its successful claim on our attention as the principle guiding deliberative discourse is evidenced in our discipline's preoccupation with analytic schemes for the validation of argument (Willard, 1976; Introduction, this volume), although there are some exceptions (Toulmin, Rieke, and Janik, 1979). The ultimate inadequacy of *method*, derived from a Cartesian view of rationality, is likewise evidenced in the resurgence of nonanalytic formulas for the validation of claims (Toulmin, Rieke, and Janik, 1979). These recent developments are familiar (Introduction, this volume) and require no elaboration beyond underscoring the necessity of an alternative to "scientific rationality":

> It is obviously true that taken from a certain perspective scientific behavior itself is rational in the sense that it proceeds systematically in accordance with

the principles and rules of theoretical reason. . . . Yet it does not follow from this that scientific rationality for that very reason would be the paradigm of all human rationality. To the contrary, it is an impoverished, demundanized, and dehumanized form of rationality to which no one will appeal directly outside the realm of pure theory and the realm of certain games. It seems legitimate to claim that the more someone's personal and social life is guided by scientific reason, the more impersonal, inhuman, and "irrational" it will be [Kockelmans, 1979, 105].

Scientific rationality, in short, epitomizes the excesses of technical reason devoid of its ontological characteristics. But if science is not the paradigm and its applicability even to science is questioned (Feyerabend, 1970), then on what view of rationality shall argument theory be premised? One possibility is to ground rationality in discourse itself (Jacobs and Jackson, this volume). Insofar as argument is a species of discourse, this possibility bears directly upon our own efforts to ensure that arguments within social, philosophic, personal, and other communities (McKerrow, 1980; see Willard, 1981a) will not lose the rationality that was proffered by science. Arguments conducted without recourse to the independent standards of scientific reason can be considered rational.

Winch (1970, 1958) presents a thesis that, in its direct concern for particular universes of discourse, has direct affinity to Toulmin's embryonic "field" notion. Winch grounds the determination of rationality in language: "Reality is not what gives language sense. What is real and what is unreal shows itself *in* the sense that language has. Further, both the distinction between the real and the unreal and the concept of agreement with reality themselves belong to our language" (Winch, 1970, 82). In particular, Winch is concerned with the attempt to impose standards of scientific rationality on the beliefs and practices of "primitive societies." In the application of such standards, the rituals and "magic" of primitive people may be judged as naive and irrational. A primary question for Winch is whether "a primitive system of magic, like that of the Azande, constitutes a coherent universe of discourse like science, in terms of which an intelligible conception of reality and clear ways of deciding what beliefs are and are not in agreement with this reality can be discerned" (1970, 83; see Maund, 1976; MacIntyre, 1970). The sense in which the beliefs of the Azande might be considered rational is not to be derived from our cultural expectations or linguistic conventions. It is instead derived from an understanding of the Azande's perception of reality—grounded in *their* language—and the standards of rationality that flow from that perception. While Winch's argument is more complex than outlined here, three implications of his position are relevant to our present concerns.

First, Winch's claims regarding language and reality provide a departure point for the thesis that scientific reason is not the sole arbiter of our rationality. If, as he suggests, there are discrete universes of discourse, each provides a distinct view of what it means to think and act in a rational manner. Second, his cultural relativism implies the absence of a single, arbitrary standard against which the rationality of our culture and others is to be judged. Arguments, whether occurring in our culture or that of the Azande, are evaluated in terms of the perceptions of reality created by the language-in-use within the respective culture. The possibility that our sense of rational argument would be violated in a primitive society may make their practice irrational by *our* standards, but not necessarily by their own. Finally, reason is allowed to assume characteristics beyond the technical. Discussing a critique of his work, Winch (1970, 106) argues that his critic has seen in the Azande magic a misguided attempt to affect the production of crops. Arguing that the critic misses the point of the rituals, Winch claims that "a Zande's crops are not just potential objects of consumption: the life he lives, his relations with his fellows, his chances for acting decently or doing evil, may all spring from his relation to his crops. Magical rites constitute a form of expression in which these possibilities and dangers may be contemplated and reflected on—and perhaps also thereby transformed and deepened."[1] Reason is interwoven with one's way of life; it is more than technique as it affirms, whether in scientific explanation or "primitive magic," that which has meaning and relevance for our beliefs and actions. Correspondingly, a theory of argument that purports to account for the way people use reason to justify their beliefs and actions must be more than an inventory of techniques.

Apel's (1979) typological characterizations of rationality provide a second point of departure for the analysis of reason's relationship to argument. Apel argues that the creation of scientific rationality has caused the a priori dismissal of other forms of explanation as prerational. In the realm of political praxis, the development of a *means-ends* or *strategic* rationality has had a similar effect on the exercise of practical reason. Both of these developments, "as paradigms of so-called *value-free* rationality have tended to render obsolete the possibility of an *ethical rationality*, i.e. of legitimizing or criticizing conventional norms and institutions on the basis of intersubjectively valid norms" (Apel, 1979, 310). The challenge to reason and hence

[1] For critiques of the context-dependent principle, see Lukes (1970) and Hollis (1970).

to argumentative discourse lies in the clear disjunction between technical and ontological reason. Value-free rationality norms, in Apel's analysis, guide deliberation in the public life. Decisions in politics, economics, and other public arenas are predicated on procedures heralded as legitimate because of their presumed value-free status.

In seeking to displace scientific rationality as the sole norm guiding deliberative affairs, Apel grounds his conception of reason in human discourse:

> Instead of suggesting that beyond the sphere of *value free scientific technological rationality*, there are only *pre-rational subjective decisions* about norms, values and aims of human actions . . . there must be presupposed a *special sphere* of *universal rules or norms of communication*, and *hence of communicative rationality*. For, it is only under this presupposition that consensus in argumentative discourse about the meaning-claims and validity-claims of science and technology can be conceived of as possible [1979, 324].

The process of reaching consensus in science or politics requires agreements embedded in the act of communication itself. If it is not agreed that consensus can be reached "through *argumentative discourse* within a *communication-community*," the application of value-free standards to deliberation is called into question; value-free rationality is not altered by this presupposition; "rather it is *complemented* by another type of rationality" (Apel, 1979, 323). This latter type can, Apel says, act as the normative base for three subtypes of rationality: hermeneutic, ethical, and dialectical. All three share a concern for the interactants in an exchange and the mutual reciprocity that results from their awareness of each other's needs. Drawing upon Habermas' analysis of the requirements of the ideal communication situation, Apel seeks to ground the rationality of scientific, ethical, and dialectical norms on the linguistic preconditions for the validation of truth, truthfulness, and rightness claims. His view of argumentation as a fundamental, originating communicative interaction emerges in this passage:

> One may show that argumentative discourse is not just one language game among others, such that its preconditions and rules are contingent in relation to other language games and such that a human being could decide to join it for a while or leave it at some point in time. One quasi-empirical way of refuting this preconception might be sketched as follows: *Consensual* communication, i.e., striving for agreement about meaning claims, truth claims, and rightness claims, is a precondition of all types of communication, even of those that primarily serve strategic purposes, e.g., negotiating and the like. Now in cases of differences or conflicts of opinion or interest, there is only one

alternative to breaking off communication . . . developing *consensual commu-nication* into argumentative discourse. Thus argumentative discourse presents itself as the *instance of critique and of legitimation* with respect to all other forms of human communicative interaction [1979, 333].

People who agree to enter into arguments do so with a commitment to the belief that, in principle, conflicts can be resolved in a deliberative manner. International symposia which bring together a wide diversity of opinions and values "*pretend* to have accepted the principles of argumentative media-tion of the interests of all affected beings" (Apel, 1979, 335–336). It is adherence to this normative principle, Apel believes, even when it is a *public fiction*, that implies respect for others and ensures the continued viability of the communication community as the vehicle for resolving public ques-tions in a rational manner.

The realization that real argumentative situations rarely achieve the po-tential implied by the standards of hermeneutic and ethical rationality leads Apel to a third subtype, *dialectical rationality*. A politician must take cog-nizance of the fact that opponents may act in strategic modes—to secure success rather than understanding, in Habermas' terminology (Habermas, 1979)—rather than in terms of ethical rationality. The contradiction be-tween the real communication situation and its ideal necessitates "a *dialecti-cal mediation of ethical rationality with strategic rationality*, under the boundary conditions of concrete historical situations" (Apel, 1979, 339). If we as a world community take our survival seriously, mediation will be aimed at a long-range goal: the realization of an ideal communication community within the historical present of a real communication situation. As Hempel (1979, 50) suggests, rationality implies goal-directed behavior. Scientific procedures are rational only insofar as they are instrumental in achieving scientific goals. Likewise, the dialectical mediation between the "is-ought" reality of our communicative condition is rational only insofar as it moves us toward the goal of an ideal communication community. This regulative principle provides the standard for assessing the status of deliberative argu-ment in the mundane world.

Habermas' contributions to argument theory are familiar (Burleson and Kline, 1979). Rather than retrace steps already taken, I shall focus on his argument for the rationality of social action. In an essay critiquing Weber's teleological approach to rationalizing action, Habermas (1979) seeks to extend the possible bases of rationality to cover cases of communication. His critical assumption regarding how arguers enter into discourse is that participants in theoretical discourse "must start from the universality of the claim to propositional truth and impute to one another a mutual knowledge of what it means to raise and to criticize truth claims. Only an identical understanding of truth, however rudimentary and implicit, guarantees the possibility of deciding a discourse with reasons; that is, of coming to a rationally motivated agreement" (Habermas, 1979, 186). Rationality, whether in theoretical or practical discourse, is premised on an understanding of the procedures by which validity claims are to be tested. Weber's model of purposive action assumes an instrumental means–ends relationship between interactants. The discussion that takes place uses empirical data to impose, in objective fashion, an agreement on the participants. A second type of action, strategic action, is a limiting case of communication. In this case, "claims to subjective truthfulness and normative rightness are suspended. The truth of statements plays a role in the private action-orientations of the individual participants, but it is just as little constitutive of the social relationship between them as are the other two validity claims" (Habermas, 1979, 196; see Habermas, 1979a, 209). It is in strategic communication that the principal forms of "real communication," to use Apel's term, undoubtedly occurs. Speakers may fake their acceptance of the presuppositions of communicative action and manipulate their audiences. They also may be deceived about their own employment of the presuppositions and engage in "systematically distorted communication" (Habermas, 1979, 1979a). In either case, the deception is hidden from the other participant in the exchange.

Where strategic action is oriented toward success, communicative action aims at achieving understanding via an intersubjectively held agreement. Three types of action—constative, expressive, and normative—seek understanding with regard to truth, truthfulness, and rightness in the external, inner, and social worlds respectively (Habermas, 1979, 198). The advantage of this triadic relationship between speaker, act, and world is that it defines for any communicative situation the parameters on which agreement must be reached if understanding is to ensue from the challenge. In reference to Willard's (1978, 1978a, 1979, 1979a, 1979b, 1980a) challenge to rationalistic argument, Habermas' formulations provide a cohesive set of possibilities for regulating interaction without denying *either* a methodical appraisal of the truth of a claim *or* the attention that may be paid to the personal perspective of the "socially situated actor." Apel's formulation adds what I believe is a needed component in Habermas' paradigm of rational communication: the dialectical tension that exists between the "real" and "ideal" speech situations. Apel locates the *force* of this tension in our self-reflective awareness of a need to be cognizant of the interests of others. Habermas is interested in explicating social types of action for analytic purposes (1979, 202). Apel usefully appends to this a practical application that seeks to explain and justify the existence of an "is–ought" gap between what our competence directs us to and what our performance invariably yields. Winch's (1970, 109) analysis is a reminder of the complexities involved in coming to an intersubjective understanding. The remedy for our cultural blindness toward the rationality inherent in primitive magic (such as an aborigine's belief that a walking stick is the incorporation of his soul) can be sought in the conjunction of Habermas' and Apel's theories of rational communication.

Arguments about the rationality of the act can proceed only insofar as we are willing to accept validity standards other than those dictated by our own culture; for example, as we extend the dialectical tension inherent in a contemporary political debate over nuclear power in the U.S. to a worldwide debate about the same issue, we cannot presume that the agreements we have reached in the limited sphere will define the parameters of rational discourse for debate in a broader context. Our use of reason will be emancipatory only as we recognize that our divergent conceptions of reality are grounded in language. Our argumentative discourse will be properly critical only as we adhere to the fundamental presuppositions inherent in validating challenged claims.

Rationality and Reasonableness

If the above conditions are realized, can we affirm that our efforts are *reasonable*? Before answering this question, it is important to note that "rationality" and "reasonableness" are not equivalent terms. Perelman (1979, 213) has a useful distinction: "We understand the expression rational deduction as conformity to the rules of logic, but we cannot speak of a reasonable deduction." Perelman connects rationality with the precision of mathematics and logic—it epitomizes technical reason. Reasonableness, on the other hand, is more akin to ontological reason. It is a social rather than a purely personal or subjective concept: "What is reasonable is, in more or less broad lines, accepted by common opinion in society" (1979, 222). Divorced from the arbitrariness of technical reason, reasonableness is subject to change as the "common opinion" of society alters; what is considered "reasonable" in one age may seem unreasonable in another. Perelman contrasts rationality and reasonableness in terms of law:

> The *rational* in law corresponds to an immutable divine standard, or to the spirit of the system, to logic and coherence to conformity with precedents, to purposefulness. Whereas the *reasonable* . . . characterizes the decision itself, that fact that it is acceptable or not by public opinion, that its consequences are socially useful or harmful, that it is felt to be equitable or biased [1979, 217].

When the force of logic yields conclusions counter to society's sense of what is reasonable, the friction between rigid adherence to the law and a "humane" interest in justice produces a re-examination of the system itself (1979, 217). The tension between the rational and the reasonable is essential: it serves as the source of progress and change as society continually revises the system of laws in accordance with the public's notion of what constitutes a reasonable decision.[2]

This coheres with Fisher's (1980, 125) view that "being reasonable requires the presence of an other." The quality of "being reasonable" is in Fisher's view more "of an attitude than an ability" that one possesses: "To say that someone is reasonable is to say that the person uses reasons and is appreciative of and tolerant toward others who use reasons to justify their views" (Fisher, 1980, 122–123, 1978). Peters (1976, 303) offers a similar sense of reasonableness: "'Reasonable' suggests a willingness to listen to arguments and relevant considerations advanced by others in public argument." The social, intersubjective nature of being reasonable implies a certain sense of impartiality in dealing with situations where the interests of others also are at stake. Peters sees the willingness to listen and to be impartial as distinct gradients in the idea "reasonable."

This thinking blends two senses of reasonableness. The first is Perelman's imputation of reasonableness to the decision that is to be made (its "fit" with socially accepted norms). The second lies in the Fisher / Peters sense of "being reasonable": the person's disposition to listen and to be impartial. How are these two senses related to rationality? If we adopt the standards of rationality formulated by Apel and Habermas, it would appear that rationally validated conclusions are also reasonable. In Apel's case the types of communicative rationality are premised on a reflexive awareness of others'

---

[2] For a recent series of essays devoted to Perelman's views, see "La Nouvelle Rhetorique: Essais en hommage a Chaim Perelman," *Revue Internationale de Philosophie* (1979).

needs. This implies a social, intersubjective stance that can be applied in two directions: toward the claim itself and toward the dispositions of the persons involved. The regulative principle bridging the gap between real and ideal situations also requires that others' needs be taken into account: one can neither judge decisions nor act toward others in a purely subjective or selfish manner. These concepts of rationality are grounded in language and tempered by an application of reason in a humane and humanizing world. Thus there is less opportunity for the type of conflict between rationality and reasonableness that Perelman envisioned. While rationality does not *entail* reasonableness, there is an expectation that the terms are compatible rather than contradictory.

Reasonableness and Good Reasons

The third question raised at the beginning of this essay was a "Does reasonableness mean that *good reasons* have been presented for belief or action? The answer to this question begins with two conclusions implicit in the foregoing analysis: (1) Ontological reason, as expressed in theories of rationality grounded in discourse, is the preferred foundation for a theory of argument and (2) the degree of a decision's reasonableness and the attitude of being reasonable are compatible with—and are expected products of—discourse that adheres to the standards of rationality adopted by a communication community. Given these as *general* operating principles, we still have not achieved a "logic of good reasons" sufficient to ensure reasonableness. Presumably, such a logic would be compatible with the presuppositions of rationality and reasonableness discussed above. But compatibility alone is not enough to justify the acceptability of the reasons themselves. The principal question that faces us is: What standard or criteria of justification should be employed in underwriting a logic of good reasons?

A caution is in order here: the relationship between reason, rationality, reasonableness, and good reasons is complicated by the imprecision of our own terminology. For example, when we speak of justification as the alternative to verification, do we imply reasons for belief or reasons for action, or both? The distinction is important, as it reflects divergent bodies of research, one investigating the cognitive basis for "knowledge" and the other determining the moral or ethical nature of our actions. Nathan underscores the difficulties and suggests that argument theorists are not alone in being imprecise or in using multiple meanings attached to justification:

We talk of one propositions' justifying another, meaning that the first proposition supports or is evidence for the second. We talk also of a man's being justified in believing a proposition. This may mean merely that he has a right or entitlement to believe a proposition which derives from its being at least probably true, or alternatively that right to believe it which derives from the fact that his believing it would be by some decision-theoretic standard better than not believing it. . . . The terminology of "justified belief" is as chaotic as the terminology of "rational belief" and "rational action" [1980, 5].

Unless otherwise noted, the following discussion will employ justification and good reasons in terms of belief rather than action. The concern will be for validating claims as worthy of belief as opposed to assessing reasons for actions. The discussion will comprise a brief review of (1) the "classical" or "traditional" analysis of belief, (2) standards of epistemic appraisal, and (3) the merits of a "plausibility thesis" as the structural components underwriting good reasons on behalf of claims.

The traditional analysis of "justified true belief" is usually cast in these terms (Swain, 1978, 89): "S has nonbasic knowledge that p if and only if (i) p is true; (ii) S believes that p; (iii) S's justification renders p evident for S; [and] (iv) there is no special counterevidence q such that q defeats S's justification." Two features of this formula are worth noting: first, it links the justifiability of p to a *truth* condition; second, the formula contains a counter (iv) to the possibility that some evidence could be brought forward to defeat the justification. Both implications would appear to flow solely from a technical conception of reason. Furthermore, the "defeasibility" injunction is logically required to insulate knowledge from contradiction, but is foreign to a world of contingent argumentative claims (see Paxon, 1978; Swain, 1978a).

The justification of p can be considered in several contexts. Those that appraise p in epistemic terms require conclusivity (strong sense) or probability (weak sense). Armstrong's derivations are instructive:

(1) "q" is a conclusive reason for believing that p if, and only if, it is the case "if q, then p." Conclusiveness of reasons is simply a matter of the *truth* of a proposition.
(2) "q" is a good reason for "p" if, and only if, it is the case that "if q, then p is (more or less) probable [1973, 97].

1 implies a standard of analyticity in accordance with the dictates of technical reason. 2 broadens the base somewhat but still perceives rational belief in terms of an independent standard of probabilities. In both cases, the emphasis is on the *epistemic* nature of p.

Lehrer (1978) offers a coherence view of *doxastic* justification closer to the standards of ontological reason. A doxastic system is "a set of subjective statements articulating what he believes, is what his beliefs must cohere with in order to be completely justified" (1978, 291). In this perspective, "S is completely justified in believing *p* if and only if, within the corrected doxastic system of *S*, *p* is believed to have a better chance of being true than the denial of *p* or any other statement which competes with *p*" (1979, 300; see Stevenson, 1975). Given the nonapodictic nature of argumentative deliberation, a doxastic perspective is compatible with a sense of *pragmatic justification* in which the aim of validation is that of providing a reasonable basis for belief. A contrast between epistemic verification and doxastic justification would imply a role for a theory of argument in both realms and would clarify the goals of particular disputes. In Habermas' system of rational "action," belief is validated when interlocutors accept, at a theoretical level, a proposition as *true*. But not all argumentation can or will be at that level or arrive at a final, irreversible claim. In those contexts a doxastic system, if extended from a subjective set to an intersubjectively shared set of beliefs, would provide a rational basis for arriving at decisions. The system also allows for new evidence that may successfully alter prior beliefs by changing the weight of the options delineated in Lehrer's definition of justification. Thus the approach is compatible with the possibility that doxastic systems, however carefully constructed, are not immune from change (see McKerrow, 1977; Stevenson, 1975). The need for technical reason at some level of analysis is not precluded by a preference for an ontological reason. As Rescher notes, "There is no rationality without an appropriate procedure for giving a *rationale*—a suitable fabric of good reasons in cases of the sort at issue" (1977, 76). Chisholm (1978) provides a "procedure" by which the relative status of reasons within a doxastic system can be appraised. In each case, the status depends on a judgment that one belief is, in his words, *epistemically preferable* to the other. Preferability does not mean that the truth value of the belief has been verified in an analytic sense. It preserves the flexibility of Lehrer's doxastic system while presenting a hierarchical scale of appraisal standards. Consider the proposition "Nuclear power is safe"; using Chisholm's formula we can derive the following logical choices [NPS = proposition] (see Chisholm, 1978, 257; Keim, 1975):

1. Believing NPS is preferable to withholding a belief in NPS.

1A. Withholding a belief in NPS is preferable to believing NPS.

2. Believing NPS is preferable to not believing NPS.

2A. Not believing NPS is preferable to believing NPS.

3. Withholding a belief in NPS is preferable to not believing NPS.

3A. Not believing NPS is preferable to withholding a belief in NPS.

Given these three statements and their respective opposites, we can establish a hierarchy of appraisal possibilities keyed to the above options:

A. NPS is certain: implies (1) plus the assumption that there is no other proposition more reasonable to accept.

B. NPS is evident: (1) plus the assumption that if other propositions are more reasonable than NPS, they are certain.

C. NPS is beyond reasonable doubt: (1).

D. NPS has some presumption in its favor: (2).

E. NPS is counterbalanced: (2) and (2A) are equal; (3) and (1A) are preferred jointly as there is no reason to embrace or reject NPS.

This hierarchical scale is adapted from Lucey's (1976) critique of Chisholm's "oppositional" format. From a negative perspective we may apply the following scale:

F. NPS is gratuitous: (1A).

G. NPS is unreasonable: (3A).

H. NPS has no presumption in its favor (2A).

A–E moves one from the realm of pure epistemic justification to a position where no choice can be made and withholding belief is the only rational recourse. From B–H one assumes a doxastic attitude on the part of the believing person. F–H are arranged in a plausible hierarchy from weak to strong rejection of belief. Taken together, A–H present a positive / negative scale that can be utilized in assessing the relative merits of propositions vying for belief. One is justified or has good reasons for acceptance or rejection on the basis of the criteria.

The set delineated above is context-independent; the determination of which criteria are applicable in a specific case is based on context-dependent considerations. This dual characteristic is similar to Toulmin's concept of "force" in that it *could* be argued that the criteria terms (evident, and so on) function as modals whose application does not vary as one moves across various logical types.[3] The duality also can be compared to Lukes' (1970, 208) critique of Winch's linguistic relativism thesis. If Winch is correct, the above criteria are context-independent *within* the formulating cul-

[3] For recent discussions of the "field" concept see Willard (1980, 1980a, 1980c, 1981a, 1981b, 1981c) and McKerrow (1980, 1980a, 1980c). Toulmin's (1972) relationship between fields and "rational enterprises" is also questioned by Haynes (1979, 419–429).

118 · REASONING AND REASONABLENESS ·

ture—they are not automatically applicable in the same sense in other cultures. Lukes argues, on the other hand, that "some criteria of rationality are universal, i.e. relevantly applicable to all beliefs in any context, while others are context-dependent, i.e. are to be discovered by investigating the context and are relevantly applicable to beliefs in that context" (Lukes, 1970, 208). A decision on the limits of universality attached to context-independent criteria is beyond the scope of this review. My purpose has been to illustrate potential commonalities and to raise an issue forced by Winch's thesis.

How fully one can determine the fit between a specific proposition ("nuclear power is safe") and the appropriate context-independent scale is virtually impossible to specify in a concrete, final sense. As Mortimore and Maund (1976, 15) suggest, "the standards of reasonableness largely concern the degree to which a reasonable man can justifiably fall short of full epistemic rationality because of its costs in terms of time, energy, resources, and forgone ends." In a fashion reminiscent of Toulmin's (1958, 1972) discussion of what it means to *claim to know*, Mortimore and Maund say that such "costs" are applied in the *research activities* that are considered normative for the particular subject area involved. From a practical standpoint, the person seeking to justify a belief in a proposition may limit the search for one of several reasons: the level of "certainty" is one that requires little proof; the implications of the proposition have a low risk factor (are not important or harmful); the monetary cost of an extended search is prohibitive; or the time constraints preclude full employment of research. Provided the person is satisfied and can satisfy an opponent, the search will yield a pragmatic justification that is acceptable even though it falls short of "full epistemic rationality"—a condition equivalent to Habermas' criteria for the ideal domain of theoretical discourse. The process may not fulfill all of the requirements intended by Habermas in validating truth but is not any the less rational in spite of its incompleteness. Its rationality lies in the same frame of self-reflexive awareness called for by Apel. The standards of a particular communication community will indicate what must be done to achieve "truth" and will specify the conditions whereby "costs" preclude the full and complete exercise of the ideal standards.

Rescher's (1977) "plausibility" thesis takes us a step further in fleshing out the activities that might be considered in underwriting a logic of good reasons. In a description of dialectic that makes use of the concepts of presumption and burden of proof, Rescher (1977, xiii) sees dialectic as a "vehicle for reasoned argumentation. In large measure dialectic is to our *factual* knowledge what logic is to our *formal* knowledge: a mechanism of rational validation." Where Chisholm would search for true or self-evidential propositions as the foundation for the claim that *p* is true, Rescher argues for the integration of "presumptive truth" within the structure of good reasons for the acceptance of a claim. Presumption must be clarified in order to assess where the burden of proof resides: "There must clearly be some class of claims (presumptions) that are allowed at least *pro tem* to enter acceptably into the framework of argumentation, because if everything were contested then the process of inquiry could not progress at all" (1977, 34). One of the chief difficulties of the "justified true belief" approach to verifying claims is its potential for infinite regress. If "p" is accepted because of "q," then what validates "q"? This led to two distinct research hypotheses, one seeking a foundation in certitude, the other attempting to escape from any formal designation of a "ground." Rescher's proposal is an alternative, one directly related to a rhetorical understanding of argumentation. Although a presumption can be overturned, its defeasibility is not a negative constraint on its utility as the stopping point in a search for good reasons justifying the acceptance of a belief in "p." Although not "true" in a final sense and hence failing to satisfy an analytic conception of knowledge, the standard of presumption does offer a sufficient basis for grounding a doxastic system of argument (see Rescher, 1976, 1979; Cornman, 1978).

Reschèr ties his concept of plausibility to the foregoing by advancing a rule that "presumption favors the most *plausible* of rival alternatives" (1977, 38; 1976). Plausibility does not refer to how probable a proposition is; rather it has reference to how well a proposition may cohere within a person's cognitive set of beliefs. An exponent of a coherentist theory of knowledge, Rescher perceives plausibility as stemming from three possible bases: (1) source reliability; (2) source evidence; and (3) systematicity (1977, 41). The first two are familiar resources: the extent to which an authority can be accepted and the probative value of the evidence are general guides to the determination of how likely the belief in question will "fit" within our present cognitive frame of beliefs. The final criterion refers, in Rescher's terms, to principles of induction: "Other things being sufficiently equal, that one of the rival theses is most plausible which scores best in point of *simplicity*, in point of *regularity*, in point of *uniformity* (with other cases), in point of *normalcy*, and the like" (1977, 41).

While Habermas provides the conditions under which rational argument can proceed, Rescher offers a theoretical stance sufficient to determine when the process ends. As noted earlier, there must be a rational procedure for determining when a controversy is over. The standards of an epistemically grounded analysis of "justified true belief," however rigorous, seem inappropriate in satisfying the present need. Their major value lies in illuminating the requirements of an analytic conception of knowledge. Lehrer's probability based doxastic system, in conjunction with the adapted scales of epistemic appraisal, offer some specificity in underwriting a logic of good reasons. Given a coherentist view of truth, in which items must fit within the cognitive system of the knower, Rescher's theory of presumptive truth possesses heuristic value both for the solution to the "foundation" problem and for the justification of argument. In particular, Rescher's theory of plausibility grounds argument in a nonanalytic set of criteria for the justification of belief. His perception of the termination of an argument answers to the infinite-regress problem faced by the traditional analysis of knowledge claims and provides a reasonable ground for decision:

> The proponent is in a "winning position" when *all* of his opponent's rebuttals—or at any rate those of them to which he has had a reasonable chance to reply when the point of termination is at hand—are covered by cogent countering limits whose component premises are *all* presumptive truths (or highly plausible theses). The opponent is in a winning position whenever *any one* of the proponent's contentions is left unprotected in point of adequate support through presumptive truths (or highly plausible theses) [1977, 44–45].

The communication community has the responsibility of imbedding a technical set of appraisal standards within the general framework of its linguistically derived standards of rationality. Only in this way will the competence displayed in the ideal situation, or the dialectical tension between the real and the ideal, be maintained. Rescher's demand is all too essential: "A shared procedure for the assessment of plausibility and the allocation of presumption thus emerges . . . as one of the critical presuppositions of rationality throughout the context of rational discussion" (1977, 45).

Attending to the weighing of facts as the basis for a rational judgment is only part of the total picture. In Meiland's (1980) view, warranting processes must go beyond the facts at hand to consider valuative and situational factors. Although an evidential relationship may exist between a proposition and reasons, the determination of belief is based on a person's voluntary choice to accept or not accept the evidence as sufficient. Meiland's (1980, 23) caution that "warranting has and must have a practical basis" is an important one, lest we be so far drawn into the intricacies of technical reason as to ignore its broader ontological nature. Fisher (1978) implicitly adheres to this caution in his criterial questions undergirding a logic of good reasons: proposed in the context of assessing values, questions of fact are supplemented by those of relevance, consequence (a direct link to the situation), consistency, and what he terms a "transcendent issue." The latter is the point at which one decides whether the belief, given its "winning" status (in Rescher's terms) or having been established as evident or presumptive (in Chisholm's) is finally judged acceptable: "Even if a prima facie case exists or a burden of proof has been established, are the values the message offers those that, in the estimation of the critic, constitute the ideal basis for human conduct?" (Fisher, 1978, 380). The transcendent question restores the evaluative process to its proper sphere within an ontological concept of reason and thereby ensures a humanizing influence in the resolution of arguments.

Conclusion

Three principal conclusions emerge from the preceding review of concepts of rationality, reasonableness, and good reasons:

1. Ontological reason, as expressed in theories of rationality grounded in discourse, is the preferred foundation for a theory of argument.

2. The degree of a decision's reasonableness and the attitude of being reasonable are compatible with—and the expected products of—discourse that adheres to the standards of rationality adopted by a communication community.

3. A procedure for assessing the reasonableness of claims is essential, but its application must occur within the framework of ontological reason. A theory of argument that emerges from these principal conclusions and the literature reviewed in this essay possesses the following features:

A. The concept of rational argument is grounded in a perception of reality formed by language.

B. Following Winch, the particular standards of rationality established within one culture are not automatically transferable to other cultures.

C. The exercise of technical rationality is conditioned by a more fundamental self-reflexive awareness of the needs of others; this adherence to a communicative rationality binds interlocutors to an agreement tht consensus can be reached through argumentative discourse.

D. Dialectic rationality, as a subtype of communicative rationality, governs the relationship between "real" and "ideal" communication situations; the regulative principle of dialectic rationality ensures forward motion toward the level of "ideal" competence standards.

E. Interaction between participants is governed by a triadic relationship between linguistic action, claim type, and placement:

> constative action validates truth claims in the external world
> expressive action validates truthfulness claims in the inner world
> normative action validates rightness claims in the social world.

Depending on the type of claim being validated, the claim's substance, personal values and perceptions of the claimant, or community values are the focal point of analysis.

F. Adherence to a standard of rationality (as proposed by Apel and Habermas) leads to the twin expectations that a decision will be judged reasonable and that the attitudes of the participants will be those of "reasonable persons."

G. An analysis of justifiable belief that is grounded in a doxastic system is preferable to one seeking absolute certainty; this rules out as inapplicable much of what occurs within the "justified true belief" debate—at least insofar as that debate seeks a self-evidential or certain foundation for establishing knowledge claims.

H. Standards of epistemic appraisal, operative within the context of a doxastic system, provide a set of criteria for determining the status of reasons offered on behalf of a claim.

I. Standards for the assessment of the plausibility of a thesis, coupled with the notion of presumptive truth, provide a vehicle for determining the epistemic status of a claim and the termination point of a controversy.

J. The application of technical reason, in the sense of warranting belief, occurs within the broader context of values and situational determinants affecting the acceptability of the claim; a claim that is justified on technical grounds is not, by reason of that alone, acceptable. Apel's regulative principle of dialectic rationality and Fisher's "transcendent issue" are key concepts which, if adhered to, insure that the dictates of technical reason are tempered by ontological realities.

While these features do not exhaust the potential components of a theory of argument, they do provide a sufficient ground for the exercise of reasoned discourse. The context presumed by the above features recognizes the perceptions of others, validates claims in accordance with intersubjectively understood and agreed-upon norms of communicative behavior, and balances the need for a rational procedure for assessing substantive claims with the equally important need to be cognizant of prevailing values.

THOMAS B. FARRELL

[6]   Knowledge in Time:
Toward an Extension of Rhetorical Form

> When any wrong statement is made, whether in public or in
> society, or in books, and well received—or at any rate, not re-
> futed—that is no reason why you should despair or think that
> there the matter will rest. You should comfort yourself with
> the reflection that the question will be afterwards gradually
> subjected to examination; light will be thrown upon it; it will
> be thought over, considered, discussed, and generally in the
> end the correct view will be reached; so that, after a time—the
> length of which will depend upon the difficulty of the sub-
> ject—everyone will come to understand what a clear head saw
> at once. . . . . In the meantime, of course, you must have
> patience [Schopenhauer, 1896, 71].

Arguments develop their meanings within history. The relationships
among claims, reasons, and issues in public arguments are constituted in
part through the changing developmental process of history itself. Whether
any public position or commitment may prove well-founded, appropriate,
even *true* can come to depend on its placement in the long run of unfolding
moments. One-time revolutionary, Jiang Qing, like some of the American
leftists of the 1930s, had the misfortune to outlive the "correctness" of her
pronouncements (Lok, 1980). History, whatever else it is, is an invention
and revision of argument, just as much of the historical process has been
reordered through a metaphor for rational contention: dialectic. What is
odd, however, is the virtual invisibility of historical speculation in recent
argumentation literature. Particularly disturbing is the removal of most
models of argument—whether formal or interactional—from the imposing effects of time and change.

While speculations about history are always perilous, there are strong intuitive reasons to press such an inquiry where argument is concerned. First, even if history does not repeat itself, the great issues of history—by rhetorical definition—are recurrent in their appearance, relevance, and meaning. The problem of social equality, the justification and morality of war, the limits of freedom and civic responsibility, the causes and control of crime: these are cases where argument has continued and will continue. As the variations and nuances of such arguments emerge, they seem to demand, yet elude, careful study. Second, at least some contributing features of an argument's meaning are historically specific. Just as the sense and reference of utterance meanings in the Platonic dialogues require that the contemporary reader attend carefully to their peculiar time and place (their indexical meanings), so must any "meaningful" document trace its rhetorical pertinence to an accumulation of such times and places: in other words, to its history. Far from being universal (in an ahistorical sense), documents like the Gettysburg Address are endlessly particular. To the extent that the meanings and ambiguities of argumentation remain worthy of investigation, reason and history are not incompatible topics. Third, since arguments within history are able to repeat and reinterpret themselves, these facts allow the unexamined features of historical meaning to be rendered problematic in the extreme. Because the motives for historical denouements have never been obvious, there are no criteria sufficient to resolve questions of conflicting historical revisions. The ever-present danger is that the argumentation process itself might prematurely be closed—on grounds that appear so obvious that they are not open to audience scrutiny. The historical definition and study of argument ought at least define some of the questions pertinent to the validation of "unfinished" arguments.

I propose, then, two questions to guide this inquiry. The first question is under what conditions is it possible to regard arguments that develop over time as recognizably *rhetorical*. The second is, assuming the historical emergence of argumentative form, how—if at all—are such arguments to be judged. My position is that rhetorical argument generally is not determined by a single author. Moreover, to understand the development of arguments within history requires the introduction of certain social-reality assumptions that are presumed to be held by interested, competent others (Farrell, 1976).

In the discussion to follow, the traditional Aristotelian view of rhetoric is introduced as a source of assumptions that provide direction to my view of argument. The most important of these assumptions is the rule-governed character of rhetoric as an art. Yet the traditional view of rhetorical form is limited insofar as it presupposes a realm of natural existence incompatible with the collective legacy of subsequent culture and history: what we might call, the modern world. After depicting this problem theoretically, an alternative conception of form will be introduced—one that is collaborative, emergent, and dependent (for the meaning and force of its claims) on the periodic successions of history itself.

But the issues I raise are also conundra. There is no guarantee that the problems of history and its "reason" can ever be laid to rest. What I have in mind is a kind of speculative approximation derived from traditional rhetorical assumptions and applied to an actual, though unfinished, discourse. This discourse is about *authority*, and I suggest that it amounts to an ongoing rhetorical argument. My evidence is recent—concerning discourse in and around American politics, circa 1976–1980—and therefore limited in reliable application. My aim is not so much to chart a formal historical logic as to offer discursive evidence that points the way toward a developmental logic of form. Such a logic would have to meet both our narrative sequential expectations of history and our traditional definitional assumptions about rhetoric; no easy task. Projects of reclamation begin with their sources, however. And the best way to find out whether traditional Aristotelian rhetoric makes sense when applied to historically constituted arguments is to look to traditional assumptions.

First and foremost in the Aristotelian view was the characterization of rhetoric as a practical activity. Rhetoric did not imitate human action like the poem or drama. Nor did it imitate and conclude the processes of nature, as did for instance farming and ship-building (Aristotle, *Physics*, II, 8). Rather, in a kind of synthesis of art and craft, rhetoric helped complete human judgments about questions of practical choice and conduct; it guided deliberate action (Grimaldi, 1958, 371–375). It did this by forming the best available arguments on either side of practical questions for interested and competent audiences (Grimaldi, 1978, 177). Rhetorical arguments had no subject matter exclusive to themselves; they concerned particular problems that touched upon and required the assistance of common knowledge. In the *Rhetoric*, the artistic proofs were each studied in terms of the general normative assumptions to which Athenian audiences would subscribe. Finally and most interestingly, each of the forms of rhetoric—epideictic, forensic, and deliberative—was seen to occupy an almost exclusive temporal habitat—present, past, and future. Simply put, Aristotle had no theory of history. The idea of an argument continuing over time, revising and replenishing itself with new audiences and interests, was alien to Aristotle's thinking. It has been observed that the failure of the classical literature to depict the historical dimensions of social problems marked "the limits not only of the realism of antiquity but of its historical consciousness as well" (Auerbach, 1953, 33). Unlike other modes of classical literature, rhetorical argument derived its meaning from its appearance in a given historical moment. But, for Aristotle in particular, the meaning of a rhetorical argument was over with the exhaustion of the moment itself—this despite the fact that he believed rhetoric to be the counterpart of dialectic. Dialectic's mission was not historical reason but the discourse of the learned theorist seeking general, ahistorical truths. The relationship between dialectic and rhetoric seems to have been topical rather than temporal: the relationship between theory and practice, general and particular, definition and accident.

Yet if classical rhetoric remains important to the student of rhetorical argument, this is because Aristotle's *stipulative* constructs for the art of rhetoric suggest fascinating contemporary variations. The notion of rhetoric enacting a practical mode of conduct remains as viable today as in Aristotle's time. As long as the principles and postulates of rhetorical theory are concerned with matters of practical conduct, there can not be an exhaustive science of rhetoric. Moreover, theorists since Aristotle have acknowledged that practical reason is an acquired higher-order methodology (Polanyi, 1962, 75; Toulmin, 1970, 21). The modes of practical reason cannot be reduced to cognitive laws, perceptual fields, or astronomic matrices; reason is emergent and governed by rules we ourselves invent, violate, and revise. And, as growing numbers of theorists increasingly recognize, rhetoric is a collaborative art. The traditional forms of practical reason (Aristotle's enthymeme and example) could not have been enacted without the presumption of certain agreements shared by auditors. To the extent that rhetoric maintains the practical, normative, emergent, and collaborative impulses thus far described, a reliable epistemic base is indispensable to argument.

Yet, what remains most problematic—and tantalizing—about classical rhetoric is Aristotle's view of form. While he did not subscribe to the rationalistic categories often attributed to him, the options, forums, and audiences of institutional life were depicted in an orderly and delimiting manner. To the extent that classical rhetorical forms required stable and static assumptions about the nature of the world and its possibilities, those assumptions are problematic today. Two revolutionary inventions make them so. One is the idea of *perspective*, which "makes the single eye the center of the visible world. Everything converges on to the eye as to the vanishing point of infinity. The visible world is arranged for the spectator as the universe was once thought to be arranged for God" (Berger, 1972, 16). This convention of European Renaissance art overturned the presumption of institutional and cultural order so often associated with the Aristotelian world. Aristotle had acknowledged that some questions were probable and contingent; but he also insisted that some were not. Moreover, the common knowledge relevant to rhetorical argument could no longer be taken for granted; its construction might even appear a somewhat forbidding task. Indeed, the success of any argument, its "realism," could be less a product of art than of chance, or tyranny.

The second invention provided the only way of overturning the partiality of perspective: the invention of *history*. History, Hegel thought, was the great leveler. Where many previously dependable realities were partial, the truth, said Hegel, "is the whole"; and the whole is a matter of *time*. Hegel illustrated this in an exacting and irritating little exercise. To those who alleged the superior confirmation of sense certainty, Hegel asked that they examine the world revealed to them at any moment and answer what the world is now. If they note that it is midnight, then write the observation down; "a truth cannot lose anything by being written down, and just as little by our preserving and keeping it. If we look again at the truth we have written down, look at it *now*, *at this noon-time*, we shall have to say that it has turned stale and become out of date" (Hegel, 1967, 151).

The inventions of perspective and history render problematic the classical conception of form as a self-contained, temporally compressed, and recognizable structure. Yet there are hints that Aristotle's thinking is capable of more than this. His conception of rhetorical argument, for instance, is unlike any other argument type described in his science of method: *The Organon*. Whereas methods of categories, interpretation, and analytic are concerned with logical distributions among terms, thoughts, or things, only rhetoric sets forth meaningful relationships among all three—things to thoughts, thoughts to terms, terms to things (Farrell, 1977, 143). The attempt of rhetoric to link ideas to actions in the haphazard world suggests more far-reaching interpretations of form:

> *The Extension.* —This consists in carrying your opponent's proposition beyond
> its natural limits; in giving it as general a signification and as wide a sense as
> possible, so as to exaggerate it; and, on the other hand, in giving your own

proposition as restrictive a sense and as narrow limits as you can, because the
more general a statement becomes, the more numerous are the objections to
which it is open [Schopenhauer, 1896, 13].

If we begin to consider history as gradually constitutive of meaning in
the endless succession of discursive utterances ("perspectives"), then rhetorical form cannot appear fully "packaged" and self-contained. We must instead perform an act of perspective-taking the phenomenologists call "horizontalizing" in order to understand what form has become (Idhe, 59).
Instead of viewing argumentative form synchronically (premise + premise
= conclusion) all simultaneously here, let us lay the developmental structure of argumentative form end to end, as befits the diachronic succession of
frames in history itself. The discourse of rhetorical argument will now be
understood to have taken on a "redoubling" character. In addition to making its appearance as a discrete, historically distinct act, each instance of
rhetorical argument will attempt to be prematurely "correct." It will purport to anticipate and co-opt forthcoming resistances, discursive and otherwise (that is, apocalyptic events). Rhetorical form will be, as Burke described it, the principle of continuity itself (1961, 39–40). Perhaps more
explicitly, form may now be understood as a narrative succession of discursive anticipations, each attempting to project, explain, and integrate that
which is subsequent. Rhetorical argument, in other words, requires that
the *given* be placed against a horizon of unrealized, unchosen alternatives—
of roads not yet taken. From the "modernist" vantage described here, then,
the prospect is not *of* rhetoric. The prospect *is* rhetoric. Moreover, the
capacity of any discourse to enter a partisan world, anticipate its prospective
resistances, and offer meaningful integration to its forthcoming results becomes the rhetorical *test* of form itself (Dewey, 1934, 207).

Having consulted some of our most traditional assumptions about rhetorical argument, it may yet be possible to detect the operations of discursive practice within the mechinations of that great leveler: history. The
question that now demands attention is whether the sense of practical reason as a normative, emergent, and collaborative impulse may be maintained in such an unusual setting. By turning to one of the few contemporary attempts to make argumentative *sense* out of history—Habermas'
recent work in critical theory—I attempt to clarify the relationship of
knowledge to the ongoing formation of historical argument. Briefly, it is
now argued that the most recent attempts of social theory to explain the
operation of practical reason in history have been quite problematic. By

assuming that social history itself simply improves in a rational developmental manner, such investigations have the unfortunate effects of closing off historic options and foreclosing prospective human choice. After discussing these problems, I introduce what are claimed to be less dogmatic hypotheses on the interrelationships among argument, history, and the "knowledge" of social collectivities.

The scholarly research of German social theorist Jürgen Habermas has gained considerable currency in the study of argumentation as a result of the recent translation of his wide-ranging volumes (1971, 1973, 1975, 1979). Habermas' earlier work grappled with the elusive problem of holding social systems (and their agents) accountable to standards of reason and morality, analogous to those elected and enacted by interpersonal communicants. While the ever-growing compass of the Habermas project proved less than satisfying, Habermas had assembled an amalgam of influences (from systems theory, ordinary language analysis, anthropology, linguistics, psychology, and beyond) that promised still more exciting syntheses for argumentation research.

I have become less and less comfortable with the most recent annexations of universal pragmatics. In an essay from his most recent work (1979), Habermas—for the first time in his *own* research—wishes to impose a biological evolutionary schema (from learning theory and anthropology) upon the somewhat more amorphous realm of cultural history. At issue, among other things, is what *kind* of argument holds the history of culture together. At times Habermas seems perilously close to suggesting a teleological, almost Aristotelian logic of cause:

> Cognitive developmental psychology has shown that in ontogenesis there are different stages of moral consciousness, stages that can be described in particular as preconventional, and postconventional patterns of problemsolving. The same patterns turn up again in the social evolution of moral and legal representations [1979, 99].

Given Habermas' avowedly Marxist leanings, it is at least surprising that the principle of coherence within history turned out to be "natural" evolution, rather than dialectical. But beyond mere incongruity, there is a Humean problem of validity here. Habermas cannot accomplish his largely analytic evolutionary schema without the kind of methodological analogies, models, and syntheses he has developed in the past; that is, without borrowing from field-dependent systems of thought that share little intrinsic commonality:

In social evolution as well, we shall not be able to classify social formations according to their state of development until we know the general structures and developmental logic of social learning processes. Corresponding to the central nervous system here are the basic cognitive structures in which technical and moral-practical knowledge are produced [Habermas, 1979, 174].

What seems most problematic about this borrowing is its tendency to shade over important differences that Habermas himself once detected among the interests of natural, social, and humane sciences. It has always been the case that analogies from one range of interests to another appear dogmatic and unsettling. At the very least, such attempts usually are outside the criteria of sufficiency that we require for a well-evidenced theory.

I offer a more modest venture into this imposing territory. If the idea of "improvement" or "betterment" or "progress" is not a utopian myth, we must assume persons who recognize that some actions are better than others, who accept responsibility for past errors, who "learn" socially, and who do the improving. These are not always the same people, but that is not the point. Social "learning" over time presupposes that the norms of arguments may be made visible, that these norms may then be consulted, and that other argumentative discourse may come to "recognize" and respond to these norms. The only optimistic alternative to the postulates I have offered accepts a dogmatic premise: that "every day, in every way, we get better and better," *automatically*. There is, it must be conceded, an element of faith in the position I am implying too. But it is the "good faith" that may be reclaimed through the sober investigation of rhetorical premises.

If rhetorical argument may be understood as a discourse that generates itself over time, then the apprehension of form (like its generation) must be something that emerges in a graduated manner. Indeed, at any given particular moment in the development of discourse, the arguers themselves are likely to see only part of the unfolding picture. Their partial views (*our* "perspectives") are like the utterances in an ongoing conversation (Burke, 1941, 94–96). These may influence the direction and shape of form without ever determining the full result. This realization may offer one contemporary way of appreciating Aristotle's observation that rhetoric deals with the probable and the contingent, things that may be one way or another. For it is the very sense of contingency in our most prominent historic conventions that must give the social theorists pause. Zarefsky's study of the Great Society is a telling example. His sympathetic analysis regards the liberal verities of the Lyndon Johnson administration as a "rhetorical proposition"—an incomplete assertion still awaiting its most propitious extension (Zarefsky, 1979, 378).

If my comments thus far have suggested at least the plausibility of viewing form through the historical constitution of argument, what now awaits analysis is the manner in which argumentative form emerges. While there are reasons for supposing that the sequence of lines and perspectives of argument may come to make formal historical sense, no one example could prove such a sweeping claim—not even an example as sweeping as the one I now propose: the concept of *authority*. I introduce *authority* now as a paradigm case for the historical construction of meaning within argumentative form. But, although its pertinence to argument is unquestioned, the idea of authority does not yield comfortably to a rhetorical interpretation. In order to establish the rhetorical pertinence of this construct, I must first show that authority admits of a historic derivation. Then I must show that the actual use of authority requires the implied consensual collaboration of others. These two facts about authority—its variation within time and its indirect dependence upon others—would give this concept special relevance to the ongoing construction of rhetorical form.

Authority is a concept that is integral to social stability and historical change, even as the character of the concept itself is quite problematic. Although there is little agreement about the nature of authority, nearly everyone acknowledges its importance to even the most ordinary conceptions of collective action. Indeed, the very idea of meaningful social action requires that one speak *on behalf of* some idea, group, or system, that utterances themselves be authorized. Bitzer puts the question broadly enough:

> . . . authorization is needed when a proposed act or message might seriously affect the well-being of others; when an act or message, regardless of consequences, is unlawful or in some sense contrary to principle; when the agent is unable to know whether his behavior is consequential, lawful, or in agreement with principle, and so needs authorization as a condition of speaking or acting in ignorance; when the agent is obliged to another person, group, or institution such that his message or action requires consent of his authorizing agency; or when a person or group claims to represent, or stand in for, another person or group [1978, 54].

But once we acknowledge the pervasiveness of authority in ordinary social discourse, we run up against serious problems of coherence. The more important recent studies of institutional authority, while helpful, mirror these difficulties.

Sennett's (1980) *Authority* wrestles with many of the emotional quandaries of that subject without offering a clear resolution. His work considers authority as one of a series of "social emotions." The other social emotions are fraternity, ritual, and solitude [*sic*]. Loosely dialectical in style, his treatment of authority seems to assume an understanding of the mass society diagnosed in his sweeping *The Fall of Public Man* (1977). Authority seems to be Sennett's idea of a "mass emotion," something that cannot be experienced by solitary individuals. The more important thesis is that there are unavoidable ambivalences (contradictions) in the emotional relationship of social beings to public authority. Drawing on an odd collection of clinical and bureaucratic examples, Sennett illustrates such flawed relationships as the paternalistic style, the autonomous style, and visible, legible authority. While his work has been criticized for deficiences of evidence and an impenetrable style (Cameron, 1980), it contains heuristic insights pertinent to the study of argument.

The paradoxes of our relationship to authority underlined by Sennett seem to derive from incompatible needs of the public and private self within the privatistic world described in *The Fall of Public Man*. Paternalism and the autonomous styles, for instance, would "ground" collective public life in unrealistic appropriations of private needs. Yet Sennett is less successful in offering a definition of authority that escapes this public–private dichotomy (power + love is as close as he ever gets to a definition). When he tries to get beyond these ambivalences of definition, the results are less than satisfying:

> Authority as a constant process of interpretation and reinterpretation makes sense in intimate affairs; it does not in public. There are structural reasons for this; the rhythm of growth and decay in a life is not the rhythm of growth and decay of society. There is an unbridgeable gap—or, to put it positively, each of us can imagine authority privately as we cannot in public. We have a principle by which to criticize society based not on abstract deduction about justice and right but on our intimate knowledge of time [Sennett, 1980, 196].

Sennett seems to be suggesting that considerations of time, change, and reinterpretation are not appropriate expectations for public life when it comes to authority. If this reading is correct, the problems are obvious. Here, without warrant, is a concept of public authority that seems static, even ahistorical. Not surprisingly, such a conception also lacks the very possibility of rhetorical reflection implied by argumentation.

Connolly's work, *The Terms of Political Discourse*, approaches the concept of authority from a radically different philosophical tradition, that of the philosophy of language. For Connolly, authority is one of a series of essentially contested concepts, concepts about which we agree to disagree, due to their normative ambiguities (1974, 22). Nonetheless, Connolly labors to establish relevant derivations, types, and functions of authority. Authority and power are seen to be coordinate concepts: either may be a source for the other, but neither is reducible to the other. Authority may depend on a person's positional legitimacy, or his or her special position to know. Authority may be grounded in special traning or expertise; or it may be "effective" but without logical foundation. Authority yet has something very important to do with the beliefs of the parties involved. These beliefs establish a presumption to act in accordance with an authority's directives, barring certain relevant considerations. Connolly's treatment provides an important logical counterpart to the rather more impressionistic diagnosis offered by Sennett. But what limits the usefulness of Connolly's analysis for our purposes is its formalism. While Connolly's arrangement of types and derivations of authority offers a helpful corrective to the *subjective* view, authority in this treatment becomes a set of logically distinct categories removed from real attitudes and interests. Perhaps this formal abstraction is a result of attempting to distinguish authority from "rational persuasion," a commitment Connolly shares with Hannah Arendt (1954, 93). Yet this is odd placement for a concept Connolly had previously described as "essentially contested."

The contrivances we employ to ground and place authority may seem less problematic if we regard this concept as an instance of rhetorical form. While authority has logical and emotional features open to characterization, it may be characterized rhetorically, insofar as it involves *the grounding of claims and utterances through the identity of the speaker*. The rhetorical complexities of authority, its language, and its historical variations are best understood through an overview of this grounding process.

The rhetorical use of authority occurs whenever the person making a claim is able to define the institutional facts that enrich and enact the claim in question. Yet, as in all performative utterances, what Searle (1969) describes as "institutional facts" must involve the compliance of others (1969, 51). Authority is, first of all, derivative from some other source. There is no such thing as an intrinsic authority. Technical expertise, to use a contemporary case, often is removed from ordinary social constituencies; but specialization requires training and the eventual perception, by *some* constituency, of competence. Political authority derives from public, or party, or historical mystification of role, or (with royalty) from the lineage of succession. In differing ways, each of these is an attempt to "overcome" history; yet each is vulnerable to history for its origin and its fate. The pontiff of Catholicism (to use a most elaborate example) still owes authority to an elaborate range of sources. He is an elected official, a trained theologian, a historical descendant of Peter, and one of the last repositories of supernatural right.

But second, every derivation of authority, however absolute and exclusionary, requires some attribution of agreement by others. When President Richard Nixon declared a state of national emergency and attempted to place the armed forces on alert in the summer of 1974, it did not matter that there may have been real reason for alarm. So widespread was suspicion of Nixon's political motives (because of Watergate) that no one believed him. Nixon's authority had diminished because (as he subsequently acknowledged) he could no longer presume a consensual base for the legitimate pronouncements of his office. As a second requirement, then, the institutional conditions that validate the utterances of authority are acknowledged through a consensus attributed to certain relevant others.

Third, even though authority exerts constraint and influence upon its "audiences," the domination exerted by this construct is always restricted to certain fields, forums, and bounded constituencies. Authority, in other words, is never unlimited in scope. The "absolute" ruler, even the shah or ayatollah who holds power over life and death, finds an exhaustion of transcendence at the edge of national boundaries. Papal pronouncements, considered "infallible," acquire such esteem in "matters of faith and morals"— and, even then, to the form of life shared by their Catholic constituencies. Authority, then, is always restricted to an agreed–upon range of competent pronouncements.

Finally and most obviously, authority is normative insofar as it has implications for human actions. As an emergent construct attributed to consenting audience constituencies, authority requires that volitional agents be capable of enacting its requests and demands. To acknowledge authority is to grant a presumption in favor of compliance. This presumption unites the fact of authority, with the prescription for some preferred mode of conduct. Whether we should pay our taxes, register for the draft, cross the picket line, or tell the painful truth in court depends—in part, at least— on the obligations implied by our consent to a structure of authority. We may—as volitional agents—dispute these obligations, or subordinate them to a higher principle. But we must, and do, contend with them.

Each of the features I have specified is a necessary condition for the rhetorical operation of authority. Interestingly enough, the requirements of emergence, audience-dependence, attributed consensus, and normative impact (or "force") were introduced some time ago as definitional constituents for what was termed "social knowledge" (Farrell, 1976). Perhaps it may now be alleged that the construct of authority itself is grounded through its social-knowledge base. Indeed, this is the only way I know that the rhetorical enactment of authority may be considered a form of *argument*. Take, as one illustration, the most basic enactment of authority as rhetoric: the command. I submit that it would be impossible to comprehend the command as a form of argument without the introduction of social knowledge assumptions. The cop says to the motorist (let us say) "Pull over." Here are the presuppositions of background importance to this command:

1. I am asking you to perform an action you are capable of performing.
2. My utterance intends that you recognize my right to influence you (toward 1).
3. You recognize this right may be justified on other grounds.

Each assumption may be resisted or disputed. The point is that the very possibility of dispute requires reflection upon such assumptions as these.

In fact, there is a large and variegated language of authority, a language that also reflects authority's grounding—its differentiated social-knowledge base. The accompanying graph overviews these important interrelationships in addition to previewing the evolving issues of authority as a rhetorical form.

Table 6.1. The Languages of Authority as Social Knowledge

	Formal	Relational	Ritual
ETHOS	commands, report charters, rules	paternalistic & autonomous style; brother, friend	apologia, vindication and endorsement
ROLE	official references	transactional & transformational; charismatic derivation of value terms;	surfacing, authorization, being "presidential"
LEGITIMACY	procedural sanctions and justifications	identification & affiliation	rituals of initiation, and confirmation; conventions, elections
IDEOLOGY	promises, criteria for competence	cultural forms of life; unity, dissensus, anomie	expectation and fulfillment; continuity, interruption, renewal; historical revision

The surface of authority as social knowledge structure is found in those traits attributed to the authority figure's own character. It might seem unusual to regard the "personhood" of an advocate as a grounding of authority, yet in Aristotle's classical lexicon of artistic proofs *ethos* defined the character of the speaker and was first among the materials available to the methods of persuasion. Traits such as intelligence (or insight, training), good will (or beneficence toward social interests), and high moral character (or the embodiment of civic virtue) represented the standards for cultural excellence in Athenian rhetoric (Aristotle, *Rhetoric*, I, 2). Needless to say, many of their practical variations can be shown to be different today. Still they are minimal attributions of audience agreement necessary to the personal authorization of discourse in public. And these are institutional conditions, as well. Whatever is trusted, respected, and honored about public figures has yet to be reduced to the machinations of source credibility.

The second level of grounding to the structure of authority is found in the stature of one's position or role. Here is a factor that is even less determined by the authority figure alone. Especially in the institutional roles that serve as our exemplars, there are precedents that define a crude type of possible and permissible action. It is no contradiction to say that one may be a less than admirable person and a brilliant heart surgeon. One may have a severely flawed moral character and be an excellent military tactician. But in any case, the authority position will usually have some acquired stature, whatever the quality of one's personal performance. And here too, the expectations of relevant constituencies, whether inherited or discontinuous, public or private, will figure prominently in defining the possibilities for institutional stature.

Much has been written about the third level of social-knowledge grounding for authority—*legitimacy* (Habermas, 1975). Here is a condition that has application to a much broader range of components, channels, and even interests than to the structure of authority. Yet the very claim to a position requires a more basic form of justification: that the person with the position, whatever his or her acquired stature, deserves the stature that the position has acquired. This is, in part, a question of procedures. The most gifted practitioner of surgery, without a medical diploma, is but an imposter. And the increasingly complicated rules of election campaigning, whatever their intrinsic merits, seem to provide blueprints for ordering a bewildering array of institutional facts. So, like the previous levels, authority holds an informal dependency relationship to legitimation. A person of dubious character in a position of questionable stature may yet refresh authority by pointing to the procedural legitimacy of entitlement.

Ultimately, the procedures of legitimacy will vary with the institution in question. And institutions are not neutral structures. There are principles of exchange and culturally specific standards of assessment that characterize every community of discourse. When the idiosyncratic procedures of legitimation are called into question, the only argumentative recourse (chosen several times in this century) is to the ideology of the public sphere. By "ideology" I do not mean the Marxist depiction of "false consciousness" (Gabel, 1975, 31). Ideology is a more intuitively grounded sense of sedimentation than the "perspectives" discussed earlier. Schurmann has defined ideology as "the manner of thinking characteristic of an organization" (1966, 18). Organizations do not reflect on their manner of thinking as a matter of course (authority being, after all, a discursive structure of domination). And when they do so reflect, the process of reflection is likely to be called by differing languages. Elites may call it *crisis*; others, excluded from the structure, may call it radical *critique* (Habermas, 1975, 2).

Taken together, then, these four levels of authoritative grounding provide an overview of the potential "resting points" for appeals to social knowledge. It would be reasonable to assume that there is a contingent relationship among these points, not unlike the contrivance of stasis in rhetorical controversy (Farrell, 1976, 10). Should one's personal reputation erode, for example, one might appeal to the role itself ("I am the President"). Or, should the stature of the office begin to suffer, one might go to the well of legitimation procedures ("I will not walk away from the mandate of 1972"). There is a "natural," and increasingly desperate, logic to the remaining alternatives; for as a matter of historic "fact," the rhetorical resources of authority are finite. They may be expanded or diminished.

The graphic sketched above also has a lateral dimension that does not require so detailed a description. On this dimension are depicted a range of languages wherein authority is enacted, expressed, or utilized. Most rigorous and straightforward, obviously, are the more denotative discursive acts labeled "semantic." Yet here as elsewhere the placement of discourse types is a rough approximation; "commands," for instance, were shown previously to depend upon more than the ethos of the speaker. Also, as the languages move from semantic to relational, to ritual dimensions, their configurations become still less precise and dependable. Paradoxically, this is as it should be. Not only do we move from denotative language performance features to the more impressionistic realm of connotation; we find— in the relational and ritualistic languages—a realm where public and private needs and interests are tightly interwoven.

Even though the graphic makes no pretence of exhausting the types and variations of authoritative language, it allows the student of argumentative form to visualize several important facets of authority. First, it can be seen .that each "surface" level of social-knowledge assumption (and authority "language") may be rendered more problematic the deeper and more relentless the scrutiny. To the radical, a simple command may become an issue of position, legitimacy, and then ideology. Analogously, the ungrounded movement from left to right (as it were) through relation and ritual may become very hazardous to the institution as a result of the noncognitive character of the affiliations involved. Second, a kind of prescribed "golden mean" relationship among levels of social knowledge might be detected. Optimally, it might be suggested that the four levels of authority depicted here (ethos of person, stature of position, procedures of legitimacy, and ideology of public sphere) ought to be both permeable to each other's influence and definition and separable, in principle, from one another for the purposes of analysis and critique. Extreme counterexamples help us recognize this middle-range relationship. In 1973, President Nixon gave a commencement speech in whch he argued that the American people had a "right to confidence" in their government. When confidence was shaken, however, presumably sinister forces were to blame (the press, those who would subvert the government, and so forth). When public ideology (here identified with "confidence") is bonded to the levels of ethos, position, and procedural legitimacy in an uncritical, obligatory manner, the resulting abuse of authority may be called "authoritarian." A counterexample in the opposite direction might occur when public ideology is acknowledged and critiqued by an institutional elite. Now discourse of authority experiences such a radical separation from its own base that it might be called anarchistic. The more tentative middle-range relationship I have described is an attempt to acknowledge the mutual importance of criticism and memory. Finally, it should be possible to devise some informal conventions of rhetorical propriety (rules) for relationships among types of language and bases of social knowledge for authority. I will not attempt a listing of such rules in the abstract. It is easier to recognize rules for language use (in politics and elsewhere) when such rules are being violated.

History as Argument: A Practical Discourse

Thus far I have offered some intuitive reasons for regarding the *form* of rhetorical argument as a phenomenon that is historically constituted. And I have suggested the case of authority as a construct that has important and unexamined argumentative features, features that came to light when the preceding social-knowledge assumptions were introduced. What remains to be illustrated is the possibility of viewing authority not ony as a case of argument but also as a construct that (like the general case of rhetorical form) may be constituted formally by the intervention of time and change.

Yet to suggest that authority is a rhetorical form of argument that acquires and abandons meaning historically is not only to take issue with existing theories of authority (Sennett, 1980; Connolly, 1974). It is also to take issue with the aims of authority itself. The whole point of authority has always been to overcome, to transcend, to "stop" history. Kings and shahs may age and die; but the royalty, the State will live forever. If democracy elevates fools to kingly heights, no matter. Fools come and go; the system is preserved. To acknowledge that authority itself—its claims and its roots— comprises a continuing rhetorical argument is to raise the unpleasant prospect that history may yet win.

This is the argument I am prepared to make. Moreover, I believe that the same social-knowledge assumptions necessary to the understanding of authority as argument also facilitate our understanding of authority as an argumentative artifact that is constituted through history. The basis for my claim comes from Olafson's exciting recent work, *The Dialectic of Action* (1979). This author offers a distinction between "communities" (the term is used loosely) that are nonhistorical and communities that have "fallen into history." The former cases are constituted, for the most part, by what he calls "cyclical agency." Life consists of multiple routines whereby patterns and habits and distributed functions are repeated in a nonreflective manner. Other than natural occurrences, or invasions from more willful neighbors, there are no recognized turning points whereby chronology and reason might intersect. As Olafson explains, ". . . the teleology of such recurring routines of action does not generate a history, in the sense developed in this chapter, because it is not cumulative" (116). In order for a community to "fall into history," it is necessary that the community's action be collective and not distributive, that its sense of agency be linear and cumulative, rather than cyclical. It is evident that societies can only "act" in this way when some mutuality of affiliative knowledge is presupposed and when this presupposition is expressed within an authoritative structure of discourse. Olafson explains that such an imputation of agency refers to

> a collective action by a group of persons, that is, the kind of action that an individual human being could not sensibly be said to be performing by himself and that can be performed only by a group of people acting jointly in a number of different and complexly interrelated ways. . . . There are, of

course, a great many important differences among collective actions with
respect to the kinds of authority that are required in order to initiate them and
the kinds of responsibility they impose upon individual members of the community that engages in them; but these need not concern us here. What *is*
important is the fact that collective actions normally require some degree of
institutionalization—some structure of authority that makes it possible for
certain individuals to initiate such collective actions and to give them the
direction they require during their execution [115].

Authority may offer a paradigm instance for the interdependence of social
history and the presuppositions of social knowledge. It remains for this
essay to suggest some important recent developments in the ongoing argument of authority.

The argument about authority has been going on for a long time in
America. Even the movement from the nineteenth-century autonomous
style to twentieth-century paternalism does not begin to encompass the
boundaries of variation in recent years. For evidence that there are elements
of a sensible ongoing argument here, I rely upon what Fisher has described
as "present data" (1980, 124). Yet I have concluded that recent political
elections offer a crude dialectical positioning of discourse that, in its exten-
siveness, expensiveness, and longevity, has no worldly parallel. Such "data"
as these, recent or not, require the most painstaking analysis. After considering some of the transitional oddities of the 1976 presidential campaign, I
analyze three subsequent "texts" in the light of my previously mentioned
"map" of authority perspectives and assumptions.* The three texts are:
Jimmy Carter's 1979 "malaise" speech, the Republican and Democratic
convention strategies, and the Carter and Reagan election-eve "debate."
Each of these texts surely deserves and will receive more extensive analysis
than is offered here. My purpose is to treat each of these discourses as per-
spectival stages in an ongoing argument about presidential authority, an
argument that doubtless was not well understood during the moments of its
unfolding.

The historical particularity of this analysis does raise an important procedural question. How can the apparent emphasis upon the singularity of the
Carter administration be reconciled to the collaborative, historical sequencing of argumentative form? I shall attempt to show that Carter began his
own authority argument as a response to the failed legitimation strategies
preceding him. During its initial stages, the Carter authority argument

*A grant from the Northwestern School of Speech Alumni Fund supported the presiden-
tial campaign research reported in this essay.

implied a kind of collaboration with the privatistic value systems of the "American people." Gradually, however, the public language of authority (along with Carter's own traditional paternalistic style) restricted this argument until it reflected only the President's institutionalized reality—his "solitude." The solitary emphasis upon Carter, therefore, reflects the limits of this stage in the authority argument. The following analysis seeks to bracket Carter's authority claims so that the fundamental insularity of these claims may be better understood.

Many scholars have noted that the 1976 campaign occurred in the midst of almost unprecedented legitimation problems. In the preceding administration there had been four attorneys general, three vice-presidents, and two presidents; and Nixon's second term had allowed the presidency to become inextricably bound up in the vagaries of Nixon's own defense. Early defenses of a "right to confidence" paled before pleas to "support the presidency." This authoritarian use of social-knowledge assumptions eventuated in suspicion of the propriety, equity, and reliability of America's institutional procedures for selecting leaders.

It is within this thematic context that the anomalies of the Carter campaign for authority may be understood. Carter grounded his vision of leadership on the fact that he was not part of the Washington power structure: In fact, his early political commercials repeatedly stressed that he was *not* a lawyer and *not* a member of the Eastern establishment. It is time, he said, "for the people to run the government for a change, and not the other way around (Carter-Rafshoon, 1976). And who was Carter? Virtually an amalgam of private-life roles: "I am a Southerner and an American. I am a farmer, a planner, a businessman, a nuclear physicist, a naval officer, a canoeist, and among other things, a lover of Bob Dylan's songs and Dylan Thomas' poetry" (Carter, 1975, 4). Here was not just an image, but an anticipated *imagery* for the antiauthoritarian campaign. Curiously, however, Carter never referred directly to his *public* role positions. Instead, he referred continually to his personal qualities. It was as if character alone had depleted the public authority of the executive branch. Now character could offer a political cure. "Trust me," Jimmy Carter said; and, with considerable hesitation, many people did.

From the view of form sketched in this essay, Carter began his argument about authority in the 1976 campaign. It was an argument with many peculiarities. For one thing, Carter made formal semantic promises about his own relational traits: "I promise," he kept saying, "never to lie." This is an odd statement, since the act of promising—if taken seriously—assumes truthfulness on the part of the speaker. Carter almost never referred to the *role* he sought (the presidency) in the traditional language of authority. "We want," he stressed, "a government [or "President" in some speeches] as good and honest, and decent, and fair, and filled with love as the American people" (Carter-Rafshoon, 1976, 2–5). The curiosities here almost defy analysis; one notices the tendency to address the public sphere itself not in terms of its genuine political interests, but rather in a projection of private ethos virtues. Carter's convention speech (Farrell, 1978, 302) and his performance in the Ford–Carter debates said almost nothing about his own ideological commitments, or even about a practical direction for governmental policy. He promised to restore "decency" to government, a claim whose background context might imply that the entire government of the United States was indecent. In general, then, Carter responded to the procedural crisis of legitimacy by stressing his own largely untested "personal qualities"; moreover, he seemed intent upon juxtaposing his almost preternatural sense of America's private morality to a less-than-flattering portrait of ordinary political life. As a response to the crisis of legitimacy, the beginning of the Carter "argument" provided a bold election strategy. But it must be added that the "perspective" afforded by the Carter beginning offered little power of anticipation, particularly when it came to the secular problem of administering actual governmental authority.

The "Malaise" Speech. There is no point in assessing the "quality" of the Carter presidency, a task that will be enacted and revised by others in the coming years. However, something might be said about the subsequent problems of authority experienced by Carter. Carter's own closest adviser, Hamilton Jordan, conceded in 1980 to Bill Moyers that the former president "did not know how to lead," if by leadership one meant "getting people to do things they didn't want to do" (Moyers, 1980). Perhaps, more charitably, it might be said that Carter encountered serious problems in grappling with the language of authority. I believe these problems eventually proved so serious that the President was forced to revise his own social-knowledge assumptions.

Not all the difficulties to which I refer were Carter's own fault. As this study has implied, the argumentative conception of authority has been revising itself for many decades. Still, here are some of the inconsistencies that might have been foreshadowed by the 1976 argument. Carter continued to follow relational rules for interpersonal language, even when these were demonstrably inappropriate to his authority position. He dramatically restricted White House ceremony traditional to his office and replaced it with a sometimes embarrassing spectacle of a half-million Americans all trying to talk to the President on the phone. He adopted an "open" foreign policy, typified by the all-too-candid ambassador to the United Nations, Andrew Young; personalized convictions and public policy became hopelessly entwined. In the first flush of victory, Carter enacted a crusade for worldwide human rights (perhaps the logical extension of his national ethos projection); then he spent New Year's Eve of 1978 toasting the Shah of Iran. Problems of consistency and direction, of ideological conviction plagued the Carter regime. Perhaps because he had asked for the most rigorous standards of competence ("I want to be tested," he said in 1976), every misstep of communication took on an ominous glare. When Carter addressed the Naval Academy in 1978, he stapled together two conflicting policy statements on the SALT II treaty (from Secretaries Vance and Brzezinski) and read them both. And when the White House acknowledged it had made a mistake in a UN vote condemning Israel, an error that might have seemed minor took on global proportions—overshadowing the one incontrovertible achievement of the Carter years: the Arab–Israeli peace accord.

As problems mounted in his administration, Carter's own hold on positional stature had begun to diminish. By 1979, crises of energy, ecology, and economy began to merge; and the failures of nature and governmental institutions began to take on the most personal connotations. With public opinion polls dropping below 30 percent approval and inflation multiplying, Carter—like Nixon before him—addressed the problem of "confidence." This speech was, in my view, the fateful turning point in the Carter authority perspective.

Carter's address on July 15, 1979, was to be devoted to the topic of energy, a problem that had obsessed the President since the first month of his administration. Congress had not acted, and special interests had resisted government sanctions. Yet the speech had originally been scheduled for delivery ten days earlier and abruptly canceled.

The intervening ten days found the President at his retreat in Camp David, surrounded by visiting opinion-leaders and increasingly wild press speculation. It was even suggested that the President was not a well man psychologically. What was designed as an appeal for political support became an almost poignant attempt to reach out for the public "qualities" the President had summoned forth in 1976.

The President began his speech with a most unusual recitation of the circumstances surrounding the creation of the speech itself: "So I decided to reach out and to listen to the voices of America. I invited to Camp David people from almost every segment of society—business and labor, teachers and preachers . . ." (Carter, 1979). More than this background depiction, however, the President went so far as to quote at length blistering criticisms of his own authority style, criticisms he seemed to acknowledge:

> This from a Southern governor: "Mr. President, you're not leading this na-
> tion, you're just managing. You don't see the people enough any more. . . .
> Don't talk to us about politics or the mechanics of government, but about an
> understanding of our common good. . . . Talk to us about blood and sweat
> and tears. If you lead, Mr. President, we will follow." . . .

Even as the President went through the list, it became clear that the President had misunderstood his sometimes-perceptive critics. He was still the figure who talked *about* his speech acts. Carter was not "talking to us about blood and sweat and tears." He was talking to us about "talking to us about blood and sweat and tears."

But there is an even more striking problem with the speech. The President turned his own remarkable self-criticism into a critical portrait of the people themselves:

> But, after listening to the American people, I have been reminded again that
> all the legislation in the world can't fix what's wrong with America. . . . The
> threat is nearly invisible in ordinary ways. It is a crisis of confidence.
>   It is a crisis that strikes at the very heart and soul and spirit of our national
> will. We can see this crisis in the growing doubt about the meaning of our
> own lives and in the loss of a unity of purpose for our nation. The erosion of
> our confidence in the future is threatening to destroy the social and the politi-
> cal fabric of America.

Later the President noted that "piling up material goods cannot fill the emptiness of lives which have no confidence or purpose." Whatever the original design of the "confidence" speech, the President's lengthy discussion of energy would not be remembered nearly so well as his revealing portrayal of a radically conflicted authority style.

This speech, despite its purposive aims, was an expressive document. It was autobiographical about its own intentions, thus of course ensuring its own failure. The authority figure does not say "I am going to try to lead you now." He or she leads. But beyond the linguistic contradictions, the President had also detached himself from his only other acknowledged source of authority: the public ideology. Admittedly, the candidate had always spoken of the public in relational ethos terms; he was its aggregate representative: a businessman, a farmer, a husband, and so forth. But now this personalized president had consulted an aggregate of opinion-leaders, jotted down notes diagnosing his own failings (in itself an odd image), and arrived at a critique of public life-style. As some of my earlier work has attempted to show, rhetoric cannot step outside its own social knowledge base (Farrell-Frentz, 1979, 244); rather, rhetoric must posit and use its own social-reality ground. With the Carter speech we have a dramatic case where discourse critiques its own foundations. To the extent that confidence is more than a political term, more than an economic term, Carter's concluding advice pays quiet homage to the limits of discourse: "Whenever you get a chance, say something good about our country." Two days later a German newspaper offered the following editorial comment: "Baron von Muenchhausen, according to his own report, succeeded in escaping from a swamp by pulling himself out by his own hair. President Carter's energy program has something of the credibility of this tale" (*Frankfurter Allgemeine Zeitung*, 1979).

Party Convention Strategies. If the ambivalences in Carter's authority argument were previewed and enacted during his 1976 campaign and 1979 speech, these same ambivalences were given a dramatic extension by the political strategies generated during the 1980 party conventions.

While I have no direct evidence that the Republican strategists choreographed their arguments in deliberate response to the Carter authority crisis, a detailed critical content analysis of speech texts and slogans produces some fascinating transitions of form. In three dramatic ways the Republicans sought to exploit and revise the Carter authority perspective. First, almost all the Republican advocates sought to revise the ethos criteria for presidential authority. Recall that this was Carter's strongest social-knowledge assumption, rooted in the continuing perception that he was and is a good, decent, and well-intentioned man. From the very beginning of the Republican oratory, it was clear that such traits as these were no longer enough. President Ford said: "No statistics can tell the jeopardy of a nation whose leaders lose faith in the future." He termed the election one of the most important in the nation's history because "our faith in ourselves is on the line." And then perhaps the most telling revision: "Our confidence in the nation's future is up to the nation's leadership to determine. If our leaders are inept and timid, we as a people will be inept and timid. If our leadership is bold and confident, America will be bold and confident"

(Campaign transcript, 1980, A). These three terms, "optimism," "boldness," and "confidence," had become decisive criteria in the search for personal leadership qualities. They were soon accompanied by other equally revealing terms: consistency, decisiveness, competence. In the speeches by Guy Vanderjagt, Kissinger, Goldwater, Bush, and—of course—Reagan himself, the public failings that Carter's inadvertent critique had detected were reunited with their source: the authority figure himself.

Second, the Republican strategy sought to revitalize the relationship between private life and public ideology. Again and again, the unusual slogan was articulated: "Family, Neighborhood, Work, Peace, and Freedom" (Campaign transcript, 1980, A). Now perhaps for segregationists, right-to-lifers, antiunion, antibusing, libertarian conservatives there are coded meanings in these terms. But perhaps not. As uttered by Jimmy Stewart and later by Reagan himself, this public homily to ordinary life sought to refresh the private sphere Carter had questioned for its materialism and loss of faith. Faith, whether found or contrived, could at least be claimed as a partisan Republican virtue.

Finally, Reagan's own acceptance speech, along with its commercial introduction, offered a powerful affirmative response to the failure of Carter's personalized authority. In one important excerpt, Reagan asked the public "not simply to 'trust me' but trust your values—our values—and hold me responsible for living up to them." Later he noted: "The trust is where it belongs—in the people. The responsibility to live up to that trust is where it belongs, in their elected leaders. That kind of relationship between the people and their elected leaders, is a special kind of compact . . ." (Campaign transcript, 1980, A). Thus began Reagan's argumentative perspective in the ongoing discourse of authority. Reagan was the autonomous leader who would maintain a distanced respect for public ideology. Rather than critique or co-opt the public prerogative, the Reagan strategy simply accepted social reality as it is.

Impressive as the Republican authority argument appeared, however, it would have been premature to conclude that Carter's discursive options were closed. Even though the Democratic convention was not nearly so cohesive in argument as that of its predecessor (due to the "open convention" debate and the failed Kennedy quest), an important revision of Carter's own authority strategy could be detected in the masterful political commercial introducing his speech and in the subsequent acceptance speech itself.

The Carter commercial began with scenes of pastoral tranquility, depicting an America of rural beauty and regional charm. But sudden cuts to urban squalor, assembly-line intensity, and frenetic congested activity seemed deliberately to frustrate the sense of calm. Carter was shown intermittently in formal ceremonial surroundings, meeting with dignitaries, behind his desk. The viewer might have wondered where is the ordinary person, so important to the outsider of 1976? The next several minutes helped answer that question. People from all walks of life offered testimony to their own expectations for the presidency. Interestingly enough, these expectations were not tailored to the Carter presidency. More often than not, they seem inconsistent even with each other: "A good President must be kind," said one. "A good President should be an effective politician," said another. "A President ought to be able to get things done," said a third; "Watch out for the farmer," and so on. Images from past presidencies emerge, some on film, some paintings. Truman and Kennedy. Of James Buchanan it was said "If ever a man deserved hanging, it was he." One president, it seems, was called a Bolshevik. No president, apparently, is loved in his own time, and the great ones were hated more than most. The body of the Carter commercial made the subliminal message clearer. Other public officials talked "candidly" of Carter. Diane Feinstein of San Francisco spoke of his support of the cities. Muriel Humphrey spoke of his importance to the Democratic party tradition. Mayor Coleman Young spoke of Carter's quiet soft-spoken manner. No ringing endorsements are offered; but one has the impression that there is much more to this private man than meets the public eye.

But it was the final statement that made the revision complete. As the screen floods with images of the Lincoln Memorial, the Washington Monument, Mount Rushmore, and so forth, we hear:

> Every four years we search for the man with every good quality imaginable. We can put him together in our minds, of course. That's not hard to do. We can always see him through the simplifying mist of memory. He would have the military genius of George Washington, the common touch of Andrew Jackson, and the determination of Grant; he would move forward into the future like Teddy Roosevelt. He would have the zest and shrewdness of FDR, the rich humor of Jack Kennedy, the feistiness of Truman, and the solidity of Ike. He would have the humaneness of Jefferson, and the quiet persistence of Abe Lincoln. But we're not electing a statue this November. We're electing a President [Campaign transcript, 1980, B].

At this moment, a montage of excerpts from the earlier interviews is repeated, and a fade shot of Jimmy Carter in the Oval Office is transfixed. The President is introduced.

In the Carter commercial, the aggregates were still there but they seem to have been transcended. The "ordinary people" from all walks of life sounded well-meaning, but their expectations are portrayed as so variegated and so vast as to defy the most gifted leader. No president, it is implied, could be all these things to all these people. The aggregate of elites understand the *real world* better and their muted support of Carter's best features seems to reflect this understanding. The final statement indulges the viewer in an eloquent fantasy of ideal leadership, only to remind us that leaders—in real life—are not statues. This commercial used the last semantic resource at Carter's disposal and used it brilliantly: the ability to define institutional reality. No longer were the private values of ordinary people the source of Carter's appeal; if my reading is correct, this ground of authority had been lost in the ambivalence over "confidence." Instead, the people were told, gently but firmly, that the *real* world is more complex, less perfect, than the world of their dreams (the "mist of memory"). Carter has been there, as have these other public officials. And in his appreciation of this institutional reality (the one he has just defined), Carter was the best real live person for an impossible task.

One of my students described the Carter argument in this commercial and in the less successful speech that followed as depicting an "ideology of reality." With each of his other authority "stases" diminishing, Carter (and his strategists) nonetheless were able to define the world of the Presidency in such a way that only an actual president could fully appreciate its complexity. "Realism" could become the single most important criterion for authority. And Reagan, by virtue of his simplistic conservatism, could simply be dismissed as not being in "the here and now." This is, I think, an accurate statement of the Carter strategy of discourse (Kfoury, 1980). While his acceptance speech was too long and lacked the eloquence of its commercial introduction, Carter did attempt to revise his authority argument in an explicitly historical direction. We are at the crossroads, he said, of a choice between "two futures." One was a future of "reality." And one was a future of fantasy and tinsel (a not-too-subtle reference to Reagan's Hollywood background). The mixed results of Carter's first term were described as a kind of painstaking investment in the more realistic future that he, the President, now promised (Campaign transcript, 1980, B). All in all, this response represented a creative revision of Carter's own problematic authority perspective. Still, it did not succeed and in order to understand why, I turn now to the last of our texts: the election-eve debate.

The Carter–Reagan Debate. In and of itself, the debate was not the sole cause for Carter's misfortune. Even had Carter maintained the strictest adherence to his convention argument, his own record was not an easy one to defend. Also, Reagan's strategy had anticipated the Carter revision. Reagan's own convention commercial was a detailed biography of the man himself. It stressed his history and his executive stature, concluding that Reagan was a "natural choice" for the presidency. In a battle of historical perspectives Carter sought to define the present but Reagan virtually owned the past; Carter never referred to tradition at all. The Reagan argument for leadership by a kind of "natural selection" was never answered; and the Reagan slogan, "The Time Is Now for Reagan," began to express less the candidate's preferability and more the candidate's inevitability. Whatever the flaws in each party's political strategy, the two conflicting perspectives that contributed to the authority argument had been imprinted on the discourse of 1980.

Ideally, a Presidential debate is a dialectical encounter of authority presuppositions. Persons, roles, aims, and even linguistic relationships are juxtaposed in a forum that emerges through the rules of the interlocutors themselves. While many have claimed that contemporary political debate structures are limited by the question–answer format and the mediated audience situation (see Kraus, 1974), our own graphic authority scheme suggests that the speech possibilities may well have expanded with these developments. In any such televised encounter, political opponents may choose whether or not to answer any question directly, what manner of address to employ in forming an answer, how to address their opponents, how to select and prioritize their vast and fragmented audiences, and—of course—what to say. The Carter–Reagan debate offered a fascinating array of possible and actual choices to enact a language of authority. Who *won* the debate (on technical grounds) therefore was less important to this study than was the unresolved question of authoritative form. In my view, the televised opposition of Carter to Reagan disclosed (as the campaign proper had foreshadowed) two radically different orientations to social reality. Carter articulated a view wherein social knowledge ("reality") could only be depicted institutionally. And Reagan, for all the constrictions of his traditional conservatism, allowed that social reality was a relational emergent—something to be recognized in the public will rather than defined and depicted by a leader. What made this juxtaposition all the more remarkable was Carter's prior dependence on a "personal relationship" with the American people. When all the other authority bases of social knowledge had eroded for Carter, this relational language was all that seemed to remain. But by restricting himself to a purely formal language of authority, Carter allowed Reagan to control all other modes of expression in the debate. And Reagan did.

Indeed Reagan's mastery of the language of authority was so extensive as to undercut whatever formal advantage the President might have had. Carter, the incumbent, sought to press his "realism" ground of authority by attacking the challenger whenever possible. But while Carter's attacks were strong, well-evidenced, even potentially lethal, they never worked.

Reagan began the debate by shaking the President's hand, a violation of the agreed-upon rules that seemed (to some observers) to unnerve the President. While Carter continued to stress the solemn complexity of presidential *reality* (he used the phrase "Oval Office" three times during his first answer), Reagan was affable. In response to sharp Carter attacks about Reagan's lack of compassion, Reagan told stories: "I talked to a man just briefly there who asked me one simple question: Do I have reason to hope that I can someday take care of my family again?" And finally, when Carter's attacks intensified, Reagan used direct address to the President. He said "There you go again!" These devices, whether intended or not, may not seem particularly important. But the contrast could not have been more striking. Carter, the once-paternalistic leader, never referred to ordinary people, but only to parts of his aggregate public: "This is a heartless kind of approach to the working families of our country, which is typical of many Republican leaders in the past." Carter, once the master of relational language, never addressed his opponent or anyone else. His one reference to another human being was to his own daughter, Amy—a sign of insularity that was greeted with less than sympathetic amusement. As such exchanges continued, the contrasts intensified. What Reagan, the autonomous figure, had been able to do was diminish whatever remaining control Carter had on the relational language of the office itself. Reagan did not talk *about* compassion, but he expressed a language of affiliation that simply erased the force of Carter's charges.

The closing statements of the candidates dramatized again the sharply differing authority perspectives. Carter offered what he called "my plan for the future." Reagan asked "It would be well if you would ask yourself, are *you* better off than *you* were four years ago?" While Reagan said "I could suggest another choice that *you* have," Carter said "Those listening to my voice will have to make a judgment about the future of this country, and I think *they* ought to remember the difference." While Carter said that in his "lonely job," "I alone have had to determine the interest of my country . . . ," Reagan said his crusade would be one "to take government off the backs of the great people of this country, and turn *you* loose again to do those things that I know *you* can do so well, because *you* did them and made this country great" (Campaign transcript, 1980, C).

During a sharply constricted period of time, two differing views of authority were exposed to one another, and one gained temporary ascendency. In order to continue, the authority argument must move *outward* toward the collaborative sense of interested others. The Carter perspective, whatever its aims and merits, had so conflicted elite and public as to return the very grounding of reality to the anonymity of official "self." In the mediated spectacle of social privatism (a situation Carter had exploited in 1976) there was really no contest in 1980. The autonomous figure appeared relationally adept and the once-relational paternalistic leader appeared alone. If what I have said thus far makes sense, however, the argument about authority can never really be over. The attempts of both candidates to develop a holistic orientation to history (holistic in that it would co-opt the opposition) represents the elite desire to finalize what can only be a transition. The time is always now; and there will always be at least two futures.

Problems of Social Judgment: Some Conclusions

From the rhetorical vantage described in this essay, questions of fact and questions of interpretation might seem difficult to separate. Nonetheless, the analysis I have attempted ought to allow us to state some tentative institutional *facts*:

First, without doubt, our criteria for the ethos dimensions of authority are shifting. While traditional traits have not been abandoned (intelligence, good will, and high moral character still count for something), there are others that link the would-be authority to the stature of position. I have discussed some of these: boldness, optimism, decisiveness, confidence, faith. Some of these are in response to the Carter failings; perhaps some are not. But what is clear is that the traditional lexicon is no longer a sufficient array for either the Neo-Aristotelian critique or source-credibility research. Second, it seems clear that the authority argument requires an ability to shift dimensions of language (horizontally), while remaining committed on social-knowledge grounds themselves (vertically). The person who shifts from ethos to position to ideology and back again is seen as confused, whereas the person who can adjust from relational to formal to ritual languages may be regarded as a "good communicator." Finally, and possibly least concrete of all, there does seem to be a kind of logical pattern to the authority argument, and perhaps to many other historical argumentative forms as well. In times of crisis, for instance, the grounding of authority seems to move steadily toward the root social-knowledge assumptions of ideology, the orientation to which seems to reflect decisively upon the competence and leadership style of the advocate in question. While one may not always approve of the interim results (I do not), this line of development does make a kind of crude historic sense. All of this testimony to form must be mitigated, however, by acknowledging the real "materials" of rhetoric: the facts of history. Wars, bombs, tides, rains are not discursively constituted, whatever the contrivances of rhetorical epistemology. If these have a logic, it has thus far defied the symmetry of our very best tropes.

The problem of judgment. It might seem as if judgment itself has become almost unmanageably tentative when viewed from the enlarged focus this essay has attempted to offer. After all, rhetorical form has now come uncomfortably near its relational counterpart—dialectic; and there prudential judgment seems all but irrelevant. Still, there are some brief strictures that deserve expression.

The encounter between speakers and audiences continues to enrich both. The test of rhetorical form, at each of its continuing junctures, is not its internal logic but rather its application, anticipation and refinement of chance and will, two uniquely rhetorical facts of social life. The public, like that very best of audiences, is but a potential, an idea that has not yet been brought into being. There is sufficient reason to act that it might be brought into existence, even if its existence would come to qualify, undermine, or refute the grounds for the analysis I have been discussing. There is also implied a sense that argument itself should never be foreclosed. In a tragic mood, history does repeat its errors; it does not "learn" (in the childlike sense presupposed by contemporary social theory). But to deny the possibility that people themselves might learn, even through the same muddied arguments, is to deny rhetoric itself. The language of authority could never "prove" anything without acknowledging the capacity of an audience to change its "mind." And then, for all the stipulative prescriptions of traditional rhetorical theory, a necessary sense of tentativeness must charge the critic the longer history is seen to run. When it is acknowledged that cultures and "life worlds" have different histories, we are thus obliged to view the history of every utterance as part of its "meaning." Much of our ethnocentric outrage seems to stem from premature closure of the other's "past." Pure "tolerance" has been critiqued. It will always be exploited. But the inferences that mark off our historical epochs are the largest unexamined rhetorical power of all.

BARBARA J. O'KEEFE AND PAMELA J. BENOIT

[7]   Children's Arguments

Examining children's communication is useful. For some people information about how children behave is intrinsically interesting. But since the child's world is in many ways quite different from the adult's, research on children's communication can stimulate theorists to seek concepts that encompass a broadened range of phenomena; in the face of the manifest differentness of children, researchers may revise their notions of what requires explanation. Hence we see research on children's arguments as both interesting in its own right and important for a general understanding of argument.

This chapter examines the role of discourse in children's disputes; our focus is on argumentative interactions rather than particular messages a child might produce. In the course of reporting results of our investigations of naturally occurring arguments among preschool children, we summarize available research on children's arguments.

Contrary to the usual practice in analyzing children's communication, our general approach is for the most part adevelopmental. We analyze children's arguments as instances of arguments in general rather than as imperfectly formed or rudimentary versions of adult arguments. Because children are different from adults, it is tempting simply to explain their differentness (usually in terms of a supposition of incompetence) without accommodating to underlying similarities in adults. Premature assumptions of developmental difference are quite dangerous, as the recent history of developmental psychology will attest. A great deal of research has been done to show that young children can in fact do perfectly well many things Piaget (and others) have claimed they are incompetent to do. For example, Shatz (1977) summarizes research that shows preschool children capable of coherent conversational behavior and listener-adapted referential communication, in contradiction to the widespread assertion that such children are too egocentric to produce appropriate messages. Flavell (1977) summarizes research which shows that infants have abilities in visual perspective-taking formerly assumed to emerge much later, in early childhood.

We are therefore wary of prematurely drawn contrasts between child and adult arguments, of conclusions about children's arguments based on research on children's presumed cognitive competencies, and of extended analysis of age-related differences in children's arguments. Our purpose is to describe children's arguments in a way that illuminates argument in general. Our analysis is presented in two sections: the first is concerned with the problem of isolating arguments as a class of phenomena; the second offers an analysis of the role and structure of discourse in children's disputes.

In Search of . . . Arguments

It should be plain to readers of this volume that current research on argument displays considerable disagreement about just what an argument is or how to define "arguments" as a class of phenomena. Ambiguity in our concepts of argument poses especially difficult problems for the study of children's arguments, if only because children's verbal disputes are often different from what might be taken as "paradigm cases" of adult argument. As a result, "boundary disputes" in the study of adult arguments can become central conceptual problems in the study of children's arguments. In this section we (1) discuss ambiguities in the concept of argument, (2) consider two alternative responses to this conceptual ambiguity, and (3) suggest an alternative conception of argumentative interactions.

Ambiguities in Concepts of Argument

O'Keefe (this volume) has displayed some of the equivocality of ordinary uses of the term "argument" and has identified two distinct senses of that term in everyday talk. One sense (which he marks as argument$_1$), as found in phrases such as "making an argument," corresponds (roughly) to claim-plus-reasons. The other sense (argument$_2$), as found in phrases such as "having an argument," corresponds (roughly) to a disputatious interaction. In the present paper we use "argument" to refer to this second sense of the term.

As O'Keefe points out, in ordinary usage "argument" (as argument$_2$) can be used to describe a very wide range of interaction types. Speakers use "argument" to refer to physical fights as well as to a variety of verbal disputes. O'Keefe recognizes (see n. 5) but does not emphasize that the connection between physical and verbal modes of dispute settlement in the everyday use of the term "argument" is not incidental.

This connection is particularly apparent in children's disputes. The following interaction between David and Chris (both age five) is typical.[1] They are at school, playing with toy animals.

(1) CHRIS: You don't got no horsie.

DAVID: Let me have a horsie. Give me another horsie. Oh.

CHRIS: Stop! You got another horsie. That's//

DAVID [Now focusing on his animals, pretending they are speaking] How you doing mon?

[Chris and David stage a mock battle with their animals.]

CHRIS: I'm going to fight you up. Uh! Uh!

DAVID: I'll bust you up.

CHRIS: I'll bust you up boy. Oh he dead.

DAVID: Hey. Let me have that pig.

CHRIS: That's my pig!

DAVID: No. Let me see that pig okay? You no//

CHRIS: Give me my pig! [Screams]

DAVID: Let me have it okay?

CHRIS: No. I want this. I want that pig.

DAVID: No. That's my pig. [Chris takes the pig.] Give me my pig back.

[Chris screams; a scuffle ensues.]

DAVID [to supervising adult]: She won't give me my pig.

The use of direct verbal appeals, physical assault, and appeals to external authority within this sequence indicates that the conduct of disputes can be pursued through a variety of means, only one of which involves direct verbal

---

[1] All examples of children's discourse offered in this paper are real (as opposed to hypothetical) examples of naturally occurring arguments. Most of our data are drawn from transcribed tape-recorded discussions among preschool children. We used two sets of transcripts. The first set was produced by the second author as data for her dissertation on discourse coherence in preschool children (Benoit, 1979). Her data were collected at a preschool in Detroit, Michigan, and included instances of interactions that were part of normal preschool activities as well as a set of interactions in which she isolated dyads of younger (two to four years old) and older (four to five years old) preschool children in a small play area. The second set of transcripts were produced by Steve Taylor as part of his dissertation on the development of turn-taking in four-, six-, and eight-year-old children (Taylor, 1977). Like Benoit, Taylor transcribed data drawn both from routine school situations and a situation loosely structured by the experimenter. References are given in the text for examples drawn from other sources. Examples 2 and 3 are hypothetical and are not intended as imitations of children's arguments.

appeals. And even when verbal appeals are produced, they may be interspersed with other modes of behavior.

It should not be supposed that this is simply "childish" behavior, to be explained away in developmental terms. In some adult communities, physical means are preferred for dispute settlement in some contexts (see, for example, Philipsen's [1975] analysis of blue-collar communication); and O'Keefe (this volume) offers a striking example of a physical fight between adults which was described in a newspaper account as "an argument." O'Keefe's analysis suggests that in ordinary usage "argument" refers to virtually any disputatious interaction. It appears that disputes may be conducted in a variety of modes, that verbal exchanges are one such mode, and that different modes of dispute may be employed concurrently or successively within the same dispute. Thus "argument," in ordinary usage, is an intrinsically fuzzy concept that can be appropriately applied to a wide range of activities.

Responses to Conceptual Ambiguity

There are two general ways of responding to the fuzziness surrounding concepts of argument. The first response (by far the most common) is to view this fuzziness as a researcher's predicament. That is, since concepts of argument are insufficient to define a clear set of phenomena for study, researchers generate other strategies for identifying objects of study. An alternative response, the response we prefer, views this fuzziness as a fact to be accepted and explained.

Fuzziness as a predicament. Researchers commonly act as though fuzziness in concepts of argument is a problem to be solved; they implicitly or explicitly adopt a research strategy in which instances of arguments are isolated for study through application of some restrictive criterion in addition to the more general concept.

This view of fuzziness as a researcher's predicament is particularly clear in O'Keefe's (this volume) suggestion of a *paradigm case* strategy for the study of arguments. After displaying the intrinsic vagueness of the concept "argument," O'Keefe suggests that analysts turn their attention to paradigm cases (clear-cut instances) of arguments. While researchers may disagree about just where to draw boundaries around the category "argument," there are probably instances that all would agree are appropriately labeled "arguments." Analysis of these paradigm cases could produce at least some consensually valid claims about arguments by focusing attention on central attributes of the category.

A paradigm case strategy would obviously be difficult to apply straightforwardly to the study of children's arguments. "Paradigm case" is an analyst's concept; it is unlikely that lay adults would find much meaning in the question "Is instance X a paradigm case of argument?" However, one may assume that if paradigm cases of adult argument exist, adult analysts are capable of recognizing them. This assumption cannot be extended directly to the study of children's arguments. In the absence of a general understanding of the variations and forms of children's arguments, it is difficult to point to a "paradigm case" of child argument. (And, if a general description of children's arguments were available, a paradigm case strategy would not be needed.)

Although O'Keefe's paradigm case strategy cannot straightforwardly be employed in studying children's arguments, a version of this strategy has been employed in research by Lein and Brenneis (1978). They asked children to role-play an argument, on the assumption that arguments are a class of speech events and that this procedure would produce the typical range of instances in this class. While Lein and Brenneis did not consciously adopt a paradigm case strategy, their procedure elicits behavior that children label "arguments;" the great similarities among the children's responses suggest that in some sense this procedure elicits children's conceptions of a "typical" argument; that is, paradigm cases.

A second type of strategy employed by researchers in response to the "fuzziness predicament" is to focus attention on some limited and well-defined *discourse genre* known to involve verbal disputes. A key feature of this research strategy is its focus on the analysis of argument within the discourse genre rather than on analysis of the discourse genre itself (as, for example, in Frake's [1972] analysis of forms of litigation employed by a group of Philippine Moslems). Examples of the use of this strategy in the study of adult arguments can be found in Enos' (1980) analysis of argument and advocacy in Hellenic litigation and Hample's (1979) analysis of argument in contemporary American courtroom proceedings.

This strategy has also been employed in research on children's arguments. For example, Goodwin (1980) has analyzed arguments produced in the context of a recurring gossip dispute activity. This discourse form, called "he-said-she-said" by participants, is commonly produced among a particular group of black, female, working-class children in west Philadelphia. In this paper Goodwin isolates and analyzes the structure of argument sequences in a number of instances of "he-said-she-said." Employing a similar research strategy, Boggs (1978) has explored the development of verbal disputing in Hawaiian children through analysis of arguments produced within a commonly occurring contradiction routine.

A third strategy employed by researchers involves the identification of arguments on the basis of *structural properties* of discourse. Among analyses of adult arguments, work by Jackson and Jacobs (1980) exemplifies this approach. They see arguments as conversational interactions organized by adjacency pairs and characterized by the attempt to withhold a preferred second-pair part and failure to withdraw or suppress a disagreeable first-pair parts (by the "projection, avoidance, production, or resolution of disagreement" [254]). This research strategy begins with some general conception of discourse structures and defines or isolates arguments on the basis of general discourse principles; arguments have in common the actualization or operation of some particular discourse structure or process.

Keller-Cohen, Chalmer, and Remler (1979) and Goodwin (1974) have employed this strategy in studies of children's arguments. Keller-Cohen and her associates have focused on the phenomenon of negation in children's interactive discourse and analyzed the various forms that simple and elaborated negation may take. Goodwin, like Jackson and Jacobs, began with the assumption that the adjacency pair is a fundamental constructional unit of conversation and examined children's conversational sequences beginning with particular types of first-pair parts: those projecting next answers that oppose prior moves (such as commands, accusations, threats).

These three strategies (paradigm case, discourse genre, and structural) are perfectly plausible responses to fuzziness; they allow research to proceed in the absence of clear concepts of argument. But these strategies are effective precisely because they restrict the field of inquiry. Thus it is important to understand exactly how each of these approaches influences characterizations of arguments.

Discourse genre approaches create clear-cut boundaries by focusing on a narrow range of events but suffer from the defect that the properties of discourse or interaction that are revealed cannot be clearly attributed to either the nature of the genre or the nature of argument. Thus in Goodwin's (1980) analysis of "he-said-she-said" the discourse structures she identifies may be characteristic of children's arguments or unique to that genre.

Structural approaches create clear-cut boundaries by emphasizing some discourse structures at the expense of other properties of interaction. Thus, for example, Jackson and Jacobs (1980, 254) propose two related criteria for arguments:

> We propose that the class of occurrences which natural language users would label arguments may be delimited by two conditions—one functional, the other structural. First, arguments are disagreement relevant speech events; they are characterized by the projection, avoidance, production, or resolution of disagreement. Argument attends to the withholding, or potential withholding, of a preferred SPP [second-pair part] of an adjacency pair and the failure to withdraw or suppress the disagreeable FPP [first-pair part]. These episodes range from instances of pure disagreement, in which participants exchange and recycle incompatible pair parts, to instances in which the basis for the disagreement becomes the substance of the argument. In treating them, we consider how an utterance may become arguable and supportable, i.e., the possible bases for argument. Second, arguments appear as a variety of structural expansions of adjacency pairs. They may involve turn expansions or sequence expansions focusing on either pair part, but they occur within the interpretive frame provided by a dominant adjacency pair.

By these criteria, Example 2 is an argument, but Example 3 is not.
(2) A: Shall I come by your office at one o'clock?
    B: You can't. You're in class.
    A: No—we're not meeting today.
    B: Oh. Okay.
(3) A: You cooked tuna casserole last week.
    B: Let's change the topic.
    A: This is an interesting-looking vegetable.
    B: I said leave it alone. If you don't like my cooking, you're welcome to the job.
    A: Hey, ease up. Just a casual observation.
    B: You jerk.

The point here is *not* that Example 3 is an argument and 2 is not. Neither is a clear-cut case of argument. They are, at best, borderline cases. But both examples are like arguments in particular ways. The point here is that our concept of argument manifests itself in a set of features of social interaction, some involving discourse organization, some involving relational considerations, some involving properties of interaction. Approaches that emphasize discourse structure to the exclusion of other properties of argument draw boundaries around instances of interaction in such a way as to include some borderline cases and arbitrarily exclude others.

Examination of examples 2 and 3 also suggests the limitations of the *paradigm case* approach. Clear-cut cases of a category are likely to display a large number of the attributes of the category, while borderline cases display fewer of those attributes. Thus it is precisely in borderline cases that a given attribute of arguments is likely to be displayed most clearly. Attending solely to paradigm cases can blind the analyst to the operation of multiple attributes and processes; thus O'Keefe points to extended disagreement as a basic characteristic of arguments on the basis of paradigm case analysis, ignoring other properties of arguments. Borderline cases are informative too, and juxtaposing borderline and clear-cut cases can display less salient attributes of arguments.

Fuzziness as a fact. One alternative to treating fuzziness as a predicament is treat it as a fact. We believe that the ideal theory of arguments would provide an adequate characterization of argument and in the course of doing so explain the fact of fuzziness itself. Such an approach requires attention to the full range of forms arguments may take, to both clear-cut and borderline cases. Such an approach requires recognition that various borderline cases are related to clear-cut instances in different ways.

Taking fuzziness as a fact suggests an analysis of argument in terms of features or attributes of arguments. There may not be a set of features that constitute necessary-and-sufficient criteria for something's being an argument, but there may be a set of "generic characteristics" of arguments— that is, a set of features that commonly (but not necessarily) appear in arguments so that an event which displays a number of these features is probably appropriately described as an "argument." This kind of approach is capable of describing arguments in general while simultaneously acknowledging that no single characteristic is necessarily common to all arguments.

This *generic-characteristic* approach has been previously used by Brockriede (1975) to analyze "argument." But, as O'Keefe (1977) has noted, Brockriede's analysis failed to distinguish argument$_1$ and argument$_2$, and thus is not entirely satisfactory. Our analysis here (as throughout the chapter) is focused on argument$_2$ and is derived from three sources: (1) our intuitions about "having an argument," (2) prior research on arguments, and (3) examination of a broad range of disputatious interactions produced by children. For purposes of identifying features of arguments, examination of children's arguments is particularly useful. From an adult analyst's perspective, children's arguments are commonly "borderline" arguments. At the same time, children's arguments are clearly related to adult arguments. Characteristics of argument generally that may be obscured in the behavior of adults may thus be more clearly displayed in child behavior.

Unfortunately, no list of generic characteristics of argument (argument$_2$) currently exists, and we are not prepared to provide one. We do wish to propose one generic characteristic of arguments, overt opposition, and to discuss the role of overt opposition in structuring arguments.

One Generic Characteristic of Arguments

We have already noted that the fuzziness of the concept of argument seems to be due, in part, to the diversity of behaviors employed within argumentative episodes. Nonetheless, arguments are organized events. For example, it is easy to see in most cases just when an argument started and when it ended. And the particular actions which occur within an argument all appear to occur relevantly given that we know an argument is occurring. In short, arguments are distinctive and coherent interactional events.

In this section we argue that the coherence of arguments is partially due to one generic property of arguments: a relationship of opposition between participants. We argue that displays of overt opposition are part of every argument and that the relationship of opposition such displays create make other displays of opposition relevant. However, since opposition itself can take many forms and since each form of opposition can be realized in a variety of ways in interaction, only opposition in its most general sense is a characteristic feature of arguments.

Overt opposition as a generic characteristic of arguments. One basic characteristic of arguments is opposition; opposition is not, in our sense, any concrete act or series of acts, but rather a type of relationship between interactants. Thus, "having an argument" is characterized by the existence of a particular relationship between participants.

"Opposition" is itself a fairly fuzzy concept. People can align themselves in opposition to each other in many different ways. Interactants can degrade or reject each other's self-identities. Interactants can align themselves in mutually inconsistent ways to some specific outcome, as in the cases of competition (in which A's winning or having is inconsistent with B's winning or having) and refusal/denial (in which A's gaining assent is inconsistent with B's unwillingness to give assent). Interactants may align themselves in inconsistent ways toward the performance of some act (as in cases in which A performs or wants to perform some act and B either does not want the act performed or does not want A to perform that act). Interactants can hold, or believe they hold, opposing beliefs. And so on.

These different forms of opposition are related types of interactional alignments. Research has already suggested connections between particular types of opposition; for example, Brown and Levinson (1978) have argued that B's opposition to A's expressed wants intrinsically involves a threat to A's face (identity). We believe that all forms of opposition are related and share a central feature: in opposition, one party impedes satisfaction of the wants of the other.

Arguments are characterized not simply by opposition but by *overt* opposition. Where A's wants are covert or where B's resistance to A's wants is concealed, arguments do not occur; arguments occur where A's wants and B's resistance are made manifest in interaction. Thus arguments begin (and continue) as overt opposition is made manifest, and arguments end when opposition is no longer manifest.

Overt manifestations of opposition. One reason that arguments take a diversity of shapes and incorporate a wide range of actions is that opposition can manifest and resolve itself in a variety of ways. Moreover, the form in which opposition is resolved does not necessarily follow from the form in which opposition is initially manifest. Analysis of typical ways in which opposition occurs suggests that there are at least four basic ways in which opposition is manifest and two ways in which opposition ceases.

Overt opposition can be created through any of the following four types of act sequences:

1. A makes known a want; B overtly impedes satisfaction of the want. The mode of B's resistance may be active or passive; B can overtly display passive resistance to A's wants by making no attempt to satisfy A's wants, by offering objections to the manner of A's expressing his wants, or by offering potential justifications for A's wants not being satisfied. Thus opposition may be created passively by objecting to conditions presupposed by a request, order, suggestion, announcement of intentions, etc. (examples 4 and 5) or by hearing but failing to respond to A's expression of want. B can offer active resistance by objecting to A's wants or directly refusing to satisfy A's wants. Opposition may be created actively when A's request, order, suggestion, announced intention, and the like is followed by a direct refusal from B (examples 6 and 7) or B's explicit denial of A's wants (Example 8).

(4) RORY: I'll be the space monster.

MATT: Space monsters hurt people and things.

(5) D: We should read a book.

A: We don't have a book. So we can't read a book.

(6) JU: Give me that.

JJ: No.

(7) D: I'm alone. I need a friend.

S: Not me. I'm not your friend.

(8) A: Oh yeah. I don't got no yellow.

D: You—you do got one.

2. A is presupposed to have a want; B overtly impedes satisfaction of the want. A can be assumed to have certain wants, either because they are fundamental and omnipresent (e.g., the want to have a positive identity; the want to not be harmed) or because B has prior knowledge of some specific want of A's. Thus A's wants can be presupposed by B and overt opposition can consist simply of acts that display resistance to A's presupposed wants. Examples of this type of overt opposition can be found in acts of physical aggression (e.g., hitting), insults (see Example 9), other negative identity claims (Example 10), threats of aggression (Example 11), prohibitions (Example 12), and so on.

(9) A: You're just a potatohead.

(10) K: Who is all the kids? You can't talk right. Robin can't talk right.

(11) K: I'll knock your head off.

(12) JEFF: Rory, you can't come to my house any more!

3. A makes known a want; B makes known a competing want. Examples of this form of opposition are straightforward: verbal or nonverbal competitions (Example 13), proposals followed by counterproposals (examples 16 and 17), competing claims of possession (Example 18), and so on.

(13) A: I goin get a big. I goin get a big one.

B: I got a bigger.

(14) DA: I take the big ones. You take the little ones. All right?

DE: Let me take the big ones too.

(15) JEFF: You be king [of the dinosaurs].

MIKE: No I wanta be stretosaurus.

(16) A: Yeah. Where these go? Oh these mine.

D: Hey, these mine!

4. B does some act; A makes known that it impedes (or has impeded) his or her wants or the wants of some third party. This pattern of opposition appears in assertions followed by disagreement (examples 17 and 18), complaints (Example 19), protests (Example 20), accusations (Example 21),

orders to desist (Example 22), reprimands (Example 23), criticism (Example 24), and so on.

(17) C: I've got your horsie. I've got your horsie.
   D: Oh yeah?
(18) C: You was playin here?
   M: Yeah. Yeah. I was playin here. Yeah. I was here before.
   C: Nah.
(19) J: God. You always want to do it so fast.
(20) DA: Move. [DA pushes K out of her way.]
   K: Hey!
(21) DA: Move up up up. My seat. I'm tellin. He won't get outa my seat.
(22) K: A bird. That's a bird.
   J: Shut up.
(23) BILLY: I'm done with these pages.
   JIMMY: You weren't supposed to do those pages.
(24) C [pretending a telephone rings]: Lug lug a ling gv a ma ma ming.
   D: You don't have a telephone.

Arguments begin when overt opposition is manifest in some form, and arguments continue while opposition continues to be manifest overtly. In the instances of children's arguments we have examined, it appears that the occurrence of any form of overt opposition makes the occurrence of any other form of overt opposition a relevant and coherent interactional move. That is, manifestation of the relationship of opposition makes any display of opposition pragmatically relevant.

Consider, for example, the following disputes.
(25) D [shows some blocks he has picked up]: Whew! [18 sec.] Look what I did!
   S: So what?
   D: So what bones? [Laughs]
   S: So what bomar?
   D: I'll kill your neck.
   S: I'll kill your bones.
   D: Oooh! [unintelligible] I—I'll
   S: And then I'll kill your jaws!
   D: Oooh! I'll kill your boobs.
   S: Oooh! Ah!
(26) C [pretending a telephone rings]: Lug lug a ling gv a ma ma ming.
   D: You don't have a telephone.
   C: Yes I do [there is a telephone pictured in a puzzle].
   D: Where is it?
   C: Right here. [Points to the telephone]
   D: Unh-uh.

    C: Uh-huh. That is a telephone. I had it.

    D: See? This is a telephone [points to another piece].

    C: Here. You have this [hands him a piece of her puzzle].

    D: No.

    C: We you not goin to have my te my blow dryer like this now.

    D: Unh-uh. I can uh I can get a dryer too.

(27) C: I beatin you [at completing a puzzle].

    D: Uh. Okay. But I gets this [a puzzle piece].

    C: See I beat you.

    D: I beat you up. I—I you better say yes okay. Okay?

    C: Yes. Okay.

In these examples, children employ moves that depart from the main lines of topical development: "So what bones," "I'll kill your neck," "We you not goin to have my te my blow dryer like this now," "But I gets this," "I beat you up." These departures consist of threats, insults, odd competitive moves, and the like. One could suppose that these moves are simply off-topic, incoherent. However, when genuine topic change occurs, opposition ceases and generally does not resume on the immediately succeeding turn. In fact, children treat these moves as perfectly straightforward. Even when they cannot or do not produce utterances that are coherent in terms of other semantic and pragmatic characteristics, the relationship of opposition makes any overt display of opposition a coherent response.

    The importance of opposition as a coherence-producing property of interaction is further evident in cases where the issue of a dispute becomes confused even though the topic remains the same. In the following example, two children become confused as to which side of the issue they support.

(28) C: When me and Amy was in here—when me and Amy was in here we told
       Bunny we was rich honey. [Laughs]

    M: Wo wu wo wah wah wah. Yup me too.

    C: You wasn't in here.

    M: Yes I was. Yes I was.

    C: I didn't see you.

    M: You wasn't.

    C: I was.

    M: You wasn't.

    C: Uh-huh. [Louder] You saw me playin with Amy. Den you say we's rich
       honey. (Didn't you Michael)?

Even when the issue becomes confused these interactants continue their dispute; displaying opposition is a relevant move as long as opposition has occurred.

Arguments end when opposition is no longer manifest. Opposition ceases in two ways: through withdrawal or through resolution. Interactants can withdraw from opposition by terminating interaction or by changing the topic (examples 29 and 30).

(29) [Rory is taking apart a Tinkertoy.]

> MATT [running up to Rory]: Don't! I made that!
>
> [Rory lays down the top and starts to walk away.]

(30) R: You want to hug each other (a little)?

> K: Shut up.
>
> R: You don't.
>
> K: You know what? I went to bed at nine—at ten o'clock.

Interactants can resolve opposition cooperatively or through the application of power. Cooperative resolution involves producing overt mutuality or agreement. Mutuality and agreement can be produced in various ways. For example, A can withdraw or modify his expression of wants (examples 31 and 32). B can withdraw or modify his resistance to A's wants (examples 33 and 34). Or interactants can re-establish mutuality through joking and similar moves (this is more common among elementary school children; see Boggs [1978]).

(31) JEFF [to Mike]: You be king [of the dinosaurs].

> MIKE: No. I wanta be stretosaurus.
>
> JEFF: Rory you be king then.

(32) SCOTT: That's my airplane.

> MATT: No, it's a flashlight. I made it.
>
> SCOTT: Okay.

(33) T: Come on. Let's go.

> D: Nope.
>
> T: Let's go.
>
> D: Wait till I come.

(34) C [to D]: Can you help me?

> D: No.
>
> C [whining, to P]: He said no.
>
> D: Yes.
>
> C: Okay.
>
> D: But I can't right now.

Opposition can also be resolved through the exploitation of power. A can be forced to withdraw his wants, B can be forced to withdraw his resistance, and either party can be forced to desist from showing overt opposition. In children's arguments, the use of power generally appears as physical force (e.g., taking, hitting), threats of force, bribes, or appeals to external authority ("I'm tellin").

Children's arguments (and, we suppose, arguments in general) begin when opposition is displayed overtly and continues while opposition continues to be manifest. Overt opposition can take many forms, both initially and as a response to overt opposition: assertions, requests, counterassertions, denials, rejections, threats, insults, prohibitions, challenges, accusations, pointing, grabbing, taking, pushing, screaming, and so on. Arguments end when opposition ceases, and cessation of opposition may appear in the production of threats, physical force, appeals to authority, bribes, agreement, revisions of requests, and so on.

Thus a superficial examination of arguments reveals substantial variability; arguments take many different forms and incorporate many different types of acts and modes of behavior (none unique to arguments). Given the diversity of forms arguments may take it may appear that arguments have no clear characteristics. This diversity in forms of argumentative interaction can be explained, in part, by assuming that one generic characteristic of arguments is a relation of opposition between interactants that makes any display of opposition by either party pragmatically relevant.

We have argued that opposition is one important generic characteristic of arguments; it is a property common to arguments generally which manifests itself in different ways in different circumstances. In at least some circumstances, opposition is the dominant property of arguments.

Opposition is not an incidental property of arguments. Rather, we have argued that the relationship of opposition is a basic structure that helps create arguments and organize behavior coherently within arguments. It is important to recognize, however, that opposition is not the only source of coherence or organization in arguments. The most superficial examination of the examples offered in this section will show that even the arguments of very young children show organization and structure beyond simple opposition; within these arguments children produce extended verbal sequences that are coherent not simply as arguments but also as discourse. In the next section we offer a more detailed description of children's arguments, a description that begins with an analysis of opposition in children's interactions and then explores the role of discourse in children's arguments.

The Role of Discourse in Children's Arguments

In this section we will examine the role of discourse in children's arguments. We will begin with an examination of opposition as a feature of children's interactions, discuss the ways children use language in producing arguments, and summarize research on the structure and organization of children's arguments. Our discussion of children's arguments will focus on arguments among preschool children, although available information on arguments among younger and older children will be incorporated in the discussion.

Opposition in Children's Interaction

Opposition is a common feature of social interaction among children. Children do not need to learn to disagree; disagreements originate spontaneously and frequently in interactions among even the youngest children. Bronson (1975) analyzed peer interactions among thirteen- to twenty-four-month-old children and found that 40 to 50 percent of the connected sequences in the encounters she examined were "disagreements." A variety of events was classed as disagreements: toy-taking (successful or unsuccessful); withdrawal of self or toy; assaults; vocal protests at peer behavior; assertions of possession of toys held by peer. The great majority of these preverbal disputes centered on toy-taking and disputed possession.

Prevalence of Arguments in Preschool Interactions. Our own research on preschool children's arguments suggests that opposition is common among two- to five-year-old children as well. We isolated instances of arguments in transcripts of children's conversations. These conversations occurred in an experimenter-structured situation. Twenty-four children enrolled in the Wayne State University Child Development Center Preschool served as subjects in this study. Children were assigned to dyads; six dyads consisted of members of the kindergarten division (five years old) and six dyads consisted of members of the prekindergarten division (two to four years old). Each dyad was brought to a small playroom, a familiar setting to all the children. Children were encouraged to play together; some children were given a set of blocks to initiate play. These twelve interactions (about fifteen minutes each) were tape-recorded and monitored by an adult observer. The interactions were transcribed from the audio tapes and observer's notes; these transcripts served as a main source of data for the analysis we report in this and the next two sections.

We isolated instances of arguments in these transcripts by searching for overt opposition in the form of verbal dispute statements. Because children sometimes fail to direct their utterances clearly to their partners and because they are sometimes unresponsive to the utterances of their partners, we selected for analysis only those sequences in which some overt verbal display of opposition was relevantly responded to by the partner.[2] Arguments were assumed to continue as long as opposition was continued, even where forms of opposition or the topic of discussion shifted. Arguments were assumed to end when overt opposition ceased, through either withdrawal or resolution.

Using these procedures, we identified fifty-six argument sequences in twelve transcripts. No dyad produced fewer than two arguments in these short play periods. The six older dyads produced twenty-one arguments (an average of 3.5 arguments per dyad); the six younger dyads produced thirty-five arguments (an average of 5.8 arguments per dyad). Arguments varied in length from two to 110 turns, with the median length of arguments being five turns for both older and younger dyads. Older and younger dyads did not differ significantly either in number of arguments produced per dyad or in number of turns devoted to arguing.

The situation in which these dyads interacted was not constructed to elicit arguments; if anything, cooperation and agreement were encouraged. Moreover, our count includes only verbally initiated disputes that displayed verbal uptake. Thus it is likely that we have underrepresented slightly the frequency of overt opposition in children's interactions. In this context, the sheer number of arguments these children produced in such short play periods is impressive and quite consistent with Bronson's findings concerning the prevalence of disagreement in toddler interactions.

One initial conclusion is obvious; as any parent can probably attest, children do not need to learn to disagree. Opposition is a natural and spontaneous occurrence in interaction; if there are age-related changes in the degree to which overt opposition occurs, opposition is probably negatively related to age. That is, rather than learning to disagree, children ultimately learn not to disagree so often.

[2] Most of the restrictions we imposed in selecting sequences for analysis were adopted so that the data we had could be treated conveniently, not for theoretical reasons. Because our data were audiotaped, we lost information about nonverbal displays of opposition, although the adult observer's notes provided some general information about the context in which disputes occurred and some of the actions that filled pauses in verbal interaction or accompanied speech. Because nonverbal behaviors were unsystematically recorded, we restricted our analysis to disputes that originated verbally. Similarly, records that essentially reflect only vocal behavior omit relevant data on nonverbal attention cues that could be used to distinguish cases of failure to hear from active ignoring. Hence we restricted our analysis to those cases in which we were sure listeners had heard and understood the initial dispute statement; we took production of a relevant response as clear evidence of listener's responsiveness.

Types of Arguments in Preschool Interactions. In comparison to younger children, two- to five-year-old children disagree about a wide range of things. For the most part, preschool children's disputes originate either when one child expresses a want that a second child refuses to satisfy or when one child says or does something that a second child finds objectionable.

Of the fifty-six arguments we identified, eighteen began when one child overtly expressed a want, either by requesting, ordering, suggesting, or stating a need, and his or her partner either refused to satisfy the want, objected to the want, or objected to the first child's expression of wants. Twelve of these arguments were produced by younger dyads, six by older dyads.

Of the fifty-six arguments produced by our dyads, twenty-seven began when one child did or said something the partner found objectionable (fifteen by younger children, twelve by older children). Of these twenty-seven sequences, sixteen involved cases in which one child stated or asserted a fact to which his or her partner objected, as displayed in denial or counter-assertion (nine by younger dyads, seven by older dyads). The other eleven arguments originated in a variety of ways. Among the older children, two arguments began when children corrected and criticized their partners' speech; one argument began when a child questioned an act performed by his partner; one argument began when one child asked a question and his partner denied a fact presupposed by the question; one argument began when one child stated an intention to which his partner objected. Among the younger children, six arguments began when children objected (by criticizing, accusing, or simply disapproving) to the nonverbal actions of their partners.

A surprisingly small number of arguments began with competing expressions ("That's mine"—"That's mine;" "I'm the mommy"—"I'm the mommy;" "I have the big one"—"I have the bigger one"); among the younger children, six arguments began this way, while only two of the older children's arguments began with competitive opposition.

Of fifty-six total arguments, only three began with unprovoked overt opposition (e.g., insults or threats). Two of these occurred in interactions among younger children. The fact that preschool-level arguments do not typically begin with insults, threats, or other forms of unprovoked opposition is somewhat misleading. Apparently the relationship of opposition is seldom created for its own sake; it generally arises from specific conflicting purposes. However, once opposition has been created, insults and threats are commonly employed to express opposition overtly. Fourteen (25 percent) of the fifty-six arguments (eleven produced by younger children, three by older children) analyzed here incorporated some type of threat or insult sequence.

Comparable data regarding the prevalence and types of arguments among older children and adults are not available, so there is no context for useful comparisons between arguers of different ages. Our data suggest that two- to four-year-old and four- to five-year-old children behave very similarly in arguments. In both younger and older dyads, request-refusal, order-refusal, or need statement-refusal sequences started a large percentage of arguments (34.3 percent and 28.6 percent for younger and older dyads, respectively), as did assertion denials (25.7 percent and 33.3 percent respectively). Thus, for both groups in our sample, about 60 percent of arguments originated in these two sources.

There are striking contrasts between the arguments of our preschool children and the primitive disputes of Bronson's toddlers. Preverbal children do not produce statements of fact; their arguments cannot arise from assertion-denial sequences. Preverbal children can certainly indicate their wants and are capable of using other people instrumentally to attain their ends. But in disputes with other toddlers they do not make requests or give orders; the other is not seen as instrumental to achieving objectives. Hence, as Bronson notes, analysis of gaze patterns in toy-possession disputes shows that toddlers look almost exclusively at the toy and only infrequently at the other child. In contrast, preschool children center their attention on each other as primary obstacles and primary means to achieving want satisfaction.

This new interactional attitude and expanded interactional competence appear to arise spontaneously with the acquisition of language. That is, it appears that competence for argument does not develop but is acquired as part of learning language. This hypothesis is supported by evidence of very early emergence of sophisticated argumentative skills like reason-giving. Garvey (1977, 73) offers a striking example that illustrates this point. This argument was produced by a girl (age thirty-four months) and a boy (age thirty-six months).

(35) [They hear a noise outside the room.]
    GIRL: It might be your mommy.
    BOY: No. She's not coming.
    GIRL: She's coming.
    BOY: No, she's not going down to pick me up. Joan is.

This is an amazingly sophisticated performance, especially given the fact that children one year younger than these are still primarily involved in nonverbal toy-taking and possession disputes.

This early emergence of skill at argument can be best understood in relation to the development of children's discourse in general.

Children's Discourse and Children's Arguments

Children's arguments occur within children's conversations; in producing arguments children call on their general conversational skills. Given that children begin producing arguments as they master language and discourse structures, it is reasonable to suppose that learning to argue is a component or product of learning to speak. In this section we first review some of the basic conversational skills of preschool children and then discuss the role of these basic skills in shaping children's arguments.

Basic Conversational Skills. The ability to have a conversation depends on four related kinds of knowledge: knowledge of the turn system, of language (including knowledge of speech act organization), of principles involved in coherence production, and of the repair system (for a general introduction to research on these four kinds of knowledge, see Coulthard [1977]). These four sets of principles combine to generate an impressive battery of conversational tactics, and each of these kinds of knowledge is mastered very early in children's development.

The turn system is the set of principles and cues used in floor allocation. It incorporates general rules (e.g., "One and only one speaker talks at a time") as well as specific verbal (e.g., grammatical markers) and nonverbal (e.g., direction of gaze) cues used to signal the end of one speaker's turn and the beginning of the next speaker's turn. Children master most of the basic principles and signals of the turn system for conversation even before they begin to talk. Caretakers impose a nonverbal turn system on their interactions with infants, and infants soon acquire the rules that make the system work (for a summary of research on turn-taking in prelinguistic interactions, see Stern [1978]). However, there are age-related differences in children's mastery of the turn-taking system. Taylor (1977), for example, found that the number of instances of talkovers, interruptions, and collaboratively produced sentences increased with age, with preschool children producing well-bounded turns (no talkovers, few interruptions, and so on) and third-grade children producing more talkovers, interruptions, and the like.

Although it is possible to have nonverbal "conversations" that mimic the structure of turns in true conversation, it is obvious that conversation is a speech event; that is, conversation involves a sequence of acts of speaking. Thus the ability to do conversation requires knowledge of language and knowledge of how language is produced as speech acts. Children begin to learn language at about twelve months, and by two and a half or so begin to produce complex multiword sentences that sound remarkably like adult speech. While the details of the language acquisition process are not relevant to this discussion (for a good summary of current thinking about language acquisition, see Clark and Clark [1977]), the fact that preschool-age children are at advanced stages in this process is relevant. The youngest preschool children have not fully mastered language, but they are quite capable of using language to accomplish their purposes. In the words of one child, aged two years ten months, "When I was a little girl I could go 'geek-geek' like that. But now I can go 'This is a chair'" (Clark and Clark, 1977, 295).

Of course, knowledge of language (in the sense of an abstract system of grammatical rules) does not by itself generate acts of speaking. Speaking occurs as acts of uttering that are organized by speaker intentions; different types of intentions produce different types of speech acts (Searle, 1969). Speech acts can be seen as falling into five general categories (Searle, 1977): representatives, in which the speaker conveys his belief that some proposition is true (e.g., assertions); directives, in which the speaker attempts to get the listener to do something (e.g., requests, orders); commissives, in which the speaker commits himself to some future course of action (e.g., promises, threats); expressives, in which the speaker expresses a psychological state about something (e.g., expressing disapproval); and declarations, in which the utterance itself brings about a new state of affairs (e.g., christening).

Bates, Camaioni, and Volterra (1976) have argued that the pragmatic intentions which generate speech acts guide children's nonverbal behavior in prelinguistic interactions; and Dore (1973), Carter (1974), and Clark and Clark (1977) have all argued that such pragmatic intentions organize the earliest utterances of language learners. Although examples of speech acts falling within each of the five general categories can be found in the speech of one- to four-year-old children, assertions and requests predominate.

But speech acts are not simply categories into which utterances fall; they are acts performed by speaking (performatives) created by sets of constitutive rules or conditions that define the legitimate and appropriate performance of a given speech act. Each speech act is defined by a set of rules, or "felicity conditions," that constitute the legitimate performance of the act. One interesting question about children's production of speech acts is whether they really know what they are producing; that is, whether they know (or display knowledge of) the felicity conditions of their speech acts. It could be the case, of course, that children produce utterances that adults interpret as particular speech acts and that children, because they lack knowledge of felicity conditions, do not in any meaningful sense intend to produce a given speech act.

We are unaware of the existence of any direct evidence regarding children's knowledge of felicity conditions, but indirect evidence that children in fact understand the pragmatic significance of their utterances and the utterances of other children can be adduced from the ways children produce coherent conversations and the ways children construct arguments.

A number of developmental theorists and researchers have portrayed children's conversations as egocentric and incoherent; the stereotype they have created suggests that children are unresponsive to their conversational partners, that children frequently produce parallel monologues, and that children do not produce topically coherent discourse. This stereotype has been the object of trenchant criticism of late. Shatz (1977) summarized research on children's conversations which indicates that in fact children do acknowledge and respond appropriately to their partners' utterances; this research contradicts the stereotype of the young child as a monologic communicator. Benoit (1979) found that even very young preschool children produced coherent conversations, in which utterances were related formally (through repetition of words or phrases), semantically (through being on-topic), and pragmatically (through producing appropriate speech acts as responses to preceding speech acts) to previous talk.

Benoit's finding that the speech of young children displays pragmatic coherence bears on the question of whether children really organize their utterances as speech acts. Jacobs and Jackson (1980) have argued, following Sinclair and Coulthard (1975), that the felicity conditions on particular speech acts define what next speech act is pragmatically relevant and what next speech act is pragmatically preferred. For example, grants are preferred and relevant responses to requests, because the felicity conditions on grants mirror the felicity conditions on requests (for a more detailed treatment of this issue, see Jackson and Jacobs [this volume]). Thus pragmatic coherence involves producing reponses that are pragmatically relevant to a prior speech act, and the ability to produce such pragmatically coherent responses suggests an implicit understanding of the underlying principles that makes such responses coherent; namely, felicity conditions on the speech acts involved. And since Benoit reports that overwhelmingly children do produce pragmatically coherent conversational turns, her results can be taken as suggesting that children have knowledge of the structure of speech acts.

An understanding of pragmatic coherence and the ways in which it is produced is particularly important for the analysis of the role of discourse in arguments, since the same principles that define agreement (production of a preferred response) also define disagreement (production of a dispreferred response). A dispreferred response to a speech act is a speech act whose felicity conditions contradict those of the act to which it responds; it is a pragmatically relevant response, since its felicity conditions are related to the felicity conditions for the speech act to which it responds. Thus, for example, a refusal is a relevant response to a request, even though it is a dispreferred response.

Frequently a conversationalist is unable or unwilling to produce either a preferred or dispreferred response. Utterances may be unintelligible or situational conditions may interfere with hearing; the speaker may assume the hearer knows an important piece of background information he or she in fact lacks; a speaker may act as if the conditions for issuing a legitimate request have been met when in fact they have not; hearers and speakers may disagree about whether the felicity conditions on a speech act have been met. In such circumstances speakers and hearers collaborate in the repair of the defectively produced utterance or illegitimately issued speech act. Repair sequences begin when the hearer indicates a defect in a prior utterance; and repair occurs when the speaker withdraws or reformulates the utterance or when the hearer withdraws the objection.

Preschool children understand and exploit the principles behind the organization of repair sequences. Repair sequences of various types are frequent in children's discourse. Children know when they do not understand and thus request clarification (examples 36 and 37); children can recognize (and object) when a speech act is based on a false presupposition or condition (examples 38 and 39).

(36) R: Can we go back and get Deekie?
    P: Yeah. After a while.
    K: Hmm.
    R: And then we'll get him. And then [after you'll] get him?
    P: Uh-hum.
    K: Him who?

R: All the kids.

K: Who is all the kids? You can't talk right. Robin can't talk right.

(37) J: I guess I goin get me a book.

K: A book?

J: I guess I goin get me a book or puzzles.

(38) R: We goin back in the gym yet?

K: No, we ain't goin back in the gym.

R: We can wait till [they] come out.

K: Nope. When they come out then it'll be lunchtime.

(39) D: Give me my horsie. [The toy is really a cow.]

C: No. That not a horsie. That's a horsie. [points to the horse]

D: Oh. This is.

Simply repeating or recycling is generally an inadequate response to the indication of a need for repair (except in cases where the hearer asks for repetition). Children in our dyads were able to respond specifically and appropriately to hearer's wants, elaborating unclear utterances (Example 37) and revising (Example 38) or withdrawing (Example 39) objectionable speech acts.

Conversational Skills and Children's Arguments. Jackson and Jacobs (1980) have pointed out that repair structures are extensively exploited in arguments. When interactants are confronted with an objectionable speech act (say, an assertion they believe to be false or a request they do not want to grant) they must say something relevant because they are obligated by the turn system and the basic rules of conversation to do so. One way to avoid giving a bald dispreferred response to the objectionable act is to treat it as defective or illegitimate. Similarly, one way of justifying disagreement is to point to defects in the act being responded to, so a dispreferred response may be supported or defended in terms of the legitimacy of the initial speech act.

The grounds for finding a speech act to be illegitimate or defective are to be found in the felicity conditions which constitute that particular speech act. Thus opposition in discourse may take the form of disagreement-relevant expansions in which failures to satisfy felicity conditions become explicit issues and serve as reasons for disagreement.

Jackson and Jacobs (1980) have shown the utility of this kind of approach in analyzing the structure of arguments produced by older children and adults. Our data indicate that preschool children have the capacity to produce such disagreement-relevant expansions, and the expansion structures we found in children's arguments are quite consistent with the general analysis offered by Jackson and Jacobs. For example, 40 and 41 show instances of reason-giving in the context of disagreement-relevant expansions that are organized around felicity conditions.

(40) RORY: I'll be the space monster.

    MATT: Space monsters hurt people and things.

    RORY: But I'll be a good space monster; good space monsters don't hurt people.

    MATT: You can't be that.

    RORY: I can too. I'm a good space monster.

    MATT: You aren't . . . too.

    RORY: I am too, Matthew, I'm a good one.

(41) MATT: Scott, don't bother me any more.

    SCOTT: I didn't bother you,

    MATT: You did too. Over at the blocks.

    SCOTT: Oooh [disagreeing].

    MATT: And you hurt me too.

Thus, preschool children seem perfectly capable of creatively generating support for their acts and support for their disagreement through expansion in terms of felicity conditions and through exploitation of repair structures in general. Even very young children show evidence of the ability to use repair organization and to construct disagreement-relevant expansions.

In general, preschool children display mastery of basic conversational knowledge and principles: they follow the turn system; they are linguistically sophisticated and not only produce an extensive range of speech acts but also give evidence of tacitly understanding felicity conditions; they produce coherent conversations; they can produce repair and disagreement-relevant expansions. They thus appear fully equipped to produce arguments, since they understand the relationship of opposition and they know how to use language to produce the speech acts that manifest, justify, and resolve opposition in the context of a sequentially produced interaction.

The conclusion to be drawn here is that while children's arguments may sometimes be little more than displays of competitive opposition or long sequences of recycled assertions and denials, children are capable of producing essentially the same range of argumentative sequences and tactics adults produce. The ability to produce arguments appears to derive from a body of general knowledge about interaction, conversational structure, and language. This knowledge is acquired very early in childhood and is exploited throughout the life span.

Structure and Strategy in Children's Arguments

So far we have examined the range of moves or tactics children may use in arguments and the basic conversational skills that allow children to generate tactics or moves. One question remains: How do children produce moves sequentially in the course of elaborating or terminating an argument?

One way of answering this question would be to look at a large number of arguments children have produced and to give a description of the typical patterns found in children's arguments. Both Boggs and Lein and Brenneis have offered descriptions of typical argument sequences.

Boggs (1978) analyzed verbal disputes of part-Hawaiian children produced as part of an assertion-contradiction routine. This routine is a common form of interaction within the children's community and may be employed seriously or playfully. Boggs found these verbal disputes follow typical patterns constructed from three sequence types. The three sequence types are: Type I: assertion, claim, or allegation followed by contradiction; Type II: challenge followed by supporting argument, allegation, or appeal to authority; and Type III: insult followed by counterinsult, threat, or trial. In general, these verbal disputes begin with a Type I sequence that is followed by a Type II or III sequence. Type II sequences are often followed by Type III sequences. In mapping the structural possibilities for verbal disputes, Boggs found that a lower-numbered sequence rarely follows a higher-numbered one. Disputes tend to escalate from contradiction to challenge, insult, counterinsult, threat, or trial.

Lein and Brenneis (1978) conducted a comparative analysis of arguments produced by children from three different speech communities: white American children from rural New England, black American children of migrant farm workers, and rural, Hindi-speaking Fiji Indian children. The arguments Lein and Brenneis analyzed did not occur naturally but were role-played in interviews. They classified argument moves into six content categories: (1) threats and bribes; (2) insults and flattery; (3) commands and moral persuasion; (4) simple assertions and negating or contradictory assertions; (5) denials and affirmations; and (6) nonword vocal signals (Brenneis and Lein, 1977). They found evidence of three basic argument patterns within each of these content categories. The first pattern, repetition, is displayed in sequences such as "I'm the strongest"—"I'm the strongest." The second pattern, inversion, involves answering with a statement denying, rejecting, or challenging a previous speaker (e.g., "Hey, give me my pencil"—"No"). The third pattern, escalation, involves each speaker making a stronger, more emphatic statement than the previous speaker (as in the case of our Example 25).

These general descriptions of patterns of moves produced within arguments are useful, but they give little insight into how arguments come to have a particular structure or into the related question of how moves are used strategically within arguments to achieve particular objectives. An alternative way of describing argument structures is to see them not as fixed forms but as emergent productions generated by strategic considerations.

When we say that arguments are emergent productions we mean that arguments are produced on a turn-by-turn basis; the structure an argument may have is not given in advance but is shaped and reshaped as speakers construct their turns sequentially. In constructing their turns arguers are guided by strategic considerations: arguments can be won or lost, and arguers want to win.

The interesting thing about arguments is that while winning can be defined in a general and abstract way as gaining either agreement or withdrawal of an objectionable move, what winning means in concrete terms must be defined within each argument. That is, the rules of the game are generated as the game is played. Different criteria for winning can be generated in different arguments. Thus, for example, Lein and Brenneis note that in some children's arguments a pattern of escalating volume in vocal production is adopted. Each child produces his turn with a louder volume than the previous speaker; when one child reaches maximum possible volume he wins the dispute because his partner is unable to produce a louder turn and is forced to withdraw. In some arguments endurance becomes the criterion; that is, children produce long repetitive series of turns where winning simply involves holding out the longest (as in Example 42).

(42) A: That's mine.
    M: That's not yours.
    A: Uh-huh.
    M: Unh-uh.
    A: Uh-huh.
    M: Unh-uh.
    A: Uh-huh [louder].
    M: Unh-uh. Unh-uh. This mine.
    A: Unh-uh.
    M: Uh-huh.
    A: This my play shoe.

Arguers may adopt a pattern of escalation in threats as, for example, in 25. Or winning may require advancing issues, as in examples 40 and 43.

(43) JEFF: Rory you can't come to my house any more!

RORY: My mom doesn't know where you live anyway.

JEFF: She does too.

RORY: She doesn't know where you live, Jeff!

JEFF: But you can't come . . . I don't want you to ever come to my house ever again!

An important feature of the production of criteria for winning and losing is that it is collaborative. Participants must collaborate in establishing a criterion: these rules are established as participants create an orderly sequence of turns; that is, as two speakers progressively raise the volume of their contributions or as insults are progressively worsened or embroidered. Participants must collaborate in maintaining a criterion: at any point a participant may break the pattern by recycling an earlier turn (see the last turn in Example 43) or by changing the character of the opposition (see the transition in Example 25 from "So what bomar?" to "I'll kill your neck"). As a result, losers can be seen as collaborating in their losses, since losing can only be defined in relation to a rule that losers have agreed to observe.

Thus the organization of children's arguments can be seen as an emergent process in which the sequential structure of turns following the initial move creates a rule participants follow in constructing turns strategically to win arguments. Participants must collaborate in establishing and maintaining criteria for evaluating turns; so in the course of an argument the criterion, and thus the structural pattern, of an argument may shift. Arguments terminate when opposition is withdrawn, and the manner of withdrawal and its meaning for the argument's outcome are determined by the success criterion established in the interaction.

Conclusion

In the introduction to this chapter we cautioned against assuming that children are incompetent arguers. We believe that our analysis of children's argument further undermines any assumption of incompetence. Even preschool children are capable communicators, and the basic skills that equip them to participate in conversation also equip them to conduct arguments. Because we have emphasized the connection between the ability to produce arguments and basic conversational skills acquired prior to and during language acquisition, we have implicitly argued that the age of the arguers is a relatively unimportant consideration for the analysis of arguments. We have juxtaposed two final examples we think make this point well. Both are examples of arguments produced when one child claims to have been at school and other children reject that claim.

(44) M: Yep. Huh, I//
    C: You you was playin here?
    M: Yeah. Yeah. I was playin here. Yeah I was here before.
    C: Nah.
    M: Yeah. Yeah.
    C: Then you didn't come in the playroom. Never. I remember you didn't. Right?
    M: Why? I cuz cuz had a go go to hospital. That's why. [M missed several days at school due to an injury.]

(45) T: Uh, that was funny when, they, we had the windows open, it goes [makes a sound like rushing wind]. [Brief laughter by T, K, and L.]
    ⌈ K: I know.
    ⌊ L: I thought you weren't there.
    K: Yeah.
    T: I was here yesterday.
    ⌈ K: You weren't.
    ⌊ L: No you weren't, cause yesterday
    ⌈   we made the flag.
    ⌊ K: We made the flag.
    L: And you weren't here when we made the flag.
    T [unsure]: I was—today's Friday, and I was here Thursday.
    L: Yeah—Thurs
    ⌈   day's the day we made the . . .
    ⌊ T: That was yesterday.
    ⌈ K: Flag.
    ⌊ L: Flag and you said you weren't here when we made the flag.
    T: You—made—Wednesday.
    L: No, we made it Thursday.
    K: Huh-uh, we didn't make it the day of [violin chorus].
    Note: Bracketed portions begin simultaneously.

These are remarkably similar arguments. Both are preceded by a child implying he was present on a particular day. In both cases, that implication is questioned and then explicitly avowed. The avowal produces denial. The denial is rejected, and the denial is then supported by reasons. The reasons offered are quite similar: "Thursday's the day we made the flag and you said you weren't here when we made the flag" versus "You may have been here but you weren't in the playroom because I was in the playroom and I remember." In both cases the child making the initial claim becomes confused and withdraws opposition (in 44, M actually offers a justification for not having been at school).

The similarity in these examples is particularly notable because Example 44 was produced by five-year-olds and Example 45 was produced by third-grade children. The primary difference between these two examples is the number of talkovers and interruptions; this difference is due to the general age-related difference in patterns of turn-taking identified by Taylor (1977).

Thus a focus on age-related differences in arguments may obscure more basic, fundamental, and important similarities across arguments regardless of the age of the participants. Consequently we think that the framework we have used to describe children's arguments might profitably be applied to the description of adult arguments as well. For example, the analysis of the role of opposition in defining relevance in arguments, the analysis of argumentative tactics in terms of the form of opposition they express, and the analysis of argument sequences in terms of the evaluative criteria they generate might help to explain what adults do when they argue. And with a more detailed description of what adults do, we might be in a better position to look for age-related differences in arguments.

MALCOLM O. SILLARS AND PATRICIA GANER

[8] Values and Beliefs: A Systematic Basis for Argumentation

Argumentation literature of the past decade clearly indicates that the logical model that had dominated the study for the preceding fifty years is moribund. In its place are a variety of approaches, all in some way linked to a postpositivistic, audience-centered communication model. However, such a communication approach can be flawed because it may lead one to the reductio ad absurdum that all argument is idiosyncratic. In the words of Gronbeck, "the new rationality may be, to some, a rule-governed system, but those systems are context—or even person determined, and hence we continually must begin anew, constructing systems of evidence and proof context by context" (1980, 10). If argumentation is totally dependent upon the whims of a particular audience, or even of a particular receiver, there can be no system of argumentative analysis, no means of generalizing about or evaluating arguments. In short, there can be no study of the process of argumentation, only the study of specific arguments.

A field approach, first enunciated by Toulmin (1958) and since adopted by many others, seems to provide a systematic basis for understanding and evaluating argument. Such an approach contends that each field has its own individual standards. The standards for evaluating and analyzing arguments are different for theology than for physics and for law than for literary criticism. While some fields, such as much of contemporary philosophy, are very close to the formal logical model, others, such as artistic argument, are far from it. The critical point, though, is that within each field there is a standard of evidence and argument to which the participants generally adhere and by which they are generally bound according to the dictates of that particular community. Each field is (in Kuhn's term) a "disciplinary matrix" with three central "constituents": "symbolic generalizations, models, and exemplars" (1974, 463). Thus each field has standards that will permit the systematic study of its own argumentation. Those standards are not fixed in some natural immutable law but are determined by the traditions and conventions of persons who participate in that argumentation and who willingly accept the standards of that field.

But what of the argumentation engaged in by a general audience on a host of personal and social issues, that communication which has been labeled "general argumentation" (Rieke and Sillars, 1975, 74) or "ordinary fields" argumentation (Willard, 1980, 351) or "social argumentation" (McKerrow, 1980, 215–217)?

When presidential candidate Ronald Reagan told the Republican National Convention and the television-viewing audience that America needed a 30 percent tax cut phased in over a three-year period to stimulate growth and decrease inflation and unemployment, he made an economic argument but he was only incidentally bound by the disciplinary matrix of the economists. The argument had to gain the adherence of people who know little and care little of the rules by which the economists play. In the same vein, the cleric must know theology but his or her congregation will respond to the sermon based upon a general standard of argumentation that is only marginally bound by the theologians' rules.

McKerrow contends that there is also a "personal argumentation" similar to that found in the social community but addressed to the individual, who is free "to ignore all standards other than the one agreed upon with a participant in an exchange of views." McKerrow claims that "there is no 'community' present" in personal argumentation (1980, 222). Although we disagree with his position because "personal argumentation" is influenced by the social values the participants hold, that issue need not be pursued here because our concern is with the public expression of general argumentation. Nor are we interested in "the essentially private, personalized ways of building units-of-inference." We wish to speak of "the essentially public, tradition-governed process of bringing forward proofs" (Gronbeck, 1980, 12).

What, then, are the standards for evaluating public argumentation? Where does one begin in an attempt to learn about the adherence individuals and groups give to those arguing factual or value claims or advocating changes in social policies? It is our contention that social values are the best starting point for evaluating public argumentation.

Such a claim is not new (see for instance Steele, 1958; Wallace, 1963;

Perelman and Olbrechts-Tyteca, 1969; Sillars, 1973; Wenzel, 1977; Eubanks, 1978; Fisher, 1978). But what are the implications of such a claim? The purpose of this paper is to examine social values as they function in public argumentation, to describe that functioning, and to determine how a clearer understanding might be applied to traditional problems of argumentation.

A social-value perspective on public argumentation could be adaptable to any relativistic perspective on the process of communication except a psychological one. The symbolic interactionist, constructivist, or ethnomethodologist should find values crucial. Only what Gronbeck calls "the age-old death trap of psychologism" (1980, 13), which depends for its effectiveness on the ability to get inside the mind of the participant, would not provide a basis for applying value analysis as we will develop it here. Social values may therefore be *the* way of providing a unified communication approach to argumentation. It is surely *a* promising one.

The Nature of Social Values

The smallest unit in a social-value system is a belief. According to Milton Rokeach, a belief is "any simple proposition, conscious or unconscious, inferred from what a person says or does, capable of being preceded by the phrase, 'I believe that. . . .' The content of a belief may describe the object of belief as true or false, correct or incorrect; evaluate it as good or bad; or advocate a certain course of action or a certain state of existence as desirable or undesirable" (1970, 113). For Rokeach a value is "a type of belief, centrally located within one's total belief system, about how one ought or ought not to behave, or about some end state of existence worth or not worth attaining" (1970, 124).

The third term in Rokeach's trilogy is attitude, a "relatively enduring organization of beliefs around an object or situation predisposing one to respond in some preferential manner" (1970, 112). However, we will not include attitude in our approach but will regard it simply as a combination of beliefs. This is not to deny the usefulness to value analysis of the attitude research that has been done because much of it can be extrapolated to values. Rokeach (1973, 18–19) has identified reasons a psychologist ought to be more interested in values than in attitudes. Our primary reason for concentration on beliefs and values is that we are interested in public argumentation and not the psychological processes of individuals where attitude research is centered. Beliefs and values can be found in actual messages or inferred directly from them; therefore those concepts are more useful to us. They can be expressed as propositions and they do not require that one get into the mind of the arguer to understand the structure of the argumentation.

Beliefs and values as used here thus constitute what McGee calls "ideographs." Says McGee, "The important fact about ideographs is that they exist in real discourse, functioning clearly and evidently as agents of political consciousness. They are not invented by observers; they come to be as a part of the real lives of the people whose motives they articulate. So, for example, 'rule of law' is a more precise, objective motive than such observer-invented terms as 'neurotic' or 'paranoid style' or 'petit bourgeois'" (1980a, 7).

"An adult," says Rokeach, "probably has tens or hundreds of thousands of beliefs, thousands of attitudes, but only dozens of values" (1970, 124). This limitation in the numbers of values makes them particularly attractive in the analysis of public argumentation because they are manageable. Our research indicates that a similar manageable situation exists with beliefs. While an individual has large numbers of beliefs from which to draw, these too are limited in a specific argumentation situation. A content analysis of a large selected sample of the 1896 presidential campaign addresses of William Jennings Bryan reveals that Bryan used not many more beliefs than he did values (thirty-three values, forty-one beliefs). When such a limitation can be observed in an extended campaign, it is reasonable to contend that in smaller argumentative situations, such as a single speech or debate, the same condition would hold.

In this paper we will be looking at beliefs and values as complementary factors in an argumentative situation. Values are *potentially* more salient because they back belief warrants. They are also easier to generalize about but, as we will note later, potentiality is not always actuality.

Values are generally more important to argumentative analysis than beliefs because they are better indicators of the shared convictions of a community. They "exist," as Wenzel notes, "in an intersubjective realm of agreements that are the fabric of a community; they exist in the actions and discourse of persons constructing, sustaining, testing and revising the rules by which they will live and act together" (1977, 153). Values are shared by the individual and the society (Rokeach, 1973, 20). They are society's way of shaping the individual and in turn are the individual's access to the society. For example, as individual parents decline to pass on to their children the Puritan value of working hard, that value is weakened and, as it is weakened, it will tend to be less reinforced by general societal values.

Values do not operate independently but rather in systems. A given value may be more important than others but the others are usually vital to the system. In any given situation the number of values that must be considered is limited. Rokeach found thirty-six (eighteen instrumental and eighteen terminal) in the American value system. One would be hard pressed, though, to find an argumentative situation that depended for its power on more than four or five values and seldom would one find a situation dependent on only one value (1973, 16). The term "value system" is better here than "value hierarchy" because placing one value over another in a hierarchy can lead to rigid linear thinking. Granted, certain individuals at certain times may prioritize in that manner but hierarchies do not appear to typify societal thinking in general.

Commonly, in public argumentation even the most critical value is adapted to the context in which it is used. In 1976, following the Nixon experience, the Carter presidential campaign could be successful with a stress on values of trustworthiness and honesty. In 1980, with Watergate memories fading and domestic economic and world conditions changing, national security and economic security seemed more important and trustworthiness less so. Carter's attempts to make trustworthiness again the issue failed. There was a national shift in values that represented not a new hierarchy but an adjustment in the value system. It was not that trustworthiness was unimportant but that its importance had been adjusted by the intensification of other values that had been less important in 1976. Such adjustments are continually taking place although the component values of the system are not fundamentally altered.

An examination of argumentation on the basis of beliefs and values should not be confused with the traditional division of claims into those of fact, value, and policy. Both values and beliefs as we use the terms are found in each of the traditional claims. Claims of fact are accepted or rejected because we believe a particular authority or because we value wisdom. Policy claims will also involve value systems. A proposal to adopt environmental restrictions on industrial development will call upon differing values, such as health or beauty versus progress. It may be that, at some future point in research, new terminology for types of claims would be useful. One might find new names for claims such as perception, ethical/aesthetic judgment, and acceptable action more clearly indicative of the roles values play in making all types of claims acceptable, but for now it is essential only that we not become confused by the use of the word "value" in two quite different senses.

Social Values in Argumentation

In recognizing the role values play in argumentation we must first understand that argumentation, necessarily, functions in a conflict situation. Social conflict, however, need not be defined (as by Coser) as "a struggle over values or claims to status, power, and scarce resources, in which the aims of the conflicting parties are not only to gain the desired values but also to neutralize, injure, or eliminate their rivals" (Jandt, 1973, vii). Conflict and cooperation are not dichotomous occurrences but rather, as Ehninger and Brockriede see them, different approaches that can and do dovetail with one another (1978, 13–15). Conflict occurs in argumentation when differences arise over beliefs and values but cooperative means of resolving those conflicts are essential to argumentation.

Such cooperation means that the parties to the process of argumentation acknowledge that some common ground exists. We would extend that to say that social values are the basis of that common ground and the greater the acknowledged common ground of values the greater the potential for conflict resolution. Certainly the potential for argumentation is greater between Jimmy Carter and Ronald Reagan than it is between either Carter or Reagan and the Ayatollah Khomeini because the former share many values they do not share with Khomeini.

Moreover, the basic willingness to consider differing values is essential in the argumentative process. As Perelman notes, "In a discussion, it is not possible to escape from a value simply by denying it. Just as someone who contests that something is a fact must give reasons for his allegation . . . so, when a value is in question, a person may disqualify it, subordinate it to others, or interpret it but may not reject all values as a whole: this would amount to leaving the realm of discussion to enter that of force" (1969, 75). For argumentation to occur, the common ground of the participants must include a willingness to recognize and consider the roles that values play in the process.

In the conflict situation, then, argumentation functions in the context of multiple points of view and its most dramatic and critical points are where the issues are joined. Much of its technical language (issue, presumption, burden of proof) reflects an attempt to identify the specific responsibilities of the participants to the resolution of conflict. By indicating more specifically how values are involved in the existence of conflict situations, it may be possible to begin to understand how values are involved in the resolution of those situations.

Let us begin by acknowledging that each conflict situation to which the argumentation process may be applied has its own context of time, persons, and issues. This context modifies the meaning and role of values. "Value statements are," in Wenzel's terms, "used to express different things in different contexts." While less impressed than Wenzel with the need to understand the speaker's intention, we agree that "we can discover their 'meaning' only by exploring each context . . . and that such a determination of meaning is necessary to enable us to identify the relevant grounds for arguing about the statement" (1977, 155). Thus a single, constant hierarchy of values that defines a society cannot be developed. Rokeach has shown that while the hierarchy has considerable stability across society it also reveals differences based upon such factors as sex, race, age, and income (1973, 55–81). More important for our purposes are studies such as one Rokeach did following the assassination of Martin Luther King, Jr., which show that circumstances cause adaptations in the value hierarchy (1973, 97–98).

Further informal information illustrates the same condition. When Rokeach's hierarchies were developed in the late 1960s, during the heated controversy over the Vietnam war, he put "a world at peace" at the top of the terminal value hierarchy. In the past four years of using the Rokeach list on a variety of college groups, it has never been higher than tenth. Surely this could not be caused merely by the less vigorous procedures being utilized. Rather, it points most directly to the fact that contexts change the relative importance of values by the demography of the audience and by the issue. We will reveal no mystical powers to anyone if we observe that a "world at peace" would undoubtedly lead the list again should America find itself in another war. Thus, although the American value system changes very slowly, time, audience, and issue bring about temporary adaptations in it. The differences appear to be of degree rather than kind because values that lose saliency because of a change of issue do not go away. They simply become less significant at the time.

Thus argumentation is rooted in conflict, conflict that is basically linked to values. The argumentative resolution of such conflict can only be brought about if the arguer sees the relation of the argument to the context in which it is found. If that recognition is absent the arguer will futilely attempt to resolve conflict because he or she will then focus on the less utilitarian values for that situation. In argumentation, therefore, values are strategically significant. Both the choice of which values to use in support of one's position and the choice of which opposing values need to be attended to become critical options for the arguer.

Since all evidence points to the fact that people do not easily or readily change their values, the arguer would seem to be faced with an impossible task. How does one argue about values when it is rare to see people acquire new values or abandon old ones? Were those the only strategies available, the chore would be difficult—but they are not the only choices. Rescher has observed that disputants have five possible options for resolving disagreements: (1) "value acquisition and abandonment"; (2) "value-redistribution" (when a value becomes more or less widely distributed within the society); (3) "value-rescaling" (changing the relative importance of one value to another); (4) "value-reemployment" (changing the range of application for a value); (5) "value-restandardization" (raising or lowering what one expects a particular value to mean when converted to specific beliefs) (1973, 14–16). Realizing how slowly values change, one can recognize that only the most traumatic changes in the environment will cause a person, and even more so a group, to abandon old values and acquire new ones. But successful argument is not limited to value acquisition and abandonment and, indeed, will usually not emphasize those objectives. Because values appear in systems which are adapted to the subject matter and context of the argumentation as well as to both the society and the individual, they will most often be adapted through "redistribution," "rescaling," "redeployment," and "restandardization."

It is probable that where the options are limited to acquisition and abandonment, argumentation is less fruitful because of the difficulties attendant upon the alteration of fixed values. In the contemporary controversy over legalized abortion its opponents have strategically seized the fundamental value of "life"; witness their identification as "Right to Life." The proponents of legalized abortion have utilized a series of arguments based on freedom, economic security, happiness, health, and the like. The value of "life" has considerable force in our society; a movement to compromise is nearly impossible because it would constitute an unacceptable solution to abortion opponents.

One can contrast that with some of the argumentation over the propriety of the death penalty. It is not unusual to find individuals arguing that *life* imprisonment is worse than the *death* penalty. In that instance, the opponent of the death penalty is not asking others to acquire or abandon a value but rather to redeploy the nature of that value. Such a conflict situation would thus appear to be somewhat easier to resolve.

We might observe here that two of Rescher's five options (redeployment and restandardization) refer rather specifically to the relation of value to belief. In short, we do not change the value but adjust the way it will be applied in a particular case. Thus arguments can gain adherence by adapting the interpretation of the value to a specific belief that at the same time reinforces the value by increasing its application. The root paradox of Christianity employs redeployment: you cannot gain your life unless you first lose it. The range of application of the value "life" is thus expanded to mean eternal life.

Value rescaling is also rather directly related to belief because here one sees an argument that does not rely on acquisition, abandonment, or redistribution of values. Rather it says "The value is important, but so are others that you need to consider." To return to the legalized-abortion argument. Its supporters do not deny the importance of life but they claim that life should have a quality which involves other values such as family, love, and economic security. A specific law or interpretation (a belief) is seen as a product of several values, thus rescaling the force of an opponent's value.

It would not be farfetched to argue that beliefs and values function similarly in their modification procedures. One could conclude that belief abandonment, for instance, is more difficult than belief restandardization. Similarity, though, does not mean equality. While they may operate in a similar functional sense, there are strategic differences in the utilization of values and beliefs. A key problem is to determine which is more important to a given argumentative situation. In some cases values are, in others beliefs. Granted, values may be more central to the belief system of an individual because they support a host of beliefs. But, in a specific argumentative situation, beliefs can be more important than values.

One example should illustrate a not-uncommon situation. In the second debate in 1976, Gerald Ford stated his belief that Eastern Europeans are free. Freedom is a value acknowledged by all Americans, but one group in particular, Americans of Eastern Europe heritage, held the belief that such freedom was nonexistent in that geographic area. The furor in that community over the Ford remark reflects the central position of that belief. The recipients of the communication were far less concerned with the values Ford had been discussing than they were with disagreements with him on a belief level.

On the other hand, basing arguments on values rather than specific beliefs can be used to unify diverse groups. McGee notes that the key terms of the Puritan revolution in England, "Religion, Liberty and Property . . . functioned to keep diverse interest groups all working for a common goal: Puritan revolution. Those who used the ideographs did not share meanings or intentions. Precisely by keeping 'propositional' content *out* of the terms, they could perform their rhetorical, 'argumentative' function" (McGee, 1980, 77). For "ideograph" read "value" and for "propositional content" read "belief" and you have a fair rendering of our point here.

Thus, whether one chooses to argue from value or belief will relate directly to the audience, the nature of the conflict, and the potential for refutation. There is no natural superiority of value over belief.

How can the arguer recognize which value or belief will gain the greatest adherence in a given situation? Rokeach argues that people arrange their beliefs on a central-peripheral dimension. The more central the belief, he contends, the more resistant it is to change but, if changed, the more widespread the repercussions (1970, 3). His contention is that our most central beliefs are terminal values (1973, 215). While that may be true in examining a person's belief system for its general structure, it is not the case when applied to a particular argumentation situation. Certain beliefs may be more important than are values. Thus, in the example cited earlier, the belief that Poland is not free is more important to Polish-Americans than is their commitment to the value of freedom, even though the commitment to freedom is inherent in the belief about Poland's freedom.

Figure 8.1 better illustrates the relationship among beliefs, attitudes, and values in a single argumentative situation. In this diagram the existence of a larger number of beliefs than attitudes, attitudes than values and the relationship among them are represented by the grouping. The fact that in a given situation one belief or value may be stronger than another is also represented by the placement.

In this diagram, B_1 of A_1 of V_1 is more central than V_2. Consequently,

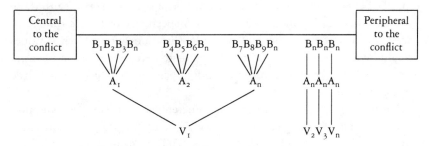

FIG. 8.1.   Beliefs, attitudes, and values in an argument.

an argument that is dependent on B_1 is likely to be more critical to the decision-making process than is an argument dependent on V_2. Moreover, it may also be more central than A_1 or V_1 if the audience for the argumentation finds it to have significant force.

Indeed, in many argumentative situations our values are dependent on the specific beliefs associated with it. Some believe in freedom for people dominated by the Soviet Union, people who work hard, people who collect guns; but not for homosexuals, children, or welfare recipients. When the belief associated in the argument with the value shifts, the strength of the value may also shift. When one argues for the legalization of marijuana, arguments about cost (of enforcement) and health ("It isn't harmful") may be much more important than the value of freedom.

There is nothing about belief and value systems which suggests that a belief because it is one of many which may be linked to a single value is necessarily less significant than that value. Both values and beliefs operate similarly as premises for arguments. Their relative significance is strategic rather than functional.

Experimental testing of this concept ought to be possible and might lead to some very interesting conclusions. For example, we might find that, in religion, greater adherence to values over beliefs is a sign of weak religious commitment. An individual who professes a strong belief in an individual church or in a specific doctrinal stance may have a deeper religious commitment than does the individual who relies on values such as spirituality or salvation. By the same token, the individual who believes in always voting a straight party ticket may have a stronger and deeper commitment to the party than does the individual who professes an allegiance to the values traditionally articulated by that party. In both instances, specific beliefs are more central to the individual than are the more generalized values.

If that is the case, then note the possibility. A speaker seeking adherence from a specific audience that has a specific point of view predicated upon specific beliefs will be more effective when he or she can identify with those audience beliefs. To the extent that such specificity of beliefs cannot be determined or found, more general identification with audience values would be most effective. The speaker needs to determine the most central factor for the greatest number of individuals upon which to base the argumentation.

Because contemporary America is so heterogeneous, speakers who present arguments to a large constituency of receivers are probably more effective in dealing with values that are less likely to cause friction than are specific belief statements. A labor leader, addressing involved union members, can argue more effectively for a twenty-billion-dollar jobs program, given that constituency, than can the president of the United States, whose constituency is broader. The president is more likely to turn to the values of work and economic security—which are less controversial. As noted earlier, when one relies on specific belief statements, the potential for both controversy and negative responses increases.

Where specific belief statements are more effective than values they remain so only if those remarks are confined to the specific audience addressed and are not communicated to another audience that does not share those same beliefs and for whom the disadvantages may outweigh the advantages. In a society of mass and virtually instantaneous communication, the problems are clearly exacerbated.

It is impossible with a diagram such as the one we have used to illustrate the fact that most of the public argumentation does not operate by single beliefs or values. One value or belief may be more salient than another but it is part of a system and, thus, other values and beliefs will influence how it is interpreted and how beliefs are modified.

Thus the person who wishes to analyze argument will need to be concerned with the values and beliefs used in a particular situation, how they link up with audiences, and how they provide a basis for belief modification. Were we to stop there, however, we would have some general observations about the role of value systems in argumentation but not recognize how they permeate every aspect of argumentation. Therefore let us examine some of the more traditional concepts of argumentation such as reason, evidence, ethos, language, and presumption to see the role value systems play.

Application

Reasoning is "the central activity of presenting the reasons in support of a claim, so as to show how those reasons succeed in giving strength to a claim" (Toulmin, Rieke and Janik, 13). The most mundane policy claim—instructors should post test grades, for example—requires that one argue values (fairness, knowledge, and the like) or argue beliefs that are linked to values (students have a right to know). In short, any argument involves reasoning and any reasoning can be driven back to a value orientation. That value orientation will most frequently and importantly serve as warrants for claims or when the warrant is a belief, values will back it. In such a role values constitute a concept that should have replaced terms such as emotion, drives, motives, and motivations long ago. Values represent the real link between the argument and the audience. They are social and public. All of the traditional concepts mentioned above attempt to describe inner states which cannot be judged.

Values are also more compatible with research in argumentation because they contribute to a holistic view of argumentation as a public social act that can be observed in the language. They may even provide a basis for differentiating an argumentative analysis of a communication situation from a persuasive analysis. Of necessity, argumentation is concerned with a unified process (Sillars and Zarefsky, 84–85) while persuasive analysis with its attitude-theory orientation has typically isolated individual aspects (credibility, fear appeals, evidence, and so on) in the sense that McBurney (1936) years ago argued that the enthymeme for Aristotle was the key to rhetoric and the enthymeme is a combination of proofs. The *Rhetoric* has an argumentation perspective though it is viewed as a handbook on persuasion. The form of the argument may change. One may choose to argue deductively or inductively, but always there will be a link to beliefs and values that can be found in the language of the argument and understood as a part of the social system of the receiver. Such an approach makes far greater sense of a phrase like "reasoned discourse" than does the explanation that argumentation is merely a modified version of logic. Indeed, the preliminary results of some research being undertaken by Rieke indicates that most of the reasons generated by people in an unplanned situation could best be characterized as arguments that merely state values. "To convert them to anything approximating traditional argument forms is an act not of description but of creativity," says Rieke.

As a part of the reason-giving which is argument, evidence also depends on values. Different individuals will accept different standards of evidence. Acceptance or rejection is dependent on the values placed on different types of evidence or the level of evidence demanded. One may, for example, insist on statistical evidence, citations from an authority with a Ph.D. in economics, or even examples from common experience to prove that a recession has been headed off. This insistence is a belief one holds and behind the belief is a value judgment. Acceptance of evidence from credible authority is based, for example, on value judgments about trustworthiness and competence. Thus the type, nature, and level of evidence are based on value judgments.

Even style has its argumentative dimension and is thus dependent on the

assessment of values. Perelman claims that one of the effects rhetorical "figures have in the presentation of data is to impose or suggest a choice . . . or
to bring about communion with the audience" (1968, 172). As noted
above, matters of both choice and audience linkage are inherently concerned with values. In that sense, when style functions argumentatively, as
it generally albeit sometimes inconspicuously does, consideration of values
is essential for the critic of that style.

A specific example may be helpful. Metaphor is, after all, a reflection of
the argument form of analogy. The acceptance of such an argument form
involves a value choice by receivers. To the extent that they reject that
argumentative form, they will reject the argumentative device of metaphor.
It will be approved of where audiences see it as reinforcing beliefs that
reflect the values held by that audience and will be rejected as "high-flown"
or "fanciful" when it is not. One person's cogent metaphor is another's
nonsense not because of the natural rationality (or lack of it) in metaphor
but because of the value system it supports.

Cox, using Perelman's and Olbrechts-Tyteca's rationale, has shown how
the argumentative concept of loci relates to the place of values in argument.
Though he does not make the point directly, Cox does present an argument
for the concept of value systems because he shows how values are refined by
loci, which in turn involves a value judgment in the selection of "*loci communes.*" Thus values interact with one another through the selection of loci
that provide a justification for an arguer's move from a value to a more
specific belief (1980b).

Fisher has provided five questions for adapting a "logic of reasons into a
logic of *good reasons* [values]: 'fact,' 'relevance,' 'consequence,' 'consistency,'
and 'transcendent issue'" (1978, 379–380). These are a useful starting
point for a more systematic means of understanding and judging such specific argument forms as sign, cause, and analogy.

The traditional argumentative concept that appears most clearly to involve values is presumption. It is clear that values determine presumption.
Handy observes a general view in the literature that "the value system of a
culture tends to maintain itself and to change much less rapidly than many
other aspects of the culture, such as its mode of economic organization"
(1969, 48–49). The combination of their relative stability and their central
role as warrants for arguments makes a society's values the only reasonable
source for understanding its presumptions.

Arbitrary views such as the designation of presumption to the status quo
make no sense when we realize that the status quo is not so stable in ad-

herence as are values. Assignment of presumption to the status quo is only possible in specific policy claims such as "The Congress should pass the Kemp–Roth bill." In all claims of fact and value and many general policy claims, such as "America should develop a better tax policy," the status quo is inoperative because the status quo is virtually impossible to identify. Thus presumption in general argumentation is not assigned; it is, like all the "available means of persuasion," found.

True, value-based presumption is more difficult to find than is an assigned presumption. But today, for instance, it is not too difficult to realize that in middle- and upper-class American society there is a presumption for the affirmative of the proposition "Overall government spending should be reduced." We know what values are strongest in the system, at least, as such an argument would begin. The arguer who has attained the ability to judge the salience of social values should have a fairly stable understanding of presumption, given the relatively enduring nature of social values.

Furthermore, enduring social values are not passive; they also influence the values of the individual. Handy notes that "the values held by a person are strongly influenced by the values he judges other people to hold" (1969, 49). Hence, an individual's choice of values to serve as warrants for claims reflects in part a societal influence. Consequently, by understanding how values operate presumptively for a society, one also has an idea of how they operate presumptively for the individual.

Whately's explanation of presumption did not use the language we have, but he clearly implied a value orientation when he wrote that "a presumption in favor of any supposition means, not (as has been sometimes erroneously imagined) a preponderance of probability in its favor, but such a preoccupation of the ground, which implies that it must stand good till some sufficient reason is adduced against it" (1963, 112). Values and beliefs constitute such "preoccupation of the ground" and the determination of "sufficient reason."

Matlon discusses the problem of applying presumption to propositions of value in the special argumentation of intercollegiate debate. However, much of what he says can be extrapolated to general argumentation and, we would argue, could be applied to presumption in all propositional forms (1978).

In argumentation, then, values form warrants for arguments, support beliefs that warrant arguments, and underlie choices that have to be made about a host of argumentation decisions such as evidence, style, reason, and presumption.

Values, whether extrinsic or intrinsic, are the most pervasive factor in the argumentative situation. They serve as underpinnings to all components of the process of general argumentation. The pervasiveness of values alone, though, does not provide it with a basis for systematic study. While the former logical perspective was too narrow and all too often misleading, it did have the advantage of clear systematization.

We hope that we have shown that argumentation, released from the confines of a logical model, need not be idiosyncratic. We would contend that value systems provide systematic grounds for argumentative analysis because they are limited in actual application and because they have both social and personal contexts. Values are individual determinations but they are also cultural reflections. One can find general linkages between arguer and audience through shared beliefs and values and need not be concerned with personal idiosyncracies.

Such significant interrelations of values into the process of argumentation clearly indicate that there is a manageable procedure whereby the process of argumentation may be analyzed. This analysis, we believe, will be based on a very traditional principle of argumentation. For us, the unifying principle is consistency.

In addition to its longstanding role in traditional argumentation (the worst thing one can do is to be perceived as inconsistent) consistency has played a major role in persuasion research. It is the core concept of balance theorists who expound a wide variety of individual theories using such terms in addition to consistency as congruity or, in a negative form, cognitive dissonance (Simons, 1976, 119–128). Consequently, there is a very healthy theoretical basis for consistency as the linchpin of a value-based theory of argumentation.

By moving our research efforts in the direction of value consistency argumentation researchers may be able to provide a basis for reviving the now moribund field of persuasion research. It may be taking more license with Miller and Burgoon's statements on the potential for persuasion research than is warranted to link their statement to our proposal. However, their view seems to fit so nicely we cannot avoid the temptation.

> We have argued that one's assessment of the current intellectual and scientific vigor of persuasion research depends upon the meaning he or she assigns to the term "persuasion research." If that meaning is restricted to the paradigms, practices, and outcomes that have traditionally been investigated by persuasion researchers, then there is probably serious cause for concern about the continued vitality of the area. . . . The problem lies not with the quality of

individual studies, but rather with the impoverished conceptual foundation imposed by the traditional view of persuasion. Because of this conceptual inadequacy, persuasion researchers have been overly restrictive in defining issues and problems, with the result being that much of the important research action has been carried out by investigators ostensibly (though not necessarily actually) concerned with other problem areas [1978, 44–45].

Holistic argumentation research, oriented to the role of values in a consistency-based system, has at least great potential to revive social control research.

Conclusion

In this chapter we have attempted to suggest an approach to argumentation that will give us a systematic basis for viewing it as a communication phenomenon. We realize that we have not answered very many specific questions, but that was not our intent. We believe our approach is a most useful one not only because it provides a unified explanation for argumentation but also because it opens up many avenues for new research which in the logical model seemed closed forever. In recent years we have heard the frequent lament about the lack of research in argumentation. That was caused not by a lack of competent researchers but by the fact that we were shackled to a closed model. To the extent that value analysis allows us more freedom to explore the factors that actually affect the argumentative process we have more opportunity to examine and reflect upon the nature of argumentation in society.

Many of the above suggestions, though, are simply concepts potentially worth considering. Research on beliefs and values can lend itself to more careful investigation than has been the case in the past. As Handy observed, "I see no reason why value phenomena cannot be inquired into using the general methods of scientific inquiry, and in that sense, value processes are natural" (1969, 17). Values certainly lend themselves to theoretical conclusions and assessments, but there is no reason they cannot lend themselves to empirical investigations as well. To the extent this is done, a more in-depth understanding of the roles of values in argumentation may be set forth. Among the areas that might be explored are those concerned with the conditions under which values are explicitly recognized and utilized, the nature of the positioning of values within a system, the relative impact of belief and value statements on argumentation both in comparison to one another and to other argumentative factors, the specific impact of values on different types of argumentative propositions or upon specific groupings, and the feasibility of various strategic choices.

Values and beliefs are key to understanding the process of argumentation; they are premises upon which arguments themselves are built. To ignore the centrality of the role of values and beliefs is to consider the role of argumentation in human discourse only partially.

PART THREE

Methodological Issues

SCOTT JACOBS and SALLY JACKSON

[9] Conversational Argument: A Discourse Analytic Approach

BETTY: Prove it.
BOB: I don't have to prove anything.
BETTY: Who says?
BOB: I do.
BETTY: Who made you the big sheriff around here?
BOB: Look, I'm the producer of this show.
BETTY: Then let's hear you produce something.
[Husband and wife co-hosts to a radio news/talk program disagreeing over the wife's answer to one of the daily quiz questions.]

[While driving home on an interstate highway the driver, Sally, signals to exit ten miles short of the customary coffee stop.]
SCOTT: Are you getting off at Altamont?
SALLY: Yeah. Getting off here you can get coffee quicker at Stuckey's. [Pause] Does that not meet with your approval?
SCOTT: No, that's cool.

A cursory inspection of the contents of ordinary conversation will quickly reveal the pervasiveness of argument. Wherever there is the potential for people to engage in conversation, there is the potential for people to imply, to make, and to have arguments (O'Keefe, 1977). Though mundane and unremarkable, arguments such as those above are essential to the fabric of everyday life.[1] Their possibility and use provide a basic condition of all

[1] The argument between Bob and Betty is a pretty clear case of having an argument. In the second example, Sally makes an argument, or at least "implies" an argument (in the sense of indirectly making an argument), so as to head off the upcoming challenge projected in Scott's question. All examples in this essay, unless otherwise indicated, come from naturally occurring conversation transcribed from audiotape recordings or from immediate memory. The following students helped supply transcripts from audiotape recordings: Arlie Daniel,

conversational exchanges as we know them. Argument regulates in important ways the shape and occurrence of other conversational events. It can be
used to obtain and avoid agreement, acceptance, or affiliation for a wide
range of conversational acts. Having an argument is something people may
anticipate and something they can work to avoid or threaten to provoke
(often by implying or making an argument). The presence of argument
signals potential or actual troubles in conversation while its absence indicates the presence of a "working agreement" in conversation (Goffman,
1959, 9–10). Thus argument, whether manifest as an event or latent as an
unexercised possibility, leaves its mark on whatever goes on in conversation.

In an ongoing study of everyday argument and interpersonal influence
processes we have been studying how conversation organizes, and is organized by, argument and what kind of knowledge individuals must possess
for conversational argument to exhibit the forms and functions we have
observed (Jackson and Jacobs, 1980, ms.; Jacobs and Jackson, 1980,
1981). We have found the concepts and techniques of discourse analysis
particularly fruitful tools for addressing these issues. This chapter elaborates the discourse analytic approach we have developed in our studies. The
first section discusses conceptual and methodological commitments informing our approach. The second section presents an empirically grounded
model of the organization of argument in conversation.

General Orientation to Conversational Argument

Our approach is grounded in a general framework for understanding the
relation of discourse to communication. Ours is more than a rhetorical
interest: we also want to know how argument is understood, how it is
communicated. From our point of view, rhetorical discourse is a subclass of
communicative discourse. Rhetoric occurs only in and through the communication process. So we have tried to relate our theory of the organization of
argument to considerations of how arguments are recognized and expressed
and how arguments enter into the coherent construction of broader conversational episodes. We have tried to relate the ways arguments regulate conversation to the ways the production of arguments communicates speaker
intentions and beliefs.

Joel Heim, Lori Merryman, and Elisa Spearman. Transcribing symbols have been kept as
simple as possible. Emphasis is indicated by underlining; "stretched" syllables by one or
more colons; short pauses by [-] and longer pauses by [pause]; interruptions by double slash
marks, //; run-on utterances by "-"; cut-offs by hyphens; and deleted material by ellipsis.

Our work reflects a general shift of attention among communication scholars to face-to-face settings and a concern for the naturalistic validity of theories. We believe that examining conversational formats for argument reveals a variety of features that are either obscured or absent in the mono-logic formats of public address and written texts or in the settings of forensic, legal, and philosophical debate.

Metatheoretic Assumptions

A variety of philosophical rationales for discourse analysis have been offered (see Donohue, Cushman and Nofsinger, 1980; Frentz and Farrell, 1976; Hawes, 1977; Sanders, 1973; Shimanoff, 1980). Our own general stand-point toward conversation and argument is most closely affiliated with the pragmatism of Mead (1932, 1934, 1938) and with developments in language-action philosophy following Austin (1975) and the later Wittgenstein (1953, 1958). We also see a general affinity between our approach and the emerging functional materialist paradigm in cognitive science (see Fodor, 1981; Harrison, 1972). While these approaches do not represent a unified philosophical position, all stress a functional approach to meaning. The rationale for our selection of specific theoretic concepts and empirical methods can be stated in terms of three metatheoretical assumptions drawn from this work.

1. Argument is a Type of Language Game

We view conversation as a collection of language games, argument being one variety (Wittgenstein, 1958, 81; 1953, &1–&11). Argument can be seen as an activity of language that is played according to an abstract system of rules which define that activity *as* argument. Argument is a language game played within other language games—negotiating the outcome of a request, issuing and receiving complaints, attacking and defending assertions. It has a subordinate function within these broader language games: it works to regulate the appearance of agreement and disagreement and thereby to coordinate individual contributions to these broader language games. One cannot imply, make, or have an argument outside these other games.

The concept of a language game highlights several aspects of conversational argument we find essential (see Weiner and Goodenough, 1977).

First, it highlights the fact that argument is a social activity definable by rules and accountable to those rules. Argument, like any game, is a public institution with public structures and public functions. Second, the concept of a game points to the fact that argument occurs by virtue of the methodical practices of the players. Natural language users have a tacit knowledge of the rules of the game and they are able to play the game by applying that knowledge. Any explanation of the ability of an individual to play a game must make reference to such competence. Third, the concept of a game suggests a useful analytic unit, the move. Making an argument can be seen as a particular move within the overall play of a language game. Fourth, the concept of a game highlights the collaborative character of argument. Games involve moves and countermoves unfolding in real time where the move of one player constrains the range of possible moves—and their effectiveness—that may be made by another player. Thus the notion of a game highlights the importance of strategy and tactics.

It should be noted that the term "game" can be used in two different ways. On the one hand, it can refer to a concrete activity, as in "George and Martha are playing a game of chess." On the other hand, it can refer to the abstract system of rules, as in "The game of poker has several variations." A parallel split can be found in the use of the term "move." Moves can be thought of as concrete events unfolding in the real-time play of a game or they can be thought of as the abstract possibilities generated by a system of rules. Our analysis trades on this ambiguity: our interest is in explaining properties and patterns of the arguments people imply, make, and have (concrete events) by deriving these features from the rules of argument (the abstract system).

We want to know how argument is played; that is our fundamental problematic. As with any game, there is a perfectly satisfying type of explanation that comes from a description of the components and rules that define the game. It is the sort of explanation that can be found in, say, a handbook on chess. We believe that any adequate theory of argument must include a similar type of account (which is not, of course, to rule out other sorts of question, such as consideration of underlying psychological processes).

A completed theory of conversational argument would lay out the elements of the game, the primary rules operating on those elements, and the overall point of the game. This system defines a range of possible moves and countermoves and entails the design features (the organizational properties) of any move. These design features provide a sense of position during play and allow players to assess the strengths, weaknesses, pitfalls, and opportunities inherent in any projected move or series of moves.

Of course, the design features of any move are open to exploitation by any participant and are not necessarily exhausted in the intent of the mover. Moves are public objects and the availability of their design features is limited only by the competence of the players. So, for example, we have found that some arguments that justify George requesting Martha to do some action may also justify Martha requesting George to do that action.[2] Or, again, we suspect that refusing a request on the grounds that one is unable to perform the action implies the respondent's willingness *in principle* to help. So, he or she may be restricted from using willingness as the basis for refusing a follow-up request that the respondent *is* able to satisfy (see Labov and Fanshel, 1977, 88).

Beyond the primary system of rules and elements, an adequate theory of conversational argument would lay out conventional patterns and strategies. The parallel is to the set of openings and defenses laid out in a chess handbook and to such strategies as "Maintain control of the center" or "Don't lose pieces without capturing pieces of equal value." Such things may not be *intrinsic* to the game—a person may be able to argue at a rudimentary level without such knowledge, just as a novice may play chess with basic knowledge of the overall point of the game and how the pieces move. However, these are commonly known aspects of the game and are features of the knowledge that a competent player would be expected to possess.

So, for example, natural language users are familiar with the conventional patterns of prepositioning supporting arguments prior to making a request (Jackson and Jacobs, 1980, 258–259; Jacobs and Jackson, 1980, 20–24) or the conventional pattern of using objections to a request as a device for inviting modification of that request toward a more acceptable proposal (Jackson and Jacobs, ms.). Likewise they are familiar with general maxims and strategies like "Be polite" or "Assess the need for a requested action against the cost to the hearer of performing the action" (Lakoff, 1977; Brown and Levinson, 1978).

Patterns and strategies like these can be said to be rational in the sense that they are rooted in the design features of moves and could be worked out

---

[2] For example:

1 C: Jon, this kitchen is a real mess. Mom shouldn't always have to be the one to clean up after you guys.

2 J: Yeaheheh. Why don't you clean it up?

See also Jacobs and Jackson (1980, 36–41).

as plans from the primary system in many particular cases. Even a chess novice may work out a conventional opening or defense. These patterns and strategies are conventional in the sense that they may be known directly by a player, without knowledge of their rationale. It is this conventional character that allows a relatively unskilled player to perform in seemingly sophisticated ways. It is also this conventional character that leads to breakdowns in performance when the player is confronted with deviations from the conventional pattern or with exceptional circumstances outside the scope of a strategy.[3]

This sort of description of argument can supply not only a straightforward answer to the question "How is this game played?"; it also supplies the basis for structural explanation of particular patterns. Take, for example, the rhetorical questions that create the confrontations outlined by Bleiberg and Churchill (1975).[4] These are so effective precisely because (1) the lead-in question–answer sequences lead the victim into contradicting a prior assertion, a fact that is exposed by the rhetorical question, and (2) the questions are so designed that their relevance is disguised from the victim. Thus the design features of the component moves can be pointed to in explaining why an argument has the force it does. From another perspective, appeal to design features provides the basis for criticism—a particular

[3] Research on children's acquisition of language skills suggests that chidren develop conventional strategies for understanding requests before they learn the primary system of interpretive rules employed by adults. These heuristics enable two- and three-year-olds to produce responses that are fortuitously appropriate to many messages directed to them (Shatz, 1978).

[4] A confrontation episode has six steps:

1. Confronted makes a declarative statement.
2. Confronter asks a yes/no question about a particular aspect of the statement.
3. Confronted picks the answer that shows that the particular aspect under question is an exception to the statement.
4. Confronter asks a second yes/no question about another particular aspect of the statement.
5. Confronted picks the answer that shows that the particular aspect under question is another exception to the statement.
6. Confronter asks a rhetorical question that contradicts the confronted's original declarative statement (276).

For example:

1. PATIENT: I don't want them [my parents] to have anything to do with my life, except [pause] // security (?)
2. DOCTOR: You live at home?
3. PATIENT: Yes.
4. DOCTOR: They pay your bills?
5. PATIENT: Yeah.
6. DOCTOR: How could they not have anything to do with your life? (274).

move or pattern of argument may be criticized in terms of the strengths and weaknesses of its design features in the same fashion that a critic approaches a game of chess.[5]

2. Argument Is Significant Communication

As stated earlier, the rhetorical function of argument (its role in the process of mutual adjustment between individuals) is grounded in the process whereby individuals communicate arguments. This relation is embodied in Mead's concept of the *significant gesture* and in the concept of a *communicative speech act* developed by language-action philosophers. Together these concepts provide a picture of how a process of cooperative adjustment in conversation is built on a process of meaning construction.

Following Mead, we see the meaning of individual acts of discourse (gestures) embedded in a social enterprise. A gesture is a phase of a social act that finds its completion in the response of another organism. This relation led Mead to suggest that the meaning of an act is to be found in the response it evokes.[6] A "conversation of gestures," then, is an ongoing process of mutual adjustment in which individual actions and reactions enter into, and gain significance from, the construction of a social activity.

For humans, this process of adjustment has the special characteristic of being carried out by self-reflexive organisms. Humans engage in what Mead called significant communication. In significant communication, the gesture not only calls out a response in another; it also calls out that response in the individual making the gesture so that he or she becomes aware of its meaning (its role within the social act). As Mead states:

> Significant symbols carried back to their origins prove to be gestures, i.e., parts of social acts through which individuals adjust their conduct to that of others. They become symbols when the act which they preface is aroused as an attitude in the other individual. They become significant symbols when the individual that uses the gesture which calls out such an attitude in another calls out the same attitude in himself. When a gesture calls out a certain attitude not only in other individuals but at the same time in the individual

[5] See Chernev (1947) or Reinfeld (1948). Note especially how interest in individual differences in competence does not in any way require the theorist to abandon explanation in terms of systemic properties.

[6] Mead never clearly distinguished between the conventionally appropriate response and the actual response a gesture evoked. As we shall see, the distinction is central to speech-act theory for the meaning an act has as an illocution and as a perlocution.

who makes the gesture, we refer to this attitude as the meaning of the gesture, or symbol [1938, 221–222].

Significant gestures are intentional. People know what they are doing. To use Goffman's distinction, significant gestures are *given* and not simply *given off* (1959, 2).

Mead's analysis of the significant gesture focused primarily on its strategic and rhetorical import—its importance was that it enabled an individual to take the role of the other and to thereby adjust her or his contribution to the conversation by anticipating the response it would call out in the other. As Mead put it:

> The function of the gesture is to make adjustment possible among the individuals implicated in any given social act with reference to the object or objects with which the act is concerned; and the significant gesture or significant symbol affords far greater facilities for such adjustment and readjustment than does the non-significant gesture, because it calls out in the individual making it the same attitude toward it (or toward its meaning) that it calls out in the other individuals participating with him in the given social act, and thus makes him conscious of their attitude toward it (as a component of his behavior) and enables him to adjust his subsequent behavior to theirs in light of that attitude. In short, the conscious or significant conversation of gestures is a much more adequate and effective mechanism of mutual adjustment within the social act—involving, as it does, the taking, by each of the individuals carrying it on, of the attitudes of the others toward himself—than is the unconscious or non-significant conversation of gestures [1934, 46].

It is clear that Mead saw the rhetorical function of language arising out of its communicative structure, but he did not extend his analysis in this direction. Mead took for granted the structure of understanding between interlocutors that emerges from a process of mutual role-taking between self-reflexive individuals. From the point of view of speech act theory, Mead supplied an analysis of *intended perlocutions*, the meaning an utterance has by its effects on an audience—instructing, persuading, getting someone to do something (see Gaines, 1979). The contribution of speech act theory has been to show how this rhetorical function of utterances is grounded in their performative structure; that is, in their nature as *illocutionary acts*.[7]

Making an argument is a type of illocutionary act that Bach and Harnish

---

[7] Most theorists have distinguished speech acts into three aspects that preserve, in one way or another, Austin's (1975) original analysis. The *locutionary act* is the aspect of an utterance that expresses a proposition. The *illocutionary act* is the sense in which one is doing something in uttering—requesting, complaining, asserting, greeting. The *perlocutionary act* is the

(1979) call communicative speech acts.[8] In seeming parallel to Mead's analysis, the illocutionary force of such acts is associated with the response of a recipient: all of the communicative illocutionary acts in Bach and Harnish's taxonomy (42–55), for example, are defined as expressing an attempt to have some conventional perlocutionary effect on a hearer. Thus making an argument would count as an attempt to get a hearer to agree with some speech act or to back down from a disagreeable speech act. However, these illocutionary acts are primarily social at the level of understanding that underlies the possibility of achieving any agreement. Strawson (1964) argues that for illocutionary acts fulfillment of the speaker's intention to express an attempt to have some effect on the hearer requires that this intention be recognized by the hearer: "The illocutionary force of an utterance is essentially something that is intended to be understood" (459). Bach and Harnish concur: "Part of the speaker's intention is that the hearer identify the very act the speaker intends to be performing, and successful communication requires fulfillment of that intention" (4). In other words, the performance of an illocutionary act is successful when what is being done is mutually recognized. An argument needs to be understood as an argument to be an argument; but notice that it doesn't need to be convincing to be an argument. The intention to have a certain perlocutionary effect need only be recognized; it doesn't need to be achieved.

Speech act theorists emphasize that the achievement of this mutual recognition occurs within the structure of reciprocal role-taking that underlies Mead's significant gestures. Communicative speech acts are intendedly interpretable. For the hearer, part of the process of recognizing a sign that is given involves taking the role of the speaker to infer that the speaker intends

---

sense in which an utterance is the cause of an effect in an audience: by requesting I may *annoy* someone, by asserting something I may *deceive* someone, by greeting someone I may *frighten* that person. All three aspects occur simultaneously in an utterance.

[8] O'Keefe (this volume) has argued that argument₁ is not a speech act, but some type of proposition—what we would consider a locution. From our point of view, making an argument is still fundamental to the analysis of arguments, since such a proposition can only be expressed in illocutionary acts and only have their status *as* arguments, by virtue of the disagreement-relevance associated with the illocutionary force of supporting or objecting to another speech act. Notice in the following example that the proposition expressed by B might count in other contexts as an argument for A's complaint (e.g., if B thought some third party was likely to disagree with A). In this case, it serves only as an explanation or elaboration since there is no disagreement-relevance understood by either party.
[A and B are talking about how cold the department offices are.]
1 A: This was bad enough on the weekends, but if it's like this *now*, I can't imagine what it'll be like up here on Saturday.
2 B: 'Cause they turn off all the heat on the weekends.

for the hearer to recognize that sign. For the speaker, part of the process of anticipating the hearer's interpretation involves taking the role of the hearer to infer the role-taking process the hearer is going through. Communication, then, involves a process of mutual orientation to the other as a self-reflexive organism—a process Grice (1957) tried to capture in his notion of a *reflexive intention* by the speaker.

This conception of argument as significant communication has two implications for our analysis. First, since the public design features of argument are a communicative accomplishment, the rules organizing the "moves" in the language game must include interpretive rules. Models for such rules can be found in Labov and Fanshel's (1977, 82–88) "Rule for Indirect Requests" and "Rule for Putting Off Requests."[9] Both rules have the achievement of mutual understanding as built-in features of the rules themselves. So the communication process becomes a constitutive feature of the game itself and not something that exists outside the game.

Second, our analysis focuses on perlocutions grounded in illocutions. For example, to convince a person to agree with an assertion or to back down from a request requires that the utterer get the recipient to recognize the argument for that assertion or against the request. We exclude, on grounds of principle, unintended and unacknowledged persuasion. Symphonies and other artistic works are not arguments (Brockriede, 1975, 179), nor are the admittedly manipulative aesthetic associations of a beer commercial (Willard, 1976, 315). We are not interested in transforming nondiscursive symbolism or the pragmatic effects of any other activity into argument in a way that bypasses their performative structure in communication.

3. *Argument Is Organized by a Social Orientation*

We locate the structure of argument in a public institution: the system of rules that define human actions as implying, making, or having arguments. Both the process of communication (the mutual recognition of an act's intent) and the resultant process of coordination (the regulation of

[9] Labov and Fanshel claim that an utterance which refers to a precondition for the valid performance of a request, to the desired action, or to its consequences or time of performance can be heard as an indirect request for action. The rule operates, however, only if the hearer can calculate what is being referred to and also infers that the speaker believes that all the other preconditions are satisfied—things a speaker must work to assure if he or she is to communicate the indirect request successfully.

agreement and disagreement) are achieved by natural language users mutually orienting to the rules of the game.

Our approach departs from the currently popular psychologistic reduction of argument to individual reasoning processes (Jackson and Jacobs, 1980, 251–252). We offer an alternative to seeing argument as "something which happens within a person" and arguing as "the way beliefs are processed within an individual's cognitive system" (Hample, 1981). Not only does the identification of argument with reasoning overlook the appearance of argument in concrete acts and interactions; it ignores the institutional structuring of individual cognitions. True, rules of argument must be known by an individual in order to play; that is, the game must be "internalized." However, psychologistic theories ignore the way in which the game of argument is experienced as existing publicly and independently of individuals in the same straightforward way that the game of chess is experienced as an objective, social object that can be described in a handbook without any transformation into a system of cognitive processes.

Patterns of argumentative discourse certainly require interpretation and reasoning by natural language users, and the cognitive resources that enable them to engage in argument is a fascinating subject. However, the processes that allow people to construct, evaluate, and make sense of arguments are not at all specific to argument. People bring to bear processes of language comprehension and problem-solving in general (Jackson, 1980). What makes argument unique is not some special reasoning faculty but the system of rules through which very general processes are adapted to a particular type of activity. Argument is not a process whereby a single individual privately arrives at a conclusion; it is a procedure whereby two or more individuals publicly arrive at agreement.

The relation we have in mind between individual and public activity has been most clearly articulated in Mead's concept of the "generalized other" and in his later principle of sociality.[10] For Mead, taking the attitude of the generalized other is essential to the organization of any significant gesture. In communicating, an individual does not simply take the perspective of

[10] Much of the discussion that follows applies as well to Perelman's concept of the Universal Audience. There are some difficult ambiguities in Perelman's concept, however, which it is not our purpose to explicate. By "Universal Audience" we understand Perelman to mean something much more abstract than simply "all of mankind"; specifically, we believe that his notion, like Mead's, is best understood as something like "abstract discourse structure." The *content* of the Universal Audience's perspective is not universally shared substantive beliefs, but universally shared discourse rules. See Perelman and Olbrechts-Tyteca (1969, 13–62).

the particular other to whom he or she speaks. The individual takes the perspective of the social institution within which both individuals are participating and assumes that his or her fellow interlocutor does the same. The prototype of this attitude is that of a player in a game. Mead argues:

> If the given human individual is to develop a self in the fullest sense, it is not sufficient for him merely to take the attitude of other human individuals toward himself and toward one another within the human social process, and to bring that social process as a whole into his individual experience merely in these terms: he must also, in the same way that he takes the attitudes of other individuals toward himself and toward one another, take their attitudes toward the various phases or aspects of the common social activity or set of social undertakings in which, as members of an organized society or social group, they are all engaged; and he must then, by generalizing these individual attitudes of that organized society or social group itself, as a whole, act toward different social projects which at any given time it is carrying out [1934, 154–155].

The fundamental importance of this attitude is that it provides the basis for communicative understanding and a standard of objectivity in argument. Speakers assess what intentions they might reasonably expect hearers to recognize and hearers assess what intentions a speaker could reasonably expect them to recognize by reference to the rules of argument. Likewise, taking the attitude of the generalized other provides individuals a basis for assessing the relevance and the adequacy of their arguments—it provides a standard of judgment participants employ irrespective of individual idiosyncracies. According to Mead: "A human organism does not become a rational being until he has achieved such an organized other in his field of social response" (1932, 87). "What I have attempted to do is to bring rationality back to a certain type of conduct, the type of conduct in which the individual puts himself in the attitude of the whole group to which he belongs" (1934, 334).

The generalized other appears from a perspective that organizes individual perspectives into an interlocking system of communicative roles. In learning one role in a game, an individual always learns the complementary roles. The concept reflects Mead's broader principle of sociality in that the relation of the perspective of one individual to another's perspective is determined by the relation of both perspectives within this third perspective (Morris, 1970, 128–32). The concept of the generalized other should not be understood as the perspective of another individual (such as an objective bystander) nor as an essentialization or averaging of the common elements of the perspectives it organizes. Rather, the generalized other should be seen as a second-order construct, a system of "transformational principles" for relating one individual perspective to another.[11]

Because the attitude of the generalized other is a perspective on social activity as an organized system, it can exist at many different levels (Mead 1932, 87). For our purposes the most pertinent level of the generalized other is that defined by language structure. According to Mead:

> Of these abstract social classes or subgroups of human individuals the one which is the most inclusive and extensive is, of course, the one defined by the logical universe of discourse (or system of universally significant symbols) determined by the participation and communicative interaction of individuals [1934, 157–158].

This level involves, for example, such categorical knowledge as the rule that a request is validly issued only if the felicity conditions are satisfied (for example, that the hearer is able to perform the action) and the way these felicity conditions are interlocked with the felicity conditions for granting a request.[12]

The generalized other becomes "particularized" by the way these rules get applied in a concrete context of argument. Adaptation to a particular interlocutor becomes a matter of constructing the relevance of his or her contextual beliefs to one's own *with respect to the categorical relevancies of language*. For example, the ability condition on a request to go to the grocery store may become particularized in consideration of whether or not the car is working, whether or not the requestee has a cold, and whether or not these

[11] In his later philosophy, Mead analyzed the generalized other in terms of his principle of sociality. His analysis was based on the implications of Einsteinian relativity theory (1932, 76–82). Instead of assuming the existence of an absolute perspective (a Minkowski-type world) as the common reality underlying different individual perspectives, the individual achieves objectivity through transformation formulae that enable him or her to organize different perspectives into a system. The importance of this notion is that the possibility of rational discourse no longer hinges on the degree of substantive commonalities between persons. Mead (1938) states: "The problem which has just been presented is that of the organization of perspectives in its most difficult form, for the perspectives in relativity are mutually exclusive, and the solution I have suggested is in terms of mind: that mind is able to organize them through a mathematical doctrine growing out of transformations found in the development of the theory of electromagnetism, that in mind we are able to pass from one perspective to another through transformations and in that manner are able to occupy different systems" (608).

[12] We have argued in detail and illustrated elsewhere (Jacobs and Jackson, 1980, 9) that grants to requests can be treated as a type of promise to comply with the request.

matters do in fact bear on the ability of the requestee to perform the action. The point here is that particular contextual beliefs "fill-in" the content of the generalized other while the generalized other supplies a structure for determining relevant contextual information.

Methodological Assumptions

Our theoretic aim is to identify systems of interpretive rules: principles that instruct natural language users in how to interpret speech acts and conversational patterns meaningfully and to produce rationally organized acts that will be interpreted by others as coherent contributions to the conversation. This theoretical aim sets up three interrelated empirical demands. First, it requires a cataloguing of the forms of expression and the patterns of discourse that are meaningful to natural language users. Second, it requires an analysis of the rules and conventions that natural language users must know in order to generate those forms and patterns. Third, it requires an explanation of the uses of the forms and patterns in terms of the properties of the discourse system. This pattern of theorizing is well illustrated by Nofsinger's (1975) analysis of the demand ticket.

Discourse analytic methods, designed to satisfy these empirical demands, differ in some important ways from more familiar methodologies. For example, because the theoretic problem is to discover a mechanism that generates a potentially infinite range of patterns, the analyst must collect data in such a way as to maximize the possibility of observing unusual and improbable patterns. This means that a random sample is unnecessary—in fact, undesirable—since what is wanted is not representativeness or typicality of observations but comprehensiveness. Likewise, since the analyst is interested in a set of abstract possibilities for language use, frequencies and probabilities of occurrence are not theoretically central as they are in interaction analysis techniques such as Markov chain analysis. A third difference between discourse analysis and other available empirical methods is that discourse analysis inevitably relies on some form of primary language analysis: the fundamental mode of demonstration is the display of concrete utterances whose properties are recognizable to any natural language user.

For the present state of theory development in conversational argument, our method of choice is some variation of "analytic induction" (Denzin, 1975). As with other forms of naturalistic methodology, discourse analysis employs conceptual devices as a presupposed part of its method. In the sections that follow we discuss the logic of analytic induction and the conceptual devices we have employed in our analysis of conversational argument.

The Method of Analytic Induction

Analytic induction, as a process, incorporates both the formulation of a hypothesis and the testing of that hypothesis. The first step in the process is the location or collection of some number of relevant examples of the phenomenon being studied. In our own efforts to produce a second-order description of the natural category of argument (Jacobs and Jackson, 1981), we began by collecting a set of naturally occurring arguments, relying on our native speaker/hearer intuitions to identify relevant cases. Our preference has generally been to collect naturalistic observations—arguments that occurred naturally, without any intervention by the analyst. There is no reason in principle why examples ought not be generated experimentally or through some systematic elicitation procedure such as interviewing, but we feel that the naturalistic validity of patterns induced from a collection is better assured if the form of the data collected cannot be attributed to manipulations by the analyst or systematic distortions in memory.

The second step in the process is the construction of a hypothesis, usually in the form of a rule, convention, or schema. The hypothesis, built inductively from the examples, must of course apply to every case. Our original collection of examples contained cases in which disagreement was openly expressed, but also cases in which disagreement was implied or not present at all. Thus we were unable to hypothesize that conversational argument was characterized by open expression of disagreement, but we were able to state as a hypothesis that in all cases the possibility of disagreement was an underlying organizational focus.

Having arrived at a hypothesis, the third step in analytic induction is to test the hypothesis through an active search for disconfirming cases. As with grammatical argument among linguists, the general procedure is to search for cases that fit the rule but shouldn't or for cases that should fit the rule but don't. For example, our hypothesis that arguments are disagreement-relevant speech events was tested by searching for cases of intuitively recognizable arguments that were not disagreement-relevant and for disagreement-relevant speech events that were not arguments. The search for disconfirming cases should be as rigorous and exhaustive as possible. One source of such cases is the analyst's intuitions as a natural language user: although constructing a hypothesis on the basis of intuitions alone is undesirable (Glaser and Strauss, 1967, chap. 1; Sacks, lecture notes, spring 1972, no. 1), supplementing observations with intuitions is perfectly reasonable, for if the analyst can construct disconfirming cases consistent with the observational evidence, we may assume that natural language users *could have* produced such cases. The fact that they have not been observed is a contingent fact of the sampling.

Should the search for disconfirming cases yield any negative instances, the method of analytic induction requires revision of the hypothesis to account for *all* cases. Our own search for counterexamples to our analysis of the natural category of argument has so far failed to turn up any cases of argument that were not disagreement-relevant, but we discovered a large number of cases of disagreement-relevant objects that were clearly not arguments. For example, inherently disagreeable speech acts such as insults and contradictions are certainly disagreement-relevant, yet they do not in themselves constitute arguments. Likewise, some cases of open disagreement never develop into arguments. So we revised our analysis, narrowing the characterization down to disagreement-relevant *expansions* of adjacency pairs. Thus an isolated act of disagreement or a disagreeable act is excluded, as our intuitions tell us they should be. This is the fourth step in the process of analytic induction, but it is not a definite end point for analysis. An analysis may be considered "complete" when the analyst arrives at a relatively durable hypothesis, but any hypothesis is continually subject to revisions forced by further observation.

Because of its suitability for descriptive analysis and its link to grounded theory, this is the method of choice for at least the initial stages of empirical exploration of any domain. But discourse analysis is not bound in any permanent way to analytic induction. Testing of rules can be done with respect to naturalistically or hypothetically generated cases, but it can also be done experimentally. Experimental testing such as Clark's (1979) analysis of requests is particularly well suited to demonstration of the psychological validity of hypothetical rules and structures. This use of experimentation is in no way inconsistent with the basic commitments of discourse analysis. The defining methodological commitments of discourse analysis are not to any particular data-collection procedure but to the goal of a descriptively adequate analysis of the communication system. In fact, we believe that this goal of descriptive adequacy is best assured by "triangulating" the results of multiple methods to counteract bias inherent in any one method (Denzin, 1970).

Conceptual Devices

Our conceptual devices have been drawn mainly from the work of speech-act theorists and conversational analysts. These devices serve as conceptual paradigms, or templates, for organizing observations into meaningful patterns.

A primary analytic unit for discourse analysis is the *speech act*. Both Austin (1975) and Searle (1969) have drawn attention to the distinction between what a person *says* and what a person *does* in an utterance. Speech-act theory emphasizes that utterances do not merely express propositions but also constitute actions organized by specific conventions of usage concerning felicity conditions.

Felicity conditions refer to categorical prerequisites to the proper or valid performance of a speech act, and every distinguishable speech-act type has its own set of such conditions. All speech acts have some form of "essential condition" that defines the act the speaker is expressing. Likewise, all presuppose some sort of "sincerity condition," which corresponds to the internal state of the speaker implied by the performance of the act (desire, intention, belief). All speech acts also presuppose one or more "preparatory conditions" which are probably most easily understood on an analogy with the stock issues that must be met in advocacy of a proposition.

Felicity conditions provide us a very powerful device for examining the relationships among individual speech acts in conversation because they specify a range of beliefs to which a speaker is committed in performing any given speech act. Thus it becomes possible to assess the bearing of one utterance on another through an inferential network supplied by the felicity conditions, even where there is no semantic connection between the contents of the two utterances. For example, one utterance may contradict the felicity condition of another or give evidence for the fulfillment of that felicity condition; or two acts may be connected through interlocking felicity conditions, as in the case of a question and its answer. Moreover, as we have argued elsewhere, the felicity conditions delimit the possible issues that may be raised in argument over a speech act. Felicity conditions provide a social framework for discourse so that individual acts in sequence can be fit into a shared, cooperative structure.

Because of the act-to-act connections made possible by felicity conditions, certain individual speech acts become conventionally bonded together to form two-act units called *adjacency pairs*. Originally noticed by Sacks and Schegloff (Sacks, lecture notes, 1967; Schegloff and Sacks, 1974), these units were considered as a conventional solution to the problem of how to produce a relevant next turn in conversation. Familiar examples of adjacency pairs are *question-answer*, *offer-accept / decline*, *request-grant / refuse*, and so on. As outlined by Schegloff and Sacks (1974, 238), these pairs have five basic features:

1. They are two speaking turns long with two parts.
2. The two parts are said by different speakers.
3. The pair parts are adjacently placed—by which is meant not that they occur contiguously but that the issuance of the first pair part establishes an ongoing relevance for the second part until its occurrence, whenever that might be. This is called a relation of "conditional relevance" (Schegloff, 1972, 107).
4. The pairs are ordered by types, so that some things (questions) are recognizable as first-pair parts and other things (answers) are recognizable as second-pair parts.
5. The pair parts are discriminatively related, so a first-pair part must receive a second-pair part of an appropriate type.

The discriminative relationship between the two pair parts is not—as Sacks and Schegloff imply—established by arbitrary surface rules but derives from the felicity conditions underlying the two acts. Thus, requests and grants have complementary, interlocking conditions that provide for the "conditional relevance" of a grant following a request.

The usefulness of adjacency pairs as a conceptual tool in the analysis of conversational argument is that they can be transformed in certain relatively well-analyzed ways to produce a vast range of socially constructed patterns in conversation (see Garvey, 1977; Jefferson, 1972; Jefferson and Schenkein, 1978; Schegloff, 1972, 1979). Specifically, adjacency pairs can be *sequentially expanded* in three ways: through preexpansion, which involves prepositioning a subordinate adjacency pair to "lead up to" the main pair (A: *"Do you believe that women have the same rights as men?"* B: *"Sure."* B: "Then why don't you do half of the housework and child-rearing?"); through embedded expansion, which involves inserting a subordinate pair between the first-pair part and the second-pair part of the main pair (A: "Would you come here and clean up this milk I spilled?" B: *"Can't you get it?"* A: *"I've gotta peel these carrots."* B: "Okay."); and through postexpansions, which involve following up the main pair with a subordinate pair (A: "I think you should do grocery shopping and laundry once in a while." B: "That is women's work." A: *"That is a wholly unacceptable response."* B: *"Okay, okay, I was just joking. Boy!"*). Individual pair parts can also be expanded through what we will call adjuncts ("You better go now *or there won't be anything open.*"). Any expansion unit can itself be expanded so that the adjacency-pair organization provides for indefinite variety and unlimited scope in the patterning of social acts.

A very general feature of adjacency-pair organization is that it exhibits a structural preference for agreement (Pomerantz, 1978). Most first-pair parts can take either of two second-pair parts, one of which is the preferred second-pair part and the other of which is the dispreferred second-pair part. Thus, for example, requests take a grant or a refusal as the second-pair part, assertions take assent or dissent, and so on.

The preferred second-pair part is associated with the intended perlocutionary effect of the first-pair part. It represents an affirmation of the felicity conditions for the first-pair part while a dispreferred second-pair part denies one or more felicity conditions. The preference for agreement operates as a principle of co-operativity: insofar as individuals participate in joint performance of social acts, they try to produce first-pair parts that can get agreement (that is, they try to perform valid speech acts), and they try to produce second-pair parts that satisfy validly performed first-pair parts (Jacobs and Jackson, 1980).

The preference for agreement also operates as a *presumption*: to say, for example, that there is a preference for a grant following a request is to say that grants are normal, expectable, and unremarkable; they therefore need no explanation. The occurrence of the request is itself sufficient motivation, or reason, for the respondent to issue a grant. Refusals, however, are by their nature accountable: if the respondent refuses, a reason or excuse is required. Likewise, agreement with assertions (whether explicit or tacit) is normal and expectable, while challenges and contradictions demand some sort of special reason. Generally, speakers are expected not to question or challenge other speakers without cause, just as speakers are expected not to say things known to be false or unsupportable (Grice, 1975).

Because of the preference for agreement, there is an intimate connection between disagreement and expansion. On the one hand, expansion of a basic pair indicates *some* deviation from the normal pattern, so disagreement becomes one of a small number of possible explanations for the deviation. On the other hand, actual or intended disagreement nearly always results in some sort of expansion to develop the account for the disagreement.

Our theoretical integration of the adjacency-pair relationship with the underlying rational organization of speech acts allows for a neat formal analysis of the regulation of disagreement through argument.

A Model of Conversational Argument

In conversation, argument takes the form of disagreement-relevant expansion. Our central empirical claim is that the struture of conversational argument results from the occurrence of disagreement in a rule system built to prefer agreement (Jackson and Jacobs, 1980). The structural properties of argument are in no way unique among conversational events, except as required by the specialized function of argument as a device for regulating disagreement. As we will show later, our characterization of argument as disagreement-relevant expansion leaves the boundaries of the concept of argument fuzzy, reflecting the fact that disagreement regulation has ramifications throughout the conversational system, not just for those episodes in which conflict is directly expressed (Jackson and Jacobs, ms.; Jacobs and Jackson, 1981).

We propose a model of conversational argument consisting of three components: the functional, the formal, and the substantive. The model is assumed to operate within the set of general conversational rules sketched above; and it is assumed that argument rules are triggered by some actual or anticipated speech act that will be referred to as the "arguable."

The Functional Component

Conversational arguments are, first and foremost, disagreement-relevant speech events. They are characterized by the projection, production, suppression, or resolution of disagreement, so that they function not only to manage cases of expressed disagreement, but also to regulate the occurrence of disagreeable speech acts. The ordinary language use of the term "argument" covers all sorts of conversational events ranging from the sort of pure disagreeableness of what Piaget (1959) called "primitive argument" to the sort of organized, orderly reason-giving recommended by argumentation texts. [13]

Examples 1, 2, and 3 display the focus and range of the natural category of argument. Example 1 is prototypical, in that it consists of reason-giving

[13] See Weddle (1978): "The brouhaha at home plate after a batter is hit by a pitch; a spat between Punch and Judy; a donnybrook—these are all arguments, but not in the sense of the term which concerns us. This book deals with sweet reason. It deals with arguing *over* something, yes, but in the sense in which arguing is *giving* arguments, not in the sense in which arguing is squabbling" (1).

under conditions of open disagreement (so that it counts as argument in both of O'Keefe's [1977] senses). Example 2 is certainly a case of *having* an argument (O'Keefe's argument $_2$), though no arguments $_1$ are *made*. Example 3 shows an argument being *made* (O'Keefe's argument $_1$) without any overt expression of disagreement (so that participants cannot be said to be *having* an argument). Elsewhere we have argued that O'Keefe's two senses of argument are unified by a common generative principle (Jacobs and Jackson, 1981); here we merely point out that an adequate theory of conversational argument must be able to accommodate cases like Examples 2 and 3 as well as prototype cases like Example 1.

Example 1. C and K are two college-age women, friends.

1 C: Why did he change from Catholic to *Lutheran*, they're *total* opposites.
2 K: No they're not, they're kind of the same.
3 C: *No they aren't* [pause] I'm a *Lutheran*.
4 K: I'm a *Catholic*. [Pause.] What's going on there [referring to an event in the street] [pause] I think they're kind of the same. [Pause.] That's cute [referring to street event]. Uh, they're both pretty close, really Chris.
5 C: I don't think so.
6 K: They both have ritual. [Pause.] Their views are pretty mu- I went to a Lutheran service one time. Well there- there's differences bu-
7 C: Well Lutherans don't believe- in- *Mar::y::* you know, like you guys do.

Example 2. S and C are getting ready to pack for departure from a visit with relatives.

1 S: Do you know where my bag is?
2 C: Yeah, it's packed away.
3 S: Whadya *mean* it's packed away?!
4 C: Just what I *said*!
5 S: Why in the *world* would you do something like that?!
6 C: Hhhhhhh [C stalks off in a huff]

Example 3. D and J are two college-age men, roommates. They are discussing which of two restaurants would be better to work at.

2 D: You'd only have five tables as opposed to six. But that can turn into a benefit because//
2 J: You do a better job.
3 D: Yeah [pause] because you have the one—the one less table makes a hell of a difference.

Of course, the examples and discussion above do not exhaust the range of conversational events which are disagreement-relevant. Ordinary language users take argumentative potential into account in planning many different types of episodes, avoiding some acts so as not to provoke disagreement, reformulating others in less disagreeable form, and even sometimes deliberately provoking disagreement for instrumental ends. Within a general theory of conversational organization, argument can be seen as a pervasive regulatory mechanism that operates in many cases to prevent overt expression of disagreement. For the ordinary language user, argument shades into other related categories of events, so our theoretic reconstruction of the commonsense concept of argument, too, has close ties to such things as conversational persuasion, explanation, clarification, and repair. Example 4, in which a clarification question hints at possible disagreement, illustrates the shading of argument into repair (compare also Example 3 with the example in footnote 8).

Example 4. A is a woman, E is a man.

1 A: Women are no more difficult to understand than men.
2 E: What?
3 A: I mean, there's nothing [pause] intrinsic in a person's *sex* that makes them hard to understand them.

Instances such as these display the communicative grounding of argument. The disagreement-relevance of an act and the propositions expressed may be ambiguous or vague, depending on the intention of a speaker, the interpretation of a hearer, and what each takes the other to understand. This can be a matter of the clarity of the perspectives of the participants themselves or the complexity (and thus the certainty) of the inferential bridge required to make, and get across, an interpretation.

What is it that characterizes the disagreement-relevance that does get communicated in argument? Within a general theory of conversation, disagreement is a relationship between two speech acts. Obviously, disagreement cannot be characterized simply in terms of overt negation, contradiction, or refutation since argument frequently involves exchange of remarks whose propositional contents are never questioned. Example 5, a hypothetical argument, shows how this is possible.

Example 5.

1 A: Come help me.
2 B: I'm busy.
3 A: I *need* you to hold this.
4 B: I need to finish this.
5 A: I always help you when you ask me.
6 B: I never ask you when you're busy.
7 A: Come on, you lazy creep!
8 B: Bug off, you shrew!

The basis for disagreement is not simply the truth or falsity of stated propositions but a contradiction between the preconditions for one speech act and another. The performance of any speech act implies that the speaker believes (or commits the speaker to believing) that all of the preconditions hold, so that the act conveys "extra" propositions. For example, in making a request, a speaker implies that she or he believes the hearer to be willing and able to perform the requested act, that the hearer would not have performed the act in the absence of the request, and so on. In refusing the request, the hearer indicts the validity of the act's performance, implying the contradiction of one or more of the preconditions. In Example 6, A's complaint is challenged for failure to meet one of the felicity conditions for complaining; it is not the proposition expressed that gets disagreement, but the act of complaining itself.

Example 6. A and B are graduate teaching assistants.

1 A: I don't understand why they—you have to pay tax here. I don't see why they don't just write a letter for you here like at Pennsylvania saying that teaching is a requirement so that they send you your money back.
2 B: Well, there's a good reason why they don't do it here, A, and I know you know what it is 'cause I told you what it is before.

Arguments regularly occur around requests, complaints, promises, offers, suggestions, and other speech acts that obligate the hearer to accept or refuse. Disagreements over the truth or falsity of direct assertions (which are possible, though not so common as one might suppose) can be seen to be a limited case of the general principle that disagreement is between speech acts (see Habermas, 1979, 26–34. *Universal* validity claims for speech acts are "truth," "truthfulness," and "rightfulness").

Any speech act can become the subject of disagreement and therefore argument, just as any utterance can become the subject of repair. But some acts, by their very nature, seem to invite argument. Acts that involve public expression of disapproval for the actions or attributes of speaker or hearer—accusations, insults, criticisms, complaints, challenges, self-deprecations—have the expression of disagreement built into their conventional properties. Insults, for example, must attack some attribute valued by the recipient of the insult in order to come off properly (Labov, 1972).[14]

Example 7.

1 A: YOU ARE A NASTY CHICK
2 B: I just had a lot to do.

[14] Both ritual insults and personal insults are built on the negative portrayals of the attributes, abilities, possessions, or relations of the addressee—especially those the addressee may be presumed to value or revere. Thus, for example, it is possible to insult a man (ritually *and* personally) through a formula like "Your mother ——" but probably not through a formula like "Your neighbor ——."

3 A: *Fine* I just want you to listen to yourself-I'm not *mad* or nothin' I'm used to it-
   if you would just listen to yourself-from now on don't bitch at me when I do it?
   When you do *the exact same thing, the same thing.*

These act types invite disagreement by contradicting one or more beliefs
that the hearer may be assumed to hold (or may be compelled—by politeness or other constraints—to publicly defend). Expression of disagreement
is part of their communicative intent. Other act types that are not inherently disagreeable can invite argument by building in contradiction of substantive beliefs known to be held by the hearer. So, for example, a speaker
can provoke an argument more or less at will by issuing an "inflammatory
remark"—one that requires public contradiction by the hearer:

Example 8. A is a former Kennedy campaign worker; he has an autographed
photograph of Kennedy on his office wall. B is an apolitical colleague.

1 B [pointing to the photograph of Kennedy]: He should be in jail, not in the
   White House.

Acts that express disagreement with a known or presumable belief of the
hearer—whether as part of the conventional structure of the act type or as
part of the unconventional background knowledge participants have about
each other's standing beliefs—promote argument by forcing the recipient
to respond in a way that either disagrees with the act or contradicts his or
her own beliefs.

The Formal Component

Argument and nonargument exist on a continuum whose one definable
end point is a basic action sequence which can be expanded indefinitely
around sources of actual or potential disagreement. As part of a general
system of rules for conversation, the organization of argument exhibits
formal variations common to all speech-act expansion. An argument episode is built up from a dominant speech-act sequence (adjacency pair) that
controls some combination of presequences, embedded sequences, postsequences, and within-turn expansions. The characterization of argument
in terms of sequential expansion is theoretically important because it
emphasizes the collaborative work that goes into having and making
arguments.

Although any formal variation can be disagreement-relevant, the different expansion forms are suited to handling disagreeableness in different
ways. Presequences can be used, for example, to establish premises prior to

issuing a first-pair part (Example 9) or to seek general assurances that the hearer will be agreeable (Example 11). In Example 9, the presequence establishes the potential availability of C for the requested action.

Example 9. E is C's grandparent. Both are visiting C's parents while C is home during Christmas vacation. E lives in another town. It is Sunday and E is getting ready to leave.

1 E: How long do you have here?
2 C: Uh, we're planning to go back Thursday or Friday.
3 E: Oh, well. Maybe you can come up for a day and visit us.
4 C: Yeah, maybe so, We'll have to see.

In Example 10, the presequence obtains a broader assurance of agreement by virtue of the mutually understood relevance of scheduling a training session. Here, J's question provides an opportunity for C to provide reasons for not going through a training session that day without having to refuse a request directly. When C provides no such reason, it is taken as C implying that he would agree to such a request.

Example 10

1 J: Are you free on Monday afternoon?
2 C: Uh, let's see. [-] Yeah.
3 J: Okay, why don't you come down at about two and I'll go through the wiring with you?

Embedded sequences, in which a subordinate pair intervenes between a first-pair part and its second-pair part, can be used to elicit arguments to support the first-pair part (Example 11), to challenge the act as invalidly performed (Example 6),[15] to set out conditions for issuing the preferred response (Example 12), or to establish premises justifying a disagreeable response (Example 13). In Example 11, B's turn in 2 amounts to an evidence demand: not really an argument against A's turn, but an exploration of the soundness of A's request; that is, an elicitation of an argument from A.

Example 11

1 A: Could you get that clipboard for me?
2 B: Why me? Can't you get it yourself?
3 A: I'm busy.
4 B: Oh all *right*.

In Example 12, the embedded sequence suggests that agreement might or might not be reached, depending on the answer to S's question in 2.

---

[15] Objections are not themselves refusals but first-pair parts to embedded sequences. They may have the practical force of a refusal should they be left unanswered. In such a case, the first-pair part is effectively invalidated (Jackson and Jacobs, 1980, 260).

Example 12. J, S, and S's husband are sitting in a restaurant looking at the menu. S has taken a long time to decide what to order.

1 J: Hey, we can still go out and get some Mexican food still.
2 S: Oh really? What time is it?
3 J: It's right down the road.
4 S: I don't know. That would mean we just start deliberating all over again, heh.

In Example 13, a series of embedded sequences following A's assertion in 2 apparently fails to obtain premises from A that would allow C to demonstrate that everyone must be baptized to be saved (compare this to Bleiberg and Churchill's confrontation sequences, footnote 4).[16]

Example 13. B and C are Mormon missionaries who have come to A's home. B is explaining that the Mormon church is different from other churches because Mormons believe everyone must be baptized.

1 B: . . . Okay? So there's one- one difference, [-] okay?// We believe every-
2 A: My church believes that too.
3 B: [pause] Uh, [-] well what do you believe?
4 A: [pause] I don't believe that.
5 C: You don't believe the Bible?
6 A: [pause] No:- not- [-] well I don't believe that uh, uh, uh, put into the context of our times that that's true.
7 C: Well:::, does Jesus Christ change from age to age? Does he change?
8 A: [pause] The world has changed.
9 C: Does Jesus Christ change?
10 A: No, but that doesn't mean that the meaning of his words doesn't.
11 C: *Oh,* but it does.
12 A: Uh- heh-heh-heh
13 C: Mrs. A, I think you need to find out what you believe, first of all. [-] You've got to find out- reach down inside yourself and find out what you believe. 'Cause it sounds like you're not even sure what you believe yourself.

The interactional consequences of embedded sequences like these have been explored in two previous analyses (Jackson and Jacobs, 1980; ms.). By specifying grounds for possible disagreement or issuing challenges to the grounds for the initial speech act, conversationalists give each other oppor-

---

[16] In sequences 5−6, 7−8, and 9−10, C appears to be setting the basis for demonstrating that everyone must be baptized, a fact in conflict with A's stated belief in 4. In each response, however, A tries to avoid giving a simple, direct answer as is needed for a pattern of confrontation to "come off" properly. In 11 and 12, C is reduced to a bald contradiction of A's claim in 10 and A marks the impasse with nervous giggling. Notice that 13 appears to be a creative effort to recoup the force of the projected confrontation by focusing not on what A says, or agrees to, but on the way A is responding and what that implies about A's statement in 4.

tunities to withdraw, modify, reformulate, or repair potentially disagreeable speech acts.

Postsequential expansion, in which a subordinate pair is placed after a second-pair part, provide opportunities for challenges to either pair part and for the refurbishing of pair parts. In Example 14, A's first turn, an apparent presequence to some sort of proposal, gets both a direct reply and a more general abortive rejection of the upcoming proposal. In the third turn, and again in the fifth turn, A challenges the basis for the rejection.

Example 14. A and B are driving past a city park that rents horses by the hour.

1 A: I wonder how much they charge to rent those horses.
2 B: I don't know. But I wouldn't want to ride them anyway.
3 A: Why not?
4 B: Oh, cause I really don't know that much about them.
5 A: So what?
6 B: Well I just wouldn't really want to ride an animal that I don't know how to control.

In Example 15, a counterproposal to the first-pair part is followed by a postexpansion designed to force a withdrawal of one or the other.

Example 15. A is in the kitchen. B is in the basement. The television is in the living room.

1 A: Turn on the last ten minutes of *As the World Turns* and we'll see if anything exciting is happening.
2 B: Go ahead.
3 A: You. I'm making lunch.
4 B: No.
5 A: Well you're *right in there*!
6 B: *No I'm not!* [Shouted loudly.]
7 A: Oh.

So postsequences serve to repair and regulate speech acts in a state of disagreement, just as presequences and embedded sequences may work to avert disagreement.

Expansion of an individual speech act can, for example, be used to anticipate disagreement by building supporting arguments into the performance of a first-pair part or be used to justify disagreement in a second-pair part. In Example 16, C expands an indirect request by referring to facts bearing on the need for the action.

Example 16

1 C: Someone's going to have to take Curtie home soon. Would you mind doing it?

Since you've got to get up early you're not going to be able to stay up late and I can. We gotta get this paper done.

So either the adjacency pair or the individual-pair parts can be expanded in such a way as to make arguments, have arguments, imply arguments, elicit arguments, or avoid arguments. Although all four types of expansion—presequences, embedded sequences, postsequences, and within-turn expansions—may be disagreement-relevant, their temporal placement with respect to the main-pair parts makes each especially well suited to particular strategic uses.

The Substantive Component

The third component of our model is a delimitation of the content of the conversational arguments people make or imply. We have pointed out that argument concerns speech acts rather than propositions. One consequence of this fact is that expansion of adjacency pairs or pair parts through arguments $_1$ must be channelized by the felicity conditions for the speech act being performed.

As indicated earlier, any speech act may be expanded so as to clarify or correct its meaning, since the meaningfulness and intelligibility of a speech act is a universal condition for communication of a speech act. Likewise, and for the same reason, speech acts can be expanded around conceptual and semantic issues raised by their propositional contents. Because issues of truth and consistency of propositional content are universal conditions for felicitous action, they are not ordinarily considered preconditions for any particular type of speech act, but of course they are. Both ordinary repair and argument can be directed at propositional aspects of speech acts, and the distinction between these two functions is not always sharp—as with Example 17.[17]

Example 17. Beth has suggested to her husband Gary that they invite another couple over for dinner.

1 G: Wuh, it seems to be okay with me.

---

[17] This example was one of a set of arguments we generated through a systematic interviewing procedure. Married couples were asked to re-enact interpersonal influence situations of various types after first describing the circumstances leading up to the episode. The example given is transcribed from actual, spontaneous dialogue, but the dialogue was stimulated not by an immediate conflict but by recollection of a past conflict. Details of the interviewing procedure and additional examples appear in Jackson and Jacobs (ms.).

2 B: You sure you don't have plans, you don't mind?

3 G: Yeah, b'what would you- what would you have?

4 B: Like chicken or- hamburger something like that-nothing expensive.

Gary's postexpansion in 3 may be just exploration of the specifics of the already-accepted proposal but, as Beth's reply indicates, it may also be a prelude to disagreement focused on cost.

Beyond matters of propositional content, the permissible bases for expansion differ greatly from one act type to another. Requests, for example, involve issues of speaker's need for some future act, the relative rights and obligations impinging on the hearer's performance of the act, and so on. Complaints, on the other hand, involve issues of harm to the speaker from a past or ongoing act, hearer's responsibility for the harm, and so on. Assertions, finally, involve issues of speaker's credibility, hearer's prior knowledge, and the like, and these are often secondarily implicated in requests, complaints, and other speech acts.

The substantive component provides for identification of a variety of distinct *fields* of conversational argument, each with its own limited set of permissible warrants. Each distinguishable speech-act type can be considered a separate field, and the felicity conditions associated with the type are its warrants. The relevance of any particular bit of proof depends on its particularization of one of the felicity conditions. This is illustrated for Examples 18–21, which are typical expansions around requests.

Example 18. Sally has requested Scott (C) to go out to their car, parked some distance from their snowbound house, to retrieve a bottle of Woolite.

1 C: Well, how bad do you need it?

2 S: Well, I don't have anything to wear for tomorrow.

3 C: Uh, hhhh okay. I guess I'll go out and get it.

4 S: I really appreciate it. [Pause] I'd certainly understand it if you didn't want to.

5 C: No, that's okay. You've got to have it.

Before granting the request, Scott elicits an argument $_1$ from Sally by asking her to address the need condition. After granting the request, Sally reopens the possibility for refusal by questioning the willingness condition, which Scott rejects with an argument for the need for the action. [18]

Example 19

1 S: You don't mean to leave this bag of garbage in here, do you?

2 C: Yes.

3 S: Ohhh no. Unacceptable. It smells worse in here now than it did before.

---

[18] Cases like this of raising arguments after an agreement appear to be a general way of expressing politeness or assuring the sincerity of the grant (Jackson and Jacobs, 1980, 261).

Here Sally explicitly questions the need to make the request in the pre-sequence and then argues for the request by appeal to the need for the action.

Example 20. S enters the house carrying a suitcase.

1 C: *Hey*, you didn't bring this back.
2 S: Bring what back?
3 C: The suitcase.
4 S: Of course not. Robeson's was closed.

After a clarification sequence, Sally answers Scott's challenge by appeal to the ability condition—she couldn't return the suitcase as requested because the store she bought it from was closed.

Example 21

1 A: Why dontcha call up the teacher?
2 B: I'm not gonna call up a teacher and ask him sumptin I'm supposed to *know*.

Here A refuses a suggestion on the grounds of relative obligations in performing the action—B has no right to bother a teacher for such information. In each of these cases, the arguments[1] for or against a request can be seen to be "warranted" by a felicity condition.

The use of the term "warrants" in this connection is deliberate, for our model presupposes that conversationalists have vast unreflective knowledge of the conditions for appropriate speech-act performance, and they apply this knowledge cooperatively to interpret the bearing of any fact on the arguable. Thus, in a sequence like Example 22, which occurred in the hearing of four or five nonparticipants, only S and C knew the exact relevance of S's "reason," but all present could see *that* S's turn was intended as a reason and assumed that some "likely story" could be constructed to connect S's utterance as a reason for refusing C's request. They assumed that, given knowledge of the particular context of mutual understandings informing S and C's exchange, such a story could be constructed along conventional routes, for example that Tuesday had something to do with S's obligations or abilities.

Example 22

1 C: Can you take the baby this afternoon?
2 S: It's Tuesday!

The substantive component of the model provides not only the routes for expansion of any speech act (via repair possibilities and felicity conditions) but also a set of interpretive principles that allow conversationalists to see *how* particular facts bear on arguments. The task of analyzing the substantive component is not as unwieldly as it might appear. Although the number of distinct speech-act verbs appearing in English is vast (Austin estimated the figure at over 10,000), most seem to fall into a small number of general classes, such as Searle's (1977) "directives" (which approximates "propositions of action" in debate terminology). For the most interesting types, such as requests, consensually validated analyses are already available (Searle, 1969, 66–67; Labov and Fanshel, 1977, 78). Moreover, Searle has provided exemplars and general conceptual categories that greatly simplify the task of analysis: the propositional content factored out, Searle's (1969, 62–63) categories include preparatory conditions, essential conditions, and sincerity conditions. In principle, this task is no more difficult than identification of stases (Kline, 1979), though the speech acts involved present novelties for the argumentation theorist. It is simply a fact that conversationalists argue not just over proposals and claims but also over complaints, insults, compliments, jokes, apologies, exhortations, and any other type of speech act.

Convergence of Functional, Formal, and Substantive Components: Enthymemes in Conversation

The rules for turn-taking in conversation have as one result that argument is a constant momentary possibility. An "argumentative" conversationalist can construct an argument $_1$ in support of or in response to any speech act whatsoever and the structural responsibilities for sequence expansion mean, in principle at least, that any speech act can be expanded indefinitely to force examination of more and more fundamental presuppositions or to provide more and more complex support for the act's validity. Yet these structural possibilities are exercised in only the most limited ways, so that most arguments are built up from fairly simple expansions rather than from complex, systematic scrutiny.

We have argued elsewhere that conversational arguments are enthymematic in that the arguments $_1$ that get produced are specifically tailored to the likely bases for disagreement by the hearer (Jackson and Jacobs, 1980). Further, we have argued that this is the result of the preference for agreement, which casts both speaker and hearer into a collaborative effort after agreement. The preference for agreement operates like a presumption—a presumption of the validity of any speech act. Disagreement requires some compelling rationale, something definite enough and significant enough to overcome this presumption. What this means is that disagreement is a local problem, not a general attitude of skepticism: disagreement is issued on some specific ground, and argument then centers around precisely that issue whose resolution is most pressing for the particular hearer.

The function of argument as disagreement-regulator converges with formal and substantive rules to promote the collaborative production of enthymemes. The formal possibilities for speech-act expansion mean that each speaker can make active contributions to the construction of the other's contributions. For example, a speaker may use presequences to elicit premises from an auditor; likewise, either speaker may issue challenges, refutations, clarification requests, and the like in response to the other's act, so that the kind and quality of support given in an argument$_1$ is jointly determined.

The substantive component, because it provides a rational delimitation of the "facts" that will bear on any speech act's validity, provides for conversationalists to judge the relevance of one another's arguments$_1$. The felicity conditions for an arguable speech act serve as the warrants for "evidence" or "reasons" offered in support of the act, and even where the exact status of a bit of evidence can't be conclusively determined, conversationalists assume that relevance, in virtue of its bearing on one of the felicity conditions. We do not see production of conversational enthymemes as any active effort by hearers to "supply premises" for the claims of speakers; rather, we find that conversational enthymemes are the result of a general pattern of *assuming* the validity of others' acts and the relevance of their proofs.

Conclusion

In this essay we have described a way of studying argument and have illustrated the sort of conclusions that can be drawn from this mode of study. Our approach, which models argument as a particular kind of language game, provides for a descriptive account that is rich and detailed yet systematic and parsimonious. We are able to represent the context-embeddedness of argument without abandoning the search for context-free structures, for speech-act structure provides the organizing principle used by both arguers and analysts to decide what aspects of context are relevant to any case of argument.

Through the method of analytic induction we have been able to build a second-order concept of argument that formally represents the naive theories of argument shared by ordinary speakers and hearers. Observed patterns of argumentation are explained in terms of their intendedly meaningful character, their purposeful use of shared social structures. The conduct of argumentation is thus shown to be reflexively organized by the interpretive principles used by arguers.

V. WILLIAM BALTHROP

[10]   Argumentation and the
Critical Stance: A Methodological Perspective

A world in which all behavior is preordained or in which novel events and explanations are either accepted or rejected categorically has little use for argument. Beliefs, customs, and actions are as they are because of the edicts of gods, the vicissitudes of fates, or the immutability of laws. Even if particular causes are espoused and courses of action exhorted, their success or failure in such a world rests not with decisions made by human beings about their own destinies but with the cosmos. Whether or not such a world ever existed is open to conjecture, but certainly the trend in Western thought has been away from such static conceptualizations of human existence toward those that grant preeminence to the relative over the absolute, to *becoming* over *being*. Becoming, however, implies far more than mere impermanence; rather, it encompasses a "mode of thinking that contemplates everything—nature, man, society, history, God himself—*sub specie temporis*, as not merely changing, but as forever evolving into something new and different. It disbelieves in all fixities, absolutes, and 'eternal' ideas" (Baumer, 1977, 20).

Disbelief in absolutes or in fixed realities does not mean, however, that human beings wander through a chaotic universe with no sense of order or purpose. If none is provided by omnipotent beings or forces, then humans will create their own, and they will do so on the basis of their experiences with sense data and with other human beings. That is, humans, through shared experiences and interaction, create their own views of what constitutes reality, and they do so on the basis of the *meanings* those experiences have for them. It is through interaction, or communication, that such realities are both created and tested (Brummett, 1976). Even these socially constructed realities are not immune to the underlying forces of change and

238

novelty; for, as Gadamer observed, "There is always a world, already interpreted, already organized in its basic relations, into which experience steps
as something new, upsetting what has led our expectations and undergoing
reorganization itself in the upheaval" (1976, 15). The impetus for change
has many sources: the ambiguity inherent in any situation that permits the
potential for different interpretations; the intrusion of some new experience
or phenomenon that cannot be accounted for within the existing construction of social reality; and, not least, the uncertainty and doubt inevitable in
a world devoid of absolutes. If an initial view of reality was created through
communication, then only through communication can it be altered. And,
as each of these potential sources for change generates the possibility of
competing interpretations, argument becomes an essential factor for resolving these conflicts and for recreating shared consensus about reality.

Therein lies the paradox of argument: it assumes dissensus, or conflict,
yet presumes understanding or agreement. Regardless of the conceptualizations of argument advanced,[1] a common perception exists that argument is
some form of discourse taking place in disagreement, whether over appropriate rules and roles accepted by partners in intimate relationships or over
appropriate policies for strategic arms limitations between geopolitical superpowers. Each participant in an argument advances claims about how
reality should be interpreted, about what a situation or an act *means*, and
why that existential claim should be accepted by others. But if argument
exists in a context characterized by disagreement, it also presumes the possibility for arriving at a shared perception of reality. That is, some motivation exists on the part of each participant to want to *understand*, to arrive at
some meaning about the experience, act, or situation that makes sense
to those involved. If participants believe the potential for agreement at
some level is nonexistent, then little motivation exists to continue that
interaction.

Understanding in this instance means much more than mere comprehension of symbols being used to transmit perceptions about how reality is or
how it should be. Rather, understanding includes an awareness and examination of the modes of thought which lead to attribution of meaning as
well as the attempts to attribute meaning to a newly experienced phenomenon or interpretation of reality. It is, I believe, this process that is consistent
with Black's discussion of criticism as "the investigation and appraisal of

[1] For a discussion of recent conceptualizations of argument, see the introductory essay in
this volume.

the activities and products of man" which "seeks as its end the understanding of man himself" (1978, 9). The process of criticism and its final product, the critique, Black wrote, "represents a particular mind at work on an object: apprehending it, examining it, coming to understand it, placing it into history" (xiv). Criticism as a way of knowing involves more than the interaction between individual and phenomenon. Instead, it involves a conscious awareness of the reasons, the motivations, for the meanings arrived at. Placing an argument in history involves an understanding of both the context from which the phenomenon emerged and the context in which it is encountered—and from which, for the critic, argument derives its current meaning.

To interact with is not the same as to engage critically, however. Interaction may be essentially immediate as one interprets and attributes meanings spontaneously without engaging in the self-reflection that permits an exploration of the reasons why these interpretations are made. To engage critically, on the other hand, is to impose a distance between the interpreter and the artifact or phenomenon and, crucially, to become aware consciously of the ways in which meanings were attributed. This conscious awareness of the searching for understanding and attribution of meaning is characteristic of the "critical stance."

This essay contends that adoption of the critical stance can be a valuable means for arriving at a deeper, richer understanding of the existential claims advanced in argument and of the argumentative process. Whether by the "naive" social actor or the "learned" scholar, use of this critical stance provides an understanding based on the interaction of the individual with the new, or the alien, *and* the conscious awareness of how one intends the world. Many specific modes for structuring and explaining the interaction with the phenomenon have been advanced in speech communication and argumentation studies—dramatism, neo-Aristotelianism, structuralism, and others. While any of these may lead to important insights in understanding any particular phenomenon, this essay is more concerned with exploring what it means to engage in the "critical stance" and in its application to the study of argument. A similar distinction was made by Hoy: "A discussion of *method* involves discussion of how to read a book or debate about the merits of different 'approaches.' A discussion of *methodology*, on the other hand, must be more abstract and philosophical; it belongs at the level of the theory of knowledge and understanding" (1978, 102). This essay, then, will consider in more detail methodological concerns about what it involves to adopt the critical stance, how that stance may be applied to argumentation studies, and, finally, what the critical stance suggests for work developing in argumentation fields.

Hermeneutics and the Critical Stance

The vision presented here of what it means to adopt the critical stance is borrowed extensively from writings in hermeneutics, especially the views of Hans-Georg Gadamer (1975; 1976; 1980). The term "hermeneutic" draws its roots from classical Greek and refers to the Delphic priest (*hermeios*) or to the god Hermes (*Hermeneuein* and *hermeneia*). Hermes was the god who transmitted knowledge beyond human understanding to mortals by translating it into language and other forms they could comprehend. Hermes was, thus, the creator of language and writing, tools by which humans seek and convey knowledge (Palmer, 1969). Palmer extended the explanation:

> This mediating and message-bringing process of "coming to understand" associated with Hermes is implicit in all of the three basic directions of meaning of *hermeneuein* and *hermeneia* in ancient usage. These three directions, using the verb form (*hermeneuein*) for purposes of example, are (1) *to express* aloud in words, that is, "to say"; (2) *to explain*, as in explaining a situation; and (3) *to translate*, as in the translation of a foreign tongue. All three meanings may be expressed by the English verb "to interpret," yet each constitutes an independent and significant meaning of interpretation. Interpretation, then, can refer to three rather different matters: an oral recitation, a reasonable explanation, and a translation from another language. . . . Yet one may note that the foundational "hermes process" is at work: in all three cases, something foreign, strange, separated in time, space or experience is made familiar, present, comprehensible; something requiring representation, explanation, or translation is somehow "brought to understanding"—is interpreted [13–14].

Hermeneutics is understood most commonly to relate to biblical exegesis or to literary interpretation. As used in this essay, however, hermeneutics refers to the philosophical investigations by which human beings are able to bridge the "gap between the familiar world in which we stand and the strange meaning that resists assimilation into the horizons of our world" (Linge, 1976, xii). As such, the critical stance becomes hermeneutical and reflects upon the conscious process by which new and unexplained phenomena are given understanding. This means that focus is not on the explanation of the unexplained only, but on the function of existing, familiar constructs in contributing to that explanation as well.

Focus on the familiar brings to conscious awareness the "foresight" or "preunderstanding" essential to any possibility for further understanding. It is impossible to begin any investigation of an alien phenomenon without some framework of knowledge from which to proceed. That framework, however, may function in either a *dogmatic* or *pragmatic* way: Functioning dogmatically, existing constructs exert such influence on interpretations of experience that those experiences serve only to reaffirm and to reify existing views of reality. The framework, in other words, leads the interpreter to discover only what he or she is already capable of understanding. When existing constructs function pragmatically, however, they become a way "into" the event, a starting point from which a genuine dialogue between the interpreter's existing forms of understanding and the phenomenon itself may commence. Rather than confirming preexistent conceptualizations of reality, such a dialogue may well force those conceptualizations to adapt and to create new explanations and perceptions of reality.

This relation between phenomenon and preunderstanding—which essentially contends that one cannot understand a particular without some awareness of the totality, and that, correspondingly, one cannot understand the totality without some awareness of the particular—is what is called the "critical" or "hermeneutical" circle (Hoy, 1978; Bleicher, 1980; Palmer, 1969; Murray, 1975). Attempting to understand the individual phenomenon, then, will fail inevitably unless one is able to inquire into the context from which the phenomenon itself emerges. In the instance of argument, analysis would involve not only an attempt to understand the language and subject matter of the argument itself but also the social grounding in which it occurred and the preunderstanding of the argument's creator. At the same time, in order to test one's understanding of the phenomenon against other possible interpretations, one must submit his or her own preunderstanding to conscious scrutiny in dialogue.

Gadamer's philosophical hermeneutics rests upon two fundamental attributes of understanding: *linguisticality* and *historicity*. Language, for Gadamer, is essential for any form of understanding to exist between human beings: "For two people to be able to understand each other in conversation . . . mastery of the language is a necessary pre-condition. Every conversation automatically presupposes that the two speakers speak the same language. Only when it is possible for two people to make themselves understood through language by talking together can the problem of understanding and agreement be even raised" (1975, 347). Whether in conversation (as when individuals conduct arguments face-to-face) or whether arguments are conducted through texts and other linguistic artifacts such as recordings, commonality of language between the two participants is essential. Even the interaction of an individual with the text is described by Gadamer as a "conversation" in which the object, or content, of the text finds meaningful expression through the interpreter; that expression, further, is possible only to the extent that a language is shared.

Language is also crucial for understanding because of the relationship between thinking and speaking:

> The hermeneutical phenomenon proves to be a special case of the general relationship between thinking and speaking, the mysterious intimacy of which is bound up with the way speech is contained, in a hidden way, in thinking. Interpretation, like conversation, is a closed circle within the dialectic of question and answer. It is a genuine historical life-situation that takes place in the medium of language and that, also in the case of the interpretation of texts, we can call a conversation. The linguistic quality of understanding is the concretion of effective-historical consciousness [Gadamer, 1975, 351].

That is, language is necessary as a transmitter of the cultural tradition within which each individual exists. At the same time, that cultural tradition or historical consciousness can exist only as a function of language.

The second pillar of Gadamer's hermeneutics, historicity, exists in a complex interaction with language and emphasizes that each instance of human action can be understood only temporally. The bulk of Gadamer's discussion of historicity concentrates upon understanding of texts. He observed that each age has to "understand a transmitted text in its own way" and that the meaning of a text for any individual interpreter "does not depend on the contingencies of the author and whom he originally wrote for" (1975, 263). Even here, however, in order to understand the significance of a text for one's own time, it is necessary to discover the *horizon* within which the text was produced initially. A horizon is "the range of vision that includes everything that can be seen from a particular vantage point" (1975, 269). It is, of course, impossible ever to reconstruct a horizon from the past because of the impossibility of removing the interpreter from his or her own horizon of contemporaneous existence. It is possible, however, to expand the interpreter's horizon to include those from the past; this expansion produces a "fusion" of the two horizons such that a broader, overarching horizon is brought into consciousness. The importance of this was explained by Hoy:

> On the one hand, fusion involves a broadening of the present horizon—as historical study is often said to dispel certain prejudices and induce tolerance. On the other, it also involves a focusing of the past horizon in such a way that other things which may have been mere adumbrations become definite factors in that horizon—perhaps because of subsequent occurrences—while other factors disappear—perhaps because certain events failed to take place [1978, 96–97].

The past, then, may be understood only through the present, which is itself conditioned historically. Additionally, one may anticipate the future, but again only through the prejudices of the present. In this sense, *all* existence and understanding is mediated historically and linguistically. One value of texts is that they function as means by which individuals—audience, source, or critic—may seek to share the horizons and interpretations of meaning from the past and into the future.

In striving for an understanding of horizons, however, one must remember that it is through the dialogue with the phenomenon or artifact that the interpretation, and hence, the fusion of horizons, occurs. Dialogue can occur only through preunderstanding by the participants in a conversation and includes not only the expectations they have about the other participant, but about the subject matter as well. This focus on subject matter and other "textual" properties is essential to combat the potential dogmatism of an interpreter's preunderstanding and to counter extreme subjectivism. In Booth's terms, concentration on the text provides a "mooring" for the critic that keeps the critical endeavor focused and prevents the development of interpretations that are not uniquely appropriate for understanding a particular phenomenon (1979, 225).

This view, however, stops far short of claiming that the text *controls* the interpretation. To grant such a claim would create the potential for one preeminent interpretation and grant an objectivity of meaning to the text it cannot acquire in a world of intersubjectively created meanings. What must be remembered is that each interpretation is a fusion of horizons, and that one of those belongs to an individual critic, functioning within his or her own preunderstanding and tradition. Each text exists only in relation to the interpreter; at the same time, the text participates in the interpretation by permitting the critic to test preunderstandings and to move, in most instances, toward a different, frequently richer, understanding. As Michael Leff explained,

The act of interpretation mediates between the experience of the critic and the forms of experience expressed in the text. To perform this act successfully, critics must vibrate what they see in the text against their own expectations and predilections. What critics are trained to look for and what they see interact in creative tension; the two elements blend and separate, progressively changing as altered conceptions of the one reshape the configuration of the other [1980, 345].

The dialogue, however, cannot be confined to the text as presented but must also engage the horizon from which it emerged. Each text serves as an asserted answer to some question assumed to exist in the background. The task of interpretation is to discover what meanings, or answers, the text provided for the horizon within which it was created and what meaning it has for another horizon in which quite different questions, hence answers, may be lurking. The latter horizon is that of the present and it is from this perspective that one enters into the critical circle to answer, "What does it mean?" (Palmer, 234–235).

The value of adopting a critical stance toward traditional perspectives of argument—what has become labeled increasingly as argument$_1$—seems clear. Such arguments, viewed as products and encountered by critics in what must surely be treated as texts, exist in public pronouncements and assume the form of documents, recordings, and so on. As do all arguments, they exist in a contingent world in which meaning cannot be separated from context, but they assume a greater immanence of textual authority than do many ordinary conversations. In discovering the horizons from which such arguments emerged, one may discover how they addressed both actual and potential consciousness. Documents from the past constitute the shared language by which interpreters may enter into the horizons of previous generations, however imperfectly, and may better understand the traditions within which individuals now exist. It is in this sense that one may discover how arguments were used to address questions of actual consciousness at the time of first expression, and how those arguments addressed issues of potential consciousness by assessing the meaning such arguments have for contemporary critics and audiences (Hyde and Smith, 1979).[2]

[2] Hyde and Smith acknowledge the influence of Lucien Goldman's book, *Cultural Creation in Modern Society*, translated by Bart Drake (St. Louis: Telos, 1976), for their interpretation of actual and potential consciousness. Actual consciousness, for Hyde and Smith, is "a result of cultural heritage, religion, life experience, political attitude, and popular art. Actual consciousness would include contemporary values as applied to contemporary situations." Potential consciousness is "determined by the maximum possible awareness of an audience, the impact of the society's understanding of its historic destiny, and that society's highest achievement in the arts" (358).

Two recent examples of critical analysis of texts are provided by Zarefsky. The first considered "The Great Society as a Rhetorical Proposition" (1979) and the second examined explanations offered by historians of factors contributing to the Civil War (1980a). In each, Zarefsky concentrated on textual material as the means for engaging in dialogue and for inquiring into the horizons from which the texts were derived. At this point, such critical analyses do not seem to differ greatly from many other critical studies published in scholarly books and journals. What does strike one as important and noteworthy in each instance, however, is the clear consideration Zarefsky displays of the preunderstanding he brings to texts under investigation. The preunderstanding in each instance is that such communications make sense *as arguments* and that the argumentative perspective is something the critic brings to the initial encounter with text. Zarefsky stated, for example, that "When we choose to impose the construct of 'argument' on the communication, we are saying that we can make sense of it by viewing it as 'reason giving' by people as justification for acts, beliefs, attitudes, and values" (1980b, 234). He went on to illustrate the specific application of that preunderstanding and its subsequent influence upon the critical questions answered:

> Now I do not contend that Johnson necessarily saw himself either as *making* arguments to justify his proposals [for a Great Society] or as *having* arguments with his opponents. Nor do I contend that the communication I examined can be designated as argument as thereby distinguished from other types of communication. Rather, it is I, the critic, who have chosen to construe Johnson's behavior as argument, in the belief that I could thereby better understand, explain, and predict the behavior investigated [1980b, 235].

The preunderstanding that led Zarefsky to interact with the texts of transcripts and documents concerning the Great Society as argument need not preclude other critics from generating interpretations that hear Johnson's utterances as pleas, promises, supplications, or whatever; each interpretation will emerge from the genuine fusion of horizons contained in and containing the text and individual critic. What is important, however, is that Johnson's utterances had to exhibit characteristics that made it possible for Zarefsky's preunderstanding to maintain itself within the dialogue. That is, textual elements had to confirm, or to make plausible, Zarefsky's interpretation of the text as argument. In paradigmatic cases of argument as text, a critic would expect to discover "a linguistically explicable claim" and "one or more overtly expressed reasons which are linguistically explicit" (O'Keefe, chap. one). These linguistically explicable reasons are what Zarefsky found in Johnson's acts and served to justify the President's claim for a reality that encompassed a "Great Society."

Application of hermeneutics, or the critical stance, may be obvious in attempting to discover what argumentative *texts* may mean, but the critical stance seems equally profitable in seeking to understand argument as *interaction in process*, or argument$_2$. After all, conversation provides the dominating metaphor for Gadamer's explanation of textual interpretation, and he has maintained that the hermeneutical problem of understanding is universal, reaching "into all the contexts that determine and condition the linguisticality of the human experience of the world" (1976, 19). A "blurring" of the traditional genres of humanistic studies and the social sciences also seems to support the value of "interpretive explanations" as increasing numbers of scholars, seeking to understand human behavior, spend their time "looking less for the sort of thing that connects planets and pendulums and more for the sort that connects chrysanthemums and swords" (Geertz, 1980, 165).

If Gadamer has moved legitimately to explain textual interpretation by extending the analogy from conversation, might it not be equally beneficial to take the analogy of textual interpretation back into an explanation of social action? Paul Ricoeur seemed to provide support for such an extension when he discussed the concept of *inscription*. Ricoeur made a distinction between speaking, "an event that appears and disappears," and writing, "a means of inscribing the content of speaking, of remembering" (1973, 93). It would seem that whether the saying is inscribed in writing or in some other form—videotape, for example—is irrelevant. What is important is that the actual event, the saying or speaking or arguing, qua event, is necessarily ephemeral. But the *meaning* of the event need not be. By its existence, however fleeting that existence may have been, something of the event's meaning will have entered into the tradition; that meaning, however, can be remembered, studied, and perhaps assume greater significance if it is inscribed or fixed in some manner. Just as ritual and icon are a way of fixing meanings and their importance into tradition, so, too, may the *textualizing of action* serve that purpose. Thus, even though an event as act or argument passes inevitably into history, a meaning of that act can be retained.

Ricoeur granted that certain aspects of meaning would be lost, or at least captured in diminished form, through inscription, but he relied upon speech-act theory to explain the utility of his approach. A speech act is composed of three levels: the locutionary or propositional act, which manifests itself in a sentence; the illocutionary act, or force of the act, which is also expressed in grammatical paradigms; and the perlocutionary action, or the doing of the act. Ricoeur argued that, to a great extent, each of these could be exteriorized into inscription, although perlocution less so than the other two.[3] Further, all action could be exteriorized by analogy:

> My claim is that action itself, action as meaningful, may become an object of science, without losing its character of meaningfulness, by virtue of a kind of objectification similar to the fixation which occurs in writing. By this objectification, action is no longer a transaction to which the discourse of action would still belong. It constitutes a delineated pattern which has to be interpreted according to its inner connections.
>
> This objectification is made *possible* by some inner traits of the action which are similar to the structure of the speech act and which make "doing" a kind of utterance. In the same way fixation by writing is made possible by a dialectic of intentional exteriorization inherent in the speech-act itself, a similar dialectic within the process of transaction prepares the detachment of *meaning* of the action from the *event* of the action [1973, 98–99].

Through such inscription and subsequent interpretation, one may adopt the critical stance toward human action in general and, it seems, toward argument as process in particular. Again, such a stance seems beneficial for the individual engaged in ordinary argument and for the scholar seeking to understand ways in which individuals construe meanings.

[3] Ricoeur's analysis is: "The locutionary act exteriorizes itself in the sentence. The sentence can be identified and reidentified as being the same sentence. A sentence becomes an enunciation (*Aus-sage*) and thus is transferred to others as being such and such a sentence with such and such a meaning [an inscription]. But the illocutionary act can also be exteriorized in grammatical paradigms (indicative, imperative, and subjunctive modes, and other procedures expressive of illocutionary force) which permit its identification and reidentification. Certainly in spoken discourse, the illocutionary force leans upon mimicry and gestural elements and upon nonarticulated aspects of discourse. . . . In this sense, the illocutionary force is less completely inscribed in grammar than is the propositional meaning. In every case, its inscription in a syntactic articulation is itself gathered up in specific paradigms which in principle make possible fixation by writing. Without a doubt we must concede that the perlocutionary act is the least inscribable aspect of discourse and that by preference it characterizes spoken langauge. But the perlocutionary action is precisely what is the least discursive in discourse. It is the discourse as stimulus. It acts, not by my interlocutor's recognition of my intention, but energetically, by direct influence upon the emotions and the affective dispositions. Thus, the propositional act, the illocutionary force, and the perlocutionary action are apt, in decreasing order, for the intentional exteriorization which makes inscription in writing possible" (94). Continuing his explanation, Ricoeur claimed that the inner traits of action in general are similar to those of the speech act, and that "In the same way fixation is made possible by a dialectic of intentional exteriorization inherent in the speech-act itself, a similar dialectic within the process of transaction prepares the detachment of the *meaning* of the action from the *event* of the action" (98–99). Also see Balthrop (1980) for a discussion of the importance of discursive form to the study of argument.

Willard's research indicates the potential of this critical stance for investigative argument as process. Granting that actors are not likely to forsake argumentative positions, Willard noted that through the interaction "actors may arrive at clear understandings of the opposing perspective and a correspondingly clear understanding of the differences which divide them" (1979, 217). It may be that individuals engaged in ordinary argument practice a form of inscription during the course of the argument. Actors might "inscribe" the meaning of an utterance—either their own or that of another participant—and commit it to memory, recalling that meaning as required during the course of the interaction. It is even possible that such inscription becomes part of a preunderstanding, in a limited way, from which individuals interpret future utterances in the argumentative process. This need not mean necessarily that individuals involved in the heat of argument function from a critical stance; rather, it indicates that at least the potential for actors to do so exists. Inscription would, in fact, seem a prerequisite for any sort of critical action or reflection to occur.[4]

Efforts of scholars to explore the ways in which individual actors use arguments and how they construe them during such interactions also seems well suited to the critical stance. Even in those instances where the researcher relies on ethnomethodological approaches, some form of inscription seems essential for the kind of extensive and continued examination required. Without inscriptions of some sort, whether informal notes or more complete forms manifest in recordings and transcripts, scholars seem susceptible to the vagaries of memory or of lapsing into the subjectivism Gadamer believed could be checked only through some concentration on textual properties or content. Willard, for instance, has relied extensively

---

[4] A process similar to that speculated about here for conversation and argument as process is described by Wolfgang Iser (1974): ". . . each intentional sentence correlative [the world presented through that particular sentence] opens up a particular horizon, which is modified, if not completely changed, by succeeding sentences. While these expectations arouse interest in what is to come, the subsequent modification of them will also have a retrospective effect on what has already been read. This may now take on a different significance from that which it had at the moment of reading.

"Whatever we have read sinks into our memory and is foreshortened. It may later be evoked again and set against a different background with the result that the reader is enabled to develop hitherto unforeseeable connections. The memory evoked, however, can never reassume its original shape, for this would mean that memory and perception were identical, which is manifestly not so. The new background brings to light new aspects of what we had committed to memory; conversely these, in turn, shed their light on the new background, thus arousing more complex anticipations. Thus, the reader, in establishing these interrelations between past, present and future, actually causes the text to reveal its potential multiplicity of connections" (278).

upon these transcriptions in his investigations of the ways in which actors make their "processes of reasoning explicit" (1979, 217).[5] Other scholars seem to provide further support for this stance in investigating the process of human behavior. Geertz argued generally that there exists "great virtue of the extension of the notion of text beyond things written on paper" (1980, 175–176) and Clark and Delia proposed investigations similar to "genre criticism" to "help uncover both the lines of inference and communication strategies" (1979, 203).[6]

Limitations to critical analysis of texts and textualizations of behavior do exist, of course, and such analysis cannot reveal all possible meanings or any one correct interpretation. The text does not acquire an immanence existing independent of the horizons from which it emerged or of those within which the critic functions. A text, then, even in the broadest of interpretations, does not contain all meanings. As Gadamer noted,

> Linguistic expressions, when they are what they can be, are not simply inexact and in need of refinement, but rather, of necessity, they always fall short of what they evoke and communicate. For in speaking there is always implied a meaning that is imposed on the vehicle of expression, that only functions as a meaning behind the meaning and that in fact could be said to lose its meaning when raised to the level of what is actually expressed [1976, 88].

Even though linguistic utterances are inherently incomplete as a representation of meaning, it is nevertheless through acceptance of the critical stance that individuals may begin to inquire about these hidden meanings and to make them understandable to oneself and to others. Hermeneutical investigation leads toward a fusion of horizons, necessary for understanding, *through* existence of the text. The text functions, as it were, as a means by which one grasps the possibility for translating meanings from one horizon into another; it is the text which functions as the shared linguistic

[5] See Willard, 1980b. In his description of research, Willard gives examples of ordinary argument and the ways actors construe meanings. In virtually every instance, he relies upon some form of transcription. In footnote 13, Willard states "I observed and hand wrote this exchange at Logan International Airport, Boston, 1978" (284).

[6] This essay also provides an example of research that gives further credence to Ricoeur's concept of a text-analogue and the way in which illocutionary acts are manifested in syntactical relations: "For instance, Ervin-Tripp has specified five forms an imperative may take: (1) interrogative ('Gotta match'), (2) imperative ('Gimme a match'), (3) imbedded imperative ('Could you gimme me [sic] a match'), (4) statement of need or desire ('I need a match'), and (5) statement of external condition ('There aren't any matches here'). . . . It should be possible to begin with alternative modes of expressing a speech act, and to specify the kinds of inferences a message recipient is likely to make from each" (203).

system and provides the potential and justification for presumed agreement in argumentative discourse.

The Critical Stance, Intersubjectivity, and Fields of Argument

If the purpose of criticism is to enhance the understanding of humankind, then the critic assumes responsibilities that go far beyond the interpretation of texts and behaviors for his or her own edification. Those arguments and instances of arguing that have meaning for individual critics are also likely to have meaning for others who happen to share the critic's *communitas*. If, through interpretation, the critic arrives at an understanding, one has the obligation as a member of a particular community to share that understanding and to promote the potentiality of a future "as it should be" which encourages the development of institutions and actions promoting the dignity of humanity and discourages those denigrating that dignity. It was in this vein, I think, that Marie Hochmuth Nichols believed that the critic's "place should be in the vanguard, not in the rear—wise-after- the-fact. He should be ready to alert a people, to warn that devices of exploitation are being exercised, by what skillful manipulations of motives men are being directed to or dissuaded from courses of action" (1955, 17). The critic, then, becomes an active participant in the creation of rhetorical, hence social, realities whether those realities focus on the issues about which humans argue or the explanations of processes by which humans argue.

In another sense, perhaps more fundamental, striving for more complete and richer understandings also demands that the critic engage in public action; that is, the critic must make interpretations accessible to other critics and would-be critics as a means for testing interpretations. Each interpretation is, of necessity, partial and constrained by the horizons encompassing the critic's own "interestedness" and historicity. Just as the adequacy of a critic's preunderstanding is tested only through dialogue with the text itself, so too can the arrived-at interpretation be tested only through a dialectic with other interpretations. Through this dialectic one approaches a kind of "truth" about an interpretation and, subsequently, that critic's construal of reality. That truth, however, is "closely connected to (although it can never be entirely reduced to) 'success'—that is, intersubjective agreement on the usefulness of the interpretations and their assumptions" (Hoy, 1978, 115; also see Brummett, 1976, 35). Most emphatically, this does not mean that there exists, or is even likely to exist, one correct interpretation of any text or text-analogue insofar as the kinds of questions which bring forth the critical assertion of understanding will demand different methods of interpretation and different emphases of horizons. Still, each interpretation, as the product of an honest dialogue with text, will make existential claims about what that text "means" in that particular context. The pragmatic usefulness of that interpretation will be indicated by the "scope, precision, and coherence of the insights that it yields" for that community (Booth, 1979, 4–5).

Yet, in examining the necessity for public statements about claims for understanding a further question arises: How can one make determinations about an interpretation's "scope, precision, and coherence?" Zarefsky provided a useful starting point when he stated that the "critic must establish that his or her interpretation is a plausible one—that is, one which deserves to be taken seriously" (1980c, 4). This statement of plausibility rests initially on the preunderstanding that a critic brings to the text and from which one begins the dialogue and on the conscious awareness by the critic as to the foundations and implications of that preunderstanding. Davis explained the importance of that awareness when he wrote

> The choice of one's modes of thought is grounded in the conceptual manifestation of one's project. To attain self-knowledge and the possibility of self-criticism each of us has to know, in depth and from as many angles as we can, the reasons why a given way of thinking carries conviction for us, as well as the reasons why other ways of thinking strike us as fundamentally unsound, even abhorrent [1978, 115–116].

That is, each critic must seek to understand as completely as practicable the horizon from which and within which he or she operates.

Once the critic is aware of the modes of thought and the horizons employed, the next test for plausibility rests within the text or text-analogue itself. As indicated previously, it is not sufficient for the critic to bring a certain perspective to the phenomenon and then to impose that perspective upon it. Rather, the critic must find those elements of linguistic expression shared by others within the community that lend support to the interpretation advanced. It is in this sense that the critic engages in dialogue with the text to arrive at a transcendent understanding.

The plausibility of an interpretation must also be discernible by others as well. The critic functions as a member of a particular public, or field, if one may. As such, he or she shares to greater or lesser degrees the language forms, beliefs, values, institutions and so on that generate common "sys-

tems of thought, shared standards for communication, and—quite by definition—shared meanings or ways of looking at and explaining phenomena"
(Willard, 1980a, 387).[7] This means that the critic's understanding must be
one others within the field of shared orientations can follow, can *understand*.
It means that others within that community must be able to engage in their
own hermeneutic experience with the text, explained by the interpretation,
through the interpretation and that the hermeneutic experience extends to
the interpretation itself as a text. For the interpretation to contribute to a
construction of reality, its audiences must then find within that interpretation some usefulness in answering the question "What does it mean?"

Another criterion for evaluating the plausibility of a critic's interpretation, although linked closely to those preceding, is that the critic must
assume some responsibility for justifying the ultimate meaning attributed
to some phenomenon to the exclusion of others. In this regard, the critic
goes "beyond" the text and explores not only why the text has taken the
form it has assumed but also why the critic's final epistemological claim is
selected in place of others. Again, this need not mean that other interpretations or epistemic claims about phenomena are inadequate or inappropriate—they may indeed be justified in terms of the horizons another critic
brings to the text or text-analogue. Rather, the coherence and strength of
any particular interpretation must be examined in terms of the questions
generating the dialectic. That is, each critical stance must be evaluated in
terms of its own internal dynamic.

The internal dynamic in question is that of the dialogue between the
critic's conscious awareness of preunderstanding and the text. A crucial part
of this dialogue is an examination of the critic's modes of thought and of the
implications of those modes for the interpretation that results from the
dialogue. The critic thus assumes the responsibility for explicating as
clearly as possible the horizons and assumptions which have influenced the
interpretation. Through one's hermeneutical inquiry with the interpretation one may then explore the consistency and honesty with which the critic
has conducted the dialogue with text. Identification and testing of assump-

[7] Others share the view that communities exist and their descriptions are similar to
Willard's although they do not specifically refer to "fields." McKerrow envisioned "argument communities" (1980); Bitzer described "public knowledge" (1978); Booth observed
that, in order for authors to be understood, "they had to obey the communal norms of their
language" (1979, 187); and, perhaps most explicit of all, Murray noted that "the author who
speaks and the critic who interprets must in some sense belong to the same world, the same
linguistic community" (1975, 73).

tions and examination of textual properties and horizons becomes one way of evaluating and, hence, of selecting between competing interpretations of phenomena (Hoy, 1978, 130).[8]

To evaluate critical interpretations on the basis of plausibility is to accept a kind of critical pluralism; each phenomenon may be approached through a variety of criticisms, each advancing plausible explanations for the epistemological vision contained within. Such pluralism is inevitable since each critic may ask different questions, may accept as "fact" certain things others may see as conjecture only, and may as a consequence arrive at different interpretations through different methods. Such pluralism is important if for no other reason than to reinforce the partiality and prejudices of one's own interpretation. As Booth commented,

> An active pluralism will reconstitute all such controversies [over critical methods]. We tell ourselves: Since any one mode [or method] will inevitably leave out, ignore, or distort the danda revealed by other modes, I *must* respect many modes if I am not to reduce the wonderful variety of human achievement . . . to the monotony of perceptions dictated by one particular mode [1979, 247–248].

It is through such pluralism, through the dialogue of interpretations, that one may discover the richness of understanding contained within human action and tradition. To the extent each interpretation is a unique and powerful explanation with pragmatic value to the community, it enters into the horizons of the text, the critic, and the community.

Even though text creators and interpreters are usually members of a shared community or field and are similar in many respects, it is important to remember that each still exists within the community *as an individual* with unique experiences and horizons. From those horizons one experiences a particular text; one's own interestedness leads to the questions one asks, to the preunderstanding from which one approaches an argument, and to the meaning the text has for an individual. In this regard, each critical endeavor is unique.

At the same time, despite individual intuition and insight that generate new and unique possibilities for understanding, standards of "correctness" or of "error", of acceptance or rejection, are forged ultimately within the crucible of community. So long as an individual functions within a given

---

[8] Presenting the standards by which a criticism was derived is not unique to hermeneutical investigation; rather, it has long been recognized by the most insightful of critics that they have a responsibility to reveal to the reader the critic's biases (Booth, 1979, 27; Campbell, 1972, 27).

field, he or she incorporates the tradition of that field into every act of understanding. Further, if the critic's interpretations are to have pragmatic value, they must in some way explain, assert, and justify a meaning for others within the community. Each critic through his or her interpretations enters into a fusion of horizons that leads to an enriched understanding; so, too, do those interpretations enter into a hermeneutical relation with others in a community to create a further fusion of horizons that permits others to share the critic's insights into his or her tradition—hence into their own. The hermeneutic circle emerges once again: each individual contributing to the meaning of community, yet each understandable only through community. It is toward that interpenetration of each and to a better understanding of both that the critical stance may contribute.

In addition to promoting *intra*field understanding, it seems plausible that adoption of the critical stance becomes an important means for increasing potential for agreement over *inter*field arguments. If each community or field employs certain assumptions, has unique ways of thinking, and construes meanings about phenomena in certain ways, it is likely that great misunderstandings will occur when disparate fields are forced into argumentative positions. Willard has claimed, for instance, that "interfield disputes are sometimes intractable if field actors back into *intuitive* defenses of their standards" (chap. 2). It would appear that actors in this situation are functioning within the natural attitude and not in one that is reflective or critical.[9] That is, the critical stance operates to counter this retreat back into intuitionism and to bring the preunderstandings within which intuition rests into conscious awareness and into dialectic relief. This does not

[9] The view of natural attitude here is that presented by Swanson (1977), and assumes "that (1) the world is comprised of persons, objects, and events having ontological status as 'real' or objective; (2) the world is intersubjective, presenting itself as essentially the same to all persons; and (3) human experience can produce factual or 'accurate' knowledge of the objective world" (209). One may adopt, within this attitude, either the mundane stance ("our experience of the world produces objective knowledge, purely factual understanding uncontaminated by our interpretation or creation of it") or the critical (which "views with skepticism some particular facet or dimension of experience . . . while regarding the wide remainder of experience as indubitable") (209). In contrast, Swanson posited the "reflective attitude" in which one "set[s] aside questions of the existence of the world. In so doing, attention is focused on that which remains—experience itself" (210). The reflective attitude, Swanson continued, "is required if we are to successfully identify those shared assumptions about the nature, origin, and limits of knowledge which define the field of rhetorical criticism" (210).

Swanson's view seems to see the critic as rooted in method, in the particular approaches individual critics use in interpretation. But in the methodological approach to criticism, one moves closer to Swanson's reflective attitude.

mean that all interfield disputes can be resolved or transcended, but critical awareness and investigation does seem to promote the possibility of such resolution.

In his companion essay on argumentative fields Willard advances the proposition that fields cannot be equated with their documents and that texts are unsure records of situated talk. Insofar as this analysis goes, it is correct. In another vein, however, as text can provide the possibility for a shared language permitting a fusion of horizons *within* a particular field, it also seems possible that a text, insofar as it is translatable, offers the potential for creating a shared linguistic expression of social reality such that a critic can begin to enter into a fusion of horizons or traditions that *transcend* interfield divisions. Through a field's texts, incomplete though they may be, the critic can begin to enter into a dialogue with the meanings contained within and lurking behind the text; that is, a dialogue with the assumptions and orientations of the field constituting the text's horizon. As Gadamer noted when discussing translation of conversation in different languages,

> the linguistic process by means of which a conversation in two different languages is made possible through translation is especially informative. Here the translator must translate the meaning to be understood into the context in which the other speaker lives. This does not, of course, mean that he is at liberty to falsify the meaning of what the other person says. Rather, the meaning must be preserved, but since it must be understood within a new linguistic world, it must be expressed within it in a new way. Thus every translation is at the same time an interpretation [1975, 346].

Any interpretation inevitably involves a heightening of certain elements and a diminishing of others according to the preunderstandings the translator brings to the interaction. However, Gadamer's concern with the subject of a conversation works to circumscribe the boundaries within which the translator may function. In fact, it is the translator's success in bringing into another language the "object that the text points to" (Gadamer, 1975, 349) that makes it possible for one field to begin to understand another. The translator or interpreter thus brings the meaning or content of some act within another linguistic field into a form his or her own field can understand. The translator becomes a kind of surrogate Hermes.

Adoption of the critical stance and subsequent public expression of resulting interpretations may well promote the possibility of incorporating elements from one field into another. Recognition of the social construction of reality and of the corresponding lack of epistemological or ontological a prioris may be enhanced by the critical stance. Further, it may bring a field's—even a culture's—own preunderstandings into conscious awareness and act to reduce the dogmatic power of such prejudices. This does not mean that all interfield disputes can be resolved or transcended, but critical awareness and investigation do seem to promote the possibility of such resolutions. It appears, indeed, that any efforts to understand assumptions and orientations of another field require adoption of the critical stance. Even if such orientations are rejected, to be able to state that one "understands" requires an entering, however incomplete, into the traditions of that field. It seems plausible that one way of entering that tradition is through the fusion of horizons made possible through interpretation of a field's texts or text-analogues.

This essay has argued that the critical stance is a legitimate and important perspective from which one who seeks to understand more completely argument—as product or process—may commence the journey. This seems so for those inhabiting social and interpersonal communities who argue over issues and relationships as "naive" actors as well as that more limited community of scholars who seek to know what argument "means" from a theoretical standpoint. Exploration of the critical stance has been directed at methodological issues rather than at specific critical methods, schools, or approaches. The view presented here acknowledges that different interpretations will emerge depending upon what it is that a critic seeks to understand. Such critical diversity, however, is not cause for alarm. Instead, such diversity is testimony to the continued vitality of human life. Each criticism with pragmatic value opens up additional horizons to each person within the community addressed, and, at the same time, calls forth a subsequent critical response. As Wayne Booth commented about a "formulation that Abrams borrowed from F. R. Leavis,"

> the most we can hope for, when we make our statement, is not a simple "yes" in reply. Rather, we should expect—and if we are really inquiring should in fact desire—the reply: "Yes, but. . . ." Yet no second speaker can sincerely say, "Yes, but . . ." without acknowledging the validity of the first voice. My *yes* (unless it is simply a polite lie) grants you your right to critical life; the *but* requests a similar grant in return [1979, 197].

This willingness to utter and to hear the genuine "Yes, but . . ." is at the heart of a critical pluralism that inspired Booth's most recent book. Further, this plurality of critical method, grounded on a shared methodology, enriches a community's understanding of self and encourages its vitality. As Booth concluded, "even after I have begun to speak what I mistakenly call '*my own* critical truth,' my continued vitality as a thinking critic rather than a phonograph record depends on my continuing capacity to take other voices into account. My life, indistinguishable from the life of my critical tribe, requires that my thought be an exchange among 'selves' rather than a mere search for ways to impose what I already know" (1979, 222–223).

Acceptance of critical pluralism and the consequent extension of such an acceptance into a community has profound implications. Questions about "What does it mean?" are likely to emerge in greater number and with greater intensity at times of uncertainty and when differing interpretations of context validate different interpretations of truth and action (Brummett, 1976, 35). A retreat into intuitionism and unquestioned acceptance of one's preunderstanding, whether personal or cultural, closes off the potential for further understanding. Alternatively, as Linge commented, "Collision with other's horizons make us aware of assumptions so deep-seated that they would otherwise remain unnoticed. This awareness of our own historicity and finitude—our consciousness of effective history—brings with it an openness to new possibilities that is the precondition of genuine under-standing" (Gadamer, 1976, xx–xxi). It is in this regard that the potential for hermeneutical investigation, for adopting the critical stance, of argu-ment holds such promise and offers the potential for continued evolution of becoming rather than a stultified form of being.

DALE HAMPLE

[11]   Modeling Argument

It is arguably the case that a discipline's maturity may be assessed accurately by inspecting its models. For instance, Hawes (1975) says that as a field of study grows it uses more math and becomes increasingly formal. Kaplan (1964) identifies several different cognitive styles in behavioral science that (while they are not necessarily listed in order of merit) reflect the order of historical development for any discipline. The styles are (1) *literary*, such as case studies; (2) *academic*, in which principles are applied to examples; (3) *eristic*, where attention is focused on proof and where scientific method appears; (4) *symbolic*, wherein mathematical formulations yield new hypotheses; (5) *postulational*, in which the validity of proofs is of more concern than the truth content of the propositions; and (6) *formal*, where several possible content domains are fitted into one postulational system. Certainly in the field of speech communication, the progression has been from the case observation and principle-extraction in the ancient rhetorical treatises to the verbal testing of those tenets in this century's rhetorical criticism, to more recent uses of statistical methodologies. This gets us halfway through Kaplan's list. What lies ahead is the increasing use of formal mathematical models.

This will be beneficial in several respects. If we provisionally define "modeling" as applying relationships found in one domain to relationships in another domain, we have the advantage of aiding comprehension and intuition by providing something more familiar—easier to think about—than the real topic of investigation (Black, 1962, 225). Theorists working with models need not worry about contradictions between equations (since they describe a real and familiar system), whereas formal impossibility could be a serious concern for someone working with equations formed of the whole cloth and applied only to the domain at hand (Ziman, 1978, 23–24). Models also have the benefit of specificity. Because their use requires explicit notice of their assumptions the assumptions become vulnerable to falsification (Barnlund, 1968, 19). Mathematical models do not allow theorists to pass over difficulties in a cloud of words (Ziman, 1978, 24–25). Models yield a precise and clear understanding of the exact character of the theories they serve: "the emptiness and shallowness of many classical theories in the social sciences is well brought out by the attempt to formulate in any exact fashion what constitutes a model of the theory. . . . The effort to make it exact will at the same time reveal the weakness of the theory" (Suppes, 1960, 296). So we may look forward to more precision in our work with a concomitantly greater risk of falsification.

There are risks to modeling as well. We may take analogies too far and draw wrong inferences about a theory's topic (Nagel, 1961, 96–97; Braithwaite, 1953, 93; Black, 1962, 223); we may become overdependent on a model and confuse it with the theory itself (Nagel, 1961, 115; Achinstein, 1965, 117); we may also short-circuit detailed theoretical work if we mistake mathematical "explanations" for causal ones, as with statistically "explained" variance (Black, 1962, 225); and we run the risk of becoming addicted to models as ends in themselves, with little regard for the prospects of deepening knowledge in a domain (Kaplan, 1964). It is facile to say that these risks can be avoided by a suitable combination of thorough empiricism and reflective thinking; our most fundamental scientific biases are often least likely to be conscious or scrutinized (Feyerabend, 1970, 212; Lakatos, 1970). But since similar objections can be made to all of Kaplan's "cognitive styles," we have little chance of removing the human element of investigation. We can only note it and pass on.

In this essay I hope to do three things. In the first part, I shall consider the nature of models generally in order to obtain at least a temporary clarity in terminology; in the second part I shall turn to a discussion of issues involved in modeling argument; and in the last part I shall present several models of argument, some of which exist in the literature and others that ought to. My exposition therefore exhibits a movement from general concerns about models to increasingly argument-related ones.

The Nature of Models

The word "model" is so variably understood as to make a consideration of definitions necessary. Chao (1962, 563–564) has reported at least thirty different meanings of the word in the scientific literature; Bunge (1973, 91) refers to the "merry confusion, prevailing in the current scientific and philosophical literature, among various senses of this word." One important philosopher says that models are *parts* of theories but later, that models *contain* theories (see Nagel, 1961, 90, 113). Suppes (1960, 292–293) notices that "model" is often used to mean "inadequate theory" while George (1970, 23) wants to use the word to mean "formalization of theory." Moor (1978) complains that computer scientists make no consistent distinctions between "program," "model," and "theory." Thus there is little future in trying to extract a single coherent meaning from ordinary usage.

Instead, let us begin with Braithwaite's well-regarded definition:

> . . . a model for a theory T is another theory M which corresponds to the theory T in respect of deductive structure. By correspondence in deductive structure between M and T is meant that there is a one–one correlation between the concepts of T and those of M which gives rise to a one–one correlation between the propositions of T and those of M which is such that if a proposition in T logically follows from a set of propositions in T, the correlate in M of the first proposition in T logically follows from the set of correlates in M of the propositions of the set in T [1962, 225; italics omitted].

Braithwaite's definition may be most clearly appreciated by imagining that work on some topic has resulted in a theory (T) that turns out to have the same equations (but with different variables) as those that express the theory (M), which describes a second domain. It does no damage to this conception to notice that there is a third set of equations, G (a general set), that expresses the same relations without using the variable names of either domain. So we have a model if G fits both domains after suitable labeling of the algebraic variables. This is *isomorphism*.

We can begin to clarify our understanding of "model" if we note that at various times T, M, or G seems to be meant by "model." The *domain* of M is also frequently intended. At the risk of appearing arbitrary, we can begin to rule out uses of "model" from which we cannot infer or construct T, M, G and subject matters for T and M. This allows us to dispense with situations where we are said to have a model with no theory, as in ad hoc adjustments to computer programs that try to generate human speech patterns (Moor, 1978; but see Simon, 1978); perhaps we ought to use "simulation" for this situation. We may also ignore usages where "model" only means the provision of a real content for an abstract, uninterpreted calculus, as in Nagel (1961, 90); this would seem to be a function of theory, not of model.

Discussions of isomorphism usually follow Braithwaite (1953, 90) in saying that the model and theory must have the same calculus or formal structure. As in the definition quoted above, isomorphism implies a one-to-one correlation of deductions possible in T, M, or G. When one complex domain models another, "the systems must therefore resemble one another as systems. . . . The resemblance is in terms of the pattern or order exhibited in each system . . ." (Kaplan, 1964, 263; also see Hempel, 1965, 435–436).

Swanson (1966) calls this the "one calculus two theories" view and makes some realistic and useful objections to it. Noticing that models have genuine heuristic merit, he wonders how this can be: "For on such an account [the one-calculus view], once the imputation of structure has been made, the isomorphism grasped and made formal, the logical consequences traced out, the model must cease to be pregnant, cease to be a source of insight" (297). There seems a need, therefore, for some asymmetry between the theory and model, some portions of the pattern that may or may not be relevant. Further, the model and theory will usually operate on different levels of abstraction; something thought to be a simple, irreducible element in T may find its isomorph in something multidimensional in M. Considering Swanson's critique in conjunction with our original definition, then, we can elaborate the importance of isomorphism between T and M: (1) Certainly there must be a basic similarity of structure in the domains of T and M; (2) this similarity ought to be apparent via G; but (3) we should expect differences between T and M (and both should therefore be different from G); and (4) the departures of T and M from G may be evidence either of a poor model or of an interesting one.

The departures of T from M suggest the common view that models function as metaphors or analogies. Although there is some dissent from the majority (Achinstein, 1964, 1965, 1972; but see Girill, 1972, and Swanson, 1966), models are usually thought to have some metaphorical force (Black, 1962; Hesse, 1966; Kaplan, 1964; Hawes, 1975, chap. 9). Ziman (1978, 23) emphasizes what I think is the central point: that models are metaphorical because they provide only *incomplete* descriptions of the domain of T. Truly, models are both isomorphic and metaphorical, and we need to recognize the tension between these two descriptors. Quite useful models give only partial guidance about T's subject matter.

This liberal attitude about the requisite degree of isomorphism is necessary, I think, to understand how models work. Braithwaite's definition seems to apply most readily to a well-developed T and M. But the whole point of using models is to find out about T's domain. Evidently T must be quite incomplete (compared to M) when the comparison begins. As results come in, it perhaps becomes apparent that the selection of M was useful and that M is, in fact, a good model of T. But, for the reasons Swanson gives, it would be pointless to *search for* a model that satisfies Braithwaite's definition; if one were to find something which exactly matched T, it would be of little practical use. So we ought to look for theories that might be (reasonably) isomorphic to T, but aren't yet (they don't satisfy Braithwaite's one-calculus definition). Proper evaluations of models ought therefore to involve judgments from a continuum for quality of fit rather than a yes/no dichotomy, which I think our original definition implies.

I have intended this discussion to be a gloss of Braithwaite's definition rather than a refutation of it. His description is generally accurate, once various emendations are made. Reasonable usages of "model" will involve T, M, G and domains for T and M, will insist on only partial isomorphism, will recognize the metaphorical function of M and its domain, and will allow qualified judgments as to the quality of M. From this it ought to be clear that a model is not a hypothesis (though of course it may suggest one). Nor is a model a paradigm, since several models may evolve within one research program.

One important usage of "model," though it may seem questionable at first, deserves to be retained. This is where a system of equations for a subject matter is called a model. Put baldly, the usage seems to indicate the relation between T and its domain rather than between T and M. That is, the equations appear to be T. A set of equations, however, can have several relations to what they represent. In the usual context in which an investigator is trying to "model" something by trying a new set of equations, we can distinguish several things: (1) the actual phenomenon being investigated; (2) the pattern the investigator perceives, enabling him or her to recognize and investigate the phenomenon; (3) the equations; (4) the hypothetical pattern the equations predict; and (5) the empirical, operationalized phenomena measured to test the model. These things correspond to (1) the domain of T; (2) T; (3) G; (4) M; and (5) the domain of M. The usage is therefore tolerable, which is important because it will be a common one in the remainder of this paper.

Up to this point, our discussion has naturally fallen into the habit of considering formal or mathematical models. However, one often finds verbal or pictorial descriptions labeled as models. Quite a few writers restrict "model" to logical or mathematical systems (among them Hanushek and Jackson, 1977, chap. 1; Atkinson, 1960; Sayre, 1965; Kaplan, 1964,

263). But Miller (1966, chap. 4) suggests that we regard models as varying from mathematical formalism on one extreme to visual aids on the
other. Barnlund (1968, 21–23) explicitly condones verbal models, and
some writers regard diagrams as models as well (see Johnson and Klare,
1961; Barnlund, 1968, 23–27).

I think that there is an insuperable difficulty to allowing solely verbal or
diagrammatic descriptions to be "models." The point of a model is to explain the domain of T; this happens, as we have seen, partly as a result of the
isomorphism between M and T. Critically, this isomorphism is not perma-
nently assumed—it must eventually be evaluated. Though it is easy to see
how to accomplish this evaluation with a set of equations—one measures
the fit of the model to data—it is hard to see how to assess discussions and
illustrations. Of course, diagrams and discussions are useful in the search
for knowledge broadly conceived, but a model is an operational tool.
McHugh (1970), for example, has given us an interesting treatment of
deviance, which is couched in terms of Toulmin's (1958) layout of argument, but I would not call McHugh's paper an example of science. It might
be *preparatory* to an actual investigation, but in it he does not even form
specific statements of hypotheses. McHugh's essay is not yet precise enough
to be testable. It might well prove to be a simple matter to convert a
discussion or diagram into operational, systematic form; then it might be
appropriate to say that a model is latent in a particular essay—but not that a
model presently exists there. This distinction between model and diagram
has been made by others (Bunge, 1973, 110; Black, 1962, 232–233;
Achinstein, 1964; 1965) and is perhaps just a consequence of recognizing
the parallel distinction between theory and description.

Development and Function

Models do not merely exist—they evolve. Morris (1970, 79; see Bunge,
1973, 93–94) recommends that investigators begin with a simple model of
a complex process, expecting to revise as data come in. Thus Morris says
that model and data form a loop (80–81); Box (1979) intends a similar idea
when he explains that model development is iterative—that the residuals
from one approximation are the starting point for the next. "The bulk of
scientific practice is thus a complex and consuming mopping-up operation
that consolidates the ground made available by the most recent theoretical

breakthrough and that provides essential preparation for the breakthrough to follow" (Kuhn, 1961, 168).

Several of the more practical philosophers of science take an essentially evolutionary view of scientific development (Kuhn, 1970b, 264; Toulmin, 1970). In an especially insightful paper, Lakatos (1970) claims that a "research programme" has both a positive and a negative heuristic. The negative heuristic is the core of the program—these are the fundamental portions of the theory and are *not* investigated. The positive heuristic consists of the implications and extensions of the core. The positive heuristic ". . . lists a chain of ever more complicated models simulating reality: the scientist's attention is riveted on building his models following instructions which are laid down in the positive part of his programme" (135). Lakatos' view emphasizes that we should expect to see a succession of models having identical core assumptions in a mature field (see Thayer, 1963, 218). His description also explains why models endure empirical failures, a topic to which we will return.

Any model's development depends on the data that generate and test it. The data requirements for generation and testing are traditionally thought to be quite different. Dreams, intuitions, and inexplicable inspiration are usually acceptable *sources* of models or theories (Morris, 1970, 77–79; Blalock, 1969; Feyerabend, 1978, 154–155). But this does not mean that they are acceptable grounds for bothering to *test* the model. There must be good reasons that nominate a model to help explain some content domain. Kordig (1978) suggests that we stop thinking in terms of discovery and justification and substitute a threefold division of initial thinking, plausibility, and acceptability. The latter two stages in a model's life require good reasons while the first may not. From the first public appearance of any model, then, it will be accompanied by supportive arguments having to do with the model's and/or theory's domain.

This is not to say that a model's fate will be determined solely by its fit to the data. Lakatos (1970) says that if a model fails in application, the usual interpretation is that the core assumptions are nonetheless accurate, but that some new variable needs to be taken into account—seemingly a matter of minor revision. The whole issue of whether "critical experiments" really exist illustrates some models' resilience to mere fact. The most appropriate fate of an anomolous finding of fact is to be ignored (Kuhn, 1961; Lakatos, 1970, 176) because it will be unlikely to yield unequivocal proof that a theory or model is wrong. Data must be *interpreted* (Longino, 1979), and bothersome data will be attributed to a failure of the experiment rather than the hypothesis (Lakatos, 1970, 100–103). Since findings of fact are multi-vocal, crucial experiments—which try to pit one model against another—are impossible. History's crucial experiments, avers Lakatos (1970, 100–103), are only recognizable with hindsight. Feyerabend (1970, 226; 1978; see Kuhn, 1970b, 232, 242) even claims that one theory's predictions can never be perfectly translated into another genuinely competitive theoretical framework (but for sounder rhetorical views see Popper, 1970, 56; and Johnstone, 1969; 1973). Kuhn (1970a, 7) says that scientists only act like philosophers when they *must* choose between theories, but this is rare.

The extremely problematic nature of an attempt to test a model is exaggerated even more when the model concerns unobservable events—like learning, feeling, and possibly arguing. Researchers interested in cognition, for example, are often at pains to remind readers that the modeled cognitive processes may or may not be isomorphic to the actual ones—that the only real points of comparison are input and output (Wyer and Carlston, 1979, 278; Radford and Burton, 1974, 326; Kelley, 1972, 171; George, 1970, 15). The strategy followed in such work is to test predictions of varying sorts under varying conditions (Hawes, 1975, 105). Self-reports or other devices may be used in the hope that our utterances may reflect inaccessible phenomena (for example, see Willard, 1979b, 22, in regard to passions). But these models can only be tested indirectly, and I think that their acceptance or rejection is probably better described broadly and rhetorically than narrowly and scientifically.

Certainly such a rhetoric will admit statistical results as one kind of good argument for or against a model. But there are other kinds of arguments that depend on the various *functions* of a model. As already mentioned, good models are heuristic and aid in comprehension. They focus attention on certain elements of a topic and imply a set of research priorities (Swanson, 1966; Black, 1962; Hawes, 1975, chap. 1). They indicate what things are to be taken as equivalent (such as all means of pressing a bar to get a food pellet—Bunge, 1973, 92) and what events invite distinctions. Models are always *reductionist*—they divide, they analyze, they differentiate their subject matter (Achinstein, 1965, 103). A model that performs these functions well has a good chance of gaining adherents, even in the face of mediocre statistical support. Researchers will then begin elaborating the model—following Lakatos' positive heuristic—in an effort to improve its predictive accuracy.

Though the usual convention is to mean *statistical* testing when we say "testing a model," we probably ought to be aware that there is more to a model's development than a historical series of predicted–observed correlations. The same personal and disciplinary biases that play critical roles in the nomination of a model continue to exert influence in its testing. A model that does a poor job of fitting the data might be abandoned, but it might also become a rehabilitation project. Readers should realize that statistical tests, though essential given today's conception of social science, are not the only topoi involved in model testing—just as isomorphism is not the only important constitutive aspect of a good model.

Issues in Modeling Argument

The preceding section has indicated some of the considerations that apply to models of any phenomena: a model ought to be isomorphic, metaphorical, data-based, mathematical, and reductionist, for example. These characteristics are related to decisions a modeler needs to make—what focus to insist on, what subject matter from which to extract the model, how isomorphic the model ought to be. Because this essay is concerned specifically with modeling argument, however, we can be more pointed and can describe questions about argument the modeler should consider. As will be apparent, the modeler's positions on these issues will go a long way toward outlining a theory of argument.

Is a Model Possible?

The last few years have witnessed a dispute over the propriety of argument diagrams. Though I have already explained that diagrams are not models, the debate over diagrams might also apply to models, and so it deserves discussion here.

To summarize the claims briefly: Willard (1976; 1979b) says that diagrams reify argument, making it seem static, concrete, and independent of its human sources. Diagrams like Toulmin's (or models like formal logic) only treat argument as a product, obscuring its more important processual nature. Burleson (1979) maintains the usefulness of applying diagrams to argument-as-product and suggests that Willard's position is overstated: even though arguments may be "fleeting and ephemeral," we may still diagram them. Kneupper (1978; 1979) explicitly endorses the wellsprings of Willard's ideas—personal construct theory and symbolic interactionism—but believes that they do not interfere with thinking that arguments have "a necessary structural character" (1979, 226) that repays diagramming.

Though I find this dispute important for what it says about argument (that it can be seen as interactive, processual, unique), Willard's arguments do not pose a serious bar to modeling. Ephemeral things can be modeled. Electrons, for instance, are apparently massless bits of energy that cannot be reliably observed; yet we model them. Political affiliation is a complex event having a multitude of causes we do not completely understand, yet we can model it. Group discussion, attitude change, learning, and therapy all have transcendent aspects, and all can be modeled. Of course, no model can completely capture argument's ephemeral character. But models by their nature focus and exclude. They are assumed to be incomplete. Willard's essays amount to descriptions of what will be left out. His claim that the only worthwhile aspects of argument are those that will be missing from a model is an empirical question which cannot be settled until we have done more modeling and have evaluated that research. Nonetheless, I would be greatly surprised if argument turned out to be impervious to scientific method.

Reductionism

As was mentioned in the preceding section, models are reductionist: they analyze and divide a phenomenon. They use the classical mode of thought, as opposed to the romantic or holistic way of understanding (Pirsig, 1974). Using the notion of reductionism, we need to mark a careful distinction between models *of* argument and models *about* argument.

A model *about* argument is one that uses argument as an undifferentiated component in a model of something else. Smith (1970, 34, chaps. 7 and 11), for example, offers a model that uses logos (l) in conjunction with pathos (p), ethos (e), and esthetikos (ae) or speech form to predict a speech's effect (E):

$$(1)\ E = f(\,l + p + e + ae\,).$$

Whatever else we might wish to say about Smith's model, we should not say that it is a model of logos. It is a model *of* speech effect and is only *about* logos.

A model *of* argument is one that displays the parts, dimensions, causes, and the like of argument. Logic, for example, would dictate that an argument be separated into premises. A motivational model might distinguish every motive appealed to by a particular argument. A developmental model might identify a series of competencies that must be successively acquired in order to argue properly. For example, B. O'Keefe and Delia (1979) report that adaptiveness and number of arguments are determined by (correlate with) cognitive complexity and construct comprehensiveness. This finding might serve as the beginning of a model *of* argument.

The distinction is important because our specialty produces studies both of and about argument. One frustration some of Willard's readers have is that he often seems to be offering an analysis only about argument. Burleson (1979, 138) accuses him of making argumentation nearly identical with communication. Indeed, Willard (1978, 121) has said ". . . argument is defined here as a specific kind of social relationship or encounter. . . . [A]ny useful understanding of argument must consistently reflect a broader theoretical framework." Pursuit of this line of thought requires a model of social intercourse; this would allow argument to placed in context and so would be about argument.

But this style of analysis is not inconsistent with a model *of* argument. For Willard, argument is a social event, but this can be reduced and so offers a chance for a model of argument:

> . . . I see inference as the starting place because it gives meaning to public systems of discourse. Public discourse is symptomatic of private processes; *groups* (fields, after all, are made up of groups) consist of *individuals* interacting with each other as they develop ongoing lines of action and attempt to coordinate them with the demands of others. I asssume, then, that understanding how an individual reasons may explain why he adopts a certain mode of discourse over others. . . [1980a, 146].

On my reading of Willard, he is reductionist when he is talking about personal construct theory but is focused on argument as a component when he treats symbolic interaction. However, Goodwin and Wenzel (1979) display a social orientation while producing an analysis *of* argument, so the shift in focus is not inherent. (They studied proverbs, and found in them evidence regarding the *structure* of everyday argumentation.)

A model *of* argument must be anatomical with regard to argument. Models are reductionist. As Barnlund (1968, 17) says, ". . . science is less concerned with the outward appearance of events than in isolating the variables that produce the events." Every model will be of and about different things. Whether a modeler produces an analysis of or about argument depends on the system level chosen for study: on one level, an analysis may be about argument, and on another be of argument. Willard's work is an illustration.

Locus of Argument

One's model of argument will surely be influenced by where one looks for argument. Our literature, self-consciously or not, proposes several answers to "Where is argument?" This issue is so fundamental that to explore it in depth would require a review of nearly everything ever written on argument. Consequently I will simply outline each of the main positions without trying to document their histories at all.

One answer is "Argument is in the speaker." This point of view emphasizes purpose and is concerned to find out how a particular argument comes to be, what influences its selection, and which forms are considered for it. A model from this vantage locates argument in the context of the rhetor. Variables important to this approach include purpose, motives, values, knowledge, education, and creativity. No doubt this list is incomplete.

A second theoretical bias is that argument resides within the receiver. Here the argument is seen as stimulated by external forces, as existing in the receiver's mind, and perhaps resulting in some observable behavior (possibly a public message, possibly not). Beliefs, attitudes, values, memorial processes, consistency schemes, and cognitive complexity are examples of likely model components. These first two viewpoints have much in common and yield similar lists of variables.

Other researchers might choose to model text, on the assumption that argument is to be found there. This procedure has the great advantage of dealing with a public document that may be studied and coded directly. In contrast, the speaker and receiver orientations depend on indicants— usually self-reports—of the variables at issue. A textual model is composed largely of its category system. A content analysis of a text might study forms of argument, types of fallacy, descriptions of evidence, use of qualifiers, or associated concerns. The text need not be merely verbal; videotapes of communication can be coded for nonverbal variables as well.

An important variant of the textual view is the insistence that argument exists in interaction. If the modeler is satisfied to reduce the conversation to a codable transcript, this view is no different from the last. However, some writers hold that important elements of the argument would be lost with transcription. Participant observation might be the preferred investigative technique for this viewpoint. Variables unique to this view could be empathy, Thou-ness, or perspective-taking. This position is probably easier to theorize about than to collect data for; the transcendent character of argument seems more likely to be the object of humane reflection than of scientific modeling.

Several other loci might be suggested: arguments might be thought to reside in a society, a symbol system, or a channel, for instance. I think that these other perspectives have to combine with one or more of those listed above in order to give a full view of argument.

It only remains to be said that one model may well encompass several of these perspectives. However, I believe that thinking about the locus of argument is a useful way to begin modeling it, and may provide a convenient way to categorize different models.

Data

The modeler must consider what data to use in order to make the model plausible (to propose it) and what data to use in testing it. Beyond the observation that the test data must be different from the nomination data—else there would be no independent test—there are few differences between these classes of evidence. I will accordingly not distinguish them in the following discussion.

Several types of data are traditionally used by argumentation specialists. The first of these is introspection. Introspection involves the thinker drawing on his or her own mental resources to propose or test a model. The value of this procedure is directly related to the nature of the data used by the thinker. Highly regarded introspection ("philosophy") tends to reveal the grounds for its claims, to use nonidiosyncratic experience as evidence, to exhibit great candor in detailing arguments, and to use familiar ways of moving from data to conclusions. Poorly regarded introspection ("mere speculation") tends to do the opposite. The details of its arguments are not available for public inspection. Whether its claims are accepted depends less on their justification than on whether prior agreement with them existed. This second kind of introspection has little value. The first type may, in principle, be useful in developing models of argument, but it must be admitted that introspection is held in low esteem by social scientists today as a method of testing empirical claims. In all likelihood, arguments from introspection will play only minor roles in winning acceptance for models.

A second source of data is publicly available resources—usually language and/or understandings common to a particular linguistic community. Methods of analysis from these bases are often quite useful in distinguishing between previously conflated meanings (see Perelman and Olbrechts-Tyteca, 1969, 411–459). For instance, Crosson, (1967, 185–189) analyzes the meanings of words related to memory in order to build a set of categories for classifying memorial processes. Most readers are familiar with D. O'Keefe's (1977) essay on the meanings of usages associated with "argument." The persuasiveness of his arguments is based on everyone's access to the data and everyone's agreement on the apparent distinctions being discussed. The fact that a model can be modified on the basis of what its terms mean (in contrast to what is being modeled) should reinforce for the reader the fact that models are human constructions, not natural growths.

A third way to provide evidence for a model is to take a convenience sample of arguments. With the recent increase in interest in discourse analysis and ethnomethodology, this procedure is becoming more prevalent and promises to appear more often in our literature. Unfortunately, it has some serious problems. The procedures followed by the investigators seem to be either to hear an interesting argument and develop a gloss for it or to look around for some snatches of conversation to illustrate a theory already held. Unlike arguments based on publicly available resources, these lack the credibility of using data known to all. Though the method of analysis *looks like* that used by ordinary language philosophers, the appearance is deceptive. One difficulty is that the authors—who tend to have years of training in argumentation and/or debate—may see things that do not exist for naive observers. Bradac and Bell (1975) found that subjects' expectations about a speaker's fluency often altered their *counts* of nonfluencies; if counts of reasonably discriminable things can be influenced by expectations, certainly our interpretations and recordings of fleeting conversations are suspect (also see Bradac, Martin, Eliot, and Tardy, 1980, for a showing that naive and expert judges rate sentence clarity differently). Professional judges may understand and participate in conversations differently (more deeply, perhaps, but still differently) than ordinary people. If we are to make serious and generalizable claims about argument models, we must use typical arguments as our evidence (see Clark, 1973), and we must clarify the means we use to identify something as an argument at all. Claims based on conversations involving experts in argumentation (such as Jacobs and Jackson, 1979) or based on one expert's impressions (in the form of *notes*) of what two naive actors said (as Willard, 1980a) have at best only suggestive value. Duncan has made a pertinent comment in another context:

> Undoubtedly, the multitude of anecdotes and examples provided in certain ethnomethodological articles significantly clarifies the communication of the author's ideas. But I can only question the feasibility of building a social science of face-to-face interaction using these devices as evidence. It seems clear that the type of information required to evaluate most hypotheses is not contained in examples or anecdotes [1979, 363].

Notice that the indictment I am making is directed against the source of the data and not the method of analysis used in these studies. Naturalistic data will prove valuable to our work, if only we have assurances that it *is* naturalistic and so generalizable. Argument sampling must be done with the same rigor as any other kind of sampling.

The last source of data to be discussed here is traditional empirical evidence, as is typically used for experiments, quasi-experiments, or surveys. The data may be direct behavioral observation or may consist of self-reports given by respondents. Texts might also be used. The quality of this type of data is a common topic in experimental methods texts, and I will not review sampling, reliability, validity, or related topics here. One concern of argument modelers may nevertheless properly be raised here: the question of how large an inference is required to get from data to model. At one extreme is my own work, to be reviewed in the next section. My model is of unobservable cognitive processes, so my data are self-reports about beliefs. Not only do I lack a direct measure of adherence to a particular belief, but I also lack any data at all that directly describe the belief processing predicted by my model. I make quite large leaps in inferring support for my model from such data. At the other extreme might be a model of text content. There the inference (about what content a text holds) is based quite directly on codings of the text. A much shorter inferential leap is required. Ceteris paribus, of course, the modeler should prefer to select operationalizations which involve minimal leaps. On the other hand, the model will have requirements of its own (textual data would have little to say about most cognitive models), and these must be respected.

This section has discussed certain issues that can be seen as preliminary to consideration of particular models. Whether models are possible, what a model's focus will be, where argument is sought, and what types of data are allowable are all questions whose answers will be strongly influenced by the prospective modeler's theoretical presuppositions. Of course, research on a model may encourage the investigator to revise some earlier beliefs, but the reader should bear in mind that theory precedes model and that a model is therefore not a phoenix.

Models of Argument

Having considered a variety of general issues related to argument models, it now remains for us to examine some actual ones. Ideally, I would select and review the formal models most representative of the main research traditions in argumentation. This is unfortunately impossible. Few models appear in our current literature; fewer are products of self-conscious modeling; even fewer can be plausibly viewed as part of research programs (in Lakatos' sense). I will not bewail the paucity of models. Instead I have chosen to show how to convert a verbal formulation into a mathematical one; to review my own model; and to discuss several psychology models we might profitably liberate.

Brockriede

We have already noticed that models and disciplines evolve in the direction of increasing formality. Several writers have discussed ways of developing models and so stimulating that evolution. Morris (1970) takes the reader clearly through the stages of building a formal model of a transportation system and in the same book March (1970) provides a list of modeling exercises that seem useful in giving instruction and experience in modeling. Blalock's (1969) slim volume is especially commendable for its description of the movement from verbal materials to mathematical equations.

I propose to attempt such a conversion, using Brockriede's (1975) "Where Is Argument?" paper as a basis. This essay was chosen because of its straightforwardness and its importance within our specialty. Because models abstract, simplify, and focus, I do not insist that the model with which we finish will completely capture the content of the original paper; more sophisticated revisions might come closer.

The first step is obviously to be as clear as possible about what is being modeled. Brockriede says that argument has six characteristics. If these six things are true of argument, if they are a sufficient description of argument, and if we model them accurately, we will have modeled argument. The six features of argument are: (1) an inferential leap from belief to belief; (2) a rationale for the leap; (3) the availability of a choice of claims; (4) the regulation of uncertainty; (5) the risk of personal confrontation; and (6) a shared frame of reference for all participants.

On the assumption that argument is processual, it is appropriate to pay attention to the time ordering within this list. Space does not permit a full explication of my reading of Brockriede's paper, but I will briefly indicate the reasons for my assignment of different concepts to different time frames. The overall function of argument seems to be uncertainty reduction; this will serve as our dependent variable, on the grounds that it is natural to evaluate a process by its ending and that its ending is evaluated by its success or failure in carrying out its function. Certain of Brockriede's ideas seem to be preconditions of argument—that is, these things must exist (at least potentially) or argument will not be possible (either for physical or definitional reasons). These exogenous variables are the existence of uncertainty (else nothing to regulate); alternate claims' existence (else no choice); disagreement or opposition of advocates (else no possibility of confrontation); and a shared reference frame (else no communication). Lastly, we can identify several items that pertain to the internal workings of the argument process: old beliefs (to move from); new beliefs (to leap toward); support for the leap (the rationale); the leap itself; and rejected beliefs (the unchosen claims). At this point in the analysis we have this ordered set of categories:

I. Conditions
   —uncertainty
   —opposition
   —alternative possible claims (C_{pre})
   —shared frame of reference (F)
II. Internal Events or Components
   —old beliefs (B)
   —leap
   —support for leap
   —new beliefs
   —rejected beliefs
III. Endpoint
   —uncertainty reduction (RU)

As a next stage in the conversion, we should diagram the events. This will help show the relations within the various categories. In my first draft of the diagram, the close associations of several of the listed components became apparent. To simplify the diagram, therefore, I combined the first two conditions into "initial uncertainty" (IU). Since it is important to produce as general a model as possible, *arrays* of beliefs are used to represent the old beliefs (B) and possible claims (C_{post}), which includes both new and rejected beliefs (that is, all that exist in C_{pre}). The leap and support for leap are represented as the implications/rationale array (R) below; this was done to focus more broadly on the general process (the model reviewed in the following part of this section shows how I would have subdivided R). Given the temporal order implied in the earlier discussion, we now have "Fig. 11.1" (which I do not intend as a causal path model):

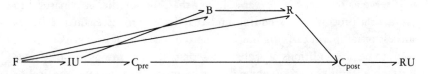

FIG. 11.1. Schematic illustration of Brockriede's essay.

The diagram may be read in this way: Participants' shared frame of reference makes it possible for them to perceive uncertainty regarding some belief or behavior. This uncertainty directly implies the existence of an array of claims about the disputed belief or behavior. At the same time, however, the uncertainty stimulates the recollection or provision of a variety of beliefs that imply (or can be made to imply) others. These implications indicate that one of the possible claims is better than the others, so it is chosen (believed, performed). This settles the original question and reduces the initial uncertainty.

Although I had been considering various possible operationalizations from the beginning (when I first read the article years ago), their importance is becoming increasingly obvious, and so I need to detail them here. F, the reference frame, is a difficult case. It might be assessed as a crude dichotomous variable (scored as 1 or 0) by simply asking participants if they understand one another. A more sophisticated device would be to have them indicate their values on one of the standard value-assessment forms available (Levitin, 1969) and take a measure of their "distances" from one another's profiles. Although I toyed with using information theory to operationalize IU, a simpler procedure is this: Within the C_{pre} array, measure the probability that each possible claim is true (from the standpoints of whatever actors are being studied). Subtract the probability of the *most likely* claim from 100 percent to obtain the measure of initial uncertainty. As with both Cs, B and R can also be measured as subjective probabilities that each belief, implication, or rationale is true. The final uncertainty reduction, RU, is obtained by subtracting the uncertainty calculated with the most probable claim in C_{post} from IU.

The last preliminary to presenting the equations is to notice that C_{post} is an interactive (multiplicative) function of B and R. That is, a particular c will be probable to the extent that its b and r are probable; their weaknesses will appear as weaknesses in adherence to c. We may now specify the equations that constitute our model of Brockriede's analysis.

The first is:

$$(2)\ \ RU = \max C_{post} - \max C_{pre}.$$

This indicates that the argument's uncertainty reduction is the amount by which the most probable postargument claim exceeds the most probable preargument claim. A related variable, IU, is given by

$$(3)\ \ IU = 100\% - \max C_{pre}.$$

In other words, IU is potentially 100 percent and will be reduced to the extent that one solution stands out among the others. If no claims are thought of, then IU will equal 100 percent as one would expect intuitively.

Max C (either before, during, or after the argument) can be directly assessed, as discussed above. If we wish to *predict* RU, however, we will need to use preargument measures to obtain a prediction of max C_{post} for use in 2. This is

$$(4)\ \ \max C_{post} = \max (F\ B\ R).$$

F appears because it "filters" the degree to which B and R can function; If $F = 0$, no claim would look probable based on reasons provided because they would be incomprehensible, while if $F = 1$, the beliefs could combine with their companion rationales to justify claims. Equation 4 may be taken to require that a calculation be performed for every possible combination of B and R units (every b multiplied by every r) and the largest product taken.

Though we do not need the variables for the diagram, it is useful to notice that final uncertainty (FU), is

$$(5)\ \ FU = 100\% - \max C_{post}.$$

This is based on the same reasoning as for IU. Furthermore,

$$(6)\ \ RU = IU - FU.$$

This is true by definition of RU. Finally, through suitable algebraic substitutions, we may specify the model in a fully candid form:

$$(7)\ \ RU = \max{(F\ B\ R)} - \max C_{pre},$$

where all the variables on the right side of the equation are measured prior to the argument.

The prediction made by 7 must, of course, be tested. After the argument is over, or during convenient pauses, the subjective probabilities for the C_{post} array can be measured to calculate a new RU or a series of them, using 2. These actual RUs can be compared with the RUs predicted from 7 to evaluate the model. Thus our development of the model is completed.

I wish to emphasize certain things about the model. First of all, it is not a restatement of Brockriede's paper: it is only a first approximation of what I thought I read there. Modeling an idea is more than just translating it into another medium of expression (though that is a useful comparison in some respects). Either Brockriede or his readers would be perfectly within their rights to object that 7 misses certain essential points and distorts others. If so, 7 ought to be revised, perhaps radically, but the project ought not be abandoned on such grounds. Secondly, 7 might prove reasonably accurate without necessarily reflecting Brockriede's paper properly. In that case, work on 7 could proceed along with a verbal restatement of the theory. The simplifications and interpretations implicit in the model might in this way influence the theory. Lastly, this example shows concretely that an equation can be a model. If one assumes that Brockriede's paper (T) accurately describes its domain, then 7 would be a general expression (G) of certain operational predictions about probabilities (M) that might or might not reflect the true state of affairs in the experimental data (the domain of M). So at least in this sense (which I think is the usual one) we may appropriately discuss equations as models.

Subjective Probabilities

I have done a series of experiments on a model that considers an argument to be a movement from one belief to another, where beliefs are measured as subjective probabilities (Hample, 1977; 1978; 1979). The model has historical but not strict mathematical connections with Bayes' Theorem; nonetheless it is better conceived as describing the operation of two different syllogisms.

A syllogism consists of two premises, P_1 and P_2, as well as a claim, C. If both premises are true, so will be the claim; similarly if both premises are probable, so will be the claim. Since each premise describes a given set of circumstances, they can both be true, can both be false, or only one may be true. The claim will be true only for those situations in which $P_1 \cap P_2$ (the intersection of the sets P_1 and P_2) is true. In other words C is a joint event. By considering the probabilities (formal logical probabilities for now), we notice that

$$(8) \quad p(C) = p(P_1 \cap P_2),$$

because $C = P_1 \cap P_2$. Assuming that P_1 and P_2 are independent—that is, that the occurrence of one does not affect the likelihood of the other—then 9 follows from 8:

$$(9) \quad p(C) = p(P_1)\, p(P_2).$$

Now consider the case of an argument viewed cognitively. The claim to the argument is some new belief, while the premises are other beliefs designed to elicit C. These premises consist of some idea, D, that provides the data for the movement to C as well as the belief that D implies C. This latter belief is conveniently regarded as the conditional probability that C is true when D is—$p(C|D)$. Given these equivalencies, 9 becomes

$$(10) \quad p(C) = p(D)\, p(C|D).$$

10 says that if subjective probabilities function like mathematical ones (a central assumption of this development), then belief in C is a multiplicative function of data (D) and warrant (if D, then C).

But our experience in the world tells us that 10 must be incomplete. C can be believed without belief in (or even acquaintance with) D. This consideration leads us to specify a second syllogism that has not-D ($\bar{D}$) as a premise. This is expressed analogously to 10:

$$(11) \quad p(C) = p(\bar{D})\, p(C|\bar{D}).$$

Both 10 and 11 may influence the level of $p(C)$.

We want one equation for the model, however, not two. If we could be certain that 10 and 11 described mutually exclusive events, we could make use of the fact that the probability of the union of sets A and B, $p(A \cup B)$, equals $p(A) + p(B)$ when A and B are mutually exclusive. Certainly D and $\bar{D}$ are mutually exclusive, but it is not clear whether the whole products are. At this point, therefore, we simply assume that the additive rule can be used, with full awareness that the assumption is questionable and may later have to be revised. Therefore,

$$(12) \quad p(C) = p(D)\, p(C|D) + p(\bar{D})\, p(C|\bar{D}).$$

One last modification needs to be made. In 12, the two syllogisms represented on the right have equal weight. This is an arbitrary assumption, and in fact I know of no good reason to suppose that the argument stimulated by the message—$p(D)\, p(C|D)$—should have exactly the same impact as the nonmessage beliefs that make up the cognitive context of the argument—$p(\bar{D})\, p(C|\bar{D})$. To repair this arbitrariness, we simply introduce variable weights for each term:

$$(13) \quad p(C) = w_1\, p(D)\, p(C|D) + w_2\, p(\bar{D})\, p(C|\bar{D}).$$

The weights—w_1 and w_2—may be hypothesized or may be empirically estimated using least squares procedures, for example.

In the studies that report data on these equations, 13 is the most accurate equation in comparisons with 12 and 10. Between half and one fourth of the experimentally observed variation in $p(C)$ is attributable to the variables specified by 13. Although w_1 and w_2 often have comparably sized effects on $p(C)$, they are often opposite in sign and rarely close to being equal (showing the artificiality of 12).

In short, 13 seems a reasonable model of argument considered cognitively. It may be adapted to slightly different conceptions of argument (for example, it might be used to explicate R in the model of Brockriede's paper), or it might be wholly replaced with a different cognitive model, depending on considerations explored in the opening parts of this paper. The point of presenting the model here has been to give an example of a model that fits our definitional criteria and is already in use within our specialty.

Adaptable Models

As we saw earlier, one traditional understanding of "model" is that an accurate description of one domain is adapted to a new subject matter. In this subsection I will select three candidates for crossapplication and sketch what I see as the possible grounds for analogy. As before, the discussion is intended to be illustrative rather than comprehensive.

The first potential model is taken from information theory, which has been influential in the overall study of communication but is not often thought of in connection with argumentation. I propose to make a small application to the idea of evidence. The basis for the crossapplication is the notion that something must be novel to be informative. By extension, a message cannot evidence a claim unless the message suggests a new thought. As Cherry (1978, 14) says, ". . . the signals must have at least some surprise value, some degree of unexpectedness, or it is a waste of time to transmit them" (also see 11–12). Whether or not a message, X, contains or implies new material depends on its context: if X is completely redundant in comparison with contextual events and messages, it has no novelty. Massey (1967, 41) gives a formula for calculating the information (I) of X once event or message Y has occurred:

$$(14) \quad I(X;Y) = \log_2 \frac{p(X|Y)}{p(X)}.$$

The most straightforward application of 14 would involve exposing subjects to a series of related messages. Each message becomes the Y context for the next. For instance, subjects could be told in sequence that a person is trustworthy, employed, indolent, honest, married, and so on. The value of I can be tested for different message series to see if I *does* depend on Y, and whether the dependency is accurately estimated by the $\log_2$ of the ratio of $p(X|Y)$ to $p(X)$. If I behaves according to 14, then informativeness can be used to predict other variables of interest—persuasiveness, knowledge, attention, or reduction of uncertainty. It might also be interesting to consider nonmessage Ys, such as source credibility or presentational style. 14, if it proves reasonably accurate, might also help us understand how several bits of evidence combine within a single argument.

A second model we might apply to argument is Dulany's (1968) theory of propositional control. Though his theory is considerably more general, it is easiest to grasp in its original context, verbal conditioning experiments (such as teaching a subject to use plural pronouns by unobtrusively reinforcing them with "good," "uh-huh," and so on). Dulany says that such "conditioning" only occurs in humans when the subject is consciously aware of what is going on. Dulany's theory is an explanation of what the subject knows about the experiment and how that knowledge affects the observed behavior ("we," "they"). The equation, which is simpler than it looks, is

$$(15) \quad R = BI = w_2 \, RHd \, RSv + w_3 \, BH \, MC.$$

R is the subject's response, and BI is his or her behavioral intention ("What

I'm trying to do"). The w's are merely weights. RHd is the subject's hypothesis about the distribution of reinforcement (his or her guess about what behavior will be rewarded), and RSv is the subjective value of the reinforcer. BH is the subject's behavioral hypothesis ("R is what I am *supposed* to do"), and MC is his or her motivation to comply with that norm or expectation. So 15 merely says that someone's intention to behave in a particular way depends on his or her awareness that a reward of some value will accrue to the behavior, and his or her willingness to obey applicable norms. Many readers are familiar with Fishbein's adaptation of this theory to the attitude–behavior relation (Fishbein and Ajzen, 1975). I propose a similar use of it, given in 16:

$$(16) \quad p(B) = w_2\, p(R)\, V(R) + w_3\, BH\, MC,$$

where p(B) is the subjective probability of a belief (the adherence to B). This is predicted by (1) the probability that the belief will result in rewards, times the value of that reinforcement, and by (2) the expectations about what one is supposed to believe, times the motivation to comply with those expectations. The w's, of course, are empirically determined weights.

Equation 16 can best be used to model two important argument phenomena. "Wishful thinking" (McGuire, 1960; see Pryor, Taylor, Buchanan and Strawn, 1980) is the tendency to believe things because they are attractive rather than justified. This inclination is broken down by 16 into affective and normative components. 16 also suggests kinds of evidence that might capitalize on wishful thinking—data relating to rewards or social demands. A second interesting application is to policy argument. By listing the advantages and disadvantages (R in 16) of some behavior as well as the likelihood that each will take place, we might obtain a value for the first predictor—p(R) V(R). We might then assess the influences of tradition, credibility, norms, and other explicit or implicit expectations to evaluate the rest of the predictor. If 16 proved accurate in this application, we would emerge with a model of policy decisions, which would of course have implications for policy advocacy.

Byrne's (1971) attraction theory can also be used as a model of argument. According to Byrne, the "law of attraction" is

$$(17) \quad A_x = m\left[\frac{\Sigma(PR_x\, M)}{\Sigma(PR_x\, M) + \Sigma(NR_x\, M)}\right] + k,$$

where A_x is attraction to some person or object X. PR_x is the positive reinforcement offered by X, and NR_x is the negative reinforcement. M stands for the magnitude or importance of a reinforcement. Both m and k are empirically determined weights. So the equation simply says that attraction is a function of the ratio of positive to total reinforcements associated with X. Equation 17 can be used to model policy arguments by letting the benefits of a program be PR_x, the costs be NR_x, and the importances or measures be M. If 17 works, then people's decisions to adopt X should be influenced by arguments directed at costs and benefits of the policy.

Readers may be struck by the similarity between 17 and our usual textbook recommendations regarding policy debate. We must avoid the temptation to devalue 17 as therefore being superficial. It is also true that 16 corresponds to some of our pedagogical admonitions regarding policy debate; so, in a sense, does 14. Even 10 often shows up in one way or another. Each formulation is quite different. Each requires a different underlying understanding of argument, and each directs our attention to a different set of variables. Most importantly, each is superior to its corresponding textbook prescription because each is directly testable.

The point of this section has been to illustrate rather than to review. Some fairly interesting models have been omitted to make room for others. Kelley (1972), for instance, uses an analysis of variance framework to explain what information points to what causal attributions. Smith (1970) contains a long list of psychology models that might be applied to communication. Within our own literature, Cronkhite (1969, 86–91) gives a formal, argument-based model of persuasion; Cox (1977) applies a subjective expected utility (SEU) model to jury deliberations; and Rabin (1978) tests Gottlieb's model of rule-guided inference against an actual Supreme Court decision. Any of these might have been singled out for detailed discussion, and readers are encouraged to inspect them.

Conclusions

Even though our literature has been cumulating for two and a half millennia, ours is in some ways a young specialty. Only in the last decade or so has argumentation begun to be recognized as a major subdivision of communication, and we continue to lag behind our siblings (interpersonal or organizational communication) in methodological sophistication. To be sure, there are valuable nonexperimental routes to knowledge about argument, and some of the leading figures in those traditions are represented in this volume. An individual argumentation scholar may well choose to restrict himself or herself to philosophical or critical methodologies, but I think our whole field should not.

Modeling is a nearly unavoidable part of the scientific approach. This is not true because science cannot be done without models, but rather because scientists find models convenient, heuristic, and illuminating. As I hope each reader can now attest, models display hidden assumptions, concretize vague slogans, and focus attention on key ideas.

This paper has had several rhetorical objectives. One—to explain the nature of modeling and how to begin it—is purely informational. But another is to persuade readers to try modeling. Hopefully the examples discussed here show the sort of general benefits argumentation students might experience from a radical increase in the use of argument models. We can expect our theories to be sharpened, both by the successful crossapplication of other disciplines' equations to our own concerns and also by the attempt to express our own theories with the precision required of mathematical propositions. We need more rigor, more concreteness, more reliability—in short, more science—in our work.

PART FOUR

Uses of Argument

CH. PERELMAN

[12] Philosophy and Rhetoric

I am very happy to have the opportunity to present to the *Wijsgerig Gezel-schap te Leuven* my ideas on the theme "Philosophy and Rhetoric."[1] The choice of the theme is already significant. I do not believe that at the time of my studies, fifty years ago, a philosopher would have treated this topic as a newsworthy subject. Rhetoric was so far away from philosophical preoc-cupations that one finds no mention of it in Lalande's *Vocabulaire de la philosophie* or in Edwards' *Encyclopedia of Philosophy*. And yet the relations between philosophy and rhetoric have a long history, going as far back as the beginning of Greek philosophy.

When, in his great poem, Parmenides opposes "the way of opinion" to the "way of truth," he opposes the rhetoricians, all those who act on opinion through speeches addressed to the great public, to philosophers who seek the truth. It is the search for truth which is the avowed ambition of philoso-phers, as we can see in the works of Socrates, of Plato, or of Aristotle. But there is hardly a philosophical truth that is not disputed.

In order to obviate this unhappy situation, the multiplicity of philoso-phies opposed to the unity of each science, the positivist philosophers, inspired by the sciences, searched for a way to limit the use of the term "truth" to controllable, demonstrable, and verifiable assertions, or at least to those which could be falsified. The positivists thus took over, in another form, the exigencies of rationalism. Before the philosophers' constant op-positions, each of them claiming to know the truth, one had to be more exacting as to the nature of their proofs. One knows that considering scho-lastic controversies, so characteristic of medieval thought, Leibniz, estab-lishing that they came to nothing, wished to put philosophical problems into equations ("calculemus") and thus come to conclusions as certain as in mathematics.

[1] Translated by Judy F. Merryman from the original French, "Philosophie et Rhéto-rique," *Tijdschrift voor Filosofie*, 3 (1979). Some minor changes from the original French text have been made by the author.

The rationalist ideal, whether that of Descartes, of Spinoza, or of Leibniz, was moreover sustained by a religious tradition, which proposed that man be inspired by a divine model. Whereas man has numerous and opposing opinions, God knows the truth, and the human ambition should strive to attain the truth which God has known through all eternity. If divine knowledge is mathematic by nature (*aei arithmei theos*), the ideal science has likewise to take mathematical form and adopt mathematical methods.

Personally, having been raised as a logician in the positivist tradition, I have always been worried by the disagreements of philosophers. Why can't philosophers agree with each other by demonstrating their theses in a manner acceptable to all? Would controversies among philosophers be due to the fact that they are not very scrupulous, not very careful, less intelligent? But how does it happen that the same person, Descartes or Leibniz, obtains good results in the sciences, whereas in philosophy their theses remain controversial? Why is this so? Does this deplorable situation result from the very nature of the philosophical enterprise? Let us note, however, that such situations exist in many other domains. It is the case in politics, in morals, in law, in religion.

To respond to these preoccupations I organized, in 1953, before the International Congress of Philosophy held in Brussels, an international symposium on the theory of proof, with the participation of a great number of eminent logicians and philosophers (*Revue internationale de Philosophie*, 1954, 27–28). The symposium included four parts, devoted respectively to deductive proof, to proof in natural sciences, to proof in law, and to proof in philosophy. It was at this symposium that Professor Gilbert Ryle presented his famous message on proofs in philosophy, where he affirmed that proofs are as foreign to philosophy as goals in a tennis match.

Why aren't there proofs in philosophy? It is because all proofs presuppose premises that can, in turn, be questioned. At last one will stop with first principles. What is the status of these latter, since it is impossible to prove them by deriving them from other premises?

In mathematics, one first considered these principles as self-evident, then one was satisfied to present them as hypotheses. Being inspired by mathematics, philosophers likewise set themselves to look for self-evident principles. Unfortunately it is not a question of subjective evidence, for what is self-evident should be self-evident for any reasoning being. But is there self-evidence in philosophy? Is not the latter characterized rather by controversies touching essential matters?

It is on account of these controversies that Friedrich Waissmann, in a study entitled "How I See Philosophy" which appeared in 1956, in the third series of the collection *Contemporary British Philosophy*, compared the activity of the philosopher to that of a lawyer: "First he makes you see all the weaknesses, disadvantages, shortcomings of a position; he brings to light inconsistencies in it or points out how unnatural some of the ideas underlying the whole theory are by pushing them to their furthest consequences; and this he does with the strongest weapons in his arsenal, reduction to absurdity and infinite regress. On the other hand, he offers you a new way of looking at things not exposed to those objections. In other words, he submits to you, like a barrister, all the facts of his case, and you are in the position of the judge. You look at them carefully, going into details, weigh the pros and cons and arrive at a verdict."[2]

Before presenting his own thesis, the philospher attacks the thesis he intends to replace, makes evident the superiority of his own, and leaves the decision up to the judgment of the listener.

This analogy with law is acceptable on the condition that one does not lose sight of the differences. The principle is less concerned with the fact that the judge is guided by rules to which he has to conform his judgment, but that there exists a judge competent to settle the conflict and that he is obliged to make a decision in a way that restores judiciary peace, guaranteed by the authority of the *res judicata*. But in philosophy, there is neither the authority of the *res judicata* nor a judge competent to settle philosophical debates. Rather, one appeals the "tribunal of reason".

In Western philosophical tradition, reason was incarnated by God, by divine reason. Human reason was only a pale reflection of divine reason, which furnishes a norm, absolute, objective, and independent of human opinions. Whether or not this norm exists is not what is important. For even if it did exist, how could we know it?

When it is a question of natural sciences, one could, a Bacon proposed, rely upon experimental control. But how does one test a philosophical theory?

Let us note in this regard that Plato appeals to dialectic and also to rhetoric, each playing a different role. I remind you that in order to take a position in the debate on the relations of philosophy with rhetoric, one must not forget that the notions of "philosophy," "rhetoric," and "dialectic" vary from one philosopher to the other,[3] each thinker adapting them to his own philosophy.

Thus Plato makes clear to us the role of dialectic in his dialogue *Eu-*

[2] Cf. Henry W. Johnstone, Jr., in *Validity and Rhetoric in Philosophical Argument* (University Park, Pa.: The Dialogue Press of Man and World, 1978), p. 22.

[3] Cf. in this regard Chap. 1 in my book *L'Empire rhétorique* (Paris: Vrin, 1977).

thyphron on piety. When we do not agree on the number of eggs in a basket, on the length of a piece of cloth, or on the weight of a jewel set in gold, it suffices that we count, measure, or weigh to settle the disagreement. Thanks to agreed-upon techniques, one easily suppresses controversy. But when it is a question of the just and the unjust, of good and bad, of beauty and ugliness—in other words, when the debate concerns values—we have to resort to dialectic.[4] As Professor J. Moreau in a suggestive article says: "Dialectic, the art of discussion, appears as the appropriate method for the solution of practical problems, those which concern the ends of action where values are engaged; it is to the test of such questions that it is used in Socratic dialogues, and this is the reason for the esteem in which it was held by Plato."[5]

In fact, dialectic serves, especially in Plato's works, to purge our mind of false opinions by showing that they lead to dead ends, to contradictions. It has an essentially negative use, clearing our mind of errors and prejudices. It prepares the way to intuition, to reminiscence, which alone will permit us to get to know the world of ideas. Rhetoric will be used by the philosopher not to learn the truth but to propagate it in order to gain adherence of those who perhaps do not have the benefit of philosophical intuition.

The thinking of Aristotle is very different, for if he admits in his *Metaphysics* that through intuition we may know the first principles, he does not believe that, thanks to intuition, one can grasp the idea of the Good. If our interlocutor came to deny the first principles, the only way to gain his acceptance would be through dialectic.[6] This will show, even to him who does not grasp them intuitively, that adhesion to these first principles is reasonable (*eulogos*). Thus in the works of Aristotle dialectic plays a positive role. But, even more, it is the only means to which one can resort in matters that are contingent. Indeed, the only principles one can grasp intuitively are those that govern changeless and eternal realities. When one passes from contemplation to action, things are very different, for action concerns the contingent, that which could be or not be, could be thus or otherwise. Reasonable action is that where the decision is preceded by deliberation, and arises from dialectic when reasons for or against guide and orient our choices.

Dialectical reasoning—which Aristotle opposes to analytical reasonings

[4] Cf. *Platon-Euthyphron*, 7 b–d.
[5] J. Moreau, *Rhétorique, dialectique et exigence première. Theorie de l'Argumentation* (Louvain: Nauwelaerts, 1963), p. 207.
[6] Aristotle, *Topics*, 101a and b.

that deduce consequences from principles in a constituted science—concerns the plausible, the probable, in the sense of "what is reasonable to admit." Aristotle finds these dialectical reasonings at work in controversies, like those he examines in his *Topics* and also in his *Rhetoric*. In *Rhetoric*, one will have recourse not only to dialectic proofs (the *logoi*) but also to the *ethos* and the *pathos*; that is to say to the authority of the speaker and by an appeal to emotions, hardly avoidable when practical matters are in dispute.

For Aristotle, the relationship of dialectic and rhetoric with philosophy will be different from what it was in Plato's works. Indeed, dialectical reasonings are the only ones that lead those who do not have a self-evident intuition to adhere to first principles, but, further, they are the only reasonings available for the establishment of reasonable theses in all domains which concern action. The (*phronēsis*) prudence, which is the quality of who deliberates by weighing the pro and the con, is a virtue, indispensable in reflective action. Rhetoric uses the same kind of arguments to persuade and to convince others.

The whole effort of Aristotle and of those who followed him to develop a theory of persuasive communication was despised and lost from sight, in the Western tradition, after Descartes. The final blow was dealt to the theory of argumentation by the extraordinary development of mathematical logic since the middle of the nineteenth century.

As we know, mathematical logic, which tends in the twentieth century to replace Aristotle's formal logic was essentially developed by mathematicians, since Boole and De Morgan and especially since the remarkable work of Frege, which was developed and popularized by Russell and Whitehead.

In order to prove, against Kant, that arithmetic is analytic, Frege studied the reasoning of mathematicians very closely in order to extract the logical principles implied. He was thus able to elaborate the theory of deduction as a point of departure for modern logic. The latter, resulting from the analysis of mathematical reasoning, will develop as a purely formal science and will consider as foreign to logic all reasoning foreign to mathematics. Mathematical logicians neglect the fact that in law, in history, in human sciences, and in philosophy one reasons all the same, even if the conclusions to which one comes in these disciplines are often controversial. But when there is a controversy, does one cease to reason? On the contrary, one turns to hypotheses and to analogies, one insists on certain methodological principles that tell us which rules to apply in similar situations. It is especially law that provides us with the chartered domain of argumentation, not the one where one proves the truth of certain theses but where one justifies decisions that, in the last instance, when they have the authority of the *res judicata*, will be assimilated to truth, *pro veritate habentur*.

The characteristics of argumentation are very different from those of deductive, demonstrative proof. A demonstration is correct or incorrect. An argument, by contrast, is strong or weak, pertinent or irrelevant. In argumentation there are no criteria for objective validity. In order to appraise an argumentation one must judge from the inside, starting from an accepted methodology at a given moment, in a given discipline, being led by what is accepted by specialists. Any initiation will bear not only upon the accepted theses, the useful tools, but also upon the methods of reasoning. Only by showing that they lead to unacceptable results will we have to modify them. (Let us note in this respect that argumentation, contrary to demonstration, is not impersonal and could not be effected by a machine.)

Indeed, all argumentation addresses itself to a mind which has to judge, to appraise. While in demonstration it is sufficient to apply rules in order to arrive at the constraining conclusion, argumentation cannot be separated from judgment. One must estimate, in their context, arguments for and against, show how arguments interact in order to strengthen or to contradict each other, in order to be capable of judging the position to which the argument leads.

The study of argumentation will lead to the development of a discipline complementary to formal logic, which I could have named dialectic but preferred to call "the new rhetoric" in order to emphasize the fact that these reasonings always address themselves to a mind, to an audience that one tries to win over to a presented thesis.

But if such is the case, will the value of argumentation be measured only by its effectiveness? This was the opinion of the rhetoricians of antiquity, and that was the reason why they were fought by philosphers like Plato. Rhetors and philosophers wanted to be *psychagogues*, educators, leaders of men, hence their rivalry, but where philosophers claimed to guide them in the name of truth, the sophists made every effort to win their acquiescence, trying everything, even the most demagogic tools, as long as they bring them success.

Plato judged demagogic rhetoric unworthy of a philosopher. But this was for him no reason to reject all rhetoric. In the *Phaedrus* (273e) he praised a rhetoric able to convince the gods themselves, those exacting, clairvoyant beings who do not let themselves be misled by any trick or falsehood.

The *new rhetoric*, contrary to that of the ancients, will be inspired by the recommendation formulated by Plato. The quality of an argument is not measured by its effectiveness alone, for it is relative to the audience to which the argument is addressed. The speech that persuades an audience of people who know nothing about the subject matter can be received with contempt by an audience of specialists. It is therefore essential to take into account not only the effectiveness of a speech but also the quality of the audience it is able to convince.

What characterizes the speeches of philosophers is that they constitute essentially a call to reason. That reason is incarnated by divinity, by some special audience, or by all men in general matters little. The philospher does not seek to win over particular groups such as the French, the Germans, fellow citizens or foreigners, the wealthy or the proletariat. Such a discourse would be ideological. On the contrary, the philosopher wishes to convince any reasonable being.

This thesis is implicit in Aristotle's *Topics*, where the techniques examined are those one can use with respect to any interlocutor, whereas in his *Rhetoric* Aristotle examines various kinds of audiences to which the orator has to adapt his argumentation, the young and the old, the rich and the poor. For him, rhetoric concerns only particular audiences, whereas the *new rhetoric* addresses itself also to the universal audience, to all those capable of participating in a philosophical dialogue, disqualifying those one considers senseless or unreasonable. It is true that in philosophy such a disqualification will be more controversial than in the sciences, where it is easier to judge that a given person is incompetent.

Let us note here that in argumentation it is easier to agree on the negative than on the positive, on what is unreasonable than on the reasonable. Contrary to the truth, which does not allow contradiction, several solutions can be reasonable. This justifies the existence of parliamentary regimes where several political parties can present different solutions to the public.

The existence of a plurality of different philosophies incites us to believe that the purpose of the philosopher, contrary to that of the scientist, is not to make us know the truth concerning a well-defined object but to present to mankind a reasonable vision of the world. It addresses itself to all humanity and not to particular groups such as voters, citizens, or believers.

Contrary to Descartes, whose *Meditations* are written in the first person, but who addresses himself to all rational beings in supposing that what appeared self-evident to him will assert itself in the same way to everybody, I believe that the discourse of the philosopher does not present necessary truths that should be accepted without discussion but is, on the contrary, submitted to all in order to be discussed, in order to give rise to objections and to provoke controversy. The debate is at the very heart of the philosophical enterprise, addressing itself to the universal audience. The philosopher undertakes to defend his theses with respect to all those who will present him pertinent objections.

Each philosopher works out his own conception of the universal audience that embodies, for him, reason. He will take, as a point of departure, the ideas which seem to him to be commonly accepted, which characterize the common sense of his society. But he is not going to restrict his purpose to that. Even the Scottish philosophy of common sense, in order to be considered a philosophy, had to be beyond this point of departure. The conceptions which rise from common sense, the commonplaces and the common values, as far as they are common, are vague and confused. To strive for justice is commonly admitted. Who will deny it? But as soon as one wants to be specific, as soon as one wants to look for criteria of a just society, disagreements appear. Everyone will admit that freedom is better than slavery, but from this commonsense truth it is a long way to the philosophy of the Stoics or to that of Spinoza.

Although the philosopher, in his effort of persuasion, can start only from commonly admitted premises, he will not restrict himself to theses of common sense. He seeks clarity and coherence, his two battle horses, but common sense is confused and incoherent. He has to clarify, by defining them, the notions he will use. But clarification implies a choice, because confusion results from the fact that the notion has a plurality of incompatible meanings. This choice can come about in different ways.

Take, for instance, the notion of liberty. One will find in the dictionary the meanings A, B, C, or D, liberty in the sense of Aristotle, of Spinoza, or of Kant. If one is satisfied with common sense, one remains confused, undetermined. But in order to choose and to justify that choice, one must deliberate, and thus argue. Aristotle noticed rightly that dialectic is indispensible in justifying the choice of a definition.

As soon as one has defined a notion and has set up the principles that govern it, the problem becomes complicated because of the existence of a plurality of values, which could be proved incompatible, like liberty and justice. If one wants to sacrifice neither the one nor the other, one must find a means of reconciling them. A philosopher will seek to work out a coherent system that would safeguard certain theses of common sense and sacrifice others. He constructs a philosophical reality that Martial Gueroult opposed to everyday reality.[7] Thus it is the whole of his system which would justify the manner in which the philosopher makes the distinction between values he favors and those that will be disqualified, considered as apparent values. The jurist will arrange, in an analogous fashion, incompatibilities which could occur in his judicial system and could be solved in various ways.

The classical method of solution, in the case of incompatibilities between values or norms, is the technique of dissociation of ideas illustrated by the traditional opposition between appearance and reality.[8] Can a vicious man be happy? The philosopher who would want to answer in the negative would have to show that the vicious man can enjoy only an apparent good fortune, true happiness being a function of virtue, or becoming identified with eternal salvation. All these techniques, as well as those of liaison as those of dissociation, rise from dialectic and from rhetoric; that is to say, from a theory of argumentation.

The mission of the philosopher is to present a reasonable vision of man, of his place in the universe, of his relations with others and, eventually, with God, of the manner in which he organizes and arranges in a hierarchy his system of values and proposes it to the adherence of all. This means that each is invited to take a position, to present criticisms and objections the philosopher must answer. This is the meaning of the philosophical dialogue. A rhetorical conception of philosophy, of a philosophy that wants to be accepted, leads inevitably to a philosophy in dialogue. It is normal that the progress of philosophy passes through controversy, through opposition of ideas and through the attempt to pass beyond this opposition. This is, perhaps, the manner in which one should understand the dialectic of Hegel.[9]

But if such is the case, one understands that dialogue can always be continued, that questions are never definitely settled. Indeed, what is allowed in one state of society, of knowledge, and of culture is not acceptable in another. To take an example concerning Belgium, it was unacceptable at the end of the last century to admit a woman to the bar in Belgium. The Supreme Court of Appeal, in a decree of November 11, 1889, ruled that "if the legislature did not exclude, by a formal disposition, women from the

[7] Cf. M. Gueroult, *Philosophie de l'histoire de la philosophie* (Paris: Aubier, 1979), v. II, 16, and Ch. Perelman, *Le réel commun et le réel philosophique, Le Champ de l'argumentation* (Brussels: Presses Universitaires de Bruxelles, 1970), pp. 253–264.

[8] Cf. Ch. Perelman and L. Olbrechts-Tyteca, *Traité de l'argumentation, la Nouvelle rhétorique* (Brussels: Editions de l'Université de Bruxelles, 1976), 89–91.

[9] Cf. Ch. Perelman, *Dialektik und Dialog, Hegel-Jahrbuch* (Verlag A. Hain, Meisenheim am Glan, 1970), pp. 11–21.

bar, it was because it admitted an axiom, so evident that it was unnecessary to state, that the administration of justice was reserved to men." It was necessary to wait for the law of April 7, 1922, before women were admitted to the bar.

What appeared evident in 1899 would appear ridiculous today. Whereas the rational to which philosophers are devoted is presented as universally and eternally valid, like the truths it takes into account, the reasonable and the unreasonable are socially and culturally dependent ideas. One understands that a conception of philosophy that links it to the reasonable, even if it is that of the universal audience as conceived by the philosopher, situates each philosophy in history, it being the manifestation of a moment, of a culture.

While diminishing in philosophy the place of intemporal truths, of universal intuitions, of constraining and absolutely valid self-evidence, one increases the role of argumentation, of dialectic, and of rhetoric.

The example of Plato and Aristotle is significant in this regard. Whereas for Plato any idea can be the object of intuition, what reduces philosophical rhetoric to the subordinate role of communication of a truth acquired independently, the fact is that for Aristotle only theoretical principles can be the object of intuition and of scientific knowledge, extending thereby enormously the field of rhetoric and of dialectic, alone capable of justifying our decisions and our choices. The realm of rhetoric will be extended still more if one stresses the fact that intuitions cannot be expressed without the language of a cultural community. Even if a philosopher, using this language, adapts it to his needs, he cannot escape the problems resulting from the fact this his thinking is historically and culturally conditioned. In consequence, he has to renounce the ambition of imitating divine reason, for he is a human being, situated, finite, and fallible. If he can have claims to universality, and by that to influence those around him, to educate them by the exaltation of universal values, he knows that this ideal is peculiar to Western culture, which was accepted in our country thanks to methods that characterize the history of philosophy since the Greeks.

It would be exciting to study in detail the argumentative and rhetorical structures of Western philosophy. Next to a general rhetoric, there is indeed a place for special rhetorics, fit for such-and-such discipline. It is thus that I published my *Logique juridique* (Dalloz, 1979²), which examines the structures of judicial argumentation. One would likewise be able to analyze the reasoning of the historian or that of the philosopher. One could try to extract the peculiar methods of each philosopher to see if there is a way of formulating a methodology of philosophical thought.

Are there any objective criteria in this matter? Can one specify in what consists a good or a bad argument in philosophy? Is not the case, to the contrary, that each philosophy would grant its favor to arguments of a determined type, as I tried to show in an article devoted to pragmatic arguments which are par excellence those of pragmatism and of utilitarianism?[10] How is discussion among different philosophies possible? How do they influence and modify what we have agreed to call "common sense"? There is a set of new perspectives which result from a view of philosophy that cannot be separated from argumentation and from rhetoric.[11]

[10]Cf. Ch. Perelman, *L'argument pragmatique*, *Le Champ de l'argumentation*. (Brussels, 1979), pp. 100−110.
[11]Cf. Philosophie, rhétorique, lieux communs, in *Bulletin de la Classe des Sciences morales et politiques de l'Académie Royale de Belgique*, VIII (1972), 144−156.

E. CULPEPPER CLARK

[13] Argument and Historical Analysis

In 1976, Theodore H. White entered a Kuhnian crisis of the personal sort. The liberal synthesis growing out of World War II no longer explained the making of an American president, much less the making of a peanut farmer from Plains, Georgia. No longer content with the journalist's appetite for "anecdote and detail," White (1978, 2) was thrown back into a search for history. He recognized that "good reporters organize facts in 'stories,' but good historians organize lives and episodes in 'arguments.'" And now White wondered whether "he was missing the 'argument,' the connection between this campaign and what was really happening in this two hundredth year of the American experiment in self-government."

As a journalist White found himself in the crosscurrents of the kind of social transition that invariably presages revisionist thinking in the hermeneutical sciences — theology, law, and history. He could still emplot the story, tell what happened and when, but he could no longer argue the story, tell what it meant, or in Hayden White's terms (1973, 11) "explicate 'the point of it all' or 'what it all adds up to' in the end." Using O'Keefe's (1977) distinction between argument as product and argument as interaction, this essay will explain how crises in the products of historiographical debate (what Theodore White had in mind when he felt he was missing the point of it all) come into being and are resolved through the transactional relationships of parties to the historiographical dispute. By discovering who the actors in this debate are, how they are situated and circumstanced in relationship to the historical record, it will be easier to see what makes for satisfactory historical explanations and why a particular mode of argument best satisfies the explanatory function of historiography.

The essay will address three questions: Who makes historical claims; What conditions must be satisfied to warrant historical claims; What method of argument best serves the warrant-making function in historical argument? The answers to these questions should provide clues to such issues as what constitutes the historical record, how historians establish

298

probability and/or plausibility in their explanations, and whether historians may be said to have a method of arguing that is field-dependent.

Making the Historical Record

When Wordsworth tells us that we come into this world "trailing clouds of glory," that "heaven lies about us in our infancy," he takes simple poetic license to acknowledge the idea that our existence is preconditioned. He might just as well have said that history lies about us in our infancy. Our being is conditioned on others having been. It is this ontological truth which leads historians to assert that theirs is the most democratic of disciplines and perhaps by virtue of that democracy the discipline least in need of examining its method.

Indeed, historians take some pride in their style and method being close to the fictive arts, while their data come from the diffuse world of everyday language and return there to be tested in the form of historical narrative. If their discipline "would-be" compact in Toulmin's sense of disciplinarity (1972, 378–395), their language (unless consciously borrowed from other disciplines) remains ordinary and open. More than any other specialized area of study, history finds close parallels in the common culture, be it the griot of Africa or the aunt who assigns herself the role of culture-bearer for the family. If the purpose of history as praxis is to sediment meanings of a culture at given points in time, professional historiography is but a more intense expression of the function of all speaking and writing; for it is through language that our individuality shades into community and a hoped-for posterity—a claim to perpetuity through memory. As Barrett observes (1978, 68), "'It is in language that each individual feels most vividly that he is only an effluence (Ausfluss) of all mankind.' A living language becomes in this way a repository of wisdom that transcends the individual's own powers if left on his own."

If historians can lay proper territorial claim to that aspect of language which enables individuals and communities to intimate their immortality, they still must come to terms with the unrepeatable nature of that language. All speaking and writing is ephemeral. Its imprint is that of "the specious present" (Becker, 1935, 241). T. S. Eliot had it in mind when he wrote:

> Time present and time past
> Are both perhaps present in time future,

> And time future contained in time past.
> If all time is eternally present
> All time is unredeemable.

Thus while historians speak the common language, the object of their speaking is past expressions of the language that are singular, unrepeatable, unredeemable. Documents do not speak, they must be spoken for. It is this interpretative act that transforms history into a process of understanding, not the object of understanding. Put another way, history recalls the past through an ongoing process of reconstruction. As Ebeling observes (1967, 26), interpretation is by its very nature "to say the same thing in a different way and, precisely by virtue of saying it in a different way, to say the same thing. If by way of pure repetition, we were to say today the same thing that was said 2,000 years ago, we would only be imagining that we were saying the same thing, while actually we would be saying something quite different."

To say that the language of the past is singular and unrepeatable is not to say that historical events cannot be re-enacted in Collingwood's sense (1956, 214–28). Each time an event is recalled, be the recollection trivial, spontaneous, unreflective, or serious and studied, the event continues a transformational development. Ricoeur explains (1971, 543), "we could say that a meaningful action is an action the *importance* of which goes 'beyond' its *relevance* to its initial situation," or in other words, "the meaning of an important event exceeds, overcomes, transcends, the social conditions of its production and may be re-enacted in new social contexts." As Studs Terkel remarked of his oral history of the Depression decade, the people interviewed were not remembering things the way they were, but the way they had come to signify themselves in the late 1960s (1970, 17). Again we see the processual, transactional nature of history. An event does not just happen and become an isolated object for investigation. As long as it is remembered or re-enacted, it continues to be transformed.

We may now ask the question of who the parties to this process of historical arguing are. I submit that there are two parties who seek the mediation of a third to posit claims on the historical record or future remembrance. The two conflicting parties may be said to be located in time past and time present, each with its own particular interests at stake. That these two parties have a stake in posterity assumes two conditions. First is Collingwood's notion (1958, 157–163) that the subject matter of history is the rational (or reasoned) actions of men and women situated and circumstanced at particular times, and second my belief that rational actions are calculated to enhance future remembrance. Not that all actions are deemed likely to attract future attention, but that situated actors want the overall patterns of their willed behavior to reflect well upon their conduct. A father wishes to be remembered affectionately by his children, a woman wishes to have it recorded that she championed the cause of women's equality. Similarly the present is future-oriented and calls upon the past to argue its case for posterity—the father drawing upon the memory of his father as a guide to future conduct, the woman searching the pages of history to justify present sacrifices in the cause. That the parties of the past and the present conflict (not in any necessarily hostile sense of that word) is given with the fact that the perceived interests of the one can never be identical with the other; indeed, as observed earlier, the very language of familial affection or human liberation changes from generation to generation.

The one who must mediate this conflict is the historian, who since the nineteenth century has become increasingly professional. In mediating the conflict the historian becomes a third situated actor in the argument as process. The historian's aim is hermeneutical; that is, to re-enact past thought in terms compatible with present understanding. It is this hermeneutical act that transforms the historian into a rhetorical agent, obligated to argue the past record in a way that makes sense, to forge, as it were, a usable past.

If the interaction of these three claimants to a product of historical argument were graphically illustrated it would look something like this:

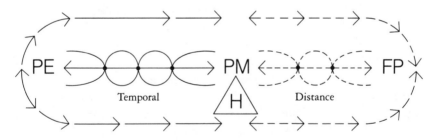

FIG. 13.1.   Linguistic possibilities qua historical tradition.

Where the enclosure represents the linguistic possibilities qua historical tradition which are available at any given moment in time to shape historical reflection; where the chain ⟨⟩⟨⟩ represents the manner in which those linguistic possibilities were tapped to derive meaning at given points in time; where the solid line ⟷ running from past event

(PE) to present moment (PM) represents the diachronic transformation of the event (or what historians would term the historiographical tradition); where the historian (H) serves as the anvil upon which a new link in the chain of interpretation is formed; and where the broken line and chain ←--+--+--→ running from the present moment (PM) to the future project (FP) represent future possibilities in the hermeneutical tradition. As observed earlier, it is the prospect of future remembrance that tempers the entire chain of an historical event.

The historian enters the historical argument through the process of selection. Being unable to follow chains of causation back to complex initial conditions, historians, like natural scientists, must be selective, and as Karl Popper observes (1966, 150), selectivity constrains one "to write that history which *interests us*." Popper's view, skeptical though it be, need not be troublesome; especially when one understands that history is not the object of understanding but rather its process. To objectify history, to attempt a comprehension of the whole complex chain of causation or even to assume such a comprehension is the ideal that governs the practice, is an impossibility that—were it attainable—would quickly void history of any meaning. Lévi-Strauss observed this truth of historiographical argument when he wrote (1966, 257–258):

> A truly total history would cancel itself out—its product would be nought. What makes history possible is that a sub-set of events is found, for a given period, to have approximately the same significance for a contingent of individuals who have not necessarily experienced the events and may even consider them at an interval of several centuries. History is therefore never history, but history-for. It is partial in the sense of being biased even when it claims not to be, for it inevitably remains partial—that is, incomplete—and this is itself a form of partiality.

The partiality of selection goes to perspectives as well as facts. For example, one cannot write the history of slavery from all its perspectives—that of the master, the abolitionist, the slave, ad infinitum. One must argue for one or the other or a third or some potential combination of views, but never for all. To argue that all perspectives have equal claim to the rectitude of historical evolution would, in Lévi-Strauss's scheme (1966, 258), be to rob American Negro slavery of any meaning whatsoever; for American slavery "as commonly conceived" would never have taken place. There would have been no right, no wrong, no winners, no losers, no subsequent significance of its ever having been. Thus, historians are locked in a Sisyphean struggle with the rock of the post hoc judgment. They are condemned to knowing who won, and while they must write in that spirit which views history as a clash of wills out of which emerges something that probably no person ever willed (Butterfield, 1965), they cannot but be aware of how the historical record has resolved and manifested itself through time. And knowing who won, the historian must inevitably select those facts and those perspectives which seem best to explain why. To do otherwise would be to write history that never occurred.

Not only do historians make the past known through the process of selection, they also have the power to know the past in ways it could never have known itself. It is one thing to select evidence from a manuscript where an author has intentionally set forth conditions. It is quite another matter to assemble data and to ask questions of that data which go beyond the ken of those whose experience the historian wishes to record. Today, cliometricians can assemble evidence which reflects everything from gross demographic patterns in the slave population to various indices of profitability in a slave economy to family stability. Psychiatrists can even put masters and slaves on the couch and probe various implications of super- and subordinate relationships. Bailyn (1979, 28) recently commented on this aspect of historical scholarship when he distinguished between "manifest" and "latent" history. He observed that prior generations of historians studied evidence that was made manifest through the intentional act of writing letters, diaries, newspapers, and their like. More recently, Bailyn observed, historians have been less content to "find" manifest evidence and more intent on "discovering" evidence that has until now been latent in such data pools as census questionnaires or slave-market records. By appropriating the methodologies of the social sciences in the process of discovery, historians become even more *rhetorical* agents as they invent ways to argue a way of knowing the record.

Finally, historians must relate what they have selected or discovered to present experience. In so doing they are aided by the assumption that human experience is at once universal to all time and specific to a given time. The relatively recent focus on black history and women's history in American universities illustrates the point. Surely one cannot argue that blacks and women were without a history, but it took the social ferment of the 1950s and 1960s to give these two groups visibility. With public concern focused on their needs and aspirations, it only remained for the historian to re-examine the historical record to find the peculiar manifestations of those needs and aspirations from the ancients to modern times. Thus perspectives of the present contribute to the fund of historical information by shedding new light on the darkened corners of our past.

Because historians serve as rhetorical agents, they are always in search of those proofs that are able to explain the past to the present in the most persuasive terms—with a natural and concomitant objective being to influence present/future understanding. In so doing, historians must balance their custodial interest in the past (preserving the past as past) and their interpretative duty (making the past known in a meaningful way to the present). This balancing act is not as difficult as it may seem; for the past as past projects itself forward even as the historian reaches back from the present. The convergence of this forward-looking past and backward-looking present is the point of historical re-creation, and it occurs naturally, almost reflexively, as the historian brings the questions and perspectives of each succeeding generation to bear on the particular event to be signified. Indeed, one of the first surprises for a graduate student in history is the realization that preceding generations of scholars did not lie; that their interpretations were grounded in the facticity of records which some persons or groups projected forward in an effort to be remembered accurately and, better still, favorably. People did cry for liberty or death; people did see conspiracies in the acts of king and Parliament; people did lash out against taxation without representation.

One has only to look at the historiography of American Negro slavery to see at work this converging phenomenon between past and present with its future implications. Historians have traditionally relied on two records (projections forward) of slavery; that handed down by the master class through plantation records and that argued through accounts of abolitionists who saw human bondage as an unmitigated evil. These two views have dominated the subsequent historical debate. The first general histories of American life, which were published in the late nineteenth century, those written by such giants as Rhodes (1900–1919) and McMaster (1883–1913), not surprisingly took the abolitionist perspective and focused on the more unsavory nature of the South's peculiar institution. This view predominated until Phillips (1918 and 1929), governed by racial prejudices of turn-of-the-century America, declared white reaction to the Negro to be the central theme of Southern history and proceeded to write about human bondage from the vantage of the slaveholder. He saw slavery as a schoolhouse of civilization for the black person, an institution for transforming savages into agents of Christian civility.

Phillips' view prevailed into mid-twentieth century. From *Birth of a Nation* to *Gone with the Wind* the popular imagination was not prone to think uncharitably of the slave regime. Moreover, historians shifted away from an examination of the institution of slavery and moved over to an attack on the abolitionists. These scholars were reacting to the inexplicable horror of World War I and the failure to win American approval for the League of Nations, both of which were viewed as a failure in diplomacy—a giving way to passion those issues reasonable people should have compromised. It was the spirit of Munich before the consequences of Munich were made known. In this light, abolitionists were seen as professional agitators who, unwilling to compromise and negotiate the vital issues of the day, brought on a tragic and bloody war. For these historians, the only thing irrepressible about the Civil War was the rhetoric of the antislavery agitation. Craven (1957, 117) summed up a generation of scholarship on the subject when he wrote: "Those who force the settlement of human problems by war can expect only an unsympathetic hearing from the future. Mere desire to do 'right' is no defense at the bar of history."

Then World War II intervened. The horrors attendant on theories of racial superiority were glimpsed in the holocaust. Moral aggression was not only called for; it worked. Myrdal's *American Dilemma* (1944) enabled Americans to see the consequences of their own racism as "separate" became an inherent denial of equal. This movement of ideology, intensified by war, began to work a transformation in the way scholars approached slavery. Beginning with Hofstadter's seminal essay, "U.B. Phillips and the Plantation Legend" (1944), historians began a critical reassessment of plantation slavery as viewed from the gardenia bush. The wave of revision reached tidal proportions with the appearance in 1956 of Stampp's *The Peculiar Institution*. Stampp not only brought historians back to a focus on the institutional aspects of the slave regime, he overturned the Phillips school through a study at once more exhaustive than Phillips' and more sensitive to human nature which expresses itself in a prejudice for freedom.

The interesting thing about Stampp's work and that of Elkins, who brought additional revisionist perspective in 1959 with publication of *Slavery: A Problem in American Institutional and Intellectual Life*, was their reliance on the same projections out of the past that had shaped earlier interpretations. Despite their more exhaustive and detailed studies, revisionists were reaching back to the same sources, slaveholders and abolitionists, that had shaped the debate at the beginning. The principal difference lay in the questions they asked of the sources. For example, when Elkins repeatedly confronted the Sambo image of the Negro in plantation records, he did not conclude, as Phillips did, that the black man was by nature a Sambo, he asked why the Negro became a Sambo, what institutional forces could have worked such a transformation? In answering the question, Elkins (1968,

103–114) used the now controversial analogy to Nazi concentration camps and the passive behavior that comes from a twisted identification with the oppressor. Stampp (1956, 97–109), too, offered psychological guesses where answers were not clear. Assuming, as did the abolitionists, that slaves surely had a preference for freedom, Stampp saw in the high incidence of farm-implement breakage reported in plantation journals signs of rebellion and sabotage, not racial indolence.

The larger consequence of the revisionists' reliance on plantation and abolitionist accounts has been the neglect of the central figure in American slavery—the Negro. No matter the sympathies of revisionists, blacks in bondage had no personality of their own. They were viewed as pawns in the larger debate between masters and antislavery agitators. Even the famous underground railroad was twisted by memory into a heroic effort on the part of white abolitionists as opposed to the blacks who actually ran it (Gara, 1961). Thus the slaves' identity was that attributed to them by white people, not the product of their own creation. Recently, historians have begun to tap into a third tradition projected out of past records—a tradition that allows blacks to speak about the community and identity they created apart from whites. Rawick has edited the nineteen volumes of slave narratives collected by the Works Projects Adminstration during the 1930s. The introductory volume, *From Sundown to Sunup: The Making of the Black Community* (1972), illustrates how these oral testimonies of ex-slaves can be used to understand slavery from the perspective of those who were enslaved. Blassingame's *The Slave Community: Plantation Life in the Antebellum South* (1972) is outstanding evidence of the historical understanding to be gained by using the autobiographical accounts of former slaves.

Thus, three distinct traditions have been projected forward from out of the past—master, abolitionist, and slave—with other variations and possibilities yet to be discovered. As rhetorical agent, the historian reaches back to interact with these traditions, asks questions of them, and interprets their voices for the present. The function of argument$_2$, then, is to mediate between this forward-looking past and backward-looking present, to provide the vital explanatory pivot which protects the past as recorded and interpreted while making it relevant to the present. As Perelman (1979, 18) describes it, "Every historian finds himself before a group of facts to be interpreted, facts which have been retained and noted because they seemed to be significant to some witness from the past, but the historian must reinterpret and place them in his own unified perspective. Because of the existence of a group of incontestable elements, of witnesses, whose interpretation and importance can be the object of controversial judgments, a dialogue among historians can take place and each new perspective brings a new dimension and new facts to this dialogue." When the historian enters this process of historical arguing a new link in the dialectical chain of interpretation is forged. "It is because of such a dialogue, and the enrichment which the historian cannot fail to procure from interlocutors [historians past and present], that the idea of a progress in historical objectivity can be conceived as the infinite march through the web of opposing theses toward a never achieved and ongoing self-protecting synthesis" (Perelman, 1979, 20–21).

Warranting Historical Claims

The fact that history as process is grounded in the ontological nature of human being seems to support the notion that the logic of historical thought does not stand in need of explanation—the logic is natural and reflexive. Recently, however, Fischer (1970, xv) argues that making explicit that which is implicit enables the historian to refine historical thinking. Acknowledging that the logic of history is neither the formal logic of the deductive inference nor the inductive patterns of a Mill or Keynes, Fischer states: "Instead, it is a process of adductive reasoning in the simple sense of adducing answers to specific questions, so that a satisfactory explanatory 'fit' is obtained. The answers may be general or particular, as the questions may require. History is, in short, a problem-solving discipline."

But the question remains: What makes certain explanations more satisfactory than others? What are the minimum conditions sufficient to warrant a historical claim? Satisfactory explanatory fits are obtained when arguments are both chronological and anthropological. Taking this proposition in its order, the first question to be addressed is what makes chronology a compelling feature of historical understanding. Any schoolchild can tell you that, often to their dismay, dates are the test of history. Lévi-Strauss (1966, 258) has written:

> The distinctive features of historical knowledge are due not to the absence of a code [or logic], which is illusory, but to its particular nature: the code consists in a chronology. There is no history without dates. . . . Dates may not be the whole of history, nor what is most interesting about it, but they are its *sine qua*

non, for history's entire originality and distinctive nature lie in apprehending the relation between *before* and *after*, which would perforce dissolve if the terms could not, at least in principle, be dated.

Dates are what give the appearance of purpose to history. Because something happens before something else, events take on the trappings of necessity rather than chance, existence comes to suppose preconditions. In the same sense, dates give an urgency to events by bracketing their existence, forming a beginning and end. For each point in the present or foreseeable future, a relevant beginning is assumed, and while an infinite regress could take historians back to the Garden of Eden, they are constrained by the criteria of relevance to find more proximate beginnings. For example, the condition of the black person in American society finds its point of departure in the fifteenth- and sixteenth-century expansion of Europe, and while one might conceivably trace its origins to Greek slavery, the lines blur and the peculiarity of modern experience is lost in gross generalization. This bracketing of time makes history appear epochal and gives to each generation its own subset of human importance. Or, as Lévi-Strauss overstates the case (1966, 254–255), "thought is powerless to extract a scheme of interpretation from events long past."

At a somewhat more abstract level chronology becomes a compelling feature of historical sense-making because the bracketing of existence within time frames confirms our sense of being. Like the alpha and omega of religion, our birth and death create an urgency and purpose to having been. It makes us see all life as an ever-changing progression and gives one a feeling of continuity with things close and discontinuity with things distant. The historicity of our own existence enables us to conceive—nay, demands that we perceive—the historicity of all existence. Indeed, failure to observe the ontological relationship of time to historical understanding, either by the false sequencing of events or by the use of synchronic analysis, works to disestablish uniquely historical claims. As Hexter (1971, 38) writes, "The problems involved in reasonably accurate determination of historical tempo have never been systematically studied, although results of the disaster of not studying them strew the historiographic landscape."

If history conforms to our sense of being through its chronological arrangement, it must also satisfy our sense of being in the human community. Historical explanations must make anthropological sense. It should be clear that "anthropological" is not being used in any particular disciplinary sense, rather as a term denoting the ability to make intelligible the behavior of humankind. The idea that we *"have* 'a nature'" and that there is a "'ground' of understanding" which proceeds from that nature is an idea essential to all hermeneutical/historical theory. Hans Jonas (1971, 499) explained this notion of the invariant nature of man in the following way: "Man *qua* man . . . is the same at all times: his hunger and thirst, his love and hate, his hope and despair, his seeking and finding, his speaking and fabling, his deceiving and truth-telling—they are familiar to us since, by either experience or disposition, we have them in ourselves. Everyone, according to this view, contains 'humankind' in himself, and thus nothing human is alien to him."

Jonas does not, however, push the notion raised by Hume in the *Inquiry* (1955, 90–93) that a uniformity of human passions explains a uniform system of nature. Rather he sees the fact of passions or feelings as creating the pathetic state essential to historical understanding. The feelings themselves are individuated and content-specific, the fact of their existence is universal.

Moreover, Jonas observes that this experience of humanness need not be, strictly speaking, inward; that is, actually experienced in order to be understood. Our awareness of being in the human community is frequently "mediated by symbols," conditioned by what we have read or heard. Jonas (1971, 519) writes: "To 'know love by love' is not to infer, from my own experience of the feeling of love, what is probably going on in someone else. I may first be awakened by *Romeo and Juliet* to the potentialities of love, by the tale of Thermopylae to the beauty of sacrificial heroism. This is itself an experience, showing me undreamt-of possibilities that may or may not become actualities of my own experience."

Thus, historical explanations are warranted insofar as they make chronological and anthropological sense. They can even enlarge on our fund of experience through the "mediation of symbols," moving us through argument from that which we know, an experience of freedom, to that which we have not know, an experience of racial enslavement. In either case the historian has the power of creating historical consciousness by engendering in the reader that sense of the "second experience," which is precisely how consciousness comes into being and which is the comparative logic of historical understanding. Buckminster Fuller (1973, 10) makes this connection between "second experience" and the historicity of thought when he writes: "And consciousness begins as an awareness to others, which other-ness-awareness requires time. And all statements by consciousness are in the comparative terms of prior observations of consciousness ('It's warmer, it's quicker, it's bigger than the other or others'). Minimal consciousness evokes time, as a nonsimultaneous sequence of experiences. Consciousness dawns with the second experience. . . . Not until the second experience did time and consciousness combine as human life."

So far the discussion has centered on a logic (as sense-making) of history which is "out there," a chronological requirement that serializes experience and an anthropological understanding that allows us to draw interpretations from the fund of all human experience. How historians go about tapping that intelligibility is the craft of their trade. In exercising that craft, the historian must answer three questions. First, how the past came into being. While knowledge of the past, as past, is necessarily imperfect, the effort to understand the past on its terms is essential. It is this effort that gives history its authenticity and its vividness—amounting to a confrontation with the historical dialectic minus the knowledge of its resolution. Second, the historian must ask how the past has manifested itself through time. The answer to this question is historiography in its broadest sense; it is the diachronic nature of history. The historian wants to know how each succeeding generation interpreted the event or events. Finally, the historian must ask how the past and its subsequent history can be made meaningful in the present, or, in terms previously explained, how the past can be rhetorically transformed in the present. Failure to satisfy these three questions, invoking as each does a different time dimension, subjects the historian to charges of being un- if not antihistorical. In such a case, the historian has failed to make historical sense.

The recent debate among historians over the book *Time on the Cross* illustrates the point. On first reading, the book was thought by many to have wrought a revolution in the historiography of American Negro slavery. Indeed, the conclusions were historiographically startling. Using the quantitative methodologies of the cliometrician, Fogel and Engerman thought they had proved slavery to be a far less anemic and brutal system than the revisionist historians had concluded. Their ten principal conclusions were profoundly disturbing to a generation who had struggled through the nation's Second Reconstruction and who, in the process, had gained a new appreciation for the abolitionist perspective. Intimidated by this new methodology, these historians began to reassess judgments that had matured over generations of historical inquiry. Other cliometricians, however, quickly detected errors in *Time on the Cross* and began to dismantle the work root and premise (Lichtman, 1974). Methodological flaws aside, and they were apparently numerous, J. H. Plumb (1975, 3) put his finger on the real rub when he wrote that "historians ought to be sufficiently well trained to beware of books which fly in the face of human reality, no matter how festooned with arithmetic."

Plumb did not stipulate what he meant by "human reality," but it seems clear that he was assuming a historical tradition with regard to slavery that gave license to certain assertions and not to others. It simply made chronological and anthropological sense that race slavery was a doomed institution and that its demise was a function of an innate drive for freedom that has characterized the ascent of Western man. It also seems clear that had Fogel and Engerman drawn different conclusions from the data, their rebuke would have been less severe, and in fact the data lent themselves to inferences far more critical of the institution of slavery than they were willing to draw. For example, the authors acknowledge a psychological dimension to slavery not addressed in their method and yet proceed to reach conclusions that demand psychological answers. When announcing their seventh conclusion, the authors assert (1974, 5):

> The belief that slave-breeding, sexual exploitation, and promiscuity destroyed the black family is a myth. The family was the basic unit of social organization under slavery. It was to the economic interest of the planters to encourage the stability of slave families and most of them did so. Most slave sales were either of whole families or of individuals who were at an age when it would have been normal for them to have left the family.

A startling conclusion until one realizes, first, that few historians have denied the importance of the family in slavery—indeed, the very importance of the family is what transformed any threat to its well-being into an unconscionable act—and, second, that the master class need destroy but one family to prove their right and power to accomplish such destruction and to induce the terrible prospect among all slaves. The statistical improbability of a nightmare actualizing itself does not lessen its grip the morning after.

Thus Fogel and Engerman flew in the face of human reality as expressed in a historical tradition. They got at the tangible, cognitive levels of the South's peculiar institution but lost the intangibles that gave the institution meaning. They did not conform to the sense-making imperatives that move from out of the past to shape the present and from out of the present to shape the past. They allowed a method for objectifying history to substitute for the mediating function of historical argument.

The Mode of Historical Arguing

We have seen that the product of historical argument derives from the process of hashing out claims made by actors situated in time and circumstanced by their interests in the historical record. We have also examined those conditions, chronological and anthropological, that warrant through experience and thereby make sense out of historical claims. It is clear from this discussion that the warrant in historical argument is not the kind of connector one finds in formal rules of inference. As White observes (1976, 15), the principle of connection for historical explanation does not consist in causal laws similar to those sought in science. "Not logic, then; and not 'free' poetry," he continues, "—neither can serve as the organon or fashioning principle of historical discourse. But rather 'experience' and the 'sense of reality.'"

The warrant in this instance is not content-free, not simply an inferential rule of connection. Its content is the fund of human experience. For this reason and others Collingwood (1956, 214–226) saw no need or reason for historians to appeal to any generalizing principle. Collingwood believed historians to be dealing with action explanations which required only that a historian re-enact an event by linking thought to the recorded action—to rethink the event. In a description of Collingwood's position, Martin (1977, 44) wrote: "Where the scientific move, in explanation, is in the direction of classification and the use of general laws, the historical move, in explanation, is in the direction of 'penetrating to the inside of events and detecting the thought which they express.' . . . The historian's move is not in the direction of generalization at all, even where generalization might be restricted to nonuniversal scope."

The appeal then is to the common sense of experience, and it occurs at that point wherein the historian becomes so suffused in the data or signs of thought as to make the historical action sufficiently intelligible. If the historian cannot rethink the given action, there is no explanation. If the historian can coherently link thought to action, there is no need for further explanation. The action to be explained is individuated and specific and must be approached from the inside (the thought content of the action) not the outside (some universal principle of generalization). Martin (1977, 44) links two passages from Collingwood to explain this critical notion:

> "For history, the object to be discovered is not the mere event, but the thought expressed in it. To discover that thought is already to understand it [i.e., the event]. After the historian has ascertained the facts, there is no further process of inquiring into their causes. When he knows what happened, he already knows why it happened" [IH, 214]. The exact meaning of this passage has been widely disputed but when it is read in conjunction with another, less cited passage, Collingwood's point becomes . . . unmistakable. "There is no such thing as the supposed further stage of . . . scientific history which discovers their causes or laws or in general explains them, because an historical fact once genuinely ascertained, grasped by the historian's re-enactment of the agent's thought in his mind, is already explained" [IH, 176–177].

So far the discussion has centered on that calculus of thought which takes place in the historian's head: linking thought to action, making sense of the historical record in terms of present understanding. But the question remains of how the historian communicates this understanding to the common reader. As Barzun (1973, 46) observes, "His [the reader's] understanding, his sense that something has been explained, derives entirely from what William James called 'the sentiment of rationality,' the impression that familiar and unfamiliar elements have been put into intelligible relation by someone who gives tokens of trustworthiness. That is intelligible to him which he finds sufficiently congruent with experience (direct or vicarious) to make him accept the neighboring strangeness and integrate it into a new imaginative experience." So the reader may be viewed as awash in that same sea of experience that creates intelligibility for the historian. It is for this reason, Barzun concludes, that the "explanatory force of common speech cannot be bettered" as a means of communicating historical understanding.

And the mode of arguing most adept at displaying the understandings of common speech, ergo historical understanding, is the *narratio*, in oratory the "statement of facts." Indeed, it was from the marriage of rhetoric and history that historiography was to achieve its distinctive style, which in the words of Lucian was "extended *narratio*" (North, 1954, 235). It is through the narrative, with its attendant stylistic devices drawn from rhetoric, that the coherence between thought and action is established. It is through narrative that data are patterned to yield claims that make sense in terms of experience. As Barzun (1972, 56) puts it, "One might say that it is by its *rhetoric* that a history communicates the precise fact found by the researcher and what he wants the reader to see."

The implications of this mode of arguing history are many. White in his *Metahistory* (1973) has gone further than most in explicating the ramifications of the various methods of emplotment. He has demonstrated forcefully that the choice of style is not barren of ideological consequences. In another essay, (1976, 23) White concludes: "If historical explanations are for the most part based on the acceptance of certain commonplaces (or, what amounts to the same thing, commonsensical generalizations about reality-in-general) which he shares with certain groups of readers, then the 'logic' of his discourse is not a logic at all, but simply the rhetorical techniques available to him for exploiting the implications of those commonplaces for explanatory purposes in his discourse."

There are two implications of narrative as an argumentative mode that should be highlighted. First, the method for establishing a historical discourse does not lend itself to the kind of "depth" analysis sought by other social sciences. Indeed the language of historical arguing spurns the denotative language of science in favor of the connotative and more evocative speech of the raconteur (Hexter, 1971, 47). Knowing what to leave out and how to pattern a story is the only way to create that sense of the second experience which is the essence of historical understanding. Barzun (1972, 56) notes; "History easily survives the right kind of superficiality and does not depend on 'depth' for its truth value. It is by its patterning, its composition in the strict sense, that understanding is conveyed and the master is made known." This is not to say that historians are blind to the possibilities inherent in the depth studies of the social sciences; it is to say that historical discourse is different in kind. Nor is a value judgment intended in the suggestion that historical discourse is superficial. It is the comparison between breadth and depth, and social sciences are as dependent on historical understanding as are historians on the social sciences. Barzun (1972, 64) puts it best when he writes that "history, on one side, and analytic studies, across the way, are preliminary to each other."

The second implication of arguing by method of emplotment is that efforts to judge historical arguments by a priori standards of formal logic miss the point. Fischer's catalog of historians' fallacies (1970) uses some formal and some not-so-formal standards to show a litany of historical errors. His putative aim is to move toward a "logic" of historical thought, and yet he gets so lost in a wilderness of historical wrongdoing as to provide no answer to his question. In truth, he seems to have wound up committing his own "fallacy of negative proof"—attempting to sustain a proof by negative evidence alone (47). Whatever the case, he misses the larger point that fallacies may be interesting but have very little to do with historical sense-making. For example, after a careful demonstration of the "logical vacuity" in a passage from Ranke, White (1976, 22) turns the table on himself, saying "My point is that, although the passage lacks any kind of logical rigor, it possesses perfect figurative coherency. The lexical and syntactical elements of the text function to invoke the image of *balance* or *harmony* which is Ranke's *ideal* of historical being." This is not to say that historians should be, or are, heedless of the common fallacies assumed in formal logic. It is to say that adherence to formal logic has no necessary relationship to the intelligibility of historical explanation. So long as the story is emplotted in such a way as to make sense, it has a formal validity; it may be false to fact or violative of logical consistency, but its form remains that which is essential to historical understanding.

We have now arrived willy-nilly at an answer to the question whether historical arguing is field-dependent. The answer is yes, but it does not derive from Toulmin's sense of compactness and disciplinarity, rather it hails from the kinds of questions history is designed to address and the method employed to answer them. To know how things came into being and how they differed in time assumes an individuality to events that can best be answered in the particular. Covering laws and principles of regularity may provide frames of reference and create perspectives. They even provide clues as to why historians select certain kinds of evidence and not others, but they cannot tell the story. And it is the story that has primacy in historical arguing. Be the historian a Marxist or an idealist, a cliometrician or psychohistorian, the essential explanatory paradigm is still the narrative. Only through the *narratio* and the stylistic devices used to emplot the story can the historian transform the warrant from its status as a general inferential rule to a connector between thought and action that is grounded in experience and appeals to common sense. Once the story is told it may become datum for some larger generalization about humankind and society, but then it is no longer history.

Conclusion

I am mindful of the tension that now sets up between the introductory problem posed by Theodore White and the manner in which I have sought to resolve that problem. Recall that White believed he could no longer *do* a *Making of the President*, that he was somehow "missing the 'argument,' the connection between this campaign and what was really happening in this two hundredth year of the American experiment in self-government." He could no longer argue "the point of it all." Taking White at his word, I used the distinction between argument as product and argument as process to throw in relief what White had in mind; for the journalist believed he could still write the story even if he could not produce some final "point of it all."

The easiest answer to this difficulty would be to say that the political pendulum had swung, thereby creating a different interest in the historical record—one that White could not comprehend fully and therefore, as historian, could not mediate. Yet the reasoning in this essay suggests that White's question is based on a false assumption: that there can be a meaningful distinction in historical arguing between product and process. If one accepts that historiographical issues are marked by actors situated and circumstanced by their role as claimants on the historical record and if there are certain chronological and anthropological conditions that must be satisfied to warrant historical claims and if the narrative is the exemplary mode of historical arguing, then the process/product distinction is not very helpful. At best the product is but a stage in improved understanding, or as Perelman (1979, 20–21) put it, a thesis in "the infinite march through the web of opposing theses toward a never achieved and ongoing self-protecting synthesis."

Here the recent turn of argumentation theorists to Habermas may be helpful. In treating Habermas' dialectical perspective on argumentation, Wenzel (1979, 88–89) points to the theory of "cognitive interests" that are embedded in various types of inquiry. Of the three interests (technical, practical, and emancipatory), the last two provide some clues for resolving White's dilemma. The *practical interest*, observes Wenzel, "describes the orientation of the cultural, historical, hermeneutic sciences that study the relation of man to man in communicative interaction with a view to maintaining and improving intersubjectivity of understanding." The end aimed at is an improved understanding, not some final point of it all. On the other hand, Habermas' notion of an *emancipatory interest* aims at just such a summary judgment. Its end is critical and evaluative; its object, at least in part, is reflection upon the findings of the historical/hermeneutical sciences. Thus White's error, as distinguished from his anguish, was to confuse the *doing* of history with the *evaluation* of history—two entirely different cognitive interests yielding different argument situations.

History, then, may be understood as the process of understanding, not its object. Its method is the recitation of data provided by actors interested in the historical record; its sense is derived from the chronological and anthropological imperatives that warrant historical claims, while its most characteristic mode of arguing is the narrative with its attendant stylistic devices. The point is that White's interest had turned from the practical to the emancipatory. He was looking for some covering law to explain what happened rather than remaining content to glean from ordinary communications insights into individuated and specific happenings.

A final note. Like Theodore White, historians are prone to the emancipatory interest. While they recognize that *doing* history is their reason for being, they lust after the critical judgment and heartily berate each other for differing evaluative theories. But in their rush to explain the point of it all, historians might do well to heed the lesson of Flaubert's comic heroes, Bouvard and Pecuchet. These clerk copyists, bored by their labors, set out to learn all that could be known from the burgeoning fields of nineteenth century inquiry. As they made their way through a welter of disciplines, each with its way of knowing, the plump Bouvard and the gaunt Pecuchet would sooner or later stumble onto the reductio in each field of inquiry. Having exhausted into confusion the possibilities of critical inquiry, they terminated their epistemic quest and returned to the copy desk—preferring at last to be *doing* if they could not know.

ROBERT P. NEWMAN

[14]   Foreign Policy: Decision
and Argument

This essay makes two assumptions. First, the tradition of British positivist philosophy, which informs much of contemporary writing on argument, is as irrelevant to significant *policy* argument as the formal logic it replaced. Second, if argument theory is to be anything other than an engrossing parlor game for academics, it will have to come to grips with the decision processes that are determining, as this is written, whether the United States will vastly expand its military expenditure, contract social services, make a test case of its *machismo* in El Salvador, and so forth.

I do not intend to argue these assumptions; others have done that. I want only to endorse Marcuse's observations for a more expansive context:

> What is this universal, larger context in which people speak and act and which gives their speech its meaning—this context which does not appear in the positivist analysis, which is *a priori* shut off by the examples as well as by the analysis itself? This larger context of experience, this real empirical world, today is still that of the gas chambers and concentration camps, of Hiroshima and Nagasaki, of American Cadillacs and German Mercedes, of the Pentagon and the Kremlin, of the nuclear cities and the Chinese communes, of Cuba, of brainwashing and massacres [Marcuse, 180].

Unfortunately, the universal, larger context is ignored in the examples of argumentation theorists such as Toulmin (1958). Whether Harry is a British subject because he was born in Bermuda or whether all Anne's sisters have red hair are banalities far removed from the concerns of policy argument. As Cooley observes, "very little appears to be at stake" in the arena of Toulmin's philosophizing (Cooley, 311).

But if argument theorists have avoided frontal attack on significant societal problems, political scientists have not. Using the terminology of decision-making, they have plunged wholeheartedly into concerns that are of great salience to academic debaters. Some of the political science contributions, however, would lead us down dangerous paths. This essay is an examination of one such contribution, with suggestions for a fundamentalist approach to argument structure in policy problems.

In hacking one's way through the jungle of current literature on decision-making and argument, it is useful to hold certain elementary precepts in mind. When we use the decision-making terminology, we are simply agreeing to focus on a certain cluster of variables in human action, as Robinson and Majak (1967, 178) put it. We can identify five such clusters: situations, participants, organizations, processes, and outcomes. The political scientists who have fostered the decision-making terminology hold that of these five the *process* is central, and one's analysis can revolve around the act of deciding. This focus is unobjectionable so long as one does not neglect the other clusters.

The act of deciding, in certain circumstances, will have regularities to it. These regularities can be teased out analogically, and one can develop models of decision-making, or models of argument, just as an engineer develops models of a river bed to serve as guides to the behavior of real rivers. But this engineering analogy itself leads to oversimplification; an engineer can at least identify and perhaps isolate all the variables with which his model is likely to deal; in complex human decisions, particularly those involving foreign policy, no one can even identify all the variables, let alone control them. This accounts for the sterility of experimental findings (Mintzberg et al., 1976; Lindblom and Cohen, 1979, 5ff). In contemporary intellectual circles there are thought to be few real discontinuities in the world; people, like things, function as systems. Hobbes told us this many years ago, but only recently have we become obsessed with the systemic nature of reality. All but the students of foreign affairs, that is; they know better. Norman D. Palmer, prestigious analyst of foreign policy at the University of Pennsylvania, notes that

> After more than half a century of debate, there is still no agreement whether International Relations is a separate discipline . . . there is little agreement regarding its nature and content. . . . Although innumerable theories of International Relations have been advanced, few, if any, have been generally accepted, even fewer have been well developed, and all attempts at developing a general theory or theories have been largely abortive. . . . Still another handicap is the changing nature and the general uncontrollability of the "laboratory" in which IR scholars must work. . . . There is still basic disagreement on the nature and role of values [Palmer, 1979, n.p.]

We have much, then, to be modest about. The seekers after architectonic theory are bound to be disappointed. But what should be the objectives of scholarship in this area? One's immediate objectives in studying foreign policy decisions and argument might be naively thought of as simple understanding: Why was this decision made, rather than some other? Why did this argument prevail, rather than some other? Intermediate objectives are also obvious and commonplace: one needs to predict what decision X will make in Y situation. But the real payoff, for practitioners as well as critics, is the long-range one: How can we improve the decision-making process? Or, in Cronkhite's plaintive terms, how, in 1968, could we devise means to decommit the sovereign (LBJ) from his fixation with escalating the war in Vietnam (Cronkhite, 1969, 113)? Ultimately this normative objective is supreme. We want to understand in order to predict and control. But we know that our successes will be partial, temporary, perhaps even controversial.

Foreign policy as a field is not substantially different from energy policy, or penal policy, or any other policy on which a state must make vital choices. What primarily distinguishes *policy* argument as such from the kind of arguments analyzed by Toulmin is the necessary factoring into *all* policy arguments of human goals or values, a necessity for which his argument layout makes no provision. Perhaps even the level at which decision and argument take place makes more difference to the process than any field-dependency. Some arguments take place, and some decisions are made, in a micro setting, by two persons arguing about whether one version of *King Kong* is better than another or whether one should keep a dinner engagement, where the decision, if any, has little impact beyond the particular dyad. Others deal with small groups, such as a company trying to decide whether to put its money in short-term bonds, where ramifications of a decision—and hence the number of variables to be considered—extend to perhaps dozens or hundreds of people. This essay is concerned with macrolevel argument, by governments, multinational corporations, or behemoth interest groups, where fateful consequences often hang in the balance and where the *purposes* of the arguers are diverse and often impenetrable. There is nothing, and will be nothing, in the arenas of foreign policy debate, approximating Habermas' ideal community; Niebuhr, in *Moral Man and Immoral Society*, should have disabused use of that. We must come to grips with a flawed decision/argument process, operating under conditions of high uncertainty, and sometimes in a crisis situation.

Arenas of Decision and Argument

It is convenient to inspect foreign policy decision and argument in three
(sometimes overlapping) arenas. Some decisions, including all crisis decisions, are made by the sovereign, which in the United States means the
president plus whatever advisers he chooses to consult. The most analyzed
decision in this arena, no doubt because it was the most fateful, was Cuba
II, or the Cuban Missile Crisis. Other decisions are made by the Congress,
both by way of appropriations and by means of legislation such as the War
Powers Act or an outright declaration of war. Still other decisions are made,
certainly in the United States, and probably in other states also, by the press
and the attentive public. There is much dispute about this, but I hold that
public opinion not only constrains the foreign policy actions of the sovereign and the legislature, it sometimes preempts them.[1] Our withdrawal
from Vietnam was such an instance; congressional action was in a real sense
dictated by public opinion.

Decisions taken by the sovereign are made in a closed setting, with a high
degree of secrecy, and with a major input of bureaucratic or nonpublic intelligence. Congressional decisions involve less secrecy and make less use of
the product of the intelligence agencies. Public decisions are made over
substantial periods of time, incorporate mostly media intelligence, and
involve many actors, including academic experts. Table 14.1 displays these
characteristics.

Table 14.1.　Decision Arenas

Arena	Degree of Secrecy	Major Source of Intelligence	Paradigm Case
Sovereign	High	Bureaucracy	Cuba II
Congress	Moderate	Mixed	Ratification of Panama Canal Treaties
Attentive Public	Zero	Media	Withdrawal from Vietnam

[1] For the best general study of electoral constraints on sovereign decisions see Gabriel
Almond, *The American People and Foreign Policy* (New York: Harcourt, 1950). For a case study
showing extreme electoral influence, see Robert P. Newman, "Lethal Rhetoric: The Selling
of the China Myths," *Quarterly Journal of Speech* (April 1975), 113.

Crisis decisions are significantly different from those made leisurely or in other arenas than the sovereign. Following Brecher (1978), I hold that a crisis is a situation where these conditions prevail: (1) a change in a state's external relationship with a potent other state; (2) a threat to security, independence, or some prime value; (3) an apparently limited time in which to take action; and (4) a possibility of war (5–24). Until the emergence of nuclear weapons with advanced delivery systems, which now make it possible for one of the superpowers to destroy civilization, crisis decisions were not as salient; if one made a mistake, there could be terrible carnage, but not annihilation. It is the possibility of annihilation that makes crisis decisions different.

Undoubtedly because of the drastic consequences of an error in a crisis decision, the arena of sovereign decision, and specifically decisions affecting nuclear war, has drawn the major attention of students of foreign policy. This paper is no exception. A decision made by the sovereign to defend Korea, or not to defend Czechoslovakia, is simply more important and more interesting than a decision to send economic aid to Haiti or to resume diplomatic relations with the Chilean junta. Congressional decisions are of course important, and may well impact on sovereign crisis decisions in such fashion as to lead to a crisis; but they are not in themselves supremely salient.

Even decisions made basically by the attentive public, such as withdrawal from Vietnam and rejection of the League of Nations, can have significant long-term effects, and warrant study; but their significance is largely in terms of establishing constraints on behavior of the sovereign.

Foreign policy decisions, because they involve interaction between vastly different political and cultural communities, and hence require decision-makers to anticipate reactions of opposite numbers who are programmed quite differently, demand a high degree of tough-minded empathy on the part of actors and sources of intelligence. Domestic decisions are less demanding in this respect. The foreign policy actor needs to know how the Russians or the Chinese will view various options; this is an order of magnitude more difficult than anticipating how the AFL-CIO will react to a decrease in unemployment compensation benefits. The expertise needed here is essentially that described by Helmer and Rescher (1960): ". . . a large store of (mostly unarticulated) background knowledge and a refined sensitivity to its relevance, through the intuitive application of which he is often able to produce trustworthy personal probabilities regarding hypotheses in his area of expertness" (21). Thus George F. Kennan and Llewellyn

Thompson have provided accurate judgments of probable Soviet behavior in various crises, and John Stewart Service and John Paton Davies accurately forecast the course of Chinese Communist foreign policy in the 1940s. The importance of tough-minded empathy on the part of decision-makers, and its frequent absence, are well described by Ralph K. White in his study of American involvement in Vietnam, *Nobody Wanted War*.

The Rational Actor

Sovereign decision-makers in the foreign policy arena are viewed through the lenses of three major models: as rational actors, as organizational processors, and as bureaucratic politicians. The concept of the rational actor in the literature on foreign policy bears no implication whatsoever of syllogistic reasoning, deduction, formal logic, entailment, or any similar concept. I will use "rational actor" to mean a decision-maker who, after deliberation, decides to adopt a particular policy because he or she believes it to be more in his or her interest than available alternatives.

More restrictive definitions are propounded by some theorists, usually those who wish to denigrate the practicality of the model. Allison (1971) states "Rationality refers to consistent, value-maximizing choice within specified constraints" (30). More elaborately, he also claims "The nation or government, conceived as a rational, unitary decision-maker, is the agent. This actor has *one* set of specified goals (the equivalent of a consistent utility function), *one* set of perceived options, and a *single* estimate of the consequences that follow from each alternative" (Allison, 1971, 32–33).

This begins to look something like a straw man. Suppose one believes that in certain (if not all) crisis situations the sovereign makes a choice among alternatives, recognizing several sets of goals held by various of his constituents, many of them in conflict with his own goals? Or must one overlook the possibility that the sovereign is prepared to examine a set of options brought to his attention by an associate or an outsider? Must the sovereign be held to reject estimates of consequences presented by competing branches of his government? And must the sovereign be thought to suppress all calculations of his personal well-being simply because he is deciding for the state?

Allison has so cribbed, cabined, and confined the concept of rational actor that he has produced an unreal abstraction. He derogates a caricature of rationality, not the way in which presidents decide or the way in which intelligent historians and internationalists and scholars of politics actually analyze decisions. The fine wit of Abraham Kaplan comes to bear on the demand for perfect consistency:

> A theory which demands only consistency of preference scales (a stable transitivity of utilities) is grossly inadequate to the political process. Political theorists have recognized at least since Burke that the decision-maker has a responsibility beyond giving the people what they want; he owes them also his own best judgment of what they *should* want. It could be said, to be sure, that rationality is not the only desideratum for political decisions, and that what I see as a problem for rationality lies, in fact, beyond its limits. But that Satan has a fine mind and is lacking only in heart is more than I am willing to admit; I believe he is a fool from beginning to end [Kaplan, 1964, 57].

The definition to which I subscribe clearly recognizes that rationality is never immune to error. Wilson, for instance, in one of the worst decisions ever foisted on the American Republic, decided on August 4, 1918, to join the Allied intervention in the Soviet Union. The fateful repercussions of that act have bedeviled us ever since. Wilson was wrong, egregiously wrong, tragically wrong. But did he not, in light of the probable costs and benefits as he saw them at the time, decide to do what seemed in the best interests of his nation?

The rational decision process encompasses several stages of analysis and argument (see Table 14.2). When foreign policy actors are first seized with a stimulus to take action of some kind, there will be argument as to the significance of the stimulus. In Cuba II, there was initial agreement as to whether Soviet IRBMs were a vital threat to U.S. defense. Kennedy, as sovereign, rapidly decided that they were. (Two decades later, confronted with intelligence that a Soviet unit in Cuba was a combat brigade, Carter waffled. At first the brigade was defined as an unacceptable threat, then it was decided otherwise.) When a crisis has been identified by the sovereign, or when a significant opportunity or problem has been delineated by Congress or the attentive public, the actors engage in a search for possible options. Obviously, this is not entirely a linear process; new options may appear at late stages of the process, attempts may be made to redefine the initial stimulus, and so forth. Once one or more plausible options have been identified, what might be called microargument begins: specific options are evaluated by argument designed to eliminate those that are weak and amplify those that are acceptable.

This is the level that corresponds to what academic debaters do. Deci-

Table 14.2.   Decision Stages

Stimulus

Classify, define:	Macroargument
Opportunity?	
Problem?	
Crisis?	

Assemble options	Search

Analyze options:	Microargument
lay out reasons for and	
against; gather evidence	

Evaluate options,	Macroargument
Select policy	

Implement policy

sion-makers ask of Option A "What reasons are there for adopting this option?" This is the stage at which argument layouts might be useful. All policy argument is inherently value-laden, and any reason for supporting a proposed policy has an axiological-teleological component. As Anderson (1970) puts it, "Each step in the process of decision making depends on the initial stipulation of values to be served" (712). Sometimes this component is not artculated, to the detriment of effective deliberation. An argument layout should force all premises to be displayed; however cogent Toulmin's layout may be for arguing about whether Peterson is a Catholic, it makes no provision for display of values.

Also, policy argument incorporates, at least implicitly, a prediction, which can be articulated: "X will accomplish goal Y." Stripped to its essentials, a microargument on a proposition of policy (a "good reason" for adopting or rejecting the proposed policy) consists of: We should do X, because it will fulfill value Y; or We should not do X, because it will have consequence Y.

Rational decision-making demands argument on all reasons for and against each policy option; this is a demanding task, never completely accomplished.

Sometimes search procedures for viable policy options fail to produce a proposal that gains the approbation of the decision group. When this occurs, design routines are invoked and the actors attempt to construct novel ways of achieving their goals (Burnstein and Berbaum, 1979). This "brainstorming" sometimes draws new personnel into the decision arena.

Finally, selection takes place; perhaps provisionally at first, but as deadlines dictate, options are foreclosed and a decision is made. In the real world this final summing up cannot be as systematic and thorough as theorists would like. And until a final decision is announced there is always the possibility that new intelligence may enter the arena, forcing reconsideration of one or more options. Actors may change their minds about previous support of a favored option; in Cuba II, this happened several times. The tortured history of SALT II in Congress shows multiple recycling and eventual forcing of the decision from Congress into the public arena.

In some situations, the decision process may proceed along the lines indicated above for cosmetic purposes only; the sovereign or the Congress may have made up their minds in advance and may go through the motions of deliberation only for window-dressing. There is strong reason to believe, for instance, that Truman decided immediately upon learning of the North Korean attack that the United States would intervene. But he had to get the military, State, and his immediate advisors on board; hence there was an ostentatious decision process. In the case of the Gulf of Tonkin resolution, deliberation was pro forma only; only Senators Morse and Gruening tried to analyze and evaluate the situation. Fulbright later, with regret, acknowledged that he had led in pressing for the resolution with no serious inspection of issues or evidence (U.S. Senate, 1968, 80).

Many of the foreign policy decisions made by Congress lack the initial steps of definition/classification and assembly of options. Specific treaties, recommendations for expenditure, resolutions such as Gulf of Tonkin, even controversial nominations with policy implications are presented to Congress ready-made by the Executive.

Because of the broad range of forums and participants, foreign policy arguments in the public arena are diffuse and chaotic. Sometimes the press fulfills its role as the fourth branch of government; on Vietnam widespread media opposition to Johnson's policies, more than academic dissent, forced reconsideration.

But it is crisis decisions, made by the sovereign, which have taken on such cosmic significance that they are given extended consideration. Let us now look at *the* paradigm case.

A Sovereign Arena Paradigm: Cuba II

In October 1962 reports began to circulate in Washington that the Soviet Union was shipping missiles to Cuba—some of them allegedly capable of reaching the United States' heartland.[2] Most of these reports came from refugees who had been at best shaky sources previously; but various Republicans, anxious to embarrass Kennedy, voiced the reports loudly. John McCone, Director of the CIA, had a gut feeling that Khrushchev might do something like this, but lacking hard evidence (U-2 photos) he did not press his suspicion. On Monday, October 15, the Defense Intelligence Agency showed Pentagon and White House officials photographs establishing beyond a doubt that the Russians were building a missile site, and the Cuban Missile Crisis began (Abel, 1966, 17–30).

Kennedy was not informed until Tuesday morning, the sixteenth. He immediately ticked off a list of names to McGeorge Bundy, his National Security Adviser, of people who were to be at a meeting that morning at 11:45. This group later was known as the ExCom, or Executive Committee of the National Security Council. It was in reality no such thing; several ExCom members were not members of the National Security Council, and several National Security Council members were not invited by Kennedy to sit on the ExCom. It was in effect a task force, composed of advisers Kennedy trusted and respected. It was to meet two or three times a day for the duration of the crisis, and it carried out the deliberations on which Kennedy depended for decision.

There was little debate over definition of the problem. Douglas Dillon, Secretary of the Treasury and a member of ExCom, had the clearest recollection: "The first reaction of the President and the others, in full agreement, was that we simply could not accept the fact of Soviet missiles in Cuba trained on the United States. Everyone round the table recognized that we were in a major crisis. We didn't know, that day, if the country would come through it with Washington intact" (Abel, 1966, 36). Later there were suggestions by Stevenson and McNamara that the challenge was not so great, that perhaps it was not a major crisis. McNamara's specific argument was "A missile is a missile. It makes no great difference whether you are killed by a missile fired from the Soviet Union or from Cuba" (Abel, 1966,

---

[2] I take my narrative from Elie Abel, *The Missile Crisis* (New York: Bantam, 1966). The best book for an understanding of Soviet actions is Herbert S. Dinerstein, *The Making of a Missile Crisis* (Baltimore: Johns Hopkins, 1976).

Table 14.3.   Flow of Cuba II Decision

Stimulus	U-2 verification of missile site construction
Classification, definition: crisis	Reached early in deliberation, but with Stevenson, McNamara dissenting

Assemble options	Nonforcible options
	    Confront Gromyko (in Washington) with photos
	    Send emissary to Khrushchev
	    Arraign Soviet before United Nations
	    Send emissary to Castro, Dorticos
	    Redefine situation: treat as no more than
	    regrettable mistake

Analyze options: reasons for and against each one	Nonforcible options rejected, selection between blockade and air strike decided on basis of blockade's lesser threat to Soviet, superior flexibility; military dissenting
Implement blockade	

32). But this argument was unavailing; majority view was clearly to define a crisis.

On Wednesday, October 17, there was already a broad spread of possible options under consideration (see Table 14.3). Sentiment then, and this included Kennedy, was for one of the forcible options, consonant with definition of the problem as a supreme crisis. Of the forcible options, the first one to engender systematic argument was the air strike; Kennedy mentioned this to Stevenson when first briefing his UN ambassador on the crisis. Opponents of the air strike led off. George Ball, later to become LBJ's tame devil's advocate on Vietnam, argued that a surprise attack would be inconsistent with American traditions. Robert Kennedy picked this up; several members recalled him saying with passion "My brother is not going to be the Tojo of the 1960s." This pointed, and ultimately successful, argument is easy to unpack:

Value premise: The United States should uphold its traditions.
Prediction: A surprise air strike would be, and would be perceived to be, in conflict with those traditions.

Dean Acheson, one of the outsiders invited to join ExCom, took sharp issue. The ranting of the China lobby in 1948–1952 to the contrary, Acheson was a hawk, vigorously anti-Communist, and remained so to his death. As Abel puts it, "He rejected the Pearl Harbor analogy with majestic scorn. For more than a century the Monroe Doctrine had made clear to all the world that the United States would not tolerate the intrusion of any European power into the Americas, Acheson said" (Abel, 1966, 52–53). Anyway, Kennedy had given the Soviet ambassador the clearest kind of warning that offensive missiles would not be tolerated in Cuba. The argument over an air strike stimulated massive staff work: what units, how many men, what equipment would be needed to wipe out the missile installations.

The other option that had considerable support in these early stages was a blockade, and much effort was made to get opinion of the best international lawyers as to its appropriateness. Both these options, corresponding to a debater's proposition of policy, were analyzed, argued about, subjected to evidential probing, related to basic American values and the political needs of the moment—in short, there was thorough deliberation.

Thursday, October 18, Dean Rusk, who had kept his peace until then, spoke up against a surprise air strike; his reasons were that it would provoke a spasm reaction in the Kremlin and that it would be costly in terms of political support both at home and in the free world. These were different arguments from those previously presented by Robert Kennedy. But Rusk did not present them as compelling arguments; his purpose was rather "to state each proposition as persuasively as he could in order that both might then be critically examined and debated" (Abel, 1966, 57). So in the afternoon ExCom session he took the opposite position: we should set a deadline of October 23, and if the missile sites were still under construction then, we should inform our allies that we would forcibly remove them; and on October 24 we would send in the Air Force. "If we don't do this," he said, "we go down with a whimper. Maybe it's better to go down with a bang."

Abel reports that every man on ExCom changed his position at least once. Bundy appears to have changed his position twice; he started out favoring a diplomatic approach, then argued for doing nothing, then supported an air strike. The most consistent bloc was the military; apparently none of the Joint Chiefs ever supported a nonforcible alternative and were usually united behind an air strike/invasion. Toward the end of the deliberations, when Kennedy had provisionally approved the blockade, the Joint Chiefs went to the airport, delayed Kennedy's departure for a long-scheduled speech in Cleveland just to plead with him for an air strike rather than the "softer" blockade.

There seems to be little doubt that ExCom deliberated extensively and that Kennedy was in control. Talk went far beyond immediate outcomes of the various options, to deal with ultimate policy goals. Should the United States use the crisis to get rid of Castro, thus fully enforcing the Monroe Doctrine? Could the missiles be removed without causing the Soviet Union to retaliate elsewhere? As we shall see, projection of consequences of the favored option, blockade, did not go far enough; perhaps, had Kennedy and his advisers had more time, they would have anticipated some of the unfortunate outcomes. But it is hard to deny that deliberation was sedulous, sustained, creative; and that the *least* advantageous options were avoided.

On the evening of Thursday, October 18, the group divided in two "teams"—George Ball heading a blockade team of seven members, Bundy heading an air-strike team of five. "Each team put its case as forcefully as it could in an exercise of comparative persuasiveness, similar to the war games played at military schools" (Abel, 1966, 65–66). After a lengthy session, a consensus began to develop in favor of blockade. The clinching argument in favor of blockade was that it would not close out the option of launching an air strike later, thus providing greater flexibility. Kennedy was not present at this meeting; at the end of it, about 10:00 P.M., the ExCom members went to the White House to report to the President. While making no final decision, Kennedy told Sorensen to start work on a speech announcing a blockade.

The decision did not change after that. There were several full-dress reviews of options, arguments, evaluations. Final approval of blockade came Saturday, October 20. Sunday the twenty-first the military members of the ExCom again petitioned for a rehearing and Kennedy met them in his living quarters before going to church. They were not persuasive. Monday the blockade was announced.

There were of course additional decisions made during the operation of the blockade. One of the most crucial was the decision to respond to a conciliatory letter from Khrushchev rather than to a belligerent one received somewhat later; this was a stroke of genius and may have been the single most fortunate decision in the whole affair. The missiles were withdrawn, and Kennedy was acclaimed a hero. One might say that the decision was rational and deliberative, by the books.

Cuba II—the Bureaucratic Process Model

But one might say something else entirely. Graham Allison has. His *Essence of Decision: Explaining the Cuban Missile Crisis*, published in 1971, sets out to undermine the previous analyses of Cuba II and to replace them with new, twin models: Bureaucratic Process and Governmental Politics.

Allison is a political scientist—which is to say, one of those who believes politics *is* a science. His book is required reading in political science courses across the country (Steel, 1972, 43). Not only does it come with the imprimatur of Harvard's John Fitzgerald Kennedy School of Government, with which Allison is affiliated, but Allison was favored in the writing of it by released time from the Rand Corporation.

The title of Allison's book is unfortunately misleading. It signals an outcome not even his hero, Kennedy, conceived as plausible, namely that he has penetrated to the *essence* of Kennedy's decision. We learn on the frontispiece from Kennedy himself that "The essence of ultimate decision remains impenetrable to the observer—often, indeed, to the decider himself." But Allison claims to have gone Kennedy one better and has found essence where ordinary mortals have to be content with looking through a glass, darkly.

And a reading of Allison confirms the implied claim of the title. Where old-style analysts looked at decision-makers as tortured indivduals trying to find their way through a tangle of options and arguments, Allison discovers, with help from the canons of modern science, that rationality is not the key to decision-making. Organizational process and governmental politics explain more than does the old-fashioned assumption that men honestly try to maximize, or at least optimize, values. His essences are men operating routinely in organizations and men struggling selfishly for power. All this is generally hedged and qualified, but Allison's thrust is clear: only when we get to the study of bureaucracy do we reach pay dirt. As one critic puts it, "With the publication of this book this approach to foreign policy now receives its definitive statement. The bureaucratic interpretation of foreign policy has become the conventional wisdom" (Krasner, 160).

The book consists of six chapters and a conclusion. Chapters 1 and 2 explain his view of the rational model of decision-making and apply it to Cuba II to show that this model is not significantly revealing. Chapters 3 and 4 explain the bureaucratic process model and apply it to Cuba II, enabling us to understand multiple mysteries that were previously inexplicable. Chapters 5 and 6 explain the organizational politics model and elucidate more dark corners.

I have already indicated my belief that Allison's definition of rationality creates a straw man that is easy for him to knock down. As part of his indictment of rational analysis of decisions, he notes that there are conflicting explanations of the start of World War I and various other conflicts coming from equally skilled scholars. If rational analysis leads to contradictory results, presumably we must reject it. If there were to be scholarly agreement on significant decisions, would that then mean that the method used was adequate? Can we ever *expect* to get agreement about, say, the main reason for World War I? The physics paradigm, misinterpreted at that, seems to underlie Allison's rejection of scholarly disagreement.

Allison then moves to the defense theorists and selects, as if he were typical, Herman "Strangelove" Kahn to demonstrate some "rational" idiocies: the commander in a nuclear war can navigate his way through a nuclear exchange, even if he is completely cut off from all information external to his own forces, by "dead reckoning" (Allison, 1971, 17). Next, the Sovietologists are inept. Equally, Henry Kissinger, Hans Morgenthau, Raymond Aron, and many other foreign policy analysts betray the rigidities and blindness of the rational model—defined as a *unitary* actor, with *one* set of goals, *one* set of perceived options, and a *single* estimate of the consequences flowing from each alternative. So much for the theory.

And Cuba II? Surprisingly, Allison's scant five-page narrative of how the ExCom came to recommend, and Kennedy to accept, the blockade option parallels closely the account I have pieced together from Abel, which is substantially the same as accounts in the other primary and secondary sources. There is no attempt in Allison's Chapter 2 to show that what appeared as purposeful deliberation was actually a cover for something else, or was a misleading patina beneath which powerful nonrational forces were at work. Allison asks, and answers, the question "Why Did the United States Respond to the Missile Deployment with a Blockade?" in a manner that would satisfy most aficionados of Cuba II. Where, then, is the problem with the rational model?

It is precisely in what the rational model leaves out, fails to bring to the surface. Chapter 3 begins the enlightenment. Point one of the enlightenment is a complaint that "Few specialists in international politics have studied organization theory" (Allison, 1971, 69). This may be partly true. And it is true, as Allison notes, that decision-makers, such as Kennedy and

his advisers, are heads of huge organizations, with standard operating procedures, vested interests in budget allocations, protected turf, and a notori-
ously sluggish way of responding to many executive initiatives. (Kennedy
was well aware of these aspects of bureaucracy. He once quipped about "a
relatively low priority project, the architectural remodeling of Lafayette
Square across from the White House, 'let's stay with it. Hell, it may be the
only thing I'll every really get done'" [Cronin, 1970, 574].) Allison *has*
studied organization theory, and hence can see verities that conventional
analysts cannot. Let's see what they are.

> . . . a government consists of a conglomerate of semi-feudal, loosely allied
> organizations, each with a life of its own. Government leaders do sit formally,
> and, to some extent, in fact, on top of this conglomerate. But governments
> perceive problems through organizational sensors. Governments define alter-
> natives and estimate consequences as their component organizations process
> information; governments act as these organizations enact routines. Govern-
> mental behavior can therefore be understood, according to [this] conceptual
> model, less as deliberate choices and more as *outputs* of large organizations
> functioning according to standard patterns of behavior [Allison, 1971, 67].

Translated, this means governments are dependent upon bureaucrati-
cally processed information in making decisions. This would surprise Hans
Morgenthau? But note what Allison does *not* say; he does not claim that
once the organization has set boundaries for a decision by defining alternatives and estimating consequences, *the decision has therefore automatically been
made*. Some unspecified initiative, some personal judgment, is presumably
left to the decision-maker. In Cuba II, Kennedy himself clearly had this
latitude; and some of the cumbersome organizations whose product he used
(DIA, JCS) found themselves on the losing end of the argument.

We will skip Allison's argument that Soviet decision-makers were dependent on their organizations to furnish information. Where else, indeed,
would they get it? We then come to a complaint that Kennedy's response to
Soviet moves—not, mind you, the initial decision to go with a blockade—
was governed by the timing and sequence of intelligence reports about the
placement of missiles. Of course. And there were many such reports. But,
as Allison (1971) notes:

> Not all this information, however, was on the desk of the estimators. Infor-
> mation does not pass from the tentacle to the top of the organization instanta-
> neously. Facts can be "in the system" without being available to the head of
> the organization. Information must be winnowed at every step up the organi-
> zational hierarchy, since the number of minutes in each day limits the number

of bits of information each individual can absorb. It is impossible for men at the top to examine every report from sources in 100 nations (25 of which had as high a priority as Cuba). But those who decide which information their boss shall see rarely see their bosses' problem [120].

There has been some sleight of hand here. When Kennedy was struggling to respond appropriately to Russian moves, twenty-five other nations had as high a priority as Cuba? Facts about Cuba and Soviet missiles were in the system, but not available to Kennedy? There is no evidence to this effect.[3]

But we do know that Allison believes organizational communication is imperfect, and the president cannot achieve a high degree of rationality because he does not have all the relevant facts, he has many distorted facts, and his knowledge of the options is incomplete. The answer to this would seem to be for Kennedy to get his intelligence people shaped up. Derogating the aim of the rational model seems a strained response.

Bureaucratic process, then, as it influences decisions, boils down to boundary-setting by restricting choices and limiting information. The sovereign still, in his own way, makes a choice.

Much of Allison's discussion of the stultifying effects of bureaucratic process bears, however not on the making of decisions but on carrying them out. The material that is unique with Allison is precisely of this sort. But the book title is to this extent a misnomer. It is not about the essence of decision but about the problems of getting decisions carried out. In Cuba II, for instance, Khrushchev's decision to place the missiles, Kennedy's decision to establish a blockade, and Khrushchev's decision to withdraw the missiles are all endangered, compromised, perverted, and ineptly carried out by bureaucratic units whose routines are ill suited to the tasks given them. Through the bureaucratic process chapters we are entertained with tidbits about the stupidities and inconsistencies of the Soviet missile operation. Some operations they camouflaged, some they didn't. Defensive, mobile missiles they took their time about; long-range offensive missiles which took much longer to emplace they speeded up. Allison concluded that the Soviet Strategic Rocket Forces and other units were blindly following standard operating procedures developed in the Eurasian heartland for totally different conditions. But how does this relate to the decision to deploy the missiles?

Kennedy suffered similar ineptitudes from his military—*after* he had

---

[3] For a somewhat different perspective on the problems of intelligence flow, see Robert P. Newman, "Communication Pathologies of Intelligence Systems," *Speech Monographs* (November 1975), 467.

made his decision. But the question of whether decision-makers are actually as much at the mercy of bureaucracies as Allison indicates has been explored at length by Art (1973). Allison seems to have overstated his case, to have ignored the options open to a sovereign when the precise implementation of decisions is highly salient to the sovereign's values. The president is the commander in chief; he can, if he is willing to take the time and effort, follow up on any decision to see that it is carried out. Kennedy, for instance, took great pains to follow the course of the blockade set up around Cuba, monitoring the actions of the Navy, directing that some ships be allowed to pass unchallenged, selecting those ships that were to be boarded, bending the blockade so that the Russians would have more time to consider their options. The hilarious confrontation between McNamara and Admiral Anderson in the Navy Flag Plot was part of this detailed following up of presidential orders. There can, indeed, be slippage between presidential intent and organizational output, but only to the extent that the sovereign fails to exert sufficient vigilance. Art (1973) summarizes the matter: "The details of implementation will, of course, influence the likelihood of success of a policy; but they become operative only after an act of positive choice. And while slippage can affect success, it cannot explain why the policy was launched. The 'detail and nuance' of actions by organizations cannot be used to denigrate the signal importance of the act of presidential choice" (478). Bureaucratic process is not the essence of decision.

Allison has here perpetrated a major misapplication of organizational theory. Building on the incremental theories of Braybrooke and Lindblom (1963), Allison describes governments as all but incapable of major, fateful decisions. Action is incremental: "The best explanation of the organizations behavior at t is $t - 1$; the best prediction of what will happen at $t + 1$ is t" (Allison, 1971, 88). For most organizations, most of the time, this may be true. But the peculiar fascination of the Cuban Missile Crisis, as of Truman's decisions to drop the bomb on Hiroshima and to defend South Korea, Johnson's decisions to invade the Dominican Republic and to escalate the war in Vietnam, Nixon's decisions to bomb Hanoi and to invade Cambodia, and the other spectacular and pregnant foreign policy decisions of the modern era, is that they were *not* incremental. They startled and terrified a trembling world precisely because they represented quantum jumps in the level of international violence (Steel, 1969). And it is these major decisions that Allison, by his choice of the Cuban Missile Crisis as a paradigm, seeks to explain. He has, in touting bureaucratic process, failed to match his theory to his example.

Cuba II—The Organizational Politics Model

Allison has another insight into how decisions are made, and another bit of the "essence" of Cuba II. This will surprise sheltered, ivory-tower academics:

> The "leaders" who sit on top of organizations are not a monolithic group. Rather, each individual in this group is, in his own right, a player in a central, competitive game. The name of the game is politics: bargaining along regularized circuits among players positioned hierarchically within the government. Government behavior can thus be understood according to a third conceptual model, not as organizational outputs but as results of these bargaining games [Allison, 1971, 144].

Here Allison takes us into a realm whose most prominent occupant is Richard Neustadt. *Presidential Power*, first published in 1960, is one of the seminal works on executive leadership. It not only caught the attention of President Kennedy, it "launched a whole growth industry in political science" (Steel, 1972, 44). Neustadt looks at the firing of General MacArthur, Truman's seizure of the steel mills, and Eisenhower's use of troops at Little Rock and concludes that the power of the president is the power to persuade the other actors in the arena of governmental politics.

Applying Neustadt's insights to Cuba II, Allison identified various pressure points where presumably internal politics pitted one actor against another, producing a pulling and hauling reminiscent of ward politics in an American town or of the rhetorical battles of Thucydides' Athenian assemblies. Secretary of State Dean Rusk, Secretary of Defense Robert McNamara, Director of the CIA John McCone, Secretary of the Treasury Douglas Dillon, Chairman of the Joint Chiefs of Staff Maxwell Taylor, and other members of ExCom came to the deliberations with different perceptions, competing ambitions, and different principles.

But Allison does not correlate the positions these arguers took with the interests of their organization, or with their personal interests. (The one exception: the military always favored maximum force.) One searches Allison in vain for an explanation of how organizational politics constituted the essence of decision. The most plausible procedure, if one wanted to justify Allison's account, would be to trace back the conflict between supporters of an air strike, who would presumably be Air Force partisans, and supporters of blockade, who could be assumed to be Navy types. If one could then show that *the politicking, rather than the argument*, determined the outcome, then perhaps organizational politics would appear more substantial a candidate for the label "essence of decision." But there is no such attempt, and should there be one, it would probably fail. "Bargaining games" between different organizations simply were not significant in determining Kennedy's decision.

Most of the furious argument in the ExCom Allison describes was between the advocates of an air strike/invasion and the advocates of a blockade. These alternatives were on the forceful end of the spectrum of possible actions. The peaceful end of the spectrum was not seriously considered after the first few days. Why? Given the dangerous possibilities of this first nuclear confrontation, could one not expect that the options of doing nothing, of exerting diplomatic pressures through the UN, of offering to trade removal of U.S. missiles in Turkey for Soviet missiles in Cuba, or of a secret approach to Castro would have been considered?

No, says Allison, for political reasons. The Republicans, in an election year, were threatening to make Cuba, and Kennedy's earlier refusal fully to support the Bay of Pigs invasion, the major issue. Kennedy was the inheritor of the McCarthyite attack on Democrats as appeasers of communism. Nixon's charges of twenty years of treason still hung in the air. Senators Keating, Goldwater, Capehart, Thurmond and others attacked Kennedy's policy of isolating Castro as a "do-nothing" policy (Allison, 1971, 188). Allison acknowledges the effects of these attacks:

> . . . it is clear that the entire circle of pressures to which he as President had to be responsive pushed him in a single direction: strong action. Indeed, the record leaves no doubt that from the outset he was determined to act forcefully. Halfway down that road of firm action, feeling the heat of the risks involved, John Kennedy raised the question of why he had ever begun. There was more than humor in Robert Kennedy's reply. "I just don't think there was any choice," he said, "and not only that, if you hadn't acted, you would have been impeached." "That's what I think," the President replied, "I would have been impeached." The nonforcible paths—avoiding military measures, resorting instead to diplomacy—could not have been more irrelevant to *his* problem [195].

A little thought will show that Allison is really saying that what turned Kennedy away from the nonforcible options was not *organizational politics at all, but politics in the widest sense.* He feared the reaction of the electorate, in the coming congressional elections and as ultimately expressed in impeachment. Here is an essence of decision, wiping out a whole range of choices, forcing the selection of military paths to the brink of nuclear warfare.

Politics was indeed influential in the Cuban Missile Crisis; but it was electoral politics, national and international politics, anti-Communist politics, not in any significant sense intragovernmental politics.

The implications of Allison's doctrines for argument are immense. If it were true that bureaucratic process and organizational politics accounted for the important crisis decisions, there is little room for deliberation. There is only room for bargaining. The belief that the extensive deliberations of ExCom really affected the outcome, leading to a blockade rather than an air strike/invasion, is only an illusion. Furthermore, if crisis decisions are primarily the product of organizational forces over which the sovereign has little control, then responsibility in politics has been eliminated. We have the ultimate cop-out: Johnson could not have acted other than he did in sending the marines into Santo Domingo because the bureaucracy, its processes and politics compelled him. Kennedy and Johnson could not have avoided involvement in Vietnam because the essence of their decisions was organizational process and politics. The leader is blameless (see Krasner).

There is yet another aspect of Allison's invidious doctrine that impacts on practitioners of deliberation. Allison appeals mightily to the "physics envy" of those who try to make sense of foreign policy problems. His process/politics models have the shining virtue of being scientific. Rationality and deliberation are hangovers of a bygone romantic age and must now yield to modern doctrines:

> The shift from Model I to the Model II and Model III forms of analysis really involves a fundamental change in intellectual style. From the basic conception of happenings as choices to be explained by reference to objectives (on analogy with the actions of individual human beings), we must move to a conception of happenings as events whose determinants are to be investigated according to the canons of modern science [Allison, 1971, 255].

The intricate reasoning that leads Allison to classify Models II and III (his organizational models) as scientific need not be reproduced here. But as if realizing that this claim might be met with some skepticism, Allison daringly *demonstrates* how his new regimen can perform. He will produce a prediction, based upon application of the new, sophisticated, scientific models to an ongoing process in the contemporary world. He wrote his book in 1971, when the Vietnam war was still a live issue:

> Strategic surrender is an important problem of international relations and diplomatic history. War termination is a new, developing area of the strategic literature. Both of these interests lead scholars to address a central question: *Why* do nations surrender *when?* . . . Thus surrender offers an interesting

issue for illustrative predictions. In spite of the risks of seeming dated, and being in error, a number of readers have persuaded me to reproduce some predictions presented in an earlier essay. The question addressed there was: Why will North Vietnam surrender when? What follows is quoted *verbatim* from a paper delivered in September, 1968 to the American Political Science Association [261].

The date was September 1968, and a competent analyst using scientific tools was seriously considering the possibility that North Vietnam would surrender? What followed in Allison's text was the conclusion that Model I, rationality, would not serve, since nations do not surrender when costs exceed benefits, as his version of rationality would dictate. Rather, they surrender sometime after that, as dictated by bureaucratic factors: "North Vietnam will surrender not when its leaders have a change of heart, but when Hanoi has a change of leaders (or a change of effective power within the central circle)" (263). How does one begin to indicate the monstrous delusion such a statement represents? One can only conclude that Allison must have been a most *un*scientific believer in the endless string of lies about Vietnam put out by the governments of John Kennedy and Lyndon Johnson.

However weak the claim of process/politics theory to essential explanatory power in Cuba II, it cannot be as weak as its final perversion in Allison's Vietnam prediction. Astrology could outperform this. Models II and III do not, in my view, have the explanatory power claimed for them; but they do remind us to attend to factors that affect the parameters within which crisis decisions are made and the difficulties of carrying out decisions. Allison, apparently, cannot use them to distinguish between chimera and catastrophe.

I have, in this essay, downplayed those occasions Allison gives the rational model credit for being useful in a "first cut" and for providing a framework for analyzing alternatives and distinguishing the preferred proposal. These grudging concessions do not in any way compensate for the overall gravamen of his work: rational analysis, and the argument that goes with it, are old-fashioned and impotent.

The Rational Model in Cuba II—A Success?

No one pretends that the rational model always works well. All the limitations and difficulties referred to at the beginning of this essay applied also in

Cuba II. One must conclude that had deliberation not been extensive and vigorous, the outcome could have been infinitely worse. Kennedy himself estimated that the chances of nuclear war were between one in three and fifty-fifty after he issued his ultimatum to Khrushchev (Sorensen, 1965, 705). Had we wiped out Soviet soldiers in Cuba, the chances would no doubt have been worse. So Cuba II was a "good" decision, far better than General LeMay would have made. But beyond that?

Allison, like Kennedy associates Sorensen, Schlesinger, and Hilsman, who have all praised their former boss for his courage and prescience in Cuba II, believes that "Here is one of the finest examples of diplomatic prudence, and perhaps the finest hour of John F. Kennedy's Presidency" (Allison, 1971, 39).

Any student of evidence will suspect bias when a member of the John F. Kennedy School of Government, embedded in the full nostalgia of Camelot and its veterans, a student and now colleague of those whose most powerful vested interest is probably maintenance of the Kennedy legend, attempts to turn a critical eye on the high point of Kennedy's presidency. It is hard to conceive any outcome other than approbation.

And one must concede immediately that Cuba II was a technically brilliant affair, that Kennedy did force Khrushchev to back down, that the missiles were removed.

But when one moves outside the aura of Camelot to get a reading on the ultimate outcome, one suspects that all may not have been as beautiful as the Kennedy forces portray. The dominant impression of a technically flawless tactical operation, of an immediate outcome favorable to the United States, begins to blur into a suspicion of long-term strategic disaster.

For one thing, we know that the Soviets were far behind the United States in numbers and capabilities of nuclear missiles at the time Kennedy took office, despite his campaign talk about a missile gap. Whether the Soviets would have been prepared to live with this smaller missile facility for an extended period we can never know. But Russia responded to Kennedy's blockade ultimatum just as one suspects we would have responded had the situation been reversed: they called it nuclear blackmail and set about building a missile-nuclear capability that would keep them from ever again being subject to such blackmail. Hence a massive increase in Soviet arms, a matching increase from our side, and on into spiraling infinity (Steel, 1972).

For another thing, the euphoria in Camelot as a result of the dazzling tactical success of Cuba II must have contributed to the willingness of both Kennedy and Johnson to raise the ante in Vietnam. As Ronald Steel puts it,

"Had the U.S. been forced to back down in Cuba, or to work out a Cuba–Turkey trade with the Russians, perhaps Washington might have awakened from the dream of American omnipotence before Lyndon Johnson launched his crusade in Vietnam" (Steel, 1973, 125–126).

Yet a third probable consequence of Cuba II was that it hastened the fall of Khrushchev. What this meant for Soviet-American relations, and for the peace of the world, is very difficult to estimate. Few scholars maintain that Khrushchev's fall was a net plus for anybody; it may well have been a distinct loss. But our rational model, performing well, allowed these unfortunate long-range consequences to come about. What went wrong?

A major effort to answer this is not possible here. But when one probes the rejection of nonforcible alternatives by ExCom and by Kennedy and asks "Why were these options foreclosed?," one is forced out to the political world, beyond the president and the Congress, to the climate generated by the beginnings of the Cold War, by the loss of China, by the trauma of Korea. One finds there partisan debate in which it becomes politically impossible for any Democrat to appear to be "soft on communism." One need not pin all this on Joe McCarthy; Patrick McCarran, Richard Nixon, Styles Bridges, and a host of spokesmen for what might be called the far right were involved. The parameters for sovereign decision had been narrowed by events in the congressional and electoral arenas.

Conclusion

This essay has focused on that arena of decision-making which holds the immediate power to destroy humankind. Within this sovereign arena, one specific decision has been analyzed: the Cuban Missile Crisis. The classic concept of rational argument, which is rejected by the most prominent contemporary decision theorist, is found nonetheless to be operative. Kennedy reacted to a stimulus, defined the situation, assembled options, gathered evidence and analyzed options, and then selected the policy that seemed to best achieve his ends.

The process was faulty, as are most human activities. Kennedy did not adequately weigh long-range goals in his analysis of options, or he had inadequate evidence of the probable effects on the Soviet Union of forcing Khrushchev to back down publicly. This failure is viewed not as a flaw in rational theory but as a consequence of the larger historical context in which the deliberation took place.

While Allison's Models II and III are rejected as irrelevant to sovereign crisis decision, no extrapolation of this rejection to congressional or electoral decision arenas is warranted. Bureaucratic process and organizational politics may be highly salient in other decision arenas. Nor is the deliberative process as traced in Cuba II held to throw light on such arguments as whether one's dormouse is torpid in the winter. The elites who conduct and the scholars who analyze argument in the foreign policy arena have found it necessary to confront crucial decisions head-on and in all their complexity. If such analysis fails to produce theory that is generalizable to all kinds of argument, this is regrettable—but foreign policy is not physics.

WALTER R. FISHER AND RICHARD A. FILLOY

[15] Argument in Drama and Literature:
An Exploration

"For although argument is a calculation and not a story, the
plot or 'myth' of a tragedy is its 'argument.'"—Richard
McKeon

Argument has been conceived traditionally in terms of clear-cut inferential
structures. So viewed, its essential constituents are *claims*, *reasons*, and *evidence*, whether conceptualized as logical product, rhetorical process, or dialectical procedure (Wenzel, 1980). Thus, unless one deduces a conclusion
from recognizable premises or infers a claim from particulars, one does not
argue. Argument is seen as the modus operandi of nonfictive genres, especially prose argumentation. Argument may appear in fictive forms of communication but it is incidental to their nature and the way they function.

Common experience tells us, however, that we do arrive at conclusions
based on "dwelling-in" dramatic and literary works (Bronowski, 1971,
77ff., 118–140; Polanyi, 17ff.; Polanyi and Prosch, 1975, 41ff.; Booth,
169). We do on occasion come to new beliefs, reaffirmations of old ones,
reorient our values, and may even be led to action. We know, in other
words, that fictive forms of communication may have rhetorical intentions
and consequences. The consequences are a result of an inferential process;
some dramatic and literary works do, in fact, argue.

Among the projects recommended in "Toward a Logic of Good Reasons," one was the exploration of the modes of proof in drama, literature,
and film (Fisher, 1974, 378). This essay undertakes that project in a limited
way by investigating the modes of proof in drama and literature, leaving
film for another enterprise. The current essay advances the logic of good
reasons project by further demonstrating that people are as much valuing as
reasoning animals, that this fact can be demonstrated by examining fictive

forms of communication, and that this behavior can be assessed in a systematic way. Specifically, we shall discuss here the relationships between rhetoric and poetic; delineate the nature of aesthetic proof in drama and literature; examine the arguments of *Death of a Salesman* and *The Great Gatsby*; propose a scheme for the assessment of aesthetic proofs; and make recommendations for further inquiry. *Salesman* and *Gatsby* were chosen because they are acclaimed forms of the genres they represent and they make parallel arguments about the American Dream (Fisher, 1973).

Rhetoric, Poetic, and Aesthetic Proof

"Rhetoric" and "poetic" are ambiguous terms. They concern theories, kinds of discourse, arts, intents, styles, and symbolic functions. We will not review all the historical arguments designed to unravel their relationships on these various levels. It is sufficient for our purposes to note those conceptions that posit overlap, the appearance of the rhetorical in the poetic, and the poetic in the rhetorical. One traditional view is that poetic forms become rhetorical when they are didactic or convey a moral. Works as diverse as Aesop's fables, Hawthorne's *The Scarlet Letter*, and Frost's "Stopping by Woods on a Snowy Evening" can be seen in this way. What distinguishes such works is generally their singularity of purpose and the explicitness of the claims they advance. These features, as qualities of argument, clearly mark the rhetorical nature of didactic literature. The attentive auditor is given little choice in understanding the aim of the work. Our intention is to show that works without such singularity and explicitness of purpose also function rhetorically. The crucial difference is that with works of the latter type the auditor must discover the claim based on experience of the work. How this discovery occurs and is verified we explain below.

Another consistent view is that, following Aristotle, rhetoric and poetic share stylistic features but differ fundamentally in form, function, or relationship to reality (Howell, 1966, 1975). While Aristotle clearly distinguishes the nature and functions of the rhetorical and poetic arts, he advises the student of rhetoric to go to the *Poetics* for "the poetical" matters of style, especially metaphor. And in regard to Thought—one of the six essential elements of drama along with Plot, Characters, Diction, Melody, and Spectacle—he says "We may assume what we said of it in our *Art of Rhetoric*, as it belongs more properly to that department of inquiry" (Aristotle, *Poetics*, ch. XIX. 1456b). Perelman and Olbrechts-Tyteca continue this line of reasoning in their *New Rhetoric*. The principal connection between rhetoric and poetic is in their concept of "presence," a process by which a speaker makes "present, by verbal magic alone, what is actually absent but what he considers important to his argument or, by making them more present, to enhance the value of some of the elements of which one has actually been made conscious" (Perelman and Olbrechts-Tyteca, 1969, 117). Among the discursive, stylistic techniques used to achieve presence are: *hypotaxis* or *demonstration, anaphora, conduplication, adjectio, amplification, sermocinatio, dialogism, onomatopoeia, personification, apostrophe,* and *prosopoeia*. "The effect of figures relating to presence," Perelman and Olbrechts-Tyteca write, "is to make the object of discourse present to mind" (174).

Perhaps the most eloquent expression of the view that rhetoric and poetic overlap is that of Fénelon. Howell describes Fénelon's *Dialogues on Eloquence* as "indisputably the best statement we have of his rhetorical theory, and the earliest statement we have of what may be said to have become the dominant modern attitude towards rhetoric" (Howell, 1951). Fénelon wrote: "Poetry differs from simple eloquence only in this: that she paints with ecstasy and with bolder strokes." Portraiture is the common means of the poet and rhetor, the duty of which is "carrying objects over into the imagination of men" (Howell, 1951, 93). Poetry, he goes on to say, "is as it were the soul of eloquence." And poetry is "the lively portraiture of things . . ." (94).

For eloquent modern statements of the view that "rhetoric and poetic are and must be closely and complementarily related," one should consult Bryant's "Uses of Rhetoric in Criticism" (Bryant, 1973, 1974) and "'Rhetoric: Its Functions and Its Scope, Redivivia'" (Bryant, 1970).

It remains to consider briefly two perspectives that provide innovations in the tradition we have outlined, those of Booth and Burke. Booth's position is clear from the first: "In writing about the rhetoric of fiction, I am not primarily interested in didactic fiction, fiction used for propaganda or instruction. My subject is the technique of non-didactic fiction, viewed as the art of communicating with readers—the rhetorical resources available to the writer of epic, novel, or short story as he tries, consciously or unconsciously, to impose his fictional world upon the reader" (Booth, 1961, Preface). He maintains "that the rhetorical dimension in literature is inescapable, evidence can be found in any successful scene, however pure, regardless of whether the author was thinking of his reader as he wrote" (105–106). Booth demonstrates the validity of this position in a masterful display of the ways authors control their readers. He concentrates especially on the rhetorical techniques of "telling" and "showing," manipulating styles of narration, and designing the characters of narrators.

No summary of Kenneth Burke's views on rhetoric and poetic can do justice to the subtlety of his thought. We can only endeavor to provide a fair sense of his direction here. His position is the most radical of those we have considered. He sees no philosophically defensible argument that can support an absolute distinction between rhetoric and poetic. Rhetoric is a symbolic function, the function of inducement (Burke, 1950, 19–46). Rhetoric arises whenever we attribute meanings to symbols; where there is meaning, there is persuasion (172). Rhetoric may be seen to operate in the experience of fictive forms of communication not only in their inducement to feel or to believe or to act in given ways, but also in regard to the appeal of the individuated forms that compose the work. "Form in literature," he writes in *Counterstatement*, "is an arousing and fulfillment of desires. A work has form in so far as one part of it leads a reader to anticipate another part, to be gratified by the sequence" (Burke, 1968, 124).

If a distinction is to be made between rhetoric and poetic, it is to be caught in these ideas: "Where a rhetorician might conceivably argue the cause of Love rather than Duty, or the other way around, in Poetics a profound dramatizing of the conflict itself would be enough; for in this field the imitation of great practical or moral problems is itself a source of gratification" (Burke, 1968, 296). Poetics is "the realm of symbolic action 'naturally' exercised for its own sake" (Burke, 1970, 409; 1978, 15–33). In other words, poetics concerns the aesthetic, consummatory function of symbols. In given works, like *The Grapes of Wrath* and the Gettysburg Address, both rhetorical and poetic functions occur. Such communications can be experienced as an inducement and a pleasure in themselves.

Our approach to the relationship between rhetoric and poetic denies none of the views we have outlined here. Our position is that a rhetorical interpretation of a work arises whenever it is considered in regard to an audience's response, the ways in which people are led to feel or to think or to act in regard to a symbolic experience. We have no quarrel with the notion that poetic discourse is rhetorical when it advances a lesson or a moral. Nor do we have difficulty with the fact that fictive and nonfictive genres share specific language forms, that one can find rhetorical features in poetic discourse and poetic features in rhetorical discourse. The difference between our approach and those of Booth and Burke is that we focus not on authorial techniques or specific individuated forms but on audience response, the mental moves made by auditors in interpreting a work. Where they stress the ways in which poetic forms are made rhetorical, we concentrate on the ways in which poetic forms are experienced rhetorically.

Let us now consider the way dramatic and literary works argue. The mode of their arguing is suggestion. Through a revelation of characters representing different value orientations in conflicts with themselves, others, and/or their environment, the auditor is induced to a felt belief, a sense of the message advanced by the work. This belief-sense of message is at first aesthetic. (An aesthetic belief is one based not on a reasoned analysis of the work's meaning but on immediate, emotional, intuitive response to the work as a representation of an enclosed, fictive world. We know that the values that Willy Loman and Jay Gatsby represent have been judged negatively, not by reasoning about them but by their fates in their worlds and our emotional satisfaction that these fates are appropriate. Works that fail to achieve this result fail as works of art.) The initial felt belief-sense of message becomes a reasoned belief-conviction, a rhetorical phenomenon, when the auditor returns to the work and recounts the elements it presented that led him or her to the interpretation. These elements, the actions and words of the characters and their results, which first provided an aesthetic sense of the work's message, also lend themselves to the reasoned account of this message, which is critical interpretation. Such elements may thus be seen as "proof" invented by the author, experienced by the auditor in seeing or reading the play or story, and used by the critic to substantiate the interpretation. Since these proofs have their origin in an aesthetic response to the work's elements, we may call them aesthetic proofs. They are outside the traditional realm of argumentative proof in that they are neither general principles that form the basis of deduction nor are they real examples that can be the basis of induction. Such proofs offer a special representation of reality somewhere between analogy and example: what they represent is not exactly our own world but it must bear a relationship to it more essential than that of analogy. In returning to a work to explain an initial interpretation, we discover the patterns among such proofs that support a conclusion and that render them part of a process of reasoning and thus within the realm of argument.

Aesthetic proof is constituted in verbal and nonverbal ways: by words and actions consistent or inconsistent with other words and actions (matters of the work's dramatic-literary probability); by considerations of whose words and actions dominate and survive, if not transcend in the conflicts between or among characters and the circumstances in which they live; and by testing the validity of characters against one's own perceptions of the nature of "real" people and "real" events—by, in other words, the work's verisimilitude. Because dramatic and literary works move by suggestion, different auditors may arrive at different interpretations. Still the range of possibilities is not infinite. Willy Loman cannot be both clear-sighted sage and deluded fool. To be legitimate, an interpretation must be based on aesthetic experiences recognizable to the auditor, it must recount the work in a way that leaves it recognizable also, and it must give a reasoned account of how aesthetic proofs are organized to create meaning.

Argument in *Death of a Salesman*

After Willy Loman is fired from his lifelong job, he visits his successful neighbor Charley to tell him the news and ask for a "loan" to pay his insurance premium. Charley, who has been the object of Willy's scorn for years, gives Willy his opinion of the business world and Willy counters with his own.

CHARLEY: The only thing you got in this world is what you can sell. And the funny thing is that you're a salesman and you don't know that.

WILLY: I've always tried to think otherwise, I guess. I always felt that if a man was impressive, and well-liked, that nothing—

CHARLEY: Why must everybody like you? Who liked J. P. Morgan? Was he impressive? In a Turkish bath he'd look like a butcher. But with his pockets on he was very well liked. . . (Miller, 1962, 1043).

In the climactic scene at the end of the play, where Biff confronts his father and brother with the truth of their existence, the following revelation occurs:

BIFF: We never told the truth for ten minutes in this house!

BIFF: And I never got anywhere because you blew me so full of hot air I could never stand taking orders from anybody!

BIFF: Pop! I'm a dime a dozen, and so are you!

WILLY: I am not a dime a dozen! I am Willy Loman, and you are Biff Loman.

BIFF: I am not a leader of men, Willy, and neither are you. You never were anything but a hardworking drummer who landed in the ash can like all the rest of them! I'm one dollar an hour, Willy! I tried seven states and couldn't raise it. . . .

WILLY: You vengeful, spiteful mutt!

BIFF: Pop, I'm nothing! I'm nothing, Pop! Can't you understand that? There's no spite in it any more. I'm just what I am, that's all.

WILLY: What're you doing? What're you doing? Why is he crying?

BIFF: Will you let me go, for Christ's sake? Will you take that phony dream and burn it before something happens? (1052).

These two quotations seem to embody two of the play's most important conclusions. In the first, Willy expresses his credo that appearance and reputation are the essential requirements for material success. Charley, consistently a voice of harsh and even mocking realism, declares this belief to be false; and indeed, Willy's whole life, as revealed by the play, supports this inference. Willy's adherence to his illusion leads to embittered destitution. It is from this position that he must confront the more profound realization expressed in the second quotation. Not only had he been wrong in his assumption about what being successful requires, he has deceived himself about his reputation and character. Moreover, he has taught his sons, to their immense cost, the same tricks of self-deception. As a result, Willy does not—nor can he ever—understand what has happened to him and his sons. Thus Willy is incapable of seeing that his misperception of the business world is a corollary of his inability (and final refusal) to confront himself realistically.

Together the two illusions that have guided Willy's life suggest a further conclusion. The price of self-deception is not merely inability to win in the business world, it also is a failure to realize that material success will not bring personal and family happiness. Willy's vision of the American Dream is material well-being founded on "respectable" work, business, or the professions, but the manual labor he scorns—being a carpenter—seems to be his most genuine source of satisfaction. His self-deception has led him to desire and expect every material sign of status and success where self-knowledge might have led to happiness and a sense of well-being with more modest but real accomplishments. This side of Willy and the general conclusion which underlies it, is expressed by Biff, who has been able to face his true self, when he says "He had the wrong dream. All, all wrong" (1054).

These conclusions, based as they are on suggestion, cannot be shown to be absolutely or exclusively those of the play. We can show, however, those elements of the work and the process of inference that led us to them. In doing so we intend to exemplify the modes of proof mentioned in the preceding section and to illustrate the type of thought that characterizes inference in the experience of fictive forms.

When we seek to recount the way in which the play argues for these conclusions, we are immediately struck by the realization that much of our inference depends not on the playwright's text but on the actors who perform it. Tone, gesture, carriage, and other aspects of stagecraft can communicate persuasively in a way words alone cannot duplicate. The performer creates much of the meaning of the play, and the immediacy of that meaning makes it especially important. The playwright includes stage directions to guide the actors and director; and they, in the performance, seek to interpret the play as the author intended. Meaning in drama is thus the product of cooperation between author and performer, and the auditor must attempt to account for the role of the performance in explaining that meaning. To do so in print and without a specific performance in mind is obviously not entirely satisfactory, for we must rely on the stage directions and use our imaginations to do the rest. We must, however, take notice of this aspect of the play's mode of argument, as it is crucial to our understanding.

The importance of appearance in the Lomans' lives, for instance, must be perceived largely in regard to their physical appearances. We must be able to see at Willy's first entrance that he is a beaten man. The directions describe his exhaustion, the "soreness of his palms," and his sigh. The ensuing despondent conversation with Linda confirms his sense of defeat about his own life and Biff's. The powerful initial impression provides the background for all his subsequent faith in appearances and reputation.

Almost immediately afterward we see Willy transported back to more hopeful times. Willy instructs his sons on polishing the car and explains his belief:

> And they know me, boys, they know me up and down New England. The finest people. And when I bring you fellas up, there'll be open season for all of us, 'cause one thing boys: I have friends. . . .

> That's why I thank Almighty God you're both built like Adonises. Because the man who makes an appearance in the business world, the man who creates personal interest, is the man who gets ahead. Be liked and you will never want . . . (1026).

The auditors, however, must contrast this brave statement with what they have just seen and arrive at a different conclusion. But even in this scene there are intimations of the falseness of this belief in the efficacy of a good appearance. Bernard comes to warn Biff that he cannot succeed on appearance alone. "Just because he printed University of Virginia on his sneakers doesn't mean they've got to graduate him, Uncle Willy!" (1026) Again, the visual contrast is important. Biff's appearance and self-confidence overwhelm Bernard, who is small, worried, and unathletic. When the play reveals the current contrasts, Biff, a confused failure, and Bernard, a confident young lawyer, give further evidence of the falseness of Willy's belief.

Other incidents in the play confirm this conclusion in similar ways. Willy assures Biff that Bill Oliver will lend him money if he has the correct appearance and manner because "personality always wins the day" (1035). But, as we later learn, Biff had no real chance of getting a loan. Remembering Biff's high school days, Willy reassures himself of Biff's promise with the words "A star like that, magnificent, can never really fade away" (1036). When Charley finally tells Willy the truth about appearance and personality, there can be little doubt that the play has supported this conclusion. The conclusion will seem correct in the play's own terms, however, only if the audience has perceived a genuine failure of these qualities. It is thus important that we see that the Lomans are physically attractive and fail nonetheless. Similarly, Willy's charm and self-confidence do not win the day, but we must see that they really do exist.

Support for the conclusion that the Lomans are self-deceiving and that this quality prevents them from understanding their true positions is similarly strong. In some cases the same incidents both support this idea and show Willy's false faith in appearances. The belief that Bill Oliver is bound to lend Biff money and that Willy ultimately will be a more successful businessman than Charley because he is better liked are examples of both self-delusion and the belief in appearances. Others of Willy's illusions reveal why he cannot understand his life. On his return home at the play's beginning he says:

> If old man Wagner was alive I'd a been in charge of New York by now! That man was a prince, he was a masterful man. But that boy of his, that Howard, he don't appreciate. When I went north the first time, the Wagner Company didn't know where New England was! (1021)

Early in the second act he says of Howard "I'll put it to him straight and simple. He'll just have to take me off the road" (1036). But when the actual interview comes, Willy's real position is revealed and he is shown pleading pathetically for any job at all. When he is fired he is shocked, but the auditor can hardly escape the conclusion that this shock is mostly the product of Willy's exaggerated idea of his value. Indeed, all of Willy's talk about his success as a salesman is undercut early in the play when he reports to Linda his sales for one trip. He begins by reporting 1200 gross and retreats gradually to 200, and then makes excuses for his performance, ending with:

Oh, I'll knock 'em dead next week. I'll go to Hartford. I'm very well-liked in Hartford. [*Pause*] You know, the trouble is, Linda, people don't seem to take to me (1027).

In these scenes the performance of Willy is crucial. As he contradicts himself, he might seem merely foolish or deceitful. He must be genuinely confused, and it must be clear that this confusion is the result of his long habit of self-deception. When performed in this way, Willy's personality and constant changeability become an argument for the consequences of self-deception.

In a parallel way, Willy cannot understand Biff's problems, because he has refused to admit they exist. He says of Biff's aimless life: "Certain men just don't get started till later in life. Like Thomas Edison, I think. Or B. F. Goodrich. One of them was deaf. I'll put my money on Biff." Yet only moments earlier he has said "Biff is a lazy bum" (1022). He really believes neither statement, but he hides behind them to avoid real understanding of Biff.

Willy consistently refuses to acknowledge the part he played in shaping Biff's character. He says of Biff at one point:

He's got spirit, personality. . . . Loaded with it. Loaded! What is he stealing? He's giving it back, isn't he? Why is he stealing? What did I tell him? I never in my life told him anything but decent things (1028).

Yet we have already seen him laughing at Biff's theft of a football, and later we see him encouraging the boys to steal from a building site. Willy tells Bernard that he is mystified by Biff's loss of initiative after high school and is eager to deny any responsibility, but we later learn that Biff found Willy in Boston with another woman and was crushed by the discovery.

Biff and Happy themselves are clearly products of Willy's mentality, and this is nowhere clearer than in the scene where they plan Biff's new business venture. Biff is reluctant to believe in the plan but his father and brother encourage him until all three are caught up in the idea.

Here too the stage directions direct the performance and are basic to interpreting the meaning. Both Biff and Happy are "lost," but in different ways. Biff, who has escaped much of his father's self-deception, has a "worn air and seems less self-assured"; it is Happy who clings to the self-deception and who is "thus more confused . . . although seemingly more content" (1022–1023). If the actors can realize this description, it will make an additional statement about the connection between self-deception and personal confusion.

The result of this personal confusion, the inability to recognize appropriate goals and to value them, is a permanent dissatisfaction with oneself. This conclusion is most clearly argued in Willy's case by the scenes in which his brother Ben appears. Ben's appearance almost always accompanies some dissatisfaction or confusion of Willy's. Ben is "utterly certain of his destiny." Willy calls him "the only man I ever met who knew the answers" (1024). But neither Willy nor his sons can live up to the ideal of Ben. His actions are too bold, and his standards are too much those of the jungle for life in the city. He comes to represent, in Willy's mind, the clear and simple solution to every problem. These solutions, however, are out of reach; they tantalize but never satisfy. These are the harvest of Willy's lifelong self-deception. The missed opportunity to go to Alaska only makes the reality of Willy's career harder to accept. The attempt to raise his sons as "fearless characters" (1031) results in Willy's encouragement of their dishonesty and adds to their ultimate unhappiness. In the end, it is with the blessing of this idealized Ben that Willy commits suicide, believing it to be an act of courage in pursuit of his dream of success.

Willy's tragic death shows the ultimate loss of self that lack of self-knowledge can bring. The case of Happy shows a less extreme but equally clear example. Happy's compulsive womanizing and his pursuit of the symbols of success have no real meaning for him, and he doesn't understand why he pursues them. As he tells Biff near the play's beginning,

> I get that any time I want, Biff. Whenever I feel disgusted. The only trouble is, it gets like bowling or something, I just keep knockin' them over and it doesn't mean anything. . . . I don't know what gets into me, maybe I just have an overdeveloped sense of competition or something, but I went and ruined her, and furthermore I can't get rid of her. . . . I hate myself for it. Because I don't want the girl, and, still, I take it and—I love it (1024).

Even after Willy's death, Happy clings to his illusions, endorsing Willy's dream to be "number-one man" and vowing to "win it for him" (1054).

Only Biff, who has had the painful realization that he is "a dime a dozen," can face his future with some peace. He will not be important or rich, but he can have "the things I love in this world. The work and the food and time to sit and smoke." For Willy and Happy those things can never be enough. They must pursue an ideal they can never achieve because they cannot see themselves as they are. The suggestion of this conclusion is built into the words and actions of the Lomans and further reinforced by the directions for performance.

Without being explicitly didactic or moralistic, *Salesman* argues for a conclusion that has relevance beyond its own characters and their actions. It suggests that the set is illusions with which Willy Loman destroys himself are built deeply into many versions of the American Dream and the dreamers are more often like Willy than like Ben. Even those who do succeed in acquiring the outward signs of success are rarely as sure of their destinies as Willy's idealized Ben. They are all too often like Happy's boss, who "builds an estate and hasn't the peace of mind to live in it" (1024). Such people are only incidental to *Salesman*, but they form the main subject of our second example, *The Great Gatsby*.

Argument in *The Great Gatsby*

Near the end of *Gatsby*, the narrator, Nick Carraway, meets Tom Buchanan, the man who was in many ways Gatsby's opposite and to a large extent responsible for his death. Carraway, in recording the meeting, observes:

> I couldn't forgive him or like him, but I saw that what he had done was, to him, entirely justified. It was all very careless and confused. They were careless people, Tom and Daisy—they smashed up things and creatures and then retreated back into their money or their vast carelessness, or whatever it was that kept them together, and let other people clean up the mess they had made. . . .
>
> I shook hands with him; it seemed silly not to, for I suddenly felt as though I were talking to a child. Then he went into the jewelry store to buy a pearl necklace—or perhaps only a pair of cuff buttons—rid of my provincial squeamishness forever [Fitzgerald, 1925, 180–181].

At the novel's conclusion, only a few hundred words later, Carraway reflects on Gatsby.

> I thought of Gatsby's wonder when he first picked out the green light at the end of Daisy's dock. He had come a long way to this blue lawn, and his dream must have seemed so close that he could hardly fail to grasp it. He did not know that it was already behind him, somewhere back in that vast obscurity beyond the city, where the dark fields of the republic rolled on under the night.
>
> Gatsby believed in the green light, the orgiastic future that year by year recedes before us. It eludes us then, but that's no matter—tomorrow we will run faster, stretch out our arms farther. . . . And one fine morning—

So we beat on, boats against the current, borne back ceaselessly into the past (182).

These observations seem to us to summarize a conclusion, or a set of related inferences suggested by the novel as a whole.

The first quotation suggests the vast privilege of the rich, a privilege that is unhealthy in its regard for dignity and worth of those other than themselves. This conclusion leads in an important way to the second quotation. Here the narrator points to the futility of clinging to a static dream and how, in such cases, the past overwhelms the future and the dream bewitches the dreamer. What links these two ideas is Gatsby himself. His idealized, romantic dream, the undivided love of a pure Daisy, is confused with the acquisition of the privileges of the world of wealth in which she lives. Thus his huge house and wealthy guests demonstrate to him that he had overcome the important obstacles to Daisy's love. The revelation of the falseness of this belief leads us to the third and main conclusion: Even the privileges of wealth cannot transform the ideal into the real. Gatsby's acquisition of every symbol of material success cannot make him a member of Daisy's world, the secure and settled world of the old rich. Nor can it turn back the clock and bring him Daisy, his dream's palpable symbol, as she was before her marriage. The American Dream, as Gatsby has (and presumably others have) dreamed it, is hollow and deceptive, implying that if one achieves the rewards of material success—wealth, power, and status—it will also provide all that one wants, including happiness and spiritual well-being. Gatsby is destroyed by his relentless pursuit of this paradoxical dream, caught by the self-centered compassionless indifference of those he would emulate.

Like the conclusions we found in *Death of a Salesman*, these can make no claims to absoluteness or exclusivity. We aim, here as there, to explain our inferences of them and illuminate the process of argument in literature.

The first inference a reader must make is one regarding the narrator's reliability (Booth). If we are to accept Nick's judgments, we must be convinced that the author intends us to view him as a competent observer, a fair judge, and a reasonable representative of our own perception of characters and events in the story. Given the importance of the readers' attitude toward Nick, the novel opens with a discussion of his carefulness and reserve in making judgments, a trait that has "opened up many curious natures" to him and that promises the audience an unusually able observer of human affairs. He is modest in establishing his credentials as an observer, asserting that "most of the confidences were unsought" (1); but the concern for their establishment is clear. We are assured of Nick's ethical normality as he confesses that his tolerance has limits and that he wishes for a world in which morality is a stabilizing force. He relates to us a set of biographical circumstances that mark him as both thoroughly trustworthy and completely stable in his values. He comes from solid stock, "prominent, well-to-do people in this Middle Western city" (2), but he is not unusually wealthy. He has been conventionally but well educated; has served his country in war; and has now, after his youthful wanderlust in the East, settled in his home town.

He stands in an ideal position for the narrator of a story about unusual people. He is not himself unusual, but circumstances have given him the opportunity to observe a special, privileged world. He has the personality to take full advantage of that opportunity while remaining essentially like his audience in values.

Having been introduced in this way, Nick must conduct himself in accordance with these characteristics throughout the novel. Thus in the novel's many unusual situations we learn not only of the occurrences but also of Nick's feelings about them. Attending Gatsby's extravagant parties, meeting Tom Buchanan's mistress Myrtle, seeing Meyer Wolfsheim, and arranging Gatsby's funeral are all situations in which Nick participates while assuring us of his reluctance, discomfort, and even disapproval. Yet in each case he conducts himself with that cautious reserve which allows him to continue as an observer. In his relations with Jordan Baker he is, by his own admission, excessively punctilious; but, as he says, "I wanted to leave things in order and not just trust that obliging and indifferent sea to sweep my refuse away" (178).

Thus readers who wish to recount the reasons for considering Gatsby's narrator a reliable guide to the story's action and meaning will find both a general claim and particulars to support it. They may then feel secure in looking to the next question. By what means, other than the sort of overt commentary cited above, does the narrator convey his conclusions and his reasons for them? One way to do this is to make a rough division between those things the narrator reports and the way in which he reports them.

Much of the book's argument is clearly derived from the reported actions and words of the characters. For instance, the view that the privilege of the rich is unhealthy is supported by a number of events. The behavior of the guests at Gatsby's parties is dramatized boorishness, a lack of a true regard for others, verified by the failure of any of them to attend his funeral. Similarly, Tom Buchanan's cavalier mistreatment of his mistress and his wife is highlighted in our final view of him unconcernedly buying jewels. Even Daisy is willing to have Gatsby take the blame for her having run over Myrtle. Numerous other examples can be given. Tom's smug and foolish racial views, Daisy's bored thrill-seeking, and Jordan's avowed carelessness are all alike in this regard. In all these cases the characters, through their own actions and words, portray themselves; the narrator merely selects and reports. However, this "showing" of support for a belief is constantly supported by the narrator's "telling" about the events.

In recording the action of Gatsby's guests, for example, Nick tells us that their laughter is "vacuous" (47), that their conversation is characterized by "casual innuendo and introductions forgotten on the spot" (40), and that they "had found little that it was necessary to whisper about in the world" (44). These and other descriptive remarks provide a tonal coloration that corroborates the meaning of the events themselves. Once we have accepted Nick as a trustworthy observer, such coloration becomes further evidence supporting the reader's conclusions. Indeed, much of the characterization is accomplished in this way rather than by direct speech or action. Before we hear him speak, we learn of Tom Buchanan that he was "one of those men who reach such an acute and limited excellence at twenty-one that everything afterwards savors of anticlimax," that he had "a rather hard mouth and supercilious manner" and "a cruel body," and that he had an air of "paternal contempt" (7). When we also learn that he is "enormously wealthy" (6) and that "Something was making him nibble at the edge of stale ideas as if his sturdy physical egotism no longer nourished his peremptory heart" (21), another support is added to our conclusion about the rich. We are also prepared to interpret correctly his subsequent treatment of Daisy and Myrtle. In a similar way we learn that Daisy has an "absurd, charming little laugh" and that a look "promising that there was no one in the world she so much wanted to see" is a mannerism of hers (9). In Daisy's flightiness we see another species of unhealthy privilege, and her ultimate irresponsibility toward Gatsby is foreshadowed. Again, in Nick's description of Jordan as "incurably dishonest" (58) and "this clean, hard, limited person who dealt in universal scepticism" (81), we see another example of the danger of privilege, and we are given a critical cue to understanding her pose of carelessness. In an argumentative sense, each element of proof strengthens others. Nick's authoritative judgments are rendered surer by the examples that support them, while the examples are clarified and given meaning by his judgments.

The same elements of proof appear in support of the notion that pursuit of a static ideal is futile, but they are rather differently arranged. There is only one significant event that supports this conclusion, Gatsby's pursuit of Daisy; but it forms the main action of the book. As such it carries great weight and is complex in its demonstration. The futility of Gatsby's quest is made clear in the climactic scene in the hotel where Daisy tells him that he wants too much and that she cannot deny that she has loved Tom. Thereafter Gatsby's world disintegrates. Still clinging to the dream, he assumes the blame for Myrtle's death and attempts to protect Daisy from Tom. Daisy, however, uses the opportunity not to elope with Gatsby but to be reconciled with Tom and leave town. By the time Tom betrays him to Wilson, Gatsby's death seems inevitable. Obviously, Daisy is no longer (if she ever was) the woman Gatsby had cherished in his dream. The auditor does not have to rely solely on the chain of events culminating in Gatsby's death to appreciate the novel's revelation of the futility of pursuing unchanging dreams.

Our first intimations of Gatsby's dream come in a conversation in which his obvious posing tempts Nick to "incredulous laughter" (66) and leaves him "more annoyed than interested" (62). As we gradually discover the precise nature of the dream, we are reminded frequently of its fantasy and hopelessness. Of the first afternoon that Daisy and Gatsby meet, Nick comments "there must have been moments even that afternoon when Daisy tumbled short of his dreams—not through her own fault, but because of the colossal vitality of his illusion" (97). Later, as Nick realizes the extent of that illusion, he attempts to warn Gatsby and again reminds the audience of the realism dreamers must eventually confront.

> "I wouldn't ask too much of her," I ventured. "You can't repeat the past."
> "Can't repeat the past?" he cried incredulously. "Why of course you can."
> He looked around him wildly, as if the past were lurking here in the shadow of his house, just out of reach of his hand [111].

During the climactic confrontation in the hotel room, we are told that Gatsby's "dead dream fought on . . . trying to touch what was no longer tangible" (135). In the same scene Nick contrasts Jordan to Daisy by saying "Jordan . . . was too wise ever to carry well-forgotten dreams from age to age" (136). And, finally, when Gatsby reveals his true past to Nick, it is "because 'Jay Gatsby' had broken up like glass against Tom's hard malice, and the long secret extravaganza was played out" (148). Even Tom, hard as he is, is judged to be driven by such an illusion, for we are told "I felt that Tom would drift on forever seeking, a little wistfully, for the dramatic turbulence of some irrecoverable football game" (6). Both Nick's overt commentary and the tonal coloration of his reports of actions reinforce the novel's claim about the pursuit of dreams; the reader who seeks to recount a perception of this claim can find a convincing combination of precept and example in support.

The basis for combining the two conclusions we have so far traced is primarily to be found in the narrator's commentary and interpretation. The events we have already mentioned form the basis for these comments and interpretations, but the confusion of the privileges of wealth with the realization of a romantic dream is a mental action and can thus only be fully recounted indirectly. Nonetheless, we are given as direct an evidence of the confusion as possible when Gatsby says of Daisy "Her voice is full of money" (120). But it is not until the narrator expands on this theme that we grasp the full import of the remark.

> That was it. I'd never understood before. It was full of money—that was the inexhaustible charm that rose and fell in it, the jingle of it, the cymbals' song of it. . . . High in a white palace the king's daughter, the golden girl . . . [120].

There are other instances where the combination is explored. In discussing Gatsby's origins, Nick explains that Gatsby's view of wealth is almost reverential. "Jay Gatsby . . . sprang from his Platonic conception of himself. He was a son of God—a phrase which, if it means anything, means just that—and he must be about his father's business, the service of a vast, vulgar, and meretricious beauty" (99). Daisy, young, healthy, and "the first 'nice' girl he had ever known" (148) becomes the embodiment of that beauty. "Gatsby was overwhelmingly aware of the youth and mystery that wealth imprisons and preserves, of the freshness of many clothes, and of Daisy, gleaming like silver, safe and proud above the hot struggles of the poor" (150). He is trapped. He has "wed his unutterable visions to her perishable breath" (112), and it only remains for him to act out the consequences of his tragic delusion.

One may obtain the symbols of achievement and satisfaction, but these are not a means to the ends they symbolize. By themselves they are hollow, and the very hollowness of the symbols becomes a cause of depravity and desperation.

Assessment of Aesthetic Proof

One tests one's interpretation of a dramatic or literary work in ways implied by our exploration of the aesthetic experience, the elements of aesthetic proof, and the arguments in *Death of a Salesman* and *The Great Gatsby*. The procedure entails four considerations. First is determining the message, the overall conclusions fostered by the work. Second is deciding whether the determination of message is justified by (a) the reliability of the narrator(s); (b) the words and actions of other characters; and (c) the descriptions of characters, scenes, and events—which are verbal in literature and both verbal and nonverbal in drama, where they may be represented physically as well as in words. Third is noting the outcomes of the various conflicts that make up the story, observing whose values seem most powerful and/or worthy, whether events are controlled by characters or forces outside them. Up to this point, the primary concern is whether the story rings true as a story in itself and what is the "truth" it makes known. Fourth is weighing this "truth," the set of conclusions advanced by the story, against one's own perceptions of the world. The questions are (a) whether the message accurately portrays the world we live in and (b) whether it provides a reliable guide to our beliefs, attitudes, values, and/or actions.

A parallel may be drawn between the four considerations involved in testing one's interpretation of a dramatic or literary work with the criterial questions that compose the logic of good reasons. The parallel is justified not only because they are both "logical" schemes but also, and more importantly, because they are both systems for assessing values. As pointed out earlier, dramatic and literary works display value-laden conflicts between or among characters, events, and/or external forces. It is also the case that dramatic and literary "messages" are value-laden. We have seen in *Salesman* and *Gatsby* that the materialistic myth of the American Dream can be a tragic delusion, leading not to happiness or well-being but to self-destruction. Both works reaffirm the values of self-knowledge and acceptance over conformity and false dreams.

The first three considerations in testing one's interpretation of a dramatic or literary work are parallel with the criterial questions of the logic of good reasons—*fact* and *relevance*. The fourth consideration, concerning the accuracy of dramatic and literary portrayal and the value of the message, coincides with the criterial questions of *consequence*, *consistency*, and *transcendent issue*. We are convinced that *Salesman* and *Gatsby* satisfy the aesthetic requirements detailed in the first three considerations, the matters of aesthetic soundness, and that this is proved by the preceding analyses of the two works.

The questions at this point are the accuracy of the portrayals of life in the two works and whether their conclusions are worthy of adherence. Based on our experiences, we judge the characters of *Salesman* and *Gatsby* to be true to life—in principle. While we have not known a "Willy Loman," a "Gatsby," or people like the Buchanans, we have "dwelled-in" their characters and found in each of them experiences familiar to our own. As Bronowski observes, "The most moving experience of literature makes us aware that we too are swept by the waves of lust and destruction that overwhelm other men. We too taste in inner agony the salt tang of cruelty that we call inhuman, and learn that it is most human. We have it in us to be murderers and con-men and perverts and the scum of the earth" (Bronowski, 1971, 75). *Salesman* and *Gatsby* provide such experience, and they ring true to the human condition.

To the question whether the central conclusions of these works are reliable/desirable guides for one's own life, we would say yes. We are reassured in this judgment because we believe that construction of a positive self-image, improvement in one's behavior toward others and society, and enhancement of the process of rhetorical transaction are all fostered by the recognition that the materialistic myth of the American Dream can be a tragic delusion and that self-knowledge and acceptance are higher values than conformity to unexamined standards. This message is confirmed in our own experiences, the experiences of others, and in the pronouncements of spiritual leaders from all segments of society. Finally, we are sure in our judgment that self-knowledge and acceptance are prerequisites to happiness and well-being, and that these values are transcendent. The fact that the conclusions themselves are familiar, while the works in which they appear are fresh and compelling, indicates both the transcendence and the immediate worth of the values.

Saul Bellow's words summarize our own view of argument in dramatic and literary works: "The artist, as Collingwood tells us, must be a prophet, 'not in the sense that he foretells things to come, but that he tells the audience, at risk of their displeasure, the secrets of their own hearts.' That is why he exists. He is spokesman of his community. . . . Art is the community's medicine for the worst disease of mind, the corruption of consciousness" (Bellow, 1973, 423).

Such is the medicine offered by *Death of a Salesman* and *The Great Gatsby*.

Further Inquiry

We have aimed to describe the nature of argument in drama and literature working through two exemplars of the sort of analysis we have in mind. We have seen in these examples the outlines of a theory of argument by aesthetic proof. It is by no means complete, but some features seem clear. Aesthetic proofs depend on our sense of the internal consistency and appropriateness of a work of fiction. These proofs are transformed into arguments by our ability to organize them into reasonable patterns suggesting conclusions. The works may then be said to argue for these conclusions. The patterns of aesthetic proof are based on similarity to the real world as we observe it but often appear in intensified form in fiction. Within the work itself, the patterns of reasoning are not linear but the result of the mutual reinforcement of different elements of proof: the words of characters accompanying non-verbal communication, actions, authorial commentary or stage directions, natural or chance occurrences, and the like. The patterns the elements of aesthetic proof form are usually first apparent to us as felt beliefs and only upon reflection are they recognizable as the products of reason. All these features, however, demand confirmation through further exploration. Our first recommendation, therefore, is that additional, more elaborate studies be done with works similar to *Death of a Salesman* and *The Great Gatsby*, such as *The Misfits* and *The Grapes of Wrath*. Investigations should be made of works in other genres: melodramas, absurdist plays, comedies, and stream-of-consciousness novels. We also recommend that attention should be given to other fictive modes of communication, including film and poetry, especially lyric poetry. Finally, we recommend a testing of the concepts of aesthetic proof and their assessment in classrooms and rhetorical criticism. With such work it may be proved beyond doubt that artists reason and make rational sense as well as illuminate our lives by "showing" and "telling."

RICHARD D. RIEKE

[16] Argumentation in the Legal Process

San Francisco police found a seventeen-year-old woman in a cheap hotel room with two sailors. She was arrested, charged with vagrancy, and about to be sentenced to county jail (where prostitutes went in those days early in this century) when the famous defense lawyer Jake Ehrlich happened into the courtroom. Curious, he learned the charges from the prosecutor and then approached the accused. He spoke to her quietly and gently and she told him she had run away from Montana when her parents died and ended up in San Francisco with no money and hopeless. The sailors had helped her. Over the prosecutor's loud objections that he was not the attorney in this case, Ehrlich announced his "client" would plead not guilty. He spent five minutes going over the story and then began his unrehearsed argument:

> From my own experience—which the court will agree has been extensive in these matters—I tell you that the City and County of San Francisco is preparing to make a prostitute of this frightened little girl. Put her through the humiliating police procedure, throw her in with those you have convicted of the oldest profession, and you can make of her, too, a woman of the streets. She should be returned to her home [Noble and Averbuch, 1955, 6].

And so they sent her back to Montana.

The modern cynic might say the story was ridiculously naive; the feminist might rail against such generally sexist behavior; sentimentalists might praise the life-saving efforts of the lawyer; the specialist in argumentation might sneer at such an illogical, unsupported, emotional so-called argument. Whatever your reaction, the story neatly opens the door for a look at argumentation in the legal process.

Most frequently, our attention is called to legal argument when we encounter the elegant phrases of an appellate court opinion on some aspect of the Constitution. No one would deny that this is an example of reasoned discourse most fully refined. But the casual encounter between an overworked public defender, a client who has been consulted only minutes before, and a jaded criminal court judge is an equally appropriate instance of what lawyers do. So, too, is the telephone call that begins "Gloria? This is Archie. Listen, I've been authorized by the insurance company to offer you five thousand dollars to settle that bent beer-truck case. What do you say?"

Lawyers deal with people who have problems, think they have problems, expect to have problems, or want to avoid problems. Lawyers reason with clients, rehearse arguments that would be presented to courts should the occasion arise, make and support claims to other lawyers representing opponents, advocate their position in trials, and argue their appeals before higher courts. Generally speaking, lawyers are professional communicators, and most of their communication involves some form of reasoning or argumentation.

Historical Relationship Between Rhetoric and Law

A symbiosis has existed between the intellectual study of rhetoric/communication and the practice of law for a long, long time—more than two thousand years. Sometimes, as in the case of an ancient Cicero or a modern Wellman, the interrelationship occurs in one person. Both of these men were accomplished forensic practitioners and erudite commentators on the theory of their communication behavior. Mostly, however, lawyers and rhetoricians have gone their separate way, relating to each other from a distance. While Aristotle's rhetorical theory embodied and systematized the process of legal decision-making, and while Cicero and Quintilian formalized the relationship between rhetoric and law, the intellectual-professional fragmentation that appeared in the medieval period set the pattern that persists today. During the Middle Ages, rhetoric contributed parts of itself to many other disciplines, sometimes retaining its identity as rhetoric, sometimes being completely lost through absorption in the new field. This was particulary true in the development of law. The practice of law broke off great chunks of the system developed in Greece and Rome and carried it on as part of law. The system of legal debate or trial along with the theories of evidence and proof were part of this, as were the processes of interpretation of law and the formulation of rational decisions through the enthymematic combination of law and fact.

By the time it emerged from the Middle Ages into the Renaissance, legal practice had an identity of its own and had developed a system of legal education quite apart from the formal study of rhetoric. Paul Hamlin (1939), in his history of legal education in Colonial New York, notes that the Inns of Court and Chancery developed control of the entry into legal practice in England by the end of the thirteenth century. On the other hand, William Phillips Sanford (1938), in his dissertation on English theories of public address, does not find rhetorical theory regaining its structure and prominence until the sixteenth century with the work of Thomas Cox, Thomas Wilson, and Richard Sherry. Eventually, preparation for law became a process of apprenticeship similar to the crafts or trades. Thus, the rhetorical characteristics of legal practice were preserved and passed on by imitation. The apprenticeship system was brought to Colonial America and persisted until the rise of law schools.

The negative correlation between the growth of law schools and the demise of interest in teaching the practice of law, including all the communication argumentation elements, is a story to long to tell here. We can give only a brief summary.

At first, it seemed as if the establishment of law schools would reinstate the formal ties between rhetorical theory and legal practice. In 1794 James Kent was appointed Professor of Law at Columbia College, and in his first lecture he said "A lawyer in a free country should have all the requisites of Quintilian's orator. He should be a person of irreproachable virtue and goodness. He should be well read in the whole circle of the arts and sciences. He should be fit for the administration of public affairs, and to govern the commonwealth by his councils . . . he ought to develop his powers of close reasoning . . . and he ought to have acquired the art of public speaking." Note that Kent included the study of reasoning within logic and mathematics, a reflection of medieval fragmentation. Note also that his advice was not taken with regard to the training of a lawyer.

In the first attempt to prescribe a course of study for law students in America, around 1756, the curriculum included work in logic and rhetoric. In the first announcement of the establishment of the Harvard Law School, it was noted that students would be permitted to study under professors in the Arts College, and John Quincy Adams, then Boylston Professor of Rhetoric and Oratory, was one of those specifically mentioned. In 1857 Columbia University established a school of jurisprudence which included in its study the reading of Aristotle's work in rhetoric and logic and Cicero's De Oratore.

Two forces combined to prevent the continuation of this trend toward educating lawyers both in the principles of law and the rhetorical elements of its practice. First, the remnants of medievalism left rhetoric with a seedy image of sophistry. Reasoning or argument was perceived as formal and having nothing to do with communication, so teaching rhetoric seemed to be nothing more than teaching Plato's trickery. Second, law schools found themselves in tough competition with the apprenticeship system. Future lawyers were hard put to see what they could learn in school that they could not learn by working with actual practitioners. And the most obvious superiority of apprenticing was learning how to do lawyering—talking with clients, settling with opponents, writing briefs and memoranda, persuading a jury. So law schools stressed the importance of learning legal principles and philosophy, denigrated the importance of learning advocacy, and gained sufficient control of bar examinations to reinforce these priorities.

Still, there were some holdouts. Yale, for example, believed that the duty of the law school was to provide a full course of preparation for the prospective lawyer, and this included the rhetoric of the law. For example, William C. Robinson was a professor at Yale who wrote *Forensic Oratory: A Manual for Advocates* (1893). He emphasized the need for law to rediscover the classic traditions of rhetoric as expressed by Aristotle, Cicero, and Quintilian. His presentation showed clear influence from the British rhetoricians Campbell, Blair, and Whately. But his was not to be the influential voice.

It was Harvard, not Yale, that set the pattern for legal education that has prevailed to this time. At Harvard, the theory was that legal education should consist of study in philosophy and principles of law. The rhetorical-communicative elements were completely rejected on the grounds that all one needed to be an effective advocate was knowledge of the law. If students wanted to spend their own time in moot courts and the like, they could only so long as it did not detract from their formal studies.

In return, specialists in argumentation and debate have been content to leave law to the law professors, for the most part. We have known that many of our students in debate classes and forensic activities go on to law school, but we have felt that undergraduate instruction in the general principles and skills of argumentation was the extent of our contribution. With occasional exceptions, the symbiotic relationship between argumentation and law has been maintained only indirectly through the experience of students who go on to become lawyers. As recently as the mid-1960s puzzled looks of incomprehension were the most common response to the announcement by a student of speech communication that he intended to study rhetorical theory in legal practice (Rieke, 1964).

Today that is no longer the case. Over the past decade or so an increasing number of communication scholars has focused attention on the communication elements in legal practice. This has led to programs at professional conventions and ultimately to communication and law interest groups. It is now possible to present a review of scholarly research in the field that reflects almost entirely the work of communication-trained researchers.

Review of Research Literature

For convenience, it is possible to group recent research into seven categories: (1) rhetorically oriented analyses of outstanding advocates, leading cases, legal pedagogy, and rhetorical theory in the concept of jurisprudence; (2) experimental or descriptive studies of selected trial factors; (3) applied studies aimed at understanding and improving the judicial instructions to juries; (4) analytic and instructional commentaries on the performance of certain lawyer communication functions; (5) experimental and descriptive studies of the use of television in the discovery and trial process; (6) systems-oriented studies of the discovery and trial process; and (7) analyses of alternatives to trial. The purpose of this review is threefold: first, to collect in one place a reasonably complete listing of the kind of work that has been done; second, to locate significant areas of research that have not attracted communication interest; and third, to suggest thereby some questions that call for future study.

Rhetorical analyses. Because specialists in argumentation have typically come from a background in rhetorical theory and criticism, and because the closing argument in a trial or the written opinion of an appellate court closely approximates a public-speaking situation, the most well-established area of legal communication research is criticism of leading advocates. Some leading forensic orators continue to attract scholarly study, as is true for Clarence Darrow. The application of Burkeian analysis to Darrow and his opponent Alexander Rorke in the case of *New York* v. *Gitlow* (Sanbonmatsu, 1971) described the importance of symbolism to establish identification between advocate and jury in the closing argument. A historical-rhetorical study of the strategies in the courtrooms of territorial Arkansas (Smith, 1977) revealed the importance of time and place in adjusting to rhetorical situations. Arguments became legal dramas in the Arkansas of the 1800s.

Leading cases will always provide raw data for some form of rhetorical analysis, whether to note the place of legal reasoning in the legal-social-cultural-political development of the country or to develop theories of legal justification, or to generate an understanding of the impact of judicial decisions on freedom of expression. The fact that so much of the national debate on school desegregation and other civil rights issues took place in the courts rather than in legislatures meant necessarily much rhetorical attention had to be aimed at legal communication (Dickens and Schwartz, 1971). When the Supreme Court of the United States specifically reversed an earlier decision regarding defendant's right to counsel, comparison of the briefs, arguments, and opinions in the two cases constituted remarkable data on the process of judicial justification (Jones, 1976). Most interesting to students of argumentation is Jones' discovery that lines of reasoning used in briefs may be clearly outside the typical scope of legal argument—bordering into legislative argument—when advocates employ anything they believe will be effective. However, these nonlegal arguments are unlikely to appear in the appellate opinions. Legislative arguments may help convince justices, but a decision is probably going to be justified by legal arguments alone.

The dramatic and emotion-filled trial of Angela Davis proved a good testing ground for well-established theories of stasis, or stock issues, as frameworks for the analysis of legal argumentation (Dicks, 1976). The equally provocative trial of Patricia Hearst gave researchers who had done advanced preparation the chance to test empirically the fundamental assumptions about the unprejudiced juror in the face of extensive pretrial publicity. Long-held assumptions about the law of evidence and the persuasibility of jurors may be challenged when scholars find reason to doubt the impact of highly prejudicial publicity (Rollings and Blascovich, 1977).

As more people in communication develop an interest in freedom of speech, there will be more analyses of cases involving the First Amendment. Examples of such studies are reviews of the concept of group libel that became more lively with the activities of the American Nazi Party (McGaffey, 1979), an analysis of obscenity on the occasion of a new position taken by the Supreme Court of the United States (Hunsaker, 1973), and a history of students' rights of expression prior to the significant Tinker case (Nichols, 1979). (The next section gives an example of how communication researchers can make a transition from essentially legalistic analysis to argumentative analyses of free-expression cases.)

A fruitful avenue of research has come from a look at the ways in which the courts demand a judicial form of justificatory argument from quasi-judicial agencies. Specifically, the courts have shown more interest in requiring the Federal Communications Commission to justify its decisions in a way that can pass the scrutiny of the judiciary (Brotman, 1980).

Legal pedagogy continues to engage communication writers. Since law schools show little interest or ability in teaching communication theories and skills to their students, undergraduate teachers are setting about to do the job (Forston, 1975; Mills, 1976; Rieke, 1978).

Rhetorical theory and the concept of jurisprudence focuses attention on the most useful theoretical postures from which to understand judicial decision-making. It still seems necessary to argue against the positivistic, rule-fact-verdict concept entertained for centuries by legal philosophers. The goal of communication writers has been to illustrate the rhetorical character of appellate opinions, thus showing the process to be a humanistic one in contrast to the appearance of formal rigor and human detachment traditionally claimed (Crable, 1976; Hample, 1979).

Selected Trial Factors. The desire to explore the trial experimentally preceded the sophisticated methodology to do it. In the 1960s researchers mostly fantasized about the prospects of holding all other variables constant while experimenting one after another with those factors thought to make a difference to juries. During the past decade, development of cooperative arrangements with the courts and the use of videotape technology has made the fantasy a reality. We can now review a series of factor studies that suggest whether or not the sex of the defendant (Snyder, 1971; Nagel and Weitzman, 1973), attractiveness of the defendant (Friend and Vinson, 1974; Efran, 1976), or the defendant's attributes (Jacobson and Berger, 1974) have any effect on the jury's decision.

Looking toward the legal audience—the jury—experimenters have questioned whether the juror's occupation (Hermann, 1970), socioeconomic status (Alder, 1973), sex (Kessler, 1975), or authoritarianism (Mitchell and Byrne, 1973) has any effect on the final decision. Evidence has been found to suggest some differences in verdict as the size of the jury is reduced (Arnold, 1976), and the effect of decision alternatives on the verdicts and social perceptions of simulated jurors has been studied (Vidmar, 1972; Padawer-Singer et al., 1977).

Witnesses have come in for their share of attention. There has long been interest in challenging some of the assumptions about the value of witness perceptions and ability to report them accurately (Marshall, 1966). Work during the past few years has added still more precise understanding of the phenomenon (Hatton et al., 1971; Farmer et al., 1977). Genuine concern comes when we learn further that if the witness does violate some aspect of the law of evidence the legal remedy—declaring the statement inadmissible and instructing the jury to disregard it—is uncertain. In fact, there is evidence that raising objections and even having them overruled may change the jury's decision (Reinard and Reynolds, 1978).

Not all studies of selected trial factors need to be performed within an experimental framework. For example, the role of oral argument in the appellate court has been examined from the perspective of communication strategies (Wasby et al., 1976). Some legal writers in the past, as well as some practitioners, have questioned the value of the oral argument. They have suggested that communication through the briefs is the critical factor. Wasby's group has illustrated the important role played in the oral presentation.

Judge's Instructions. The final act of a trial is the instruction of the jury on the law. While this is, too, a trial factor, it is distinct in that it is the one time the judge speaks at length; its function is to inform the jurors the limits within which they may decide rather than to persuade them to any particular decision. The research has been more didactic than inquisitive. The legal profession has turned to specialists in language and communication to assess the extent to which jurors comprehend instructions, and the results have shown serious problems (Buchanan et al., 1978; Pryor et al., 1980). Currently work is under way in an effort to find a way to express the instructions so that jurors understand what they must do without, at the same time, doing violence to the legal requirements (Charrow and Charrow, 1980).

Lawyer Communication Functions. The trial, with all its pretrial activities, is the consummate instance of legal argumentation. The interpersonal communication that occurs during preparation of a case as in the interviews between lawyer and client or prospective witness has been found lacking in a number of communication principles (Thomas and Insalata, 1964; Goodpaster, 1975; Goldsmith, 1980). Plea bargaining and legal negotiation have not received much scholarly attention. However, Quimby (1977) has examined the specific bargaining that led to the nolo contendere plea of Spiro Agnew, a case with many sensitive points since it involved a criminal charge against the vice-president of the United States.

Jury selection or voir dire is increasingly seen as more than a procedural process of discovering prejudice. Behavioral scientists suggest that they can show lawyers how to use their questions of prospective jurors to discover bases for persuasion (Fried et al., 1975). Lawyers offer advice, for example, on the forty-four most common blunders of jury selection (Baum, 1979).

Similarly, the opening statement, specifically excluded from the label "argument" in legal parlance, is now receiving the attention one would expect when it is perceived as an important step in making a case to a jury. For instance, the role of primacy in persuasion is seen as giving importance to the opening statement (Sams, 1978).

Law-trained writers give considerable attention to the strategies of cross-examination. For example Schwartz (1973) devotes a thousand pages to the subject in his extensive *Proof, Persuasion, and Cross-Examination*. The continuing series of volumes from the Institute of Continuing Legal Education (Holmes, 1973; 1978) provides advice from successful practitioners on how to cross-examine various special witnesses as well as how to go about the overall case-building process. These volumes give particular attention to expert witnesses, effective opening statements and closing arguments, and the development of evidence.

Television and the Trial. Two issues of interest to specialists in argumentation have come out of the advanced technology in television broadcasting and videotape recording. The increased use of pretrial depositions and the delays caused by the need to assemble a large number of witnesses in a courtroom at one time have raised the question of whether or not a trial can be assembled piece by piece on videotape and then presented to jurors as if it were a television program. Lawyers and judges have been concerned that arguments thus presented would yield different verdicts than those presented live. Furthermore, questions of excluding inadmissible testimony by electronic editing of tape needed to be compared with the current practice of instructing jurors to disregard them. In an extended series of experimental studies, Miller and Fontes (1979) have reported that no significant differences can be expected in verdicts between live and videotape trials. They have also shed some light on the importance or insignificance of exclusion of certain aspects of inadmissible testimony.

The second issue investigated by communication scholars has been the prospect of allowing television to broadcast actual trial proceedings. Most particularly, when the State of Florida allowed this to be done experimentally, Craig (1979) and Pryor and his colleagues (1979) observed the results and reported them. They have discussed the strengths and weaknesses of such access to trials by the broadcast media.

Working closely with the legal profession, the Communication and Law

Project at Kent State University under the direction of Carl Moore has produced some applied studies on the use of videotape testimony. The project has also provided a forum for the interaction of communication scholars, judges, and lawyers (Moore, 1979; 1979a; 1979b).

Systems Studies of the Trial. Recently some researchers have become increasingly critical of the experimental approach to the study of trial factors. They have suggested that such piecemeal studies leave an unclear picture of the trial process as a whole. This movement parallels similar dissatisfaction with limited variable studies of other communication phenomena such as persuasion or group decision-making. Two alternative approaches have been suggested.

Bennett (1978; 1979; 1981) views the trial as an exercise in storytelling and rhetorical transformation. Thus the case presented by plaintiff or prosecution must interrelate various elements of the case and trial so that they stand as an integrated narrative capable of surviving the typical tests people apply to drama or prose fiction: do the characters, actions, motivations, and the like hang together in a credible and sensible whole? Similarly, the defense must construct a counter story that may prove to be more believable than the opposition's story.

Barber (1981) views the trial from the perspective of general systems theory. Working with both pretrial depositions and trial examinations, she employs the methodology of interaction analysis to describe the processes as a whole.

Alternatives to trial. While no formal communication based research has yet been done on the various alternative ways to resolve disputes in contrast to the trial or pretrial negotiations, legal writers have clearly invited it. Johnson and his colleagues (1977) have described a number of paths through which legal problems can be diverted away from trials. They focus on the use of mediation and arbitration to generate mutual dispute resolution.

Evaluation of the Research. In the last ten or fifteen years the symbiosis between communication studies and legal practice has become significantly stronger as the law has shown increasing interest in what communication research can do and as communication scholars have accepted the challenge to do the research. That much of the research reviewed here (and this has by no means been an exhaustive review) is poorly conceived or executed should be no surprise. That much of the research reviewed here shows too great a tendency to look at those aspects of law that most resemble public speaking or mass communication should also be no surprise. It is understandable and even forgivable that communication researchers would start their investigation where their experience most prepared them to do so. This form of the drunkard's search, however, will be forgiven only so long. It is clearly time for the examination of more difficult communication aspects of legal practice, even if that requires the development of new perspectives and methodologies. Let's examine some of the possibilities.

Look back at the categories in the review and notice the gaps. The judge's instruction on the law is a communication task directly related to setting parmeters of reasoned decision-making. The research reported to date has been limited to the not-so-surprising discovery that jurors have not understood them and that, therefore, they could be written more clearly. Linguists have undertaken the task of trying to write the instructions so that they can be understood while keeping within the confines of the law. Researchers at Florida State University are experimenting with an adaptation of programmed instruction methodology to generate what they call "process instructions." These will encourage jurors to consider each case issue by issue. But we still know surprisingly little about the reasoning process that takes place in the jury room. To what extent do jurors do their reasoning the way lawyers do? To what extent do jurors generate quite another form of reasoning that satisfies their needs and is more consistent with their typical modes of argumentation? What can we learn, and therefore what can we tell lawyers, about the actual process of reasoned decision making that jurors do? Then what can we say about the efficacy of judges' instructions?

Most astounding is the absence of communication-related research into lawyer communication functions. To bring the history of the relationship between rhetoric and law up to date, we have passed through the first stage in which law training and the training of an orator were the same; we have endured a long period in which the two disciplines went in separate directions; from time to time we are still engaged in still a third stage in which those who have experience in teaching speech and coaching debate believe that on that basis alone they can teach lawyers how to do trial advocacy, and more and more we are discovering this to be an inadequate background. Now, specialists in argumentation stand in a kind of limbo: we know we must do our homework—do the research necessary to relate our knowledge in argumentation to the specific field of law—but we have not done that work yet. At the same time, lawyers are coming to us asking for what help and instruction we can offer. It is a precarious time. If we charge in and try to teach legal communication without the research background, speech communication will be exposed as having nothing of value to offer and another period of neglect can ensue. On the other hand, if we accept the challenge to do the research before presuming to teach, a solid relationship can be expected.

An example of research that promises to provide some of the specific information that will be of direct use to legal practitioners is that reported by Parkinson (1981) on verbal behavior in relation to courtroom success. Working with actual transcripts and examining linguistic elements displayed by principals in each case, the researcher concludes that "Attorneys who select a speech-delivery style that is appropriate to their message content and intent are more successful than attorneys who use a style that is incongruous with their message" (32). While this may not be an unexpected outcome, the ability of the study to specify elements of appropriate style makes the conclusion important.

There is room for research from various methodologies. Experimental studies of trial factors have been tried and can be continued with more sophisticated research questions, designs, and statistical measures. Systems-based studies have only just begun, and perhaps these promise a more holistic understanding of the role of the advocate in a trial. Specific investigations from a practical, argumentation-based perspective into such elements as direct and cross-examination, presentation of nontestimonial evidence, or overall case strategy would be useful. There is much room for increased understanding of the function of the closing argument. Here, rather than rhetorical criticism of leading advocates, research is required to learn more about the day-by-day work of the ordinary advocate.

Alternatives to trial, including the use of videotape technology, is an unexplored area suitable for argumentation research. Traditionally, the concept of argument or argumentation has been defined narrowly to exclude such communication behaviors as bargaining, negotiating, arbitrating, and mediating. This restricted definition seems to have discouraged research into trial alternatives. Since there is reason to believe that popular conceptions of reasoning include negotiation, arbitration, and the like (Rieke, 1980), and since the work would directly contribute to an improved understanding of legal decision-making, it should be done.

In summary, there are mutual benefits to be derived from an expansion of the already established program of research into legal communication by specialists in argumentation. For argumentation, there is an opportunity to learn how argumentation functions in the specialized field or forum of law. For law, there is a promise that expertise thus gained can be shared with those in practice to increase their proficiency in lawyering and thus increase the effectiveness of the legal system.

Argumentation and the First Amendment

This review of research literature has included studies aimed at understanding judicial behavior with regard to freedom of expression, and it has included research designed to increase our understanding of the reasoning used in appellate court opinions. No research has been found that explores judicial argumentation through the medium of opinions on free expression, and that deserves special comment.

First, consider some background. Interest among speech-communication scholars in problems of freedom of expression is growing. Interest groups have existed for some time, and more classes in the First Amendment are being taught. Reasonably, many of the people working in argumentation and law also have an interest in freedom of expression. Furthermore, legal scholars tend to believe that decisions dealing with the First Amendment constitute paradigm examples of judicial reasoning in general. It makes sense, then, that one way to develop an extensive body of literature on the reasoning of appellate courts is to focus on First Amendment cases, thereby contributing to the literature on freedom of expression as well.

There is an impediment. Work on the freedom-of-expression problems tends to be more legal than rhetorical. That is to say, articles and books take their lead from legal scholarship and adopt a case-by-case approach with attention to legal traditions such as rule-fact-decision. When we turn our attention to free speech and press we try to become lawyers and forget our rhetorical backgrounds. Thomas Emerson's idea of "tests" for First Amendment decisions (1963; 1966; 1970) epitomizes this legalistic thinking.

Why we do this is hard to understand in the face of a half-century of work by legal philosophers such as Cardozo (1921), Frank (1949), Llewellyn (1960), Hart (1961), and Gottlieb (1968), who have shown the inherent fallacies in the formal logic model and have suggested in its place a much more rhetorical model. They have argued in the same vein as Toulmin (1958; 1972), Perelman (1979), and Johnstone (1978) have with regard to formal logic in general.

The correction seems obvious. Research into First Amendment decisions needs to be done from the perspective of modern argumentation theory. Rieke and Newell (1981) suggest some ways in which this can be done. Transpose the legal concept of rule or test into the argumentation concept of warrant. Look then at the lines of reasoning used by courts to justify their decisions. Warrants can be organized according to the kind of issue addressed. While the specifics change, appellate courts are faced with a fairly redundant set of issues that can be conceptualized as levels of argument. A partial list includes these: Level 1, jurisdiction (Should this court be hearing this case?); Level 2, interpretation (How does the First Amendment apply to this case?); and Level 3, prioritization (What priorities must be weighed in deciding this case?).

With these guidelines, specific decisions can be discussed, for example, at the first level, *Lanemark Communications, Inc.*, v. *Commonwealth of Virginia* (1978) exposes the warrant that the judiciary has jurisdiction to criticize state laws repugnant to the Constitution of the United States. This then can be contrasted with *Dennis* v. *United States* (1951), where the negative of that warrant was used.

On the second level, for example, *United States* v. *O'Brien* (1968) can be studied for the warrant that some actions or behaviors such as burning a draft card, even though they are done to communicate a point, do not merit First Amendment protection. This can be studied in contrast to the arguments used to justify as expression the wearing of a swastika armband.

Finally, on Level 3 the court might use a warrant that even inaccurate facts are protected if the subject is newsworthy, as some suggested in *Time Inc.* v. *Hill* (1967), which can be contrasted with a trial court that awarded a former Miss Wyoming $26.5 million for an inaccurate story that appeared in *Penthouse* magazine, apparently on the theory that some inaccuracies are more harmful than others.

This is only a suggestion of the kinds of analyses that might combine the development of understanding of judicial reasoning with a knowledge of the ways courts deal with conflicts over freedom of expression. This is clearly an area of potential research.

Summary.

Ancient writers instinctively knew that solving problems through law involved people reasoning together, communicating. Although the history of that relationship is checkered, the contemporary scene reveals work by lawers and argumentation scholars suggesting the emergence of a permanent bond. If both sides work together with vigor and good will, the bond will come to pass.

Reference List
Notes on Contributors
Index

Reference List

Abbreviations Commonly Used in This Reference List

AJS	*American Journal of Sociology*
CE	*Communication Education*
CM	*Communication Monographs*
CQ	*Communication Quarterly*
CSSA	Central States Speech Association
CSSJ	*Central States Speech Journal*
HCR	*Human Communication Research*
ICA	International Communication Association
JAFA	*Journal of the American Forensic Association*
QJPS	*Quarterly Journal of Public Speaking*
QJS	*Quarterly Journal of Speech*
QJSE	*Quarterly Journal of Speech Education*
SCA	Speech Communication Association
SM	*Speech Monographs*
SSCJ	*Southern Speech Communication Journal*
SSJ	*Southern Speech Journal*
WJSC	*Western Journal of Speech Communication*
WSC	*Western Speech Communication*
WSCA	Western Speech Communication Association

Abel, E. (1966). *The missile crisis*. Bantam.

Achinstein, P. (1964). Models, analogies, and theories. *Philosophy of Science*, 31: 328–350.

———. (1965). Theoretical models. *British Journal for the Philosophy of Science*, 16: 102–120.

———. (1972). Models and analogies: A reply to Girill. *Philosophy of Science*, 39: 235–240.

Adams-Weber, J. (1979). *Personal construct theory: Concepts and applications*. Wiley.

Alden, R. M. (1900). *The art of debate*. Holt.

Alder, F. (1973). Socioeconomic factors influencing jury verdicts. *New York University Review of Law and Social Change*, 3: 1–10.

Allison, G. (1971). *Essence of decision: Explaining the Cuban missile crisis*. Little, Brown.

Anderson, C. W. (1979). The place of principles in policy analysis. *American Political Science Review*, 73: 711–713.

Anderson, J. M. & Dovre, P. J. (1968). *Readings in argumentation*. Allyn & Bacon.

Anderson, J. P. (1977). Practical reasoning in action. In Douglas & Johnson.

Anderson, R. L. & Mortensen, C. D. (1967). Logic and marketplace argumentation. *QJS*, 53: 143–151.

Apel, K. O. (1979). Types of rationality today: The continuum of reason between science and ethics. In Geraets.

Applegate, J. L. & Delia, J. G. (1980). Person-centered speech, psychological development, and the contexts of language use. In R. St. Clair & H. Giles, eds., *The social and psychological contexts of language*. Erlbaum.

Arendt, H. (1954). What is authority? In H. Arendt, *Between past and future: Six exercises in political thought*. Viking.

Aristotle. (n.d.). *Topics*. 101a–101b.

———. (1932). *The rhetoric*, L. Cooper, ed. Appleton.

———. (1941). *The physics*. In R. McKeon, ed., *The basic works of Aristotle*. Random.

———. (1954). *Poetics*, I. Bywater, trans. Modern Library.

———. (1954a). *Rhetoric*, R. Roberts, trans. Modern Library.

———. (1968). *De Anima*, D. W. Hamlyn, trans. Oxford.

Armstrong, D. M. (1973). *Belief, knowledge and truth*. Cambridge.

Arnold, C. C. (1970). Perelman's new rhetoric. *QJS*, 56: 87–92.

Arnold, W. E. (1976). Membership satisfaction and the decision making in six member and twelve member juries. *JAFA*, 12: 130–137.

Art, R. J. (1973). Bureaucratic politics and American foreign policy: A critique. *Policy Sciences*, 4: 467–490.

Atkinson, R. C. (1960). The use of models in experimental psychology. *Synthese*, 12: 162–171.

Attwell, P. (1974). Ethnomethodology since Garfinkle. *Theory and Society*, 1: 179–210.

Auerbach, E. (1953). *Mimesis*. Princeton.

Aune, J. A. (1979). The contribution of Habermas to rhetorical validity. *JAFA*, 16: 104–111.

Austin, J. L. (1975). *How to do things with words*, 2nd ed., J. O. Urmson & M. Sbisa, eds. Harvard.

Bach, K. & Harnish, R. M. (1979). *Linguistic communication and speech acts*. MIT.

Bailyn, B. (1977). Commentary on papers presented at the Smithsonian Institution's sixth international symposium, Washington, D.C. In Lichtman and Challinor.

Baird, A. C. (1924). Argumentation as a humanistic subject. *QJS*, 10: 258–264.

———. (1928). *Public discussion and debate*. Ginn.

———. (1943). *Discussion: Principles and types*. McGraw-Hill.

Baker, G. P. (1895). *Principles in argumentation*. Ginn.

Baker, G. P. & Huntington, H. B. (1905). *The principles of argumentation*. Ginn.

Balthrop, B. (1980). Argument as linguistic opportunity: A search for form and function. In Rhodes & Newell.

Banty, C. R. (1981). Public arguing in the regulation of health and safety. *WJSC*, 45: 71–87.

Barber, S. J. (1981). *A systems perspective of the interaction present in three selected legal cases*. Unpublished doctoral dissertation, University of Utah.

Barnlund, D. C. (1968). Introduction. In D. C. Barnlund, ed., *Interpersonal communication: Survey and studies*. Houghton Mifflin.

Barrett, W. (1979). *The illusion of technique*. Anchor/Doubleday.

Bartley, W. W. (1962). *The retreat to commitment*. Knopf.

————. (1964). Rationality versus the theory of rationality. In M. Bunge, ed., *The critical approach*. Free Press.

Barzun, J. (1972). History: The muse and her doctors. *American Historical Review*, 77: 36–64.

Bates, E., ed. (1976). *Language and context: The acquisition of pragmatics*. Academic Press.

Bates, E., Camaioni, L., & Volterra, V. (1976). Sensorimotor performatives. In Bates.

Baum, D. B. (1979). *Advanced trial strategy 1979*. Practicing Law Institute.

Baumer, F. L. (1977). *Modern European thought: Continuity and change in ideas, 1600–1950*. Macmillan.

Becker, C. (1935). *Everyman his own historian*. Crofts.

Bellow, S. (1973). Culture now. In A. M. Eastman et al., eds., *The Norton reader: An anthology of expository prose*, 3rd ed. Norton.

Benn, S. I., & Mortimore, G. W., eds. (1976). *Rationality and the social sciences*. Routledge & Kegan Paul.

Bennett, W. L. (1978). Story telling in criminal trials: A model of social judgment. *QJS*, 64: 1–22.

————. (1979). Rhetorical transformation of evidence in criminal trials: Creating grounds for legal judgment. *QJS*, 65: 311–323.

———— & Feldman, M. S. (1981). *Reconstructing reality in the courtroom*. Rutgers.

Benoit, P. (1979). A descriptive study of coherence in naturally-occurring and experimentally structured conversations of preschool children. Unpublished doctoral dissertation, Wayne State University.

Berger, J. (1972). *Ways of seeing*. British Broadcasting Co. & Penguin.

Berger, P. L., & Kellner, H. (1970). Marriage and the construction of reality. In Dreitzel.

Bergman, P. B. (1978). A practical approach to cross-examination: Safety first. *UCLA Law Review*, 25: 547–576.

Bitzer, L. (1978). Rhetoric and public knowledge. In Burks.

Black, E. (1978). *Rhetorical criticism: A study in method*. Wisconsin.

Black, M. (1962). *Models and metaphors: Studies in language and philosophy*. Cornell.

Blalock, H. M., Jr. (1969). *Theory construction: From verbal to mathematical formulations*. Prentice-Hall.

Blassingame, J. (1972). *The slave community: Plantation life in the antebellum South*. Oxford.

Bleiberg, S., & Churchill, L. (1975). Notes on confrontation in conversation. *Journal of Psycholinguistic Research*, 4: 273–278.

Bleicher, J. (1980). *Contemporary hermeneutics: Hermeneutics as method, philosophy and critique*. Routledge & Kegan Paul.

Bliese, J. R. E. (1979). Richard Weaver's axiology of argument. *SSCJ*, 44: 275–288.

Blumer, H. (1969). *Symbolic interactionism: Perspective and method*. Prentice-Hall.

Bock, K. (1956). *The acceptance of histories: Toward a perspective for social science*. California.

Boggs, S. T. (1978). The development of verbal disputing in part-Hawaiian children. *Language in Society*, 7: 325–344.

Booth, W. C. (1961). *The rhetoric of fiction*. Chicago.

————. (1974). *Modern dogma and the rhetoric of assent*. Notre Dame.

————. (1979). *Critical understanding: The powers and limits of pluralism*. Chicago.

Bostrum, R. N. (1966). Motivation and argument. In Miller & Nilsen.

Bowers, J. W. (1966). Language and argument. In Miller & Nilsen.

Box, G. E. P. (1979). Robustness in the strategy of scientific model building. In R. L. Launer & G. N. Wilkinson, eds., *Robustness in statistics*. Academic Press.

Bradac, J. J., & Bell, M. A. (1975). The effects of observer expectations, task ambiguity, and medium of presentation on low- and high-inference judgments of communicative behavior. *HCR*, 1: 123–132.

Bradac, J. J., Sandell, K. L., & Wenner, L. A. (1979). The phenomenology of evidence: Information-source utility in decision making. *CQ*, 27: 35–46.

Bradac, J. J. et al. (1980). Cognitive processing of sentences: Studies of linguistic intuition. ICA Convention Paper.

Braithwaite, R. B. (1953). *Scientific explanation*. Cambridge.

———. (1962). Models in the empirical sciences. In Nagel, Suppes, & Tarski.

Braybrooke, D., & Lindblom, C. E. (1963). *A strategy of decision*. Free Press.

Brecher, M., ed. (1978). *Studies in crisis behavior*. Transaction Books.

Brenneis, D., & Lein, L. (1977). "You fruithead": A sociolinguistic approach to children's dispute settlement. In S. Ervin-Tripp & C. Mitchell-Kernan, eds., *Child discourse*. Academic Press.

Brock, B. L. et al. (1973). *Public policy decision-making*. Harper.

Brockriede, W. (1975). Where is argument? *JAFA*, 11: 179–182.

———. (1977). Characteristics of arguments and arguing. *JAFA*, 13: 129–132.

Brockriede, W., & Ehninger, D. (1960). Toulmin on argument: An interpretation and application. *QJS*, 46: 44–53.

Bronowski, J. (1971). *The identity of man*, rev. ed. Natural History Press.

Bronson, W. (1975). Developments in behavior with age-mates during the second year of life. In M. Lewis & L. Rosenblum, *Friendship and peer relations*. Wiley.

Brotman, S. N. (1980). Judicial review of the F.C.C.: The developing legacy of Greater Boston. *Journal of Communication*, 30: 31–36.

Brown, P., & Levinson, S. (1978). Universals in language usage: Politeness Phenomena. In Goody.

Brown, R. H. (1977). *A poetic for sociology: Toward a logic of discovery for the human sciences*. Cambridge.

Brummett, B. (1976). Some implications of "process" or "intersubjectivity": Postmodern rhetoric. *Philosophy and Rhetoric*, 9: 21–51.

Bruyn, S. T. (1966). *The human perspective in sociology*. Prentice-Hall.

Bryant, D. C. (1970). Introduction—uses of rhetoric in criticism. In D. C. Bryant, ed., *Rhetoric and poetic*. Iowa.

———. (1973). "Rhetoric: Its functions and its scope" *rediviva*. In D. C. Bryant, ed., *Rhetorical dimensions in criticism*. Louisiana.

———. (1978). Literature and politics. In Burks.

Buchanan, R. W. et al. (1978). Legal communication: An investigation of juror comprehension of pattern instructions. *CQ*, 26: 31–35.

Bunge, M. (1973). *Method, model and matter*. Reidel.

Burke, K. (1941). *Philosophy of literary form*. Vintage.

———. (1950). *A rhetoric of motives*. Prentice-Hall.

———. (1961). *The rhetoric of religion*. California.

————. (1968). *Counterstatement*. California.

————. (1968a). Rhetoric and poetics. In K. Burke, *Language as symbolic action: Essays on life, literature, and method*. California.

————. (1970). Poetics and communication. In H. E. Kiefer & M. K. Munitz, eds., *Perspectives in education, religion, and the arts*. SUNY.

————. (1978). Rhetoric, poetics, and philosophy. In Burks.

Burks, D. M., ed. (1978). *Rhetoric, philosophy and literature: An exploration*. Purdue.

Burleson, B. R. (1979). The justification of message strategies: A developmental analysis of interpersonal reasoning. SCA Convention Paper.

————. (1979a). On the analysis and criticism of arguments: Some theoretical and methodological considerations. *JAFA*, 15: 137–147.

————. (1979b). On the foundations of rationality: Toulmin, Habermas, and the *a priori* of reason. *JAFA*, 16: 112–127.

————. (1980). Argument and constructivism: The cognitive-developmental component. SCA Convention Paper.

————. (1980a). The place of non-discursive symbolism, formal characterizations, and hermeneutics in argument analysis and criticism. *JAFA*, 16: 222–231.

————. (1981). A cognitive-developmental perspective on social reasoning processes. *WJSC*, 45: 133–147.

Burleson, B. R., & Kline, S. L. (1979). Habermas' theory of communication: A critical explication. *QJS*, 65: 412–428.

Burnstein, E., & Berbaum, M. L. (1979). *Policy decisions by governmental groups: An information-processing analysis*. Research Center for Group Dynamics, Institute for Social Research, University of Michigan.

Butterfield, H. (1965). *The Whig interpretation of history*. Norton.

Burne, D. (1971). *The attraction paradigm*. Academic Press.

Cameron, J. M. (1980). Take me to your leader. *New York Review of Books*, 27: 16.

Campaign Transcripts, A, B, C, ed. T. B. Farrell (1980).

Campbell, K. K. (1972). *Critiques of contemporary rhetoric*. Wadsworth.

Campbell, P. M. (1980). The *Gorgias*: Dramatic form as argument. *CSSJ*, 31: 1–16.

Cappella, J. N. (1975). An introduction to the literature of causal modeling. *HCR*, 1: 362–377.

Cardozo, B. N. (1921). *The nature of the judicial process*. Yale.

Carleton, W. M. (1978). What is rhetorical knowledge? *QJS*, 64: 313–328.

Carter, A. L. (1974). The development of communication in the sensorimotor period: A case study. Unpublished doctoral dissertation, University of California at Berkeley.

Carter, J. (1975). *Why not the best?* Bantam.

————. (1979). Address to nation (July 15, 1979). *Chicago Tribune*, July 17, 1979, 12.

Cassirer, E. (1946). *Language and myth*. Harper.

Chandler, M. J. (1977). Social cognition: A selective review of current research. In W. F. Overton & J. McCarthy, eds., *Knowledge and development, Vol. I: Advances in theory and research*. Plenum Press.

Chao, Y. R. (1962). Models in linguistics and models in general. In Nagel, Suppes, & Tarski.

Charrow, R. P., & Charrow, V. R. (1979). A psycholinguistic study of legal language and its comprehensibility. *Columbia Law Review*, 7: 1306–1379.

Chernev, I. (1947). *The Russians play chess*. Dover.

Cherry, C. (1978). *On human communication: A review, a survey, and a criticism*, 3rd ed. MIT.

Chisholm, R. M. (1976). Knowledge and belief: "de Dicto" and "de Re." *Philosophical Studies*, 29: 1–20.

———. (1978). On the nature of empirical evidence. In Pappas & Swain.

Cicourel, A. V. (1964). *Method and measurement in sociology*. Free Press.

———. (1970). Basic and normative rules in the negotiation of status and role. In Dreitzel.

———. (1974). *Cognitive sociology: Language and meaning in social interaction*. Free Press.

Clark, H. H. (1973). The language-as-fixed-effect fallacy: A critique of langauge statistics in psychological research. *Journal of Verbal Learning and Verbal Behavior*, 12: 335–359.

———. (1979). Responding to indirect speech acts. *Cognitive Psychology*, 11: 430–477.

Clark, H. H., & Clark, E. (1977). *Psychology and language: An introduction to psycholinguistics*. Harcourt.

Clark, R. A., & Delia, J. G. (1976). The development of functional persuasive skills in childhood and early adolescence. *Child Development*, 47: 1008–1014.

———. (1977). Cognitive complexity, social perspective taking, and functional persuasive skills in second- to ninth-grade children. *HCR*, 3: 128–134.

———. (1979). *Topoi* and rhetorical competence. *QJS*, 65: 187–206.

Cohen, M. R. (1944). *A preface to logic*. Holt.

Cohen; M. R., & Nagel, E. (1934). *An introduction to logic and scientific method*. Harcourt.

Collingwood, R. G. (1956). *The idea of history*, T. M. Knox, ed. Oxford.

Colodny, R. G., ed. (1972). *Paradigms and paradoxes: The philosophical challenge of the quantum domain*. Pittsburgh.

Connolly, W. E. (1974). *The terms of political discourse*. Heath.

Cooley, J. C. (1942). *A primer of formal logic*. Macmillan.

———. (1959). On Mr. Toulmin's revolution in logic. *Journal of Philosophy*, 56: 297–319.

Copi, I. M. (1954). *Symbolic logic*. Macmillan.

———. (1972). *Introduction to logic*, 4th ed. Macmillan.

Cornman, J. W. (1978). Foundational versus nonfoundational theories of empirical justification. In Pappas & Swain.

Cottrell, L. (1933). Roles in marital adjustment. *Publications of the American Sociological Society*, 27: 107–115.

Coulthard, M. (1977). *An introduction to discourse analysis*. Longmans.

Cowan, J. L. (1972). The uses of argument—An apology for logic. In D. Ehninger, ed., *Contemporary rhetoric*. Scott, Foresman.

Cox, J. R. (1977). Deliberation under uncertainty: A game simulation of oral argumentation in decision-making. *JAFA*, 14: 61–72.

———. (1977a). Editorial note. *JAFA*, 13: 117.

———. (1980). *Loci Communes* and Thoreau's arguments for wilderness in "Walking" (1851). *SSCJ*, 46: 1–16.

———. (1981). Argument and the "definition of the situation." *CSSJ*, 32: 197–205.

Crable, R. E. (1976). Models of argumentation and judicial judgment. *JAFA*, 12: 113–120.

———. (1979). Logic, argument, and the criteria for reasoning "correctly." SCA Convention Paper.

Craig, R. S. (1979). Cameras in the courtroom. *Journalism Quarterly*, 56: 703–710.

Craven, A. (1957). *The coming of the Civil War*. Scribner.

Crocker, L. (1944). *Argumentation and debate*. American Book.

Crockett, W. H. (1965). Cognitive complexity and impression formation. In B. Maher, ed., *Progress in experimental personality research*, Vol. 2. Academic Press.

Cronin, T. E. (1970). "Everybody believes in democracy until he gets to the White House . . .": An examination of White House-departmental relations. *Law and Contemporary Problems*, 35: 573–625.

Cronkhite, G. L. (1964). Logic, emotion, and the paradigm of persuasion. *QJS*, 50: 13–18.

———. (1969). Out of the ivory palaces. . . . In R. J. Kibler & L. L. Barker, eds., *Conceptual frontiers in speech-communication*. SCA.

———. (1969a). *Persuasion: Speech and behavioral change*. Bobbs-Merrill.

Crosson, F. J. (1967). Memory, models, and meaning. In Crosson & Sayre.

Crosson, F. J., & Sayre, K. M., eds. (1967). *Philosophy and cybernetics*. Notre Dame.

Davis, W. A. (1978). *The act of interpretation: A critique of literary reason*. Chicago.

Dearin, R. D. (1969). The philosophical basis of Chaim Perelman's theory of rhetoric. *QJS*, 55: 213–224.

———. (1970). Chaim Perelman's theory of rhetoric. Unpublished doctoral dissertation, University of Illinois.

———. (1970a). Perelman's "universal audience" as a rhetorical concept. SCA Convention Paper.

Delia, J. G. (1970). The logic fallacy, cognitive theory, and the enthymene: A search for the foundations of reasoned discourse. *QJS*, 56: 140–148.

———. (1976). Change of meaning processes in impression formation. *CM*, 43: 142–157.

Delia, J. G., & Clark, R. A. (1977). Cognitive complexity, social perception, and the development of listener-adapted communication in six-, eight-, and twelve-year old boys. *CM*, 44: 326–345.

Delia, J. G., & O'Keefe, B. J. (1979). Constructivism: the development of communication in children. In E. Wartella, ed., *Children communicating*. Sage.

Delia, J. G., O'Keefe, B. J., & O'Keefe, D. J. (1981). The constructivist approach to human communication. In F. E. X. Dance, ed., *Comparative theories of human communication*. Harper.

Dennis v. *United States*, 341 U.S. 494 (1951).

Denzin, N. K. (1970). *The research act: A theoretical introduction to sociological methods*. Aldine.

Dewey, J. (1934). *Art as experience*. Capricorn.

Dick, R. C. (1972). *Argumentation and rational debating*. Brown.

Dickens, M., & Schwartz, R. E. (1971). Oral argument before the Supreme Court: Marshall v. Davis in the school segregation cases. *QJS*, 57: 32–42.

Dicks, V. I. (1976). Courtroom controversy: A stasis/stock issue analysis of the Angela Davis trial. *JAFA*, 13: 77–83.

Dilthey, W. (1913–1967). *Gesammelte schriften*, 14 vols. Vandenhoeck & Ruprecht.

Donohue, W. A., Cushman, D. P., & Nofsinger, R. E., Jr. (1980). Creating and confronting social order: A comparison of rules perspectives. *WJSC*, 44: 5–19.

Dore, J. (1973). The development of speech acts. Unpublished doctoral dissertation, City University of New York.

Douglas, J. D., ed. (1970). *Understanding everyday life*. Aldine.

Douglas, J. D., & Johnson, J. M., eds. (1977). *Existential sociology*. Cambridge.

Dovre, P. J. (1965). Historical-critical research in debate. *JAFA*, 2: 72−79.

Dreitzel, H. P., ed. (1970). *Recent sociology, no. 2: Patterns of communicative behavior*. Macmillan.

Dulany, D. E. (1968). Awareness, rules, and propositional control: A confrontation with S-R behavior theory. In T. R. Dixon & D. L. Horton, eds., *Verbal behavior and general behavior theory*. Prentice-Hall.

Duncan, S., Jr. (1979). Face-to-face interaction. In D. Aaronson & R. W. Rieber, eds., *Psycholinguistic research: Implications and applications*. Erlbaum.

Eaton, R. M. (1931). *General logic*. Scribners.

Ebeling, G. (1967). *The problem of historicity*. Fortress Press.

Efran, M. G. (1976). The effect of physical appearance on the judgment of guilt, interpersonal attraction, and severity of recommended punishment in a simulated jury task. *Journal of Research in Personality*, 8: 45−54.

Ehninger, D. (1968). Validity as moral obligation. *SSJ*, 33: 215−222.

──────. (1970). Argument as method: Its nature, its limitations and its uses. *SM*, 37: 101−110.

Ehninger, D. & Brockriede, W. (1963). *Decision by debate*. Dodd.

──────. (1978). *Decision by debate*, 2nd ed.

Elkins, S. (1968). *Slavery: A problem in American institutional life*, 2nd ed. Chicago.

Emerson, J. P. (1970). Behavior in private places: Sustaining definitions of reality in gynecological examinations. In Dreitzel.

──────. (1970a). Nothing unusual is happening. In T. Shibutani, ed., *Human nature and collective behavior*. Prentice-Hall.

Emerson, T. I. (1963). Toward a general theory of the first amendment. *Yale Law Journal*, 72: 877.

──────. (1966). *Toward a general theory of the First Amendment*. Random.

──────. (1970). *The system of freedom of expression*. Random.

Enos, R. L. (1980). Emerging notions of argument and advocacy in Hellenic litigation: Antiphon's *On the murder of Herodes*. *JAFA*, 17: 182−191.

Eubanks, R. T. (1978). Axiological issues in rhetorical inquiry. *SSCJ*, 44: 11−24.

Eubanks, R. T., & Baker, V. L. (1962). Toward an axiology of rhetoric. *QJS*, 48: 157−168.

Farmer, L. C. et al. (1977). The effect of the method of presenting trial testimony on juror decisional process. In Sales.

Farrell, T. B. (1976). Knowledge, consensus, and rhetorical theory. *QJS*, 62: 1−14.

──────. (1977). Validity and rationality: The rhetorical constituents of argumentative form. *JAFA*, 13: 142−149.

──────. (1978). Political conventions as legitimation ritual. *CM*, 45: 293−305.

──────. (1979). Habermas on argumentation theory: Some emerging topics. *JAFA*, 16: 77−82.

Farrell, T. B., & Frentz, T. (1979). Communication and meaning: A language-action synthesis. *Philosophy and Rhetoric*, 12: 215−255.

Feinberg, G. (1972). Philosophical implications of contemporary particle physics. In Colodny.

Festinger, L. (1954). A theory of social comparison processes. *Human Relations*, 7: 117−140.

Feyerabend, P. K. (1970). Against method: Outline of an anarchistic theory of knowledge.

In M. Radner & S. Winokur, eds., *Minnesota Studies in the Philosophy of Science*, Vol. 4. Minnesota.

———. (1970a). Consolations for the specialist. In Lakatos & Musgrave.

———. (1978). *Against method*. Verso.

Feys, R. (1961). Logique. In R. Klibansky, ed., *Philosophy in the mid-century*. La Nuova Italia Editrice.

Fine, A. (1972). Some conceptual problems of quantum theory. In Colodny.

Fischer, D. H. (1970). *Historians' fallacies: Toward a logic of historical thought*. Harper.

Fishbein, M., & Ajzen, I. (1975). *Belief, attitude, intention and behavior*. Addison-Wesley.

Fisher, W. R. (1973). Reaffirmation and subversion of the American Dream. *QJS*, 59: 160–167.

———. (1978). Toward a logic of good reasons. *QJS*, 64: 376–384.

———. (1980). Rationality and the logic of good reasons. *Philosophy and Rhetoric*, 13: 121–130.

———. (1980a). Rhetorical fiction and the presidency. *QJS*, 66: 119–126.

Fisher, W. R., & Sayles, E. M. (1966). The nature and functions of argument. In Miller & Nilsen.

Fitzgerald, F. S. (1925). *The great Gatsby*. Scribners.

Flavell, J. (1977). The development of knowledge about visual perception. In Keasey.

Flavell, J. H. et al. (1968). *The development of role-taking and communication skills in children*. Wiley.

Fodor, J. A. (1981). The mind-body problem. *Scientific American*, 244: 114–123.

Fogel, R. W., & Engerman, S. L. (1974). *Time on the cross*. Little, Brown.

Forston, R. (1975). Communication perspectives in the legal process. In R. L. Applbaum et al., comps., *Speech communication: A basic anthology*. Macmillan.

Foster, W. T. (1908). *Argumentation and debating*. Houghton Mifflin.

Foucalt, M. (1972). *The archaeology of knowledge*, A.M.S. Smith, trans. Harvard.

Frake, C. (1972). "Struck by speech": The Yakan concept of litigation. In Gumperz & Hymes.

Frank, J. (1949). *Law and the modern mind*. Coward-McCann.

Freeley, A. J. (1966). *Argumentation and debate*, 2nd ed. Wadsworth.

Frentz, T. S., & Farrell, T. B. (1976). Language-Action: a paradigm for communication. *QJS*, 62: 333–349.

Fried, M. et al. (1975). Juror selection: An analysis of *voir dire*. In R. J. Simon, ed., *The jury system in America*. Sage.

Friend, R. M., & Vinson, M. (1974). Leaning over backwards: Jurors' responses to defendant's attractiveness. *Journal of Communication*, 24: 124–129.

Fuller, R. B. (1973). *Intuition*. Anchor/Doubleday.

Gabel, J. (1975). *False consciousness*. Harper.

Gadamer, H. G. (1975). *Truth and method*, G. Barden & J. Cumming, trans. Seabury.

———. (1976). *Philosophical hermeneutics*, D. E. Linge, ed. and trans. California.

———. (1979). Historical transformation of reason. In Geraets.

———. (1980). *Dialogue and dialectic: Eight hermeneutical studies on Plato*, P. C. Smith, trans. Yale.

Gaines, R. N. (1979). Doing by saying: Toward a theory of perlocutions. *QJS*, 65: 207–217.

Gara, L. (1961). *The liberty line: The legend of the underground railroad*. Kentucky.

Garfinkle, H. (1967). *Studies in ethnomethodology.* Prentice-Hall.

Garfinkle, H., & Sacks, H. (1970). On formal structures of practical actions. In J. C. McKinney & E. Tiryakian, eds., *Theoretical sociology: Perspectives and developments.* Appleton.

Garvey, C. (1977). Contingent queries. In M. Lewis & L. A. Rosenblum, eds., *Interaction, conversation, and the development of language.* Wiley.

————. (1977a). *Play.* Harvard.

Geertz, C. (1980). Blurred genres: The refiguration of social thought. *The American Scholar,* 49: 165–179.

Gellner, E. (1959). *Words and things.* Penguin.

George, F. (1970). *Models of thinking.* Schenkman.

Geraets, T. F., ed. (1979). *Rationality today.* Ottawa.

Girill, T. R. (1972). Analogies and models revisited. *Philosophy of Science,* 39: 241–244.

Glaser, B. G., & Strauss, A. L. (1967). *The discovery of grounded theory: Strategies for qualitative research.* Aldine.

Goffman, E. (1959). *The presentation of self in everyday life.* Anchor Books.

Goldman, L. (1976). *Cultural creation in modern society,* B. Drake, trans. Telos.

Goldsmith, J. (1980). The initial attorney/client consultation: a case history. *SSCJ,* XLV: 394–407.

Goodpaster, G. S. (1975). The human arts of lawyering: interviewing and counseling. *J. of Legal Education,* 27: 5–32.

Goodwin, M. (1974). Aspects of the social organization of children's arguments: Some procedures and resources for restructuring positions. American Anthropological Assn. Convention Paper.

————. (1980). He-said-she-said: Formal cultural procedures for the construction of a group gossip activity. *American Ethnologist,* 7: 674–695.

Goodwin, P. D., & Wenzel, J. W. (1979). Proverbs and practical reasoning: A study in socio-logic. *QJS,* 65: 289–302.

Goody, E. N., ed. (1978). *Questions and politeness: Strategies in social interaction.* Cambridge.

Gottlieb, A. (1968). *The logic of choice—an investigation of the concepts of rule and rationality.* Macmillan.

Gouldner, A. (1976). *The dialectic of ideology and technology.* Seabury.

Graham, G. M. (1924). Logic and argumentation. *QJSE,* 10: 350–363.

Grice, H. P. (1957). Meaning. *Philosophical Review,* 66: 377–388.

————. (1975). Logic and conversation. In P. Cole & J. Morgan, eds., *Syntax and semantics,* Vol. 3: Speech acts. Academic Press.

Griffin-Collart, E., ed. (1979). La Nouvelle Rhétorique: Essais en hommage à Chaim Perelman. *Revue Internationale de Philosophie,* 33: 3–385.

Grimaldi, W. M. A. (1958). Rhetoric and the philosophy of Aristotle. *Classical Journal,* 53: 371–375.

————. (1978). Rhetoric and truth: A note on Aristotle. *Rhetoric* 1355a 21–24. *Philosophy and Rhetoric,* 11: 173–177.

Gronbeck, B. (1972). Four approaches to studying argument in graduate programs. *JAFA,* 9: 350–354.

————. (1980). From argument to argumentation: Fifteen years of identity crisis. In Rhodes & Newell.

Gueroult, M. (1979). *Philosophie de l'histoire de la philosophie,* Vol. 2. Aubier.

Gumperz, J. J. (1972). Introduction. In Gumperz & Hymes.

Gumperz, J. J., & Hymes, D., eds. (1972). *Directions in sociolinguistics: The ethnography of communication*. Holt.

Gurvitch, G. (1971). *The social frameworks of knowledge*, M. Thompson & K. Thompson, trans. Blackwell.

Gurwitsch, A. (1964). *The field of consciousness*. Duquesne.

———. (1966). *Studies in phenomenology and psychology*. Northwestern.

Gusdorf, G. (1965). *Speaking*, P. T. Brockelman, trans. Northwestern.

Habermas, J. (1971). *Knowledge and practice*. Beacon.

———. (1973). *Theory and practice*. Beacon.

———. (1975). *Legitimation crisis*. Beacon.

———. (1979). Aspects of the rationality of action, T. McCarthy, trans. In Geraets.

———. (1979a). *Communication and the evolution of society*, T. McCarthy, trans. Beacon.

Hamlin, P. (1939). *Legal education in colonial New York*. NYU.

Hample, D. (1977). Testing a model of value argument and evidence. *CM*, 44: 106–120.

———. (1977a). The Toulmin model and the syllogism. *JAFA*, 14: 1–9.

———. (1978). Predicting immediate belief change and adherence to argument claims. *CM*, 45: 219–228.

———. (1979). Motives in law: An adaptation of legal realism. *JAFA*, 15: 156–168.

———. (1979a). Predicting belief and belief change using a cognitive theory of argument and evidence. *CM*, 46: 142–146.

———. (1980). The cognitive context of argument. ICA Convention Paper.

———. (1980a). A cognitive view of argument. *JAFA*, 16: 151–158.

———. (1981). The cognitive context of argument. *WJSC*, 45: 148–158.

Handy, R. (1969). *Value theory and the behavioral sciences*. Thomas.

Hanushek, E. A., & Jackson, J. E. (1977). *Statistical methods for social scientists*. Academic Press.

Hardwig, J. (1973). The achievement of moral rationality. *Philosophy & Rhetoric*, 6: 171–185.

Harré, R. (1974). The conditions for a social psychology of childhood. In Richards.

Harrison, B. (1972). *Meaning and structure: An essay in the philosophy of language*. Harper.

Hart, H. L. A. (1961). *The concept of law*. Oxford.

Haskell, R. E., & Hauser, G. A. (1978). Rhetorical structure: Truth and method in Weaver's epistemology. *QJS*, 64: 233–245.

Hatton, D. E. et al. (1971). The effects of biasing information and dogmatism upon witness testimony. *Psychonomic Science*, 23: 425–427.

Hawes, L. C. (1975). *Pragmatics of analoguing: Theory and model construction in communication*. Addison-Wesley.

———. (1977). Toward a hermeneutic phenomenology of communication. *CQ*, 25: 30–41.

Haynes, M. (1979). Evolution and reason: Toward a theory of the growth of knowledge. In Geraets.

Heath, R. L. (1976). Variability in value system priorities as decision-making adaptation to situational differences. *CM*, 43: 325–333.

Hegel, G. W. F. (1967). *The phenomenology of mind*. Harper Torchbooks.

Helmer, O., & Rescher, N. (1960). *On the epistemology of the inexact sciences*. Rand.

Hempel, C. G. (1965). *Aspects of scientific explanation*. Free Press.

390 · REFERENCE LIST ·

———. (1979). Scientific rationality: Analytic vs. pragmatic perspective. In Geraets.

Hepp, M. H. (1956). *Thinking things through*. Scribner.

Herman, P. J. (1970). Occupations of jurors as an influence on their verdict. *The Forum*, 5: 150.

Hesse, M. B. (1966). *Models and analogies in science*. Notre Dame.

Hewes, D. E. (1975). Finite stochastic modeling of communication processes: An introduction and some basic readings. *HCR*, 1: 271–282.

Hexter, J. H. (1971). *Doing history*. Indiana.

Hirsch, E. D. (1967). *Validity in interpretation*. Yale.

Hochmuth, M. (1955). *History and criticism of American public address*, Vol. III. Longmans.

Hochmuth, M., & Murphy, R. (1954). Rhetorical and elocutionary training in nineteenth-century colleges. In K. R. Wallace, ed., *History of speech education in America*.

Hofstadter, R. (1944). U. B. Phillips and the plantation legend. *Journal of Negro History*, 29: 109–124.

Hollis, M. (1970). The limits of irrationality. In Wilson.

Holmes, G. W., ed. (n.d.). *Persuasion: The key to success in trial*. Institute of Continuing Legal Education, U. of Michigan.

———. (1973). *Approaches to advocacy*. Institute of Continuing Legal Education, U. of Michigan.

Hospers, J. (1953). *An Introduction to philosophical analysis*. Prentice-Hall.

Howell, W. S., trans. (1951). *Fénelon's dialogues on eloquence*. Princeton.

———. (1966). Rhetoric and poetics: A plea for the two literatures. In L. Wallach, ed., *The classical tradition*. Cornell.

———. (1975). Kenneth Burke's 'lexicon rhetoricae': A critical examination. *Poetics, rhetoric, and logic: studies in the basic disciplines of criticism*. Cornell.

Hoy, D. C. (1978). *The critical circle: Literature and history in contemporary hermeneutics*. California.

Hume, D. (1955). *An inquiry concerning human understanding*. C. W. Hendel, ed. Liberal Arts Press.

Hunsaker, D. M. (1973). Upsetting the pornographer's applecart: A critical review of *Miller* v. *California*. WSCA Convention Paper.

Hyde, M. J., & Smith, C. R. (1979). Hermeneutics and rhetoric: A seen but unobserved relationship. *QJS*, 65: 347–363.

Ihde, D. (1977). *Experimental phenomenology*. Capricorn.

Iser, W. (1974). *The implied reader: Patterns of communication in prose fiction from Bunyan to Beckett*. Johns Hopkins.

Jackson, S. (1980). Review of *Thinking; Readings in cognitive science*, edited by P. N. Johnson-Laird & P. C. Wason. *JAFA*, 17: 66–72.

Jackson S., & Jacobs, S. (1978). Adjacency pairs and the sequential description of arguments. SCA Convention Paper.

———. (1980). Structure of conversational argument: Pragmatic bases for the enthymeme. *QJS*, 66: 251–265.

———. (1981). The collaborative production of proposals in conversational argument and persuasion: A study in disagreement regulation. *JAFA*, 18: 77–90.

Jacobs, S. & Jackson, S. (1979). Collaborative aspects of argument production. SCA Convention Paper.

———. (1979a). The social production of influence. CSSA Convention Paper.

Matlon, R. J. (1978). Debating propositions of value. *JAFA*, 14: 194–204.

Massey, J. L. (1967). Information, machines and men. In Crosson & Sayre.

Maund, J. B. (1976). Rationality of belief—Intercultural comparisons. In Benn & Mortimore.

Mead, G. H. (1932). *The philosophy of the present*, A. E. Murphy, ed. Open Court.

———. (1934). *Mind, self and society: From the standpoint of a social behaviorist*, C. W. Morris, ed. Chicago.

———. (1938). *The philosophy of the act*, C. W. Morris, ed. Chicago.

Mehan, H. & Wood, H. (1975). *The reality of ethnomethodology*. Wiley.

Meiland, J. W. (1980). What ought we to believe? or the Ethics of belief revisited. *American Philosophical Quarterly*, 17: 15–24.

Miller, A. (1962). *Death of a salesman*. In H. M. Block & R. G. Shedd, eds., *Masters of modern drama*. Random.

Miller, G. R. (1966). *Speech communication: A behavioral approach*. Bobbs-Merrill.

Miller, G. R., & Burgoon, M. (1978). Persuasion research: Review and commentary. In B. D. Ruben, ed., *Communication Yearbook 2*. Transaction Books.

Miller, G. R., & Fontes, N. E. (1979). *Real versus reel: What's the verdict*. (Final report, NSF-RANN Grant).

Miller, G. R., & Nilsen, T. R., eds. (1966). *Perspectives on argumentation*. Scott-Foresman.

Mills, G. E. (1968). *Reason in controversy*, 2nd ed. Allyn & Bacon.

———. (1976). Legal argumentation: Research and teaching. *WSC*, 40: 83–90.

Mills, G. E., & Petrie, H. G. (1968). The role of logic in rhetoric. *QJS*, 54: 260–267.

Minas, A. C. (1977). Why "paradigms" don't prove anything. *Philosophy and Rhetoric*, 10: 217–231.

Mintzberg, H., Raisinghani, D., & Théorêt, A. (1976). The structure of "unstructured" decision processes. *Administrative Science Quarterly*, 21: 246–275.

Mitchell, H. F., & Byrne, D. (1973). The defendant's dilemma: Effects of juror's attitudes and authoritarianism on judicial decisions. *Journal of Personality and Social Psychology*, 25: 123–129.

Monge, P. R. (1973). Theory construction in the study of communication: The system paradigm. *Journal of Communication*, 23: 5–16.

Moor, J. H. (1978). Three myths of computer science. *British Journal for the Philosophy of Science*, 29: 213–222.

Moore, C. M. et al. (1979). *Use of videotape in the legal environment: Annotated bibliography*. Kent State University Communication and Law Project.

———. (1979a). *Videotape testimony: A practical guide to process and procedure*. Kent State University Communication and Law Project.

———. (1979b). *Videotape testimony and evidence: Advantages, disadvantages and recommended uses*. Kent State University Communication and Law Project.

Moreau, J. (1963). *Rhétorique, dialectique et exigence premiere. Théorie de l'argumentation*. Neuwelaerts.

Morris, C. (1970). *The pragmatic movement in American philosophy*. Braziller.

Morris, W. T. (1970). On the art of modeling. In Stogdill.

Mortimore, G. W., & Maund, J. B. (1976). Rationality in belief. In Benn & Mortimore.

Mudd, C. S. (1959). The enthymeme and logical validity. *QJS*, 45: 409–414.

Murray, M. (1975). *Modern critical theory: A phenomenological introduction*. Martinus Nijhoff.

———. (1980). Structure and strategy in conversational influence. SCA Convention Paper.

———. (1981). Argument as a natural category: The routine grounds for arguing in conversation. *WJSC*, 45: 118–132.

Jacobson, S. K., & Berger, C. (1974). Communication and justice: Defendant attributes and their effects on the severity of his sentence. *SM*, 41: 282–286.

Jandt, F. E. (1973). *Conflict resolution through communication*. Harper.

Jaspers, K. (1974). Three essays. In M. Natanson, *Phenomenology, role, and reason*. Thomas.

Jefferson, G. (1972). Side sequences. In Sudnow.

Jefferson, G., & Schenkein, J. (1978). Some sequential negotiations in conversation: Unexpanded and expanded versions of projected action sequences. In Schenkein.

Johnson, E. (1977). *Outside the courts*. National Center for State Courts.

Johnson, F. C., & Klare, G. R. (1961). General models of communication research: A survey of the developments of a decade. *Journal of Communication*, 11: 13–26, 45.

Johnson, J. M. (1977). Behind the rational appearances: Fusion of thinking and feeling in sociological research. In Douglas & Johnson.

———. Ethnomethodology and existential sociology. In Douglas & Johnson.

Johnstone, H. W., Jr. (1964). Self-refutation and validity. *The Monist*, 48: 467–485.

———. (1965). Some reflections on argument. In Natanson & Johnstone.

———. (1969). Truth, communication and rhetoric in philosophy. *Revue Internationale de Philosophie*, 90: 404–409.

———. (1973). Rationality and rhetoric in philosophy. *QJS*, 59: 381–389.

———. (1978). *Validity and rhetoric in philosophical argument*. Dialogue Press of Man and World.

Jonas, H. (1971). Change and permanence: On the possibility of understanding history. *Social Research*, 38: 498–528.

Jones, S. B. (1976). Justification in judicial opinions: A case study. *JAFA*, 12: 121–129.

Junker, B. H. (1960). *Field work: An introduction to the social sciences*. Chicago.

Kallmeyer, W., & Schutze, F. (1976). Konversationsanalyse. *Studium Linquistick*, 1: 1–28.

Kaplan, A. (1964). *The conduct of inquiry: Methodology for behavioral science*. Chandler.

———. (1964a). Some limitations on rationality. In C. J. Friedrich, ed., *Rational decision*. Atherton.

Keasey, C. B., ed. (1977). *Nebraska symposium on motivation, 1977: Social cognitive development*. Nebraska.

Keim, R. (1975). Epistemic values and epistemic viewpoints. In Lehrer.

Keller-Cohen, D., Chalmer, K. C., & Remler, J. E. (1979). The development of discourse negation in the nonnative child. In E. Ochst & B. Schieffelin, eds., *Developmental pragmatics*. Academic Press.

Kellerman, K. (1980). The concept of evidence: A critical review. *JAFA*, 16: 159–172.

Kelley, H. H. (1972). Causal schemata and the attribution process. In E. E. Jones et al., eds., *Attribution: Perceiving the causes of behavior*. General Learning Press.

Kelly, G. A. (1955). *A theory of personality*. Norton.

Kessler, J. et al. (1975). The effect of juror sex on the decision-making of jurors in a simulated case. SCA Convention Paper.

Ketcham, V. A. (1914). *The theory and practice of argumentation and debate*. Macmillan.

Kfoury, R. (1980). The ideology of reality. Unpublished manuscript.

Kline, S. L. (1979). Toward a contemporary linguistic interpretation of the concept of stasis. *JAFA*, 16: 95–103.

Kluback, W., & Becker, M. (1979). The significance of Chaim Perelman's philosophy of rhetoric. *Revue Internationale de Philosophie*, 33: 33–46.

Kluckhohn, F. (1940). The participant-observer technique in small communities. *AJS*, 46.

Kneupper, C. W. (1978). On argument and diagrams. *JAFA*, 14: 181–186.

———. (1979). Paradigms and problems: Alternative constructivist/interactionist implications for argumentation theory. *JAFA*, 15: 220–227.

———. (1980). Rhetoric, argument, and social reality: A social constructivist view. *JAFA*, 16: 173–181.

Kockelmans, J. (1979). Sociology and the problem of rationality. In Geraets.

Kordig C. R. (1978). Discovery and justification. *Philosophy of Science*, 45: 110–117.

Kramer, C. (1977). Cross-examination of the medical expert. *Trial*, Dec.: 26–27.

Krasner, S. D. (1972). Are bureaucracies important? (Or Allison Wonderland). *Foreign Policy*, No. 7: 159–179.

Kraus, S., ed. (1974). *The great debates*. Indiana.

Kruger, A. N. (1960). *Modern debate: Its logic and strategy*. McGraw-Hill.

———. The nature of controversial statements. *Philosophy and Rhetoric*, 8: 137–158.

Kuhn, T. S. (1961). The function of measurement in modern physical science. *Isis*, 52: 161–193.

———. (1970). Logic of discovery or psychology of research? In Lakatos & Musgrave.

———. (1970a). Reflections on my critics. In Lakatos and Musgrave.

———. (1970b). *The structure of scientific revolutions*, 2nd ed. Chicago.

———. (1974). Second thoughts on paradigms. In F. Suppe, ed., *The structure of scientific theories*. Illinois.

Labov, W. (1972). Rules for ritual insult. In Sudnow.

Labov, W. & Fanshel, D. (1977). *Therapeutic discourse: Psychotherapy as conversation*. Academic Press.

Lakatos, I. (1970). Falsification and the methodology of scientific research programmes. In Lakatos & Musgrave.

Lakatos, I., & Musgrave, A., eds. *Criticism and the growth of knowledge*. Cambridge.

Lakoff, R. (1977). What you can do with words: Politeness, pragmatics, and performatives. In Rogers, Wall & Murphy. *Landmark Communications, Inc.* v. *Commonwealth of Virginia*, 56Led 2dl (1978).

Laudan, L. (1977). *Progress and its problems*. California.

Laycock, C., & Scales, R. L. (1913). *Argumentation and debate*. Macmillan.

Lee, A. M. (1966). *Multivalent man*. Braziller.

Leff, M. C. (1980). Interpretation and the art of the rhetorical critic. *WJSC*, 44: 337–349.

Lehrer, K., ed. (1975). *Analysis and metaphysics: Essays in honor of R. M. Chisholm*. Reidel.

Lehrer, K. (1978). Systematic justification: Selections from *Knowledge*. In Pappas & Swain.

Lein, L., & Brenneis, D. (1978). Children's disputes in three speech communities. *Language in Society*, 7: 299–323.

Levi-Strauss, C. (1966). *The savage mind*. Chicago.

Levitin, T. (1969). Values. In J. P. Robinson & P. R. Shaver, eds., *Measures of social psychological attitudes*. Michigan Survey Research Center.

Lichtman, A. J. (1974). A benign institution? *New Republic*, 171: 22–24.

Lichtman, A. J., & Challinor, J. R., eds. (1979). *Kin and communities: Families in America*. Smithsonian.

Lindblom, C. E., & Cohen, D. K. (1979). *Usable knowledge*. Yale.

Lindeman, E. C. (1924). *Social discovery: An approach to the study of functional groups*.

Linge, D. E. (1976). Editor's introduction. In Gadamer.

Livesley, W. J., & Bromley, D. B. (1973) *Person perception in childhood and adolescence*

Llewellyn, K. N. (1960). *The common law tradition*. Little, Brown.

Lok, P. (1980). Curtains for a leading lady. *Macleans'*: 93.

Longino, H. E. (1979). Evidence and hypothesis: An analysis of evidential relation *phy of Science*, 46: 35–56.

Loreau, M. (1965). Rhetoric as the logic of the behavioral sciences, L. I. Watkins Brandes, trans. *QJS*, 51: 455–464.

Lucey, K. (1976). Scales of epistemic appraisal. *Philosophical Studies*, 29: 169–1

Luck, J. I., ed. (1973). *Proceedings: National conference on argumentation*. Texas Ch

Lukes, S. (1970). Some problems about rationality. In Wilson.

MacEwen, E. J. (1898). *Essentials of argumentation*. Heath.

MacIntyre, A. (1970). The idea of a social science. In Wilson.

McBath, J. H. (1963). *Argumentation and debate*, 2nd ed. Holt.

McBurney, J. A. (1936). The place of the enthymeme in rhetorical theory. *SM*

McBurney, J. H., & Mills, G. E. (1964). *Argumentation and debate: Techniques of* Macmillan.

McCarthy, T. (1979). Rationality and discourse. In Geraets.

McElligott, J. N. (1868). *The American debater*. Ivison, Phinney, Blakeman.

McGaffey, R. (1979). Group libel revisited. *QJS*, 65: 157–170.

McGee, M. C. (1980). The "Ideograph": A link between rhetoric and ideolo 1–16.

———. (1980a). The "Ideograph" as a unit of analysis in political argument. Newell.

McGuire, W. J. (1960). A syllogistic analysis of cognitive relationships. In C. M J. Rosenberg, eds., *Attitude organization and change*. Yale.

McHugh, P. (1970). A common-sense conception of deviance. In J. D. Dou *viance and respectability: The social construction of moral meanings*. Basic B

McKerrow, R. E. (1973). Rhetorical logoi: The search for a universal criteri SCA Convention Paper.

———. (1977). Rhetorical validity: An analysis of three perspectives on *JAFA*, 13: 133–141.

———. (1980). Argument communities: A quest for distinctions. In Rhod

———. (1980a). On fields and rational enterprises: A reply to Willard. Newell.

———. (1980b). Reason and validity: Selected claims. SCA Convention Pa

———. (1980c). Validating arguments: A phenomenological perspective. tion Paper.

McMaster, J. B. (1883–1913). *A history of the people of the United States, from the Civil War*. Appleton.

Manicas, P. T. (1966). On Toulmin's contribution to logic and argumenta 83–94.

March, J. G. (1970). Appendix: Problems in model-building. In Stogdill.

Marcuse, H. (1964). *One-dimensional man*. Beacon.

Marshall, J. (1966). *Law and psychology in conflict*. Bobbs-Merrill.

Martin, R. (1977). *Historical explanation: Re-enactment and practical inference.*

Myrdal, G. (1944). *An American dilemma: The Negro problem and modern democracy*. Harper.

Nagel, E. (1961). *The structure of science*. Harcourt.

Nagel, E., Suppes, P., & Tarski, A., eds. (1962). *Logic, methodology and philosophy of science*. Stanford.

Nagel, S., & Weitzman, L. J. (1973). Sex and the unbiased jury. *Case and comments*, 78: 28–31.

Natanson, M. (1965). The claims of immediacy. In Natanson & Johnstone.

Natanson, M., & Johnstone, H. W., Jr., eds. (1965). *Philosophy, rhetoric, and argumentation*. Penn State.

Nathan, N. M. C. (1980). *Evidence and assurance*. Cambridge.

Nichols, E. R., & Baccus, J. H. (1936). *Modern debating*. Norton.

Nichols, J. E. (1979). The pre-Tinker history of freedom of student press and speech. *Journalism Quarterly*, 56: 727–733.

Nixon, R. M. (1972). Radio address on the philosophy of government, October 21, 1972.

Noble, J. W., & Averbuch, B. (1955). *Never plead guilty*. Bantam.

Nofsinger, R. E., Jr. (1975). The demand ticket: A conversational device for getting the floor. *SM*, 42: 1–9.

North, H. F. (1956). Rhetoric and historiography. *QJS*, 42: 234–242.

O'Keefe, B. J., & Delia, J. G. (1979). Construct comprehensiveness and cognitive complexity as predictors of the number of strategic adaptations of argument and appeals in a persuasive message. *CM*, 46: 231–240.

O'Keefe, D. J. (1977). Two concepts of argument. *JAFA*, 13: 121–128.

———. (1980). Is argument a speech act? SCA Convention Paper.

Olafson, F. A. (1979). *The dialectic of action*. Chicago.

O'Neil, J. M., & McBurney, J. H. (1932). *The working principles of argument*. Macmillan.

Padawer-Singer, A. M. et al. (1977). An experimental study of twelve vs. six member juries under unanimous and nonunanimous decisions. In Sales.

Palmer, N. D. (1979). Some continuing problems in international relations research. *International Studies Notes*, Spring.

Palmer, R. E. (1969). *Hermeneutics: Interpretation theory in Schleiermacher, Dilthey, Heidegger, and Gadamer*. Northwestern.

Pappas, G. S., & Swain, M., eds. (1978). *Essays on knowledge and justification*. Cornell.

Parkinson, M. G. (1981). Verbal behavior and courtroom success. *CE*, 30: 22–32.

Pattee, G. K. (1920). *Practical argumentation*. Century.

Paxson, T. D., Jr. (1978). Professor Swain's account of knowledge. In Pappas & Swain.

Pellegrini, A. M., & Stirling, B. (1936). *Argumentation and public discussion*. Heath.

Pelsma, J. R. (1937). *Essentials of debate*. Crowell.

Perelman, C. (1952). Logique et rhétorique. In C. Perelman & L. Olbrechts-Tyteca, *Rhétorique et Philosophie*. Presses Universitaires de France.

———. (1963). *The idea of justice and the problem of argument*, J. Petrie, trans. Routledge & Kegan Paul.

———. (1965). Act and person in argument, W. Sacksteder, trans. In Natanson & Johnstone.

———. (1968). Recherches interdisciplinaires sur l'argumentation. *Logique et Analyse*, 11: 502–511.

———. (1968a). Reply to Mr. Zaner. *Philosophy and Rhetoric*, 1: 168–170.

———. (1970). *Dialectic und dialog, Hegel-jahrbuch.* Verlag A. Hain.

———. (1970a). The new rhetoric: A theory of practical reasoning, E. Griffin-Collart & O. Bird, trans. In *The Great Ideas Today.* Encyclopaedia Britannica.

———. (1970b). Le réel commun et le réel philosophique, *Le Champ de l'argumentation.* Presses Universitaires de Bruxelles.

———. (1977). *L'Empire rhétorique.* Vrin.

———. (1979). L'argument pragmatique, *Le Champ de l'argumentation.* Presses Universitaires de Bruxelles.

———. (1979a). *Historical meaning and categories.* Translator's manuscript prepared at the National Center for the Humanities.

———. (1979b). *The new rhetoric and the humanities.* Reidel.

———. (1979c). The rational and the reasonable. In Geraets.

Perelman, C., & Olbrechts-Tyteca, L. (1957). The new rhetoric, F. B. Sullivan, trans. *Philosophy Today,* 1: 8.

———. (1958). *La nouvelle rhétorique: traité de l'argumentation.* Presses Universitaires de France.

———. (1969). *The new rhetoric: A treatise on argumentation,* J. Wilkinson & P. Weaver, trans. Notre Dame (1971). Paperback ed.

Perry, F. M. (1906). *Argumentation.* American Book.

Peters, R. S. (1976). The development of reason. In Benn & Mortimore.

Petrie, H. G. (1969). Does logic have any relevance to argumentation? *JAFA,* 6: 55–60.

Philipsen, G. (1975). Speaking "Like a man" in Teamsterville: Culture patterns of role enactment in an urban neighborhood. *QJS,* 61: 13–22.

Phillips, U. B. (1918). *American Negro slavery.* Appleton.

———. (1929). *Life and labor in the old South.* Little, Brown.

Philosophie, rhétorique, lieux communs (1972). *Bulletin de la Classe des Sciences morales et politiques de l'Academie Royale de Belgique,* 8: 144–156.

Piaget, J. (1959). *The language and thought of the child,* 3rd ed. Routledge & Kegan Paul.

Pirsig, R. M. (1974). *Zen and the art of motorcycle maintenance.* Bantam.

Plato. (n.d.). *Euthphron.* 7b–d.

Plumb, J. H. (1975). How freedom took root in slavery. *New York Review of Books,* 22: 3–4.

Polanyi, M. (1962). *Personal knowledge.* Harper Torchbooks.

———. (1967). Tacit knowing. In Polanyi, M., *The tacit dimension.* Anchor.

Polanyi, M., & Prosch, H. (1975). *Meaning.* Chicago.

Pomerantz, A. (1978). Compliment responses: Notes on the cooperation of multiple constraints. In Schenkein.

Popper, K. R. (1966). *The poverty of historicism.* Basic Books.

———. (1970). Normal science and its dangers. In Lakatos & Musgrave.

Pospesel, H. (1971). *Arguments: Deductive logical exercises.* Prentice-Hall.

Preiser, S. E. (1977). Cross examination of lay witnesses. *Trial,* Dec.: 22–25.

Pryor, B. et al. (1979). The Florida experiment: An analysis of on-the-scene responses to cameras in the courtroom. *SSCJ,* 45: 12–26.

———. (1980). An affective-cognitive consistency explanation for comprehension of standard jury instructions. *CM,* 47: 68–76.

Psathas, G., ed. (1973). *Phenomenological sociology.* Wiley.

Quasthoff, U. (1978). The uses of stereotype in everyday argument. *Journal of Pragmatics*, 2: 1–48.

Quimby, R. W. (1977). Agnew's plea bargain: Between rhetorics of consensus and confrontation. *CSSJ*, 28: 163–172.

Rabin, D. A. (1978). Gottlieb's model of rule-guided reasoning: An analysis of *Griswold* v. *Connecticut*. *JAFA*, 15: 77–90.

Radford, J., & Burton, A. (1974). *Thinking: Its nature and development*. Wiley.

Rafshoon, G., producer (1976). *Carter-Rafshoon 1976 primary commercials*. Gerald Rafshoon Advertising.

Rawick, G. (1972). *Sundown to sunup: The making of the black community* (Contributions in Afro-American and African Studies, No. 11). Greenwood.

Ray, J., & Zavos, H. (1966). Reasoning and argument: Some special problems and types. In Miller & Nilsen.

Reimer, H. (1937). Socialization in the prison community. *American Prison Association Proceedings*, n.v.: 151–155.

Reinard, J. C., & Reynolds, R. A. (1978). The effects of inadmissable testimony objections and rulings on jury decisions. *JAFA*, 15: 91–109.

Reinfeld, F., ed. (1948). *Hypermodern chess: The games of Aron Nimzovich*. Dover.

Rescher, N. (1973). The study of value change. In E. Lazlo & J. B. Wilbur, eds., *Value theory in philosophy and social science*. Gordon & Breach.

———. (1976). *Plausible reasoning*. Van Gorcum, Assen.

———. (1977). *Dialectics: A controversy-oriented approach to the theory of knowledge*. SUNY.

———. (1979). *Cognitive systematization*. Rowman & Littlefield.

Rhodes, J., & Newell, S., eds. (1980). *Proceedings of the summer conference on argumentation*. SCA/AFA.

Rhodes, J. F. (1900–1919). *History of the United States from the compromise of 1850* (7 vols.). Macmillan.

Richards, M. P. M., ed. (1974). *The integration of a child into a social world*. Cambridge.

Ricoeur, P. (1965). *Fallible man*, C. A. Kelbley, trans. Northwestern.

———. (1965a) *History and truth*, C. A. Kelbley, trans. Northwestern.

———. (1966). *Freedom and nature: The voluntary and involuntary*, E. V. Kohak, trans. Northwestern.

———. (1967). *Husserl: An analysis of his phenomenology*, E. G. Ballard & L. E. Embree, trans. Northwestern.

———. (1970). *Freud and philosophy*, D. Savage, trans. Yale.

———. (1971). The model of the text: Meaningful action considered as a text. *Social Research*, 38; 529–562.

———. (1973). the model of the text: Meaningful action considered as a text. *New Literary History*, 5: 91–117.

Rieke, R. (1964). Rhetorical theory in American legal practice. Unpublished doctoral dissertation, Ohio State University.

———. (1978). The role of legal communication studies in contemporary departments of communication. *Assoc. for Comm. Administration Bulletin*, no. 24: 31–33.

———. (1980). Human reasoning theory for modern communication. East-west Comm. Conf. Paper.

Rieke, R., & Newell, S. (1981). Toward a general theory of Emerson's general theory of the First Amendment. WSCA Convention Paper.

Rieke, R., & Sillars, M. O. (1975). *Argumentation and the decision making process*. Wiley.

Robinson, J. R., & Majak, R. R. (1967). The theory of decision-making. In J. C. Charlesworth, ed., *Contemporary political analysis*. Free Press.

Robinson, W. C. (1893). *Forensic oratory: A manual for advocates*. Little, Brown.

Rogers, A., Wall, B., & Murphy, J. P., eds. (1977). *Proceedings of the Texas conference on performatives, presuppositions and implicatures*. Center for Applied Linguistics.

Rokeach, M. (1970). *Beliefs, attitudes and values*. Jossey-Bass.

———. (1973). *The nature of human values*. Free Press.

Rollings, H. E., & Blascovich, J. (1977). The case of Patricia Hearst: Pre-trial publicity and opinions. Journal of Communication, 27: 58–65.

Rowell, E. Z. (1932). Prolegomena to argumentation. *QJS*, 18; 1–13, 224–248, 381–405, 585–606.

———. (1934). The conviction-persuasion duality. *QJS*, 20: 469–489.

Ryan, J. (1974). *Early language development: Toward a communicational analysis*. In Richards.

Sacks, H. (1972). Lecture notes, spring 1972, no. 1. Unpublished manuscript.

Sales, B., ed. (1977). *Psychology in the legal process*. Spectrum.

Sams, M. J., ed. (1978). *Advanced negligence trial strategy*. Practicing Law Institute.

Sanbonmatsu, A. (1971). Darrow and Rorke's use of Burkeian identification strategies in *New York vs. Gitlow* (1920). *SM*, 38: 36–48.

Sanders, R. E. (1973). The question of a paradigm for the study of speech-using behavior. *QJS*, 59: 1–10.

Sanford, W. P. (1938). *English theories of public address, 1530–1828*. Hedrick.

Sayre, K. M. (1965). *Recognition: A study in the philosophy of artificial intelligence*. Notre Dame.

Schegloff, E. A. (1972). Notes on a conversational practice: Formulating place. In Sudnow.

———. (1972a). Sequencing in conversational openings. In J. A. Fishman, ed., *Advances in the sociology of language*, Vol. 2. Mouton.

———. (1979). Identification and recognition in telephone conversation openings. In G. Psathas, ed., *Everyday language: Studies in ethnomethodology*. Halstead.

Schegloff, E. A., & Sacks, H. (1974). Opening up closings. In R. Turner, ed., *Ethnomethodology: Selected readings*. Penguin.

Scheler, M. (1973). *Formalism in ethics and non-formal ethics of values*. Trans. M. S. Frings. Northwestern.

Schenkein, J., ed. (1978). *Studies in the organization of conversational interaction*. Academic Press.

Schopenhauer, A. (1896). *Essays of Schopenhauer*. Wiley.

Schurmann, F. (1966). *Ideology and organization in Communist China*. California.

Schutz, A. (1945). On multiple realities. *Philosophy & Phenomenological Research*, 5: 533–574.

———. (1953). Common sense and scientific interpretation of human action. *Philosophy & Phenomenological Research*, 14: 1–37.

———. (1954). Concept and theory formation in the social sciences. *Journal of Philosophy*, 51: 257–273.

———. Symbol, reality, and society. In L. Bryson et al., eds., *Symbols and society*. Harper.

————. (1962). *Collected papers I: The problem of social reality*, M. Natanson, ed. Martinus Nijhoff.

————. (1964) *Collected papers II: Studies in social theory*, A. Broderson, ed. Martinus Nijhoff.

————. (1966) *Collected papers III: Studies in phenomenological philosophy*, I. Schutz, ed. Martinus Nijhoff.

————. (1967). *The phenomenology of the social world*, G. Walsh & F. Lehnert, trans. Northwestern.

————. (1970). On phenomenology and social relations. Chicago.

————. (1970a). *Reflections on the problem of relevance*, R. Zaner, ed. Yale.

Schutz, A., & Luckmann, T. (1973). *The structures of the life world*, R. M. Zaner & T Engelhardt, Jr., trans. Northwestern.

Schwartz, H., & Jacobs, J. (1979). *Qualitative sociology: A method to the madness*. Free Press.

Schwartz, L. (1973). *Proof, persuasion and cross-examination*, 2 vols. Executive Reports Corp.

Schwartz, M. S., & Schwartz, C. G. (1955). Problems in participant observations. *AJS*, 60: 350–351.

Scriven. M. (1959). Truisms as the grounds for historical explanations. In P. Gardiner, ed., *Theories of history*. Free Press.

Scult, A. (1976). Perelman's universal audience: One perspective. *CSSJ*, 27: 176–180.

Searle, J. R. (1969). *Speech acts*. Cambridge.

————. (1977). A classification of illocutionary acts. In Rogers, Wall & Murphy.

Seibert, D. R. (1980). Proof beyond a reasonable doubt as proof to a reasonable degree of certainty. *JAFA*, 16: 213–221.

Sennett, R. (1978). *The fall of public man*. Vintage.

————. (1980). *Authority*. Knopf.

Settekorn, W. (1977). Pragmatique et rhétorique discursive. *Journal of Pragmatics*, 1: 195–209.

Shatz, M. (1977). The relationship between cognitive processes and the development of communication skills. In Keasey.

————. (1978). On the development of communicative understandings: An early strategy for interpreting and responding to messages. *Cognitive Psychology*, 10: 271–301.

Shaw, W. C. (1922). *The art of debate*. Allyn.

Shepard, D. (1966). Rhetoric and formal argument. *WJSC*, 30: 241–247.

Shibutani, T. (1961). *Society and personality*. Prentice-Hall.

Shimanoff, S. B. (1980). *Communication rules: Theory and research*. Sage.

Shotter, J. (1974). The development of personal powers. In Richards.

Shurter, W. D. (1908). *Science and the art of debate*. Neale.

Sillars, M. O. (1973). Audiences, social values and the analysis of argument. *Speech Teacher*, 22: 291–303.

Sillars, M. O., & Zarefsky, D. (1975). Future goals and roles of forensics. In J. H. McBath, ed., *Forensics as communication*. National Textbook.

Simmons, J. R. (1960). The nature of argumentation. *SM*, 27: 348–350.

Simon, H. A. (1978). On the forms of mental representation. In C. W. Savage, ed., *Minnesota Studies in the Philosophy of Science*, Vol. 9. Minnesota.

Simons, H. W. (1976). *Persuasion: Understanding, practice, and analysis*. Addison-Wesley.

Sinclair, J., & Coulthard, M. (1975). *Towards an analysis of discourse: The English used by teachers and pupils*. Oxford.

Smith, C. R., & Hunsaker, D. M. (1972). *The bases of argument*. Bobbs-Merrill.

Smith, R. G. (1970). *Speech-communication: Theory and models*. Harper.

Smith, S. A. (1977). Rhetorical strategies in the courtrooms of territorial Arkansas. *SSCJ*, 42: 318–333.

Snyder, E. C. (1971). Sex role differential and juror decisions. *Sociology and Social Research*, 55: 442–448.

Sorenson, T. (1965). *Kennedy*. Harper.

Spector, M. (1962). Models and theories. *British Journal for the Philosophy of Science*, 16: 121–142.

Sproule, J. M. (1980). *Argument: Language and influence*. McGraw-Hill.

Stampp, K. (1956). *The peculiar institution: Slavery in the antebellum South*. Random.

Steel, R. (1969). Endgame. *New York Review*. March 13, 1969, 15–22.

———. (1972). Cooling it. *New York Review*. October 19, 1972, 43–46.

———. (1973). *Imperialists and other heroes*. Vintage.

Steele, E. (1958). Social values in public address. *Western Speech*, 22: 38–42.

Stern, D. (1978). *The first relationship*. Harvard.

Stevenson, J. T. (1975). On doxastic responsibility. In Lehrer.

Stich, S. P., & Nisbett, R. E. (1980). Justification and the psychology of human reasoning. *Philosophy of Science*, 47: 188–202.

Stogdill, R. M., ed. (1970). *The process of model-building in the behavioral sciences*. Norton.

Strawson, P. (1964). Intention and convention in speech acts. *Philosophical Review*, 73: 439–460.

Sudnow, D., ed. (1972). *Studies in social interaction*. Free Press.

Suppes, P. (1960). A comparison of the meaning and uses of models in mathematics and the empirical sciences. *Synthese*, 12: 287–300.

Swain, M. (1978). Knowledge, causality, and justification. In Pappas & Swain.

———. (1978a). Some revisions of "knowledge, causality, and justification." In Pappas & Swain.

Swanson, D. L. (1977). A reflective view of the epistemology of critical inquiry. *CM*, 44: 207–219.

———. (1977a). The requirements of critical justifications. *CM*, 44: 306–320.

Swanson, J.W. (1966). On models. *British Journal for the Philosophy of Science*, 17: 297–311.

Taylor, D. M. (1970). *Explanation and meaning*. Cambridge.

Taylor, S. (1977). The acquisition of the roles of conversation: A structural developmental perspective and methodological comparison. Unpublished doctoral dissertation, University of Illinois at Urbana-Champaign.

Terkel, Studs (1970). *Hard times: An oral history of the great depression*. Avon.

Thayer, L. O. (1963). On theory-building in communication: Some conceptual problems. *Journal of Communication*, 13: 217–235.

Thomas, W. I., & Znaniecki, F. (1918–1920). *The Polish peasant in Europe and America*. Chicago.

Thompson, W. N. (1971). *Modern argumentation and debate*. Harper.

Thompson, W., & Insalata, S. J. (1964). Communication from attorney to client. *Journal of Communication*, 14: 22–33.

Thonsson, L., & Baird, A. C. (1948). *Speech criticism*. Ronald.

Tillich, P. (1953–1960). *Systematic theology*. Chicago.

Time, Inc. v. *Hill*. 385 U.S. 374 (1967).

Toulmin, S. E. (1958). *The uses of argument*. Cambridge.

———. (1963). *Foresight and understanding*. Harper.

———. (1964). *An examination of the place of reason in ethics*. Cambridge.

———. (1969). *The uses of argument*. Cambridge.

———. (1970). Does the distinction between normal and revolutionary science hold water? In Lakatos & Musgrave.

———. (1970a). Reasons and causes. In R. Borger & F. Cioffi, eds., *Explanation in the behavioral sciences: Confrontations*. Cambridge.

———. (1972). *Human understanding*. Princeton.

———. (1977). The structure of scientific theories. In F. Suppe, ed., *The structure of scientific theories*, 2nd ed. Illinois.

Toulmin, S. E., Rieke, R., & Janik, A. (1979). *An introduction to reasoning*. Macmillan.

U.S. Senate, Committee on Foreign Relations. 90th Congress, 2nd session (1968). *The Gulf of Tonkin, the 1964 incidents: Hearings with Robert S. McNamara*, February 20, 1968). GPO.

United States v. *O'Brien*, 391 U.S. 367 (1968).

Utterback, W. E. (1925). Aristotle's contribution to the psychology of argument. *QJS*, 11: 218–225.

Vidmar, N. (1972). Effects of decision alternatives on the verdicts and social perceptions of simulated jurors. *Journal of Personality and Social Psychology*, 22: 211–218.

Wagner, R. H. (1936). *Handbook of argumentation*. Nelson.

Wallace, K. C. (1963). The substance of rhetoric: Good reasons. *QJS*, 49: 239–249.

Waller, W., & Hill, R. (1951). *The family—A dynamic interpretation*. Dryden.

Warr, P. B., & Knapper, C. (1968). *The perception of people and events*. Wiley.

Wasby, S. et al. (1976). The functions of oral argument in the U.S. Supreme Court. *QJS*, 62: 410–424.

Weber, M. (1949). *The methodology of the social sciences*, E. A. Shils & H. A. Finch, trans. Free Press.

Weddle, P. (1978). *Argument: A guide to critical thinking*. McGraw-Hill.

Weimer, W. B. (1979). *Notes on the methodology of scientific research*. Erlbaum.

Weiner, S. L., & Goodenough, D. R. (1977). A move toward a psychology of conversation. In R. O. Freedle, *Discourse production and comprehension*. Ablex.

Wenzel, J. W. (1977). Toward a rationale for value-centered argument. *JAFA*, 13: 150–158.

———. (1979). Jürgen Habermas and the dialectical perspective on argumentation. *JAFA*, 16: 83–94.

———. Three senses of argument. SCA Convention Paper.

———. Perspectives on argument. In Rhodes & Newell.

Werner, H. (1957). *Comparative psychology of mental development*. International Universities.

Whately, R. (1963). *Elements of rhetoric*. D. Ehninger, ed. Southern Illinois.

White, H. (1973). *Metahistory: The historical imagination in nineteenth-century Europe*. Johns Hopkins.

White, H., & Manuel, F. E. (1976). Rhetoric and history. Clark Library Seminar Paper.

White, T. H. (1978). *In search of history: A personal adventure*. Harper.

Whyte, W. F. (1955). *Street corner society*, 2nd ed. Chicago.

Wichelns, H. A. (1925). Analysis and synthesis in argumentation. *QJS*, 11: 266–272.

Willard, C. A. (1976). On the utility of descriptive diagrams for the analysis and criticism of arguments. *CM*, 64: 308–319.

———. (1978). A reformulation of the concept of argument: The constructivist/interactionist foundations of a sociology of argument. *JAFA*, 14: 121–140.

———. (1978a). Argument as non-discursive symbolism. *JAFA*, 14: 187–193.

———. (1978b). *The logic of choice: An investigation of the concepts of rule and rationality* by Gidon Gottlieb. *JAFA*, 15: 124–132.

———. (1978c). Contributions of argumentation to accounts of moral judgment. SCA Convention Paper.

———. (1979). The epistemic functions of argument: Reasoning and decision-making from a constructivist/interactionist point of view. *JAFA*, 15: 169–191.

———. (1979a). Argument as epistemic II: A constructivist/interactionist view of reasons and reasoning. *JAFA*, 15: 211–219.

———. (1979b). Propositional argument is to argument what talking about passion is to passion. *JAFA*, 16: 21–28.

———. (1979c). Solomon's *The Passions*. *JAFA*, 16: 71–76.

———. (1980). Some questions about Toulmin's view of argument fields. In Rhodes & Newell.

———. (1980a). Würzburg revisited: Some reasons why the deduction-induction squabble is irrelevant to argumentation. In Rhodes & Newell.

———. (1980b). Some speculations on evidence. In Rhodes & Newell.

———. (1980c). A theory of argumentation. Unpublished manuscript. Department of Speech Communication, University of Pittsburgh.

———. (1981). The status of the nondiscursiveness thesis. *JAFA*, 17: 190–214.

———. (1981a). Argument fields and theories of logical types. *JAFA*, 17: 129–145.

———. (1981b). Essays in argumentation. Unpublished manuscript, Department of Speech Communication, University of Pittsburgh.

———. (1981c). Field theory: A Cartesian meditation. SCA/AFA Summer Conference on Argumentation II.

———. (1981d). Positivism is alive and muddled in the sphere of policy research: A reply to Nehnevajsa. Conference on Knowledge Use Convention Paper.

Willhoft, W. O. (1931). *Modern debate practice*. Prentice-Hall.

Wilson, B. R., ed. (1970). *Rationality*. Harper.

Winans, J. A., & Utterback, W. E. (1930). *Argumentation*. Century.

Winch, P. (1958). *The idea of a social science*. Routledge & Kegan Paul.

———. (1970). Understanding a primitive society. In Wilson.

Wittgenstein, L. (1953). *Philosophical investigations*, G. E. M. Anscombe, & R. Rhees, eds., trans. Blackwell.

———. (1958). *The blue and brown books*. Blackwell.

Woolbert, C. H. (1917). Conviction and persuasion: Some considerations of theory. *QJPS*, 3: 249–264.

Wyer, R. S., Jr., & Carlston, D. E. (1979). *Social cognition, inference, and attribution*. Erlbaum.

Yost, M. (1917). Argument from the point of view of sociology. QJPS, 3: 109–127.

Zarefsky, D. (1979). The Great Society as a rhetorical proposition. *QJS*, 65: 364–378.

———, ed. (1979a). *Special issue devoted to Jürgen Habermas. JAFA*, 16: 77–148.

———. (1980). Causal argument among historians: The case of the American Civil War. *SSCJ*, 45: 187–205.

———. (1980a). Product, process, or point of view. In Rhodes & Newell.

———. (1980b). Rhetorical analysis as argument: A search for standards of validity. SCA Convention Paper.

Ziegelmueller, G. W., & Rhodes, J., eds. (1981). *Dimensions of argument: Proceedings of the 1981 Summer Conference on Argumentation*. Speech Communication Association.

Ziman, J. (1978). *Reliable Knowledge*. Cambridge.

Zimmerman, D. H., & Pollner, M. (1970). The everyday world as phenomenon. In Douglas.

Znaniecki, F. (1940). *The social role of the man of knowledge*. Columbia.

———. (1952). *Cultural sciences*. Illinois.

———. (1955). *Social relations and social roles*. Chandler.

———. (1968). *The method of sociology*. Octagon.

Zyskind, H. (1979). Introduction. In Perelman, *The new rhetoric and the humanities*.

Notes on Contributors

V. WILLIAM BALTHROP is Assistant Professor of Speech Communication at the University of North Carolina at Chapel Hill. He has twice received the American Forensic Association's Research Award, most recently for "Argument as Linguistic Opportunity: A Search for Form and Function" (1980). He has also been editor of *Speaker and Gavel*.

PAMELA BENOIT is Visiting Assistant Professor of Speech Communication at Bowling Green State University.

E. CULPEPPER CLARK is Associate Professor and Chairman of the Department of Communication Studies at the University of Alabama in Birmingham. He is the author of *Francis Warrington Dawson and the Politics of Restoration: South Carolina, 1874–1889* and has published articles on historical method in communication and history journals. He has served on the editorial board of the *Journal of the American Forensic Association* and has chaired the Forensic Division of the Speech Communication Association.

J. ROBERT COX is Associate Professor of Speech Communication at the University of North Carolina at Chapel Hill. He was guest editor of the *Journal of the American Forensic Association*'s issue on "Argumentation Theory" (1977). He served as a planner for the AFA/SCA Conference on Argumentation in 1979 and 1981.

RAY D. DEARIN is Professor of Speech at Iowa State University. His essays on rhetorical theory and criticism and argumentation (including "The Philosophical Basis of Chaim Perelman's Theory of Rhetoric") have appeared in a number of anthologies in contemporary rhetoric, as well as the *Quarterly Journal of Speech*, *Central States Speech Journal* and *Communication Education*.

THOMAS B. FARRELL is Associate Professor of Communication Studies at Northwestern University. Among his publications in the philosophy of rhetoric and communication are "Knowledge, Consensus, and Rhetorical Theory," "Social Knowledge II," "Communication and Meaning: A Language-Action Synthesis," and "Language-Action: A Paradigm for Communication" (which received a distinguished monograph award in 1977).

RICHARD A. FILLOY is Assistant Professor of Communication Arts and Sciences at the University of Southern California.

WALTER R. FISHER is a Professor in the Department of Communication Arts and Sciences, University of Southern California. He specializes in criticism and contemporary rhetorical theory, especially problems in logic and ethics. Among his publications are *Rhetoric: A Tradition in Transition*, "Toward a Logic of Good Reason," and "Rationality and the Logic of Good Reason."

PATRICIA M. GANER is Professor of Speech Communication and Director of Forensics at Cypress College.

DALE HAMPLE is Associate Professor of Communication Arts and Sciences at Western Illinois University. His articles dealing with the cognitive processes associated with arguing and reasoning have appeared in *Communication Monographs* and the *Journal of the American Forensic Association*.

SALLY JACKSON is Assistant Professor of Speech Communication at the University of Nebraska at Lincoln. With co-author Scott Jacobs, she was awarded the Speech Communication Association Golden Anniversary Monograph Award for her article, "Structure of Conversational Argument: Pragmatic Bases for the Enthymeme" (*Quarterly Journal of Speech*, 1980).

SCOTT JACOBS is Assistant Professor of Speech Communication at the University of Nebraska at Lincoln. He has written several articles in the area of conversational argument, one of which (with co-author Sally Jackson), "Structure of Conversational Argument: Pragmatic Bases for the Enthymeme" (*Quarterly Journal of Speech*, 1980), was awarded the Speech Communication Association Golden Anniversary Monograph Award. He is also a recipient of the 1981 Karl R. Wallace Memorial Fund Award.

HENRY W. JOHNSTONE, JR. is Professor of Philosophy at the Pennsylvania State University. He is author of numerous articles on the role of argumentation in philosophy. His books include *Philosophy and Argument*, *The Problem of the Self*, and *Validity and Rhetoric in Philosophical Argument*. With

Maurice Natanson, he is a contributor to and co-editor of *Philosophy, Rhetoric, and Argumentation.* From 1968 to 1976 he was editor of *Philosophy and Rhetoric.*

RAY E. MCKERROW is Associate Professor and chairman of the Department of Speech Communication at the University of Maine at Orono. His articles on the philosophy of argumentation have appeared in the *Journal of History of Ideas, Philosophy and Rhetoric,* and the *Journal of the American Forensic Association.* He received the AFA Research Award for "Communities of Argument: A Quest for Distinctions" (1979). He is also editor of *Explorations in Rhetoric: Studies in Honor of Douglas Ehninger.*

ROBERT P. NEWMAN is Professor of Speech at the University of Pittsburgh. He has written extensively on argumentation and the decision process, including "Communication Pathologies of Intelligence Systems," *Speech Monographs* (1975) and "Truman's Self-Inflicted Wound: The China White Paper of 1949," *Prologue—The Magazine of the National Archives* (1982). He has also published *Recognition of Communist China? A Study in Argument* and (with Dale R. Newman) *Evidence.*

BARBARA O'KEEFE is Assistant Professor of Speech Communication at the University of Illinois, Urbana-Champaign.

DANIEL J. O'KEEFE is Assistant Professor of Speech Communication at the University of Illinois, Urbana-Champaign. His articles in the area of argumentation and human communication have appeared in *Communication Monographs, Quarterly Journal of Speech, Journal for the Theory of Social Behavior, Rhetoric Society Quarterly,* and the *Journal of the American Forensic Association.* His essay, "Two Concepts of Argument," received the 1977 AFA outstanding monograph award in argumentation.

CHAIM PERELMAN is Professor Emeritus and Director of the Center for the Philosophy of Law, University of Brussells. He has organized and held offices in many international philosophical societies and congresses. His books include *The Idea of Justice and the Problem of the Self; The New Rhetoric: A Treatise on Argumentation* (with L. Olbrechts-Tyteca); *The New Rhetoric and the Humanities; Justice, Law, and Argument*; and *The Realm of Rhetoric.* In 1962 he was awarded the Prix Franqui, the highest award given by the Belgian Government for scholarly or scientific work. A special issue of *Revue Internationale de Philosophie,* "La Nouvelle Rhetorique: Essais en hommage à Chaim Perelman," appeared in 1979.

RICHARD D. RIEKE is Professor of Communication at the University of Utah. He has written extensively in the areas of argumentation and processes in reasoning in both children and adults. His books include *Teaching Oral Communication in Elementary Schools* (with Willbrand), *An Introduction to Reasoning* (with Toulmin and Janik), *Argumentation and the Decision-Making Process* (with Sillars), and *The Rhetoric of Black Americans* (with Golden).

MALCOLM O. SILLARS is Professor of Communication at the University of Utah. His articles include "Rhetoric as Act;" "Audiences, Social Values, and the Analysis of Argument;" and "Persistent Problems in Rhetorical Criticism." He is co-author (with Rieke) of *Argumentation and the Decision-Making Process*. He has received the Delta Sigma Rho–Tau Kappa Alpha Distinguished Alumni Award and the Winon-Wichelns Award for *The Rhetoric of Protest and Reform* ("The Rhetoric of the Petition in Boots"). He has also served as an Associate Editor of *Quarterly Journal of Speech* and *Western Journal of Speech Communication*.

CHARLES ARTHUR WILLARD is Assistant Professor of Rhetoric and Communication at the University of Pittsburgh. His essays have appeared in *Communication Monographs* and the *Journal of the American Forensic Association*; his article "Reformulation of the Concept of Argument" received the American Forensic Association's "Best Monograph" award in 1978. His books include *Argumentation and the Social Grounds of Knowledge*. He is also an Associate Editor of the *Journal of the American Forensic Association*.

Index

Abstraction: levels of, 262

Action: types of, 111

Actor-performer: role in meaning creation of texts, 349–50, 356–57; performance as argument, 352

Adjacency pairs: as argument, 61, 156, 161; defined, 221–23; expansion of, 222–23, 228–29, 230–32

Adjustment: process of mutual, 211–12

Agency: cyclical nature of, 139–40; quasi-judicial, 368–69

Agreement: definitions of, 239–40, 243–44; factors of, 239–40, 242, 244, 249, 250; preference for, 223, 235–36, 239–40. *See also* Disagreement

Allison, G., 323–24; *The Essence of Decision Making*, 331–39

Analogy: role of, in logic, 291–92

Analytic induction: applied to conversational argument, 219–20; defined, 219

Apel, K., 108–10, 111–12, 113–14, 117

Applied formalism: argumentation as, xviii–xxii; criticisms of, xxii–xxvi, xxxiii, xxxvii–xxxviii

Apprenticeship: in legal practice, 365–66

Arbitrariness: reduction of, in models, 280

Argument: ambiguities in concept of, xxviii, 154–83, 249–50; among children, 154–83; bases of, 6, 96, 105–6, 108, 114; characteristics of, xxi, xxv, xxxii, 61, 107, 112, 156, 157–59, 162–63, 165, 168, 170–73, 180–81, 210–11, 219–20, 224, 235–36, 274–75, 343; classifications of, 3, 4, 6–9, 155; and communication, xiv, xxvi, xxxiv, 96, 107–12, 156, 158–59, 161, 166, 170, 205–16, 224–36, 298, 365–66, 370; constructivist/interactionist view of, xxvii, xxviii, 24–77, 177, 212–18, 238–39; definitions of, xiv, xxvi–xxviii, xxix, xxxvi–xxxvii, 6–7, 155, 159, 214–15, 249–50, 274–75, 298, 316; as disagreement, 219–20, 224, 235–36; fields of, xxiii–xxv; forms

of, xxv, xxvi–xxviii, xxix, xxxiv, 9–11, 22, 168, 274–75, 298, 316, 343, 346–47, 352, 357; functions of, xx, 74, 274–75; hermeneutical aspects of, 238–40, 242, 244–48, 301; and history, 123–24, 301; in literature, 348–59; and logic, xx; and models, xxvii, xxxviii, 105, 224–36, 265; and philosophy, xiv, xlv, 101; policy, 318–20; and rationality, 22, 109; resolution of, 167–68, 180–81. *See also* Argument₁; Argument₂; Argument making; Children's argument; Conversational argument; Critic of argument; Fields of argument; Historical argument; Legal argument; Modeling argument; Ontological arguments; Philosophical argument; Policy argument: Quasi-logical argument; Rhetorical argument

Argument₁: characteristics of, xxxvi, 19, 157; and communication, xxvi–xxvii, 3–4, 11–12, 15–18; and conversational argument, 224–25, 234–36; defined, 5, 15, 155; as distinct from argument making, 12–20; as distinct from argument₂, 5, 11–12, 22; forms of, xxvii; hermeneutical aspects of, 245; importance of study, xxvii–xxviii; paradigm cases of, 11–12, 15–17

Argument₂: and argument₁, xxvi–xxix, 4–5, 10–12, 22; characteristics of, 4, 9–10, 22–23, 157; and conversational argument, 224–25; criticisms of, xxix, xxxviii, 22; defined, xxvi–xxvii, xxxvi–xxxvii, 4, 9–10, 155; hermeneutical aspects of, 247, 249; and history, 306–7; importance of study, xxvi–xxviii, xxxvi–xxxvii; paradigm cases of, 9–10

Argumentation, 91–92, 189–91, 196, 197–98, 200–201; bases of, 24, 73–74; characteristics of, xvi, 81–83, 86, 92–93, 184, 292; and communication, 82–83, 86, 92–93, 184–86, 196; effectiveness of, xvi–xvii, 292–93; as field of study, xiii, xxi, 24, 51, 74–76, 184, 283–84; forms of, xxvii–

Argumentation (*continued*)
  xxviii, xxxiv, 79, 94, 185–201, 240, 292;
  hermeneutical aspects of, 249; history of
  study of, xliii–xliv; importance of audience,
  184, 193–95, 292–93; importance of study
  of, xii, xix–xx, xxxiii, 94, 363–64; and
  logic, xviii, 78–80, 82–85, 87–88, 91–
  92, 184, 195–96, 292; and rhetoric, 79,
  81–82, 87–88, 92–93, 292–93, 295–97;
  and values, 187–201. *See also* Fields; Fields
  of argument
Argumentation analysis, 82, 368–69
Argumentative form, 131, 135
Argument criticism, 50–52
Argument diagrams: controversy over, 267–
  68; and models, 267–68, 275, 276. *See also*
  Toulmin model of argument
Argument fields. *See* Fields; Fields of argument
Argument making: as distinct from argument₁
  and argument₂, 12–17, 18–22
Argument models. *See* Argument, and models;
  Modeling argument; Models about argu-
  ment; Models of argument
Argument validity, 95, 100; and rhetorical va-
  lidity, 83–84, 88; standards of, 84–85,
  91–92
Aristotle: classical traditions of rhetorical the-
  ory, 83, 86–87, 97–98, 124–26, 130, 196,
  290–91, 344–45, 365–66; view of dialec-
  tic, 290–91, 294–95; view of form, 126–
  27; *The Rhetoric*, 87, 124, 196, 290, 293;
  Topics, 87, 290, 293
Artist: purpose of, 361
"As if" maxim, 35–36, 39, 58, 76
Association: quasi-logical argument as, 80, 85.
  See also Dissociation
Asthetic belief: defined, 347
Asthetic proofs: defined, 347–48; function of,
  in argument, 347–48, 362; in literature,
  347, 357–59, 360–61, 362
Attitude: defined, 186; relation to belief,
  186–87, 193–94
Attraction theory: defined, 282–83
Audience: concern for, in argumentation theory,
  xxii–xxiv, xxvi–xxvii, xxxvi–xxxvii, 79–
  81, 84–86, 92, 193–95; definition of fields
  as, 39–40, 44–46, 72; importance of values
  of, 195–97; particular, 86–87; universal,
  xxiv, 86–87. *See also* Universal audience
Aune, J., xxxii–xxxiii
Authoritarian: abuse of authority, 138
Authority, 132–33, 136–38, 141, 147–49; argument about, 125, 140–52; definitions of,
  131–36, 138; and rhetoric, 125, 131, 133–
  35, 137–39; role of, in field study, 39–41,
  46; role of, in history, 131, 133–34; and

  social knowledge, 132, 134–40. *See also*
  Credibility; Ethos; Legitimacy
Authorization, 131

Balthrop, B., xl, 21; and critical stance perspective, xxxviii–xxxix
Bartley, W.: concept of retreat to community,
  42–43
Becoming: concept of, 238
Belief: defined, xxxix, 186–87, 193–94; as factor in argumentative situation, 187; relation
  to attitudes, 186, 193–94; relation to values,
  186–87, 191–94
Benoit, P., 175–76
Bilateral communication: defined, 99–100; humanizing nature of, 101–2; role of rhetoric
  in, 100–101
Bilaterality: of communication, 95, 100–102;
  defined, 69, 95; as means of maintaining humanity, 99, 101–2; and notion of force,
  101–2; as standard of argument validity,
  95, 100
Bitzer, L.: concept of authorization, 131
Black, E.: rhetorical criticism as understanding,
  239–40
Boggs, S., 179
Booth, W.: and critical pluralism, 254; rhetoric
  and poetics relationship, 345
Borderline cases: children's arguments as, 157–
  58; compared to paradigm cases, 157; concept of, 155–56. *See also* Paradigm case
Borrowing: interfield nature of, 62, 70–72; obligations of, 71–72
Bracketing: importance of, to historical study,
  308
Braithwaite, R.: definition of models, 261–63
Brockriede, W.: characteristics of argument,
  157, 274–76
Bronson, W.: study of child interaction, 169–
  70, 172
Burden of proof: relation to dialectic, 118–19;
  relation to presumption, 119
Bureaucracy: role of, in decision making, 333–35
Bureaucratic process model of decision making:
  bureaucratic role in decision making, 332–
  34; explained, 331–35; policy implementation problems in bureaucracy, 334–35; value
  of model, 339, 341–42
Burke, K.: relationship of rhetoric and poetics,
  346–47
Burleson, B.: characteristics of argument, 15–
  16, 22; defense of argument models, 4, 22,
  267–68

Carter, J., 188–89; and authority argument,
  140–49

Cartesian rationality: as paradigm case, 106
CBA. *See* Cost-benefit analysis
Change: sources of, in society, 238–39
Children's arguments: as borderline arguments, 157–58; development of competence in, 172–78, 181–82; difference from adult arguments, 154–55, 159–60, 162, 175, 183; elaboration and termination of, 179–81; emergent nature of, 180–81; expansion in, 177–78; felicity conditions in, 174–76; over opposition in, 162–68; prevalence of, 169–71; repair sequences in, 176–77; speech acts in, 173–74; structure and strategy in, 179–81; types of, 171–73, 179–80; usefulness of, for argument study, 154, 157–58. *See also* Speech acts; Speech act theory
Children's communication: cognitive development of conversational skills, 154–55; and communicative competence, 173–78, 181–82; difference from adult communication, 154–55, 175; importance of, 154–55; opposition as feature of, 168–73. *See also* Communication
Chronology: importance of, in historical understanding, 306–7
Cicero: and classical traditions of rhetoric, 364–66
Claims: role of beliefs and values in, 188–92,195
Classical rhetorical theory. *See* Graeco-Roman rhetoric
Closure: defined, 69–70; in field study, 72–73
Cognitive development: role of, in argument field study, 34–35, 64
Cognitive interests: types of, 316
Cohesion: between fields, 29–30
Common case (analysis of argument): difference from paradigm case, 8
Common ground: social value as basis of, 189
Communication, 95–97, 100, 313; as approach to argument study, 186, 200; bilaterality and, 99–102; community notion of, 117, 120, 214–15; defined, 213–14; difference from critical stance, 240; as maintenance of humanity, 95–96, 98–99, 101–2; rationality in, 109, 110–11, 113–14; reflective nature of, 98–99, 100; relation to legal practice, 364–67, 369–70; rhetorical functions of, 100–101, 211–12; role of language in, 95, 97, 206; as test of reality, 238–39; types of, 109–10, 111. *See also* Bilateral communication; Children's communication; Unilateral communication
Communication theorists' view of argument, 91–94
Communicative speech act: concept of, 211. *See also* Speech acts; Speech act theory

Community: cyclical agencies and, 139; need for authority in, 139–40; notion of, 139; role of, in argumentation, 185; role of, in field disputes, 255–56; role of values in, 187–88; as test of plausible interpretations, 254–56
Conclusiveness: as truth of proposition, 115
Confidence: relation to ideology, 138
Conflict: definitions of, 189; role of, in argumentation, 189–91
Conflict situations: role of values in, 189–90
Connolly, W.: concept of authority, 133
Consciousness: creation of, 309–10
Consistency: role of, in argumentation research, 198–99
Constructivism: as school of thought, 38–39
Constructivist view of argument: argument as process, 92–94. *See also* Argument, constructivist/interactionist view of
Context: importance of, 190–91, 240, 242; role of, in argumentation, xxiii, 82, 92, 190–91
Conversation: as metaphor for textual interpretation, 246–47. *See also* Dialogue
Conversational argument: characteristics of, 211, 224, 226, 235–36; as disagreement, 219–20, 223–26; importance of concept, 205–7; model of, 224–36; modes of inquiry for, 206, 218–20, 222–24; permissible warrants of, 233–34; range of, 224–26; types of, 234–35
Conversational discourse: as basis for argumentation study, xli–xliii. *See also* Discourse
Conversation of gestures: defined, 211
Conviction: as goal of argumentation, xvi–xvii, xxi; association with formal logic, xxiv; difference from persuasion, xxv–xxvi
Conviction-persuasion duality: concept of, xv–xvii, 85–87
Cooley, J.: criticisms of Toulmin, 318
Cooperation: role of, in argumentation, 189
Cost-benefit analysis (CBA), 29, 36, 43, 54–56, 62, 68–70, 72; and notion of closure, 72–73; as paradigm case for argument study, 25, 33; defined, 33, 38, 43, 64–65; role of ethics in, 67–69; role of intuition in, 64–65
Cox, R., 238; concept of loci, 197
Crable, R., 80; standards of argument validity, 91–92
Credibility: of literature narrator, 355–56; role of value judgments in, 196–97. *See also* Authority; Ethos
Crisis decisions: characteristics of, 321–22, 324–26; compared to incremental decisions, 336; empirical example of decision making steps involved in Cuban missile crisis, 327–

Crisis decisions (*continued*)
28. *See also* Cuban missile crisis; Foreign policy decisions

Critical decision making: role of argument in, xx–xxi

Critical interpretation: derived from aesthetic proofs, 347–48

Critical pluralism: defined, 254; value of, 257–58

Critical stance: defined, xxxix, 240–42; hermeneutical aspects of, xl, 241–42, 253–54, 255–56; and promotion of understanding, 240, 247, 249, 255–57; values of, in argumentation, xxxix, 240, 245–49, 256–58. *See also* Hermeneutical circle

Criticism: characteristics of, as field, 53, 55–56, 58–60; defined, 47–48, 76, 239–40; hermeneutical views of, 49–50, 56; as mode of epistemology, 47–49, 51, 53; uniqueness of, 240, 254–55; values of, 251–52. *See also* Argument criticism; Rhetorical criticism

Critic of argument: concept of, 240, 244–45; responsibilities of, 251–53

Cross examination: strategies of, 371

Cuban missile crisis: composition of decision making body involved in, 327–29; decision viewed as bureaucratic process, 331–39; decision viewed as rational actor, 339–41; decision viewed as sovereign arena, 327–30; discussion of blockade option, 328–30, 340–42; discussion of decision making options in, 327–41; flow of decision making process, 328 (table); forceable options available, 327–28, 329–30. *See also* Crisis decisions; Foreign policy decisions

Data: requirements of, for argument models, 265–66, 271–72; types of, used by argument theorists, 271–74. *See also* Evidence

Death of a Salesman: argument in, 348–54

Debate: as analytic thought device, xviii; as decision making tool, xv; as form of argumentation, xvi; as paradigm of critical decision making, xx–xxi; as problem solving device in non-scientific spheres, xvii–xix; role of logic in, xix–xx

Decision arenas: types of, 321 (table)

Decision making, 331; defined, 318–19. *See also* Group decision making processes

Decisions, of foreign policy. *See* Foreign policy decisions

Decision stages: role of argument in, 324 (table)

Deduction: as departure from modern logic, 291

Defendant: effect of characteristics of, on jury decisions, 369

Demonstration: difference from argument, 292

Descriptive methodology: critical techniques for, xxxviii–xxxix

Determinism: as distinct from invariance, 61

Dialectic: defined, 118–19, 126, 289–90; and history, 123; and notion of choice, 294–95; Plato's view of, 289–90; relation to philosophy, 289–91, 296–97; relation to rhetoric, 126, 289–91, 295–97; role of, in dissociation, 294–95; role of intuition in, 289–90, 295–96; and truth, 118–19, 251–52; and values, 289–90

Dialectical rationality: as subtype of value-free rationality, 110, 121. *See also* Ethical rationality; Rationality; Value-free rationality

Dialectical reasoning: difference from analytical reasoning, 290–91. *See also* Reasoning

Dialogue: concept of, 244; function of, for historians, 306–7; importance of, in understanding, 244, 252–54; interpretation as product of, 251–52; role of horizon in, 244–45; role of text in, 244–47. *See also* Conversation; Interpretation

Didactic literature: rhetorical nature of, 344–45

Disagreement: and conversational argument, 223, 226–27, 236; difference from argument, 235–36; options for, 224–36; options for resolution of, 191; relation to expansion, 223, 228–29, 231–32, 235–36; relation to speech acts, 226–28, 231, 233. *See also* Agreement

Disciplinary fields: criticism as, 58–59; difference from ordinary fields, 30, 37–38; epistemological functions of, 30, 38; use of cost-benefit analysis in, 29. *See also* Fields; Fields of argument; Ordinary fields

Discourse: and relation to communication, 206; role of, in children's arguments, 168–81. *See also* Communication; Conversation

Discourse analysis: limits of, for argument models, 272–73; methodological concerns of, 218–20, 222–23; philosophical rationales for, 207, 218; role of, in argument study, 156, 206, 272

Discourse genre: as research strategy for argument study, 160–61

Dissociation: role of argumentation in, 294–95

Documents: as distinct from fields, 55. *See also* Historical documents; Texts

Domain: of models, 261–63

Domains of objectivity: concept of, 25–26, 27; relation to fields, 37, 46, 59

Doxastic system (of justification): as rational basis for decisions, 116–17, 120

Drama: as creator of meaning, 349–50; as portrayer of value-laden conflicts, 360–61

Ehninger, D.: tests of argument validity, 84
Electronic media: role of, in legal proceedings, 371–72. *See also* Televised trials; Videotaped trials
Emotion: involvement in argument, 82, 85–87
Empathy: role of, in foreign policy decisions, 322–23
Enthymemes: in conversation, 235–36; as key to rhetoric, 196
Epistemics: defined, 24, 72; relation to field theory, 73–74
Equations: in argument models, 263, 276–79, 282; as evaluation of isomorphism, 264; syllogistic generation of, 278–80; weighting of variables in, 280
Ethical rationality: use of, in argumentative discourse, 108–10. *See also* Dialectical rationality; Rationality; Value-free rationality
Ethics: role of, in field theory, 62–63, 65–66
Ethos: relation to authority, 136, 138, 145, 151–52; as binding element of fields, 45. *See also* Authority; Credibility
Evaluation: as critical procedure, 50–51; contrasted to explication, 51, 58–59
Evidence: standards of, 196. *See also* Data
Expansion (units of): as form of opposition, 177–78; permissible bases of, 232–33; post-sequential, 231; relation to adjacency pairs, 222–23; relation to disagreement, 223, 228–29, 231–32, 235–36; as regulator of argument, 232–33. *See also* Conversational argument; Speech acts; Speech act theory

Fallacies. *See* Logical fallacies
Family unit: as argument field, 34
Felicity conditions, 27; children's knowledge of, 175; defined, 221; importance of, in discourse analysis, 221–22; relation to adjacency pairs, 222–23; relation to generalized other, 217–18; relation to speech acts, 174–76, 221–22, 232; role of, in argument, 176–77, 223. *See also* Conversational argument; Speech acts; Speech act theory
Fiction (Fictive literature): example of *Death of a Salesman*, 348–54; example of *The Great Gatsby*, 354–59; as mode of rhetorical communication, 343, 360–61; as suggestive argument, 347, 354, 357
Fields: accomplished nature of, 38–39, 46, 56, 259; as analytic distinction, 47, 58–61, 67–68; and borrowing from other fields, 61–62, 70–72; characteristics of, 28–47, 67; and closure, 70, 72; concept of unity, 28–29, 39–40, 46; constraints of, 38; context-embedded nature of, 46–47, 53, 54,

61, 76; defined, 28–37; defined, as audience, 39–40, 44–45, 72, 76; and definition of the situation, 46–47, 49; and disputes, 41–42, 62, 66, 254–57; as distinct from documents, 47, 55–57, 256; as framework of assumptions, 47, 53–55, 59; as schools of thought, 38–39, 42, 46, 54; as sociological entities, 28–31, 46, 47, 54, 58, 67, 75; as synonymous with group, 29–30, 37, 46; recurring themes in, 28–29, 48–49, 54–55, 58, 61; rhetorical nature of, 39–40, 44–45, 72, 76; role of authority in, 39–41; value of critical stance in transcendence of, 254–57. *See also* Argumentation, as field of study; Fields of argument; Interfield disputes
Fields of argument: concept of, xxiii, xxxvii, xlvi, 24–26; epistemological perspectives of, xl–xli, 74; importance of, xlvi–xlvii; methodological concerns of, 34–35, 47, 74. *See also* Argumentation, as field of study; Fields; Interfield disputes
Field studies, 42, 47; concept of, 24; disputes in, 62; role of hierarchy in, 43, 67; social interaction perspective toward, 37
Field theory, 26, 35, 53, 58; concept of, 184–85; empirical differences in, 28; foundations of, 41–42, 259; as psychological perspective, 33–37, 46; relation to epistemics, 61–75; relation to ethics, 62–63; role of, in argument study, 31, 184; as study of objectifying, 31–33, 46, 75. *See also* Fields; Fields of argument
Figures of style (stylistic techniques): as means of creating presence, 345
First amendment: analysis of legal cases concerning, 367–68, 376; role of argumentation in, 375–76
Fisher, W.: views on reasoning, 113, 197
Fisher, W., and Filloy, R.: relationship of rhetoric to poetics, 346–47
Force: and bilaterality and philosophical argument, 101–2
Foreign policy decisions: characteristics of congressional, public, and sovereign input in, 321–22; constraints on, 322; objectives for study of, as argument field, 319–20; role of empathy in, 322–23; role of intuition in, 322–23. *See also* Crisis decisions; Cuban missile crisis
Foresight: as basis of internal dynamic, 253–54; dogmatic and pragmatic aspects of, 242; role of, in dialogue, 244–45; role of text in, 245–47, 249; role in understanding, 242. *See also* Pre-understanding
Form: defined, 125–28; emergent nature of, 130; and rhetoric, 127, 128, 138–39

Formalism: disputed between fields, 65–66, 69–70, 72

Foucalt, M., 44–45; concept of domains of objectivity, 25–26

Frame of reference: as argument variable, 274–76; difficulty of study of, 276–77

Freedom, 52; as American value, 192; loss of, when entering fields, 38

Functions of models. *See* Models, functions of

Fusion (of horizons): defined, 243–44; necessity of, for understanding, 250, 256–57; role of interpretation in, 244–47. *See also* Horizon

Fuzziness: as fact in argument study, 157, 159; and paradigm cases, 159–60; responses to, 159–62

Gadamer, H.: and attributes of philosophical hermeneutics, 52, 241–43; explanations of textual interpretations, 246–47, 256; notion of historicity, 56; view of critical understanding, 52; view of linguistic context, 56–57, 250

Generalized other: defined, 215–17; levels of, 217–18; relation to notion of fields, 31, 36

Generic characteristics: as approach to study of argument, 157–58; example of overt opposition as, 162–68

Goffman, E.: and concept of perspective-taking, 52

Good reasons: criteria for, 114; hierarchical nature of, 117; and reasonableness, 114–21

Goodwin, M.: and discourse genre, 160

Graeco-Roman rhetoric: conception of argument in, 79–80, 92; difference from New rhetoric, 79–80, 85. *See also* Aristotle, classical traditions of rhetorical theory; New rhetoric

Great Gatsby, The: argument in, 354–59

Gronbeck, B.: concept of new rationality, 184

Group decision making processes: steps involved in, 324–26. *See also* Decision making

Habermas, J.: contributions to argument study, xxxii–xxxiii, 110–12, 117, 128–29, 136, 316; criticisms of theory, 129–30

Hegel, G.: and concept of dialectic, 295–96; and notion of history, 127

Hermeneutical circle: defined, 242, 244; value of, 256–58. *See also* Critical stance

Hermeneutical rationality: use of, in argumentative discourse, 109–10

Hermeneutics: and attributes of understanding, 242–43; definition of, 241–42, 301; and fusion of horizons, 55–56, 243–44; and mediation of symbols, 57, 309; relation to literary interpretation, 241–42; role of, in history,

301, 306–10; role of, in study of argument, 24, 247; as study of texts, 52, 55–56; as view of criticism, 49–50, 51–52, 241. *See also* Critical stance; Philosophical hermeneutics

Hermes: and etymology of philosophical hermeneutics, 241–42, 256

Heuristics: role of, in model evaluation, 265

Historian: aspect of post hoc judgment, 302–3; example of role of, in slavery, 303–7; goals of, in study of historical argument, 301, 310, 312–13; persuasive functions of, 303–4, 309–10; and process on making historical sense, 300–301; as rhetorical agent, 301–4, 306–7; role of, in historical argument, 300–303

Historical argument: diagram of, 301; as explanation, 312–13; field dependent nature of, 315; process of, 300, 312–15, 317; relation to knowledge, 128–29, 151–52

Historical documents: temporality of, 124. *See also* Texts

Historical method: process of, 299, 301, 313

Historical objectivity: as obtained through dialogue of historians, 306–7

Historical record: role of, in historical argument, 299, 313, 314

Historical re-creation: as goal for historian, 312–13; nature of, 300–301, 304

Historical sense: process outlined, 309–10

Historical understanding: role of communication in, 312–13, 314; conditions for, 307–10

Historicity: as basic attribute of philosophical hermeneutics, 242–43; as constraint on interpretation, 251–52; as function of language, 243–44; as temporal understanding, 243–44

Historiography: need for, in argumentation study, 298–99

History: and authority, 131, 138–39; and dialectic, 123; link to rhetoric, 313–14; nature of, 300–303; object of, 312–13; ontological assumptions of, 307; as preliminary to analytic study, 314–15; as process of understanding, 127, 302, 307, 316–17; and recurrence of argument, 123–24

Horizon: of argument, 245–46; defined, 243–44; need for understanding of personal, 252, 253–54; as test of plausible interpretation, 254, 258; text as basis of, 245–46. *See also* Fusion

Horizontalizing: and understanding of form, 128

Humanity: defined, 96–97; maintenance of, 98–99

Identity: as basis for quasi-logical argument, 83
Ideographs: role of beliefs and values in, 187, 193
Ideology: and authority, 137, 138, 151–52; definitions of, 137
Illocutionary acts: argument as, 212–14. *See also* Speech acts; Speech act theory
Immediacy: and risk of selfhood, xxx–xxxi
Importation. *See* Borrowing
Incompatibility: defined, 81–82. *See also* Logical contradiction
Incrementalism: and bureaucratic action, 335
Inferential leaps: minimization of, in argument models, 273
Information theory: applied to argumentation, 280–81
Inscription: relation to critical stance, 247–49
Intention: role in speech acts, 174
Interaction analysis: as methodology for systems approach to trials, 372–73
Interface: as characteristic of communication, 96–97, 101
Interfield disputes: bases of, 41–42, 67, 74; borrowing and, 71–72; resolution of, 43, 62, 66–69, 76; role of argumentation concepts in understanding, 43–44. *See also* Fields; Fields of argument
Internal dynamic: defined, as evaluation of interpretation, 253–54
Interpretation: definitions of, 49, 56, 241–42; documents of fields and need for, 55–56, 58; evaluation of, 251–52, 253–54; as fusion of horizons, 244–45, 251–52; need for shared public understanding of, 252–53; possible biases of historical, 300, 302–5; as product of dialogue, 251–52; role of text in, 244–45; uniqueness of, 56, 254–55. *See also* Selectivity
Introspection: use of, in argument models, 271–72
Intuition: as element of foreign policy decisions, 322–23; role of, in cost-benefit analysis, 64–65; role of, in field practices, 43, 63, 64
Invariance: as distinct from determinism, 61; nonproductive nature of, 67–68
Isomorphism: in models, 261–62, 267–68; problems of, 264–66

Jacobs, S., and Jackson, S., 175; argument as illocutionary act, xxviii; criteria for arguments, 156; criticism of psychological theories, xxxiv–xxxv; repair structures in argument, 177–78; structural properties of argument, 161
Johnstone, H., 69; concept of personhood in argument, xxix

Judge: impact of instructions on jury decision, 370
Jurisprudence: role of rhetorical theory in, 369
Jury: factors in selection of, 370–71; needed research on reasoning processes of, 373
Justification: and authority, 41; doxastic, 116; types of, 114–17

Kant, E., 291, 294; criticisms of ethical theory, 63, 66
Kaplan, A.: criticisms of rational actor models, 324
Kelly, G.: personal construct theory, 53, 68–69; view of freedom, 38, 52
Kneupper, C.: defense of argument diagrams, 267–68
Knowing: perspective-taking and, 52; relation to domain of objectivity, 27
Knowledge: and need for public data, xxxvi, xxxviii; relation to historical argument, 128–29; role of, in children's interaction, 173–78; types of, xxxvi; views of, xli, xlii
Kuhn, T.: notion of community, 45–46, 53

Lakatos, I.: heuristic view of models, 265
Language: children's knowledge of, 173–74, 178; as cultural transmitter, 243–44; importance of common, for understanding, 242–43; nature of, 86–87, 137, 151–52, 299–300; range of, for authority, 137, 142–43, 149–53; relationship to magic, 107–8; relation to argument, 82–83, 95–96; role of, in historiography, 299, 313–14; types of, 137–38, 149–52; variations of, for authority, 137–38. *See also* Communication; Discourse
Language-Action philosophers, 207; concept of communicative speech act, 211
Language games, 33; argument as, 207–11, 214–16; breakdowns in, 209–10; confrontations in, 209–11; roles in, 216–17; rules of, 207–10
Laudan, L., 70; notion of cognitive progress, 58, 59–60
Law: historical relationship between rhetoric and, 364–67
Lawyers: use of argumentation, 363–64
Leadership: President Carter's problems with, 142–49. *See also* Authority
Legal argument: compared to legislative argument, 368
Legal communication: functions of, 370–71
Legal communication research: evaluation of, 372–74
Legalistic analysis: and transition to argumentative analysis, 368–69

Legal pedagogy: communication scholars interest in, 369
Legal trial: as public speaking situation, 367
Legitimacy: relation to authority, 136, 138; problems of, in 1976 presidential campaign, 141–48. *See also* Authority
Lein, L., and Brenneis, D., 179–80; research on children's argument, 160
Linguisticality: as basic attribute of philosophical hermeneutics, 242–43
Literary criticism: difference from argument criticism, 52
Loci communes, 80; role of, in argument, 197
Loci of inquiry, in argument theory: audience centered, xxxviii; in social interactions, xxxiv, xxxvi
Locus of argument: bases of, 270–71; as means to model argument, 271
Logic, xxi–xxv, 80–83, 87, 113, 125; distinguished from rhetoric, 85, 313–14; formal, xix–xxi, 80–81, 90, 91–92; and formal knowledge, 118–19; and good reasons, 197, 360–61; inappropriateness of, for historical argument, 314–15; informal, 80–81; place of, in rhetoric, 87, 89–90, 93–94; as practical art, xix–xx, xxi, xxiv; and questions of validity, 83–84, 88, 91–92; role of, in argumentation, xix–xx, 78–79, 80–81, 83, 87, 89–93; as system for value assessment, 360–61. *See also* Quasi-logical argument
Logical contradiction: as basis for quasi-logical argument, 82–83; defined, 81–82; difference from incompatibility, 81–82. *See also* Incompatibility
Logical fallacies, 88; role of, in historical argument, 314–15
Logical positivism: criticisms of, 318; role of, in rhetorical theory, 287
Logos: form of message and impact on audience, xviii

McGee, M., 192–93; and ideographs, 187
McKerrow, R., 88–89, 185; notion of argument validity, 84–85; objectification in argument, xxxii–xxxiii
Macroargument: role of, in foreign policy decisions, 325
Magic: concept of, 107; primitive, 108–12; rites of, 108
Man: defined, 98; humanization of, 98–99
Marcuse, H.: criticism of logical positivism, 318
Mathematical logic: conceptual problems of, 291–92
Mathematical relations: argument based on, 83
Mathematical science: compared to philosophical inquiry, 288

Mead, G., 9, 40, 46; concept of generalized other, 215; concept of significant communication, 211; concept of significant gesture, 211
Meaning, 190, 248; creation of, in drama, 349–50; impact of inscription on, 247–48; role of argument in assigning, 239–40, 245–46, 250; shared, as basis if social reality, 238–39; social construction of, 207
Medium: role of, in communication, 97–98, 101
Message: as essential to field definition, 45–46
Metaphor, 197; argument model as incomplete, 262
Method: compared to methodology, 240–41; importance in Cartesian rationality, 106
Methodology: compared to method, 240–41. *See also* Descriptive methodology
Microargument: role of, in foreign policy decisions, 325
Miller, G., and Burgoon, M.: and persuasion research, 199–200
Mills, G., and Petrie, H.: role of belief and emotion in argument, 87–88
Model conversion: stages involved in and diagram of, 274–76
Model development: nature of and data requirements for, 264–67; resources for use in, 274–75
Modeler: decisions to consider, 268–69; resources for, 274–75
Modeling: accuracy in, 279; argument, issues in, 267–75; benefits of, 259–60, 267–68, 278–79, 284; defined, 259; operationalization of, 276–77; and prediction, 277–78
Modeling argument: argument characteristics as basis for, 268–72, 274–75; considerations in, 267–75, 277–80; data possibilities of, 271–74; definitions of, 278–79; equations in, 276–77; Hample's example of, 274–78; link to formal logic, 278–79; resources for use in, 274–75. *See also* Argument, and models; Models about argument; Models of argument
Model of conversational argument: formal components of, 224–28; functional components of, 228–32; as interpretive principle, 234–35; substantive components of, 232–36
Models: considerations of, 267–68; data requirements for, 265–66; definitions of, 259, 261–62, 280–81; as distinct from diagrams, 264; domain of, 261, 262–65; evaluations of, 262–63; evolution of, 264–65; formal, 259, 263–64; functions of, 259–60, 264–68; human construction of, 272, 279–83; limits of, 268–69; nature of, 260–68, 280–83; support for, 265–66, 268–69;

risks of, 259–60; tests of, 265–67; types of, 263–64, 266–69, 283; uniqueness of, as research technique, 261–63

Models about argument: defined, 268–69; difference from models of argument, 268–69. *See also* Argument, and models; Modeling argument

Models of argument: defined, 268–69; difference from models about argument, 268–69; examples of construction of, 278–83; nature of, 269–70. *See also* Argument, and models; Modeling argument; Toulmin model of argument

Multiple realities argument: concept of, 48; role of, in field study, 49

Narratio (Narration): defined, 313; implications of, as mode of argument, 314–15

Narrator: as portrayer of argument in literature, 356–59; role in meaning creation of texts, 356–57

Natanson, M.: risk, selfhood, and immediacy in argument, xxx–xxxi

New rhetoric: and concept of universal audience, 93; consideration of audience in, 85–87, 292–93; difference from Graeco-Roman rhetoric, 79–80, 85, 88; as replacement for formal logic, 88–90; as study of argumentation, 79, 292

Nondiscursive forms of argument: as supplement to discursive forms, xxvii–xxviii, xxxiv

Nonverbal communication: role of, in argumentation, 10, 13–14, 21–22; role of, in children's interaction, 173–74

Objectification: concept of, xxxii–xxxiii, xxxvi–xxxvii; possibilities of, through argument, 248

Objectifying: defined, 31, 53; relation to "as if" maxim, 39; relation to field theory, 31, 46, 48; relation to texts, 55–56

Objectivity: defined, 34–35; difference from objectifying, 34–35; as subjective accomplishment, 61

Observer-critic: and attribution of meaning, xxxvii–xxxviii; role of, in argumentation theory, xxxvi–xxxvii

O'Keefe, D., 155–60

Olafson, F.: notion of community, 139

Olbrechts-Tyteca, L. *See* Perelman, C. *See also* New rhetoric

Ontological argument: concept of, 96

Ontological reason: compared to technical reason, 108–9, 116; defined, 105–6, 112; as foundation for argument theory, 114, 121. *See also* Reason

Ontology: assumptions of man, 308–19; existence as pre-conditioned, 299, 307–9; need for, in historical study, 299, 308–10

Opposition: concept of, 162–64, 166, 170; development of competence for, 172; as feature in children's interaction, 168–81; forms of, 162–63, 168, 177–78; overt, as characteristic of argument, 163, 183; resolution of, 167–68; types of overt manifestations of, 163–66, 171–73

Oral argument: role of, in legal process, 370

Order: human need for, 238–39

Ordinary fields: difference from disciplinary fields, 30, 37–38; relation to domains of objectivity, 37–38. *See also* Disciplinary fields; Fields; Fields of argument

Organizational politics model of decision making: defined, 336–37; difference from partisan politics, 337–38; value of model, 339, 341–42

Palmer, R.: etymology of hermeneutics, 241

Paradigm case, 106–9; benefits of, 20–22; and borderline cases, 7–8, 14, 21, 157; characteristics of, 8–11, 21–22; as clarification of argumentation concepts, 7, 8, 9–17, 155–59; defined, 21, 160; examples of, 7–17, 25, 131, 155–59; limitations of, as mode of inquiry, 157; limitations of, in study of children's argument, 160. *See also* Borderline cases

Participant observation: defined, 35; relation to perspective-taking, 35–36, 55; value of, in argument study, 271

Partisan politics: role of, in foreign policy decisions, 337–38

Perelman, C.: concept of presence, 344–45; concept of universal audience, 86; consideration of audience in argument theory, xxiv, 85–88; criticism of applied formalism, xxii; descriptive study of argument, xxii–xxiii; and discursive forms of argument, xxvii–xxviii; discussion of role of historian, 306–7; distinction between rationality and reasonableness, 112–14; emotive meaning of argument, 86–87; implications of quasi-logical argumentative techniques, 83–94; nonformal reasoning, 79–80; role of values in argumentation, 189, 197; theory of new rhetoric, 78–80; view of formal logic in argumentation, 80–84, 87–88; view of role of rhetoric in argument, 81–82. *See also* New rhetoric; Universal audience

Personal argumentation: concept of, 185

Personal construct theory: relation to field theory, 53, 68–69

Personhood: and argument assessment, xxx; and argument associated with acts of people, xxxix–xxx; defined, xxxii; importance of, in argument, xxx–xxxi; and person-making, xxxi; and risk in argument, xxx–xxxi; role of, in argumentation theory, xxix–xxxiii

Perspective: concept of, 127; emergent nature of, 130; and horizontalizing, 128

Perspective-taking: defined, 34; as mode of knowing, 53, 55; relation to socialization into argument fields, 34–35, 55

Persuasion: argument as, 79, 86–87, 94; distinctions between argument and, 7–8; logic and, 80–81, 87–88; research in, 198–200; role of, in foreign policy decisions, 336–37; standards of, xliv; as supplement to rational appeals, xv–xvii

Philosopher: cultural and historical conditioning of, 295–96; importance of audience for, 292–94; purpose of, 289, 292–95; and value conflicts, 294–95

Philosophical argument: and bilateral communication, 101; and notion of force, 101–2; validity of, 95, 100

Philosophical hermeneutics: as theoretical basis for argument study, xxvii, xxviii, xl, xli. See also Hermeneutics

Philosophical positions: on argument, xii–xlv

Philosophical theory: tests of, 289

Philosophy: purpose of study of, 288–89, 292–93; and quasi-logical argument, 88–89; relation to rhetoric, 287, 289–91, 295–96; and value conflicts, 294–95

Philosophy of science: and explanations of progress, 31–32; relationship to field theory, 26

Piaget, J., 34, 154

Plato: view of dialectic, 289–90; view of rhetoric, 292–93

Plausibility: concept of, 118–19; shared assessment of, 120, 252–53; sources of, 119–20, 252; tests of, 252–54

Playwright: role in meaning creation of text, 349–50

Poetics: relationship to rhetoric, 344–45

Policy argument: and prediction, 325–26; values in, 324–25. See also Macroargument; Microargument

Policy debate: application to argument models, 283

Power: relation to authority, 133

Pragmatic coherence: in children's interaction, 175–76

Prediction: in argument models, 283

Preferability: concept of, 116

Presence: defined, 344–45

Presumption, 68; and dialectic, 118; and rationality, 120; role of, in argumentation, 197–98; and truth, 119–20

Pre-trial publicity: impact on jurors, 368–69

Pre-understanding: as basis of plausible interpretation, 252; importance of awareness of, 252. See also Foresight

Probability: compared to plausibility, 119; as standard of argument validity, 115

Processual view of argument: concept of, xxvi–xxix; second order descriptions of, xxxiii–xxxv, xxxviii–xxxix

Progress: and closure, 70; explanations of, 31–33, 59–60; in fields, 42

Psychological monism, xvii–xix

Psychological processes: role of, in argument theory, xxxiv–xxxv, 93

Psychologistic concepts: as argument theory basis, xxxvii; as inadequate for argument study, 215

Public argumentation: defined, 185; role of values in, 185–200; standards for, 185–87

Public scrutiny: as test of critical understanding, 251–53

Quasi-judicial agencies: decision making in, 368–69

Quasi-logical argument: bases of, 82–83; characteristics of, 78–84; criticisms of, 91; and implications for argumentation theory, 83–94; and logic, 80–87

Quintilian: classical traditions of rhetoric, 364–66

Rational actor: defined, 323; model of, xliii

Rational argument: characteristics of, 22

Rationality: bases of, xxxv–xxxvi, 107, 109, 112, 114, 121; characteristics of, xliv, 110–12, 117; role of, in decision making, 323–26, 331, 338; role of, in field study, 32, 40; and logic, 112–14, 120; and reason, 106–12; and reason-giving, xxxiii–xxxiv, xxxv, xliii–xliv, 116; and reasonableness, 112–14; social influences on, xxxv, 110–11; standards of, xxxiii, xxxiv–xxxv; study of, xli–xliii. See also Dialectical rationality; Ethical rationality; Value-free rationality

Rational model of decision making: criticisms of, 332–33; defined, 322, 323–26

Reader: involvement of, in literature, 358–59, 361

Reagan, R., 140, 149, 185

Realistic criticism: and hermeneutical views of criticism, 49–50; objections to, 50–51, 58–60

Reality: perceptions of, 242; role of argument in social construction of, 238–39

Reason: grounded in discourse, 109–12; nature of, 105, 108, 126; ontological, 105; relation to rationality, 106–12; technical, 105, 108; traditional forms of, 126. *See also* Ontological reason; Technical reason

Reasonable: and decision making, 120; defined, 113

Reasonableness: and good reasons, 114–21; ontological nature of, 112–14; and rationality, 112–13, 114; senses of, 113–14; standards of, 118

Reasoned belief: as rhetorical phenomenon, 347

Reason-giving explanations, xl; as standard of rationality, xxxiii, xxxv, xliii

Reasoning: role of, in argument, 195–96. *See also* Dialectical reasoning

Reductionism: role of, in argument study, xxi–xxiii

Reflection: processes of, 137

Reflective communication, 98–100

Rescher, N., 117–21, 191

Research traditions, 42, 60

Repair sequences, 176, 177. *See also* Speech acts; Speech act theory

Rhetoric, 90, 126, 290, 291, 293–96, 364–67; as art, 124–26; and bilaterality, 100–101; and communication, 82–83, 100–101, 206; in fictive literature, 343–45; and history, 124, 313–14; importance of audience, 81, 84–85, 292–93; and logic, 83–85, 87, 88, 93, 94, 313–14, 365–66; and notion of form, 126–27; relationship to dialectic, 126, 291; relationship to philosophy, 287, 289, 296–97; relationship to poetics, 344–47; role of, in argumentation, 81–82, 92, 100–101, 124–25, 211. *See also* New rhetoric

Rhetorical agents: historians as, 301–7

Rhetorical analyses: of legal cases, 367–68

Rhetorical argument: characteristics of, 125, 128, 130; defined, 127–28; and form, 138–39; and history, 126, 138–39

Rhetorical criticism: relation to argument criticism, 50–51

Rhetorical form, 128, 130; authority as example of, 131, 133; historical constitution of, 138–39; relation to dialectic, 152

Rhetorical processes: relation to notion of fields, 39–40, 42–46

Rhetorical propriety: and relation to authority and social knowledge, 138

Rhetorical reason: supremacy to formal logic, 80

Rhetorical situations: importance of, in legal argument, 368

Rhetorical theory: relation to legal processes, 369, 372

Rhetorical validity, 85; compared to argument validity, 83–84, 92; concept of, 92

Ricoeur, P., 247–48, 300

Ridicule: as technique of argument, 82

Risk: nature of, in argument, xxx–xxxi; and personhood, xxix–xxxiii; as product of objectification, xxxii–xxxiii

Rokeach, M.: definition of attitude, belief, and value, 186–87; concept of value analysis, 193; notion of value hierarchies, 190

Roles: importance of, in language games, 216–17; relation to generalized other, 216–17; relation to authority, 136, 138, 151–52

Sacks, H., and Schegloff, E.: concept of adjacency pairs, 222

Scheler, M., 64–67; criticisms of Kant, 63, 66; ethical considerations of field theory, 62–64

Schools of thought: fields as, 38–39, 46

Schurmann, F.: definition of ideology, 137

Schutz, A., 52

Scientific rationality: role of, in argument, 107; criticisms of, 108–9; defined, 106–7

Searle, J., 37, 133, 174; and speech act theory, 11–12, 234–35

Second experience: concept of, 309–10; creation of, 313–14

Selectivity: examples of, in historical account of slavery, 303–7; necessity of, in historical argument, 302–3. *See also* Interpretation

Self-evidence: and philosophy, 288

Self-reports: as indirect test of models, 266–67; as source of data for argument models, 273

Sennett, R.: concept of social emotion, 132; definition of authority, 132

Sentiment of rationality: defined, 313

Sequence types: typical patterns of, in children's argument, 179

Shatz, M., 175

Significant communication: argument as, 211–14

Significant gesture: defined, 211–12; relation to generalized other, 214–15

Simmons, J.: and distinction of argument₁ and argument₂, 94

Simulation: in models, 261

Sincerity conditions: defined, 221. *See also* Speech acts; Speech act theory

Slavery: as example of historical argument, 303–7; as illustration of historical understanding, 310–12; role of rhetoric in, 304–5

Social comparisons: process of, 34–35

Social emotion: and authority, 132

Social institutions: role of, in argument study, 214–18

Social interaction: as means of field study, 37
Social knowledge: appeals to, 137; as grounding for structure of authority, 134–39, 151–52; levels of, 136–38; rhetorical propriety and, 138, 144–45
Social learning: concept of, 130
Social values: function of, in public argumentation, 185–86; and influence on individual values, 198–99; nature of, 186–89, 190, 193–94, 198; role of, in argumentation, 189–95; salience of, 198; and social conflict, 189. *See also* Values
Socialization: into argument fields, 34–35
Sociological disputes: compared to rational disputes in the sciences, 26, 27, 60–61
Source credibility: relation to authority, 136, 138. *See also* Authority; Credibility; Ethos
Sovereign arena model of decision making: compared to bureaucratic process model, 334–35
Speaker: as defining character of fields, 44–45
Speech acts: and adjacency pairs, 221–22, 223; role of, in argument, 11–12, 228, 231–32; children's knowledge of, 174–75; defined, 174–75; expansion of, 177–78; as expressions of disagreement, 226–29; and felicity conditions, 174–76, 221; levels of, 234–35, 247–48; quantity of, 234–35; repair sequences, 176; types of, 226–28, 233; as units of discourse analysis, 221, 223
Speech act theory: as basis for argumentation theory, xxviii, 212–14; defined, 221; illocutionary acts, 212–13, 217–18; intended perlocutions, 212–13
Speech communication: as mode of explaining interaction, 240
Speech style: impact in legal arena, 374
Stasis: tests of, in legal argument, 368
Statistical tests: of models, 266–67
Strategic rationality: defined, 108–9; and ethical and dialectical rationality, 110
Structural properties of discourse: influence on characterizations of argument, 161–62. *See also* Speech acts; Speech act theory
Syllogism: components and use of, 278–80
Symbolic interaction: as means of entry into fields, 35
Symbolism: argument as symbolic justification, xxvii–xxviii; importance of, in legal argument, 367
Symbols: meaning and, 211–12; as mediator of awareness, 309–10; role of, in argumentation, 91–92; significant, 211–12, 217

Tautology: relation to quasi-logical argument, 82

Technical reason: compared to ontological reason, 108–9, 116; defined, 105–6; and justification, 115; and rationality, 112, 120–21. *See also* Reason
Televised trials: strengths and weaknesses of, 371–72. *See also* Electronic media
Texts: argument as, 245–46; as basis for hermeneutical study, 52, 55–56; as basis for internal dynamic, 253–54; as boundary, 244–47, 250, 256–57; and concept of extention, 250; as data source for argument models, 273; as test of plausibility, 252–54; value of, in understanding, 55–56, 58, 244, 250–53, 256–57. *See also* Interpretation
Theory: predictions from, 265–66; relation to models, 261–62
Theory construction: role of, in argumentation, xxvi–xxxix; foundations of, xxvi–xxxvi; methodological issues in, xxxvi–xxxix
Theory of proof: role of, in philosophical inquiry, 288
Theory of propositional control: applied to argument models, 281–82
Thought: discovery of, as historian goal, 312–13
Time: and form of rhetorical argument, 139; and history, 127
Toulmin, S., 25, 27, 29, 40, 68, 74–75; and concept of force, 117; criticism of applied formalism, xxii; and descriptive study of argument, xxii–xxiii; field approach to argument study, xxiii, 107, 184
Toulmin model of argument: as characteristic of argument$_1$, 18–19; criticisms of, 19–21, 267–68, 318, 320, 324–25; defense of, 4, 19. *See also* Modeling argument; Models of argument
Transitivity: as basis for quasi-logical inquiry, 83
Trial factors: experimental tests of, 369–70; systems approach to study of, 372
Trust: role of, in concept of fields, 40, 41–42
Truth: dialectic and discovery of, 251–52; as goal of philosophical inquiry, 287–88; importance of audience in determining, xxiii; intersubjective nature of, 251–52; and justification, 115; notion of, in argumentation, xix–xx, 101; role of, in rhetorical inquiry, 85, 287–88
Turn system: children's knowledge of, 173, 178; defined, 173; and emergent nature of argument, 180. *See also* Speech acts; Speech act theory

Understanding: defined, xxxvii; role of text in promotion of, 55–56, 58, 244, 250–53, 256–57

Unilateral communication: compared to bilateral communication, 99–101; concept of, 99; as means of maintaining humanity, 101–2; and notion of force, 102

Unity: concept of, 28; sources of, 39–40

Universal audience: compared to particular audience, 86; concept of, 86, 89, 90, 93, 293; criticism of, 89; role of, in new rhetoric, 293; role of, in philosophy, 293–94; temporal nature of, 296

Universal pragmatics: concept of, 129

Validity, of argument: bilaterality as standard of, 95, 100. *See also* Argument validity

Value analysis: usefulness of, in argument research, 186, 200–201

Value-free rationality: as paradigm case, and subtypes of, 108–9. *See also* Rationality

Values: acquisition of, 187, 191; characteristics of, 187–91; defined, 186; forms of adaptation of, 191–92, 194; importance of, in argumentation, 187–89, 191, 193–95, 196–201; importance of, in rhetoric, xxiv–xxv, 195–96; need for research on, 200–201; relation to belief, 186, 192–94; relation to context, in public argumentation, 188, 193–95; relation to presumption, 197–98; relation to reasoning, 195–96; relation to social community, 187–88. *See also* Social values

Value system: nature of, 187, 190; role of, in resolution of disagreement, 191; as systemic grounds for argument analysis, 199

Variables in argument models: types of, 274–75. *See also* Modeling argument; Models

Verbal models (pictorial): as distinct from argument model, 298; usefulness of, 264. *See also* Modeling argument; Models

Verdict (legal): effect of defendant characteristics on, 369–70; effect of jury size on, 369–70

Verstehen, 24; defined, 35–36

Videotaped trials: impact of, in legal arena, 371–72; needed research concerning, 374. *See also* Electronic media

Vietnam: relation to Cuban missile crisis, 338–41

Warrant (legal): role of, in free expression study, 375–76

Warranting: concept of, 120–21

Warrants: of claims, 187, 195–96; of historical cliams, 307–12; relation to felicity conditions, 233–34, 236; values as, 197–98

Weltanschauungen, 28–29, 49–50

We-ness: relation to family units, 34

Wenzel, J., 78, 190, 316; criticism of universal audience, 89–90; views of argument, xxviii, 5–6, 11, 93

Whatley, R.: influence on legal rhetoric, 366; ridicule as technique of argument, 82; view of presumption, 198

Willard, C.: and argument fields, 185, 255–56; and critical stance, 248–50; criticisms of argument diagrams, 19, 21, 92–93, 267–68; criticisms of quasi-logical argument, 86, 90–92; definition of argument, 79–80, 92–93, 269–70; nondiscursive forms of argument, xxvii–xxviii, 6, 8, 15, 16; non-justificational approach to argument, xl

Will-intellect dualism: and conviction-persuasion dichotomy, 85–87

Winch, P., 107–8, 112, 117

Witness: value of testimony, in legal arena, 369–70

Zarefski, D., 130–31; and critical textual analysis, 245–46; and interpretation, 251–52

Ziman, J.: metaphorical view of argument models, 262

Znanieki, F.: concept of humanistic coefficient, 36

Zyskind, H., 6; and argument as behavioral matter, 82, 86–87